The Stranglers
1977-1990

A MUSICAL CRITIQUE

Mark Finnigan
&
David Rodgers

The Stranglers
1977-1990

A MUSICAL CRITIQUE

Mark Finnigan
&
David Rodgers

WYMER
PUBLISHING
Bedford, England

First published in Great Britain in 2023
by Wymer Publishing
www.wymerpublishing.co.uk
Tel: 01234 326691
Wymer Publishing is a trading name of Wymer (UK) Ltd

Copyright © Wymer Publishing.

ISBN: 978-1-915246-42-4

The Author hereby asserts their rights to be identified
as the author of this work in accordance with sections
77 to 78 of the Copyright, Designs & Patents Act 1988.

All rights reserved. No part of this publication may be
reproduced or transmitted in any form or by any means,
electronic or mechanical, including photocopying, or any
information storage and retrieval system, without written
permission from the publisher.

This publication is sold subject to the condition that it shall not,
by way of trade or otherwise, be lent, re-sold, hired out or
otherwise circulated without the publishers prior consent in any
form of binding or cover other than that in which it is published
and without a similar condition including this condition
being imposed on the subsequent purchaser.

Every effort has been made to trace the copyright holders of the
photographs in this book but some were unreachable. We would
be grateful if the photographers concerned would contact us.

Typeset and Design by Andy Bishop / Tusseheia Creative
Printed by CMP, Dorset, England

A catalogue record for this book is available from the British Library.

Wymer Publishing would like to
thank the following people for pre-ordering this book:

Tim Bagnall
Steve Bell
Jim Brown
Neil Chamberlain
Colin Davies
Paul Davies
John Diamond
Jim Dorman
John Dowling
Brian Edwards (Didsbury)
Brian Edwards (Milton Keynes)
David Elmer
Graham Fisher
Tam Getty
Jamie Godwin
David Higginson
Paul Hills
Dexter Hockley
Mark Honan
Kevin Jones
Carolyn Lee
Cliff Loveday
Ian March
Alan McNiven
Philip Meek
Christopher Moock
Alan Mulholland
Pete Rickman
Peter Slater
Howard Sloane
Ewan Smith
Alan Spacagna
Mark Turner
Robert Tyler
Norman Vazquez
Ian Walker
Douglas Weldy
Stephen Whiteside

Contents

Preface	9
Key Musical Terms	11
Rattus Norvegicus IV	15
No More Heroes	41
Black and White	71
The Raven	103
The Gospel According to the Meninblack	131
La Folie	159
Feline	185
Aural Sculpture	211
Dreamtime	241
Ten	267
Overall Musical Conclusion	291
Final thoughts	293
Appendices	297
Solo Albums and Collaborations	327
Live albums Compilations, Session Albums and Bootlegs	
The Authors' Journey.	333
Acknowledgements	339
Bibliography	339

Preface

This book has been co-written with Mark providing contextual and lyrical analysis (in black text) followed by David's musical analysis for each song (grey text). We have endeavoured to avoid repetition but, essentially the songs represent our own opinions so there will be instances of differences of opinion between us.

This book is about our individual personal responses to the songs which will not necessarily tally with what has been said over the years by the band or anyone else. Our personal opinions have generated enthusiastic debates between us, and our intention is that this book will generate a wider debate about the music of the band.

The idea to co-write a book about the music of The Stranglers was conceived as we were digesting the very sad news of Dave Greenfield's death from Covid-19 in March 2020. This book is therefore dedicated to the memory of Dave Greenfield and Jet Black who, along with Hugh Cornwell and Jean-Jacques Burnel, have given us so much fulfilment in our lives.

Mark Finnigan and David Rodgers

Key Musical Terms

This book aims to find the answer to the question of why the music of The Stranglers has had a profound influence on many peoples' lives, so we will analyse the music and lyrics of the band in considerable detail. But any in-depth analysis requires some degree of musical detail so there may well be passages in the book where readers with limited musical experience will find challenging language. This overview of key musical terms that characterise all popular music attempts to clarify and support the analyses of the songs to follow.

Most music of any genre will have all the following elements present to a greater or lesser degree:

Melody

Tempo

Rhythm

Chords and keys

Structure

Time signatures

Texture

The actual sound of the instruments and voices

The first three elements: Melody, tempo (speed of the music) and rhythm are common concepts, but the other five elements may require more detailed definition.

Chords and keys

At a basic level, chords are essentially what accompanies the melody. When Eric Clapton sings the melody to 'Tears in Heaven', he is accompanying the melody with guitar chords. When Paul McCartney is singing the melody to 'Let it Be', he is accompanying the melody with piano chords. Chords can be played in a variety of ways. For example, in 'Let it Be' the piano chords are played in a block (all the notes played together) for each chord whereas in Adele's 'Someone Like You', the piano chords are broken up as individual notes but are still chords.

These are also known as arpeggios which became a common feature of Dave Greenfield's playing. When guitarists and keyboard players accompany singers, most of the time they will play the chords whilst the bass guitarist is often inextricably linked to the chords, playing a single note that is a main or root note of the chord.

The actual chords played in most popular songs are very limited. There are, essentially, six main chords which constitute approximately ninety per cent of all chords used in popular music and also the majority of all the classical music of composers such as Mozart and Bach. Status Quo were infamous for composing three chord songs and almost all Rock n' Roll songs from the fifties used three of the same six main chords which were arranged in a specific pattern known as the

12 bar blues chords.

All bands/artists use these chords, but some artists more than others use different chords as well that are often close to/related to the six main chords. Some artists used different chords that deviated a long way away from each other and we will see that The Stranglers were rare amongst their contemporaries as they often used unconventional chord patterns.

Usually, the chord patterns determine the 'key' of the music. Many songs change key at the end, for example in 'I Will Always Love You', or 'My Heart Will Go On', when the music all moves higher or lower but essentially stays the same.

The Stranglers very rarely changed key in this way, but they often changed key and introduced new chord patterns so their music moved off at tangents. Unsurprisingly, when bands like The Stranglers move off in these new directions during songs, this is usually too much for our conditioned ears to cope with, so these songs may not be as commercially successful as those which are based on the predictability and conventionality of the six main chords. A good example of a song that bucks the trend of conventionality and moves off at tangents with new, unrelated chord patterns in different keys is 'Bohemian Rhapsody'.

Some artists very occasionally deliberately play notes that don't fit with each other so the sound clashes which is also known as dissonance or a discord. The end of The Beatles' 'A Day In The Life' is an example where the whole orchestra play random notes that are unrelated to each other to form clashing or dissonance.

When one plays a C and an F sharp at the same time or just after each other, this provides a clash and is called a tritone and was also known as the Devil's interval from the 1600s when the sound of these two notes was said to be the work of the devil. Black Sabbath used this relationship on their dark and unsettling song 'Black Sabbath', and The Stranglers also made use of this relationship.

Structure

Structure refers to the way a song is assembled by using different sections. The most common song structure since the 1970s is to have an intro, then a verse, often a bridge (or linking section) and then a chorus. The verse, bridge and chorus are all then repeated and there might be either a guitar solo or a new section with different melodies and chords followed by another chorus to finish.

Artists that deviate from common song structures carry the risk of songs being less commercial because, as was the case with the use of the main six chords, our ears are tuned to expecting to hear these structures. Furthermore, the verse/bridge/chorus structure is so commonly used because the verse will usually prepare us with a restrained mood and the bridge will help to move from this restraint into exposure of contrasting stronger emotions in the chorus.

'Don't Look Back in Anger' by Oasis is a clear example of the verse being sung lower with restraint, followed by the bridge which is gaining emotional momentum to lead us into the climax of the chorus. Although there will be many album tracks from more experimental or prog rock bands that use unconventional song structures, there are fewer chart hits that deviate from the conventional structures. The most glaring example is, once again, 'Bohemian Rhapsody' where new sections keep appearing and there is only one repeat of the soft piano section, otherwise all the following sections are completely new. It is also worth noting that there is no section where the restrained emotion of the verse prepares us for a chorus as each section carries its own completely different emotion.

The Stranglers, however, did play with many unconventional song structures and the consequent unrelated emotions that resulted from this in a significant number of their songs. The Stranglers singles overall tended to be more structurally conventional, but even these songs had nuances of unconventional structural approaches. But it is their album tracks where we find fascinating structures.

Time signatures

All popular music has a time signature. This is the number of beats in every bar and the vast majority will have four beats in every bar. Some will have three beats in every bar which is the Waltz rhythm. Very occasionally, a piece like Dave Brubeck's 'Take Five' will be based around a different time signature with this piece having five beats in the bar, hence the title. As with structure, many experimental and prog rock bands will experiment with changes of time signature during songs. But chart hits that have time signatures that change during the song are few and far between. 'Say a Little Prayer', 'Money', 'Happiness is a Warm Gun' and several Genesis and Radiohead songs are examples but a prominent hit that clearly utilises time signature changes is The Stranglers' 'Golden Brown'. The band had been experimenting with time signature changes from their first album.

Texture

Texture refers to way the different instruments and voices combine to create the overall sound. At one extreme, Adele's opening to 'Someone Like You' has a light texture with just the piano playing soft arpeggio chords and then a solo vocal melody enters. At the other extreme, many heavy rock songs still have chords and melodies but played in a different way to provide very heavy textures.

Songs often change texture as they progress so every backing vocal or every added guitar part will increase the texture. Not all texture uses chords and many songs like 'Another One Bites The Dust' and 'Smoke On The Water' are more based on riffs which are melodies that repeat. Many songs like 'Smoke On The Water' will combine riffs (at the start) and chords (when the vocals enter).

The Stranglers were at the forefront of on alternative textural approach where each of the three melodic instrumentalists (guitar, bass and keyboard) played different melodies at the same time thus providing a multi-melodic layering texture which created a more complex overall sound. When a vocal melody was added, there were sometimes four different melodies being played at the same time and this highly unusual approach to the overall texture of a song was a key part of their originality.

The sound

All music is made up of different sounds, sometimes referred to as timbres. If a flute and a trumpet play the same note one would instantly differentiate between the soft, fluttery sound of the flute and the bright, harsher sound of the trumpet. An electric guitar can have many different electronic effects applied to change the sound and a keyboard will have many different sounds which can be controlled at the touch of a button. The way an instrument is played will also affect the sound so, for example, a guitarist can pick or strum the strings and can vibrate or bend the strings, all affecting the sound being produced.

There are many different drum and bass guitar sounds. All four band members of The Stranglers had distinct sounds that merged together to provide an instantly recognisable and highly original overall sound when they first appeared in the late seventies. And every singer has a unique vocal sound with many singers changing their vocal sound or tone depending on the mood of the song. This was certainly the case with Hugh Cornwell and JJ Burnel.

The Stranglers experimentation with chords and keys, structures, rhythm and time signatures, textures and the overall sound combined to cement their originality as both a band that would have many hit singles but also unconventional album tracks. Most chart singles, including The Stranglers' biggest hits, tended to rely on the more conventional use of these elements and this book will shine a light on the lesser-known tracks of the band as well as analysing their most popular songs in detail.

David Rodgers

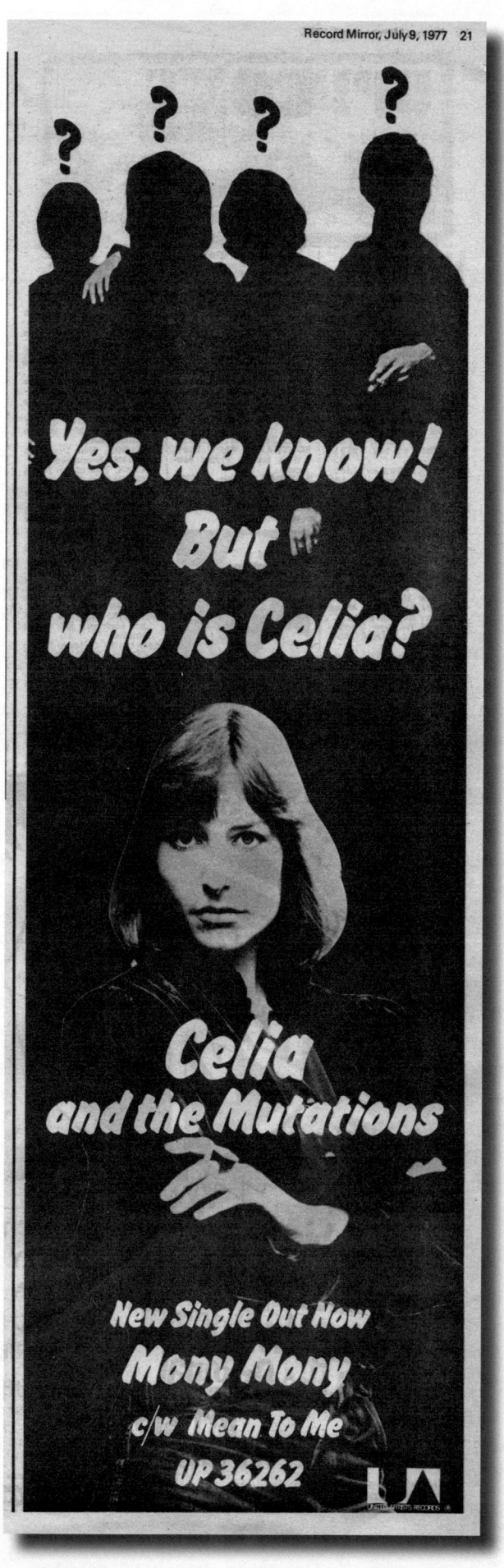

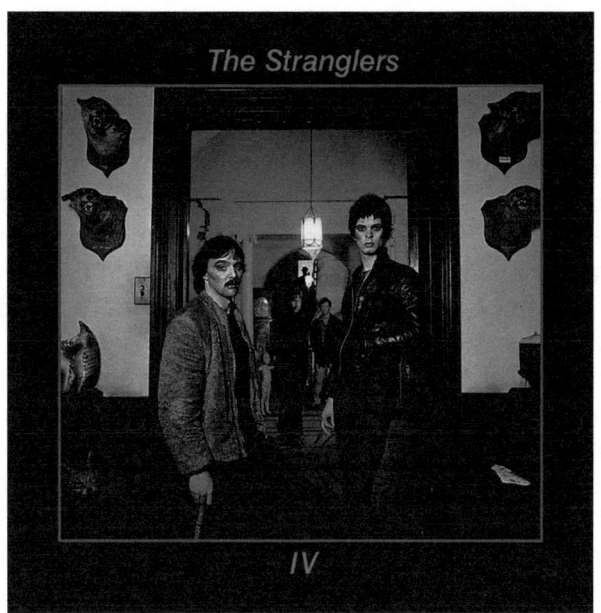

Rattus Norvegicus IV

In the early part of the New Year 1977 a group of four hungry for success musicians arrived in TW studios in Fulham. They had a long list of songs already finely honed and arranged from three years of touring. They had a major record deal and were chomping at the bit to kick off their recording career. Within a couple of weeks, they had produced one of the best and most influential debut albums of all time.

In the recording studio it was simply a matter of now getting them down on tape with the right sound and mix. A live concert debut album had been discussed and shows had even been recorded to possibly facilitate the idea. Thankfully the idea was dropped, and Martin Rushent and Alan Winstanley producer and engineer had the task of capturing that live sound but in the studio. Normally a producer would be expected to make suggestions about arrangements, song structure and a whole lot more but Rushent had little to do, in as the works were already complete. Any further suggestions would have been unnecessary tinkering and could have damaged the precious goods. Rushent was astute enough to realise this and got the band to basically play the songs live with a few overdubs when required.

Most of the songs were inspired by rock 'n' roll's traditional muse: touring, girlfriends and life on the streets. Set against the backdrop of the Britain's urban decay in the late seventies these high octane, musically complex songs with twisted social realism stories scored a bullseye with the country's disgruntled youth.

The taster for what was about to hit the public came in late January 1977 with the release of the single '(Get A) Grip (On Yourself)'. It stormed into the chart at number 44[1] but failed to progress further due to an 'error' by the chart compilers which took all the momentum out of a track that appeared destined to be pushing for the top 20.

The sales of the single were attributed to another band and the single was killed stone dead. This was an issue that was to hit the band again later in their career. 'Errors' by chart compliers BRMB were not uncommon to bands labelled punk rock the most famous incident being The Sex Pistols being denied the number one slot in June 1977 with their single 'God Save the Queen'. It has since been uncovered that this particular incident was not an accident but a deliberate plot. No wonder most new wave artists appeared paranoid.

The album was released in mid-April and this time there was no chart shenanigans and it smashed into the album charts at number 4. It was to stay in the charts for 34 weeks.[2] The chart placing was boasted by the release of a free 7 inch single with the first 10,000 copies. The tracks featured on the single were 'Choosey Susie' and 'Peasant in the Big Shitty (Live)'.

To keep momentum going another single was pulled from the album — the lyrically controversial 'Peaches'. In its album form the song would have received zero airplay. To get over this problem the record company released a radio edit of the single removing the offending words and replacing them with similar sounding words but less controversial.

Radio edit vinyl versions of 'Peaches' have become a much sort after collector's item for hard core fans and still today exchanges hands for big money. The notoriety of the 'Peaches' and its killer riff would have probably ensured a hit but to be absolutely sure the song was coupled with previously unreleased live favourite 'Go Buddy Go'. "Buddy" was given double a side status and received a lot of radio play. The tactics worked as the band got their first Top 10 single reaching number 8 and spending 14 weeks in the charts.[3] It also gained them their first appearance on national institution *Top of the Pops*.

The album garnered a rave review in music newspaper *Sounds*, journalist Chas de Whalley using the headline Hot Rattus (a pun on Frank Zappa's second solo album *Hot Rats*) and gave the album four stars out of five and perceptively commented 'Stranglers: there roots lie deep on the dark side of psychedelia.' De Whalley was a long-time champion of the band and one of the few music journalists to be on their side. He also in the first line of his review demolished the punk label 'I think the album will surprise a lot of people. After all (by chance, coincidence and a spot of media manipulation no less) The Stranglers have long been branded punks.'[4]

The Journalist's substantive point was that the band were wrongly labelled as punks and that people would be surprised at their technical excellence. The review goes on to talk about the Gothic nature of the music. He was meaning Gothic in its original sense not Goth the music genre which was a few years off being conceived but as we will see The Stranglers have a key if so far unrecognised role in its conception. The review also referenced The Doors as a legitimate influence on the band but as we know this comparison was misused and did become an inaccurate musical millstone round their neck.

So what is the album called? Some refer to it as Stranglers IV or IV due to that being on the front cover. To the harden fan it is just Rattus, but the official title is *Rattus Norvegicus IV*. The front cover and inside sleeve and back cover with its rodent at sunset are striking and iconic. The band in the cover photo are pictured win an interesting variety of sartorial choices. The colour black was not yet de rigour. They look like four desperate individuals who have run away to join a freak show circus. There is an element of danger and uncertainty when you appraise the band in the picture.

The setting for the photos was a curiously decorated house in Blackheath, London.[5] The backdrop is incredibly atmospheric and the lighting and the shadows giving it a genuine gothic feel. The way band line up in the photo with Cornwall and Black barely visible is odd and unsettling. It is hardly promoting the whole band, but it gives the impression of the band being outsiders and different from the norm, outside the rock mainstream and outside the punk elite. Greenfield and Burnel dominate the foreground. Burnel in makeup and leathers and Greenfield in his Afghan jacket and sporting a moustache, an incongruous pair looking for all the world like they are bouncers for a fetish club.

Then there is the man in black mannequin at the back. A prediction of what is to come perhaps? Had the band got their career that well planned they knew what future albums in four years would be about? Well, no it's a coincidence but with hindsight an unnerving one. However, the suggestion that it was all part of a plan has over the years has become common currency with fans and all added to the myth and mystic of the band.

The famous Stranglers name logo is also present for the second time, it had been used on the "Grip" single but in the album's case only on the back cover in another act of contrary mischief. From this point on it would nearly always take pride of place on the front of all subsequent albums.

The sales of the album confirmed what a hot property the band had become and as was the practice in those days the record company and the band's management sort to make hay whilst the sun shines. The result was a gruelling touring schedule and then back into the studio at the earliest opportunity to record a follow up and get it in the shops as quickly as possible.

The band had plenty of material ready but not enough for a full album so as well as touring *Rattus Norvegicus IV* to death they had to find time to write new material. In those days there were no two or three year plans round an album and tour like there are for name bands now. The business plan then was to get in the studio, bang out the songs, get it in the shops and tour like your life depended on it. Then six months later do the same thing all over again with new songs that are in the same style as the last album.

The model had been in operation since the dawn of rock 'n' roll and by the sixties had been perfected and was seen as the normal way to work a band. The record industry's thinking and fear was that rock acts were transient things and what sells today might not sell tomorrow, therefore squeeze every last drop out of an act as quickly as possible whilst the band are a hot property. Even The Beatles fell victim to this approach doing twelve albums in seven years. Despite The Beatles and other acts such as The Rolling Stones and Pink Floyd proving longevity was perfectly possible the industry by the late seventies had not taken this on board.

The Stranglers were the hot act at the beginning of 1977 and whether they liked it or not they were now part of this commercial machine. They might not have admitted at the time, but it must have in years to come taken a toll on the band in terms of health, both mental and physical and their creatively. Unlike all their peers from punk days the line-up of the band stayed the same until 1990 which was an amazing achievement given all the pressures they were under emotionally and commercially let alone the need to keep producing material.

So, in the summer of 1977 they duly returned to the studio less than three months after Rattus's release to finish the already half recorded follow up. The band's career was moving along at furious pace.

Sometimes

As an opener to an album and effectively an opener to a career (let's ignore '(Get A) Grip (On Yourself)' for a minute) you'd be pushed to find a song as challenging and vibrant. It's a dynamic entrance that delivers the band's musical and lyrical manifesto. It's pacey, melodic, and aggressive. Immediately grabbing the listener's attention. The keyboards and bass are most noticeable as they are high in the mix, but guitar and drums fight their corner and are critical to the overall sound. Then add in the controversial lyrical content and you most definitely have the listener's attention.

The gruff angry vocal delivery combined with the confrontational in your face attitude and the determination to expose an unsavoury and taboo subject gave the band a social realism that was to dominate their style for at least the first two albums. The tune itself makes it clear this wasn't *Sniffin' Glue's* famous 'learn three chords and now form a band' approach. With this opener The Stranglers were quite clearly in the building with their aggressive, brutal, beauty.

The band made the choice to ride the punk wave rather than protest or deny being part of the genre despite it being too simplistic a label to describe their music. Instead, they played up to the *News of the World* version of punk whenever they could. The next lazy label was the comparison to The Doors largely based on Chas De Whalley and others reviews who early on seemed to constantly reference the Doors.[6] These journalistic references centred on the organ sound used by both bands. It's as if no other band ever used a Hammond organ in the sixties and seventies! To be fair, the band were fans with Cornwall in particular being a huge fan of Doors guitarist Robbie Krieger.[7] The solo on 'Sometimes' does to these untutored ears echo Krieger's style but, as Cornwall would soon prove, he had a creative style of his own. It is true that both Jet Black and John Densmore began life as jazz drummers, something that effected their playing throughout their careers but that hardly signifies a strong link between the styles of both bands. One of the key, but not the sole differences between the two is the bass. The Doors were always shy about their use of bass guitar even though they used it throughout their career. The Stranglers embraced and championed the instrument often using it as a lead instrument to drive a song.

Cornwell's lyrics are controversial as they detail his response to discovering his girlfriend was cheating on him, his response was to slap her. His defence was that he was merely reflecting reality and documenting an event in his life. He wasn't condoning his actions but neither was he apologising. Further studying of the lyrics demonstrate that the vast majority of the words aren't gender specific it only becomes clear he is talking about hitting his girlfriend halfway into the song when he sings 'Beat you honey till you drop' To most people the depiction of an incident of domestic violence was lost and it was viewed as a celebration of casual violent behaviour that inhabited 1970s Britain. Fans had little idea it was a portrayal of domestic violence against women from the perpetrators point of view.

1977 saw football hooliganism high up on the social and political agenda and very much in the forefront of the national consciousness. Punk surged into the national consciousness and was associated with violence by the majority of the population. The band exploited this to gain them notoriety and attracted people seeking the thrill of violence. Whilst many interpreted the song as being about general 'aggro' and a call to storm the barricades, others of course spotted the references and labelled the band misogynists.

*****

The influence of Greenfield's Hohner Cembalet keyboard riff on the overall sound is immediately established with the opening riff. Greenfield used two other keyboards, the Hammond organ and the Mini Moog synth and it is the contrasting nature of these sounds were to play a central role in the overall sound, alongside the mid frequency aggressive sounding bass, the thinner, slightly distorted guitar and the tightly tuned, slightly jazzy drums.

Although this sound was something new to 1977, The actual music to their opening track on *Rattus Norvegicus IV* does not suggest any unconventional approach and, by and large, this a typical foot stomping pub rock song. But there are some small clues in the song that will point us from the outset of their musical canon to the musical complexities and originality to come.

The chords deployed are conventional throughout. The opening part of the song is based on repeating bass and keyboard riffs over one chord rather than on chordal patterns. The second section moves to a chord pattern which uses five chords, all of which belong to the six main chords for the key of the song. Vocal melodies are conventional with the shape often moving by step and the instrumental melodies are generally conventional but there is a moment of note in the main instrumental section halfway through the song at 2:26 where the keyboard plays two notes (F sharp and C sharp) that really clash with the guitar solo. This clashing of notes, known as dissonance, is to become a key musical feature of the band.

The structure of 'Sometimes' is relatively conventional. On other songs on *Rattus Norvegicus IV* the band played around with more complex structures, and this developed even more on subsequent albums. But there is an interesting moment on 'Sometimes' where the middle "You're way past your station" section that was first played at 1:20 – 1:32 and was eight bars long is then repeated at 3:03 - 3:27 and is now doubled in length and has two extra lines of lyrics. But it is not just a simple repeat. The vocal melody is repeated but the backing chords on the guitar, keyboards and bass are doubled in length, now being played for two bars each chord whereas in the 1:20 section each chord was only played for one bar.

The song is 4:53 long with less than one third of it containing vocals. To have well over three minutes of instrumental music points at the Prog rock influence, but the band were clearly presenting themselves as a chart band with the shorter 'Grip' and 'Peaches' being their first single releases. This combination of longer songs with substantial instrumental passages allied to shorter, more radio friendly songs were a feature that infused many of their albums. These instrumental passages in 'Sometimes' also carry some clues to the complexities that are to come.

Whilst the opening instrumental has a fairly conventional musical texture with the bass and the guitar playing a standard, repeating riff, there are the two different keyboard sounds playing the riff which are in harmony with each other which can be heard clearly when listening on headphones as the smoother organ sound on the lower harmony is panned to the left headphone whilst the Hohner Cembalet sound on the higher harmony is panned to the right headphone. This higher harmony is then played with two notes instead of one (creating a 3-part harmony) when the riff is repeated.

It is the instrumental section at 1:33 where other features create more complexity with regards to the texture of the song. The guitar plays a solo whilst the keyboards continue to play the riff in harmony as at the start. This layering of different melodies being played at the same time is to become a crucial feature of the band. And this notion develops apace at 2:23 where the keyboard breaks from the riff to start soloing. But the guitar carries on, so we now have two completely different solos at the same time, the guitar being lower in pitch with the keyboard being higher.

This instrumental section changes at 2:50 when the opening keyboard riff returns with both the right and left panned harmonies and the guitar plays another harmony of the same riff but with a few embellishments. So, we now have 4-part harmony of the riff.

Cornwell's solo incorporates cross rhythms at two minutes where he plays a motif that has a feel of 3 beats to the bar whereas the rest of the band are continuing their four beats to the bar. This was to become a rhythmic device that the band employed judiciously but with great effect.

Dave Greenfield's trademark keyboard rising and falling arpeggios were immediately unfurled in this opening song at the end of the main section and again during the middle section.

It will become apparent in future songs that each member of the band has a style of playing that is almost unique. In 'Sometimes' we see elements of this from the guitar and keyboards, whereas the drums and bass seem happy to bide their time for musical fireworks to come in subsequent songs on the album. The individuality of each member's style of playing will, over the course of the next two years, combine with complex effect to create a highly original sound.

Goodbye Toulouse

The frantic pace continues with the second track. The music is Cornwell's and the lyrics are courtesy of Burnel. However, it's Cornwell who sings it which is unusual for the band as normally the singer was whoever wrote the lyrics. The reason behind this decision was that the bass line was so frenetic Burnel couldn't play and sing at the same time. The song begins with an organ sound that initially suggests a magical moment and morphs into mimicking a siren and this announces a fast and furious instrumental assault that gives the impression the band are racing to the end of the song as fast as possible thus giving the impression of an emergency. Speed in what was considered punk music was de rigour, The Ramones were the kings of this technique, but this song wasn't a copy of the style of their New York peers, it was plainly something different and rather more complex.

The lyrics are based on a prophecy of Nostradamus one of which is supposed to predict the destruction of the city of Toulouse. The words reflect this jeopardy and have a clear apocalyptic feel as does the music. The title itself 'Goodbye Toulouse' means bidding farewell to the city because of Nostradamus's predicted act of God. However, this is rather simplistic deduction when looking at all the lyrics.

As we will see throughout this book The Stranglers lyrics are multi-layered and there is more than one interpretation to many songs numerous of which work on several different levels. In the last verse for instance Burnel introduces us to a woman: "Paula looked down on me from her high balcony, Toulouse". The idea of a woman and a balcony suggest Romeo and Juliet so potentially we are looking at Burnel's lover from the city of Toulouse. Romeo and Juliet also suggest tragedy of lovers but also the city in the title. Burnel knew the effect of what he was doing when making these references, he is toying with the listener. He goes onto say he will return someday which now suggests the city isn't going to be wiped from the earth and he is in actual fact saying a temporary goodbye to the city and his lover.

However, the apocalyptic lyrical themes of the song is backed up by the finishing keyboard effect which recreates the sound of an explosion and therefore the destruction of the titular city. So effectively the listener is confused but it's a brilliantly delicious confusion that Burnel and the band had chosen to make, they clearly want the listener to think and be creative in their interpretations and feelings about the band's songs.

*****

Musically, this is a different type of song to the opening track, and it displays more unconventional approaches. It is the bass now that drives the song with an urgent melodic, almost lead guitar style of playing that was to become such a crucial and much-loved part of the musical palette of the band. When the vocal starts, the bass continues to play its own melody of sorts, so we again have a sense of two different melodies being played at the same time. And as keyboards do not want to miss out on this melodic layering, when the main verse repeats at 0:32, a new organ melody appears. This song is therefore beginning the textural approach for what is to come a unique element in later albums with the multi-melodic layering.

The main vocal melody has a strong shape and could easily be adapted into a more ballad or even jazz style and the chorus 'Goodbye Toulouse' melody is a very simple rising stepwise melody that provides an effective foil to the verse.

The chords suggest an unconventionality that is reinforced by the relationship between the second and third chords which form the tritone, also known as the 'devil's interval' from the 1600s. Black Sabbath, masters of dark moods frequently employed this two-note relationship. which will be widely used by The Stranglers on future songs. Whilst the chords overall are essentially conventional, the relationship between those first three chords create an unsettling feel that chimes with the subject matter.

The drums play a snare on every beat and also have 'off beat' cymbals at times. These two features became a significant part of Jet Black's playing and often gave the listener an extra texture to cope with on top of the riffs on guitar, bass and keyboards.

Structurally, like its predecessor 'Sometimes', 'Goodbye Toulouse' has large sections of the middle of the song as instrumental which will become a key feature for the band. This enables the band to highlight the dual role that many of their earlier songs displayed: to support the subject matter with appropriate melodies, chords and so forth whilst adding a further dimension with instrumental sections that often moved away at tangents to the vocal sections. There seemed to be a deliberate attempt from the band to achieve parity in these two approaches, thus creating an original approach.

Texturally, the section at 1:22 is fascinating as it commences with the guitar playing a riff which is panned in the left headphone. The same riff is then overdubbed, panned in the right headphone but starting one bar later whilst the left panned solo continues, deploying a musical device the same as when singing Frere Jacques and this is called a canon. The bass and keyboards continue their melodic playing at the same time as these two guitars thus creating a rich mix of multi-melodic layering.

Another interesting musical feature of this song was the time signature. Most musicians of a certain rock vintage will know that the band's biggest hit, 'Golden Brown' has an unconventional time signature. But we will see many examples of the band experimenting with different beats in the bar and their first example of this was here at 1:15 - 1:22 where the 3/4 time signature of the rest of the song is interspersed with 2/4 time signatures.

The backing vocals sung in harmony in the chorus were to become a staple musical feature of the band and were also a key feature of the opening song, 'Sometimes'. The Punk bands were dismissing backing vocal harmonies as a 'Bohemian Rhapsody' type musical excess as they moved on the whole, towards a more direct single vocal with other vocals occasionally joining in but in unison, not in harmony. It is no surprise that these 'old men' were regarded very suspiciously by the punk elite when they were immediately introducing longer instrumentals, changes of time signature, dissonant clashing of notes, unconventional drumming, weird textures where different melodies were stacked up at the same time and now, vocal harmonies. And that punk defying list derives from just the first two songs on the album.

London Lady

The energy and pace doesn't let up as 'London Lady' storms out of the blocks led by Cornwell's now distinctive, distorted yet thin sounding guitar. The song had already appeared as the B-side to "Grip so although it's a very strong song it is a little surprising to find it on the album when the band had so many songs in their repertoire already recorded. This embarrassment of riches would be put to use on the second album, released just a few months later.

The story behind the lyrics is fascinating and has led to much debate. Myths, denials and serious 'put downs' surround the song. If we take the lyrics at face value, they are clearly about a woman Burnel had at least a one night stand with 'Why did you lay me? He clearly has a problem with the woman and is very disparaging about having sex with her comparing it to "making love to the Mersey tunnel with a sausage".

The clear implication here is that she is promiscuous with a long list of lovers in the past. There are other disparaging references to her with thinly veiled or not veiled at all comments about her age and looks. If this wasn't enough there is also a reference to trouble at the music venue Dingwalls in London again the clear implication is the titular woman was the cause of this incident.

Undoubtedly it is sexist with its judgment of a woman for her looks and sexual preferences. This isn't an interpretation in hindsight or a 21st Century 'Me to' view of the subject matter. The band were actually called out by the music press. So, what is the truth behind the tirade of insults directed at this lady? This is easier said than done. The events are surrounded by claims, counter claims, and a merging of several stories into one. Some say it's about a groupie who used to frequent Dingwalls. Others claiming it's about music journalist Caroline Coon. Coon tackles this on her website and whilst not directly admitting or denying the lyrics are about her, she doesn't mince her words about the song.

'In fact, the song is a woman-hating fantasy with lyrics indicative of what clinicians call small penis anxiety; and evidence of the sexism and misogyny that contaminates the male dominated music industry to this day'.[8]

The 'Dingwalls bullshit' could refer to Burnel's infamous fight with the Clash's Paul Simeone in 1976 at a Ramones gig at Dingwalls. The background being The Stranglers had got the prestigious slot of supporting the Ramones ahead of The Clash and the Sex Pistols This event appeared to be the pivotal point where the national music press turned against the band. Choosing instead to talk up the Clash and the Pistols and marginalise The Stranglers.

Coon was a member of that part of the music press and also in a relationship with Clash bass player Paul Simeone.[9] Whatever the truth it does demonstrates the rivalry in nascent punk scene.

Petty jealousies abounded and minor incidents became major apocryphal ones as the scene mushroomed. 'London Lady' recalls these events and by doing so adds fuel to the myth making fire. There is no doubt that The Stranglers in their early days were better than any other band at capturing and documented the early punk scene and the dark seedy side of London life. Many other groups were concerned with wider societal or international issues whilst the outsiders from Guilford reflected accurately their surroundings and the life they actually lived. Being the bad boys of punk, whatever the reality was publicity for the band and, of course, 'There is no such thing as bad publicity'. The band's later career emphatically challenged this age-old wisdom attributed to P T Barnum.

*****

Musically, this song was one of the closest moments on the album where the band displayed traits of a typical punk song with limited power chords, very prominent guitars and shouting, aggressive vocals with little discernible melody. It was also one of the least prominent keyboard inputs in a Strangler's song so the texture of the song, like the melody and chords, portrays a conventionality. The discordant guitar solo is typical of pub/punk rock and very much less typical of most of Cornwell's more melodic solos.

It is one of the bands shortest songs at 2:33 but giving a feeling of a helter-skelter of a musical experience due, in part, to some structural additions to the song with three sub sections adding to the restless power of the song – it keeps coming back in slightly different disconcerting guises to demand more of the listener than one might imagine.

Princess of the Streets

A change in style and pace after the frantic first three numbers with a traditional slow blues number. Allowing listeners to regain their breath after the high octane burst of the previous songs. Written and sung by Burnel about a former girlfriend, the legendary Choosey Susie. The bassist starts the song with the gruff growling but melodic bass riff.

Burnel was a lover of the blues and enjoyed using this musical style when writing as other songs in his cannon demonstrate but these tended to be up-tempo numbers e.g. 'Go Buddy Go'. This then is a rare example of the band writing a slow blues number – rare but not unique.

If you're looking for another slow blues, try the song 'Tits' on the B-side of the free 7-inch single with *Black and White* is the only other example of a Stranglers slow blues over the period covered by this book. It may appear strange that the band recorded a song in this style particularly in the febrile atmosphere of the 1977 music scene but remember they started out as a band playing their own material but also a great many cover versions to try and keep the punters happy. Many of those cover versions were popular standard blues numbers and simply a means to end by helping them to get more gigs. It is therefore no surprise that the blues would inform some of their song writing.

The lyrical tone is set immediately with the first line "She's gone and left me" perhaps the most used Blues trope in musical history. Burnel continues in the same vein throughout the song so the lyrics are as traditional twelve bar blues as one can get.

Potentially by using such a clichéd lyrical theme one could think the band were about to mock the genre but in reality, it's such a great song it acts as a tribute to the genre. The band play the blues straight reflecting their love of the genre. As in a lot of songs from this musical field the protagonist might love his lost woman, but he is not averse to blaming her for his strife.

Nor is Burnel afraid of insulting his beloved Choosey, referring to her as a 'piece of meat' as well as stating 'She's no lady'. The song added more fuel to the bonfire of misogyny the critics were building. Despite some of his choices of phrase Burnel clearly loves his muse and recognises she has the power in the relationship by being able to get him to cry and sigh. As with all good blues the lecherous side of the narrator is well articulated with the description of his lover's blue jeans leather jacket and high heels clothing that clearly excites the singer.

The title itself is interesting and again it follows a Blues tradition. 'Princess of the Street' to most people would conjure up an image of a prostitute, a fallen woman working as a sex worker which is a common theme in the blues tradition. In addition, in the mid-seventies CB radio had taken off and the slang for a sex worker was a 'pavement princess' these are two cultural items that could have fuelled the title.

Whether Burnel's muse fits into this bracket we don't know. However, using this as a title about his lost love is a back handed compliment with him only able to get the upper hand in the relationship when she is not there to defend herself. Burnel is metaphorically stabbing her in the back just as he accuses her of doing to him in the song. Using the term princess tells us whatever he says about the woman in the song he is devoted to her, and the term also happens to bestow a royal status upon her with the streets of London as her realm. The word street or streets also implies someone who tough and aware of the realities of life.

Burnel's writing style is a straightforward narrative which is a form of writing he has continued to adopt throughout his career. He also plays with the listener by keeping us guessing in terms of the meaning of the song title and uses direct images which can be shocking and tasteless to outrage the establishment and challenge the status quo of accepted morality.

It's another song that led to more misogynist accusations being laid at the band's door. These accusations may well appear to hold water but one look at the back catalogue of many blues and classic rock artists and you will find a litany of sexist songs that are well loved and part and parcel of mainstream culture and have faced little of the criticism The Stranglers have had to face. The Rolling Stones with 'Brown Sugar', The Beatles with 'I Saw Her Standing There' and Chuck Berry's 'Sweet Little Sixteen' all have highly questionable sentiments but are considered classics and part of our cultural norms. In addition, these songs are endlessly played on the radio, at wedding discos and by a plethora of covers bands. Moral equivalency may not be a defence but if The Stranglers get called out so should The Beatles and The Stones.

*****

After the musical hyperventilation of "London Lady, it is time to release the tension with the immediate slower, lighter texture and swing rhythm of 'Princess of the Streets'. The texture is bass only to start with, with less aggression in the sound to begin with, but there is still much prominence and bristling intent to the bass.

The vocal delivery was also completely different with a now discernible melody. This song is clearly rooted in blues with the bass employing the blues scale in the intro. The guitar also plays blues riffs whilst the keyboard has the trademark arpeggios but much slower than usual.

The drums also maintain a sparseness that was often employed and, once again, add a texture to the song where the rhythmic momentum is provided more by the keyboards in the first verse.

The vocal melody, guitar and keyboards do, once again, create a feeling of a multi-melodic texture as all three seem to be vying for melodic supremacy to some extent in the opening verse more so than would be the case for a typical blues band accompanying their singer. Prior to the vocals entering, the bass also displays melodic moments to compete with the guitar and keyboards. This probably would not be to the liking of traditional blues aficionados, but it does reinforce the unique textural approach of the band.

The shape of the melody has a typical blues feel and the rhythm of the melody follows a similar path to both 'Sometimes' and 'Goodbye Toulouse' where the verse sections display quicker notes, and the following sections display longer contrasting notes. The chords used are conventional for the style and the structure also has a conventionality but also follows on from the first two songs where instrumental sections play an important role in the song. For the guitar solo to be played twice is a reinforcement of this structural approach. The song benefits from this repetition and to finish the song with the guitar solo once again gives parity to the instrumental approach.

This guitar solo is, unlike in the previous song 'London Lady', another example of Cornwell's well-crafted melodic soloing first heard during 'Sometimes' and was to become a key feature of the band's sound. The use of backing vocals in the chorus "She's no la-dy" reinforces the trend that was present in the first two songs. So, although the song is a simple minor key blues style, the distinctive styles and sounds of each instrument allied to Burnel's more languid vocal, dreamy yet still with a slight menace, embed a typically Stranglers overall sound whilst creating a satisfying contrast not only to the previous song but also to side A's triumphal closer that is about come.

Hanging Around

A classic Stranglers song, and always in the set list. It was mooted as a possible single but with The *No More Heroes* album in the can so soon after *Rattus Norvegicus IV* it meant the idea was shelved. A great shame as it had huge chart potential and was a more obvious choice of single than 'Grip' or 'Peaches'.

Most of the lyrics are Cornwall's but the song is crowned by Burnel's crucial last verse that continues the series of images of London's night life seamy side, a world inhabited by colourful characters, misfits, and drug dealers. It perfectly illustrates the bands musicality and savvy street credibility. The start of the song was instantly recognisable from the iconic beats on the hi-hat which has become a signature moment for fans, something everyone recognises as the intro to a classic. Cornwall often used to tease the audience as they cheered in recognition stopping the song two beats in saying "How do you know what song it is from that?"

The lyrics are a brilliant observation that vividly capture the punk scene and related sub-cultures. There is a series of characters introduced to us as Cornwell paints a lurid picture of a nightclub entrance on a backstreet in London. There's an air of danger and sleaziness as the characters go about their business. The vignettes Cornwell paints encourages us to use our imagination to flesh out the life stories of the characters. "The big girl in the red dress", possibly a sex worker, is brassy, confident, and drunk on barley wine, a cheap but strong intoxicant. Close to her there are the tough hustlers trying to sell their drugs or maybe they're pimps trying to sell the pleasures of the flesh. The reality of who these characters and what they do doesn't matter it's an impressionistic view which actively encourages us as listeners to fill in the gaps.

In the second verse Cornwell brings Jesus into the scene and this was the first time he uses a religious reference in a song. Using religious imagery in songs was to become a trademark of his style.

The 'Christ' reference adds a surreal edge to the night scene being painted. The point being that if Christ was going to be anywhere in London in 1977, he was going to be on the Court Road with the lowlife, the poor, the prostitutes, and the criminals just like he was in the bible. We also have the suggestion that Christ partakes in the available narcotics as he is "High above the ground". An alternative interpretation is the word 'Christ' could be an exclamation or expletive about the scene being described. Again, the exact interpretation of this image doesn't matter as both work and stay within the spirit of the song.

The sense of menace and secrecy is captured effectively by the repeated phrase "Their eyes are on the ground." In other words don't catch anyone's eye as it might lead to a violent confrontation. Another favourite lyrical trick of Cornwell's used here is to slightly alter an established saying to subtly change its meaning or emphasis.

The "monkey on his shoulder" line is a minor alteration to the saying 'Monkey on your back'. The meaning is still basically the same i.e., the person has a difficult, possibly insoluble problem. By being on his shoulder the problem appears more obvious and immediate to observers. It adds to the dark brooding scene he has already created. The final verse is Burnel's, Cornwell was struggling with an additional lyric, so the bass player took the vibe of the song and sketched out a scene of the secret gay and leather scene at The Coleheme pub he had witnessed. It fits the rest of the song perfectly and Burnel elaborated on the verse in an interview, saying punters travel by bus with their leather gear in rucksacks so as not to reveal their secret passion.[10]

The completion of the song with the last verse also importantly demonstrated the dynamism and almost telepathic nature of the writing partnership between the two front men at this time in their career. This song remains a firm favourite of the fans and the band can't get off stage without playing it. Everyone likes a good singalong, and the simplicity of this song combines that as well as combining the four disparate instrumental sounds to stunning effect.

*****

The intro lets each sound enter one by one, first the drums with that simple hi-hat, followed by the organ chord played twice. This chord is held for a precise amount of time, not staccato but with a slight gap before the next time it is played. The guitar then enters with the now established thinly distorted sound followed by the (also established) contrasting aggressive sound of the bass.

This song has limited melodic shape as the verses are more spoken than sung and the chorus has a simple narrow range of notes. Chordally the song is also conventional, and the texture is, overall, unchanging with a typically conventional drum pattern. But Cornwall's delivery, the memorable hook line, reinforced by the backing vocals and the perfect union of the four disparate sounds creates an indelible impression.

There are several moments that stray from the overall conventionality and reinforce the strength of the song. Although the drum pattern is conventional, one can't keep the jazz influenced Jet Black down for long and the instrumental break at 0:58 to take us into the chorus with his snare drum dominated fills is typical of his multifaceted playing. This short instrumental section also serves the purpose to transition us seamlessly into a new key for the chorus which provides a contrast due to the sung vocals and the vocal harmonies.

Greenfield's established arpeggio runs are also present here and are becoming an important yet consistent textural contrast between sections whenever they are used. The subtle transition back to the original key for the next verse is an early example that reinforces the bands' command of their ability to use key changes as an important compositional tool when providing contrasting sections. Cornwell's vocal line here "One of them comes closer" is spoken with slightly more urgency, personifying Cornwell's restless and edgy mood.

After the second chorus the guitar solo commences at 2:37. This important section is, once again, defining the band as songwriters who give equal weighting to the instrumental sections as they do to the vocal sections and probably explains to some extent why they gave songwriting credits for every song to the entire band. As will be evident in their later albums, the songs often became the domain of one songwriter, but in these early songs, the prominence of the instrumental sections and the overall sound created by the four disparate instrumentalists reinforced their 'all for one' approach.

The instrumental section here involves a classic interplay where the keyboards imitate the guitar four beats after the guitar, rather like the musical canon 'Frere Jacques' moment in 'Goodbye Toulouse' but the imitation is only short lived, and the two instruments then develop their own different solos at the same time. This idea (repeated every four bars) of starting with a clear link then moving away is fascinating and, of course, is becoming a trademark multi-melodic layering textural approach.

For the second half of this instrumental section, the guitar and keyboards have no link and undertake their own completely different solos and, once again, this seems to work effortlessly. Why does Cornwell play a low F# at 3:10 and 3:17 and Greenfield gives him just that second of space for us to hear the low resonance on its own? Simple, slightly clashing, yet beautiful. As the instrumental enters its final stage, Greenfield and Cornwell play off each other, both flying around in swirling movements, with the contrast between Cornwell's edgy yet thinly distorted guitar and Greenfield's waspish Cembalet sound also becoming a cornerstone of the holistic band sound.

The ending to the song sees Greenfield and Cornwell play a cross rhythmed riff, where their triplets go against the normal straight four beat rhythms of the drums and bass until the last time when they also join in to unify the rhythm. But when the final chord is struck, Black plays a very subtle jazz influenced low tom drum roll which seems to capture a moment — the song feels live and powerful yet Black is disdainfully hanging around. The holistic effect of the simplicity of the song unified by the four disparate sounds and the extra instrumental jewels provides a clear highlight for the album.

Peaches

This was the first Stranglers song to enter the public consciousness and for many fans it was their entry point into the band. People were excited almost intoxicated on hearing the song for the first time because it so unusual. The jerky, slowly unsettling and dangerous sounds did not sound like any kind of popular music including the new sound of punk. The listening experience was also enhanced by band already being known, even at this point in their career as rebels kicking against the establishment. They clearly didn't care what people thought and releasing this song as a single cemented that stance.

The band gave the public a stark choice and positively dared people to vilify and hate them or take a risk and embrace them on a new, strange, and exciting musical journey. The latter won but for many fans their first exposure to the song was via the expletive deleted radio edit. However, the sound of Cornwell's lecherous growl still made its point and combined with Burnel's titanic bass riff made the track compellingly addictive.

The song was written after Cornwell and Burnel attended a reggae sound system party. They lent the organisers the band's PA and took the opportunity to explore the sights, sounds and hospitality associated with reggae. They returned to their abode early in morning and inspired by what they had experienced, wrote the song in a couple of hours.[11]

Cornwell's verse vocals are entirely spoken albeit in a lascivious crowing tone. Only in the chorus refrain do we find anything like a melody. Some commentators have suggested because the lyrics are spoken it means that the song is a sort of proto rap, but this feels like a bridge too far in terms of a concept. There are, however, later tracks in the band's career where this idea is more valid e.g. Just Like 'Nothing on Earth' and parts of 'Nuclear Device'. What is clear though is that it was a very unusual song to have a hit single with.

The grimy voyeuristic and lecherous nature of the lyrics give an added cutting edge to the song. Use of words like clitoris and phrases like "well what a bummer" enhanced their rebellious, contrary credentials. The lyrics were obviously tongue in cheek and meant to be funny in a 'Carry on at the Beach' or an aural representation of saucy seaside postcards.

It wasn't a threat to western civilisation but instead it was a cheeky amusing take on that age old male hobby of girl watching intended to bring a smile and sense of recognition to peoples' faces and wind up any prudes. The band argued they were only reflecting an accepted form of behaviour in wider society. Cornwell's scat singing at the end where his voice makes a lecherous sound perhaps akin to someone engaged in a sexual act and about to orgasm is a riotous end to this unconventional hit single. This is the song that introduced the band to a wider public not all of whom were fans and who were shocked and horrified by the language and attitude.

As well as crossing over culturally because of its notoriety it crosses boundaries in other ways. The reggae vibe of the song is a confirmation of the punky reggae alliance that existed in the late seventies and proves the band were genuinely part of this scene and its influence despite being ostracised by punk royalty and its press lackeys. Over the years the song has become embedded in mainstream culture being used numerous times on TV pieces about beaches and most notably as the theme for a BBC2 Keith Floyd cooking programme *Floyd on Food* in the eighties and nineties.

Floyd was actually a huge fan of The Stranglers and insisted their music was used for his programmes. The riff that drives the song is probably the most recognisable riff in the band's back catalogue and this recognition helped to propel their career forward. However, at the same time it is a curse as this fun, crude moment has become inextricably linked to the group and meant those with only a passing interest in the band or music general thought it represented completely their musical style. Those who did scratch below the surface of 'Peaches' were to be rewarded with growing musical and lyrical complexity as the albums progressed.

The song was released as a single following the release of the album a few weeks earlier. It was a huge hit reaching No.8 and helped provided further sales to the already successful album.[12] Being such a big hit was quite an achievement given the controversial lyrics, the radio edit mix and a song that actually defies conventional song structure. A clever ruse by the band/record company to ensure they had a hit the single was to make the release a double A-side coupling 'Peaches' with the live favourite 'Go Buddy Go'.

*****

Whilst the memorable bass line allied to the vocals and sparse guitar, keyboards and drums gave a memorable overall sound, one can argue that 'Peaches' is not one of the strongest songs from the album.

It is a riff-based song with no real chords and is essentially very simple. The melody of the main riff is based on a typical blues scale, but it is the rhythm of this melody with its use of rests/gaps that provides the memorability. This melody is first played by the bass and after ten seconds, most of the melodic contribution to the song has been exposed as the second half of the riff becomes the main vocal hook line and the only part of the song that is sung. The texture of the song is very simple with the prominent bass riff also being played with the same notes in unison on both guitar and suitably brooding organ sound throughout. A crucial addition to this sparse texture is the two quick guitar chords, the second being a 'hammer on' and they are repeated almost throughout the song. The structure is also very conventional thus proving that hit singles are often very formulaic in terms of melody, chords, structure and texture. What makes many hits stand out is the indefinable notion of the distinctive overall sound, often with a catchy hook line melody, and this was certainly the case with 'Peaches'.

There are some less noticeable musical moments worthy of consideration. The very first drum fill that we hear just before the main beat where there are six snare drumbeats. The first four snares, however, are squashed into one beat thus creating a cross rhythm with the rest of the song which has a swing rhythm of three beats into one. This cross rhythmic fill is repeated at various points of the song and is another example of Black's unconventional and jazz influenced approach.

The consistency of the sparse texture provides the ideal backdrop for Cornwell's typically lairy spoken voice apart from the main "Walking on the beaches" sung phrase which copies the bass part. Another interesting musical moment is when Cornwell says, "the whole summer" and the first two notes of the three-note riff being played in unison by the bass, guitar and organ form the tritone/Devil's interval that was first heard in 'Goodbye Toulouse'. The jarring relationship of the three notes here is repeated but on lower notes and adds to the rather undesirable, menacing mood.

The slightly disturbing mood is enhanced by the spoken backing vocals (high and low) which keep popping up throughout the song, and the choice of organ sound for the solo which continues underneath the spoken "Down on the beaches" line with the continuing backing vocals. This is followed by the rather hilarious "Hmmm, hmmm" vocals and the return of the tritone riff. The ending sees the main riff repeated with the guitar playing a harmony on top of it for the only time in the song then some finger clicks, the cross rhythmed snare fill and a final emphatic chord to complete one of the simplest musical arrangements that the band undertook. But this simplicity supports the quirky yet coarse, voyeuristic nature of the song which clearly appealed to the 1977 chart buying public.

(Get A) Grip (On Yourself)

Having opened side two with the lewd laid back holiday groove of 'Peaches', normal service is resumed with the punchy pacey '(Get A) Grip (On Yourself)'. Led by a memorable keyboard melody and driving bass line. This is the song that launched the band's recording career being the band's first single a few months before *Rattus Norvegicus IV* was released and was therefore for many fans their introduction to the group. Notable also for the use of saxophone which the band were to use occasionally on individual tracks up until fully embracing a brass section on the *Aural Sculpture* album. It was remixed and released as a single in 1989 to support the *Singles (U.A. Years)* compilation. For this release the song was known as 'Grip '89 (Get A) Grip (On Yourself)' and actually surpassed the chart performance of the original by hitting No.33 in the Top Forty.[13]

Lyrically this is familiar rock 'n' roll territory, a tale of life on the road. Cornwell opines about the downside of life on tour particularly the poverty but keeps admonishing himself for these complaints with the repeated refrain "Just get a grip on yourself" urging himself get on with enjoying this way of life.

The first verse refers to what would be his preferred mode of transport, the Morry Thou or Morris Thousand. A car the singer wants to use as a tour vehicle but can't afford. In verse two, one might think Cornwell could be unintentionally predicting his later run in with the law when he talks about a two way stretch inside. It could also be a reference to one of Cornwell's heroes Peter Sellers who made a movie in 1960 called *Two Way Stretch*. In reality he is suggesting rock 'n' roll is a kind of prison sentence that has to be endured.

The third verse carries on the prison motif which has been a common theme in rock music since Jerry Lee Lewis and Elvis and before that with the blues. Crime and rock music have been familiar bedfellows over the years, from 'Jailhouse Rock' to 'I Fought the Law' to 'Jailbreak' – the list of songs is endless. Cornwell is more than happy to add his own two penn'orth to this traditional rock music theme.

The third verse also introduces us to another familiar Stranglers lyrical obsession for the first time, namely aliens. At the same time, he adds an even more surreal edge to the image suggesting the extra-terrestrial should play some rock guitar. The alien image can be interpreted as people who find the band's music alien and distasteful or the image could equally be the result of a vivid imagination inspired by an acid trip or just Cornwell's love of the surreal. Whatever Cornwell originally meant; all interpretations seem to work here. The message to the 'alien' is just relax and enjoy the music.

*****

Many musical elements that will come familiar throughout the bands career are present here: The arpeggio keyboard, the driving growling busy melodic bass, the galloping drums, the thin metallic sheen of largely rhythm guitar, and backing vocals.

In addition, there is the recurring sax refrain courtesy of Eric Clarke. Another unexpected timbre is Greenfield's heavy otherworldly sounding synth break later in the song and these low rasping Mini Moog sounds were to become commonplace and add depth and variety to the array of synth sounds whilst complimenting Burnel's more mid-range frequency bass.

The dichotomy of the band being seen as a punk band but displaying many musical features that are alien to the genre are present here. The main opening riff is on a keyboard sound that would not be seen as typically Punk and then the guitar is very low in the mix as the keyboards, bass and drums are all much more prominent. The use of backing vocal 'Uhhs' (rather than Ahhs) and the use of a saxophone are further anomalies whereas Cornwell spits out the mainly spoken vocal in a more punk fashion.

The main feature of the overall sound is the keyboard arpeggios which are present for a large part of the song, and are of the two different arpeggio parts, both running up and down but slightly different, one panned to the right headphone/speaker, and the other panned to the left. This provides a chordal approach to the song in contrast to the previous track, 'Peaches'.

The bass throughout veers between holding root notes and departing onto trademark florid 'walking bass' runs as if Burnel is straining at the leash, for example at the first chorus when Cornwell sings "But the money's no good" and Burnel immediately answers with a vibrant walking bass moment. This agitated bass playing becomes even more apparent when Burnel is forced to play a pedal point (holding the same note whilst the chords on guitar and keyboards change) during the vocal Uhhs apart from a brief glorious moment of chromaticism at the end of the first and third phrases.

After four repeating Uhh phrases, it is all too much for him to hold any longer and he departs into a manic walking bass whilst the keyboard plays an equally frantic riff based solo, thus both instruments are driving on with constant quavers at the same time. This is another example of where the multi-melodic layering texture is beginning to take hold in many of their songs, especially during the instrumentals. This will shift during the third and fourth albums to being a regular feature during the vocal sections as well.

After the vocal line "Just get a grip on yourself" in the second chorus, the keyboard plays the riff in harmony, a typically trademark moment. Another interesting moment is when the "Uhhs" are sung to the melody of the opening keyboard riff, but the chords have now changed as has the key of the music from G to D, a clever subtle change and another early example of the bands' innovative approach to use of chords and key changes.

The low rasping keyboard section is followed by a slightly different higher keyboard riff (at 2:15) on the original sound) which creates a cross rhythm (or polyrhythm) with the rest of the music where Greenfield is playing in threes (triplets) whilst the rest of the band is maintaining the standard four beat pattern.

The song structure is typical of most other songs on the album where the instrumental sections are as crucial to the song as the vocal sections. Nearly two thirds of the song is instrumental assuming one regards the vocal Uhhs as more of a texture than a main vocal and, considering that this was the band's first single release, the intent to place both instrumental and vocal sections on equal footing is clear.

The end section sees more frenetic activity from all three instruments, the bass plays the frantic walking bass again, but the keyboard becomes more rhythmically chordal and the guitar, with altered chords, becomes more prominent. The drums, meanwhile, have stayed resolutely the same throughout the song, with the bass and snare on every beat, a favourite Jet Black rhythm.

The final held chord just moves quietly away on the fade out from the main chord on both bass and guitar, giving a slightly more relaxed final moment than the rest of the song demanded. Whilst 'Grip' has a constant driving rhythm, and prominently pounding bass and arpeggio keyboards allied to the growling vocal delivery, there is a melodious feel to the music at times reinforced by the backing vocals and saxophone, and it is the combination of these different elements that make this a highlight of the album as well as further establishing the band's trademark original overall sound.

Ugly

A very unusual song that challenges conventional song-writing rules and pushes the bounds of taste and morality. The music is wild, and the lyrics are delivered in places in a way that defies punctuation and syntax conventions making it essentially a stream of consciousness. The words themselves are controversial featuring drug use, murder, misogyny, and racism. Given the subject matter and the unhinged music the closest musical reference to any other song is the Velvet Underground's 'Sister Ray'.

Like 'Sister Ray' the song has a great dumb riff to pull you in and then as Cornwell describes the music "was very much freeform in the middle."[14] The Velvets took seventeen minutes to make their point The Stranglers just over four minutes to create the same effect!

The song works on several levels and was initially a fans' favourite probably because it appeared to personify punk with its shock value through the use of bad language, questionable subject matter, simple riffs and shouted vocals.

It is an example of the band using what was considered a punk style and attitude to further their cause with a clone of a punk song. The lyrics are a stream of consciousness, an internal conversation featuring intrusive thoughts being vocalised. Controversial ideas and thoughts materialise in the human mind all the time and are not usually articulated for fear of causing offence and moral outrage.

In this instance they are actually articulated, and the thoughts are shocking to the listener. To appreciate the thinking behind the song the listener needs to imagine vocalising every thought they ever had and then contemplate the chaos, astonishment and shock such thoughts would actually cause when heard by other people. If as a listener one is able to do this one can appreciate the purpose of song and the meaning of the lyrics in the correct context. Burnel's vocal delivery is effectively mimicking a person with Tourette's syndrome.

Lyrically the song starts with Burnel referencing the poem *Ozymandias* by Shelley. The main thrust of that poem is the decline of great rulers, who over time have become obscure nonentities however great they once were. Perhaps Burnel is musing on and predicting what the band's fate will be in later years.

At the start of the song the lyrics are sung in what can only be described a clumsy meter with Burnel using the ugliest sounding voice imaginable. This combination makes the understanding or clearly hearing the words very difficult, but it is possible. However later in the song Burnel drops any traditional phrasing and punctuation making the interpretation much more difficult.

If one was to look at the lyrics unpunctuated, each individual would make their own personal sense and meaning from them. This is simply because it is habit and logically to try and punctuate a collection of words to find a meaning. Each person would produce different meanings and language nuances. When Burnel wrote the lyrics he effectively produced a series of random thoughts and words and then with his vocal delivery he created his own stream of consciousness.

After the oblique Shelley reference at the start which will have confused many the lyrics start to get a little more conventional and comprehensible even though Burnel's raucous vocal and odd phrasing masks the understanding. We learn he has had sex with a woman. He then totally shocks the listener by singing 'I guess I shouldn't have Strangled her to death' – to most people a shocking random misogynist image. However, given his Shelley reference in the first line it's a reference to another great English poet the dramatic monologist Robert Browning who in his poem *Porphyria's Lover* wanted to preserve his lover's beauty in the dawn light by strangling her to death.

Burnel goes onto describe having his drink spiked with LSD/acid but then goes on a free form though process turning the LSD/acid into sulphuric acid. Then he jumps to another random thought about a woman having acne and we finally get to the word ugly. The narrator at first expresses sympathy for 'ugly' people. But the song lyric then switches again to say that only the rich are good looking but that's only because they are wealthy rather than ascetically good looking. As the listener digests this and starts to think these statements are offensive and subjective Burnel is a head of the game shouting "Don't tell me aesthetics are subjective". As if he has read or predicted the listener's thoughts.

Having offended women, the singer then lashes out at Jews with a historical anti-Semitic stereotype by overtly referring to all Jews as being moneyed. It's a clumsy lazy reference but fits in with the idea that if one actually articulates verbally intrusive, stream of consciousness thoughts they can be highly offensive.

Finally, we go into the off the wall musical and lyrical chant 'Muscle. Power'. These are perhaps the two things Burnel doesn't think of as ugly because they are about physical strength and are the main virtues of his beloved karate.

To many commentators it was a nasty song with little merit and just confirmed to a large part of the music press that the band were foul-mouthed yobs with no respect for women or society. In some ways, this might have been alleged to be true but to judge the song purely at this level is to again miss the point.

The references to tripping in the lyrics give us the clue that the protagonist, Burnel is hallucinating and expressing his trip experience with the song. Not all LSD-induced hazes were beautiful technicoloured dreams popularised by hippies in the sixties. This was the late 1970s and life was tough, dirty, and confrontational and there were a lot of people having bad acid trips famously Fleetwood Mac's Peter Green and Pink Floyd's Syd Barrett succumbing to long term mental health issues exasperated by bad LSD experiences.

'Ugly' works on so many levels but on a superficial level it's what the moral majority might define as punk, fast, full of bad language and what the *Daily Mail* would deem, immoral and amoral sentiments. Add into that the obvious nihilism of the song and it confirms the establishment's view that this subculture is public enemy No.1. We should also never forget there is also a huge amount of humour behind the lyrics, the vocal delivery, and the music. The song is entitled 'Ugly' and those three elements of the song are all ugly. What could be funnier than that? Not everyone got the joke.

*****

Musically, this song is, along with 'London Lady', the closest the band came to a true punk sound on their debut album. Burnel's aggressive vocal certainly creates an imposing, anarchic atmosphere. However, scratching below the vocals, an analysis of the music points to some interesting moments that were to be developed and honed on the following three albums with highly creative results.

Primarily, there is an ambiguity of key to the song overall. Whilst the first, main section seems reasonably clearly in the key of 'B' the next (instrumental) section has moved into another key. We return to the original section and key but then the final section moves into a third different key and this section rather abruptly finishes the song. The overall effect is one of instability which, of course, dovetails with the disturbed lyrics and vocal delivery.

The band were to go on to further experiment with sudden destabilising key changes. This, of course, does not lend itself to commercial chart success so the band's hit singles tend to be more predictable in their choice of key relationships. The most significant musical moments in 'Ugly' come in the two instrumental sections. The first one at 1:02 has the bass repeating two notes, whilst the guitar and keyboard play chords to fit those two notes (E and D) but they immediately move to other chords thus challenging the listener with a more clashing, dissonant moment.

After another shouted vocal phrase, the challenge to the listener is further exacerbated by, firstly, the bass, freed from the leash, embarking on a fast-moving embellished bass line and then a low rasping keyboard solo that arrives on top of this bass line and the repeating chords. As if that wasn't enough, Greenfield even points to the future concepts by adding some otherworldly spooky sounds to the already hectic mix. This is messily chaotic but, in the context of what is to come, a challenge that the growing band's legion of followers were going to accept and revel in over the next three albums.

The ending section also has links to the section at 1:02 as the bass keeps repeating two notes but the guitar and keyboard playing those two notes and then two different notes thus following a similar idea to the first instrumental. There is also a frantic keyboard riff to further place us on edge whilst the vocals repeat "Muscle. Power" before the song comes to a sudden end. Black's drumming throughout didn't need many of his idiosyncratic fill-like rhythms, he maintained a conventional pattern whilst the music around him exploded into chaos.

The song structure has a chaotic whole, largely due to the instrumental sections, once again reinforcing the importance of instrumental sections to the overall effect of the song. The texture was also clearly pointing towards the multi-melodic layering approach in these sections and the use of fluidity of key and subsequent clashing effects of the juxtaposition of the chords was also pointing the way forward.

Down in the Sewer
(a) Falling (b) Down in the Sewer (c) Trying to get out again (d) Rats Rally

At nearly eight minutes with four distinct movements segueing into each other, creating anticipation, tension and release it is the band's first magnum opus. Sound effects are critical to the atmosphere and tone from the fading cry of the falling narrator to the metallic synth sound for the rats' sharp teeth and their eerie squeaking as they rally to the final emptying of the sewer with a giant burping plug hole sound. The track itself is a highly effective end to the album which is enhanced by this inspired sound effect at the end to the song. The belch of the plug hole is so final that there is nothing more that can follow.

Lyrically it is rooted in sci-fi horror and was influenced by James Herbert's horror novel *The Rats*. The parallels between the novel, author, song, and the band are stark. Herbert's novel is set in a decaying capital city and suburbs a theme that the band constantly reflected in their songs. Cornwell muses about creating a new breed of 'survivor' rats and the premise of Herbert's book is very similar, a new breed of deadly super rat shaped by experimentation. Herbert, like the band, suffered harsh criticism and strong public outrage for his graphic descriptions of violence and death.

Having been introduced to the rat by the album's title and cover artwork on the final track the listener at last gets a song about rats to complete the concept. The rat of course has become synonymous with the band ever since. The sewer is a metaphor for the city and, in particular, London. Cornwell is clearly using the rats as a symbol for the darker, less savoury side of life.

Rats and rat imagery have a long tradition of terror in literature being Winston Smith's nemesis in room 101 in Orwell's *1984* and another example being the giant rats that were a centrepiece of a classic episode of the seminal BBC series *Doomwatch* in 1970. There has been something of a historical obsession with rats in Britain which can be back hundreds of years to the plague and Black Death.

The band's bond with the brown rodents was now sealed. Rats like the band are viewed by the majority as unwelcome outsiders. Seen as vermin and facing extermination wherever they inhabit and many in 1977 wished for the band perhaps not to be exterminated but to be kept as outsiders and not granted any kind of acceptance. It is no coincidence given its symbolism that the band have chosen to keep the rat motif as part of the band's image.

*****

Musically, a fascinating end to their debut album. It is nearly eight minutes long and about six and a half minutes of it is instrumental with the vocal sections being spoken. Although the band divided the song up into four parts, the structure gives the listener lengthy instrumental sections that meander into each other to give an extended experience. The middle spoken vocal section has considerable repetition of the main riff, but the flanking instrumental sections combine the various riffs to great effect. The structure is approximately two minutes of various riffs followed by one and a half minutes of spoken vocal, followed by one minute of an organ solo, one minute of repeats of the original riffs and the two minutes of an ending with new ideas. There is an appropriate balance of repetition, development, and new material to this structure within a framework more akin to a final movement of a classical symphony rather than a typical Verse/Chorus pop song.

This structure was not as influential as other songs from the album in developing their overall style as it did not initiate other similar eight-minute songs, the closest probably being 'Toiler on the Sea' at five and a half minutes. But it did help to establish the band as serious instrumentalists. The song, therefore, was another example from the album of the band having a less than secure relationship with punk from a musical point of view. The links are more with Prog rock here as the punk movement embodied a move away from the instrumental and soloing excesses of the Prog rock bands of the seventies.

This was also one of the principal songs that gave rise to the notion that Dave Greenfield was heavily influenced by Ray Manzarek of The Doors: a lazy comparison as it seems to be based mainly on the organ sound and the fact that there were some long solos with occasional arpeggios. The

Doors comparison has some merit in two other songs due to The Stranglers using similar guitar, organ and drum sounds and they were the two hit single cover versions of 'Walk on By' and '96 Tears'.

Greenfield and Manzarek had different styles and Greenfield used the sounds of his three keyboards in almost equal measure whereas Manzarek was essentially organ based. Greenfield had stated that he was influenced by Jon Lord (Deep Purple) and Rick Wakeman (Yes) but there is little to suggest that he based his style on anyone in particular although Greenfield had marvelled at Jon Lord's heavy Hammond organ sound.

There is a sense of uniqueness in all these great keyboard players and Greenfield's ability to produce memorable riff after riff, as well as contributing to composing many chordally complex and creative songs (one of which, 'Golden Brown', won an Ivor Novello award) within the overall sound of a unique band that were pushing the boundaries of creativity comfortably places him amongst this pantheon. His frequent use of clashing/ dissonance was a further example of his individual style.

The song itself also established the band's preference in the first half of their career of each album possessing some longer songs with extended instrumental sections, and the solos were more melodic rather than aiming to be virtuosic as was the case with many prog rock songs. 'Sewer' gives us one of Cornwell's most memorable guitar riffs at 0:39 that would be more at home amongst Hank Marvin and The Shadows melodiousness than the punk bands. There is a case for arguing that the comparison with The Doors ought to focus more on the influence of Doors guitarist Robby Krieger on Cornwell. Nevertheless, the guitar and organ sounds do give the song something of a sixties feel.

The song bursts into life right from the start with no atmospheric preamble. The main riff after ten seconds played in unison on bass and keyboard is catchy in its blues style, but we are soon introduced to a complex moment at thirty-one seconds where a simple three-note riff is played upwards by the keyboards and, at the same time, downwards by the bass with the guitar joining in on other notes. Furthermore, because it is a three-note riff, it is an early example of the band deploying a rhythmic displacement where, although the drums continue to suggest four beats in the bar, the other instruments are, at the same time, suggesting three beats in the bar for these few seconds. The band experimented more and more with rhythmic and time signature complexities in the coming albums. A keyboard solo of just over a minute was the longest actual solo (as opposed to riff-based sections) from the band until their hit single cover of 'Walk on By'.

It is the ending of the song that is, perhaps, the most memorable moment as the band embarks upon a series of different chord sequences that evoke images of Clint Eastwood riding into a gun battle due to the chords that the band deploy and, of course, that sixties sounding organ. The drums using the galloping snare also evoke sixties images in a similar style to '7 And 7 Is' by the band Love. The speeding up of the tempo adds to the feeling of adventure and brings the song to a close.

The chords were generally conventional, but the sense of movement is exacerbated by some less conventional moments, for example at 1:06 where the devil's interval tritone is again deployed and when this is repeated at 1:36 it immediately moves to a new keyboard riff that suggests a change of key, but the chord pattern skilfully moves back a few bars later with Burnel's bludgeoning bass riff. The change from the minor key to the major at 6:47 is another such example of subtle shifts. The fact that the song never changes key from B minor until this change to B major is testament to the ability of the band to maintain interest through a plethora of contrasting riffs rather than having to move key to sustain interest. The texture of the song also stays reasonably constant throughout, similar to the chords and keys in that the changes are subtle. The quality of the riffs and the instrumental prowess emphatically draws the album to a close.

Musical Summary

Rattus Norvegicus IV was the beginning of the fascinating journey and the sound that exploded from it was different to anything else in 1977 and, indeed, since. 'Peaches' was their biggest hit from the album, but it was their most simple song in terms of the texture, chords and melody. But it was that thunderous mid frequency picked bass sound very high in the mix that immediately caught the ear for the 1977 record buying public and there was no let up from the bass throughout the album.

The drums were more studious with controlled fills and the guitar was thinner sounding overall to a lot of harder rock or punk bands. But it was the keyboards that ultimately took the band to a different sonic level than any other band at the time. Greenfield's three-pronged armoury of the Hohner Cembalet, the Hammond organ and the Mini Moog synth provided many contrasting sounds/timbres, often within the same song.

The four band members' distinct styles of playing created a unique sound and whilst the drums and guitar did not command as much attention, they are crucial to that overall sound. Cornwell's style was clearly more melodic than thrashing out standard distorted chords. His solos were already melodically strong with 'Sometimes', 'Princess of the Streets' and 'Down in the Sewer' whereas the more riff driven solos in 'Goodbye Toulouse' and 'Hanging Around' created the multi-melodic layering approach with Greenfield.

There were riffs everywhere from the guitar, keyboards and the bass and this was, again, what set them apart from other bands. Black's drumming was, at times, conventional, and allowed the other three band members the space to develop melodic enterprise. But his moments where he utilised more unconventional drum patterns were to become a crucial part of many of the band's songs.

Many of the songs themselves seemed to be vehicles for their styles of playing, for example, 'Peaches' and 'Down in the Sewer'. Even 'Sometimes' relies heavily as a song on the forceful bass riff, the keyboard arpeggios and the interplay between the keyboards and the guitar during the instrumentals and most of this could also be applied to 'Goodbye Toulouse' and 'Princess of the Streets'. 'Hanging Around' and 'Sometimes' showcased the trademark sound with aplomb yet 'Goodbye Toulouse' and 'Grip' were two of the most important songs from a perspective of development of musical elements as was 'Ugly' with its dissonance and textural interest to support its aggressive vitality.

Half the vocal melodies were spoken or shouted, and this, along with the aggressive sound prompted by the bass, identified the band with the punk image but the overall musicality of the band was many miles away from traditional punk.

Most of the chords were conventional using the main six chords and the two (flattened third and seventh) blues chords but there were moments where the band were pointing the way forward with the use of challenging chord patterns, for example in 'Goodbye Toulouse' with the use of the tritone/Devil's interval. This dark sounding tritone also appeared in both 'Peaches' and 'Down in the Sewer', no surprise for a band that had a rat as its emblem.

Melody notes occasionally clashed with the chords as in Greenfield's solo in 'Sometimes' and the instrumental sections in 'Ugly' also had clashing notes. There was occasional ambiguity or fluidity of key as in 'Ugly' and the key change in 'Hanging Around' was highly effective as was the change of chords when the backing vocals sang the opening keyboard riff in 'Grip'. None of these features were particularly groundbreaking in themselves but, taken as a whole, there were plenty of signposts suggesting future experimentation.

Structure was the musical element that carried the most influence on the debut album. The use of long instrumentals immediately established the band as being significantly different to other bands as their song structures moved away from the common verse/chorus structure. Even though songs like 'Grip', 'Hanging Around' and 'Goodbye Toulouse' had clear climatic choruses following the preparational verses, the prominence of the instrumental sections moved the songs into another structural dimension. And every song on the album carried instrumental sections that combined repeating riffs and/or solos and this contributed to well over half the length of the entire music.

Despite this, there were very few atmospheric build ups that occupied the songs of many Prog bands. Pink Floyd for example would often have several minutes of atmospheric build up within their songs whereas *Rattus Norvegicus IV* displayed a directness with the key riffs immediately entering in 'Sometimes', 'Down in the Sewer', 'Peaches', 'Grip' and 'Ugly'. This forthright feel to their songs allied to the instrumental passages often being riff based resulted in tight structures with more contrasting sections than in many songs. There was rarely a sense of 'filling' songs between vocal sections with a quick solo or a repeat of previous chorus.

Texturally, the instrumental sections in 'Sometimes' and 'Hanging Around' where Cornwell and Greenfield play different melodies at the same time are sowing the seeds for the bands' use of multi-melodic layering textures. The main vocal sections in 'Princess of the Streets' and 'Goodbye Toulouse' are also creating a feel for this texture as the vocal is being accompanied by riffs that have a melodiousness rather than conventional chords. 'Ugly' also has multi-melodic riffs during the instrumental sections.

Most of the album saw conventional textures for a rock band and most of the songs maintained similar textures as they developed. But having an innovative keyboard player and a classically trained bass guitarist who both moved towards melodic riffs as often as playing conventional chords and bass notes opened a new world to textures. Cornwell also adopted a melodic riff-based approach at times and there were also fleeting moments from Greenfield of his desire to play two different riffs at the same time but more of this was to come later. Indeed, a lot more was still to come regarding chords/keys, structure and texture. But for now, the unique band sound had been established and the seeds of innovation were well and truly sowed.

Summary

Rattus Norvegicus IV, to give its full name was a stunning debut – it caught the zeitgeist of Britain in the late seventies and in particular London and it's developing new music culture. It was the beginning of a fascinating journey and the sound that exploded from it was different to anything else in 1977. Many critics would point to The Sex Pistols and The Clash's debut albums from the same year being more in touch with the times and street culture. *Rattus Norvegicus IV* was at least the equal if not better than both those debuts in reflecting the times.

It is so evocative of the time, you can almost smell and taste the decaying London of the late seventies. This malaise was not just in the capital but in all cities across the land. In an act of serendipity worthy of a prophecy of Nostradamus the Victorian sewers the band had brought to life on the album's closing track literally started to collapse in the country's major cities. Just a coincidence of course but a wonderful metaphor for the state of the nation which this album perfectly reflects indeed in 2023 the same malaise and issues effects the cities of the day, thus making the band's debut a timeless classic.

Lyrically the songs were on the whole straightforward stories, a reportage of touring and life on the streets with Burnel and Cornwell pull no punches, telling us exactly how they see it. Both writers take the stance that they are reporting the facts as they see them and not making any judgements. However, if we are objective, Burnel in particular, was judgemental in many of his words one obvious example being 'London Lady'. This approach by the writers can be seen as rather simplistic and brutal however as we have seen many of the other songs have hidden lyrical depths and layers of meaning e.g., 'Ugly', 'Goodbye Toulouse' and 'Hanging Around'.

The idea of the words working on several levels was a theme they would keep developing and truly master on later albums. As has been demonstrated many of the lyrics were shocking and controversial but another area worthy of note is that there was a great deal of humour in many of the words. At times it was a very dark humour and at others it was cheesy double-entendres which weren't to everyone's taste. However juxtaposing dark and lightweight humour against such dense, tough, and claustrophobic music meant many, including most of the music press didn't get the jokes. As their career progressed the band refined their humour and indulged regularly in puns and other word play to make their point.

With the country in decline The Stranglers articulated this degeneration with their exciting dangerous and complex music. Musically the band were way ahead of their peers, and they exploited this to the full voicing their ideas musically and lyrically. They had set their stall out to storm the barricades of conventional popular music and they weren't going to back down. The band may have appeared parochial with their tales of London life, but they had also signalled with songs like 'Goodbye Toulouse' and 'Down in the Sewer' that musically and subject matter wise they had wider horizons.

To many Stranglers fans this is 'the' album, to be surpassed by any of their subsequent releases. Commercially it is their most successful album of their career receiving platinum status in the UK. Artistically it is a triumph and acts as a manifesto for their later career. All the elements developed later in their career are present.

Every track is a master work whether it be the complex music of tracks like 'Goodbye Toulouse', the straight head aggressive rock of 'London Lady' or the slow blues of 'Princess of the Streets'. All the tracks on the album were completely realised and essential listening, each one in their own way unforgettable classics. The songs all demonstrated stunning musicianship, strong melodies, and complex arrangements and allied with the edgy lyrics and the sheer energy of the performances it couldn't fail to make a lasting impression on the record buying public. This was an album conceived and created by life on the streets, it's dirty and loud but magnificent and proud.

The issue now was how to follow up now they has kicked down the door. This wasn't going to be a problem they had songs in the can already and just needed a few new numbers to complete an album. With a band as creatively on fire as The Stranglers and a management chomping at the bit to take full advantage of buzz and huge commercial potential the band had created. 1977 already a busy year for the band was just about to get busier.

B-sides and free EP given away with the album
Choosey Susie

One side of a free EP given away with the album and another song about Burnel's muse and lover the titular 'Choosey Susie'. It's a pleasant melody led as ever by Greenfield's keyboards but nothing remarkable by the high standards of the band. It's easy to see why it didn't make the cut, close but no cigar. Burnel's vocal delivery is his angry punk voice which injects some passion and urgency into proceedings. He assumes the role of band leader as he does on several other songs from this period when he cues in Cornwell's guitar solo with the words "Take it from me Hugh" By doing this he is not only appearing to call the shots but it gives the song a live feel which was then representative of the band's way of recording in studio at that time where the music was laid down live with very little overdubs.

It's worth noting that there was serious talk of the first album being a live album called 'Dead on Arrival'. Ultimately the right decision was made. Live albums can capture the essence of a band, or they can also do it a disservice by sounding dated a few years later. With the quality of material, the band had a live debut wouldn't have done the band or material justice. It seems producer Martin Rushent was instrumental on the debut being a studio recording albeit it basically a live in the studio recording.

Lyrically Burnel gives the song an edge with nothing left to the imagination as he relates a tale of him and Susie making love until they're weak and until they bleed. The edge is sharpened when he delivers the implied threat "You remember what happened to the last wife" It also suggests how much she has got into his mind, and this is backed up by the fact that Susie leaves him early in evening when Burnel wants her to stay for a night of passion. Clearly Choosey knew her own mind and was a free spirit.

*****

Like 'Go Buddy Go', 'Choosey Susie' has a raw live feel relating to their early pub rock days. The structure of the song is conventional with a main section repeated three times, interspersed with the opening instrumental section. There is also a guitar solo and, as was also the case with 'Go Buddy Go', the overall sound has the guitar higher in the mix than was to be the case later and for this song, The drums were also slightly higher in the mix. The bass had already been established more in the forefront than in other bands and this was due as much to the middle and treble EQ than the actual mix.

The keyboard was less prominent than it was to become for the album and the lack of a keyboard solo in this song reduced Greenfield's role to that of a background, filling texture. This was soon to be turned on its head as Greenfield's chordal, accompanying lines were to become a central part of the sound on almost every track on *Rattus Norvegicus IV*. 'London Lady' was an exception, and that song had a similar Pub Rock feel to these two songs. The chords were conventional with a stepwise chordal pattern at the end of the main section providing the contrast from the main four chords that occupy most of the song.

The main melody was reasonably well shaped considering that much of the bands' vocals at this time were less discernibly melodic, being more spoken or shouted. There was none of the multi-melodic texturing that was to become commonplace with the only slightly unconventional moment being the half bar time signature on "Until we're weak" at the end of the main section. Like 'Go Buddy Go', "Choosey Susie was a pleasingly energetic song showing deference to their early roots but little in the way musically of what was to come.

Peasant in the Big Shitty (Live) (B-side of 'Choosey Susie' free single)

Coupled with Choosey Susie on the free 7-inch single given away with the first 10,000 copies of the album and is a live recording of a track that was later appear on *No More Heroes*. For that reason the detailed analysis of the song will be done in that chapter. This live recording is from the originally proposed idea to make the first album a live recording. Record at the Nashville pub, London, December 1976.

Go Buddy Go (Double A-side single with 'Peaches')

A double A side with 'Peaches' it's a traditional rock 'n' roll song delivered with vigour. The band were able to perform the song on *Top of the Pops* instead of 'Peaches' thus getting vital exposure. Buddy received a great deal of radio play justifying the record company tactic of a double A-side and effectively guaranteeing the band a hit single.

The song was and still is a live favourite and was wholly written by Burnel. There is nothing particularly inventive musical about the song, but it illustrates the band's musical roots and showed they could mix it with the best of them when it came to straight rock 'n' roll. Early Stranglers live performances relied a great deal on covers so it's not surprising their early original tracks would reflect the styles of music of cover versions.

Also, the band were part of the pre punk pub rock scene where bands like Dr Feelgood and Eddie and the Hot Rods plied their trade with turbo charged rhythm and blues. Another influence particularly on Burnel and his style of writing was the fact that he shared a flat with Dr Feelgood guitarist Wilco Johnson around this time and hard to imagine there wasn't any cross fertilisation of influences and styles.

Lyrically a straightforward tale of a night at a local dance hall. There is a feel of an American high school hop in the story with girls dancing in line. American rock 'n' roll vibe is further pursued with the Chuck Berry lyric "No siree". Burnel also again plays band leader by calling in Greenfield's Jerry Lee Lewis styled solo. The story follows Burnel and his friend Buddy trying to pull girls at the dance. The song ends with Burnel failing in his mission but friend Buddy being successful. Later in their career Burnel and Greenfield followed their love of this genre with a side project called The Purple Helmets who played classic blues and rock 'n' roll covers. They gigged extensively and recorded a couple of albums.

*****

Chordally the song is highly conventional and, to begin with, uses the twelve bar blues chord pattern with the last part of the pattern being a reasonably common variation. The Middle "Elbow rooming his way" section is contrasting but still uses common chords. The melody has an effectively shaped lower range for this section after the higher melody of the main section, but the overall feel is of classic Pub Rock boogie and the texture of the song remains the same throughout, reinforcing the Rock boogie.

The song structure is standard except for the combined length of the two solos which move the song closer to four minutes and was a feature that had already been established on the *Rattus Norvegicus IV* album. The emphatic run down at the end of Greenfield's first solo has a particular 'joie de vivre' in keeping with the mood. The chorus hook line has an effective sing-along quality allied to the simplicity of the song which was looking back to their early pub rock days rather than forward to the musical experimentation that was to follow.

Footnotes

1. Official Charts website

2. Official Charts website

3. Official Charts website

4. *Sounds* magazine 16th April 1977 Simon Dell archive

5. Trevor Rogers Photography trevorrogersphotography.com

6. *Sounds* magazine 16th April 1977 Simon Dell archive

7. *Song by Song* – Hugh Cornwell and Jim Drury

8. Caroline Coon's website CarolineCoon.com

9. oneweekoneband.tumblr.com/post/103161433169/caroline-coon

10 The Stranglers Chris Twomey's band biog on line on thestranglers website

11. *Song by Song* – Hugh Cornwell and Jim Drury

12. Official Charts website

13. Official Charts website

14. *Song by Song* – Hugh Cornwell and Jim Dury

Stranglers
Doncaster

TO PARAPHRASE Johnathan Richman, I still love the Sixties, and I still love the Old World. Despite my interest in the New Wave, the Doors are still my favourite band, and 'Forever Changes' is still my favourite elpee. That's why I was initially attracted to the Stranglers; yes, kids, the spirit of good ol' 'psychedelia' lives on in their music.

Their gig at Doncaster's house of flickers, the Gaumont, was a goody. They played such numbers as 'Ugly', 'Go, Buddy, Go', which I can never hear without being reminded of 'Little Old Lady From Pasadena' ("Go, Granny, Go"), 'Schoolma'am', 'Peaches' — a bad song, period, and 'I Feel Like A Wog'. The latter selection is interesting; for days after I first heard it I was haunted by it. Lyrically the Stranglers haven't distinguished themselves yet, but on 'Wog', a vignette about paranoia, they actually use inarticulacy to very good effect. Good music, too; when they are at their best ('Down in the Sewer', 'Peasant in the Big Shitty', dopey lyrics notwithstanding, 'Schoolma'am', etc), they can't be beaten...the throbbing rhythm section, the spectral guitar, the calliope-like organ flourishes straight out of 'Something Wicked This Way Comes'... Just blur your eyes and let the music transport you; you're watching the Doors at the Whiskey, the Velvets at the Dom...

The Stranglers don't look like a chart-topping band, though. They are really as grisly and unappetising as specimens from a Reader's Wives page. Burnel does his best to come on sullen and mean, in which consists the whole art and duty of punkhood, but doesn't convince; and his singing — the word is a euphemism — isn't too good, either. Cornwell looks like he arrived at the theatre on an old push-bike. Jet and Dave, frankly, look too old and pudgy to playing to a set of identikit 'anarchists' fresh out of secondary school.

But they are a fine, fine band. To hell with it. Oh, half way through 'Go, Buddy, Go' Jean Jacques and Hugh leapt into the audience and conducted a little business...that was interesting; but the best part of the set, during a second reading of the same song, was when all the kids down front went apeshit and clambered up onstage to dance around and play their imaginary guitars and so on. A beautiful celebration of youthful energy — touching, even. — PETE SCOTT.

Stranglers/Dictators
Roundhouse

"MEXICAN JUMPIN' bean music!" Thus spake Handsome Dick Manitoba, introducing himself and his band, The Dictators for the last of five consecutive engagements in support to the Stranglers. Nice turn of phrase, young Dick, but he undersells himself and his buddies not a little bit. Nah, I've known a Mexican jumping bean or two in my time but they were *never* like this.

Seen three shows out of five and — no thanks to London Transport — would've clocked in an even higher number if I could. God bless The Dictators — they're fast, they're funny, they can play as hot as any premier punkometal outfit you'd care to mention, have really excellent original material, *and* a stage act that can't fail with anyone who enjoys watching rock 'n' roll. And sure, during the unreeling of such key-works as 'Master Race Rock', 'Exposed', 'Young, Fast, Scientific' and 'Disease', it quickly becomes apparent that the Dictators aren't totally *prostrate* before the rock 'n' roll altar, that there's a strong element of afffectionate rib-digging involved ('And I think Lou Reed is *a creep!*' scoffs the narrator of 'Two Tube Man') in these chaps' schtick. But they're not comedians; they're The Dictators and they're the freshest breath of air to cross the Atlantic since Talking Heads. They're the Dictators and, music/quality-wise they've finally made an offer I don't *want* to refuse, a neat mingling of the two sides of the band evinced by their recordings. The rough 'n' ready hammerhead relish of the first album mated with the sheer professionalism of their second. I didn't know what was happening almost — one minute I was laughing with them, then savouring the tunes . . . and all the while I had the itchiest of feet.

Ah, the Stranglers — it was *their* record-breaking residency, after all. I hadn't seen them in over six months and I have to confess that when they first came on, all stiff-legged and po-faced I couldn't help but smile — seemed as if they'd become *exactly* the kind of tight-arsed 'artist man' The Dictators had been lampooning only twenty minutes before.

Hang on though — I don't aim this to be a 'classic' example of the build-up/knock-em-downery of which my wretched profession is so frequently accused. As far as I'm concerned the Stranglers will always deserve acknowledging as perhaps the only major '77 act to really have earned their high record sales by having gone out and played to the kids more frequently and more thoroughly than any of their contemporaries.

Seems to me though that the endless roadwork has rubbed off some of the fine finishes I used to enjoy so much — old favourites ('Hangin' Around' was, I think, a particularly keen example) that used to move me waybackwhen have become faster, heavier and coarser, with assault and battery replacing pursuit and flattery.

Mind you, the mixture as of now *did* get the required crowd adrenalin on the move and a heck of a lot of people left as damp as they'd arrived — and where rains was the first offender the latter was good old pore juice. — GIOVANNI DADOMO.

A Musical Critique

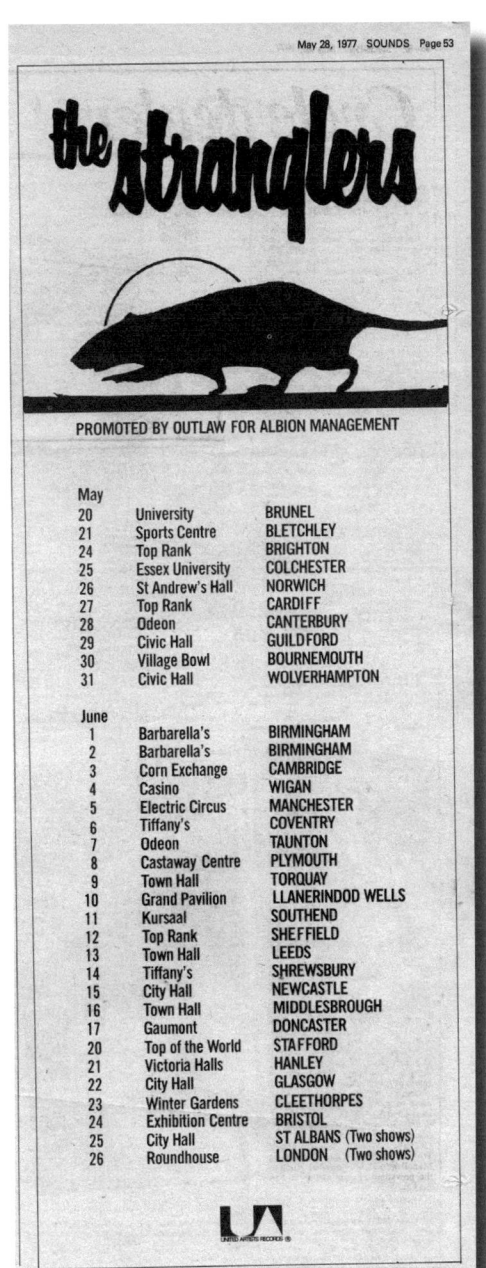

The Stranglers
No More Heroes
c/w In The Shadows

New Single Available Now   UP 36300

No More Heroes

In September 1977 the follow up to *Rattus Norvegicus IV* hit the racks lees than six months after their debut album. The record company was keen to follow up the momentum of the first album, so they pressed for an immediate follow up. Two albums in one year was not unusual in the late 1970s especially after the new wave explosion The expectation was huge and the band had a lot to live up to after such a stunning debut. The task of following up the debut was made easier by the fact that the band still had quality songs left over the first album recording sessions. It can be seen as a continuation of their debut album as four of the songs on the album were left over from the first album sessions and given that the new songs were recording in the same studio added to the feeling of continuity.

The album was trailed in the summer with a double A-sided single featuring two brand new tracks 'Something Better Change' and 'Straighten Out'. The single peaked at number 9[1] the band's second foray into the Top Ten. Then a week before the album was released the title track was put out with the non-album track 'In the Shadows' as the B-side. The Top Ten was breached again with the song hitting the dizzy heights of number 8.[2]

By the end of 1977 the band had had three top ten single hits and two top five albums in the space of less than a year. The record company was putting its commercial muscle behind the band even going so far as to shot promo videos for the singles a highly unusual step for any band in those days.

The album was released on 23rd September and crashed into the charts at number two and stayed in the charts for eighteen weeks.[3] Initially the album flew out of the shops and resulted in a higher chart position than their debut, but sales tailed off, meaning it spent fewer weeks in the chart. Historically the album is the band's second-best seller in their history with *Rattus Norvegicus IV* holding the number one spot.

The album arrived just as its predecessor was slipping down the charts, but it meant the band had two albums in the top 30, a stunning achievement for a new band. The Stranglers never hit the top spot in their career in either albums or singles but missing the top spot didn't really matter as 1977 had been a spectacular year for them. In late September they were the biggest sellers of the new musical movement. A few weeks later The Sex Pistols hit number one in the album charts and became the first punk band to attain this height. What no one realised at the time was this was to be the Pistols only creative statement whereas their commercial and cultural rivals in the punk wars, The Stranglers had barely started.

The cover design is stunning and was the work of designer Paul Henry and photographer Trevor Rogers[4] who had also designed the cover for *Rattus Norvegicus IV*. The artwork has a wreath of red carnation with the title and the band name in the middle of the wreath. The back cover has separate pictures of the band that have been placed through filters and solarised by Eamonn O'Keefe[5] making their faces appear like they were in a Dr Who episode coloured green, red or blue. There is a jagged design that frames and links the pictures given the impression of flames or electricity. The inner sleeve has a stage photo of the band in full flow. The stage lighting links into the colours used on the back sleeve. The other side of the inner sleeve has a magnificent picture of the wreath with our new friend and about to become career spanning icon a rather large Rattus Norvegicus. Having such a big image of such a reviled and unfashionable animal is meant to shock and adds to the unsettling feel of the whole album. The artwork is genuinely thought provoking and shocking. The use of a wreath is obviously a representation of death and ultimately decay, subjects the band were immersing themselves in at this time.

The flowers are not poppies or red roses as is often thought they are red carnations. Red carnations symbolise love and affection and are traditional funeral flowers. The classic Stranglers logo which has now become iconic is not present this time it would take until *The Raven* for it to appear again on an album and from then on it would be ever present on original albums. There was a mock-up of another potential sleeve featuring Burnel centre stage on the tomb of Leon Trotsky. Quite rightly the rest of the band vetoed this vanity project and opted for the iconic artwork we know and love.

Placing Burnel as the main man would have been misleading and denied the band the gang mentality and image they had carefully built up. The band wasn't about individuals it was a collective project, and it was plain to anybody who knew the music well that the band were quite obviously a group whose individual contributions added up to a greater sum than all the individual parts. They weren't someone's backing band they were four equal partners, and this was reflected in the equal split they agreed over royalties. The Stranglers appear to be almost unique in this approach, most bands don't share money. Even if a band gives writing credits equally on the record sleeves the money is rarely shared equally The Stranglers were an unusual example in this respect.

Musically the band built on the ideas of their debut but began to show an even more experimental but still melodic direction. Whilst doing this the group ensured there was more than a fair share of immediate up-tempo numbers to please the punks. Conversely the synthesiser started to inform the sound more and push the band even further away from what was seen as punk. Lyrically tales of the grimy London underground scene still dominate, and the atmosphere of post-industrial decay positively seeps from its pores. The rotting underbelly of the UK in Silver Jubilee year exposed for all to see without doubt the most punk of all their albums in attitude and style.

Production wise it's possible to discern more influence and ideas from producer Martin Rushent. The band had to write new material, so he was able to be in at the genesis of new material and make suggestions which shows through on tracks like 'I Feel Like a Wog' and 'School Mam'. Obviously, people were quick to compare it with their debut and reviews were certainly not as good. Although retrospective reviews viewed it more favourably, with one review on the Allmusic website asserting it was better than *Rattus Norvegicus IV*.

To most fans such an assertion is pushing things too far however in one area the album is probably the leader over its predecessor and that was it was even more controversial. This is quite an achievement given the subject matter of much of their debut but with songs like the aforementioned 'School Mam', 'I Feel Like a Wog' and 'Bring on the Nubiles' on the new album the nastiness was right in your face and shocked and frightened the country's moral majority.

With *No More Heroes* they were coming to the public as a known quantity thanks to 'Peaches' and the large sales of their debut album. With *Rattus Norvegicus IV* they were an unknown quantity and had sneaked under the radar with only those in the know noting the controversy. This time the band had a target on their back, and they revelled in attention and notoriety.

I Feel Like a Wog

As we have already seen The Stranglers were a band that called it as they saw it and were not afraid to be contrary, controversial, challenge conventions and contest society's accepted values. First track on the album and they are in the listener's face again. Played at a frantic pace driven by the bass this number takes no prisoners musically or lyrically. It became a firm favourite live because of its pace, quirky changes, angry delivery, and controversial lyrics.

It is an anti-racist song, or more accurately an attempt at an anti-racist song but unfortunately fails at the first hurdle. An all-white band using the word 'Wog' disables it immediately, Despite Cornwell arguing in *Song by Song* the word Wog is an acronym of the term **W**ily **O**riental **G**entleman which was a term allegedly invented by the British Empire to describe the people it subjugated. This is a spurious argument and though oft repeated it is not in fact true.

Even if this entomology of the word was true the sentiments behind it were still racist and it was a term imposed on ethnic groups by those in power over them. The true entomology comes from a shortening of Gollywog to Wog, A Gollywog was a racist stereotype cartoon character created by the artist Florence Kate Upton in the late nineteenth century. It was used in children's books and later became the symbol for *Robertson's* jam. It is the British equivalent of the word nigger. It is an inherently a racist term. Its use as a symbol in 1977 was being questioned but the image and toys of Gollywogs were everywhere, a sign of its general acceptance. The song has the following words in the chorus "Golly gee, golly gosh, don't call me your Golly Wog". Using such words can only lead to questioning Cornwell's original assertion about the origins of the word as he clearly using it in the context of the word Gollywog.

Witnessing the song being played live in the early eighties it was clear that much of the crowd missed the anti-racist sentiment and a minority revelled in shouting 'Wog' during the chorus therefore despite the anti-racist sentiment of the lyric the song fails in its intent because much of the band's audience missed the point and saw it as a song celebrating racial insults.

The same fate befell other attempts at anti-racism in other forms of media at the same time. Two situation comedies of the mid-seventies *Til Death Us Do Part* and *Love Thy Neighbour* tried to make the same point in a similar way but unfortunately the laughter was generally because of the racist slurs used rather than laughing at the stupidity and ignorance of the racist characters using them. Cornwell should at least be applauded for his sentiment and dealing with the issue head on even if the execution was flawed and misguided. A letter to *Sounds* music paper by Stranglers fan Joan Geoffroy on 25th February 1978 captured one black person's feelings on hearing the song and therefore its inherent weaknesses.

Rattus offencivus

"THANK YOU, Mark Gregory, for writing to Sounds (11/2/78) about The Stranglers LP track "I Feel Like a Wog". I am a Stranglers fan, and I am black and I went to see them on their tour last autumn. At the time I wasn't too familiar with their music, I had just heard the four singles, that's all. So I was taken completely by surprise when Hugh Cornwell said "This next one's called "I Feel Like A Wog" – (I think it's a bloody stupid title, anyway; how the hell do they know what it's like to be black?)

I was totally shattered, upset and furious (I'm not being dramatic, I'm being truthful) and by the time I could even bring myself to even listen to the song it was half over; however I did manage to suss out that it is not a racialist song. The realisation, didn't stop me from feeling miserable for days after, 'cos it is no joke seeing smug self-satisfied expressions on the faces of some of the people in the audience when they heard him use the word 'wog'.

It's no good people telling me that names don't hurt because they're just words. They hurt like hell." [6]

It should also be remembered that Rock Against Racism was a thriving movement at the time so the issue was very much news, and it could be argued they should have written a better anti-racist song given the media spotlight racism was getting.

The Stranglers weren't the only band to get their response wrong at this time. In 1979 Northern Irish punk band Stiff Little Fingers recorded a song called 'White Noise' for their first album. It was an anti-racist song, but it used the clumsy device of putting every racist slur for every ethnic group you can think of including the Irish into the lyrics.

Sadly, all most people could see and hear were the racist terms and not the sentiment. The song's failure was compounded when it earned Stiff Little Fingers a ban from playing Newcastle City Hall because the band were wrongly deemed racists by the council. A sad, ironic end to a well-intentioned song with a flawed delivery.

The Stranglers learned from the controversy around this song and on later albums they made the points with more subtly and with clever word play.

Burnel reflects on these early direct lyrical approaches later in the band's career with the song 'Never to Look Back' where he outlines being accused of being fascist but responds saying he never was. It is done in a sensitive and thoughtful way as this part of the lyric shows: "I had a black shirt, but I was never one".

The point being The Stranglers were the men in black but and literally wore black shirts and although it has been a symbol of fascism not everyone wearing a black shirt is a fascist. It is another example of people jumping to simplistic and inaccurate conclusions. The band weren't fascists or racists.

In 1977 the punk and new music was flirting with Nazi and fascist imagery. Siouxsie Sioux worn a swastika arm band and Sid Vicious wore a swastika T-shirt. Siouxsie later explained it was about a rebellion against parents who were forever going on about the war. What could upset them more than wearing the enemies' insignia? Some fans of punk adopted this approach and dressed using Nazi symbols and insignia. It didn't necessarily mean they were racist but to be honest it was true in many cases. Others were probably just ignorant or naïve, for example the band Sham 69, whose populist approach picked up a racist right wing following. Attracting such a following was a disaster for the band, virtually destroying well-meaning but naïve lead singer Jimmy Pursey as their gigs descended into violence between the Fascists and anti-fascists.

Siouxsie atoned for her early punk indiscretion by recording the single 'Israel' in 1980. All these band's including The Stranglers were playing with fire with their heavy handed and misunderstood approach to tackling racism. Finally in 1979 the most effective way to combat racism in music arrived with the multiethnic Two-Tone movement that confronted racism head on but did it in an effective credible way the most credible part being the bands were multi-ethnic, with a feminist stance and from the inner cities not white middle-class men from the suburbs.

*****

The two long chromatic notes give an immediate sense of expectation before the whole band crash in with immense force and energy in the key of E where Burnel can use the lowest note of the bass to add a surging depth to the sound. The restless feel is relentless and encapsulates the sentiment of the lyrics. Whilst Black maintains the snare on every beat, a drum pattern established on *Rattus Norvegicus IV*, Burnel's typically energetic bass riff, based on only three notes, propels the song forward whilst Greenfield has a simple two chord riff but played slightly differently, panned left and right.

This vibrant constancy enables Cornwell to attack with sustained punctuated distorted discords on guitar and this sonic platform never relents, providing the perfect mood for the ensuing vocal growling. This song was a departure from the previous album with its prominence of clashing/dissonant notes and chords. The clashing became a part of the bands' musical make-up and whilst we had seen moments of this on *Rattus Norvegicus IV*, 'I Feel Like a Wog' deploys this as central idea with its use on much of the guitar and, later, the keyboard as well. The impact of this results in a more aggressive and disconcerting feel than anything from *Rattus Norvegicus IV*. The song 'Ugly' was close in its aggressive intensity but the relentless constancy of the bass riff here clearly establishes the home key so the dissonance can pour forth above this base which provides a sense of grounding for the listener that was absent in 'Ugly'. This disconcerting musical aggression provides a strong opening statement for the album.

The song is mainly riff based with some implied conventional chords. The short instrumental section that follows "to do with their time" is an important moment as not only does the clashing dissonance intensify, the multi-melodic layering textures from the opening album are apparent here. The bass riff simply rises by one note, but the guitar engages in a highly dissonant moment where a riff descends sequentially whilst the keyboard adds extra dissonance with a more rhythmic response to the guitar's melody. These disconcerting instrumental moments challenge yet beguile the listener, but only briefly as the original instrumentation soon returns. But it creates an effect of lashing out at the listener before letting them settle down again and was to become a common part of the bands musical psyche. This section also relates to the structural ideas that were established on their opening album where instrumental sections carried equal weight to their vocal sections. This song is slightly different in that the instrumental sections are shorter with more spoken vocals than for any songs from *Rattus Norvegicus IV*.

When this brief instrumental is repeated after "Sho sho sho shoes" the guitar has been developed into a higher sequence with suitable keyboard adaptation, thus creating even more urgency and tension in the song. This takes the song into a chorus of sorts where the bass riff are keyboards are now higher in pitch supporting "Don't call me" expanding even more urgency and drive into the proceedings. When the tension is released, and we return to the verse the band are not content to reproduce the original texture but now have a robust low keyboard sound doubling up the same notes as the bass.

Rhythmically, the end of many of the vocal phrases, first heard with "Yo yo yo yo yo", accent a triplet rhythm on the vocals and keyboards which, again, helps to propel the song as the bass and drums maintain the previous driving rhythm underneath the triplets and is indicative of their growing mastery of rhythmic ideas. The abrupt ending follows some more discordant guitar chords, played quicker this time, and perfectly embodies the disconcertion that has been building during the adrenaline rush of the song. A challenging and vibrant opening song.

Bitching

A Burnel song with an incredibly catchy, simple but rough around the edges tune that demonstrated their innate ability to juxtapose an aggressive playing and lead singing style with strong melodies and honeyed backing vocals. The end result was devastatingly effective and something the band seemed to be able to do at will at this point in their career thus pleasing their young punk audience but at the same time drawing in an older fan base who knew their rock history. Cornwell's guitar intro and Greenfield's solo mimic the sound if not the music of Jonathan Richmond's 'Roadrunner' which in turn was inspired by The Velvet Underground's 'Sister Ray'.

The melody makes the song strong enough to merit being considered as single fodder, but its length and the use of choice language would have derailed that. The BBC would have banned a song with the word 'bitching' repeated so many times then add in the repeated use of 'screwed' and a ban would have been guaranteed. It was never considered as a single but was a live favourite because of the memorable tune and taboo words. To many people taboo words and phrases in songs was what punk was all about and that wasn't just the general public scared by tabloid reports but also many punks themselves. Punk had only gained national recognition because of the 'filth and fury' swearing incident by the Pistols on the *Bill Grundy Show*. Without that event punk would not have entered the public consciousness as much as it did, if at all.

The subject matter is the back biting of the London music scene and the stresses of touring. The lyrics paint a picture of the band in a pub or bar chatting and gossiping about the situations and scrapes they have gotten themselves into. Add into this the band's standing in the punk community and there is plenty of subject material to put into a song which seems to be basically a list of complaints.

The Stranglers age and musicianship set them apart from the scene and given their recent commercial success there was a great deal of jealousy around and band suffered many barbed comments from other bands and the music press. In addition, the band had a following of people who could handle themselves. Firstly, a gang of Hell's Angels and then the Finchley Boys added to the punk glitterati dislike of the band.

Then throw into the mix Burnel knocking out punk pinup boy Paul Simonon of the Clash in a bar brawl and the band were effectively persona non grata with punk's inner circle. The hip fashionable journalist of the time such as Julie Burchill, Caroline Coon and Tony Parson's hadn't a good word to say about them and peppered reviews with snide comments and accusations. All these circumstances went into Burnel's cutting angry lyrics which just seemed to flow out of him in an angry howl.

The lyrics are also interesting because they reference characters and places important to the band. For example, in the second verse "the Grainger man" and the "Phelan man" were two pub landlords who supported the band by giving them gigs at their establishments. Fred Grainger was landlord at the famous Hope and Anchor and Bill Phelan was the boss of The Duke of Lancaster both legendary venues that gave many bands particularly punk groups their first big gigs in London. The same verse also mentions "The Windsor C" (Castle) which was another pub on the gig circuit.[7] The verse also mentions the infamous trip and gigs in Amsterdam which led to scrapes with the Dutch Hell's Angels. Being Amsterdam, the band were able to partake in the local customs including smoking marijuana; "Strange smoke perfume round the peacock guys". Life on the road with The Stranglers was nothing if not interesting.

As a footnote the "Bar bitching" refrain could be seen as a reference to barbiturate prescription drugs whose illicit use exploded in the 1970s. Barbiturates were a cheap substitute for class A drugs in low doses they were a downer but taken in a high dose they had the opposite effect and acted as a stimulant. It's no wonder they were popular and were widely used illicitly by people in the music business and wider society. The band would certainly have been aware of this and the reference maybe unintended, but it demonstrates an innate ability to reflect street culture.

*****

The chordal guitar that opens the song provides a suitable contrast to the previous keyboard and bass driven song and Black's snare work that soon follows provides an interesting complex off-beat foil to Burnel's high pitched opening riff. The keyboards then enter signalling the bass to assume its normal lower range.

The separate entry of the instruments had been introduced on 'Hanging Around' and this intro also promises much but the chords become rooted on chord one of the key, with a brief foray to the second most common chord and the limitation of chordal fluidity with no riffs to drive the song unlike 'I Feel Like a Wog', results in a lack of forward momentum.

The solos also struggle to take shape due to this chordal lack of moment although Cornwell provides some strong melodic quality towards the end of his solo. 'Bitching' was the second longest track on the album and the lack of momentum leads to question marks over whether the song with its five choruses may be too long. The structure develops from *Rattus Norvegicus IV* where the instrumental sections, in this case the two solos, are central to the song and there is a 'middle eight' section at 2:41 which is also a departure from conventional middle eights as it appears late into the song when most songs of this type would be entering a closing section. Whilst this enables the organ to solo and then the guitar takes over with an effective melodious riff, one feels that placing the middle eight after the first guitar solo would have resulted in a leaner yet more effective song where the chords are severely limited and there are few riffs to drive the song. But there is no doubt that the overall aggressive groove appeals to many fans.

Dead Ringer

A Cornwell lyric but sung by Greenfield. The atmosphere of the music suggests a classic tale of paranoia with added menace coming from Greenfield as a suitably sinister sounding vocalist. He was a master of this type of voice and could create a genuinely unsettling atmosphere by uttering one syllable. In hindsight the band should have used him rather more on lead vocals as he could have used his style to add and improve certain songs from this period, 'In the Shadows' or 'School Mam' spring to mind as suitable for Greenfield.

Instrumentally it's what was quickly becoming classic Stranglers and more complex than it initially appears. There are brilliantly crafted bits of stop, start tension when the instruments leave the listener hanging and then shock when the stop is punctuated by the disturbing vocal or a small instrumental run. It signals a new kind of musical approach from the band that would come more to fruition on *Black and White*. It demonstrates a band who are totally at home with each other and again points the way to further experimentation later in their career. Greenfield's unique vocal style is complimented by the chanted backing vocals on the refrain "Then you're a Dead Ringer" and add to the tension and air of paranoia.

A series of nonspecific images which Cornwell observed were about the bands who changed their image and rode in on the back of punk to make their reputation and money.[8] It would be difficult to gage this if you just heard the song cold without the back story. Just the sound of Greenfield's voice suggests a disturbing unpleasant narrative when in fact the actual meaning according to the writer is more mundane.

It's a classic example of the bands multi layered meanings. Cornwell also gives us the made-up phrase "conkeroonee stringer" which allegedly means conker stringer and is the writer equating the punk scene to a playground and playground bragging rights? Making up new phrases is an endearing signature of Cornwell's writing style and always stimulates interest and debate. The song finishes with three words "Productivity, credibility, impossibility", inviting us to fill in the gaps i.e., "Too much productivity makes credibility an impossibility".

This was the band's issue in late 1977 they had been incredibly productive but was it good enough quality and therefore was their credibility being threatened. Cornwell outlined these fears in 2001: "If we're producing all this music are we losing credibility?"[9] The lyrics lack development, and a little more work could have painted a clearer picture. However, the fact they are just impressionistic, sparse word sketches allows multiple interpretations and this is something Cornwell does deliberately and revels in giving his topics a bit more mystery.

On the other hand, if you have a target you want to hit, the listener needs a few more specifics. Because of the sketchy lyrics this leads the song more open to the interpretation, so for example Greenfield's threatening vocal delivery allied to some of the lyrics "Haven't I seen you somewhere else before" conjures up images of a deranged stalker. Not at all what Cornwell was thinking of in the original lyric but the performance of the song, the general darkness of the album and the subject matter of an deceive the listener into drawing such a conclusion.

The dictionary definition of dead ringer is "an exact duplicate" and it has become an idiom for describing people who look alike. The entomology traces back to horse racing where a horse would be presented at a race with a false lineage and name for dishonest purposes. Such horses were known as 'ringers' and the word 'dead' preceding doesn't mean deceased in this case but means exact as in 'dead on'.

Cornwell's analogy of punk bands recreating themselves is stunningly appropriate and accurate given this information. Another theory of the origin of the word builds on the deceased definition when people presumed dead were buried but just in case string was attached to their limbs which was them attached to a bell which they could ring if they actually weren't dead. This definition takes us back to the sinister and macabre which is the prevailing atmosphere of the track. The final related point is that the novel *Twins* was published in 1977 (the year the album was produced) was based on the true story of strange deaths of identical twins Cyril and Stewart Marcus. The novel later became e a film in 1988 called *Dead Ringers*. Is this serendipity or synchronicity? To be honest it doesn't matter but by making such links and explaining the lyrical idioms is fabulously stimulating and the band intentionally and unintentionally were about intellectual stimulation.

*****

Following the previous chord-based song, 'Dead Ringer's' riffs immediately re-establish the multiple melodic texture as well as continuing the clashing dissonance introduced in 'I Feel Like a Wog'. Burnel's growling low bass riff is in the same lowest 'E' key as 'I Feel Like a Wog' and Black's off beat, ride cymbal accompaniment helps to accentuate the swing rhythm. But the ensuing clashing chords between guitar and keyboards ensure that once Greenfield's twisted vocal tone enters, any potentially swing rhythm induced jazz feel is immediately extinguished.
This is Greenfield's debut on lead vocals and provides another contrast to the overall sound.

The brooding feel is an effective contrast to the more aggressive previous two songs and the song also benefits from an expansive melody itself, shaped with an octave range. The bass continues the riff, and the guitar is now playing a spindly low riff of its own whilst the keyboard chords provide more dissonance with the delayed effect adding more texture.

Furthermore, Black's drumming is really pointing the way forwards to future songs with a fascinating two bar pattern, the second of which resembles a fill, but it carries on throughout most of the song and the multi-melodic texture is to the fore. The "Hey you're a dead ringer" short chorus contrasts the main verse section by being chordal, but the irregular chord pattern adds to the quirkiness and unsettling nature of the song that was already established in the verse.

Greenfield's low growling glissando at the end of each phrase in the verse followed by a prolonged low growl at the end of the second chorus add to the menace and the guitar solo that follows this is particularly chordally dissonant and is also a cross rhythm which creates an even more unsettled feel. Greenfield's solo is not one of his most melodic but the rhythmic accents towards the end on drums bass and guitar add to the idiosyncratic feeling. This is ratcheted up further at the end with Greenfield's "productivity" low rasping and the band employing rests in the music to knock us even further off kilter.

The song structure is also important as it is the first example of a long instrumental that serves to finish the song and, in this case, accounts for forty percent of the overall song. This unconventional structure will be deployed on future songs and reinforces the significance of instrumental sections. It also creates a brevity that leaves us wanting a repeat of the chorus and possibly also the verse thus affecting our traditional equilibrium. The option for a long instrumental ending on 'Bitching' was less likely due to the lack of chordal fluidity. As was the case with 'I Feel Like a Wog', 'Dead Ringer' is a challenging yet highly effective song, predominantly due to the clashing dissonance and the structure.

Dagenham Dave

Burnel wrote the words and Cornwell the music. The music is based around Cornwell's straightforward aggressive guitar chords with Burnel delivering the words in a gruff shouting style that mirrors many new wave singers of that time. However, there are a couple of interesting surprises with the spoken section at the denouement of the tale followed then by Greenfield's long quirky outro showcasing exceptionally creative use of his synthesiser and sound to represent the titular protagonist struggles with his mind.

This is another of Burnel's story driven lyrics an approach that dominated his lyric writing style at this time. It relates the story of the eponymous hero of the title. He was the band's number one fan in the early days and his sad decent into mental health problems and eventual suicide. Despite dealing with a tragic death the song is not sentimental it comes across as a muscular celebration of a very tough, self-educated man with many internal demons. The story was that Dave was never the same after feeling he had been usurped as the band's main fan and confidant by the Finchley Boys.

He ended up picking a fight with the whole gang that led to him being badly hurt because he wouldn't give up. Then his girlfriend upped and left him and sadly not long after he committed suicide by jumping off a bridge into the River Thames.

The lack of sentimentally in the song and references to the river endlessly flowing on helps cements the message of the song, 'Dagenham Dave' has gone, celebrate his life but things moves on. This also serves as a metaphor for the band's situation at the time. They needed to move on both musically and out of the pressure cooker atmosphere of the insular scene that had grown up around them. To develop and seek wider horizons they needed to free themselves from groups like the Finchley Boys. Although ultra-loyal fans they were holding the band back artistically as was the whole punk scene they had been pulled into.

The last verse mostly spoken shows the bass player's sensitive side as he ponders Dave's reason for taking his own life and finishes with the line according to the lyric sites, "A howling of bulls" which corrupts the usual accepted saying which would have been a "howling of wolves". Both versions are an accurate descriptions of the song's protagonist. If we opt for the more unusual 'bulls' interpretation the one thing we have learned from the previous verse was that Dave was a bull, maybe one in a china shop but a physically strong man who is best represented as a bull who fights to the very end.

*****

In contrast to the previous riff-based song we return to a simple chord rock song for the most part using the main three conventional chords in the key of E, enabling the bass once again to growl at its lowest pitch. The bass is, also once again, very high in the mix. The sad subject matter was, perhaps, the catalyst for such a straightforward musical approach so the instrumental creativeness that was appearing on other tracks was kept under wraps here with all four instruments content to play in a very conventional way until the keyboard solo with a change of key after the third chorus moves the songs into another dimension aided by a strange, disconcerting keyboard sound.

This lasts for over a minute and also brings the song to an end which results in the structure being similar to 'Dead Ringer' although 'Dagenham Dave' has a middle eight section after the second chorus. Burnel's tone carries slightly less aggression than in "Bitching and there is more discernible melody in the vocal delivery. The tone of the middle eight carries an emotive reflective resonance which is then released on "Like the howling of bulls". A simple yet fitting tribute.

Bring on the Nubiles

'Bring on the Nubiles' was as the title would suggest another controversial song and another attempt to antagonise the moral majority and the punk elite. It certainly did that, women's groups and sections of the music press began to challenge the band's approach and views on women. The song can be seen as a high-octane 'Peaches' without the humour and whilst on that track the group got the benefit of the doubt — for many the sexism joke had anyway worn thin.

Over the years Cornwell has defended the song saying it was meant to be humorous and maybe it was initially meant to be funny given that the lyrics were so outrageous. Of course, the only other possibility is that he means the sentiments expressed in the words. Cornwell has always been prepared to deal with taboo subjects and part of his motivation on this song is to not hide the meaning. As mentioned in an earlier chapter, rock 'n' roll has throughout its history has dabbled with the age of consent but more often than not tried to disguise the meaning with coy less direct lyrics, 'Sweet Little Sixteen' by Chuck Berry being just one famous example. However other contemporaries of the band like Motörhead and Ted Nugent were almost as direct both penning a song called 'Jailbait'. However, The Stranglers went further by daring to use the word "fuck" in their song. It was the height of punk and bands were pushing the boundaries to see what they could get away with and in this febrile atmosphere Cornwell jumped in with both feet, as if he had been dared to do so.

The word nubile itself is defined as a woman just at the age of consent. Many found this distasteful particularly as they were seen as the old men of punk. The topic has however a long history and has been dealt with by playwrights and authors throughout history. Nabrakov's *Lolita* being a prime example and a book that inspired the international smash hit 'Don't Stand so Close to Me' by new wave contemporaries The Police.

The protagonist in the song is dehumanised by the jerky robotic vocal delivered in an angry aggressive tone. This delivery coupled with the use of violent sexual images like "nail you to the floor" presents the character as a sexual predator. There are potentially some tender phrases in the lyrics, but any pretence of tenderness is destroyed by the vocal delivery and tone.

By dealing with the subject in this most direct way, whether it is meant to be humorous or not meant they were again courting controversy and were in danger of becoming famous for being notorious rather than famous for their music.

The band were at another crossroads. What did they want to be known for? Their music or their notoriety? The truth in 2023 is they are probably known for both with their notoriety fading gradually with the passage of time but like Uranium notoriety has a very long half-life and people still remember the controversy.

The song was later re-recorded some years later in the style of a smooth jazz number entitled 'Cocktail Nubiles'. This particular version will be dealt with in a future chapter.

*****

The Stranglers 1977-1990

Page 12 SOUNDS September 17, 1977

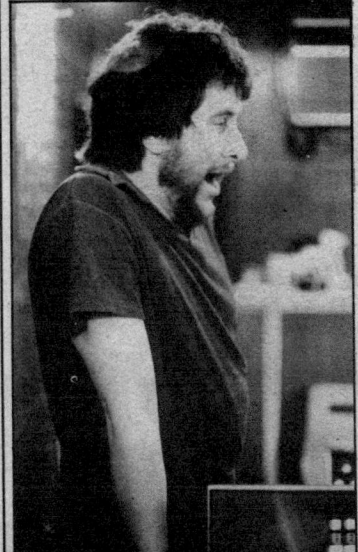

Jet Black
(that's him on the left)

sits about, rolls cigarettes, opens beer cans, drinks coffee...

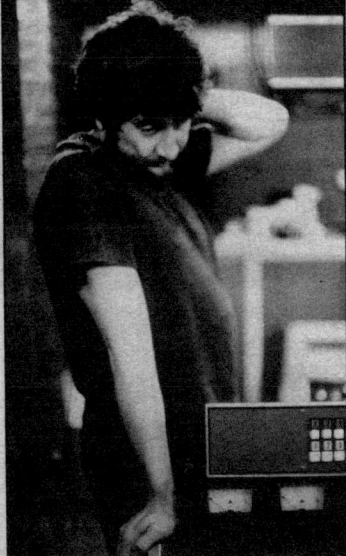

...and mopes around the studio while the other three Stranglers and producer Martin Rushent search for that unique sewersound.

Chas De Whalley searches for words

Chris Gabrin takes searching pix

TW STUDIOS are tucked away behind a drab shopfront off London's Fulham Palace Road. To gain entry you have to go round the side, through a used car lot and down three crumbling steps. The building looks so ramshackle it's difficult to tell whether it's in a state of terminal collapse or whether it's being shored up at the eleventh hour.

It's a far cry from the slick recording establishments you might find in the West End. You can hear the music out in the street, but it still comes as a surprise to push open the battered white door and stumble straight onto the mixing desk.

No lap of luxury this. There is hardly room to swing a cat in the tiny control room. And there are few chairs. The walls are painted some shade of dirty brown. The ceiling tiles are battered and broken while the air conditioner, if it's working at all, fills the square concrete cell with a hum as pervasive as the tobacco smoke in the air.

But as a recording studio, as a place to capture those rock'n'roll vibes piping hot as and when they happen, TW and its twenty four tracks are highly regarded in London circles. Despite its lack of facilities, TW comes out top of the pile for its atmosphere and intimacy.

Even on those terms, however, the place has its drawbacks. Like if you've been drinking too much you'll have to step out into the cold to hang a rat. Once you're there, (up the steps over the rubble and turn right, okay?) you'll find there's no door on the bog. And should have been foolish enough to sample some of Fulham's awe-inspiring array of takeaway food, you'll discover there's no bog paper on the roll either.

What a bummer!

WHILE YOU and I spent the first week of July basking in the sun or staring longingly out of an office window, the Stranglers were locked away in this grubby little pit. Working on their second album even as their first 'Rattus Norvegicus' crested the New Wave and their double headed single 'Peaches/Go Buddy Go' became THE Summer Hit of Seventy Seven. For ten days the toasts of the nation might just as well have called TW home.

But if it wasn't actually home the Stranglers were still receiving visitors. A steady flow of well-wishers. Like the dressing room of a successful football team an hour before the match. Stranglers people like Steve, Dennis and Leigh from Finchley (first the band's fans, now their personal friends, these three young guys recently promoted the Stranglers at a secret North London Youth Club benefit). Stranglers' comrades in arms like Dick and Sheds from the road crew. Representatives from the record company United Artists.

And while the boys were at work the control room was filled with a friendly and relaxed atmosphere that was jaunty even to the point of being jovial. The Stranglers know this studio inside out. They recorded everything they've released there and its seedy backstreet ambience suits their moods. Perfectly at ease, the Stranglers were working under little strain.

Unlike producer Martin Rushent, Chain-smoking with a look of genuine harassment on his face.

"THAT'S GREAT JJ. If you really want drum spill all over the track, you're doing a really great job."

At the mixing desk Rushent sits with a smile of playful sarcasm hiding his exasperation. On the other side of the glass Jean Jacques Burnel bounces past the amplifiers and tiptoes through the trailing leads with his face fixed in an impish grin. He thrashes at Jet Black's kit with all the energy and skill of a three-year-old with a tin drum.

Martin Rushent groans again in mock despair, but Jean Jacques pretends he can't hear. Secretly watching the window along his sly black fringe he crashes the cymbals with renewed vigour. *Le gamin francais* raises titters and smiles as usual. Even the producer has difficulty supressing a snigger.

But Dave Greenfield is not amused. He stands at his keyboards, fingers poised, headphones over his ears, ready and waiting to lay down a lil' overdub. He shoots Rushent a look of mild irritation as Jean Jacques bashes on.

The bearded producer takes the hint immediately.

"Okay, Jean. Dave's ready to do this take. If you don't cut that crap out immediately, I won't let you go home tonight. Come back in here."

Burnel recognises the tone of authority and, obediently he lays down the sticks. But, as he appears at the console door, with the hangdog expression of a truant summoned to the headmaster's study, he looks like there's still a dodge or two up his sleeve. Dennis the Menace with a history book in the seat of his pants.

"Oh Martin. It's getting late, man. Recording's supposed to be fun. You're too much of a slave driver."

"And you're a c----. Stop giving me a hard time' eh." quips out man. "I don't need to take that from you."

The room bursts into laughter. Rushent has this 'Look-I-could-get-just-a-little-pissed-off-with-you-guys' rap that always begins with the line 'I don't have to take that from you'. And it's invariably a show stopper. Jean Jacques played for that point and he won it in a game of verbal tennis the two strike up every time they meet.

Backchat and banter, mental muscle flexing and friendly rivalry make up the twenty fifth track in any Stranglers mix and as the hours drag on, the sun shines bright outside but the tapes continue to roll down below, the jokes and the pokes serve to keep the corporate pecker up, the band cheerful and relaxed and the morale high.

Making records, you see, isn't the most exciting thing in the world. Unless you're personally involved, a recording session can be a remarkably tedious experience. And even if it is you that's got your head in the bucket screaming your thoughts to the world or else lacing your vanillas with electricity, the process is hardly one big party.

For the Stranglers, the same as any other band, it means work. And like every other aspect of rock'n'roll it is money earned under extremely high pressure. Short bursts of high activity, real mental energy squeezed into a thirty second organ break the same way as the whole working day might be compressed into sixty minutes on a stage. The action is exhausting and the subsequent inaction sometimes deadly boring.

Just ask Jet Black what it's like and, reaching for his rolling tobacco, he'll tell you how he spends two thirds of his time simply sitting about. Rolling cigarettes, opening beer cans, drinking coffee and ... sitting about.

There's not that much for him to do, you see. After the basic group

CONTINUES PAGE 14

A Musical Critique

The Stranglers

FROM PAGE 12

backing tracks have been laid down Jet has few if any overdubs to see to.

So he sits at the back, next to the mixing desk, and chips in short and pithily but with fatherly wisdom as the Stranglers and their producer toss ideas around off tape. Otherwise he is silent for hours on end.

So while Dave Greenfield sucks on his Sherlock Holmes pipe and rattles through books of crossword puzzles; while Hugh Cornwell talks knowledgably about cricket, discusses the virtues of Strangler schoolgirl fans or reads socialist book club paperbacks about prisons; while Jean Jacques Burnel bounces between serious conversation and comic riot, Jet Black leans back, puts his hands behind his head and closes his eyes in repose.

You asleep Jet?

"Nah. I'm thinking about my holiday." The bearded face breaks into a smile. "I'm going to Tenerife next week. It's the first holiday I've had for years."

In the beginning there were the Guildford Stranglers and they starved for nearly two years. Then they signed a record deal with United Artists last December and since they have been moving at a pace that would cripple most other bands. Their debut album 'IV (Rattus Norvegicus)' was recorded at the TW studios in little more than a fortnight.

They had little rest since, for they were out working on a gruelling schedule that culminated in the 'Rats On The Road' tour and those two triumphant shows at the Roundhouse. Less than a week later they were back down in Fulham hard at work on the follow-up 'No More Heroes'. They seemed to be what we music critics call a 'creative peak'. In fact where I expected to find them tired and drained after the months on tour the Stranglers were bubbling with ideas and motorvatin' with their foot hard down on the floor.

In seven days they cut eleven tracks for the LP.

And gave short measure to none.

A QUICK look on the label of a Stranglers record will credit no one individual with songwriting credits. The experienced ear can often pick out individual authorship (except for the man from the NME who thought Hugh Cornwell was responsible for the voice as well as the lyrics of 'Princess Of The Streets') but the songs as such are conceived by the band as a whole. Sitting in the dressing room, riding in the car, playing in the studio they pick up on phrases in conversation and marry them to a riff or a beat someone has in their heads.

New numbers are normally rehearsed at soundchecks. But if nothing seems to be working out after twenty minutes or so, that number is dumped unceremoniously. A hard system, perhaps, and one which might trample on a few egos from time to time. But it is one which makes the Stranglers an unusually cohesive and committed band.

The strength of purpose carries over on to record. Few can have failed to notice the actual sound of the Stranglers. It's full, round and rich in texture. A Fleetwood Mac fan with an expensive stereo might even grant it decktime — an honour bestowed on few New Wave bands. There is a quality about the Stranglers recorded sound that creates a vivid, almost psychedelic tension in the jagged nature of the music itself.

Fanfares for Martin Rushent (although he would be the last to claim it was all his doing). This bearded young man with the wit of a used car salesman and a line for every occasion is United Artists 'house' producer and he learned his trade working with just about everybody from Shirley Bassey to Stretch and beyond.

Not automatically the sort of person you'd expect to click with the Stranglers. A bit too Recordbiz at first sight. Talks of 'artistes' and 'acts' and such. Rushent admits that he found the four Stranglers a little perplexing when he first saw them. Now, though, he is open handed in his praise of the band as a whole and as individual musicians.

The claims he makes of Hugh Cornwell's abilities as a guitarist are awe-inspiring. But then Martin ought to know. He started off playing the six string in public himself. He knows it all from a musician's point of view. Which is maybe why despite and because of the playfully insulting banter, Rushent and the four Stranglers get on.

They were a winning combination at work on 'No More Heroes', and they knew it.

But to imply that the songs were the Stranglers contribution and the sound purely Rushent's would be to over-simplify the situation. Even falsify it. Admittedly it's Jean Jaques Burnel's unique bass tone and that eerily unreal vocal timbre that's the key to the Stranglers' Sewertone. And it's in Rushent's department to get it down

Dave Greenfield & Martin Rushent

through to you. Of grabbing your attention. We experiment, but we don't go over the top. But even if we do it doesn't matter."

The adventurous imagination department. The suggestions department. The 'why not an echo on the guitar?' department is staffed by Stranglers and Rushent respects their judgement one hundred per cent. He says they're probably the easiest band he has ever worked with precisely because they are not afraid to speak their minds. In plain simple English or even in the vernacular.

'That's great, you know. Because when you get down to it the sound and emotion of a record is only as good as the ingredients your artiste puts into it. All the producer does is mix the cake. So if you're working with a band that doesn't know what they want you're in real trouble.

So what are the Stranglers looking for?

"Well, it obviously differs from track to track," ponders Jet Black, always the man for a serious appraisal of anything. "But, basically, when we come into the studio we have a preconceived idea of what we want.

"It's a certain sound we get live when we've got a good sound and the acoustics are right. That's what we're looking for."

Hugh

on tape. He freely concedes that he uses the sophisticated modern studio at full stretch to earn his money.

"But we use the equipment in unorthodox ways that would be frowned upon by whoever designed them originally. As far as I'm concerned, the idea is to recreate the vibe I get off the band at a live gig and to compensate for the fact that you can't actually see the band playing in your front room. What tricks are used are to make the right noise. If somebody notices any of them merely as effects then I think I've failed."

But it's them Stranglers 'oo think it all up first.

"We want to sound like ourselves," Jean Jacques Burnel insisted. "We don't want a Ramones sound like most of the other bands these days. We want to explore ways of getting

> 'We don't want a Ramones sound like most of the other bands these days. We want to explore ways of getting through to you.'

JJ

PUNK PURISTS may knock the Stranglers for those operatic productions. They might even claim the Stranglers aren't even a New Wave band at all and use that sound gushing from their speakers as evidence backing their case.

Certain critics will doubtless brand the 'No More Heroes' album 'another case of middle class angst from those sexist hedonistic and existentialist Stranglers'. But this is still a democracy and idiots are allowed their opinions.

The Stranglers hearts are firmly with the 'new politics' of rock even if they approach it from up the fire escape and criticise its back yard while supporting its facade.

Already classic Stranglers numbers like 'Feel Like A Wog', 'Dagenham Dave', 'No More Heroes', and 'Peasant In The Big Shitty' — all on the new album — are by no means songs of selfish appetite. They question the status quo as strongly as the Clash, and only 'Something Better Change' could be criticised as mere sloganry. They question the motives and the integrity of the revolutionaries too. 'Dead Ringer' quite shamelessly points the finger at some of the big punk politicians.

But what about the X Certificate porn of 'Schoolman' or the decadence of that brand new tune 'Bring On The Nubiles'? Our Feminist friends won't buy those two, that's for sure.

The Stranglers are ready to pull the sheets off anybody — YOU even — and if that doesn't give them New Wave credibility then the Boring Old Farts are right. The whole thing is nothing but a Fashion.

or on the end of a skewer

Another song that is riff-based to begin with and then the conventional chords take prominence. It is also a fourth song out of five on the album in the key of E thus, once again, utilising the bass's lowest range. There are none of the clashing notes that were present on the previous similar riff-based songs, 'I Feel Like a Wog' and Dead Ringer' although the alien sound effects create a similar disconcerting mood. The structure does not possess the longer instrumental sections that were present in the previous two songs but there are two short instrumental breaks that showcase Greenfield's growing interest with otherworldly sounds and these sounds permeate through the song, aided by the Dalek like vocal effects on 'Bring on the Nubiles'. The second keyboard solo adds to the alien palette with a series of SFX sounds rather than melodies and is a precursor to the keyboard solo in 'Nice 'N Sleazy'.

The vocal melody is in unison with the riff on bass and keyboards thus reinforcing the simplicity of the song and drawing us more towards the unequivocal lyrical content. There is a strong rhythmic drive to the main riff with the use of rests helping Cornwell to deliver the staccato vocal delivery.

A simple, quick song and whilst many will see the lyrical content as being too outrageous, it is difficult not to be uplifted by the infectious groove.

Something Better Change

Side one closes with a song which was the closest to writing a punk anthem the band ever came to, with Burnel giving a metaphorical two fingers to the establishment and indeed anyone else who didn't embrace the new cultural, musical and fashion movement. Or if you like it could be the bass player arguing with his girlfriend, either way it works on both levels and captured the mood of the time. It's a great song a stonking piece of rock 'n' roll rebellion with a killer melody and a feeling of arrogant swagger and anger. Quite rightly chosen as a single to trail the album and consolidate the Top Ten success of 'Peaches'. It gave the band their second top 10 hit[10] and cemented their position as serious musical contenders who were more than a novelty one hit wonder act.

The adrenaline fuelled start of the song with the instruments building to set up Burnel's a guttural howl "OOH!" It is an incredibly powerful intro and an iconic moment of the punk movement. That one primeval roar sums up the emotion of the time articulating in one sound the feeling of the country's disenfranchised youth. More meaningful and to the point than the plethora of words, songs and political pontificating that were swamping the music world at the time. Amazingly the energy and anger is maintained in the rest in the song by the jerky angular melody in tandem with Burnel's Tourette's like delivery

The song has a live feel with Burnel's ad-libs to Cornwell ("Yeah change it Hugh!") and Greenfield ("Go Dave") before their instrumental breaks giving a feeling of gig excitement. It's an established rock 'n' roll convention most people will be familiar with, Paul McCartney doing the same in The Beatles with songs like 'Back in the USSR' and 'Get Back'. It's also Burnel again asserting himself as band leader for a song he sings. The singer's voice is even snarlier than usual because he is singing about cultural rebellion and his tone is dripping with sarcasm and 'don't give a fuck' attitude. However, in the lead up to the chorus with the "Something happening" line Burnel breaks into a tuneful voice for a couple of lines a nod to the future and his more melodic voice.

The song was left over from the *Rattus Norvegicus IV* sessions but obviously not because it lacked quality. Perhaps realising they had a sure fire hit and that the song didn't fit in with the vibe of the first collection, the song was kept back. The group were in such a rich vein of form they could even afford to donate the searing 'Straighten Out' (analysed later in this chapter) to be coupled with it on the single and potentially condemn another quality song to flip side obscurity. In actual fact it was promoted as a double A-side, but it was 'Something Better Change' that got the airplay.

*****

Back to the chordal texture for the final track on side one and a symmetry as songs one three and five were more riff based whereas songs two four and six are more chord based. The verse/chorus structure is also highly conventional for most of the song although the reasonably long guitar solo and the two shorter instrumental breaks towards the end of the song reinforce bands' preoccupation with combining vocal and instrumental textures on equal footing. Although Burnel's vocal tone is bristling with aggression, there is a clear melody. The first phrase is based around the bass riff but the two distinct bridge vocal phrases contrast effectively and this, allied to the clarity of structure led to his song being wisely chosen as a single.

A departure from E into the more studious key of G flat and the very first bar heralds an anticipatory guitar riff that is soon left behind never, unfortunately, to be heard again. However, the organ chords that soon join in add to the sense of expectation. As the drums and bass then explode into the mix there is no doubt the exuberance that is to follow has already been emphatically established. The guitar distorted chords remain higher in the mix than in previous songs and the overall sound for the entire song feels like a 'one take' live mix where all four instruments are sharing the energy. The fact that the guitar is panned hard left whilst the organ is panned far right throughout the song adds to the projection of the four separate instruments standing out.

Burnel's use of inversions (playing a note of the chord that is not the main note) in his main riff and on "Ain't got time to wait" add a piquancy of interest to the chords and, of course, Greenfield's fast rising arpeggios on the "Something's happening" bridge move the song into an even more powerful gear.

Cornwell's guitar solo commences with typically melodious phrases albeit with distortion and, as it descends towards the end into more of a thrash, Burnel replaces his inverted note into the main/root note (at 2:09) propelling us towards the climax. The keyboard rising chordal riff from the introduction helps, this time, to signal the climax and the final riff adds the flattened second chord which is to become a crucial chord on the seventh album *Feline*, albeit creating a completely different mood. The final held organ chord is guillotined by the shouted "Change" accompanied by the band all coming off together. The simplicity of the message of the song delivered with Burnel's aggressive tone is combined with the rawness of the live feel alongside the clarity of melodic contrast and the structure so it was no surprise that the song was an early hit for the band and remains a hugely popular singalong with fans today.

No More Heroes

The title track was the second single from the album and kicks off side two giving the band their third top ten hit in a row.[11] To many fans it defines the band and it has also has moved into mainstream consciousness during the last forty-five years, most recently being used in the trailer for the BBC series *SAS Rogue Heroes*. It's also the song the band have played most live.[12]

It has a timeless quality; the tune is exquisite, and the witty lyrics still resonate today. The start of the song has become iconic a short bass solo makes it instantly recognisable – the rest of the band kick in to set up Cornwell with the greatest opening line in rock history. From that point on the quality doesn't falter until the song is done three minutes later with its crescendo ending.

Released in the summer of '77 it again takes advantage of the punk maelstrom that enveloped that Jubilee year. Lyrically it works on several levels with Cornwell bemoaning the fact that all his heroes are now dead, but one can also approach the lyric from the completely opposite side and read it as anti the idea of having heroes at all. If one takes this interpretation, it very much fits the non-elitist ethos of punk. It's another example of Cornwell's lyrics being multi-facetted with no straightforward explanation.

All bands wishing to appear punk adopted antihero and anti-elitism stances. The Stranglers did it with their famous sabotaging of the BBC's *Rock Goes to College*. Denouncing elitist organisations as they left the stage. Other bands were less spectacular but still subversive even it was a small gesture like Paul Weller sporting an 'I am nothing' badge. The Clash refused to do *Top of the Pops* because bands were only allowed to mime. The Stranglers more effective approach was to appear on the show and make their point when asked to mime by subverting the medium by deliberately messing with the format. When they appeared on the show to support 'No More Heroes' they swapped instruments and mimed very badly with Black famously and hilariously doing his rock god impression on guitar.

As well as the hilariously savage opening line "Whatever happen to, Leon Trotsky? He got an ice pick that made his ears burn", Cornwell invented the word Shakespearoes simply to get a rhyme with "hero". Despite the word being initially a functional technique to make the song lyrics scan it has become a cult word that people drop into conversations.

So, what is a Shakespearoe? Fans and critics had their own views. The idea of it describing a sycophant is popular but there are many other interpretations positive and negative. Perhaps the best clue to helping secure a definition is the following line "They watched their Rome burn". A reference to Nero, the psychotic murdering Roman emperor who allegedly played his fiddle whilst the great city burned. By placing this line after the Shakespearoes line it suggest a person who is ineffective, who procrastinates when they should be decisive, abdicates responsibility and is frightened to act because of the consequences for them, in other words certainly not a hero. The substantive point being that all heroes have their flaws. Whatever Cornwell meant by the word shakespearoe, if indeed he meant anything at all, it is a wonderful sounding, evocative word that just nails the dry wit vibe of the song. Sadly, the word hasn't made it into the Oxford English dictionary yet.

Elsewhere the lyrics list a series of famous people from Sancho Panza, the Mexican revolutionary leader; the Great Emyr, the artistic forger and controversial American stand-up comedian Lenny Bruce, cutting edge and boundary pushing comedian. It is Lenny Bruce not Lenin who is referenced. Many jumped to the conclusion it must be Lenin as Trotsky was mentioned in the first line. These days at gigs the band and Cornwell in his solo shows make it clear by singing "Dear old Lenny Bruce".

As a song it's a classic and has entered into the popular consciousness. An interesting footnote to the song's story occurred in 1995 when Britpop band Elastic 'borrowed' the tune for their hit 'Waking Up'. The Stranglers' publishers sued, and the case was settled out of court with a royalty and co-writing agreement.

*****

The song that most defines the band and, yet there is much simplicity to the actual music with regards to the chords, melodies and texture. The song brings together many of the trademark features with prominent bass and keyboards, fast rising arpeggios and one minute fifteen of instrumental in the middle of the song. But almost any chart hit needs a strong hook line and the title itself is so emphatic, with the message in keeping with the 1977 mood, that allying this to these trademark musical features was always likely to result in a memorable song that will be forever remembered.

The opening bass is a fans' folklore and whilst it does not really prepare us for what is to come, there is a uniqueness about it that belies convention yet propels us into the main groove. Burnel states the main keynote of G, then plays that G an octave higher whilst moving back to the low G but the higher notes now descend in a frenetic whirl. These descending notes never quite reach the lower G but seem to give up when they are so tantalisingly near and splurge out holding a discord, refusing to resolve thus maintaining the anticipatory edge. All the instruments then enter at once and the keyboard riff is simple and uses arpeggios in its construction, but it is Greenfield's trademark sound on the Hohner Cembalet keyboard that is memorable.

Once the vocals begin, the final two chords that formed the four-chord pattern of the preceding instrumental are now flipped the other way round. The arpeggio keyboard riff continues whilst Cornwell sings the verse using only two notes for his melody. When the bridge arrives, "Whatever happened to the heroes" the vocal melody is now more expansive and the keyboards race into the fast, rising arpeggios that were also utilised on the bridge of the previous song, 'Something Better Change'. There is only one chorus of "No more Heroes anymore" sung twice before the middle instrumental section where Cornwell delivers a less melodious solo than in some of the previous songs, but here it captures the indignant mood before Greenfield answers it with a more structured solo where, after a brief fast rising arpeggio moment, he settles into an elongated triplet rhythm section over the standard straight rhythm being played by the rest of the band.

There follows a longer pitched section before moving up in pitch again and then, the coup de grace where a simple repeating A, B flat, A, G, is played over the bridge chords that have been used for the entire keyboard solo but then at 2:23 the band move back to the verse chords whilst Greenfield continues repeating this riff. A moment that defies words.

After another verse, bridge, and double lengthened chorus the end section is another structural example of the band using a new instrumental section to end a song. In this case, they use the riff that had been heard briefly at the end of the bridge phrases and this section further strengthens the belligerent mood. Burnel, who has hitherto been playing a supporting role following his introductory burst, plays this riff, Greenfield plays a continuous high notes riff and Cornwell plays rising long held distorted notes on the last beat of every bar rising by step from F to D before repeating the D note to bring us to an emphatic and glorious end.

Peasant in the Big Shitty

One of the key tracks on the album that signpost the way to the band's future musical innovation and experimentation. The unusual time signatures, the weird sounding vocals and the multiple melodies make it standout and if you want a rock musical label its Prog. However just because it's unusual does not necessarily mean it's a good listening experience.

But this is where the band have excelled in their career because when they did become musically complex, they created extremely listenable music that pushed the envelope of popular music. They were rarely experimental just for the sake of it and if they were, they tended to end up as B-sides. It should also be noted that for a band that now had such a high commercial profile such experimentation was risky.

"Peasant" was an old song and was briefly considered for *Rattus Norvegicus IV* but was deemed rightly not to fit the feel of that album. Although sung by Greenfield it is in fact a Burnel song. The complex bass part meant, just like with 'Goodbye Toulouse' he had it all on with his instrument, never mind singing as well. This time Greenfield stepped up to the mic and although rather busy in the song himself with the keyboard melodies he carries off the vocals with aplomb with his now distinctive vocals, a kind of Captain Beefheart rasp and it was this vox that most people latch onto in the song initially.

This does the song and the other musicians a disservice as the crucial part of the song is Black's drumming giving the song an unsettling feel, which the rest of the band embrace and although coming from different directions the instruments mesh to form a sonic masterpiece. The band realised they were onto something, and such experimentation informed their work for most of the next four albums.

Lyrically for once it's a Burnel song not about a woman! The song appears to be describing a bad trip and the paranoia associated with that. Greenfield's unique vocal style perfectly embodying the sinister inner voice that can be a symptom of a paranoid mind. Several colours are mentioned in the song which supports the idea of a psychedelic trip. The title brings us back to a common Stranglers theme, their love hate relationship with London.

The title obviously expresses the writers' thoughts about the metropolis and other references in the song present a picture of a decaying conurbation, for example the phrase "The day is sticky yellow" hardly suggest a health environment. It may also suggest pollution in a big city which was a massive issue in the seventies. Seeing himself as a peasant the lowest of the low medieval society is a metaphor for the crushing oppressive nature of the city.

The whole atmosphere of the song, the words and music is confusion which could be related to a drug stupor as well as a sick city. The final verse refers to garlic and fear, adding to idea of paranoia and introduces the suggestion of vampire hallucinations, the city not as an animal but as a vampire sucking the life out of its inhabitants.

*****

An important song that demonstrates how the band were placing structurally and texturally conventional songs ('Something Better Change' and 'No More Heroes') side by side with highly unconventional songs. The structure here has no sense of a verse leading to a chorus but has the main section being interrupted by two new sections, the second one being instrumental, that have suddenly moved a long way away from the main section. A return to the main section is then interrupted by another unrelated instrumental section to finish. Texturally, the song deploys the multi-melodic layering approach from the outset, and when Greenfield solos the bass and the guitar continue playing different melodic riffs. This texture is further reinforced with no chords as such for the main section or the second "You're not real" section.

Another key unconventional element at play here is the time signature. The band had experimented with changing time signatures with 'Goodbye Toulouse' from *Rattus Norvegicus IV*, but this is the first time where the rhythm to most of the song is based on an irregular time signature. The drums commence proceedings and immediately alternate each bar between four beats and five beats per bar. This unsettling effect is heightened by Black's off beat accents during each five-beat bar. The bass and keyboards enter in unison on the main riff covering the nine beats of the two bars, but, immediately upon the first repeat, Greenfield employs an additional high harmony.

On the third playing, two guitar riffs enter, panned left and right, both with an enigmatic feel. Greenfield's spoken vocal plays on the mysterious nature and the use of effects like the portamento on "alright" and "like that" and additional echo and reverb allied to the panning, the multi layered melodic riffs and the irregular time signature, further exacerbate the unnerving atmosphere.

The song takes an unexpected musical turn into a new key following the keyboard solo and second verse where a bass riff, with much off beat unison with the drums, accompanies the "You're not real" vocal. This is now sung with Cornwell adding a vocal harmony which is panned hard left but when he sings "Oh know you're not" the panning moves towards the centre. When this phrase is repeated, it is panned hard right this time and moves to the centre again. The overall effect maintains the disconcerting effect that had been established from the outset and, when listening with headphones, invades the headspace, getting under the skin as it were.

The music takes another sudden turn into an instrumental in a different key at 2:03. This major key creates a less menacing atmosphere with guitar and keyboard soloing over a descending scalic bass before returning rather abruptly to the main verse section. Extended portamentos and effects on the now severely disturbed vocal and Cornwell's backing "Just a peasant in the big shitty" add a sense of closure as we expect a fade out. But the twists and turns have not finished yet as the ending suddenly moves into a new section with three beats per bar before a messy final 'come off' by the band, reinforcing the disconcerting feel.

This song has a huge significance on the band's future direction with changes of time signature, use of vocal effects and sudden new sections in different keys as well as continuing to give prominence to instrumental sections and clashing notes. Traditional rock and punk fans were rightly eulogizing over the superb singalongs of the previous two songs, but this track was developing those disparate and unconventional ideas that had started to appear on previous songs into a coherent whole and established the band as having a two-pronged musical attack of the expected and the unexpected.

Burning Up Time

The band's homage to speed their drug of choice in the early days. Lyrically it's a straightforward, Burnel's description of an away day romp travelling on the Brighton Belle train to his girlfriend's (Choosey Susie) in Brighton. He cleverly uses the term Brighton Belle to describe his girlfriend which is also the name of the iconic electric train which ran between London and Brighton between 1933 and 1972 and a bit like the Flying Scotsman entered into public consciousness. The lyrics also reference uber fans the Finchley boys who unofficially did band security and also fuelled themselves with alcohol and speed. The theme running through the song is that old rock 'n' roll adage live fast die young and leave a good-looking corpse it.

Musically it takes two of punk's main virtues, speed and brevity and clocks in at under two and a half minutes. Cornwell's careering guitar lead is genuinely unsettling and sets up Burnel to uses his shouted vocals to glorious effect. Greenfield in contrast plays a sweet-sounding melody, the polar opposite of his two comrades on guitars that is until towards the end where he gives us an electronic maelstrom of a solo. The song has a disturbing end with what we can only assume is a potential paedophile offering a young girl sweets. "Hello little girl, are you on your own? Does you mummy know where you are? Would you like a sweetie?"

The ending appears to have been bolted on as it seems totally unrelated to the rest of the song. It may be just a naked attempt at provocation which was something the band were now masters of. 'Stranger danger' in the 70s was a major concern and public information films were shown regularly on TV warning of the perils of strangers. It is worth noting that then and now statistically most danger to children comes from people they know. The most famous 'danger' films were the cartoon cat series of films called *Charlie Says* featuring a boy and his pet cat, Charlie warning of perils youngsters might encounter. One of these cartoons featured a stranger with sweeties. Parents drumming into their children the menaces of outsiders and this put stranger danger at the forefront of public consciousness. The band knowingly tapped into this consciousness and were perceptive and calculating enough to realise it would add to their reputation and notoriety. Classic Stranglers, musically and attitude wise.

*****

After the unpredictability of the previous track, we are back on familiar ground with an up-tempo track that flatters to deceive at the start as the opening keyboard riff is clearly in a major key and the bright Cembalet sound suggests a more polite mood than the one that soon thunders in with Burnel's shouted delivery and then sets the frenetic atmosphere for the rest of the song.

It quickly moves through four short sections and the distorted guitar riff after "Other peoples' bad times" deploys a pleasing simplistic aggressiveness. The keyboard solo has a strong shape and more cross rhythms and then Burnel's previous vocal energy manifests itself into a brief bass surge where the energy is maintained, especially as the vocal delivery has all but ceased after one minute ten seconds.

The long instrumental final section develops from the previously mentioned guitar riff, using a scalic rising series of bass notes, mirroring the descending bass line from the instrumental in the previous song, whilst the guitar plays a repeating variant of the riff. There is another guitar riff being played in the background which then comes to the fore with keyboards adding ballast to the sound.

The main guitar riff now fragments to play just one note, then two notes, then three and so on. It is debatable whether Cornwell's menacing whispering adds to or intrudes upon this final section. The unconventional song structure of the four short sections that are then all repeated followed by a keyboard solo and then then a long instrumental end section is another example of a song giving equal weighting to instrumental passages with unexpected twists to end the song. The texture is a mixture of chords and being riff dominated and the chords never completely settle into the main key of A as the "Like a meteor" short section suggests a key change.

The long end section never settles into a key either, thus reinforcing an unsettling feel. This fluidity or ambiguity of key was growing during the first album with examples of subtle shifts going into the chorus of 'Hanging Around' and the shifting under the opening keyboard riff of Grip being two examples. The fluidity will become a common feature and will stand the band apart from many other bands.

English Towns

Yet another Burnel lyric but sung by Cornwell and reminds us that it is sometimes easy to forget that Burnel was probably the dominant writer in the band in 1977, certainly in terms of recorded tracks. Being a good-looking young man and in a band, he was never short of female company and takes that traditional rock 'n' roll path of writing about his conquests on the road.

There were so many that he talks about, thousands of lovers that he can barely distinguish and compares them to the faceless high-rise blocks found in the titular English Towns the band found themselves in during their long tours. Burnel calls the tower blocks "Ivory towers" but he isn't of course referring to aloof seats of learning but to the ubiquitous white high-rise dwellings that like academic ivory towers divorce their inhabitants from wider society. It's a nice juxtaposition and demonstrates that even in an almost throwaway song the band were working on several levels of meaning. Elsewhere the line "seeking pleasure seeking fame" neatly sums up Burnel's 1977 modus operandi.

Musically Greenfield saves a basic track with his flowing melody line and Hugh adds a nice off kilter guitar line towards the end to give the track a bit more interest. In terms of the vocals, it's Cornwell's classic gruff croon, a style that he was starting to perfect. There was less of a snarl in his delivery, and it was becoming voice he would settle on to use on the band's best work.

Not a bad song but not up to the band's usual high standards. It's a bit of an album filler however to be fair it didn't outstay its welcome at only two minutes thirteen second longs. It was a popular live number and indeed many fans will argue it's one of their personal favourites.

*****

The fluidity of key continues as the main section suggests B but the second "I can see their" section shifts to E but the shifts to this section and back to the main section are barely noticeable. The structure is also continuing the trend of stating the main sections early and then having more instrumental focus later in the song. But in 'English Towns' there is no real development of new ideas into the instrumental sections so the predictable playing by all the instruments creates a highly conventional texture, and the repeat of the lyrics towards the end results in a less interesting outcome than in the previous songs. The instrumental section at 1:18 with the repeat of the guitar riff and a keyboard solo in the background highlights the multi-melodic layering textural approach.

Cornwell's vocal line is more melodious despite the negativity of the subject matter and the key shift helps the song to move along in a contrastingly gratifying way. This song clearly carries the least menacing mood on side two. There are also further examples of the band playing triplet figures in unison towards the end after "In a thousand girls" but, overall, the song cannot live up to the stronger singalongs or the unexpected musical riff-packed instrumentals that preceded it.

School Mam

The inspiration whether subconsciously or directly, for the song is the Velvet Underground's 'The Gift'.[13] Musically the tune tries to mirror the Velvets as it rambles hypnotically for seven minutes with several interesting musical highlight. On 'The Gift' John Cale used a spoken word approach to narrate a wickedly sinister and shocking story of a man wrapping himself in a box and having himself delivered to his lover as a gift. The story ends badly when she uses a knife to open the suspicious package and inadvertently stabs him to death. Cornwell matches the narration approach, but the quality of the lyrics/story aren't in the same league as the Velvets. Cornwell recites a sexual fantasy in a leering drawl which is full of innuendo and lurid Imagery.

The story is about a teacher and his pupil having sex and being spied on via CCTV by the prim and proper, sexually repressed principal the School Mam of the title. The couple orgasm as does the principal, but the excitement of her voyeurism cause her to have a heart attack. The added irony being it is the first and last time she climaxes having never had sex before. There is undoubted humour in the lyrics and of course they are meant to be provocative. The sexual liaison is done without sexual language so it's not shocking in that way in fact Cornwell tell us to "use your imagination" instead of using a graphic copulating like he had in 'Bring on the Nubiles'. The shocking thing to most people now would be the sexual relationship between the teacher and who we assume to be a sixth form girl. A liaison that today would be deemed illegal.[14] This was not true in 1977 and there were many cases of teachers having relationships with sixth formers and many went on to marry and have children.

Cornwell as a very young man was briefly a teacher in a private sixth form girl's college. However, we get the impression he hasn't got much sympathy for the teaching profession and with a type of jealous glee he brings his guns to bare on the profession with jibes about long holidays, monthly salary cheques and free milk. So, teachers or those involved in education therefore struggle with the song because of the constant jibes at their profession but it's nothing personal just the band's now familiar tactic of questioning accepted.

Towards the end of the song the lyrics have an improvised feel as the singer embarks on a tortuous mental arithmetic route to reach fifty with plenty of witty, smutty asides on the journey to his half century.

Producer Rushent added in playground sound effects to set the tone of a school, and this is almost the highlight of the tune as it is a deliberately dull dirge, lacking any real musical high spots. The song was a big live favourite in the early days, and it was played on what was to be Cornwell's final tour in 1990. When the song was played live Cornwell famously simulated an orgasm in a very graphic way by, pardon the pun, jerking his neck and using saliva to simulate semen yet another example of the band ruffling feathers of an establishment.

*****

The opening guitar riff with low octave effect promises much but the following groove, where the drums steadfastly remain on toms, never changes. The guitar opens with an angular solo that is intended to jar across the steady repetitiveness of the bass and the drums. The keyboard has very little input across the whole track and any creative guitar work ceases after the opening solo and is replaced with low pulsing distorted chord notes. The bass tries to inject movement as the verses progress, but we are, sadly, here to listen to the lyrical message and the music lacks any forward momentum.

The "Oooey" section employs a tritone/devil's interval relationship to reinforce the dark mood, but we then return to the previous musical elements. The music could easily have been improvised in a couple of run-throughs by such creative performers, so we are left to wonder why we had to be subjected to over seven minutes of repetition.

The long closing song from *Rattus Norvegicus IV*, 'Down in the Sewer', with all its different musical substance and sense of movement throughout the different sections brought the album to such a climax whereas here the album peters out from a musical perspective, not helped by the previous song which also had limitations.

The Stranglers 1977-1990

A Musical Critique

Musical Summary

Not surprisingly considering that four of the songs were recorded at the same time as the *Rattus Norvegicus IV* songs, the sense of continuity was present regarding the overall sound. But the engineering had a slightly tighter, less ambient sound and Burnel's aggressively mid EQ bass tone was, perhaps, even more to the fore, maybe with the band realising that this was central to the difference in sound between them and other bands.

Greenfield's three different keyboards were also, again, central to the overall sound. There was much to admire from the drum and guitar contributions and the sense of the ensemble of all four instruments creating the unique Stranglers sound was reinforced. The contribution of the highly unconventional drum patterns to 'Dead Ringer' and 'Peasant in the Big Shitty' was important as this was the more experimental side to the band that was to permeate through into more songs to great effect.

It was interesting to note that "Peasant", the stronger of the two songs, was left over from the *Rattus Norvegicus IV* sessions. Maybe the band believed that such musical experimentation was not suitable at the time of their debut. It is a blessing that the band saw the potential for this song as the contrasting compositional style was, perhaps the most significant realisation during their early years and elevated them from a direction of being mainly Pub Rockers. Vocally, Cornwell and Burnel continued their aggressive tones, with, as before many of the melodies shouted. The addition of Greenfield's voice on two of the tracks added another dark and menacing tone to the overall sound.

The band's use of chords and keys had more of the clashing/dissonant notes with 'I Feel Like a Wog', 'Peasant in the Big Shitty' and 'School Mam' being examples of songs that were largely defined by the dissonance, something that had less influence on *Rattus Norvegicus IV*. The fluidity of key, as mentioned during the analyses of 'Burning up Time' and 'English Towns', continued to move the songs into different sections, in these instances seamlessly or sometimes, as in the instrumental sections of 'Peasant in the Big Shitty' and the endings of 'Dagenham Dave' and 'Burning up Time', with a more sudden lurch into a distant key to change the mood. Most of the chord patterns used were conventional.

The unconventional structures that had permeated through *Rattus Norvegicus IV* where new instrumental sections played an important role in developing songs were continued here and most of the songs had endings where new instrumental ideas helped to maintain momentum. Furthermore, there wasn't a single fade out on the album which helped to reinforce this notion. The two most conventional structures were the two hit singles, 'Something Better Change' and 'No More Heroes' where the verse and bridge sections helped to prepare the way for the more climactic choruses.

The song lengths of *No More Heroes* show that only two out of eleven songs were close to the four-minute mark, in contrast to *Rattus Norvegicus IV* with seven out of nine songs. The two lengthy songs, 'Bitching' and 'School Mam', are also two of the weaker songs from the album and were from the initial *Rattus Norvegicus IV* sessions. So, the band clearly moved towards shorter songs, and some will argue that some of the songs lacked a sense of completeness, especially when comparing them to the songs on *Rattus Norvegicus IV*.

The solos, whilst still present on almost every song, were shorter and carried less of the interplay between guitar and keyboards that had occupied a significant part of *Rattus Norvegicus IV*. The lyrical messages were nastier, and it seemed that the band made deliberate attempts to trim the instrumental excesses to result in shorter songs with more punch to support the bluntly controversial lyrics.

Texturally, the songs were a mixture of being riff-based and chordal and the multi-melodic layering textures of 'Dead Ringer' and 'Peasant in the Big Shitty' reinforced the experimental approach to texture that had been bubbling on *Rattus Norvegicus IV*.

The band had so many melodies created by instrumental sections that songs like 'Peasant in the big Shitty' and 'I Feel Like a Wog' never suffered from a lack of a melodic vocal line.

The nine-beat time signature of 'Peasant in the Big Shitty' was the first example of a Stranglers song being based around such an unconventional rhythm and, along with the drum groove in 'Dead Ringer' was a highly effective foil to the energetically driving riff-based songs like 'I Feel

Like a Wog', 'Burning up Time' and 'Bring on the Nubiles'. 'Something Better Change' was a strong sing-along and, of course, the musical masterpiece of its time, 'No More Heroes' resulted in an album that, musically, maintained the bands reputation.

The songs were weaker than on *Rattus Norvegicus IV*, but the more simplistic aggression resulted in a reaffirmation of the qualities of the band in the eyes of their fans. The extra tracks that were not on the album were, overall, strong on quality and some would argue that the album could have been further elevated had one or two of these bolstered the second half of side two by replacing the weaker songs.

Album Summary

No More Heroes is a very popular album with long term fans but despite that perhaps the most dated of the pre 1984 albums. The main reason for this was nearly half the album were tracks left over from the debut. 'Peasant in the Big Shitty' and 'Something Better Change'. were two stunning songs but perhaps didn't quite fit the all-round feel of Rattus. The other remaining songs 'School Mam' and 'Bitching' didn't make the debut album simply because they weren't strong enough and using them on *No More Heroes* emphasises this point.

The music of some of the newly written tunes was highly inventive 'Dead Ringer', 'Bring on the Nubiles' and 'I Feel like a Wog', whatever their lyrical failings, pushed the band's musical envelope. However, this was not the case of all the new songs and tracks like 'English Towns' and 'Burning Up Time' have an element of the perfunctory about them. They are reasonable tunes but there is nothing particularly special or innovative about them. Both these tracks are the band almost doing and impression of themselves chucking in musical and lyrical elements willy-nilly to make it Stranglesque. 'Dagenham Dave' on the other hand at least had a good narrative with interesting images and an off the wall musical break going for it.

Rattus Norvegicus IV was a genuine surprise when it arrived and that is part of the reason it has remained timeless. When *No More Heroes* appeared six months later it had a strong element of more of the same. A *Rattus Norvegicus IV* part two about it so therefore it lost the element of surprise. The band also did what was expected of them in terms of being obviously controversial. On their debut the controversial parts were genuinely shocking on *No More Heroes* it appears there more for effect rather than to be unsettling and challenging.

In addition, the subject matter was also very much the same as its predecessor and there was now an element of fatigue setting in with more songs about the London scene. The band were realising this and even when the album was high in the charts in late 1977, they were plotting their next move and direction with new recordings taking them on a different creative route.

All this said there were some great tunes on the album the title track is a timeless iconic classic, 'Something Better Change' a great tune that captures the mood of the times perfectly. Add in 'Dagenham Dave', 'Peasant in the Big Shitty' and 'Dead Ringer' and you have half an album of great songs. If only they had a little bit more perspective and been more patient with recording and added in 'Straighten Out' and '5 Minutes' (recorded at the end of 1977 thus missing the cut) instead of 'Bitching' and 'English Towns' (which could have been B-sides instead) and you would have something to rival *Rattus Norvegicus IV*.

'Bring on the Nubiles' and 'I Feel Like a Wog' whilst musically incredibly vibrant and innovative they are let down by overtly deliberately provocative lyrics, a tactic which had worked on *Rattus Norvegicus IV* because it was a surprise and very well executed this time it felt far to premeditated.

By today's standards the album was rush recorded and released A bit more time, patience and critical appraisal of the material would have made it an undoubted classic. Instead, we have a very good album released too close to the seminal debut to be regarded as a classic. The reason for the fast follow was record company desperate to build on the band's initial success and current hot property status. Artistic consideration barely entered their thoughts, more of the same and make it quick.

Meanwhile the band were moving on creatively keen to be more experimental but still make listenable and thought-provoking music. Martin Rushent their producer wasn't taken with this new approach and whilst staying on board for the next recording the beautiful relationship was coming to an end.

The Stranglers 1977-1990

Page 32 SOUNDS September 24, 1977

Heroes or zeros?

THE STRANGLERS
'No More Heroes'
(United Artists UGA 30200)***

AHHH — BUT these are testing times ... now the very real euphoria has subsided, the scales have fallen from my eyes: not recantation, but re-evaluation. Timely sift and sort. Now I'm blinded I can really see ...

Oh, the Stranglers, such nice boys. But they *need* to be nasty, so squalid. And they do it so well. Look at Hugh Cornwell, standing on stage, posture saying: 'C'mon man, c'man get me, g'wan, I dar ya ...' They want to get up your nose. They want to shock. They want to confront you with the seamy white underbelly ...

OK, OK, OK. So why did 'Rattus Norvegicus' sell so well, then? Because they're bright and talented enough to translate their aggression and studied venom into direct musical terms: an instantly recognisable sound [which'll be hard to break away from] that scrapes under your skin and lodges there, even better as an irritant. You can't escape it. And of course they're heavy metal macho cross-over — perfect for the time when there wasn't much punk product and most were unconverted but ... curious. And it was brilliantly produced, and their constant playing paid dividends, and it was right in there with the then zeitgeist — all that stuff about rats and angry, suitably 'change' oriented lyrix ...

Well here we are with new product, all tarted up in a hideous — successful indeed as kitsch — chintzy chocolate-box style sleeve. Inside, on cue, a rat appears — very reassuring. The themes of utter negativity, seediness, sleazo inputs continue, only, by the great law of Alice Cooper, a little more hysterical, more strident, just nastier. Oh look: more titles for 'liberals' to get fussed about: 'I Feel Like A Wog', 'Bring On The Nubiles', and some creepy-crawlies: 'Peasant In The Big Shitty', 'School Mam'. Sort of like 'Plague Of The Zombies'.

Oh, you guessed: I don't like the album. I've tried very hard [really: for all the 'right' reasons] but I still think it sucks. No, this isn't a critic's Set-'Em-Up-And-Shoot-'Em-Down exercise, nor a virulent manifestation of putative — new wave elitism — the Stranglers convinced me they had something when I heard 'Grip' thundering out over Portobello Road and couldn't rest until I'd found out who it was.

I got no axe to grind — but what I hear now turns me right off.

It'll sell. Half the album is full of very strong material: songs which are ridiculously catchy and well-constructed, and, oh yeah, they stay in the head ... 'No More Heroes', 'Dagenham Dave', 'Bitching', and the best, 'Burning Up Time'. The rhythm section is simply very tight, relentless, while the organ that fleshes the sound out [and *does* bring to mind Seeds/Doors at 45 comparisons] holds some kind of magical power with its hypnotic swell, sinister undertone. Oh yes, they can do it ...

But it sounds so *assembled*, somehow. And the material isn't as consistent as last time around; some of the songs, 'Dead Ringer', 'School Mam', 'Peasant In The Big Shitty' are plain awkward, embarrasing in parts ... A problem is Cornwell's lyrix/stance, and the band's intrinsic and deep coldness. No amount of 'intellectual' rationalisation can get round the fact that too many lyrix are dumb. Dumb — and Cornwell patently isn't. Like at the end of 'Burning Up Time', he goes into this 'Hellow little girl, want a sweetie ...' routine, and blows it. 'Bitching', with its 'Why don't all go get screwed' refrain. Or the platitudes of 'Something Better Change'. Or the end of 'School Mam' ... The rest of the band meshes so closely that his voice is given more prominence: under close security, it seems forced, trying to be tough, macho, too hard.

And the subject matter. 'Wog', 'Nubiles', 'Bitching'; point taken. Holding up a mirror, confrontation etc. (although 'Nubiles' comes over most as being adolescent) — but who needs them as moralisers? Agreed that having your face rubbed in a cess-pit can, on certain occasions, be salutary (shock/emetic). Beyond a point, reached on this album, it seems more redundant, self-indulgent. I mean we know already that England's 'going down the toilet', we've been told often enough. What to *do* about it? Because the Stranglers offer nothing positive, not even in their music. Look: the Pistols tell you we're being flushed too, but their music has a kick, a bounce, a tension that gives you energy, makes you want to do something. Some sort of life out of decay ...

The Stranglers rumble along relentlessly, zomboid, with sledgehammer blows driving their message home ... they move, but they can be so wooden. Like a skimming coffin lid ...

I suppose they got up my nose, didn't they? So they win in the end. Some pyrrhic victory, though. The music's powerful enough to get some reaction (always better than none) but what comes off this album, with its deliberate unrelenting wallowing, is the chill of death. No life force, nothing vital. Not so that it's frightening, just dull and irritating, ultimately. And it doesn't make it as a statement, even though its all taken so seriously.

Oh well — you can take it or leave it. They need this review like a hole in the head, so do you — no doubt you'll all buy it anyway. I know it isn't aimed at me, but it sounds as though everyone's intelligence is being insulted, yours, mine, and that of this record's creators... — JON SAVAGE.

STRANGLERS: so assembled

Extra tracks: Standalone singles and b sides

Straighten Out (Double A-side single with 'Something Better Change')

A furious frenetic song that begins with a frazzling bass run and a post apocalyptical cry by Cornwell worthy of Jaz of Killing Joke. The verses sprint along courtesy of the frenzied bass work. The pressure lets up slightly for the chorus as the vocals become more laid back and the backing vocals harmonise. Greenfield let's rip with a devastating solo and then the vocals return for a frantic finish and fade out but this time the laid-back chorus becomes a desperate chant.

In terms of lyrics there is a collection of disturbing images which feature allusions to religion, one of Cornwell's favourite topics, cannibalism a theme explored throughout their career and potential revolution by young people. Society at that time was seen as broken with much social unrest in the country. Despite the enforced joy of the Silver Jubilee there were riots on the streets in 1977 – the Notting Hill carnival disturbance being a prime example.

Lyrically Cornwell represents society's breakdown. By referring to "cracks in the wall" Cornwell isn't sure why he references cannibalism in the first verse[15] but it's not much of a leap to say by using an image of cannibalism he is depicting a broken, dog eat dog society. The line about little boys and little girls destroying their toys is a call for young people to take direct action. The title itself, 'Straighten Out', implies that these ills need to be resolved. Some might also see a drugs reference in the title, addicts talk about coming off drugs as being straight or straightening out and another view would be a reference to a criminal leaving their past life behind and 'Going straight'. The band yet again working in a complex way. Cornwell and Burnel were throughout their career clever enough to imply multiple layers to their lyrics.

The song is full of menacing because of the delivery regardless of what the lyrics mean, it's a frightening collection of images designed to shock and unsettle. The song was used as the flip to 'Something Better Change', officially as another double A-side. In reality it was 'Something Change' that got the airplay most probably because radio would have shied away from such a provocative opening line so effectively the song was lost to daytime radio airplay. With hindsight it was a waste of a great song which would have fitted well on *No More Heroes* and even better on *Black and White* and would certainly have enhanced both collections.

If it had been written by The Clash the press would have never stopped lauding it as a song that captured the cultural zeitgeist. The song did make it onto the *Live (X Cert)* album thus getting more much deserved exposure and was another well-loved live song. The track is also one of the first example of the band moving on from punk. It takes the attitude and anger but the subject matter and the technically expertise take us into a darker place and towards a musical genre that would soon become known as Post Punk.

*****

A song which uses conventional chords and a conventional structure with the short verse, bridge, chorus repeated three times followed by an organ solo and an ending which gives a vehicle to Burnel's exuberant bass runs, the change on the fade out where his constant rhythm moves higher, being particularly imposing. The texture of the song is also highly conventional. Apart from the introductory and closing bass pyrotechnics, all the instruments display a conventional approach to this typical fast paced rock song.

It is a well-crafted song with the melody in particular displaying the contrasts of the high-pitched bridge following the low pitching verse and the chorus is in between in pitch, but the rhythm is now a stark contrast with much longer notes to the short notes of the verse. This serves the song well and the appealing hook line reinforces the lyrical message. One could argue that word painting is at play here with the long and reasonably 'straight' shape of the "Straighten out" chorus melody.

5 Minutes

A single released in early 1978 and recorded after the album was released in late December 1977. Written by Burnel. It's lyrically and musically another step in the new direction the band was perusing. The subject matter and it's dense, harsh, and in your face track, a musical maelstrom hardly a formula for commercial success.

Burnel's frenetic bass playing personifies the anger of the song. The track careers along like a runaway train, and it doesn't take any prisoners because as the words suggest "If you hassle me mister I might just lose my head" it's not for the faint-hearted. Yet despite this the song made No. 11[16] just one place away from it making four consecutive Top 10 hits for the band.

The lyrics tell the grisly tale of the rape of a former girlfriend of Burnel's by a gang of men. It happened in a flat he was living in at the time but on the night happened to be away when the attack occurred. Concerned for his own safety Burnel left the premises and became effectively homeless, forced to sleep rough at the recording studio the band were using, Bear Shank Lodge. The lyrics are delivered in a blistering broadside of a voice and represents Burnel's most effective use of his punk vocal style. The tone and style scream anger and the need for revenge. Burnel's true feelings and emotions are reflected in the lyrics despite reports that the rapists were black Burnel refused to condemn all black people as racists would call him to do.

This is in marked contrast to Liam Neeson's 2019 remarks when promoting his movie *Cold Pursuit* where following experiencing a similar incident, he admitted that immediately after the event he had racist feelings and wanted to kill a black person at random even going so far as to admit stalking the streets with a weapon looking for revenge.

Burnel deals with the racists calling for him to hate all black people extremely effectively with the line "Some say that I should hate them all, But I say that wouldn't help at all" and followed it up in press interviews later "I just wanted to find those guys, I didn't use it as an excuse for hating all black people. How would you?"[17]

He was also sensitive enough not to mention specifically the attackers' ethnicity in the song, unfortunately reviewers did that for him. Burnel was fully aware that mentioning the perpetrators race could stir up racial hatred and responsibly chose to deliberately not directly refer to ethnicity. In the late seventies Britain was experiencing a surge in support for the racist National Front political party and racial tension was high. The singer is very clear it's only the perpetrators he is after not an ethnic group.

The bass players raw emotion, frustration and anger are ably demonstrated when he appears to inadvertently use his other native French to express his emotion in spoken word in the outro "Et si j'les trouve, Mon pauvre chouchou, enculés! J'les aurai! J'les aurai!" which translates to "if I find them, my poor darling, motherfuckers! I will have them! I will have them!" Another example of classic Stranglers subversion not too many bands get the word motherfuckers albeit in a foreign language into the top 20.

Using French may have been a rouse to get the word into the song, but it also shows Burnel's emotion and anger, by reverting to his parents' first language to express extreme emotion without suffering moral outrage from middle England.

'5 Minutes' sees the band beginning to build on the change in direction signified by tracks like 'Straighten Out' and 'In the Shadows'. Burnel's lyric writing was still mostly in the story telling mould, but the subject matter was far more serious. This isn't a life on the road song or just a description of London's exotic life. It deals with a serious and dark issue in a righteously indignant way but at the same time manages to stay rational.

There are some familiar themes in there, the rotting edifice of London city life, the title refers to the fact the rape took place in a notorious part of London whilst five minutes away you'd be in the richest part of the city. The music was darker and moodier, and this is summed up by the single picture cover a black sleeve with just digital display red titles for the song and the band at the top and bottom.

The lyrics were printed on the back using the same format, the red display signalling the danger and menace of the song and its content. The video was equally dark shot in shadow at awkward angles in a studio that looks like a slaughterhouse. However, the film does look professional and was a step up from the videos the band had filmed earlier in the year.

★★★★★

A majestically powerful song with a secure verse/chorus structure that not only has keyboard and guitar solos, but also has a middle section that is then unconventionally repeated to great effect at the end. The successful chart position of the song is due to the direct message and strong hook line but, once again, the band are developing a song structure that is subtly different to the norm but more interesting for it.

The foundations are laid by the repeated low keyboard chord on top of the simple repeating bass drum on every beat. This enables the initial guitar riff to move away from a traditional key with its use of the sharpened fourth to create a clashing, dissonant feel. The bass has a restless feel of improvisation at the start before they all settle on reinforcing the same chord which is the only chord used for the verse.

However, all three melodic instruments continue to engage in fills: guitar panned right, keyboard left and bass in the middle, reinforcing the multi-melodic layering texture on top of Black's now trademark bass and snare on every beat, thus resulting in an energetic and aggressive wall of sound. The chorus see a change of chord but there are only two chords in total for the chorus and this simplistic static use of chords enables the reinforcement of the wall of sound.

Burnel's use of an inversion for the second of these chords could, in other circumstances, have weakened this wall but here it seems to add to the powerful force. Black also adds to the belligerent mood in the chorus with his fast snare rolls after each "Almost there".

The middle "Some say that I should" section after the short keyboard solo has more chordal movement which destabilises the sense of key that was clearly established in the main sections, thus providing an effective contrast as does the vocal melody that has now moved to a lower range and, in doing so, sounds almost reflective compared with the verse and chorus until Burnel emphatically abandons this reflection with the final "That's all that's all" phrase. This is followed by a guitar break that is based on the sharpened fourth riff from the introduction and again reinforces Cornwell's ability to use dissonance to enhance a song and creating a more foreboding mood.

The ending sees the return of the middle section with Burnel launching into French and the fluid chords of this section result in a final chord that does not belong to the main key of the song and is therefore unsettling, as is the guitar feedback and the clock ticking. This reinforces the aggressive perfection that was established by Cornwell's dissonant guitar allied to Burnel and Greenfield both agitated in their playing to create the multi-melodic layering whilst Black provided the glue and extra snare filled impetus. All of which provides flawless accompaniment to Burnel's melody which, despite the obvious confrontational vocal tone, has a strong melodic shape that is almost forgotten amongst the hostile mood.

Rok it To the Moon (B-side of '5 Minutes')

Strange as it may seem, but this is a key track in the band's musically development. Most fans probably haven't even heard the track or may have played it once as it was the B-side. Once was probably enough for most fans as it isn't the most accessible or particularly outstanding of songs. Closer listening reveals the track as the stepping stone away from the mire punk rock was becoming into the world of post punk experimentation and beyond.

It's the first time the band actually really experiment in the studio and use the studio as another instrument rather than simply for recording their existing live set. A variety of studio effects are used including what appear to be tapes running backwards and lots of sci-fi electronic bleeps and whistles from Greenfield's keyboards which had first appeared on 'I Feel Like a Wog' and 'Bring on the Nubiles'.

On this track he gets free reign to whip up a storm and this type of sound would inform the band's sound for the up-and-coming album, *Black and White* and collections beyond that. Cornwell's lyrics are treated to given them a staccato feel. The feel of the music is of an urgent jerky stomp. The band even recorded a video for the track using the same stage set as the '5 Minutes' video. A video effect makes the group's look like they are playing light sabres from *Star Wars* instead of their instruments. *Star Wars* had only just been released for a month in Britain when the single was released and was taking the country by storm. Whether it was planned or not is a moot point but if it wasn't it highlights the Midas touch in terms of mirroring cultural events the band had at this point.

The words are set in the near future where Cornwell predicts a dystopian future for the world as early as 1988. It's a prophecy and something the band had used as a theme before with 'Goodbye Toulouse'. He paints a scene of world hunger and people resorting to cannibalism, as we have seen already a popular Stranglers subject throughout their career. The escape for the narrator is to fly to the moon and watch the planet and human race self-destruct from there.

As ever with Cornwell there are little puns and knowing jokes in there. The spelling of the title as 'Rok it' instead of 'rocket' is a nice little pun and a dig at traditional rock bands particular hard rock bands who were forever talking about rocking things e.g., "rock 'til yer drop" "rock this town".

There is also a nice line using the album and hit single title "No more heroes". The phrase is juxtaposed to not having T-bone steak which is clearly a humorous reference but nails the point made earlier in the song about food shortages. The next line follows through the theme saying there will be no more bread or cake. A famous reference to French Queen Marie Antoinette who allegedly told starving peasants to eat cake if they had no bread. Lyrically there is clearly a green agenda before it was fashionable or well known.

*****

The opening keyboard two note chord over the hi-hat immediately exudes an air of the otherworldly, almost towards the famous Hitchcock *Psycho* mood. Cornwall then introduces a rhythmically energetically jarring three note riff completely at odds with the keyboards to reinforce the sense of the unbelievable. This is clearly going to be a different musical ride to its A side, '5 Minutes'.

Over the relentless constant quaver guitar, bass guitar and bass drum rhythm, Cornwall further disengages the journey with his vocal melody especially with a very clashing/dissonant last note of the phrase. The structure is relatively straightforward as the jarring chordal relationships are enough to provide an unconventional experience found in the bass and guitar notes which are not centred around a traditional relationship and create an ambiguity of key.

The "I'm gonna rok it to the moon" chorus changes the key in an even more abrupt fashion. This rocket is not set for a smooth ride. All the while, Greenfield has abandoned any pretence to play along and is set on reinforcing the otherworldly atmosphere with constant sound effects that are augmented by the tape reversing effect.

After the second chorus, the constant driving rhythm continues over a new set of dissonant notes enabling Cornwall's guitar solo to be rhythmically diverse and melodically angular and has the tape reversing effect, reminiscent of The Beatles' *Revolver* album.

The climactic final chord is, again, dissonant to previous tonal centres and Greenfield has the final say as his effects complete the journey into the world of the infamous sixties children's TV show *The Clangers*. The entire song challenges us as listeners with its unpredictable chordal, melodic and key relationships. This unpredictability allied to the effects is certainly a barometer of what is to come on the following three albums. Many listeners, even ardent fans, will find this too challenging but, for some, the song is a fascinating foil to '5 Minutes'.

For both this song and '5 Minutes', this was also possibly the first time that the band experimented with tape speed for the song pushing it into a microtone between standard 440 Hz tuning and thus making it challenging to play along with as the standard tuning of a piano or guitar would be slightly different.

In the Shadows

Although recorded around the time of the *No More Heroes* album and used as a B-side to the first single from the album it appeared as a track on the next album *Black on White*. The song is appraised in the chapter on that album.

Footnotes

1. Official Charts website

2. Official Charts website

3. Official Charts website

4. trevorrogersphotography.com/, Album cover sleeve notes and Progrography website

5. trevorrogersphotography.com/

6. *Sounds* magazine 11/2/78 Simon Dell Archive

7. Burning Up Time website and Facebook page

8. *Song by Song* – Hugh Cornwell and Jim Drury

9. *Song by Song* – Hugh Cornwell and Jim Drury

10. Official Charts Website

11 Official Charts website

12. setlist.fm website

13. *Song by Song* – Hugh Cornwell and Jim Drury

14. In 1977 sexual relations between a teacher and a pupil over 16 was not illegal. Since 2001 a teacher having a sexual relationship with a pupil who is over 16 is illegal. Sexual Offences Act 2001

15. *Song by Song* – Hugh Cornwell and Jim Drury

16. Official Chat Website

17 JJ Burnel interview

Stranglers arrested

TWO OF the STRANGLERS were arrested in Brighton last week after a gig at the Brighton Top Rank. There was some trouble at the gig between the police and Hells Angels, two of whom were arrested. When the Stranglers learnt of the arrest Jean Jacques Burnel and Jet Black went down to the police station to try and bail them out.

Burnel, Black and a friend who had gone with them were then charged with disorderly conduct and held in the cells overnight. They were bailed out on £75 each and will appear in court on November 15.

Page 60 SOUNDS May 20, 1978

THE STRANGLERS

TOUR DATES
20th May   Brighton Centre
26th May   Glasgow Apollo
30th May   Bingley Hall Stafford

BLACK AND WHITE ALBUM

Album UAK 30222 / Cassette TCK 30222

Black and White

There was no let-up in the bands recording schedule, before Christmas 1977 they were recording standalone single '5 Minutes'/'Rok it to the Moon' which on release reached No. 11 in the UK charts.[1] Early in 1978 they were back in the studio recording their third album. By May it was in the shops less than nine months after the release of *No More Heroes*, making it three albums in less than eighteen months an astonishing schedule by today's standards and even for the late seventies it was going some.

Martin Rushent was at the console again but this time the recording was done at Bear Shank Lodge, which sounds like it should be located in the Rocky Mountains of America but was in fact in Northamptonshire. The tracks were laid down in February and March when famously there was snow on the ground and such imagery was one of the factors that led to the albums name. The finishing touches were done back at their old haunt TW Studios.

The album was trailed by the single 'Nice 'N Sleazy' released in late April. It peaked at Number 18[2] which must have been a slight disappointment given the band's recent run of hits and it being such a brilliantly innovative and catchy song. The album was released on 12th May and peaked at No.2 and stayed in the charts for eighteen weeks.[3]

The first 75,000 came with a free EP featuring the tracks 'Walk on By', 'Mean to Me' and 'Tits'. Bizarrely 'Walk on By' was then released as a single in July allegedly due to fan demands and whilst a respectable hit reaching No.21[4] the fact there were 75,000 copies out there already must have hindered its chart placing.

On the surface the chart performances were good but actual sales were not as good as the first two albums. It's clear that as the band were beginning to spread their wings musically and lyrical and become far more complex and wide ranging in both areas. This meant to some extent they started to lose fans particularly those who preferred the in your face attack and rawness of many of the band's earlier songs.

John Robb in 2011 magazine *Louder than War* rightly refers to it as the first Post Punk album. At the time it wasn't recognised as such. It was The Stranglers and to most people it therefore must be punk with a bit of a twist. Reviews in the music press were more discerning but not all thought that it was a step forward for the band. Not one review saw it as the start of a new genre which of course is understandable particularly in the confusion and ferment of the music scene in the late seventies. Historically musical innovation and invention are seldom properly recognised or appreciated at the time, The Stranglers were the proverbial prophets without honour.

Looking back forty-four years later it is clear that *Black and White* was the start of a new musical movement that moved punk out of the dead end it had turned into. So, what is different about the album and why is it so important and influential? Firstly, musically it is a huge step away from much of the material on the first two albums. The first two albums had their experimental side but at the same time the tracks the band were best known for were their hits, their straight-ahead album filler rock numbers and their flirtations with high octane rhythm and blues.

On *Black and White* every track demonstrated a band pushing musical boundaries. It was without doubt a challenge to many fans of the first two albums. It even challenged band producer Martin Rushent who in an interview years later was disparaging about much of the material the band were coming up with and wanted the band to continue to mine the seam of *Rattus Norvegicus IV* and *No More Heroes*.

"I liked some of them and some of them I had problems with. I like 'Toiler on the Sea' and 'Nice 'N Sleazy'. There were others like 'Tank' I had a problem with. Because I admit I love the first two albums so much I loved that style of music for the rest of my life and been very happy with it".[5]

He stayed on board for the album but the band to their credit trusted their judgement and stuck with what they wanted to do.

Musically, Greenfield used the Mini Moog synth more than in the previous two albums and this resulted in a more atmospheric soundscape at times yet his trusted organ and Cembalet sounds were still in force so the versatility that he created resulted in keyboards generally being even more prevalent than before with bristling arpeggios once again sitting side by side with solos and memorable riffs.

Cornwell continued the conventional chordal approach, but his melodic riffs were growing in importance and creativity and alongside Burnel's continuing explosive melodic bass work and the keyboards, the band were employing more of the multi-melodic layering textures that had previously only been fleeting in appearance.

Black's drumming also assumed greater importance on several tracks with his idiosyncratic patterns leading to a greater rhythmic complexity, especially when partnered with tempo and time signature changes. Structurally, the continuation of different instrumental sections in songs maintained the unconventionality had already been established on *Rattus Norvegicus IV* and *No More Heroes* and most of the songs retained a brevity and gave the impression of having very little in the way of 'filler' sections.

The vocal tones were starting to move away from the more aggressive and shouted delivery which resulted in more shaped melodies. The use of more complex chords with less use of the conventional chordal patterns was growing as was the dissonance. Every one of these musical features was pointing the way forward for the band and away from the norms of punk and pub rock.

Lyrically Cornwell developed as well choosing to leave behind the street life and parochial punk scene they had brilliantly documented on their first two albums recognising such subject matter was a cultural dead end that was now being worked by every up and coming 'punk' band. The Stranglers turned their attention to world affairs, cold war paranoia, dystopian nightmares, Japanese philosophy, and psychotic personalities. They had of course already dallied with the prophecies of Nostradamus but with their third album they immersed themselves fully into the nascent post nuclear apocalyptic counterculture of the late seventies.

We didn't know or realise it at the time, but The Stranglers ushered in the post punk movement and *Black and White* was the movement's first definitive statement. In the ensuing forty years history has been somewhat rewritten with other bands being credited with inventing the post punk movement post.

Simply summed up post punk that took punk's energy and irreverence but moved it away from rough, fast, three chord rants and pushed the music and lyrical boundaries to widen the definition and acceptance of what popular music could be. PIL, Wire, Siouxsie and The Banshees and Gang of Four, to name but four of the pretenders to the crown. All great innovative bands who changed the musical landscape, but all owe The Stranglers a debt as it was the Meninblack who kicked down the door to what we now call post punk.

The Stranglers innovation, legacy and contribution to this movement has largely remain uncredited, forgotten or even been erased from musical history, Reviewers, and even historic reappraisals of the scene, with the notable exception of John Robb, seem content to emphasis the band's notoriety rather than their innovation whilst at the same time choosing to give the plaudits to other bands.

There was originally supposed to be a concept behind the album, with one side sung by Cornwell and one side by Burnel. This didn't quite come off but if we consider the original vinyl version of the album the printed record label calls one side 'black side' which has very dark songs and then on the flip printed 'white side' on the label with some slightly lighter or less dark tracks.

If one follows the album's title the black side should be played first so therefore the opening track should be 'Curfew'. At the time there was debate between fans on which side to play first. However, if they had consulted the pre-recorded cassette released at the same time as the vinyl and looked at track listing on the back of the cassette box and in the inner sleeve, they would have discovered it's the white side that is meant to be played first therefore making 'Tank' the opening track. The compact disc reissues released years later confirmed this running correct order by starting with the white side.

The artwork reflects the contrast implicit in the title. The band dresses in all black save for a white sleeve on Burnel and white panels on Greenfield's shoes against an all-white back drop. There is no album title or band name on the front cover. The back cover is all black apart from the band's name at the top and minimal record label information in white. The inner sleeve printed the white side lyrics in black on a white background and vice versa for the black side. The striking and effective design was done by Kevin Sparrow and the iconic cover photo was taken by Ruan.

As well as a punishing recording schedule the band continued to tour relentlessly. There was a first visit to the USA. The band might have had new musical horizons, but they still maintained or more accurately were dogged by their notorious reputation which to be honest they were doing little to try and lose. The launch event for the album in Iceland being a prime example, where the band chose to settle a couple of scores with journalists by subjecting the scribes to humiliating scenarios.

The recording and touring schedule made the time around the recording and promotion of the album difficult and put band relationships under pressure particularly the relationship between Cornwell and Burnel. Cocaine and heroin were becoming part of the two protagonist's lives and the potential for a split seemed high.

Certainly, there appeared to be strong rumours in certain parts of the music press even if nothing was overtly said. The result of the tension whether planed or not was a sabbatical with the next full band release of original material being sixteen months later in September 1979. The band had released three albums in the first sixteen months of their recording career in an effort to keep them current.

As alluded to earlier, taking such a long layoff could have been commercial suicide. So, whether it was planned or just merely happened, it was an inspired decision that probably kept the band going. The time was used productively with Burnel and Cornwell working on their own material which would later be released as solo/collaboration albums the following year.

A live album *Live (X Cert)* was put together featuring tracks from their Battersea Park gig in '78 and the Roundhouse shows from '77 was released in early '79 to ensure there was some profile for the band as well as the solo offerings.

Martin Rushent produced *Live (X Cert)* but was unhappy with his own work commenting, "I don't think I captured them."[6] Rushent had just about kept going on *Black and White* but by the time it came to *The Raven* realised it was time to depart. Tired of the arguments between Cornwell and Burnel and triggered by the recording of the track 'Meninblack' he walked away from the band commenting later, "For their sake they needed a new mentor".[7]

Tank

An explosive opening salvo with a song that charges along at breakneck speed the sound of the song is a metaphoric tank smashing anything that gets in its path. The pace and exciting dynamics are thrilling and it's no wonder that since the song's unveiling it has been a firm live favourite. The lyrics are about the armed forces and the instrumentation and sound effects add to this feel with military drum rolls on the snare, explosive sound effects and booming bass.

On the surface the sound, pace and snatches of lyrics give the impression of an exciting tune which could be used as an army recruiting campaign, 'Join the army and see the world' as the 1970s army recruiting posters used say. The real message is rather different. Cornwell takes on the persona of a new recruit seduced by military hardware, be it a tank or a self-loading rifle.

Initially we are invited to put the narrator's love of weapons down to youthful enthusiasm and the wide-eyed naivety of being given the keys to a military kit sweet shop. At the end the darker side of the armed services is made clear with the listener made to confront the reality that the protagonist is a trained killer. The extended shout of "maim" serves to emphasise the darkness of what he has become. The way the word "maim" is expressed with an excited glee tells us the narrator is a little bit too excited about the prospect of harming people, he likes his work a bit too much. Join the Army, see the world and kill people.

Interestingly Burnel in the NME in 1978 seems to claim it isn't anti armed forces and a celebration comparing the rush of driving a tank to riding a motorbike. Yet again the band were working on several levels of understanding and never afraid to be contrary by chucking the metaphorical cat amongst the pigeons.

The subject matter was a new departure for the band and perhaps the first time a band from the new musical movement had taken a side swipe at a military institution. Criticism of the armed forces became ubiquitous in the punk and post punk world. Bands as diverse as The Skids, The Gang of Four, Stiff Little Fingers and of course The Clash forged their careers with songs about the armed forces. Military fatigues became de rigor for most bands, but The Stranglers as ever were content to plough their own furrow in terms of a sartorial image. Not for them the cliché of the army surplus greatcoat and camouflage, instead the band – ever ones to adopt a contrary approach – opted to dress in all black. The clue to their future couture being the cover of the album with its stark contrasting photograph of four black clad figures against a brilliant white background. The Meninblack had arrived.

The instrumental end of the song is interesting giving a musical metaphor for the tank running out of gas as the instruments slow down and finish the song with a grinding halt. The tank is empty and maybe the armed forces referred to in the song are as well, originally full of promise and excitement but ultimately the realisation there is a darker truth.

*****

A tighter, more clinical mix from the previous two albums is evident from the outset. This is not however detrimental to the overall impact, as the opening song has impact in spades. A furious pace is immediately established with the lengthy drum roll followed by a bass performance that is one for the ages.

One of Burnel's finest moments with many melodious fast paced runs throughout, but the result is somewhat more subtle than in previous albums and due, in part to the more sensitive mix and less aggressive bass EQ. In short, the bass blends in more to the overall sound as do the other instruments The song is strong enough for the instruments to support it rather than, at times in the first two albums where sections of some songs seemed to be vehicles for the bands' instrumental prowess.

There are the immediate trademark arpeggios on the Cembalet but more subtlety in the verse where the organ feels more mellow and supporting. The drums are softer sounding compared, for example, with the opening songs on the previous two albums, with a little more reverb giving the impression that they are a slightly lower in the mix, but the guitar is slightly more prominent although, once again, with a tone that blends in rather than standing out. The vocal melody in the verse is more shaped and with a less aggressive tone than was the norm on the first two albums and this further reinforces the blending in of the overall sound.

The song has a typically tight structure where, against the norms of the time, the second chorus is cut short to move into a different section in a new key which reinforces the notion established on the opening two albums of lengthy instrumentals being central to the overall impact of the song as the key change has moved this section into a new direction as important to the overall song as the verse and chorus sections. This section provides the opportunity for a robustly rasping keyboard Mini Moog solo for twelve bars, followed by a bass solo which is moving us back into the original key, It is accompanied by explosion effects which, to some opinions, could have been lessened in the mix to hear more of the intricacies of the music where the low synth sound and the bass seem to compete for the limelight but in a way that enhances the power of the music.

The wondrous bass line also comes to the fore in the "Drive drive" chorus which has a different shape for three out of the four repeats, but it never intrudes until the instrumental. The final chorus sees even more of Burnel's fireworks especially with the fourth "Drive drive" phrase and the following sprawling keyboard solo also possesses great shape in a mode (Dorian) that suggests some clashing dissonance and segues neatly into effects as the song comes to an aptly stuttering end. Jet Black has the last word with a trademark cross rhythmed brief snare fill before an emphatic final chord.

The chords are conventional throughout but the change of key into the instrumental section raises the unconventionality of the song which supports the structural idea of highlighting new sections. The energy of this strong song is clear yet there is a subtle shift in vocal melodic feel and general wash of sound compared to the first two albums. Same difference, and emphatically so. And... that bass.

Nice 'N Sleazy

A hit single and a *Top of the Pops* appearance but the band's lowest chart placing since '(Get A) Grip (On Yourself)'. Maybe it was too off the wall with the otherworldly almost insane synth break, jerky rhythm, and existentialist musing. This is a piece of musical genius, combining complex musical ideas, which meld into a remarkably memorable catchy song relating a life on the road tale with religious imagery. Another controversial move by the band in their unerring aim to provoke, question and entertain.

The song has a pseudo reggae feel with Cornwell's compact crunchy sounding rhythm guitar providing stability for the others to come together with their individual virtuoso magic and combine to create yet again marvellous synergy. The opening of the song featuring Black unaccompanied on the drums provides a rhythm pattern that makes the song instantly recognisable, no mean feat for a drum pattern but something he had already achieved earlier in their career with the pattern for 'Peasant in the Big Shitty'.

On the surface the lyrics are about the band's experiences with Hell's Angels in Amsterdam. The Hell's Angels had adopted the band in their early days and the band had many experiences in Britain and Europe with various Chapters. Cornwell's lyrics are a type of existential impressionism using biblical image to paint a picture of a tribe of people searching for the Promised Land. If one dips into the lyrics, you can't fail to see the link. For example, the complete final verse is packed with biblical references at the same time the same words reference the Hell's Angels:

'An angel came from outside

Had no halo, had no father

With a coat of many colours

He spoke of brothers many

Wine and women, song a plenty

He began to write a chapter in history'

Angel, halo, and a reference to the prophet Joseph plus an implied reference to the prophetic land of milk and honey, need we say more. With such references, the song although about the Hell's Angels is also quiescently about faith and religion.

Elsewhere the song implies desert travel, another reference to the search for a Promised Land. If final evidence were needed the lyric references a preacher, implying the cleric is a charlatan but hugely influential. The song positively drips with religious imagery and Cornwall demolishes the institution with his delivery and clever word play. Without doubt an iconoclastic song. That said there is an obvious narrative around the biker gang references like "chapter", a Hell's Angel club. And "A coat of many colours" refers to the jackets the bikers wear which are adorned and decorating. The "brothers many" line refers to the whole biker gang and finally the "Wine women and song a plenty" is the notorious partying these gangs got up to.

By writing in this style Cornwell is mimicking biblical verse the lyrics are working on at least two different plains. Perhaps the key is the pronunciation of the word "History" as in the study of past events, or does he say "His story" two separate words as in a man's story. In fact, if you listen carefully the pronunciation falls between two stools being neither "history" nor "his story" but a fudge which makes it impossible to decide the exact enunciation. This is deliberate and Cornwell's clever way of demonstrating the song has more than one meaning.

The title 'Nice 'N Sleazy' is a play on the phrase nice and easy (also a famous Frank Sinatra big band jazz number) and nails the lifestyle of the Hell's Angels in a single phrase but again it also refers to the way religions find it so easy to manipulate gullible people with fear and unrealistic promises. By replacing the word "easy" with "sleazy" suggests the dirty underhand way faiths religious or otherwise control their followers. The attack on faith is also carried by the "Angel with no halo", a swipe at religious leaders, as angel with no halo of course suggests Lucifer, the devil which of course neatly brings us back to the Hell's Angels.

Cornwell's sardonic, menacing delivery is vital to the song's overall feel of seething anger. At times he spits out the words at critical times. In just over three minutes, the band deliver on every front controversial subject, musical invention and a Top 20 hit to boot. The atonal synthesizer break perfectly represents the unsettling, controversial feel of the song. The band were in a category of their own in terms of the Top 20 hit makers. An iconic song which has been used as a soundtrack to provide an unsettling atmosphere for TV reports.

*****

There are links to 'Peaches' with the reggae influenced groove and memorable prominent bass line but there are some subtle differences. The vocal delivery is far more restrained which is no surprise considering the difference in lyrical message. 'Nice N' Sleazy' is, however, a far more complex song and it is the drum pattern that sets the tone here. There is essentially a six-beat intro before the guitar enters with hi-hat only for beats one and two followed by bass and snare and the open hi-hat on the offbeat of beat four.

However, when the vocal commences, it is an unusual ten beat first phrase, but the drum pattern keeps repeating as a four-beat pattern. So now when the second phrase "We used our hands" appears, the pattern is halfway through so beats three and four (including the offbeat open hi-hat) are now on beats one and two. At no point however does this break the flow of the song. This creative drum pattern infuses and elevates the entire song as had been the case with 'Peasant in the Big Shitty' from the previous album.

Such distinctive patterns were to become widespread and crucial to future songs for the next two albums as well as *Black and White* but, sadly, these influential rhythms were to fade alarmingly from the fifth album onwards.

Structurally the song continues to demonstrate unconventionality as the second verse does not appear until the end of the song. There is also a now trademark long instrumental section which is different to any previous section by the band as the solo is composed entirely of sound effects on the Mini Moog synth which certainly gives the song a unique focus.

The sparseness of the texture to this song effectively contrasts with the wall of sound opener, Tank. Each instrument is so clear due to this sparseness and Cornwell's brooding staccato, almost rhythmically robotic, vocal is also very prominent enabling the memorable lyrical content to really infuse our consciousness. We feel as though we are in room with Cornwell intruding into our personal space as he begins "To write a chapter, in his story". No backing vocals here necessary as the one voice is very much in our headspace.

The keyboard effects that dominate the middle section of the song are, as with all the other sounds and vocal, clearly prominent. These effects and unusual structural elements were possible reasons why the song did not chart particularly highly. But that is of little significance when their appearance on *Top Of The Pops* influenced legions of young people to believe in this sound that had been established with 'Peaches' but had taken an even more challenging twist with the synth sound effects. The new wave was in full flow with bands like The Police, The Jam and even Dire straits all having distinctive new sounds, but nothing was as brooding and disconcerting as the 'Nice 'N Sleazy' sound.

Outside Tokyo

An exquisitely unforgettable song which perfectly illustrates how the band complement each other. A sublimely haunting keyboard led song where in terms of accompaniment the rest of the band perform their 'less is more' roles to perfection.

The lines of the song see Cornwell philosophically musing on the concept of time and the way it is measured he posits the idea of time as a finite commodity and that it was invented. He surmises when watches, the device time is measured with sell out, time will end. Clearly a bizarre statement as this couldn't possibly be the case, time isn't a commodity which can be bought and sold and won't end when all the watches have been sold. Time isn't like that. Or is it?

We constantly use inaccurate language when talking about time or the concept of time. Who hasn't used phrases like 'buying time' or 'time saving'? We are talking about time in a metaphorical concept when we use such phrases, not in terms of time being a concept of physics. Cornwell is using it in a metaphorical way and by raising the issue of the end of time it invites us to think more about time and muse about how we measure it and how we perceive it. We all have different perception of time, depending on the kind of activity we are involved in, it can appear to be fast or slow. Or we talk about running out of time, a wholly inaccurate understanding of the concept but we all know what we mean when we say it.

Setting the song in Tokyo or outside Tokyo is no accident it places the song in the centre of the world digital watch making industry and the electronics giant *Seiko* which along with the car industry was helping turbo charge Japan's economy in the 1970s. In 1978 Britain a land of strikes, high inflation and unreliable cars was being seduced by digital watches and cheap efficient cars ushering in a new era of troubled economic times for the UK. The song is just as relevant today just swap the digital watch of the song for today's smartphone. A timeless song.

*****

Melodically the album is a clear departure from the previous two albums as the opening two songs have had discernible melodies even though the rhythm of 'Nice 'N Sleazy' was very rigid. 'Outside Tokyo' further advances the melodious feel and, along with other elements of the song, pushes the album further away from the realms of punk that permeated large parts of the opening two albums. In some ways, 'Outside Tokyo' is a precursor to 'Golden Brown' with its keyboard dominated texture, 3/4 time signature, soft rhythmic feel and strong lilting melodies, but, in other ways, the two songs are very different.

This is only their second slow tempo song, after *Rattus Norvegicus IV*'s 'Princess of the Streets', and their first foray into a song being solely with a waltz feel in the 3/4 time signature. However, there is a sumptuous rhythmic moment on the "If people wanted proof" phrase where the expected and hitherto eight bar phrase is extended by an extra bar to nine. The lyric message discusses the conventions of time and at this moment the band are musically challenging the conventional approach to time. Black also adds a further intricacy on the rhythm by regularly accenting the final (third) beat of the bar with an open hi-hat. This accenting of weaker beats in the bar is becoming a feature of Black's playing and often, as is the case in this song, adds a subtle impetus to the song.

Texturally, the song is also fascinating as there is the simple yet highly effective repeating guitar riff from the introduction with two soft sighing sliding notes following the main riff. Burnel provides another sublime bass part that is highly melodic and clashes at times with the vocal melody, yet these clashes add to the general soporific, almost hypnotic atmosphere that suggests not all is sweetness and light. This is heightened using the descending semi tonal chords at the end of the verse "They'd like to buy one".

Greenfield keeps the song ticking over with his waltz playing. Once again, we are witnessing the sum of the band's parts blending highly effectively but this time with their softest, most equable song to date. The vocal here is key as the smooth tone and rhythmic constancy blends the melodic rumbles of the bass, the percussive keyboard waltz, the occasional distorted guitar riff, and the strangely accented simple drum pattern into such a satisfying whole.

The keyboard solo further unites the song by having a melodious shape whilst the bass and the guitar provide a 3-part multi-melodic layering texture but then all three instruments all hold their notes for the same, considerable length of time at the end of each phrase. The second half of this instrumental section becomes more animated by omitting the held notes. The slightly clashing feel created during this section is reinforcing the band's approach to challenging the listener with unconventionality that appeared with the synth effects in the previous song and will become a dominant feature of the album.

Such a wonderfully balanced song in a different style lasting a shade over two minutes so structurally there is continuity with the importance of the instrumental sections as the introduction and keyboard solo accounting for nearly half the song. Despite the change in style, the unmistakable individual instrumental sounds add further continuity with both the bass and guitar sounds refusing to adopt softer tones. This song points the way forward to further triumphs for a band that is clearly at ease with this reflective style.

Sweden (All Quiet on the Eastern Front)
Sverige (Jag Ar Insnoad Pa Ostfronten)*

*Swedish language version of Sweden (All Quiet on the Eastern Front) release as a single in Sweden

In less than three minutes this song packs in an amazing amount of interesting lyrical and musical ideas. A Swedish language version was recorded and released as a single in that country. A bizarre video was shot for the song as it was also considered for a single release in Britain. The video features Cornwell, Burnel and Greenfield conducting what appears to be an autopsy on Black. The drummer loses his head during the procedure which appears to be a metaphor for the band's legendary trip to Sweden in 1977 where amongst many other events the drummer became very angry when refused service in a restaurant and put a table through a plate glass window during an altercation. The drummer losing his head in anger!

The video is also worth a mention because it had a concept and storyline rather than just showing the group playing. This was the first time they had produced a video with a concept, and it was also highly unusual for any band in 1978 to film a video in the first place and having a clear concept and storyline was extremely rare.

As a single it would have been an odd choice the subject matter i.e., attacking a whole country for being boring, the stop-start nature of the music and the strange conceptual promotional video. However, the tune is catchy with memorable keyboards leading the way as the rest of the band lock together to propel the song along. Cornwell's vocals are delivered in a staccato fashion except when he croons the slower chorus. The use of stops in the song is unusual and serves to emphasise the quiet from the title and the idea of boredom expressed in the lyrics.

Effectively the song is a list of reasons why Sweden is tedious. Cornwell had lived there whilst studying for an unfinished PhD in Biochemistry and original band member Hans Wärmling was Swedish so one may ask what's not to like? The band had had a very difficult time in the country. Whilst gigging there a gang of rockers – The Raggare[8] – who didn't like punk took great exception to The Stranglers. The guitarist exacted his revenge with this biting lyric.

In his assault we learn the there is nothing to do, very little happens, and the only interesting thing is the clouds. The full title gives the song a cold war feel. Sweden might have been boring but in 1978 it was the front line of the cold war. Whilst things were all quiet in 1978, a reference and play on words of the famous communique of the First World War 'All quiet on the Western Front', things always had the potential for a major incident to occur. The reference to Big Brother adds to the feeling of tension and the potential of war with a totalitarian regime.

Cornwell is also suggesting that despite its famous liberal approach to life Sweden could be an oppressive place to live. With the phrase "hypochondriac tombstone", he also criticises and stereotypes the population for feigning illness. Interestingly most British peoples' view of Sweden in the 1970s was at odds with Cornwell's. It was perceived as far more interesting, viewed as the land of efficiency with Volvo and SAAB plus it was renowned for its liberal attitude to sex and pornography. The people were viewed as beautiful, and this was personified by seventies Swedish cultural icons such as Bjorn Borg, Britt Ekland and ABBA. To many British people it was perceived as exciting and exotic.

The band's sense of humour and mischievousness is crystallised in the song and to finish the job they recorded the song in Swedish. Cornwell's time in the country and command of the language enabling him to do this with a swagger and his tongue firmly in his cheek. The final kiss off was then to release this version in the titular country. The fairy tale ending didn't occur as the single sank without trace, the population probably wising up that they were being mocked. A final footnote is that Cornwell sings the clouds line of the song in English suggesting a mistake was made during the take.

*****

Arguably their most complex song musically thus far with a bewildering mix of chord sequences that are constantly suggesting changes of key. The subject matter may explore boredom, but the chords are anything but. The initial bass line suggests one chord every bar but when the vocals enter, the rate of change of chord is doubled even though the chords remain virtually the same. This device was first exposed in their very first album song, 'Sometimes'.

In the next "Too much time to think" section, there is a different final chord when the phrase is repeated. The vocal melody is then shortened by omitting "to think" and then two very distant chords on "Cos it's all quiet" take us into a chordal no man's land followed by a ten-beat pause. Furthermore, after a straight repeat and a twelve beat pause this time, we are propelled into a completely new section with a new, ambiguous (again) key and a change of tempo.

The chord sequence is played twice, the second time with the "Cumulous" vocal melody but then the chords are subtly altered to taking us into the keyboard solo and the tempo gradually increases, a seldom used feature that helped Dexy's Midnight Runners develop their career with 'Come on Eileen' four years later.

Later in the solo, Burnel again deploys inversions before he and Black suddenly stop, leaving the guitar chords on their own accompany the arpeggios which have been present through the song. As the main vocal section returns and we approach the end, the keyboard arpeggios become even more agitated whilst the backing vocals retain their prominence that were first exposed in the main opening section. The tempo is a little slower than it was for the same section at the start, but the song lacks nothing in drive and intensity as all the instruments are suddenly cut short by "All quiet".

The structure to the song is reasonably conventional with two repeats of the main section followed by the instrumental section and a further repeat of the main section. But the strength of this song lies in the flow that the band manage to create despite the implausible chordal relationships, tempo changes and long pauses. The drums and guitar form a supportive accompaniment for this song, whilst the keyboard and bass are more dynamic, but never intruding in the evolving chordal journey. Once again, the band have struck a highly impressive balance of musical interest and performance virtuosity to accompany memorable lyrical phrases.

Hey (Rise of the Robots)

Building on the pace set by Sweden the band career into the song led by Cornwell's abrasive rhythm guitar riff. From then on, it's a nonstop sprint for two minutes until the abrupt ending. The group showing that they had taken a couple of things from punk brevity and pace but so much more was added by the band musically in the two minutes. One notable part being the guest appearance of former X-Ray Spex saxophonist Laura Logic whose contribution adds to the disturbing manic edge of the song.

The song deals with increasing use of robots and artificial Intelligence (AI) in society to replace human functions and ultimately the idea that robots with AI will take over the world. In 1978 this wasn't a particularly new idea in fact the idea has a long history in culture some experts suggest the idea was first mooted in Mary Shelley's *Frankenstein*. Certainly, popular culture like cinema has explored the idea with *Forbidden Planet* and *2001: A Space Odyssey* being prime examples of malevolent AI. In 1978 the biggest news in world industry was the FIAT factory in Turin using robots instead of humans to build cars. A famous TV advert at the time showed the factory in action using music by Rossini's 'Barber of Seville' interspersed with robotic bleeps and finished with the tagline 'Hand built by Robots'.

The Versatran Series F mentioned in the words is a car assembly robot and Cornwell's lyrics are rooted in the idea of the factory robot, and what captains of industry would see as their advantages over humans e.g., they don't get bored, and they work harder. Cornwell's familiar word play is present in this work musing on the idea that robots might make demands and want a union and an oil break. The oil break reference refers to Britain's troubled industrial relations in the seventies where unions fighting for more breaks was a real issue. By suggesting this he brings the AI idea to the fore and indeed the whole of the lyric assumes that there is an Artificial Intelligence capacity to the robots. The lyric also finishes with the implied threat that they don't get angry with their bosses yet. The use of yet suggests this is going to be a problem in the future.

He also deals with the humanisation of the robots pointing out they are fashioned into men. Again, the humanising of robots has a long history, the point being that by doing this we as humans feel more comfortable with a perfect logical entity if it looks like us.

Cornwell's delivery is crucial to the track as part of the words are delivered in a way that mimics what we have come to understand as a robotic voice. The effect is also emphasised by his use of words of a short length effectively making a voice people in 1978 would recognise as robotic. Cornwell then reorders the words and with this technique consolidates the idea of a robot singing.

The song is a warning which is even more present in this day and age as we stand on the edge of an AI revolution. In 1978 musical contemporaries of the band Kraftwerk were exploring robotic technology which took them down the road of magnificent cold detached music with the robotics and AI being the centre of their musical manifesto. The Stranglers chose a different route content to use technology but not to make it their reason for being, a magnificent blend of the human and the technical.

*****

After the calm comes the storm and this white side to the album is fast becoming genre defying. The frenzied atmosphere supports the subject matter with the ambiguous key during the first part of the song allied to some metallic timbres/sounds and the high-pitched random saxophone helping to sustain the feeling of disorder.

This is the first time on the album where there is no discernible melodic shape but the chorus "Rise, just watch them rise" does provide shape and a significant change with the singalong long held note "Rise" sung with many voices contrasting to the verses call and response of shorter lengthened notes alongside a clear sense of key and strong chordal relationship of chords one and five. But the end of the chorus, "Series A" moves us suddenly back into the realms of the more uncontrollable verse. The instrumental section provides further multi-melodic layering with the guitar, bass and keyboards frenetically adding to the sense of disorder.

Perhaps not as consummate a piece of music as the other tracks on the white side, but "Hey" does provide a beneficial energetic diversion.

Toiler on the Sea

Instantly recognisable from the first beat as Burnel's exigent bass leads us on a voyage of discovery. Without doubt one of the band's signature tunes and another song that since its inception has been a mainstay of their live sets. They band opened Cornwell's last ever gig with the song. Sadly, that version is a little insipid and didn't benefit from having an extra guitarist John Ellis on board. One can't help thinking that such performances confirmed Cornwell's decision to depart. The definitive version is found on this album. The feel of the song is hugely energetic and gives Cornwell a solid foundation to showcase some wonderful guitar. Vocally the singer adopts a relaxed crooning voice to relate his tale of lost love. The essence to the song is it melodic long instrumental introduction and outro which sandwich the pinnacle of excitement when the seagulls appear in the narrative.

The song is loosely based on Victor Hugo's novel *Toilers on the Sea*[9], a story of shipwreck, salvage, unrequited love, and tragedy. In 2001 *Song by Song* Cornwell acknowledges the book as the songs inspiration but then describes the plot wrongly and basically outlines the plot of the song.[10] A key scene in the book involves a shipwreck in the fog which is a scenario Cornwell uses in his lyrics. The song uses nautical imagery to illustrate Cornwell's relationship with a woman.

Ships are always personified as being women and when Cornwell adds some straightforward sexual imagery using seafaring terms such as "hold" and "dock" and the meaning of that part of the song is easy to decipher. The relationship ends in the third verse and the writer again uses popular imagery of being wrecked on rocks to illustrate and described its demise. However, there is a rekindling of the love in the last verse, but it fizzles out and the narrator describes the end of the affair by using the idea of getting lost in the fog.

The third verse also has some rather more enigmatic images of seabirds and aliens which allude to troubles outside the relationship, as well as within it culminating in the classic repeated cry "A flock of seagulls!" This point is signalled musically by Greenfield's screeching synth mimicking squawking seagulls (This line inspired the name for eighties act A Flock of Seagulls). The line is meant as a wakeup call and realisation that there is work to be done and maybe this relationship can be saved, and other issues can be resolved. The aliens that the writer fights with mentioned in this verse are not extra-terrestrial but humans that inhabit the place where the writer has been metaphorically shipwrecked. When two alien cultures meet there is always a tension.

The song fades out with the faders being slowly pushed down to give a tidal sound and extinguish the song and the relationship. This sonic effect also illustrates the ending of Hugo's book where the protagonists tragically ends his life wait for the tide to drown him. It is probably serendipity or maybe it's synchronicity but the very popular *The Fall and Rise of Reginald Perrin* TV series originally shown between 1976 and 1979 had a key scene based on the same idea except the drowning was faked. It is not a great leap to say Cornwell would have been aware of this and with Hugo's novel had used the idea.

*****

This emphatic closer to the white side follows on from 'Down in the Sewer' with its memorable guitar and keyboard riffs for nearly two minutes to open the song but thereafter bears little resemblance to "Sewer". The instruments again enter one by one, firstly Burnel's energetic growling bass essentially on a single note is followed by a short two chord riff sequenced downward by Cornwell followed by the drums before a swirling keyboard riff that is simplicity itself, descending in scale before it is repeated on higher notes with another keyboard in harmony. Low rumbling synth effects help to set the aquatic mood then Cornwell produces one of his finest moments with a series of beautifully crafted riffs. The fast, driving tempo and Greenfields arpeggios help to convey the perfect backdrop for Cornwell's more thoughtful slower rhythms to accompany the melodic shape.

Following a brief section of chordal togetherness at 1:32, we enter the verse chords that prepare us for the vocal to come. At this point the guitar and bass are playing a new riff in a new key (that will become the key to the verse) in unison whilst the keyboard embarks on a solo but the focus is split between the solo and the riff which is then harmonised by Cornwell, so we now have a multi-melodic layering texture which contrasts the previous textures. This, allied to the unobtrusive key changes provides an impressive accompaniment to the band's melodic instrumental prowess.

Cornwell delivers the main vocal section with a strong melodic shape and his most mellow tone to date for a high-pitched song. 'Outside Tokyo' also possessed such a tone but with a low pitch and slow tempo, so the vocal delivery here is a new departure for the band and was soon to become far more commonplace with both Cornwell and Burnel, a key example being the title track to the following album where Burnel deployed a mellow tone for a song that had many similarities to "Toiler".

Another memorable new instrumental section bridges the two verses where the band play the new riff in harmonies. This riff is rhythmically constant with fast quaver notes throughout and thus provides yet more contrast within the song to the other instrumental sections.

After the second verse and repeat of the bridging instrumental section, there is a new vocal section "And when we reached the land" where the music is clearly becoming climactic and the key, which has hitherto been well defined, is now obscured as the bass, guitar and vocals keep repeating whereas the synth ascends with a bubbling effects type sound which climaxes with "A flock of seagulls" as the keyboards maintain the effect whilst the rest of the band play the drum rhythmic pattern in unison.

There is an immediate release of tension as the main verse section reappears and sails purposefully on through the water to finish with wave like sound effects and more multi-melodic layering from the bass, keyboard, guitar, and fragments of the vocal melody as the song slowly fades away, evoking imagery of the ships sailing off into the sunset.

The overall structure of an introduction, a main section that is then repeated, followed by a contrasting section and then a repeat of the main section with some development was known as Sonata Form in classical music and was the main structure used by Mozart and his contemporaries. This became a common structure for the band over the next few albums and provided an effective contrast to their more verse/chorus structures on albums this providing a subtle difference to most other bands who were overusing the latter structure.

This structure on "Toiler" enabled the band to highlight the equal weighting of instrumental and vocal sections. This feature, allied to such melodic prowess from both the instrumental and vocal sections as well as the reinforcement of the multi-melodic layering and the key shifts, showcases the band at the height of their powers.

Curfew

'Curfew' opens the black side of the album a song that subversively creeps up on you. The listener needs to be on their guard as the first part of the song could lure them into the trap of thinking that this will be a straightforward up-tempo number. The song propels along, then bang, out of the blue you're hit with unusual musical passages in odd time signatures and a domineering vocal relating a war time crisis.

The song recounts the tale of the perennial Cold War nightmare – a Russian invasion of Western Europe. Burnel casts himself as a frantic army officer issuing orders to a shell-shocked population. His voice sounds almost Dalek like and therefore extremely assertive as he hectors frightened citizens, demanding they stay off the streets. The song also posits some interesting scenarios that were current in the late seventies but are all but forgotten, but they are still scenarios that are current today.

The lyrics make it clear that Scotland is an independent country which of course is a major political debate today, but it is often forgotten that in the late seventies the same debate was raging and dominated news coverage. In 1978 the Scotland Act was going through parliament just as the album was being recorded. A referendum was called for the following year to ascertain whether the Scots wanted a limited legislative assembly. It wasn't a vote on granting the country independence. Voters rejected proposal partly because it didn't go far enough and for others it went too far. So Burnel in a couple lines references a major political argument that still has resonance. It is a perfect example of the band being able to drop a subtle point within the raging mayhem of the musical backing and vocal delivery.

The song also reflects Burnel's European obsession which he was also exploring around the same time with the recording of his solo album *Euroman Cometh*. He was particularly harsh on Germany who he believed had been seduced by the American dream. Elsewhere he paints a picture of a chaotic England with no power supply and having been routed by the Eastern Bloc forces. Westminster the centre of government has been destroyed meaning politicians have to flee to independent Scotland in attempt to unite what remains of the English army with the Scots. The song refers to the "men from the Steppes" which in 1978 would have involved Russian soldiers and soldiers from the Soviet Bloc countries like Poland, Hungary and Czechoslovakia and of course there would have been soldiers from the Ukraine which at that time was part of Russia.

The parallels with today's geopolitical situation are stark. Burnel isn't a Nostradamus but he has always been an intelligent and creative thinker. At the time he was given little credit for his farsighted appraisal of the political scene in Europe. Elsewhere in the newly created post punk world bands like PIL, Killing Joke began their careers trading in apocalyptic visions of the world and like Burnel many of their lyrics were insightful and prophetic. Even in mainstream pop world the subject was high on the agenda with the release of one of the most successful albums of the late seventies, *War of the Worlds* by Jeff Wayne.

Two of the key lines are found in the chorus "Grey becomes black and white" and the end of the chorus "Black and white becomes" this line is left unresolved but the temptation in the listener's mind is to finish it with "grey". The idea being that nothing is black and white particularly in war where frontiers and morality become blurred into grey areas. It's also a metaphor for the album itself.

The concept of the album was originally along the lines of brighter songs on the white side and darker numbers on the black side. As we have seen there is some dark material on the white side and with 'Outside Tokyo' a slow waltz with a philosophical point. The album was blurring the boundaries it had set itself with the stark title. It was also part of the albums idea to have a side of Cornwell singing the songs and then a side of Burnel as lead vocalist.[11] As we know this idea became blurred with Burnel only singing two songs Greenfield one and Cornwell the rest. Black and white becomes grey.

*****

The structure contrasts with the previous song and follows a familiar pattern where there is an independent intro prior to the verse and chorus, and this is all repeated. There is then a contrasting middle instrumental section before the other sections are all repeated, once again highlighting the effective combination of vocal and instrumental sections. But there are considerable musical complexities that surfaced on "Sweden" and these are now raised even further with this commanding opening to the black side.

The opening guitar has extensive chorus effects and this, alongside the unconventional second chord in the sequence, immediately reinforces the darkness and unpredictability of the (black) mood. But it is the verse section that truly establishes this piece as a tour de force. The chord sequence becomes even darker with two tritone/devil's interval relationships. Furthermore, the time signature has now moved into a very unusual 7/4. Moreover, cross rhythms are established as the keyboards bass and guitar accent beat groupings of 3,3,3,5 whilst the drums keep as normal a 7/4 beat as can be expected.

Because the other instruments are playing constant half beats, the 3,3,3,5 adds up to fourteen which is the seven beats played as half beats. So, the listener has to contend with these irregularly accented beats as well as the 7/4 time signature. Greenfield's rasping synth sound adds a sense of panic to Burnel's shouted vocals which resoundingly captures the disconcerting mood.

The chorus "It becomes Black and white" returns us to more conventional norms with a clear sense of key, 4/4 time signature and a simple two chord pattern, although the guitar, bass and keyboards all play riffs based around these two chords rather than merely the chords themselves. This multi-melodic layering helps to maintain the momentum of the song, as does the sung vocal which has a strong memorable shape and is sung in unison by Cornwell and Burnel apart from the last notes which is harmonised. Rich contrast and only fifty seconds into the song. The introductory chords, verse and chorus are all then repeated to soak up the contrast.

A new instrumental section follows where the chordal tritone idea from the verse is slightly altered (no longer fifths but fourths now) by the guitar and bass and now they play different notes to each other, extinguishing the fragile sense of key. Meanwhile Greenfield embarks upon a descending chromatic swirling solo moving the song even further into a tonal no man's land which, of course, is totally in keeping with the intended effect of the disconcerting mood. As if all that wasn't enough, the fourth of the six repeats of this two-bar sequence covertly add an extra beat to the bar, thus making it a five-beat bar.

The ending sees Burnel's bass line expanding to the higher register for a solo and then the final four chords see the verse tritone chords return one last time, powerfully played with the final chord held, bringing to a close a superbly unsettling musical journey in little over three minutes.

Threatened

'Threatened' and 'Curfew' share similar ideas and were actually written around the same time. They are packed full of musical innovations as if they are throwing down the gauntlet to listeners and daring them to widen their musical boundaries. It's not just showing off though, it clearly works, and it builds on the musicianship exhibited in the first two album. Another album track that has become a live favourite the band opened their set with it in 1980/81.

A deceptively quiet start that gives little indication of the mayhem to come except we have as the listener the nagging suspicion that this quiet beginning somehow cannot last after all it is The Stranglers! The tension builds and then the quiet start is jettisoned as the band crash full on into the song. Burnel's vocals come on-stream but in the other channel Cornwell is constantly singing "Malfunction, malfunctioning" the effect is stunning as it gives the impression that Cornwell is singing another totally different song. This phrase wasn't on the original lyric sheet, and this gave the song an extra mystery.

The song's meaning is multi-layered, talking in the *NME* Burnel said the song was about aesthetics and the fact he didn't always have an opinion on things. In the interview he mentions being asked about a building and as to whether it's beautiful or not where is only opinion he has is whether it threaten him or not. So hence we get the first verse:

I don't' think things can be

Pretty or ugly

All that you can say is

If your existence

Is not threatened in any way

The "Bring me a piece of my mummy she was quite close to me" line he attributes to him wanting to have sex with his mother. By referring to his mother as 'a piece' he is using the same turn of phrase he used in 'Princess of the Street' where he referred to 'Choosey Susie' as a "piece of meat". Given the band's relationship with the press and the group's notoriety it is tempting to assume there was an element of provocation about Burnel's assertions.[12]

Another take or layer to the meaning of the song and given the sinister sounding backing track is that Burnel appears to be inhabiting the mind of a serial killer which links back all the way to 'Ugly'. The vocal style is intimidating and very different from punky roar of previous Burnel efforts. The phrase "Not threatened in anyway" is repeated several times but the tone of voice belies this sentiment.

The song moves to a conclusion with Burnel listing a series of 'accidental' deaths. He finishes the lyrics with a chilling request for "a piece of my mummy" which given the content of the previous lines could relate to murdering or wanting to murder his mother. The line resonates with Alfred Hitchcock's iconic film *Psycho* where psychopath Norman Bates murders his mother and others. He kills his mother as she was overbearing and domineering but she then inhabits his mind urging him to kill. The song has close similarities to The Doors song 'The End' and Burnel was a huge Doors fan. In that song the protagonist is a killer and wants to have sex with his mother. Further evidence is provided by Cornwell's urgent "Malfunction, malfunctioning" which could refer to the malfunctioning mind of a psychopath.

This subject matter wasn't new in the post punk scene Talking Heads released their iconic song 'Psycho Killer' in late 1977 just as The Stranglers were beginning to write and record *Black and White*. The Talking Head's song had a long history and had been around since the band's inception in the mid-70s and was a staple of their live set so Burnel would have been aware of its existence and would certainly have been fully aware after the song was performed live on *The Old Grey Whistle Test* on the 31st January 1978.

This may not have been the original intention of the song, but it gives us another example of the different number of levels the music and lyrics work on.

*****

The overall sound is shifting on the black side as Greenfield uses far more of the Mini Moog Synth than the Cembalet or the Hammond organ and this, along with the growing clashing/dissonance casts a forbidding mood. The structure of 'Threatened' enables much of this to grow as the song builds upon the notion of the importance of different sections that are instrumentals. We only have just over one minute of vocal for a song that lasts over three and a half minutes and there is no one section that is a straight repeat. The second "You are quite safe" verse develops into an extended section with "Threatened in any way" repeated and with new chords. The following "Man killed by" section is also a development of the main verse section. The instrumental section between the first two main sections also contains new material. In short, the structure is highly unconventional yet effectively balanced with the main ideas being constantly fused with new ideas.

Cornwell immediately creates a dark mood by beginning with the tritone/devil's interval relationship that permeated through the previous song. His use of string muting during the first guitar riff is interesting as there is random muting of certain strings and then others are left to ring out more whilst Black creates a ticking time bomb with his hi-hat and Greenfield is adding simple synth riffs. Burnel changes the mood with a dissonant bass riff enabling Black to expand the drum pattern to the well-used snare and bass drum on every beat. There are frequent changes to chord patterns and riffs where the music continues to cast a 'threatening' spell with more dissonances created by the multi-melodic layering texture where the riffs never quite fit with one another (further exacerbating the dark mood) on all three melodic instruments.

There is a semblance of chordal order established for the verse, almost a settling down, and we soon realise why as there are imposing vocal melodies to follow. Whilst Burnel's main vocal is simple, based on two notes, Cornwell sings "Malfunctioning" with a more shaped counter melody throughout the main section and Greenfield also adds to the melodic layering with another shapely riff, but played low with a slightly menacing swell. Another instrumental section with melodic layering and strong dissonance is followed by a repeat of the main section. This is then followed by the vocal repeating "Threatened in any way" where all the instruments drop out other than the drums and single repeating low pitched guitar notes. The emphasis is clearly on the vocal message and this textural contrast does indeed threaten our sensibilities.

The new "Man killed by" vocal section see the two voices start in unison, but the end of the phrase sees one voice shaped higher and the other voice moving lower, again, providing a clashing dissonance. All the instruments then drop out whilst Burnel delivers the chilling "Bring me a piece" line completely unaccompanied with a dark passion thus creating a climax by reducing the texture as far as possible.

We return to the instrumental section from before with the synth rasping into a solo before all the instruments suddenly stop. These extreme textural contrasts based on the multi-melodic layered approach allied to the synth sounds, the progressive structure and the dissonance that invades the piece from the very start really do unnerve the listener. Once again, the band has challenged us, and the result is gloriously perturbing.

In the Shadows

Recorded during the *No More Heroes* session and used as a B-side for a single then adding the song to the album appears a strange decision. It was also a track that producer Martin Rushent wasn't keen on. The band worked on it themselves initially without Rushent and on hearing it he was less than impressed. Some reports had the original version at over ten minutes long and the track was edited down to just under five minutes. It signified the band working in a new way going for timbre and atmospherics.

The track is led by the bass with the other instruments providing an atmospheric backdrop. The track has a definite dub feel with the atmospherics coming in and out of focus over a strong bass and drum sound which again emphasise the band were open minded to other musical ideas that were current and had the musical expertise to execute the idea but add something of their own to it.

Lyrically it's a series of frightened images about walking in a city at night. Paranoia sets in when there's movement and noise in the shadows. The question is asked about what it might be but the mystery and the fear remains. City centre streets in the seventies were dangerous places in a different way than they are now. Things were very tribal – being a recognisable punk could get you beaten up. Attending a gig in the city or another town could see you targeted because you were out of town. CCTV didn't exist and city streets at night although heavily populated saw nothing like the volume of people we see today in the big cities. A lone punk could be easily isolated and picked off by random gangs of thugs looking for some aggro. Just as it is today the danger to women was even worse. This was also the time when the Yorkshire Ripper Peter Sutcliffe was stalking the streets. For over five years from the mid-seventies until the early eighties Sutcliffe held the north of England and possibly the whole country to ransom. His reign of terror was a national obsession and reported almost daily in the news. It's impossible not imagine that this informed some of Cornwell's lyrics.

Other bands wrote about inner city violence perhaps the most surprising was The Cure who closed side one of their first album *Three Imaginary Boys* with the 'Subway Song' which had clear links with 'In the Shadows' with the bass leading the melody and atmospheric instrumental backing and vocals. The lyrical themes are very alike, and Robert Smith's vocals are expressed in a similar way to Cornwell's. The denouement of each song is different however. In Smith's the victim dare not turn around and the song finishes with an ear splitting scream from the female victim whilst Cornwell on the other hand advises us to "look around you", so we can avoid the danger and as the track finishes there appears to be no harm to the traveller. Cornwell's lyrics are presented almost as a form of advice to a naïve visitor.

The track is another comment on London and its dysfunctional nature. The minimal melody and random sounds of the instrumentation perfectly conjuring up a sense of urban decay, deprivation and danger.

*****

The heavily effected bass leads us into another dark atmosphere and the drums play a very prominent role in the overall mix. Every bar ends with different fills of which there is no set order. This creates an improvisatory feel to the song and the synth sound effects and guitar add to this feel with random interjections.

There are few keyboard contributions other than the synth sound effects whilst the guitar is often absent but then interjects with sustained notes or brief semblances of riffs. The very first triplet riff on the guitar which creates a cross rhythm is highly effective and leaves us craving for more but, alas, the guitar becomes more sporadic.

Burnel's bass riff is the only constant, and apart from a brief section of held bass notes at 2:05, this riff carries on throughout the entire song, with the occasional fragmentation. Consequently, the structure to the song feels like one long continuing improvised section, with the brief release of the held bass note section. The overall texture, unlike the previous song, remains reasonably consistent for most of the song with a lack of chords but unlike 'Threatened', the multi-melodic layering is not developed due to the sporadic presence of the keyboard and guitar.

The vocal is very low in pitch for the most part, the shape being based on the bass riff, and it also has effects that help to blend in with the overall soundscape. The result is indeed dark and atmospheric, but it is difficult to be completely won over by a series of atmospheric effects and laboured melody for this second longest song on the album, when the previous tracks provided such complete and satisfying musical entities.

Do You Wanna?

Sung by Greenfield but a lyric of Cornwell's it is an angular musical piece with what appears to be stream of consciousness free form lyrics. The music also has an improvised feel and the fact that it segues into the next track perhaps suggest the band weren't quite sure how to finish it. There is a kind of word association in them within the start of each line by being associated with the end of the line. For example, one line starts "Do you wanna stay at home", and finishes "On the range?" Home on the range being a famous country and western song. There appears to be no narrative. They are a collection of random questions posed to a woman, it is a woman because she is asked does she want to be a beauty queen and later on whether she wants to blow her hymen.

In what feels like a non sequitur the song also refers to the Jubilee of 1977, one of punk's iconic moments. The line is a criticism of the establishment, pointing out that Jubilees historically, were associated with the release of prisoners. For example, under Hebrew law in biblical times prisoners were released. In 1977 no prisoners were released specifically because a Jubilee had been declared.

Cornwell makes the same point during his between song patter from the stage at Battersea Park on the *Live (X cert)* album. The final line appears to be a Cornwell double entendre when he talks about a hole in his muffler and one suspects he isn't referring to a scarf. Some of the images in the song were going to see the sexist charges laid at their door again. The band always protested they had a sense of humour that followed the Carry On and saucy seaside postcard tradition and it informed many of their lyrics. Unfortunately for the band most critics didn't buy this, and the sexist label persisted.

The real truth is probably, as always, is somewhere in between the two there is genuine humour in many of their lyrics and much of it in the saucy *Carry On* style but if we are honest such humour is at time's sexist, on the other side it's hard see any irony or humour in 'Bring on the Nubiles' given the hard core lyrics and delivery.

'Do You Wanna?' is sung by Greenfield in his now familiar creepy, spine-chilling style which gives another edge to the already jagged muscular music. The song finishes as it segues effortlessly into 'Death and Night and Blood'.

*****

The structure once again continues in an unconventional way with another short song that has many different sections, with little in the way of straight repeats. But the bass and drums are very prominent for every section and there is a random feel to the bass as well as the spoken vocal so the sections almost merge into one whole with only the powerful synth defining one of the sections.

The tempo is quicker following the slow brooding previous song. There is still an ominous menace to the piece though as the bass and guitar play completely clashing riffs to each other whilst Black's drum pattern continues in the previous song's vein with random fills on the second half of each bar, this time making more use of the tightly tuned mid toms.

The anarchic result is totally in keeping with the black side of the album. Greenfield takes over the vocal reins with a typically snarling spoken feel adding to the anarchy. The keyboards, however, are absent until forty seconds into the piece after the "let out all the prisoners" in the chorus of sorts, when they explode with powerful held chords.

There is enough random dissonance from the guitar and bass on top of the interestingly dysfunctional drum pattern during the main verses to enable Greenfield to concentrate on his vocal duties, but his repeating held chords in the second chorus come in at the start of the section so are played for longer and then add glue to the final instrumental section where they initially enter in a different key but then move back to the original key.

This is probably the bands most dissonant song and whilst the overall result feels a little lacking in completeness due to the lack of identity for each section, there is interest in the merging together of such different ideas and the segue into the next track helps to establish an identity to the second half of the black side.

Death and Night and Blood (Yukio)

An inspired segue way brings this song onto the musical horizon. The bass leads us into the song whilst the other instruments provide a solid interesting unsettling backing. Towards the end of the song, they play off each other in classic Stranglers fashion but frustratingly the song fades out as this is occurring.

It makes one wonder how much of the track went on and where it went musically and lyrically after the fade out. Fading the track suggests the band and Rushent didn't think what followed particularly worked, and they were possibly struggling to end the song properly. The chanted chorus answering Burnel's narrative is particularly effective. It is equivalent of the Greek chorus in literature with the chorus sounding out warnings to the narrator of the song.

The subject of the song is easily identified — the clue is in the title. Yukio Mishima was a Japanese author, poet, and playwright as well as being an actor, model, and nationalist with a panache for sadomasochist sex. He was fascinated by the associations between sex and death, He was effectively a fascist and died of suicide when he failed to incite a revolution with the Japanese security forces.

In actual fact his attempt at suicide initially failed and he had to rely on a devoted follower to finish the job by eventually decapitating him. To the casually curious he is an interesting character whether you agree with his philosophies or not. Burnel was interested in him because of his love of Japanese culture stimulated by his Karate training which has since become a lifelong obsession. The lyrics led to accusations of fascism but an interest in a philosophy doesn't mean one becomes a follower of what you are interested. Are all historians who study Hitler Nazis? Unfortunately the music press wasn't always able to make that distinction. Singing a song about a philosophy doesn't make you a supporter of the viewpoint.

The key lines in terms of the fascism accusation were in the first verse when Burnel alludes to torchlight parades which was a Nazi modus operandi and finishing the line with "there I came" gives the torchlight march a sexual ritual element. Burnel is putting himself in Mishima's body and relating the obsession. Burnel was without doubt interested in Mishima's fascination with a strong human body and sadomasochism and to his credit was not afraid to nail those colours to the mast.

However, one shouldn't confuse an interest with a belief. The brain exposed line refers to Mishima's death when he disembowelled himself in the ritual suicide Hari Kari with a samurai sword. He had ordered one of his followers to decapitate him to finish the job unfortunately the follower botched the attempt and had to use more blows to kill him. The references to a black leather jacket enclosing his brain served to emphasise further fascist accusations.

The subject matter was unique and clearly controversial. It needs to be emphasised no one else in the music world was going anywhere near such ideas. Without doubt dealing with a Japanese fascist was contentious particularly as it appeared there was no judgement about the ideas. However, Burnel does make a judgement with the line "your rotten thoughts Yuk!" Is a rejection of the philosophy and conveniently forgot by those wishing to criticise him.

The group weren't making it easy from themselves, but they were relying on critics and fans to have a bit of intelligence. With the critics they were to be sadly disappointed with the responses. If overtly leftist political bands like the Gang of Four had written a song about Mishima and his belief's it wouldn't have led to any questioning. The Stranglers as a band never allied themselves to any political beliefs and wrote songs about things that intrigued them and then add this to their notoriety and the judgements about the group were made without any extended thought or research.

*****

The segue into the song from 'Do you Wanna?' is an interesting moment. The bass has played two repeating notes at the end of 'Do you Wanna?' (A and G) so there is a chordal link as the keyboards and guitar play D to C at the start of 'Death and Night and Blood'. However, Burnel immediately plunges into a bass solo with considerable dissonances whilst Black strikes up a different groove to introduce the new song. This groove however, is off kilter to a traditional rock beat (where the snare plays on beats two and four) as the snare here is playing on beats one and three. Black has, of course, constantly reconstructed rhythms at various times throughout all three albums and particularly so during *Black and White*. He does not 'correct' this rhythm until half a minute later, on "When I saw that" with a subtly that doesn't interrupt the flow and can go unnoticed.

During the verse, Burnel repeats the same two final notes of the previous song, albeit with a different groove now. The vocal melody here is supported with a conventional chord pattern although Burnel's repeating of the two notes does add interest to the chordal palette, but this song is altogether far less dissonant than the previous track once Burnel's introductory bass settles to the two notes. Even though the constant backing shouted vocals "Death and night and blood" add grotesque aggression to the song, Burnel delivers the rather shapely melody with almost a mocking tone, exacerbated by the glissando on "Looove".

The second section "Hey little baby" continues in this mocking vein and shaped melody, and we are left to wonder where the band wanted to pitch the mood of this song. Without the shouted backing vocals, this is the least dark moment on the black side so the juxtapositions of the subject matter and backing vocals against the vocal tone, shaped melodies and lack of dissonance are of interest. But the structure is lacking here.

The two main sections are repeated three times, but the backing vocals are dominant and as they only cease for a few seconds during the second section, they start to feel a little obtrusive, so the song suffers from a lack of contrast. After these three repeats the final instrumental section lacks interest in comparison to the previous instrumental sections the earlier songs on the black side, 'Curfew' and "Threatened.

This song sees a return to a chordal texture following the more multi-melodic layering of the previous song and the chordless texture of 'In the Shadows'. The opening two songs on the black side combined the two textures to stunning effect but here we are lamenting the lack of contrast. Unfortunately, this was also the case for 'Do You Wanna?' and 'In the Shadows'.

Enough Time

The original album and black side closes with apocalyptic 'Enough Time'. The instrumentation suitably matches its bleak theme being dark and foreboding in nature. As Cornwell begins to sing Greenfield's synth nagging away in the background giving an onomatopoeic impression of nuclear fallout raining down. Cornwell's vocal mixes desperation and disgust as he ponders the desperate state he faces.

A post nuclear holocaust world where the sun is blocked out, and the sea has evaporated. In terms of population millions have had their faces disfigured and lost their sight. This scene of horror takes us to the bridge of the song where Greenfield uses his keyboards to emulate a Morse code message which might be the first middle eight to use such a device as a musical instrument it's effectively a one note solo, minimalist in the extreme! The message says 'SOS. This is planet earth. We are fucked. Please advise.'[13]

Pointing the way to an up-and-coming obsession, extra-terrestrial life forms. Following this the song moves into an extended piece which doesn't really go anywhere. It builds up the tension relentlessly but ultimately disappoints as the song is ended by slowing down the tape until it grinds to halt. The backing vocals are speeded up over this slow down to give a similar effect to the Meninblack voice. It's a disappointing end and leaves a promising song without a proper ending,

The subject matter was a familiar Stranglers theme, the end of the world in a nuclear Armageddon, which they had already used on this album with 'Curfew' and on their debut with 'Goodbye Toulouse' and was to become obsession with the post punk bands that were crawling from the musical wreckage of punk.

A Musical Critique

*****

There is a brooding feel to this final song which never resolves to moments of musical unity and this restlessness captures the mood that we cannot 'rest easily'. The sustained notes are a particular feature that help to create the brooding feel, giving us time to digest the bleak, black message of the song, such messages have been attacking us for the entire side.

The first two chords are a semitone apart but the first of the chords utilises the tritone/devil's interval in relation to the home key. The main vocal section is disconcerting musically as Greenfield's thin high pitched synth riff holds the pulse together as we move from two bars of four beats to one bar of three beats and this repeats three times before two bars of four beats takes us into the more standard chorus section.

But Burnel is growling along with a lack of clear beat pattern and Cornwell's guitar, very low in the mix, is even more dissonant, feeling like it belongs to a different world. Black makes matters even more unsettling with his sporadic beat patterns, often with the snare on the off beats, and Cornwell's vocal phrases start towards the end of the keyboard riff, so we are left in an interesting rudderless state with regards to the sense of rhythmic continuity. The vocal melody starts in a low range with a reasonably well shaped melody and reflective tone, then rises in the same vein before Cornwell delivers with venom on "What when your face", thus continuing the many different vocal tones that have been adopted across the whole album.

The chorus binds the piece together after the dysfunctional verse with the two intro chords used and a clear sense of rhythmic pattern, but the twisted backing vocals and sustained notes help to retain the apocalyptic mood.

The Morse code section has more dissonance with a repeating bass riff, and guitar and keyboard chords all unrelated to each other. The final section briefly repeats the strange 4,4,3 time signature before the pieces descends into chaos with the continuation of unrelated instrumental random ideas whilst the backing vocals are speeded up to create an otherworldly effect whilst the overall music tape speed is slowed down right at the end.

Whilst the song achieves its fateful mood thus ensuring closure to the black side, there are question marks over the quality of the song which, considering to the lack of contrast in the songs that immediately preceded it, results arguably in a musically unconvincing end to the album.

Musical Summary

The band had moved on from the rawer sound of the first two albums and any semblance of traditional Punk sounds were minimal. Perhaps 'Hey! (Rise of the Robots)' and 'Tank' still had links, but both those songs had such musicality that the new wave label, fluid as it was, seemed to be a more apt description.

Instead, there was a growing challenge from a musically dissonant angle which had been briefly present on their first two albums but now, was completely permeating the black side as were the multi-melodic layering textures and the unconventional rhythms and time signatures. Structurally the songs were also highly accomplished and varied, with a continuation of having instrumental sections contained new material which moved the songs into new areas that set the band apart from other similar artists.

As a result, there was so much development and contrast of material packed into songs like "Sweden", 'Curfew' and 'Threatened'. The structures to 'Nice 'N Sleazy', 'Tank' and 'Toiler on the Sea' also contained deviations from the norm for such songs, yet these three strong songs needed very little structural tinkering anyway. There were hardly any moments where the songs trod water with a repeat of chords waiting for the next verse or with aimless solos to merely provide a break from the vocals. There were fewer solos on the album with the instrumentals being more riff based. The final four songs on the black side were not quite as strong structurally which was due to less contrasting ideas in these songs but, taken as a whole, the black side blended to produce a dark dissonance that befitted the loose concept.

The white side was an exceptionally strong set of standalone songs with great contrast between them all, and some superb musicality from all four band members resulted in the band's unique sound providing strong links from the first two albums. This sum of the separate parts was more of the same from the first two albums, and fans revelled in this even though the band were clearly looking forward and not back with regards to the already mentioned dissonance, multi-melodic textures, and unconventional rhythmic patterns, but also with their vocal melodic development ('Outside Tokyo', 'Toiler on the Sea', "Sweden") and their reflective moods ('Outside Tokyo').

Many fans will regard *Rattus Norvegicus IV* and *No More Heroes* as the band's greatest albums. However, the unique Stranglers sound was new and unleashed with these albums and this quite justifiably resulted in fans latching onto these albums with such excitement and conviction. But the songs were, overall, stronger on *Black and White* and the subtle maturity of the above musical ideas allied to the slightly tighter, superb production and mix that lost none of the bands combined energy, resulted in such a profound album.

Bands will often struggle to attain consistency of songwriting following their debut album (or albums in the case of The Stranglers) as they will now have to produce songs to order having filled their debuts with songs written from years previously. But *Black and White* gloriously bucked that trend with so many ideas and moods. Almost every song had a different vocal delivery or tone or combination of tones, and this greatly supported the subject matter. For these combined musical reasons, many saw this as the first post punk album, but coming from a band that was only ever tenuously related to punk that seems like a moot point. What is unequivocal is that *Black and White* was a truly groundbreaking and accomplished album.

A Musical Critique

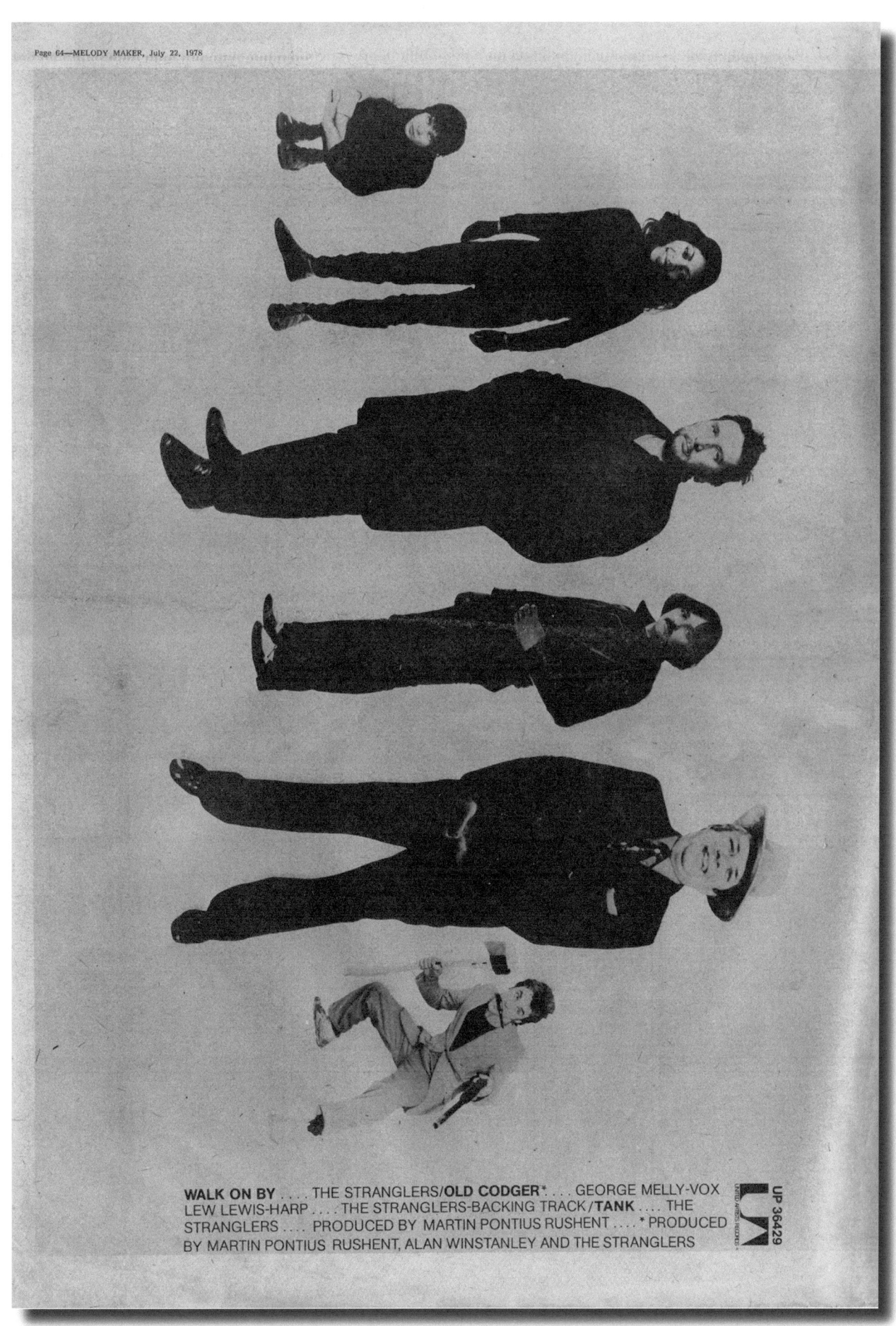

The Stranglers 1977-1990

May 13, 1978 SOUNDS Page 45

**THE STRANGLERS
'Black and White'
(United Artists
UAK 30222)*****

Lewd lullabies

"Superstitions are instinctive, and all that is instinctive is founded in the very nature of things, to which fact the sceptics of all times have given insufficient attention" — Elithas Levi.

FALLING hypnotised prey to this sacreligious seduction, spinning carnivalesque delirium; untie this infernal knotted talisman! Allow me to ponder unpossessed upon this melodrama. Eruptive charged pandemonium oozes sickly throughout sinister chants and beckoning rythmic paths.

*'What's gonna happen when the sky goes black?
What will you do when the sea comes back?''*

Hollowed, echoing warnings of impending doom with saccharine, euphemistic offerings of sacrificial salvation. The force is available only to those with the power to use it. From 'Death and Night and Blood' *'and we decided that to die there was no greater love . . .
. . . I will force my body to be my weapon and my statement.'*

Eerie, necromatic suggestions coercing (unknowing?) disciples of black and white and red. No seeds of living green. Do I read what isn't written? Or react to dangling possibilities?

The law of extreme opposites is presupposed clearly through this haunting atmosphere: dramatic dynamic duelling deliciously deranged diction; shouting silhouettes; literary luminaries lurking.

'Black And White' fights through this statosphere with sharpened daggers gleaming. Is there no respectable end to the Magick these four conjure up from dark depths? Though subtleties differentiate the 'funky' Black side and the 'pop' White side, adjectives from the mouth of the alluring Jean Jacques himself, the soul-swiping songs never loosen their grip.

All this obliquely coloured description of an album (free white single of songs not on LP for first 75,000)? More it should be called a culmination of the senses, an appeal to the mysterious and inexplicable. Yet they still maintain as songs, well planned, well written, emphasised by recording wonders. They comfortably embody themselves on the brain. Blessed blasphemy bequeathes bastardised behaviour.

Erotically evil euphony excels ethnic etymology. Sing for me insufferable Stranglers! I shall lecherously languish in your lewd lullabies.

DONNA McALLISTER

Album summary

At the time the album was labelled "New Wave", fluid as that term was, it seemed to be a more apt description of their music rather than punk rock. Of course, as time has passed the label post punk has become the generic term to refer to music with roots in punk but with more farsighted horizons lyrically and musically.

The album was a listening challenge particularly because it was unashamedly less accessible and less commercial in terms of its sound and to some extent because of the subject matter of the songs. Cult Japanese artists, Cold War invasion. AI and 19th century French novels hadn't real featured on their first two albums. The band were now encompassing the whole world and more with their new direction. There had been innovation on the preceding albums but nothing like the extent found on *Black and White*.

The band's new approach completely dominates the black side of the album resulting in every respect to some very dark and complex songs. Although as demonstrated earlier in the chapter it can be argued they sometimes struggled to fully articulate and finish this vision on the final three tracks. In terms of the white side the band produced an exceptionally strong set of standalone, contrasting songs enhanced by some stunning musicality from all four band members. The result as a whole was to produce a unique sound that still had superficial links to the first two albums but was a step up and a step away from their past. A new era was dawning for the band. An era that would see them pushing boundaries even further in terms of concepts and musically, whilst still remaining listenable and relevant.

Many fans dating from the band's early career would agree with Martin Rushent and regard *Rattus Norvegicus IV* and *No More Heroes* as the gold standard and therefore the band's greatest works. After all they did launch the unique Stranglers sound and kick start their career. This results in many fans from this era seeing *Black and White* as a bit of a disappointment and sales at the time reflected this. But *Black and White* was a game changer, the songs were unusual and not what fans had come to expect but in many ways, they were much stronger songs particularly when compared to a great deal of *No More Heroes*. The musical ideas on *Black and White* were much more ambitious, and the production and mix was tighter which allowed the songs to realise their potential. The band had lost none of its energy but with tweaks in the right places the result was a profound genre inventing and genre defining album.

Although some fans deserted the band at this point many new fans were attracted to the new artistically edgier version of The Stranglers with their world view, they now wanted to articulate. This was really the first time the band had had to write an album to order. *Rattus Norvegicus IV* was in the bag when they went into the studio and there was enough left over to provide nearly half of *No More Heroes*. With *Black and White* there was nothing apart from "In the Shadows in the can.

The band jumped at the opportunity to be creative from scratch despite the huge pressure. They made a conscious decision to build on the musical chops they had honed over their early years in the career and at the same time opted to go for musical experimentation and create an album of songs that was diverse and challenging but still showcased their musically virtuosity. They widen their horizons lyrically leaving behind the kitchen sink dramas of the early punk scene and write instead about an eclectic mix of topics which reflected the dark atmosphere of the late seventies.

Even when they wrote about more commercial topics there was a twist. Burnel and Cornwell were developing as writers and their educated minds came to the fore. Their lyrics worked on several layers maybe sometime unintentionally, but their use of imagery allowed fans' imagination to flourish. Almost every song had a different vocal delivery or tone or combination of tones, and this greatly supported the subject matter. Many bands struggle to attain consistency of songwriting following their initial couple of albums having filled their first albums with songs they had written years previously. By the time of the third album bands have a blank sheet to fill. This is very often when the song quality suffers meaning the album then bombs and ultimately this leads to a group being dropped by the record company meaning and a premature end to a promising career. *Black and White* and The Stranglers gloriously buck this trend as the band turn their imaginative ideas and moods into stunning tunes.

This album was the first post punk album and set the agenda for the up-and-coming bands like Joy Division, The Cure, Teardrop Explodes and many more. Some will cite Magazine, Siouxsie and the Banshees, Wire and PIL as the founders of the genre but chronology and of course their previous works puts The Stranglers first with the other bands, admittedly all working in insolation of each other, in second position.

Magazine were recording their debut at the same time but it was released a month after *Black and White*. PIL and the Banshees' first efforts along with Wire's second album wouldn't arrive for another six month or so at the end of 1978 with their recordings starting months after The Stranglers released *Black and White*. It might not be a competition and the benefit of hindsight might be driving this assertion but contemporary critics' panache for writing the band out of the history based on their notoriety and conflict with key journalist should not get in the way of the facts. The record should be set straight and proper credit given to the band for forging a new type of music.

The question facing the band was how on earth they would follow up such an innovative masterpiece. The omens weren't good. Cornwell and Burnel were at each other's throats,[14] and the cycle of recording and touring had put everyone on edge. Drug use was more prevalent, there were issues with management, and they were losing their Midas touch producer. Whether by design or accident the band survived. Solo projects and a break from each other's company saw them fresh and raring to go in 1979.

Extra tracks: Free single and B sides

Walk on By (*Black and White* bonus single given away with the album and later released as a single)

A tune that has a special place in their hearts for many Stranglers fans even though it is a cover. On their tour of the UK in 2022 the song was dusted down yet again receiving a rapturous reception as ever from fans. It was written by easy listening gurus Burt Bacharach and Hal David. Originally a big hit for Dionne Warwick and adopted by The Stranglers in the early part of their career when to get gigs you had to have your fair share of covers. The band melded the song into the same style as the original numbers they were writing in the mid to late seventies, so much so that when some fans heard it, they thought it was a Stranglers original.

The group added pace to the song as it seems at least twice as fast as Warwick's version, but it wasn't done to disrespect the song like some punk bands did with old classics it was to inject the song with more energy and life.

As well as adding their own stamp to the song the band kept the spirit of the original with sweet sounding backing and lead vocals. Greenfield also mimicked Bacharach trademark horn sound on his organ. Bacharach himself was said to be impressed by the groups take on his standard.

*****

This cover version was a substantial hit and yet four minutes of the song that lasts well over six minutes is devoted in equal parts to a keyboard solo and then a guitar solo. The main sung section whilst showcasing the band's unique sound does not involve any instrumental excesses and the band closely adheres to the chords and melody of the original. But the solos themselves are both impeccably shaped and take us on sumptuous journeys.

Firstly, Greenfield commences with an expansive run down as Cornwell delivers the memorable "stroll in the trees" line but this is short lived as after ten seconds the sound changes into a tight, slightly subdued organ sound, with mid EQ and less treble. The riffs are constricted in terms of range but there is a pleasing rhythmic flow. After two minutes, the sustained keynote of A then takes us into a wider ranged and higher pitched section where the rhythms are more defined. Burnel now seems to be straining at the leash as he punctuates the keyboard solo with his constant fills for the last two beats of each bar. Greenfield meanwhile heightens the rhythmic feel with his cross rhythms at 2:27 and then wonderfully displaces the rhythm with a repeating riff across the other instruments at 2:37.

Meanwhile, Black has joined the bass in filling in during the second half of each bar and Greenfield uses this feverish backdrop to alternate between more reverbed and some dryer timbres as well as becoming more dissonant in his solo. This finishes off with a two-bar fast descending riff played four times before everyone calms down to let the guitar take centre stage. And Cornwell certainly does not disappoint us with such melodic prowess. His fingers don't move as fast as Blackmore or Page, but the playing here is equally as memorable. 3:43 and 3:58 prepare us for the triumphs at 4:13 and then, not to be outdone by Greenfield, produces another indelible rhythmically displaced moment at 4:28.

The riff that follows this is moving in a higher sequence and is a perfect riposte to the previous moment. 4:53 is the crowning moment where Black introduces a triplet rhythm and Cornwell soon joins in with a variation of the displaced riff from 4:28. The bass and keyboards are of course continuing in the standard four beats to the bar, and we can only marvel at such togetherness. The band emphatically laid down their own stamp onto the song with the fascinating long solos whilst remaining true to the original in many ways.

Presumably this version had been honed over the early years of their existence when they played various cover versions to pad out their set list. And the soloing on the *Black and White* album had been reduced as the band was moving towards more riff based instrumental sections, so this song is not particularly representative of where the band now stood.

The comparison with The Doors was based mainly on this song and 'Down in the Sewer' and it is easy to see why. And surely, bands that perform cover versions are going to be even more linked to classic bands from recent eras? But there was far more in evidence with this particular cover version: the unique band sound and the musicality were all too evident and for this reason, the song was and still is a favourite with fans.

Mean to Me (*Black and White* bonus single given away with the album)

A high-speed rock 'n' roll number which was also record by Celia Gollin with the band backing her and released as a B-side to her single 'Mony Mony' under the moniker name Celia and The Mutations. The idea came from the band's manager Dai Davies as a way of launching her career. Unfortunately, the single wasn't a hit. Burnel played on her second single 'You Better Believe Me'/'Round and Round' which again sank without trace. Cornwell wrote the lyrics which are the traditional blues fare of a woman leaving her man and him wanting revenge.

*****

A throwback song to their early pub rock days where the twelve-bar blues chord structure is closely adhered to, apart from bar ten where a flat seventh chord replaces the standard fourth chord. But this is an alternative chord that is also used reasonably frequently in blues music. The instrumental playing from all four band members here is in keeping with fast blues song traditions and both the keyboard and guitar solos also lend themselves to this style, albeit at the manic end of the scale.

There is even the stop chorus after the guitar solo and a vocal melody with an appropriate combination of shape and repetition of certain notes to further cement the style. But overall, this is, along with 'Walk on By', an enjoyable romp that requires far less of the listener than the dark dissonance of the *Black and White* album.

Tits (*Black and White* bonus single given away with the album)

Recorded live at the Hope and Anchor in November 1977. A song the band wrote to try and win audiences over with humour. The real humour is not the actual lyrics of the song but Cornwell's mockney double entendre banter and the joke solos of all the band members. Cornwell's final quip to the audience "Now you know why no one came to see us two years ago." Tell us all we need to know. The song famously won the audience over when played at the Roundhouse when they supported Patti Smith. I wonder what Patti thought?

*****

Comical mockery or mildly vulgar depending on one's taste. One listen is enough to this demented twelve-bar blues where they briefly sing a nonsense chorus about the female anatomy. Cornwell then narrates about very little and introduces each band member in turn to play a solo with varying degrees of deliberate ineptness. Greenfield can't help but add a flourish of quality, but Burnel's one note and Cornwell's disintegration do induce considerable laughter and are well worth listening to... once.

Shut Up (B-side to 'Nice 'N Sleazy')

Just over a minute in length it takes the punk virtues of pace, aggression and melody to give us a whirlwind view of a 'domestic' between Burnel and his then girlfriend. All the band get a bar or two to show off their chops. It's a perfect example of the band's subversive nature, tarred with the description as a punk band, why not play up to the name and beat the movement at its own game?

*****

Another song with a throw back to their pub rock days with an obvious punk leaning. The intro has a trademark Burnel run finishing on an obscure chord for the key, followed by Black's fast snare roll. The energetic keyboard solo changes the key and takes us to the abrupt ending to the song in just over one minute of pleasant frenzy.

Old Codger (B-side to 'Walk on By')

The Lyrics were written by Cornwell specifically for George Melly. The band played the backing track with the assistance of Lew Lewis on harmonica. Melly as well as being old was a jazz singer, critic, writer and openly bisexual at a time when the world was less tolerant and inclusive. He also happily described himself as an anarchist and was always keen to subvert the accepted the norm.

The band appeared in his *Arena* documentary *The Journey* where Melly referred to them as punks and when he met the band on camera, they did their best Sid Vicious looks into the camera. Melly saw them as the future of Dadaism, describing them as 'The Dada surrealists of the punk movement'. Yet more reasons why the wider world considered them as punk and still consider them as punk whilst conveniently forgetting the first part of Melly's assertion.

When Melly turned up for the session, he surprised the musicians by quite happily rolling joints for everyone not something the band associated with someone from the older generation however much of an anarchist they claimed to be.

The lyrics describe an old man's obsession for a younger boy and would today now raise eyebrows, but Melly was more than pleased to sing them.

The musicians became friends with the old jazzer and kept in contact for several years, Cornwell even making an appearance on the Channel 4 art quiz *Gallery* fronted by Melly in 1990. The host when introducing Cornwell described him as 'Actor, songwriter and musician and member of the pop group The Stranglers'. At last, the punk moniker had disappeared. Also worthy of note is the order in which he describes Cornwell's talents with actor being the first descriptor. It shows the frontman was spreading his wings and within a few months he had left the band.

*****

This humorous little blues ditty has minimal expansiveness from the band with the drum beat completely repetitive with not one single fill, the guitar and keyboards in the background playing the chords and the constant traditional walking bass. The main section consists of only one chord and the two other chords in the second section are both conventional for the style. The harmonica played by Lew Lewis adds further authenticity to the style. Melly's bawdy vocal style provides the focus for the song.

Footnotes

1. Official Chart Website

2. Official Chart Website

3. Official Chart Website

4. Official Chart Website

5. Martin Rushent interview in *The Stranglers Rattus Norvegicus IV and No More Heroes* by Chris Wade

6. Martin Rushent interview in *The Stranglers Rattus Norvegicus IV and No More Heroes* by Chris Wade

7. Martin Rushent interview in *The Stranglers Rattus Norvegicus IV and No More Heroes* by Chris Wade

8. *Song by Song* – Hugh Cornwell and Jim Drury

9. *Song by Song* – Hugh Cornwell and Jim Drury

10. *Toilers on the Sea* by Victor Hugo originally published in 1866, Present day Publisher Legare Street Press (26 Oct. 2022)

11. *Song by Song* – Hugh Cornwell and Jim Drury

12. *NME* February 10th 1979

13. Morse code message meaning revealed by Jean Jacques Burnel in stranglers-ratter.blogspot.com May 2013

14. Martin Rushent interview in The Stranglers Rattus Norvegicus IV and No More Heroes by Chris Wade

Stranglers still tied in a knot

THE STRANGLERS' London date on their British tour was still in doubt at the beginning of this week.

They originally planned to play two nights at Alexandra Palace early in June, but the Greater London Council refused permission for the gig to take place.

The latest plan is for them to play an open-air gig at Queens Park Rangers Football Club at Loftus Road, Shepherds Bush, on June 10. However, permission for this gig has still not been forthcoming from the GLC.

Quite what the GLC have against the Stranglers is not clear, but it does seem as if the band's plans to play in London are being consistently thwarted.

The planned dates at Alexandra Palace were not refused on security grounds. A spokesperson for the band told SOUNDS that the didn't know why the Alexandra Palace dates were refused, but he thought that the GLC didn't want to be seen to be encouraging new wave bands around the time of the metropolitan elections (being held this week) and that the T-shirt incident at London's Rainbow over a year ago still rankled with the authorities.

In that incident Hugh Cornwell persisted in wearing what the GLC decided was an 'obscene' T-shirt, despite warnings from the authorities, and the curtain was lowered on the group's performance.

A decision on the Queens Park Rangers date is expected later this week.

The Stranglers' new album, 'Black And White' released on May 12, is to be issued in different form as a cassette.

The cassette version is to include an additional track, 'Mean To Me', which is only available elsewhere as a track on the free white single given away with the first 75,000 LPs.

Advance orders for The Stranglers' third album exceeded 53,000 in one week.

Stranglers left hanging around

THE STRANGLERS have finally given up trying to play a London concert on their present British tour.

Planned concerts at Alexandra Palace have had to be cancelled after objections from the Greater London Council. A licence was originally sought back in February by promoter Harvey Goldsmith, but the GLC apparently objected on three grounds. The first was the now notorious T-shirt incident at the Rainbow, which the GLC seem to have remembered longer than anyone else; the second was the band's rumoured abuse of the GLC; and the third was the safety problems caused by having 6,000 people standing at the gig. The GLC were not impressd by the fact that the Stranglers have already played to a capacity audience of 5,000 at Leeds with no problems.

As the GLC didn't want to enter into any correspondence over the gig, it's hard to understand just what their attitude to the Stranglers is, but those who remember the interview with Bernard Brook Partridge of the council in SOUNDS last year may get the general picture.

The final stumbling block came when the GLC refused to give a decision until after the local elections. When a fresh application was made, the same objections were reportedly raised.

The Stranglers are obviously annoyed about what they see as 'big brother' tactics by the GLC. Drummer Jet Black said this week: "Why us? ELO and Dylan can play London, the Stranglers can't. What's going on?

The band have raised the matter with their local MP, Nick Scott from Kensington.

An alternative gig at Queens Park Rangers football club had to be abandoned when it became impossible to organise the event in time. This left indoor venues like Hammersmith Odeon, but the demand for tickets would have meant playing a week of concerts, which is not practicable at present.

So thanks to the GLC, London fans wishing to see the Stranglers will have to travel outside London. They can either go to Brighton this Saturday or to Stafford Bingley Hall on May 30. Tickets for the Bingley Hall concert are available from Harvey Goldsmith's box office at Chappels and the price of the ticket will include a coach trip to the concert and back. The cost of the coaches is being for by the Stranglers.

The Raven

September 1979 saw the band release their fourth album in a two- and half-year recording career. Add into that time the two solo/collaboration projects by Burnel and Cornwell and the *Live (X Cert)* (see the appendix section for an appraisal of these albums) making this period an incredibly busy and artistically productive start to their career.

The new album marked a true beginning to a new phase in their history. Despite being so busy in their first few years of their recording career it had actually been sixteen months since the band had last released any original material. Back then this was a long time for a band to be out or circulation. Only established 'rock dinosaurs' like Pink Floyd and Led Zeppelin kept out of the limelight for that long. A live album, *Live (X Cert)* was released in February '79 to keep fans happy and give the band some profile. During this hiatus there were rumours of a split which was furthered fuelled by the two solo projects.

The band announced they were back with energetic, poppy and short leadoff single 'Duchess' in the summer of 1979. It seemed a guaranteed top 10 hit but stalled at number 14[1] partly due to the promotional video banned by the BBC. The video featured the band dressed as choirboys singing in a church. At the time this was deemed offensive and with the controversial Monty Python's *Life of Brian* about to hit the cinemas the establishment was very sensitive to anything that might be deemed offensive to Christianity.

Looking back, it was a ridiculous decision but with Aunty Beeb extremely wary of anything to do or anything considered punk the banning was a fait accompli. The band's reputation for controversy was now starting to hurt. In the past this notoriety had assisted their progress and reputation now these forces seemed to turn against the band and the next two years they struggled to deal with this change of fortune.

The album had been recorded in Paris in the summer of 1979 and was mixed at Air Studios in London. It marks the end of their relationship with Martin Rushent producer of the first three albums. He had started to doubt the band on *Black and White* and although initially on board apparently flipped over the track Meninblack and at some of the band's behaviour.

The record was therefore credited as being self-produced with engineer Alan Winstanley. The mix was done by Winstanley and Steve Churchyard. Many will argue that this album sees the band at the heights of their creative powers. There has been a clear journey so far and *Black and White* had been seen as a leap forward for the band from their original pub/punk rock musical and lyrical content into a fascinating more complex musical entity. *The Raven* was to be another great leap forward, only two and a half years after the release of their debut with the band now at the pinnacle of their creative powers.

The cover artwork was stark and attention grabbing. A huge picture of a Raven dominates the front. Initial copies had a 3D photograph by Toppan and subsequent copies had a 2D photo by Chris Ryan. On the back the band pose on a replica of a Viking Long ship in a photograph by Paul Cox. The Viking boat is known as The Hugin and is on display at Pegwell Bay in Kent.[2]

A cursory glance at the track listing with titles like 'Longships' and 'The Raven' and you could be forgiven for thinking the record was about to be a concept album about the Vikings. The raven after all was a bird that was sacred to Norse people and Longships were their mode of transport when they invaded other lands.

However, that's really a far as the concept goes. The rest of the songs dealt with contemporary world issues, culture that interested the band, ethical issues, and conspiracy theories. Additional clues to these themes are given not just by song titles but by the inner cover artwork provided by the design company Shoot that Tiger! The lyrics are reproduced on the inner sleeve and each song has a picture or photograph to illustrate it. It's a brilliant device, coordinated by John Pasche[3] and helps the listener unlock the mystery of the song or come up with their own off the wall interpretation of the meaning, either way it's fun and very intellectually stimulating.

The lyrical themes build on and expand the subjects the band started to explore on *Black and White*. The group had now clearly moved away from the small-town characters and situations of seamy London life they captured so well on the first two albums. The mood was still dark and brooding but the menace now had a world view to it.

In terms of performance, it was a top 10 hit peaking at number 4, but it only stayed in the charts for eight weeks[4] despite a huge advertising campaign including a very short TV advert. The limited-edition 3D cover helped boast initial sales but not enough for them to match or better their previous best chart placing.

Things were not helped when some Raven sales were for some bizarre reason credited to The Police and their *Reggatta de Blanc* album.[5] Whatever the reasons this was an underperformance in terms of all the previous Stranglers studio albums and even the *Live (X Cert)* album was a top ten hit and managed ten weeks in the charts.[6] *Black and White* had some fans complaining it wasn't punk enough and was a bit weird. It wasn't about life on the streets of London but more about issues in far flung places like Sweden and Japan. Such a change in emphasis probably led to some of the band's hard-core punks defecting after the third album.

The Raven was musically and lyrically a further push away from these narrow confines of what many fans considered punk to be. There is a lush, sumptuous sound on much of *The Raven* which would also have disturbed many of the original punk fan base. However, the band kept a very large loyal hard core and the change in musical emphasis also brought in new fans like the co-authors of this book.

In an effort to keep the album high in the charts another single 'Nuclear Device (The Wizard of Aus)' was released in October. The single failed to crack the upper reaches of the charts stalling at number 36, the first time since debut single '(Get a) Grip (of Yourself)' in 1977 that a single release had not made the top 30.[7] The subject matter of the single was considered controversial dealing with the corruption of Joh Bjelke-Peterson and mining uranium for nuclear fuel amongst other things. The inner sleeve of the album saw Peterson in a less than flattering cartoon pose which when his lawyers found out was removed from the sleeve. Given all this ferment, controversy, lack of air play and unusual musical features, it's not surprising the single was a relative failure.

To give them their credit the record company were undeterred and pushed out another single, 'Don't Bring Harry' within a month of issuing 'Nuclear Device'. This time the release was made more attractive by making it an EP with a previously unreleased live version of 'In the Shadows', the track 'Wired' from Cornwell's *Nosferatu* album, and a previously unreleased live version of 'Crabs', one of the tracks off Burnel's solo *Euroman Cometh* album.

In addition, the EP came at a bargain price of 99 pence and given Christmas was approaching an ironic Christmas cover featuring turkeys strung up in a butcher's window. It was released in early November which in those days was probably a couple of weeks too early to be thinking of a Christmas push for number one. This is of course, is in marked contrast to today when Christmas appears to start in mid-September and doing anything about it in early November is considered far too late!

In addition, the band got a slot on *Top of the Pops*, despite the single initially charting outside the top forty. How could it fail? Well sadly it did the and after their appearance of the nation's favourite pop show it actually went down in the charts which was almost unheard after a *Top of the Pops* appearance. It therefore failed completely to pierce the all-important top forty peaking at 41[8] and then quickly sunk without trace.

Then to add to the bands woes in early January 1980 Cornwell received a two-month custodial sentences for possession of heroin and cocaine amongst other things. Cornwell appealed but this was rejected, and he went to prison on 21st March 1980 for a sentence that turned out to be five weeks. The band's activity was effectively put on hold. Tour dates were cancelled in the USA and the Far East. However, something was salvaged and the other three members got friends to rally round and play The Rainbow in London on two nights, 4th and 5th of April. The night of the 4th was recorded and can be heard on the release, Stranglers and Friends Live in Concert. (See appendices for an appraisal of this album) It was originally released in 1995 then reissued in 2002.

Whilst Cornwell was awaiting the result of the appeal. The record company and the band didn't let the grass grow under their feet; another song 'Bear Cage' was quickly recorded. The company had the foresight to get the band to record a video in case the record was a hit and their lead singer was indisposed at Her Majesty's pleasure and unable to make TV appearances. It was coupled with *The Raven* track 'Shah Shah a Go Go' and released on 7th March 1980, two weeks before Cornwell's failed appeal.

It was initially promoted as a double A-side, but it was 'Bear Cage' that got the radio play. (The track was later added to *The Raven* as a bonus track when the album was reissued in 2001). Frustratingly the top 40 was breached but only up to number 36 again.[9] This failure to have a big hit single was in danger of becoming a trend and with Cornwell in jail the band had reached a precarious point in their career.

Longships

Is a rousing instrumental and given its title it evokes travel, discovery and adventure at a breakneck speed, powering along as if it were crashing through a stormy sea. The drums adding serious amounts of ballast with a sound that sounds like depth charges exploding under water as the band race on a voyage of artistic discovery.

The Viking longships, for it is them we are talking about, were the height of technology in the 9th Century. So much so their design and techniques are still used by boat builders across the world today. They were prosecutors of war and equivalent of a cruise missile today. The symbolism with the band is not difficult to see. Four musical Vikings setting sail to plunder record company coffers and discover new musical horizons. To the fans the track feels like the band calling its army of followers to arms. As if it's telling the audience to take their place and get ready for the upcoming experience. Stranglers' fans were some of the most loyal in the business and over the years it almost feels that they would go to war for their band. In some cases, you could argue that some of the band's more fanatical followers have literally fought for The Stranglers' honour.

The music was written by Cornwell, but it appears he was unable to come up with any words. Whether by accident or design the piece doesn't need them as the title and the music tell us all we need to know and urging the listener to strap in for the musical journey that is to follow. Not since Led Zeppelin's 'Immigrant Song' had a piece about Vikings sound so cool and exciting.

*****

The short overture is a wall of sound with no textural contrasts preparing us for what is to come and creating the imagery of the Viking ship sailing powerfully off on the start of its journey. In a quick 3/4 time signature, the drums are to the fore whilst the bass plays constant root notes to the chords for most of the piece. The bass sound has slightly less mid EQ edge and the swirling synth and reverbed guitar sound create a less distinct individual instrumental sound in comparison to the last album's opener, 'Tank'.

The guitar plays a repeating riff for most of the time whilst the chords played by the synth and supported by the bass are reasonably conventional until a twist in the middle section at 0:25 where the tritone is introduced as was the case for the previous three albums. The chords for this section are unconventionally fluid giving rise to the imagery of the ship encountering some more turbulent waters, but order is restored as a riff from the first section returns with the powerful low toms to fade out as the ship sails into the distance. The original vinyl album provided a segue into the following track.

The Raven

So, after the approach journey by 'Longships' the listeners are in place for the experience to begin. The first song on the album written by Burnel is the mighty and magnificent 'The Raven'. A magical, evocative, musically driving track that totally encapsulates the genius of the band. It is a prime example of how tight and locked together they are as musicians as if they were within each other's musical pockets.

Lyrically there is a lot going on in the song, its heavy in symbolism, and it feels Burnel is being autobiographical as well as pulling in elements of Viking mysticism. It also alludes to and builds on the bass player's interest in Europe which he conceptualised in his *Euroman Cometh* album. The raven was a sacred bird to the Vikings, a pathfinder and news bringer. It was believed to be the eyes and ears of Viking god Odin. Pictures and carvings of the bird adorned Viking armour, shields, and ships. Raven banners were carried into battle, and it was seen as a great dishonour for a banner to be lost to the enemy.

In the song Burnel is effectively having a conversation with the deity asking for guidance. He is lost and asks for help but recognises the raven's world isn't the right place for him and perhaps with a hint of jealousy intones "Your world has never been my own" ultimately realising he will have to make his own journey in his particular world. Linked to this are references to reincarnation and being a Viking in a past life who had the raven as a friend and a guide who can suggest actions but ultimately, it's the writer that has to make the choice.

There are elements of self-reflection and regret from the narrator contained in the song when he mentions behaving occasionally like a child. This may refer to Burnel's at times, notoriously unruly behaviour reported weekly in the music press and intermittently spilling out into the daily national press. Other elements in the song suggest changes in direction which illustrate what was happening with the band at this time.

Musically they were changing direction from cold harsh restrictive sea of punk to warmer calmer more comfortable luxurious waters of an established band doing exactly what they wanted with their music. The fact most of song is delivered in a softly textured voice gives it gravitas of a standalone poem and therefore making the words matter more. Burnel breaks the vocal shackles in the final verse with a soaring refrain "And when they find me all alone, the world will never be my own" the voice mimicking the bird soaring in the skies.

The song fades out as if the band, like a raven having visited the listener are now on their travels again flying to distant lands and we are left with siren like keyboards sounding like a warning, a warning of what new aural challenges are to come.

*****

There is a clarity of texture and sound that effectively contrasts from 'Longships' as the wall of sound is now replaced by the simple two note bass riff with a conventional drum pattern and no other instrumentation. This contrast is heightened by the album segue, yet continuity is maintained by the bass riff being in the same key as 'Longships'. But simplicity is short lived as the multi-melodic layering texture that was occasionally used on the first two albums and far more extensively on *Black and White* arrives here as the synth engages in a low rasping slow descending riff whilst the guitar has a much thinner sound and higher pitch for its riff, and the bass occupies more middle ground with changing notes to the same rhythm.

There is clashing/dissonance between these three parts as none of them are sharing the same key. This, however, is a preamble to the stunning synth riff that now enters and helps to define the song. Synth, bass, and guitar are all now firmly established in the same key and the simplicity of the synth riff creates a microcosm of the album to come where clarity and complexity will become willing companions.

The following section at 1:00 becomes the main vocal section and there is a subtle change from minor to major key suggesting an image of the ship having ploughed through troubled waters to now have the fog clear and the raven encircling the ship. There is word painting as the "Fly straight" vocals enter to, essentially, a one note melody with just the last note of the phrase dropping. This is also Burnel's first deployment of his breathy tone, and it supports the lyrical message here whilst reinforcing the notion of the band as having developed from various aggressive vocal tones that had previously dominated their songs. Cornwell had already moved into this new area on *Black and White* with 'Outside Tokyo' and, to a lesser extent, 'Toiler on the Sea' and "Sweden".

There is a clarity of texture in the main section as the repeating guitar and keyboard riffs are not merely filling out with the chords but have identities of their own, which, although being a respectful accompaniment to the vocal melody, is crucial to how the band stands out from other bands. Individual instrumental creativity on the album either blends in or stands out but rarely does it go through the motions. An example of this sensitivity is where the guitar riff after "The things they said" swells with a beautiful riff yet still embodies the flow of the music. The main section is repeated and the there is such a strong unity of movement here from the band with equality and creativity from all four instruments again reinforcing the imagery of the ship powerfully moving on.

The structure has similarities to 'Toiler on the Sea' and to the Sonata Form structure of the classical composers where there is a lengthy opening instrumental section, a main section repeated, a contrasting climactic middle section, a return to the main vocal section then a lengthy instrumental section to finish. This also reinforces the intent to continue this album in the same vein as the previous albums with giving equal weight to the instrumental sections.

The middle section at 1:53 has sub sections where, initially, the synth and the guitar have multi-melodic layering riffs followed by the entry of the vocal "And when you" and a harmony very low in the mix. The guitar is providing more multi-melodic layering here with a new rhythmically constant riff whilst the synth plays in unison with the main vocal. A key change follows which soon becomes another multi-melodic layering moment with both synth and guitar embarking on riff-based solos followed by the vocals returning with the layered guitar from before. The wealth of melodic ideas in this section alone, lasting just over one minute, is enough to comprise an entire song in itself.

More repeats of the main section followed by the opening synth riff with the instruments fading as a swirling synth sound takes prominence to end the song, once again creating images of watching the ship sail off into the wind. A glorious musical journey that builds on the instrumental prowess and the multi-melodic textures from previous albums and adds more melodic invention from the instruments and the vocals than before to announce the album as such a creative force.

Dead Loss Angeles

Another track powerfully propelled by an immense bass riff, in fact two basses — with the second one played by Cornwell — which give the song a deep heavy undertow both sonically and metaphorically.

The piece is a scathing attack on the city of angels. Our first clue is the title itself with the clever word play of 'Dead **Loss** Angeles'. This kind of word play as we have already seen is a typical Cornwell trait giving the song humour whilst at the same time perfectly making his opinions clear.

Cornwell goes on to rail against what he sees as the fake nature of the city. He comments on everything that flows into his head about the place. The fake beaches built on concrete inhabited by plastic peaches which harks back to the band's first hit single 'Peaches' but Cornwell isn't happy as the peaches are fake. 'Peaches' was originally used by the band for bikini clad women on a beach. The implication here is that the peaches are surgically enhanced and therefore not real. The use of the soft fruit as image also works in another way as outside LA California is famous for growing 'Peaches'. In this case maybe genetically modified ones to fit the 'plastic peaches' idea mentioned by Cornwell. To complete the association, John Steinbeck's iconic novel *Grapes of Wrath* is set in California and deals with the trials and tribulations of migrant peach pickers. Someone as well read as Cornwell would have undoubtedly been aware of this, and by using peaches in his imagery he skilful links several cultural ideas which include the band's and California's history.

Android Americans suggest robotic people with no ability to think for themselves. The whole city is compared to nothing more than a giant theme park. The city is soft and superficial with the writer comparing it to a marshmallow and calling the whole city shallow. The song also references the Le Brea Pit which is a huge natural tar pit in LA. It is famous for its ability to preserve dead animals from thousands of years ago almost intact. The Mastodon (a type of Mammoth) in the song refers to the most famous fossil pulled from the pits. Cornwell speculates the Mammoth will need glasses to shield its eyes from metaphorical shit in LA.

Given the Masterton is a decaying fossil it's another swipe at the city who the writer views as crumbling and rotting. The pits can catch fire given their chemical composition and by referencing this event in the song we are given the impression of LA ablaze in an almost biblical way. The image is completed by bringing in the city's ever-present danger from earthquakes. The singer paints another apocalyptic biblical picture calling the city a modern-day Babylon.

The bible's *Book of Revelations* foretells the destruction of Babylon by earthquake. Babylon in the bible means anywhere that isn't doing God's bidding. So, although it's LA, the city of angels named and shamed in the song it actually means any city that is not built on genuine values and virtues. Oh course this isn't the first time the band had dealt with the destruction of a city. On their first album Toulouse is laid waste to in the track 'Goodbye Toulouse'. The sickness of cities has been a recurring theme in the band's career. To illustrate his contempt Cornwell spits out the words in an aggressive spoken fashion and allied to urgency and rhythm of the delivery they reinforce the singer's contempt.

Around this time the band had toured in America and famously took every opportunity to criticise America and Americans. Fans who saw the tour in 1979 witnessed exactly this at a gig in San Diego where they refused to play their hits and bad mouthed a bemused American audience.[10] An ill-advised attempt by the band to gain notoriety and get publicity, after all it had worked in the UK.

Unfortunately, such an approach was never going to break the USA. It soon became apparent this tactic was backfiring on them and was another early sign that notoriety, contrariness and their sometimes-thuggish behaviour was beginning to work against the band.

As a final note it's Interesting to note after name checking LA negatively in the title and then venting his spleen throughout the whole song on its duplicity, ironically on his collaborative album *Nosferatu,* which was recorded in LA, Cornwell's sleeve credits refer to the record being recorded in "Undead Los Angles". Cornwell had a lot of musician friends in the city including his *Nosferatu* collaborator Robert Williams and members of Devo. Clearly not everything was bad about the city.

*****

Following the expansive musical landscape of the previous track, 'Dead Loss Angeles' is a more concise song with a conventional structure of a main section repeated, a largely instrumental middle section followed by a return to the main section. This is similar structurally in some ways to the previous track but more condensed with less instrumental ideas. A new development of two basses but no guitar creates another clarity of texture where the second bass sits effectively on top of the main bass riff in the intro with a rhythmically sparse rising riff.

The clarity of texture in the main section is now challenged as there are three extra keyboard tracks adding to the two basses, a two-chord organ riff, constant off beat chords and a low rasping sustained synth sound. It is a credit to the engineers, Alan Winstanley and Steve Churchyard, that the abundance of low sounds did not adversely affect the overall sound. Even though there is clear melodic link between the vocal melody and the main bass riff, mild dissonance is created by the juxtaposition of these sounds with the vocal line which has the same repeating first note but then the following notes move higher. This dissonance is reinforced by the final note of the section, a bass guitar pitch bend reinforcing the tritone.

The instrumental section at 1:03, however, changes the dimension of the song. There is an absence of chords with the main bass playing a repeating riff whilst the other bass plays another sparse but rhythmic melody, the synth improvising and the vocal repeating "from the la Brea pit" So we have no chords and four melodic ideas to create a forceful multi-melodic layering texture aided by its dissonance as there is no real sense of a home key, which is a continuation of moments from the black side from the previous album. 1:32 sees a resolution of the musical chaos with a return to the original bass riff with a clear sense of home key to accompany a keyboard solo.

Following a return of the main vocal section, the final dissonant pitch bend note is sustained giving further emphasis to the dysfunctionality of the subject matter.

The first three tracks are giving a clear indication of the subtle change in overall sound which had been developed on their third album *Black and White* but has now shifted again to a less harsh timbral standout for each instrument. The drums are still as prominent in the mix, but the snare now has slightly less 'crack'. The bass has less middle EQ and the guitar has more effects to create a warmer sound. Most significant is the keyboard where the harsh tone of the Hohner Cembalet has disappeared and the synth has taken centre stage with a greater array of different sounds thus being the catalyst for comparisons with the synth-based bands that were growing in 1979. The overall effect of these four instruments created a warmer, more blending sound.

Ice

Having signalled a music direction with the preceding tracks the genie was well and truly out of the bottle with the next incredibly complex song, both musically and lyrically. Live the band often segued 'Shah Shah a Go Go' into 'Ice' which means the magnificent, crafted opening has to be ditched. However, the band do play the song as a standalone song occasionally, so it gets to appear in its whole sonic glory.

On first hearing the lyrics seem impenetrable. Listeners were thrown initially by the symbolism of the lyrics and words that were outside the common usage of the English language. The biggest clue to cracking the lyrical code was the image on the inner sleeve of a Samurai soldier cutting himself with a ceremonial sword. The keyword to the song is "Hagakure" which is repeatedly used in the chorus. Further investigation reveals Hagakure was the name of the 17th Century practical guide for the samurai warrior.[11] The Hagakure manual was used to indoctrinate Japanese soldiers in World War Two. The most notorious result of this and one of the key principles of the manual was that surrender meant dishonour and death in battle was preferable.

If this can't be achieved, then death by ritual suicide was required. Such a philosophy hugely increased casualties on both sides of the conflict during the war. Obviously, this simplifies a complex way of life but that is the essence. It reflects Burnel's huge interest in Japanese culture. That interest of course includes the bass player's lifelong devotion to Karate. The song builds on the subject matter discussed in *Black and White's* 'Death and Night and Blood'. The protagonist of that song, Yukio Mishima was a devoted disciple of Hagakure.

The track is loaded with symbolism, the title 'Ice' is a commonly used metaphor for death. The cherry blossom referred to in the song is a Japanese flower which symbolises both birth and death, beauty and violence and represents Samurai life. The perfume referenced in the line "Hagakure with perfume" is another reference to cherry blossom and its associated symbolism with the Samurai way of life. The line "I need cold air not your treason" is another death reference and illustrates the idea that death is preferable to dishonour.

The percussive effects which serve to punctuate the song and create tension are crucial to the song's overall atmosphere. The breaking glass effect was achieved using glass bottles and glasses and apparently took some time before the band were happy with the sound. Although dealing with a challenging controversial subject the lush nature of this song almost has the potential to be a single, but the delicious musical complexities just take it out of reach.

*****

The twin features of instrumental sections and multi-melodic layering textures are to the fore here. The structure sees three independent instrumental sections and the main section is, instrumentally, anything but an accompaniment. These sections last for well over half the song with the longest section forming the intro and this can be divided into four sub sections with the last being the accompaniment for the main vocal section. The second instrumental section follow the vocal section sung twice and third instrumental section also has two sub sections and follows the third vocal section. A fourth repeat of the main section takes us into the fade out ending.

There is an abundance of melodic material that occupies the instrumental sections, and there is parity amidst the creativity from all three melodic instruments here. The opening sees the bass and guitar vying for the melodic attention and establishing the multi-melodic layering then a drum roll soon enters adding an even more complex texture to the sound. This is the first time that Black has set his unconventional stamp upon the album and the remainder of the album will see much more of his creative drum patterns.

A contrasting chordal texture at 0:15 is followed by a high bass riff at 0:30 sounding more like a cello. This takes us to the main verse section at 0:43 where we have a rhythmically constant high pitched synth riff with a staccato sound which helps to define the song, over the repeating bass line, but the guitar provides a dissonance with punctuated reasonably low distorted chords. And that is just the intro.

The entry of the vocals reinforces this multi-melodic layered approach where no instrument is merely filling in with standard playing. Even the drums display a rhythm that is out of the ordinary. This is a clear moment where the band are united yet so individualistic in their playing whilst accompanying a melody. This feature has been developing through the previous albums and this texture will also be dominant in other songs on *The Raven*.

A change of chords at the end of the section is followed by the second instrumental section at 1:30 in a new key. The main section returns with another key change followed by the third instrumental section at 2:03 which is more dissonant with melodic layering again to the fore alongside extra glass or ice breaking sounds.

The final main vocal section adds new higher thin sounding guitar riffs that develop into a solo on top of the "Hagakure with perfume" vocal melody as the original guitar, bass and main synth riff continue to play their melodic lines thus creating five melodies layered on each other to fade out the song. Burnel's clipped, restrained vocal tone allied to the thin sounding main synth riff, similar thin sounding guitar riffs, melodic yet restrained tone of the bass and unconventional drum patterns creates an overall lightweight mood that will not necessarily appeal to the harder rock-based fans, but the melodic creativity and originality of the overall sound is a great force in this song.

Baroque Bordello

Baroque Bordello retains the musical shift of the band with its complexities. Cornwell adopts a rich soft crooning vocal style for the sumptuous metaphors he presents. The heavenly, swooning backing vocals and luscious instrumentation give the song a dream like feel to which perfectly fit the illusory line of images paraded for the listener.

The lyrics conjure up a luxurious brothel where clients can get the sexual experience of a lifetime. The words articulate what we can only assume is a Cornwell fantasy constructing images that one suspects have been thought about and honed over many years to create his perfect sexual fantasy. The scenario described is a long way from the seedy sex vignettes of the first couple of albums e.g., 'Ugly', 'Princess of the Streets' and 'School Mam'.

This again emphasises the shift the band were making with their lyrics as well as the new direction of their music. The lyrics list a series of sensual fantasy images. The scenarios are not explicit, but they are meant to be sexual and require the listener to picture the scene and fill in the details themselves.

By doing this Cornwell creates a genuinely erotic scenario rather than a pornographic one. With genuinely erotic writing a writer sets the scene, and the reader completes the picture with their own mind and imagination. Cornwell is completely successful in this goal as he weaves his words to create a picture and we listeners gleefully fill in the gaps.

The title is fascinating and operates on a number of levels. Baroque is a word used to describe extravagant art, architecture, and music. A dictionary definition talks of "Artistic expression that conveys drama, movement and tension". Baroque art and architecture arrived in the 17th century and it's not hard to picture Cornwell's Bordello in all its grandeur huge frescos, statues, and marble pillars but perhaps a whiff of faded glamour as he alludes to with the phrase "picturesque decay".

The song might be a sensuous masterpiece but at the same time we can't help but think about the murky world of the sex worker. The images Cornwell describes are fantasy and luxury related but the reality of the sex trade for workers even at the 'high' end is not such a lush paradise. Indeed, he refers to finding heaven and hell in the same place so everything isn't okay in what appears to be this garden of luxury. Building on this further he goes on to suggest that any love that might be found will have to remain secret after all the clients are engaging in illicit sex which can't be acknowledged in the outside or real world for fear of damage to the clients' reputation.

*****

Another structure where the instrumental sections are fundamental to the song. There is a one-and-a-half-minute introductory instrumental section followed by the main vocal section sung twice, with a short instrumental section in between, a keyboard solo and then a new vocal idea to end the song. So far, there has not been any structure on the album that relies on verse and bridge sections to prepare for a climactic chorus. Instead, the band has used instrumental sections to provide the necessary contrast from the main vocal sections. The prevalence of multi-melodic layering textures also links this song to the previous tracks.

The opening instrumental section suggests imagery which was also the case for 'Longships', 'The Raven' and 'Ice'. In this case an atmosphere of doubt or trepidation is exposed as the second of the two opening organ chords is a minor fourth chord, used occasionally in popular music to create a more sombre, emotive twist. The fading in of the bass, hi-hat and then the guitar add to the trepidation before a change to a more confusing mood at 0:28 as the bass and guitar embark on rhythmically continuous riffs over an unconventional chord sequence creating a dissonant feel.

The atmosphere then changes again at 0:43 into a more resplendent mood in keeping with the opulence of the bordello. One can imagine here walking through the doors to the establishment as the multi-melodic layering grows with the bass playing the most prominent melody whilst the guitar is slightly more rhythmically sporadic with its higher pitched riffs. The improvisatory keyboard is deploying a harpsichord sound, in keeping with the baroque notion as the harpsichord was, along with the organ, the main keyboard of this period in classical music, the piano having not yet been invented. The music then changes once again to become the accompaniment for the main vocal section to follow and this is another set of new multi-layered melodies. The whole of this instrumental opening section has frequently changed mood with many different melodic ideas producing a complexity to reinforce the band's creative instrumental powers.

The complexity does not abate as the vocals enter. There is a sense of rhythmic displacement as Cornwell sings the first phrase commencing on beat two, the second phrase commencing on beat one, the third phrase one beat four and the final phrase on beat three. Meanwhile, Black's rhythmic pattern has an irregular fill on beat three of the first bar rather than the convention of being at the end of the second or fourth bar. This is becoming a trademark of some of Blacks drum patterns and, along with the vocal phrases, adds to the feel of rhythmic displacement despite the music remaining in four beats to the bar. The drum pattern also enhances the complexity of the texture and there are now, along with the vocal melody, five different musical strands on top of each other. Features of baroque architecture include twisted elements, elaborate decoration, and occasional bizarre and uneven approaches so the band have unequivocally applied musical ideas to support this.

Cornwell's vocal tone is his most equable yet, which supports the elaborate atmosphere as do the heavenly backing vocal "Ahhs" that follow in the short instrumental section that also uses dissonance. The repeat of the main vocal section is necessary due to the abundance of melodic ideas that have permeated through the song so far, once again showing the band to be masters of structural decision making as there has been no instance on side one of repetition causing songs to stall yet ample evidence of new ideas helping the songs to move on.

The harpsichord solo seems judicious to embed the opulence, giving way to the bass to embellish the earlier riff from the verse to take us into the new, final section which, again sees five different musical strands layered as the bass is joined by a new unconventional tom-based drum pattern in tandem with the vocal "Baroque bor-de-llo" and additional keyboard and guitar riffs. Some may consider this overall sound rather chaotic but, for many, the ever-expanding multi-melodic layering journey that has been growing throughout the albums is now developing with such a fascinating intensity.

Nuclear Device (The Wizard of Aus)

The closing song to side one and the pace doesn't let up. The song begins with the main riff of the Australian folk song 'Waltzing Matilda' hurriedly delivered by a synth that seems to have a jokey human whistle pre-set. Matilda is now as it was then seen as the unofficial national anthem of Australia. In fact, in 1979 Australia's official nation anthem was 'God Save the Queen' and not The Sex Pistols' version either!

Australia was in the midst of a colonial hangover and still working at throwing off the shackles of British Imperialism. The use of 'Matilda' is a musical joke the band using a traditional well-known tune not to mock Australians but to mock Joh Bjelke-Peterson the so-called Wizard of Aus in the song title. Cornwell snarls out the words and combined with the aggressive music it clearly suggests that they all the band have something on their minds, and they are going to say it as they see it.

Lyrically, again there is word play in the title. The protagonist Joh Bjelke-Peterson is christened the Wizard of Aus. That's Aus as in Australia and not Oz the make-believe land at the end of the yellow brick road but the intended pun is brilliantly subversive, mocking the state Governor suggesting he is living in a fantasy world.

Bjelke-Peterson can be seen as a wizard as he appeared to be above laws and conventions and seemed to be able to weave his magic and spellbind his critics with his rhetoric and sheer brass neck. This enabled this ultra-conservative shameless politician to engineer all kinds of schemes and tricks to maintain and increase his power and wealth. He was a small time Donald Trump, but this didn't stop him holding huge power in his home state.

The band had personal reasons to target Bjelke-Peterson, whilst on tour in Australia they criticised his state regime and heavies were brought in by Bjelke-Peterson to disrupt their concerts with the end result, according to Burnel talking to Canadian magazine *Toro* in 1979, "We had to flee over the state line". He also carried on to quip "But a wonderful inspiration for the song".

The lyrics are a collection of observations about the political shenanigans of the Queensland Trump. In effect it is a protest song for the band and the people of Queensland against their scheming self-serving populist leader. In the verses Cornwell highlights the mining and selling of uranium without care for the environment, the aboriginal people who lived there and the ethics of it being sold to be used to create weapons. He then lays into the state governor's gerrymandering the election boundaries so his National party could stay in power with only twenty per cent of the vote. Cornwell then took aim at Bjelke-Peterson's treatment of two other groups, civil liberties protesters, and sex workers.

Draconian laws to prevent people from protesting and then laws allegedly to target prostitution. The laws whilst claiming to outlaw prostitution just pushed it underground, thus effectively giving the corrupt police force who were in Bjelke-Peterson's pocket, license to run it and exploit the sex workers. Cornwall's final accusation is that the state governor wanted to secede from Australia and set up his own independent state.

The singer rounds off his accusation stating that money and power was the motivation for this policy. In the late eighties and early nineties justice was almost done when top police officials were jailed. Bjelke-Peterson was forced to resign from government and faced criminal charges. A jury failed to come to a verdict and following further proceedings it was then ruled he was too old for a retrial. However, by now his reputation and his beloved National political party were in tatters.

The song ends with what might now be called a rap or a freestyle lyric. The use of the word Abo to refer to Aborigine people dates the piece. It wasn't meant in any offensive way as the song is strongly supportive of Aboriginal rights in the face of Bjelke-Peterson's onslaught. It's a fact that as a whole, society was then far more ignorant and insensitive to racial slurs than it is now. Perhaps in a perverse attempt to put this right when the band play the song live the band introduced the white Australian stereotype names 'Bruce' and 'Sheila' to accompany the bass drum break in the chorus. This is a long-established live performance tradition that has been adopted by audiences with band encouragement for many years possibly as far back as the 1980s.

The rest of the outro refers to the effects of nuclear fallout on the wildlife, another pertinent point for Australia a country that had experienced nuclear testing on its own shores and nearby in the Pacific Ocean at the behest of its then colonial masters in the fifties and yet now here was one of their own politicians seeking to encourage and profit from the nuclear industry.

*****

Following the multi-melodic layering that has dominated the previous three songs, there is now a return to the less complex chordal texture. There is also a return to a structure that seems more linked to a common verse chorus structure with less emphasis on long instrumental sections. For these reasons, the song was chosen as the follow up to the successful 'Duchess' as the second single from the album. However, it is no surprise that the song was a chart failure.

Structurally, although the verse is clearly preparing us for a chorus, the hook line "Nuclear device" is not melodic enough for chart hits and only appears twice, the second time being well under halfway through the song. The first appearance of this hook line is followed by a short instrumental interlude where a six-beat phrase is played with the final beat is Black's low tom, followed by a repeat but this time for seven beats with two toms on the final two beats. This adds to the interest and thrust of the song but fails to grasp the necessary structural commerciality. This is then followed by a new "If I could get lucky" section which, again, is of limited melodic impact as the shape is simply ascending through a chord.

Furthermore, this section is clearly leading to a return of the verse, so the structure has further deviated from the feel of a traditional verse/chorus. The repeats of what is essentially four different sections are followed by an effective melodic synth riff instrumental section and then there is no repeat of the verse or hook line, but an extended section based on the "If I could get lucky" followed by a final section that is extremely unconventional. In short, the structure suggests verse/chorus but is far more complex than the convention.

The lack of memorable melody in this unconventional structure is accompanied by a series of chords that are also unconventional. There is no reliance on the main four chords and the sections are not linked by the chords thus reinforcing the lack of a progressive relationship between verse and chorus. 'Duchess' by comparison was largely built upon the three main chords (1,4,5) and this, allied to a clearer structure where the sections progressed into each other, and more memorably shaped melodies resulted in its commercial success. Furthermore, Cornwell's growling vocal tone delivering the antipodean political message is also contrary to commercial norms.

The uncommercial musical features do result, however, in a strong song within the framework of the album. Clearly the band are moving away from formulaic songs into more creative territory and for many fans this was a highly welcome move. This created complications in the years ahead but for now, there is no doubt that side one of the Raven was a creative triumph with the coup de grace being the highly unusual 3/4 time of the final fade out section with one of Black's unconventional drum patterns gluing together a return to the multi-melodic layering of the main vocal, bass, synth, and fragmented backing vocals.

Shah Shah A Go Go

Side two opens with a Muslim street call to prayer. Then the music sets a sombre foreboding disturbing tone. The listener knows the song will be about a weighty subject before the words even start. In classic Stranglers fashion the instruments fade in separately building the tension. The bass part is outrageous, and you can picture Burnel wrestling with his guitar to tame the beast of a riff. Cornwell starts to deliver his story in an urgent style as if he is rushing to spread the news. When he has finished the instrumental at end of the song takes us into another world and the music at this moment morphs into the main groove from 'Ice' which meant that live the band could meld the two songs together to provide the audience with a segued piece of sonic genius.

This part of the song is also a musical metaphor of showing a revolution i.e., a complete change.

The words tell the story of the beginning of the Iranian revolution in 1979. The style is reportage and places the singer, Cornwell, as a foreign correspondent for a news station. The stance isn't neutral, in fact it is highly critical of Iran's then leader the Shah, but it attempts to report both sides. At the time of writing, the first half of 1979, the jury was still out on the new regime which later became known as the Islamic Revolution. This was a time of ferment and confusion in Iran and Cornwell reflects this in his lyrics. The first two verses list the charge sheet against the Shah. Cornwell the reporter accuses him and his followers of luxurious excesses whilst the majority of people in Iran lived in poverty and worked hard to maintain his lavish lifestyle. The end of verse two tells us this can't continue and that ultimately the Shah and his acolytes will fall from power.

The third verse introduces us to the other protagonist in the revolution — Ayatollah Khomeini the 'Priest in Paris France' — who precipitated the revolution from exile by flooding Iran with tapes preaching revolution hence the line "sold cassettes for 60p". The tapes were incredibly successful and were a major part in motivating Iran's population. By early 1979 the Shah's position was untenable, and he left the country to go into exile. Khomeini immediately returned from exile and assumed control.

The song was written at a key time in the revolution as events were unfolding in early 1979. The album was recorded in June 1979 in Paris meaning the band's and Khomeini's time of being in Paris didn't coincide, however at this time Paris was still a hot bed of activity around the revolution. The Ayatollah arrived back in Iran in February and despite declaring an Islamic republic in April the result of the revolution was far from a done deal as there were many opposition forces to the new regime. Cornwell takes a non-judgemental stance on the new regime with a closing line about the fluid situation. Khomeini claimed he was going to set people free, and our correspondence response is "we shall see we shall see".

The lyrics are a very simple explanation of extremely complex events, but they aren't completely judgemental and are balanced and a genuine attempt to sum up a world-shattering event. The news at the time were full of the events so it's not totally surprising the band chose to tackle this difficult and complex world event. It marks another area of development for the band. *Black and White* had seen them start to look at issues outside their parochial sphere of southern England, for example 'Curfew', the cold war tale about imaginary invasion scenarios but this time it was a world event unfolding in front of all our eyes on television.

The band had not dealt with such a weighty and immediate subject before. Not long after, punk band The Angelic Upstarts attempted to deal with a similar issue in the same region, releasing a song called 'Guns for the Afghan Rebels' in 1981. The title tells us the Upstarts nailed their colours firmly to the mast but given what has happened in Afghanistan since, history has not been kind to their sentiment although the idea of arming the Afghans against the USSR following their invasion in 1979 was at the time a populist idea.

At the time there was little or no knowledge that many of these fighters would become the Taliban. The Stranglers song on the other hand, with their far more considered view stands up rather well and combined with the music could be considered timeless. Whilst this point might not be particularly significant it does demonstrate that as well as musically being head and shoulders above their peers, they were brave enough to set their sights on the most challenging subject matter and not bat an eyelid and deal with it intelligently.

This willingness to grasp thorny issues and controversial topics can be related back to the band's involvement in punk. If punk influenced The Stranglers in any way, it was to give them that contrary attitude to the status quo. Pop bands didn't write about nasty things or world events. Punk changed all that meaning the new wave of groups were not afraid to provoke and to challenge in fact they relished and embraced the prospect. The Stranglers took this notion and ran with it.

The inner sleeve has an interesting update or stop press addition on the revolution which occurred after the song had been recorded. Next to the lyrics is the very latest newspaper report from Iran written after the song was recorded with the headline "Iran bans' opium music" which suggests after the recording of the song things began to become much clearer very quickly about the new regime's agenda.

Cornwell had said, "We shall see" and by the time of the album's release in September the world was beginning to see. The lyric sleeve quotes Nostradamus, the 15th century mystic who appears, four hundred years before it happened, to have predicted the revolution. Nostradamus was popular reading with the band and had inspired the track 'Goodbye Toulouse' on the first album. The Stranglers were nothing if not well read.

*****

The structure has a long opening instrumental section followed by the main vocal section sung three times with another long instrumental section to finish. The three vocal sections in total last less than a quarter of the length of the song providing further evidence of the importance of instrumental sections to a song.

As the call to prayer fades out at the start, the fuzzy, sustained synth sound fades in with three notes (F, E flat, D) that are commonly associated with middle eastern music. Black's regular pattern of bass drum on every beat enter whilst the bass guitar plays in octaves giving the intro considerable drive and a somewhat unwieldy, powerful feel. The power increases for the second half of the intro with a key change for Cornwell's dissonant solo on his thin distorted sound. This dissonance is further enhanced by the swirling synth that has melodic intent even though the sustained sound disguises a clear melody.

Meanwhile Black plays another fascinating unconventional pattern that feels like a fill and includes a cymbal crash on beat two and a half. The bass restrains from much melodic interplay and continues, for the main, to help drive the song with its octave pattern but the overall texture has a multi-melodic layered feel with Black's drums adding to the individualism within a coherent whole.

The main vocal section returns to a chordal texture with Cornwell's vocal melody for the most part being based around two notes a semitone apart from each other. This is not a creatively strong section but moves the song effectively along as the political lyrical message now takes centre stage following the robustly original sounding musical intro. Burnel does however provide an interesting melodic surge underneath "Shah Shah".

The instrumental section following the three main vocal sections commences with a new four note synth riff that repeats lower then higher four times followed by a return to the vocal "Shah Shah" but this time with added twisted backing vocals before the four note synth riff re-enters. The piercing sound of this riff is accompanied by the swirling synth that has been present throughout so the keyboards are dominating the overall sound here. But the other three instrumentals still have their sense of individuality, and the chords never settle creating an overall distorted, disconcerting effect. This disconcertion is further developed by all the instruments moving higher in pitch but still unrelated to each other creating an effect not dissimilar to The Beatles final dissonant orchestral surge in 'A Day in the Life'.

But the difference here is that the upward climactic moment gradually subsides as the instruments begin their descent into a repeat of the main groove from 'Ice' on side one. Cornwell adds an angular solo which returns us to the multi-melodic layering that started the song. This enabled the band to segue the two songs together when playing live and here gives a sense of continuity of instrumental ideas from side one to side two.

Although there is no particular reason for a return to musical ideas from 'Ice', the creativity that ensues is highly effective as it completes the dissonant musical journey with the two long instrumentals flanking the song.

Don't Bring Harry

One of the best songs ever written about drug addiction and particularly heroin addiction. Musically it's a surprise as it is the first Stranglers song to feature an acoustic piano as the only keyboard part. The backing by the rest of the band is subtle and sparse and allows Burnel to intone in a deep almost whispered baritone the object of his malaise.

The instrumentation and production of the song brilliantly recreates the fog of the addiction with its laid-back bare approach. Burnel's vocal delivery gives the impression of someone who has just woken up in a dishevelled bedsit after a night of burning the candle at both ends, not wanting to get out of bed or face the daylight.

There is no dual meaning to the song it's about the trials of addiction and the dreadful pain of the body needing another fix. The main image of the song is to personify heroin as a 'friend' called Harry who is in fact a malevolent playmate always trying to tempt the narrator to indulge. The title suggest that friend Harry is brought to the narrator by another friend.

Drugs were very much part of the group's culture at the time, and it's confirmed in Cornwell's biography *A Multitude of Sins* and the *Song by Song* anthology that he and Burnel took drugs together on multiple occasions. The song implies peer pressure and opportunity were part of the problem and in that kind of atmosphere it was all too easy to slip into addiction.

The singer feels imprisoned by the drug but feels powerless to do anything about it except maybe summoning up the energy to score again and feel better for a while. Anyone who has suffered from addiction or lived with someone who is an addict will totally relate to this powerlessness. The lyric sheet features a drawing of an elephant with a big H on it. The link is obvious, heroin is the elephant in the room that nobody will talk about.

Amazingly it was chosen as a Christmas single and formed part of a four-track EP. Great song that it is, it was never a viable single despite a cheap price and previously unreleased tracks packaged with it. Even more amazingly it wasn't banned by the BBC. The Stranglers had form with the BBC. It wasn't so long after the incident where the band had destroyed a *Rock Goes To College* broadcast by downing tools after a couple of songs citing they wouldn't play for an elitist institution. The bone of contention being the bands nonstudent and under eighteen fans had been refused entrance to the gig itself.

In addition to this incident there was the radio version of 'Peaches' and the corporation's banning of the 'Duchess' video. Obviously, no one at the BBC had listened to the words of "Harry" carefully or rather more unlikely maybe the Beeb thought a song about addiction should be supported. Anyway, in an amazing surprise it received airplay and even more amazingly granted the band a *Top of the Pops* performance even though the song was outside the Top 40. Sadly, as already alluded to the song bucked the usual trend after an appearance and went down. With hindsight a more up-tempo song would have been more successful.

Also worth of note the band recorded a version of the song in French entitled 'N'emmenes pas Harry'. Interestingly being in a different language the lethargic feeling of the original is enhanced and meaning is still clear to a non-French speaker. The other difference is there is a bass drum introduction from Black which effectively counts in the song. It's a moot point amongst fans as to whether this benefits the song or not.

*****

A severe contrast from anything else on the album and any previous Stranglers song, and this serves the album well as the plaintive piano introduction immediately catches the ear following the complex instrumental fireworks of the previous song. 'Outside Tokyo' from the previous album had, for the first time, ballad-like qualities with the keyboard taking prominence but that song still had the other instruments contributing in considerable measure to the overall sound. In 'Don't Bring Harry' the other instruments are, for most of the song, providing background supportive roles but the song sounds nothing like an Elton John ballad.

A principal reason for this is that the piano part has its own melodic impetus rather than providing mere accompaniment and it is this lilting piano part that could form the basis for an effectively atmospheric piece of music even without a vocal melody. The first bar has a clearly defined melody, and this is developed with, for example, the flurries after "It might not come today".

Many piano ballad parts will have melodic interjections, but these will usually be in the gaps where the vocals are resting. In 'Don't Bring Harry' the piano is contributing a separate melodic idea at the same time as the vocal melody thus continuing the multi-melodic layering that was infusing most of the songs on the album. But unlike most other moments where the tempi were faster and the songs were driven by the different simultaneous melodies, here this texture creates the soporific mood alongside Burnel's low pitched, breathy vocal tone.

Despite the melodic interplay between the piano and the vocal, the song is chord-based and it is these chord patterns that also help to rise the individuality of this song beyond the conventions of a typical piano ballad. The third bar of the pattern sees the tritone/devil's interval relationship which adds a sense of unease and insecurity to the lethargic mood that wholeheartedly supports the lyrical intent. The unease is further enhanced by the unusual entering of Burnel's first vocal phrase near the end of the second bar suggesting that the drugs are taking their toll by reducing the speech to a sporadic unpredictable fog.

The main section is divided into two halves with the "I don't know where" phrase providing an effective melodic and chordal contrast to move the song forward. The whole section is repeated and followed by the "Don't Bring Harry" chorus which creates even more out of focus feeling as the four chords are now particularly unconventional and Cornwell again demonstrates his talent for adding a suitable yet creative texture with his piercing guitar arpeggios.

This creativity is developed further with the ensuing melodically angular, and a rhythmically strong guitar solo carrying the sense of voices cutting through into the mind. The bass arrives for the first time during the chorus and the dissonant first phrase with the sustained final note also gives the impression of the mind wandering. It is yet another example of Burnel adding a creative melodic layer to the overall sound rather than settling for a conventional bass line that would follow the chords. He does become more conventional for the other sections but plays the same rhythm as Cornwell at times during the guitar solo which adds further subtle rhythmic impetus.

Black, meanwhile, maintains a respectful simple rim click based pattern but the chorus does see judicious use of cymbals on beats two, two and a half, and three to create a further texture. The repeats of the vocal sections create an overall structure that is, typically for the band, bordering on the unconventional as the only repeat of the chorus arrives to finish the song.

Choosing this song as a single was unwise as the low pitched discombobulated vocal allied to the unconventional chord patterns were at variance with chart friendly songs. But the highly creative piano and guitar parts supporting the strong vocal melody created such an original song that was an important moment in the band's development. It added another dimension to the raft of originality already on the album and its successor, 'Golden Brown', became an undisputed triumph.

Duchess

At less than two and half minutes long 'Duchess' romps along as a song. The first single off the album It was another hit for the group but peaking at 15[12] there was slight disappointment given the band's singles chart track record up to this point. Having the band dress as choir boys for the video is significant as the backing vocals are church like. Dressing up as choir boys was seen as disrespectful and resulted in a BBC ban which obviously didn't help its chart position.

Reviews of the song also saw a bit of a back lash with celebrity critics Lesley Judd (Blue Peter presenter) and David Willkie (Olympic swimming gold medallist) on the TV show *Jukebox Jury* accused the band of going commercial and soft as did other more qualified critics in the music press. The view of the song being commercial may have foundation and it can't be denied that it is catchy. However, there is considerable interest in the musicality of the song and much to be admired and the sounds of the instruments are recognisably full-on Stranglers but wrapped in a commercial sheen.

The lyrics are a mixture of the impressionistic with elements of a narrative. Like all good pop songs, it leaves the listener free to make up their own meaning whether the songwriter intended it or not. 'Duchess' is a song about a real-life minor aristocrat that Cornwell had a brief affair with. The title and references to her being an heiress clearly supports the idea that the song is about a member of the ruling class.

Cornwell himself in his book *Song by Song* made it clear this is what he was writing about. However, there is other interpretation of the song that is almost the exact opposite to Cornwell's stated meaning, and it fits the lyrical imagery just as well. It could just as easily be a tale of a working-class matriarch know as Duchess, a Peggy Mitchell character from the East End who has just been widowed.[13]

A woman of power in her family and the local community but not formally titled. The image of a terrace and broken-down TV suggest poverty. The picture standing still, and the quiet empty house are images of death. It's the death of her husband we are talking about as other lyrics talk about her needing a man. The men come in the forms of "Rodneys wanting to win the cup". Rodney is a stereotypical name of an upper-class man often portrayed as a twit. However, it could equally be a working-class character as we were only a two years away from the iconic working class character Rodney Trotter in the BBC TV comedy series *Only Fools and Horses*. Around the same time there was another working-class Rodney who was at this time in the twilight of his career. But a working-class hero from the East End and that was footballer Rodney Marsh of QPR, Manchester City and Fulham. As a footballer he was certainly a man who as the lyrics suggest would have wanted to win the cup. It is of course rather fanciful to suggest this, but it is all part and parcel of why good pop and rock music works.

All listeners have their own interpretations of lyrics regardless of the songwriter's original intention. Differing lyrical interpretation of a song have always been fun and stimulating even when the song writer has told you exactly what it means. It's the same experience of mishearing the lyrics and then singing along with the wrong words and it can be disappointing when you hear the real words or in this case the real meaning.

In terms of Cornwell's meaning winning the cup is unmistakably about Duchess's potential suitors gaining her hand in marriage. Whether she is working, or upper-class Duchess is clearly a catch. A consummate piece of pop music with a soap opera twist all in two and a half minutes.

As a footnote one of The Stranglers peers, Squeeze based a whole career on kitchen sink drama songs with similar songs like 'Up the Junction', 'Take me I'm Yours' and 'Labelled with Love' to name but a few. The lineage of songs of this genre goes all the way back to London diarists The Kinks.

*****

The only serious choice for a single from the album was a reasonable success and this is largely due to the well-shaped melodies that have effective contrasts between sections as well as the chords used. The three main chords (one, four and five) form most of the song as opposed to the two following choices for singles, 'Nuclear Device' and 'Don't Bring Harry' which, as already mentioned, had unconventional chord patterns. The high-pitched vocal melody also accentuates the strength of the melodic shape, and the instrumental backing adds further to the commercial feel with a seemingly conventional drum pattern and synth arpeggios that give drive and distinction to the upbeat tempo. Add to this Cornwell's less aggressive vocal tone and the overall effect is to create the band's least edgy single to date. This did not please everyone, especially the diehard punk and rock-based fans and the release of 'Duchess' prior to the album signalled the change of approach.

The structure is reasonably conventional with the main section in two halves being played twice, a new section after the instrumental break involving the backing vocals and the return to the second half of the main section to finish. The song is also notable for being only two and a half minutes long with virtually no melodic instrumental sections as the instrumental break in the middle highlights the synth arpeggios but with no discernible melody as such. This is not, however, detrimental to the song as there is much to appreciate.

The powerful opening chords are interspersed with drum fills that are similar but changing each time from less of the toms to more of the snare and this is typical of Black's studious playing where every beat of the fills seems to have been carefully considered, as is the snare fill on the fourth beat of every bar for the first half of the main section. Greenfield's fast paced arpeggios are highly impressive and are central to the forward trust of the song and there is another low pitched four note synth riff on the second bar of the main section that adds depth to the sound.

Burnel's constant fast bass also helps to add drive and his movement away from the root notes on, for example, "God forbid" and "Standing still" are, unsurprisingly, moments to savour. The backing vocals on the "Du-chess, du-chess" section provide a further texture as they build up into four part harmonies.

The backing vocals had been previously used during the second half of the main section as "Ahhs" in a mock angelic state with the band revelling in this moment for the promotional video as choirboys. Cornwell's guitar is hardly noticeable as he maintains a supportive chordal role throughout, but with the synth, bass and drums providing so much drive, this is typical of the band's unity and vision that it is the song that dictates the prominence of instruments. Cornwell's guitar work throughout the album was highly impressive in this regard.

The song is also a strong contrast from the previous two songs on side two and the immediate burst of energy following the beautiful lethargy of 'Don't Bring Harry' gives balance to the side, and this was also important considering what was to come. Despite the commerciality of the song, there is an impressive originality with an instrumental drive encapsulating the band's unmistakable sound which separated the band from any other artists of the time.

Meninblack

This song divides fans, and the evidence suggests most fans dislike or downright hate it but there are some, admittedly a small minority who do genuinely like it. The backing track is from another song 'Two Sunspots' played at half speed. 'Two Sunspots' would eventually appear on the next album *The Gospel According to the Meninblack*. The slower speed gives the track ballast particularly with the slow heavy drum sound, so much so that the bass guitar was left off. Cornwell added a twangy doom laden Black Sabbathesque guitar part. The feel of the sound is funereal and sinister given the subject matter it was entirely appropriate.

Apocryphally this is the track that finished the group's relationship with producer Martin Rushent. Originally the session was booked to record the aforementioned 'Two Sunspots' as a single. The band had arrived early and were experimenting with the track and already had the half speed 'Two Sunspots' in the can and were busy adding ideas. Rushent arrived later heard the result, wasn't impressed, flipped his wig and left the building never to be seen again.[14]

It was a sad end to a relationship that had lasted three classic albums. With the band becoming more confident in the studio and keen to pursue their own ideas and trust their own judgement, added to even more complex musical ideas, it was destined the relationship wouldn't go on forever. The band then began to produce themselves with assistance. Even name producer and mid-eighties 'hot' producer Laurie Latham shared the credits on 1984's *Aural Sculpture*.

It wasn't until 1990's *10* with Roy Thomas Baker only one producer was credited for a whole album.

The studio high pitched vocals were done by putting Burnel's voice through a harmoniser and thus the Meninblack alien voice was created a sound you will still hear at the beginning of any Stranglers concert as they take the stage. The song was performed live on the 1981 tour as a final encore song with Burnel using some effects to achieve the high pitch and there is a live recording from an American tour on YouTube without a harmoniser so there are no effects on the vocals and therefore lack the high pitch of the studio version.[15] Despite this it's worth a listen to hear a rare live outing for this track that was controversial in terms of its merit and popularity with fans and also for its subject matter.

'Meninblack' is a taster for what is to come. It's the first time in their career the band had signposted what was to come on the next album. It was a technique they were to employ later in their career. It is very unusual for a band on their latest album to overtly suggest the concept that would inform their next work. It was planned as interviews and articles in the band run magazine *Strangled* made it quite clear what was coming in the future.

Whether you like the song or not it is pivotal in the Strangers history. By the 1979 the colour black was featuring heavily in the band's image. Their drummer was called Jet Black, one album used the colour in its title and all their album covers and inner sleeves up to this point were dominated by the colour black. Their music was often defined in words associated with black or deliberately described as black. The band had up to this point often dressed but not exclusively in black. So that darkest of colours loomed large in the band's philosophy and image.

From 1979 the black motif was stepped up even more, from this point on the band would acquire the moniker The Men In Black which has been used in headlines, stories and reviews ever since. It's integral to the next album's title and was used in the names of two songs on that album. One of those songs 'Waltzinblack' became the bands intro music for gigs and is still used today after over forty years since its inception. From now on the band exclusively dressed in black for gigs and promotion. In 1982 Black and Cornwell made a short documentary for the South West regional TV on the colour black. Part of the film explained the Men in Black conspiracy with our two heroes playing the sinister officials. The band's music was used to provide part of the soundtrack and the script was narrated by Black. The colour has become the iconic symbol and concept of the band.

The concept of the Meninblack is a conspiracy theory based around UFO sightings and alleged alien abduction. The theory goes that anyone reporting either of these phenomena then received a visit from mysterious government officials who then warned them to keep quiet or something unpleasant would happen to them. The theory can be sourced back to the 1940s when UFO sightings started to make the news. However, it really took off amongst the Ufologists in the seventies and eighties. The theory gathered such a pace that it led to the Hollywood blockbuster films beginning in the late nineties.

The Stranglers were the first people to popularise the Meninblack conspiracy and place it in the public domain. There had been one small reference in a Blue Öyster Cult song a few years earlier, but no one had written a whole song around the theory, let alone produced a whole album round the notion. The public perception of UFOs had also hugely increased at exactly this time with Stephen Spielberg's 1978 Hollywood blockbuster *Close Encounters of the Third Kind*. An encounter of the third kind is defined as actually seeing an alien. Given such interest in aliens it's not difficult to see now the band then constructed their Meninblack theory.

The band were obsessed with the idea in the early eighties. Band magazine *Strangled* was full of articles and references by band members about UFOs and the mythical Men in Black. In terms of the song's lyrics the band expound their own theory suggesting that the titular men may in fact be aliens themselves and have manipulated the human race over centuries so they can use them as food. This concept potentially borrows from the sixties Hollywood film *Soylent Green* staring Edward G Robinson and Charlton Heston, where humans are euthanised to produce food for the population.

Another potential stimulus was the early seventies sci-fi series *UFO* where the premise was a dying alien race seeks out humans so they can harvest their organs to save their species. All these ideas fed into the Meninblack theory. Fans added to the theory via correspondence in *Strangled* and one popular idea to emerge was that the concept had been planned since 1977 because on the shadowy figure seen on the *Rattus Norvegicus IV* album cover which does actually look like the cartoon representation of the MeninBlack. There were no denials from the band at time but they later confirmed this was just a coincidence but realised at that time it made sense to say nothing and keep the mystery around the project flowing.

*****

The slowed down backing track to 'Two Sunspots' that appeared on the following album provides a suitably otherworldly backdrop to the alien's message in conjunction with the synth swirling spaceship-like sounds. The guitar riffs also add to the alien effect because the trademark thin, slightly distorted sound here is deployed with low notes and a relaxed slow rhythm along with the melodic shape that is, unsurprisingly, unconventionally angular and floating without having a true sense of key.

The unconventional chord patterns add to the alien mood but there is little discernible change to the dynamics or the texture throughout the song giving rise to the argument that the song is a minute too long although the overall hypnotic feel is an engaging idea.

Although there is a sense of development, by the "We don't approve of artificial food" change of chords, this is subtle, and the overall structural feel is not defined. We are only just over halfway through the song at this point and the following two and a half minutes could have been shortened. It does point the way forward to the concept of the next album and also enables side 2 to have reflection prior to the dynamic ending.

Genetix

A single beat of one bar of the music of the drum pattern is enough for every Stranglers fan to recognise this iconic song. Sung by Greenfield but with a lyric written by Cornwell. The keyboard player fulfilling his evolving role as at least a track an album as a lead singer. Again, another song that builds and builds with many distinct parts It became the traditional set finale being a natural candidate because of the dramatic crescendo at the end of the song.

Lyrically the song deals with the dangers and ethics of genetic engineering. We are left in no doubt about the band's feeling on the subject and this was a time when cloning animals and animal organs was years away. Towards the close of the song Cornwell comes in as a second vocalist to intone Gregor Mendel's first law of genetics in a warning tone. Then the band drive with an ever-building tension to the musical crescendo and big finish of the song. The song has a climactic ending with Greenfield's final decaying chord emphatically signalling the end of the album. Because of the definitive ending it made the song a natural set finisher for many years.

The spelling of the title is interesting, the lyrical references i.e., gene experimentation and Gregor Mendel the scientist who articulated the laws of genetics means you would expect the song to be called and spelt Genetics. However, the spelling on the lyric sheet and on the cover is 'Genetix'. A simple spelling mistake? Well probably but by putting the 'x' instead of 'ics' gives the title a sinister feeling.

Live Greenfield's vocals were treated with a vocoder and gave the impression of a sinister, stereotypical mad scientist complete with a cod German accent. Interestingly *Marvel Comics* in the early nineties launched a superhero team using The Stranglers spelling, Genetix. A cartoon strip about a group of heroes with superpowers related to genetic mutations they have.

*****

The single musical idea of the previous track is contrasted with a return to the complex multi-melodic layering texture and equally complex structure with a multitude of ideas for the final track.

The band are, again, reinforcing the importance of instrumental sections with nearly four minutes of the five minutes twenty length of song being instrumental. Even within the main vocal section that is played three times, there are instrumental breaks that last for six bars between each four-bar vocal phrase. There is a new instrumental section between the second and third playing of the main section and then another new instrumental section after the third playing of the main section. This is followed by a completely different section which combines vocal and instrumental ideas to finish the song.

The opening sees another unconventional Black-tom dominated drum pattern that repeats throughout most of the main part of the song. The fill is dominated by the toms with the hi-hat on the offbeat towards the end of the bar. This provides rhythmic complexity and the guitar riff that fades in is more rhythmically constant. Greenfield's vocal has a reasonably simple melodic shape but the keyboard, guitar and bass riffs that play in this section form a rich variety of different rhythms and melodic ideas. The chords are implied, but the multi-melodic layering texture is at its height here and is further augmented by Black's rhythm that almost suggests a melodic strand in itself.

For those not associated with the band's music, this song could represent a chaotic mess. But, for those who have journeyed from the first two albums with moments like this, followed by an increasing number of occasions where this texture has dominated songs on *Black and White* and *The Raven*, we are witnessing a glorious culmination of melodic complexity where the separate identities of the four band members shine through to produce a unified whole. Greenfield has reassured us with a return to the comfort of the Cembalet but has added low held synth notes as well. The instrumental phrases that intersperse with the four bar vocal phrases provide further variety and being six bars long they add even more unconventionality to the music as do the fluid chord patterns that suggest a home key but never cement it.

The new instrumental section that follows the repeat of the main section sees a melodic dialogue between the bass and the guitar with the drums and the synth providing more constant rhythms on toms and a clipped percussive sound respectively.

2:45 sees a bass solo where Burnel is at his melodious best, using the whole range of the instrument whilst there are two supporting guitar melodic strands and the Cembalet continues to solo but lower in the mix and Black has continued with the second rhythmic pattern. At 3:24 Burnel settles his way down to a repeating low G note and the rest of the band now fall in line with a conventionality based around the G chord, including the first time that Black has played a standard drum pattern. This is the first time that we have a clear suggestion of a home key (the rest of the song was loosely based around A), yet this also provides a sense of anticipation.

Block harmony backing vocals suddenly enter singing "Gene Regulation" and this is now a simple chordal texture for all the instruments in contrast to the complexities of the multi-melodic layering that preceded it.

Furthermore, when the harmony vocals repeat, the bass launches into a solo whilst Cornwell speaks the laws of genetics moving the song towards its climax. Following the laws of "9 to 3 to 3 to 1" a powerful instrumental finale sees the band move towards rhythmic unity with the final chords although the individualism still shines through. Greenfield has the final say with his octave sliding portamento which reinforces the thoughts that had gathered on the previous song and points the way forward to the concept of the following album. A highly complex song that is a fitting album finale for a band at the height of their creative powers.

Musical Summary

There had been growing moments on the previous album where the multi-melodic layering combined with the conventional chordal texture and now side one of *The Raven* emphatically combined both to produce a complexity previously unattained.

Side two had a more chordal approach with the middle three songs but the final song, 'Genetix', reinforced the transformation. The sheer quantity and quality of melodic inventiveness in the instrumental sections throughout the entire album was astounding and the structures reinforced the importance of instrumental sections being integral to the songs with even more such sections with new ideas than had been the case on the previous albums.

Of the eight songs where there was a clear drum pattern (discounting 'Don't Bring Harry', 'Meninblack' and 'Longships') four of these; 'Ice', 'Baroque Bordello', 'Shah Shah a Go Go' and 'Genetix', had highly unconventional drum patterns that drove the songs and a further two: 'Nuclear Device' and 'Duchess', had moments of unconventionality.

Black's drumming was therefore as crucial to the complexity of the overall sound as any other band member. Greenfield moved away from the Hohner Cembalet until the final song and the Hammond organ was also far less evident, being replaced by a plethora of different timbres on his new Oberheim.

Burnel's bass sound was less aggressively mid frequency and Cornwell played less power chords and more melodic riffs. The vocal melodies had less singable hook lines, and all these musical elements, combined with the more measured vocal tones adopted by Cornwell and Burnel moved the album further away from the bands' pub rock roots and headlong into a more experimental complex sound to accompany the more elaborate lyrical ideas. This was not to all fans liking and the more punk based fans had the simple decision to embrace the changes or to move on. For many, this album is their crowning achievement.

Retrospectively, the crowning achievement is that, within the space of two years, the band had produced three distinctly different periods, all of which were highly successful, and which showed a desire and unquestioned ability to develop their musical creativity.

Album Summary

The Raven marked a massive step forward from the band both musically and lyrically. It built on the foundations laid down on *Black and White* and ran with it and then expanding them into a brave new musical world that set out to challenge and stimulate the listener and asking them to draw their own conclusions. The band were acting like guides playing the role of the mythical raven of the album's title and taking the listener to new places and situations but ultimately leaving them to make up our own minds as to what to think about these new vistas.

Lyrically the topics tackled were wide ranging, complex and controversial. A quick roll call of the subjects demonstrates this on side one you find songs about Viking mythology, urban decay, ritual suicide, sexual fantasy and political corruption. On side two the Iranian revolution, heroin addition, alien conspiracy theories and genetic engineering. Phew! There was only 'Duchess' that comes close to being conventional subject matter and even that has an edge. It's not surprising this was the only hit single off the album. The other songs chosen to try and scale the charts showcased political corruption, drug abuse and violent rebellion hardly topics that would crack the top 10. There seemed nothing that the band wouldn't tackle and nothing was safe from their appraising musical gaze.

The band were incredibly self-assured at this stage. They felt confident enough to work without a producer and had musical ideas and ability to burn. The next album was already planned. The band had a high profile, and they were seen in the industry as commercial bankers. There was a growing feeling the band had matured from a commercial, shock Punk singles band to a serious album band. Live they were on fire at this time. Prior to the release of *The Raven* the band supported The Who at Wembley Stadium. They premiered the album at the gig to rave reviews and stole the show in front of the headliner's noses. There was a swagger and confidence to their demeanour, they talked the talk and walked the walk. They knew absolutely what they wanted and knew how to get it. At this point The Stranglers seemed untouchable.

But despite this strong self-belief, artistic and commercial peak there were some cracks appearing. They had had three relative failures at getting hit singles. Not disastrous but it was in danger of becoming a trend and a sign that the fan base was large and loyal but not big enough to cross over into mega stardom. The fan base was changing, *The Raven* brought in new fans but also saw many original punk fans deserting them. The band would argue they weren't interested in any of this whether it be stardom or chart performance. They had tried to widen their fan base by touring America but had failed to make an impression. Another worrying element at this time was the increasing use of hard drugs like cocaine and heroin which could only go one way if it continued. However, by the end of spring 1980 the band were chomping at the bit to work — Cornwell was out of jail, there was a new single to make and a tour to support it. What could go wrong?

Page 2 SOUNDS June 28, 1980

Stranglers in jail on 'riot' charge

THE STRANGLERS found themselves on the wrong end of the law yet again last weekend when they were all arrested in Nice after a gig at the University turned into a riot. Keyboard player Dave Greenfield was later released but the other three — Hugh Cornwell, Jet Black and Jean-Jacques Burnel, — were all charged with inciting a riot and held in prison.

The band's manager Ian Grant was flying to France at the beginning of this week to arrange bail but at press time it was still not clear whether the band would have to remain in France until the trial came up and whether their upcoming British dates would have to be postponed.

The trouble started last Friday when the Stranglers arrived to play the gig at Nice University and claimed that both the power supply and the PA were inadequate for them. They decided to carry on with the gig but the power supply failed three times and the third time it happened the band left the stage for good. Jet Black was alleged to have told the angry audience to "take it out on the university, not us, and ask for your money back", which Jean-Jacques Burnel kindly translated into French.

The audience did demand their money back and proceeded to wreck the theatre causing damage estimated by university authorities at £10,000.

The band meanwhile had already left the university and gone for a meal. When they returned to their hotel the police swooped and took them all into custody.

The following day they were brought before an examining magistrate to determine if there was a case for them to answer. A tape of the gig was playing to the magistrate who confessed he wasn't able to understand any of it and demanded a translation.

The band were then taken back to the police cells for a second night and brought before the magistrate again on Sunday. He freed Dave Greenfield who had said nothing throughout the gig but charged the remaining three and sent them back into police custody. A trial date has not yet been fixed.

The tape containing the 'evidence' of the gig was made by Radio Monte Carlo without the permission of the band and the band's management will be suing the radio station for unauthorised taping of the concert as well as the promoters for failing to supply adequate power or PA.

Extra Tracks: Singles and b sides

Fools Rush Out (B-side to 'Duchess')

The B-side to 'Duchess' and another example of The Stranglers trait for putting good songs on the B-sides of their singles. It's short at two and a half minutes and the production values are lower than the tracks you might find on an album. There was certainly potential in the track the verse is interesting as when the band get to the "One of them" lines the emphasis changes and becomes staccato like, with the vocals more urgent than previously before, returning back to the more laid-back feel at the start of the song. Unfortunately, the ideas fail to be fully realised.

Lyrically it's Cornwell using one of his favourite lyrical devices of taking a well-known saying and turning it on its head. The original saying is "Fools rush in where angels fear to tread" and dates from the poem *An essay on Criticism* by Alexander Pope in 1711.It was also the title of a popular song written in 1940 and recorded over the years by a veritable legion of big name stars the most famous version being by Rick Nelson.

The saying means people without good judgement have no hesitation in trying to deal with a situation which the wisest would avoid. By saying "Fools rush out" Cornwell turns the saying around and then adds to the idiom by stating "angels got the better of them", implying that the fools have been taught a lesson. The religious image is kept up when he adds "hope there is a place in heaven for them". The rest of the lyrics list situations and experiences that 'fools' may experience and learn from e.g. another famous saying "crying wolf" (calling for help when it is not needed).

We can assume the fools are known to Cornwell and the lyrics probably relate to people who have annoyed him over the years — for example the band's managers and possibly band members. Again, the words are mostly impressionistic and don't relate a story, just series of scenarios and images. Like the music the lyrics are undeveloped although they certainly provoke thought but are a little undercooked to make complete sense.

There is certainly the potential for this song to be a longer more polished piece. Maybe there wasn't time to finish it properly or the band just weren't feeling the love. It's an archetypal B-side not really a candidate for the album but with a bit more love and work it could have been a contender.

*****

A return to the multi-melodic texture with the vocal melody entering straight away and accompanied by a bass riff and guitar and keyboard playing similar riffs. None of these riffs particularly carry conviction and the vocal melody is reasonably shaped but not strong enough to gel the disparate riffs together. The return to the harsher Cembalet keyboard sound does not enhance the overall sound here as the band have moved away from the more live, aggressive, and reverbed overall sound to a clearer band sound so the Cembalet struggles to blend in. The new "One of them" section tries to add a more forceful thrust and has partial success, but the melodic shape is lacking. The structure is conventional apart from a short additional instrumental section at 0:59 where a sudden shift to 3/4 time accompanies a guitar riff that descend with unconventional chords. More repeats and a fade out over the return of the 3/4 instrumental section brings the song to an unconvincing close.

Yellowcake UF6 (B-side to 'Nuclear Device (Wizard of Aus)')

To many fans the only interesting thing about this track is its name. So, let's go there first, Yellowcake UF 6 or Urania is a type of Uranium the element that is used to create nuclear power so it's a perfect name for the B-side to 'Nuclear Device (Wizard of Aus)'). It's not a song but just an instrumental backing track played backwards. The original song was called 'Social Secs' which was a song the band were working on at the time of *The Raven*.

That track was an attack on the social secretaries at colleges and universities following the bands infamously truncated *Rock Goes to College* gig. Having heard a demo of 'Social Secs' it was a tune that lacked any real inspiration and didn't really go anywhere so flipping it on its head was actual an inspired decision.

The lyrical content of 'Social Secs' seems rather petty given the issues band were addressing on *The Raven*. They had widened their horizons to international events and thought-provoking philosophies so a song about a polytechnic's s entertainment committee's shortcomings seemed to lack ambition and gravitas. In need of a B-side, it made sense to reverse the tape and see what happened.

Coincidentally The Skids, a band The Stranglers actively supported by giving them prestigious support slots early in their career, were doing exactly the same thing in Rockfield Studios/ Wales at the same time in 1979. Their resulting track 'Peaceful Times' was good enough to make their seminal album *Days in Europa*. In fact, so good it has become The Skids' walk on music at their gigs. 'Yellowcake UF6' was never going to attain those heights but the title and recording technique demonstrated innovation.

The backwards tape experiment for The Stranglers produced an interesting vibe and some great sonic effects which now could potentially make interesting samples. However, unlike The Skids there is no inspired added vocal track. Stimulating but definitely no more than a B-side.

*****

An instrumental using backward recording effect throughout. Initially many will find the piece to be the same sound throughout and a rather pointless studio exercise, but repeated listens will result for some in a compelling, hypnotic piece that divides into various sections. The main section at 0:16 is driven by the bass followed by a second section at 0:34 with the chords sounding more dissonant with more prominent synth then a third section at 1:16 with the same sense of key as the first section which duly returns at 1:31 followed by a guitar solo of sorts, another return to the first section with a higher added guitar riff, and then a return to the guitar solo with drums to fade. The differences between the sections are subtle due to the reversing creating a dominant sound. But these subtle changes can entice the listener with the result being a long way away from the direct complexities in *The Raven* album.

In the Shadows (Live), Crabs (Live) and Wired

(Additional tracks on 'Don't Bring Harry' EP)

All these tracks were released as part of the 'Don't Bring Harry' EP. Only 'In the Shadows' is a Stranglers track whilst the other two are from Burnel's and Cornwell's sabbaticals from the band. 'In the Shadows' already had two studio releases one as the flip side to 'No More Heroes' and then the same version appeared on 1978's *Black and White* album. This version stems from the Hope and Anchor live recordings from 1977.

We have already dealt with the merits of the song earlier however this version is even more sleazy, dangerous, and atmospheric than the studio version and showcases Burnel's 'barracuda' bass at its best and most untamed form. A brooding unsettling break in their restlessly fast and furious live set in 1977.

'Crabs' was a song on Burnel's solo album *Euroman Cometh*. This live version of the song beefs up the original album version. The use of real drums in conjunction with a drum machine and a full band showing off their musical chops really brings the song alive making the studio version appear rather tame. Lyrically, it is of its time with Burnel bemoaning a former squeeze giving him an STD. It's not exactly empathetically delivered by the bass man and added to the accusations of sexism associated with the band. However, such subject matter wasn't unique to members of The Stranglers. Heavy metal bands such as AC/DC and Motörhead were dealing with the same subject with a similar lack of empathy.

'Wired' is a cut from Cornwell's collaborative album with Robert Williams, *Nosferatu*.

Instrumentally and lyrically it perfectly creates the feeling of a drug induced trip. The unusual instrumentation, particularly the percussion, ambient space and stereo effects give the track the feeling of enhanced sensory perception and paranoia associated with being high on narcotics. Cornwell's vocal adds to the atmosphere with its unhinged and off the wall delivery. The songs long instrumental run out finishes with a call and response routine between various instruments as if they're having a conversation or even a disagreement.

Bear Cage

When the album was reissued on CD this standalone single was included. It makes perfect sense as although it was recorded separately it fits into the feeling of the album, whilst along with the album track 'Meninblack' signals the arrival of the next album. It's the first Stranglers' single to be released as a 12-inch with an extended mix which to many fans is far superior to the rather short, less than three minutes, cluttered 7-inch single mix. The 12-inch came in a record company die cut sleeve which was rather disappointing. There was a 12-inch picture sleeve but in a clerical error it was sent to shops a week after the single was released. Most shops had sold the 1- inch with a regulation record company die cut sleeve before the picture sleeve arrived and the late arriving sleeves were mostly discarded by record shops. So, if you have the 12-inch in a picture sleeve you have a rarity.

The song has a heavy beat which makes it potentially danceable and being on a 12-inch format which in 1980 was almost totally the preserve of disco suggests the record company were thinking along these lines. There are some interesting musical dynamics in the song particular on the extended mix where Burnel and Black in the rhythm section create a groove.

The feeling off the song is cold war paranoia. The lyrics written by Cornwell are firmly set in Germany with the G M B H backing vocal being the acronym for a German limited company. The lyrics also mention the Mark, then the German currency.

The use of the bear image suggests the threat of Russia and Greenfield's decaying keyboard sound imitate rain, again suggesting nuclear fallout descending on central Europe. The keyboard player had done a similar thing on *Black and White* with his work on the track 'Enough Time'.

In 1980 nuclear war was a genuine fear and informed everyone's thinking. In the 1990s the threat disappeared but sadly in 2023 following the attack on the Ukraine by the Russian Bear the threat is back with a vengeance.

Germany or West Germany (Federal Germany Republic) as it was then known was right on the frontline, the western front. Readers will also realise the link to another cold was song on the *Black and White* LP, 'Sweden (All Quiet on the Eastern Front)'. The enemy on the West German border was Communist East Germany (GDR), backed and controlled by Russia.

The lyrical allusions to private enterprise and limited companies (G M B H) make the conflict with the opposite ideology, communism, all the more immediate and starker. The GDR is acknowledged in the song when the city of Dresden is referred to in a positive light but it's not a call for communism but more a call for a united Germany. The narrator wants to return and spend summer there like he did in the united Germany of his youth. He would prefer to do this than to visit the western European cosmopolitan cities Brussels and Amsterdam. The German reunification alluded to in the lyrics appeared a long way off, nigh an impossible dream 1980. However, as we know just over ten years later this was to become a reality. The line about drawing lines on maps is a clear reference to divided Germany and what then appeared an impossible dream.

*****

The simple verse chorus structure with no extra instrumental sections and the conventional chords were suitable reasons for 'Bear Cage' to be released as a single. But the song is built around another of Black's creative yet idiosyncratic drum patterns with a snare roll in the middle of the repeating four beats, which does not lend itself towards commerciality.

Furthermore, there is only one chord for most of the song and this also affects the suitability for chart success as there is, subconsciously, little sense of development to the chart buying public.

A Musical Critique

Page 60 SOUNDS March 22, 1980

RELEASED!

DON'T GO DOWN TO THE WOODS TODAY...

the stranglers
NEW SINGLE HAS BEEN RELEASED

"BEAR CAGE"

c/w
"SHAH SHAH A GO GO"
TAKEN FROM THE ALBUM "THE RAVEN" UAG 30262 CASSETTE TCK 30262

IN CUDDLY PICTURE BAG

BP344
UA
UNITED ARTISTS RECORDS

The drum pattern repeats continuously throughout for most of the song and is accompanied from the start by a restrained repeating bass riff, shimmering descending synth effects and conventional guitar power chords which, like the bass, is low in the mix as the drums are, arguably, a little too high. The vocal therefore has plenty of space to occupy and, whilst the melody is reasonably well shaped, the low pitch and ponderous tone also do not lend the song towards commerciality.

The first chorus subsection, "Gee (G), I'm" sees no change in any of the instrumentation and the vocal melody returns to the low first note of the verse so any feeling of forward momentum is absent. There is an additional stepwise rising synth part for the second verse, but this is too subtle to alter the dominance of the drums.

The second chorus subsection, "Bear...ear cage" has contrast as the chords now move and the backing vocals enter to add a welcome extra texture, but the melody is functional and not particularly strong, so it is no surprise that the single failed to succeed. There is, however, considerable merit in the overall idea and the song development. Interestingly, when played live the song has a rawer feel that enables the song to have more energy than its plodding studio version. If this original version had desires to create a dance-like groove, it sadly misfired.

Footnotes

1. Official Chart Website

2. visitkent Website

3. John Pasche website

4. Official Chart Website

5. The Stranglers Chris Twomey's band biog on line on thestranglers website

6. Official Chart Website

7. Official Chart Website

8. Official Chart Website

9. Official Chart Website

10. Eyewitness report from Mags and George Proctor 1978

11. Hagakure: The Book of The Samurai Yamamoto Tsunetomo – originally published in the early 18th Century reprinted 2001 and translated by A S Wilson

12. Official Chart Website

13. Fictional TV character in long-running BBC TV series, *Eastenders*

14. *Song by Song* - Hugh Cornwell and Jim Drury

15. The authors witnessed a performance of the song Meninblack at Manchester Apollo 1981 and although unconfirmed got the impression Burnel was using helium rather than a harmonizer to obtain the high-pitched vocals

April 12, 1980 SOUNDS Page 11

LAUGH A MINUTE Hazel O'Connor

Hugh Cornwell 'not about to top himself'

DID YOU see 'Law And Order' or 'The Glass House' on tv last week? If you didn't, I can tell you they gave a pretty grim picture of prison life both sides of the Atlantic. Stranglers fans must thus be pretty damn worried about how young Hugh Cornwell is faring right now. Jaws spoke to Hazel O'Connor, budding actress and singer who's recently been to visit him in Pentonville Prison to see whether he was still intact.

She told us that he's healthy, very calm, his eyes are bright and he's still smiling. In fact, Hugh says it's just like being back at school. (Must enjoy the discipline, knoworrimean?). He's the only detainee with one collar turned out and one turned in (the most rattus norvegicus of the lot, I dare say), and he's currently being employed in a catering capacity, serving out food to fellow inmates. This does give him the chance to cheat on the grub, but we're assured he doesn't.

He's changed cells three times already since he went inside, as it seems there's a rota system in operation which moves you on up till you get expelled at the end of your sentence. The chap's in good spirits, as he won't have to stay in for the whole two months, just four more weeks and he should be out on remission. An ongoing 'things could be worse' situation. Hugh misses his guitar, like any creative genius (shame, we could have had 'Down In The Sewer' Part II), but since it would be half-inched even if he had one, he's not so worried.

Hazel herself, having completed her 'Breaking Glass' movie, is now sweating it out waiting to see what the film distributors are going to do about releasing it. It's a case of split personalities as regards record companies, too, as Hazel was with Albion, then went to Arista, and has her film soundtrack emerging on A&M. Confusing, huh?

She has a band together now, comprising Wesley McGoo, Bob Carter, Ed Casey (ex-999), Chris Fay and Charlie Casey, and they're currently re-working songs which were written by Hazel two years ago. From now on they're out on the road, doing the promotion for the film, going over to the States in the summer, and hopefully avoiding the chat show syndrome. Films and music should speak for themselves, says Hazel. That's what we like to hear.

BETTY PAGE

The Stranglers 1977-1990

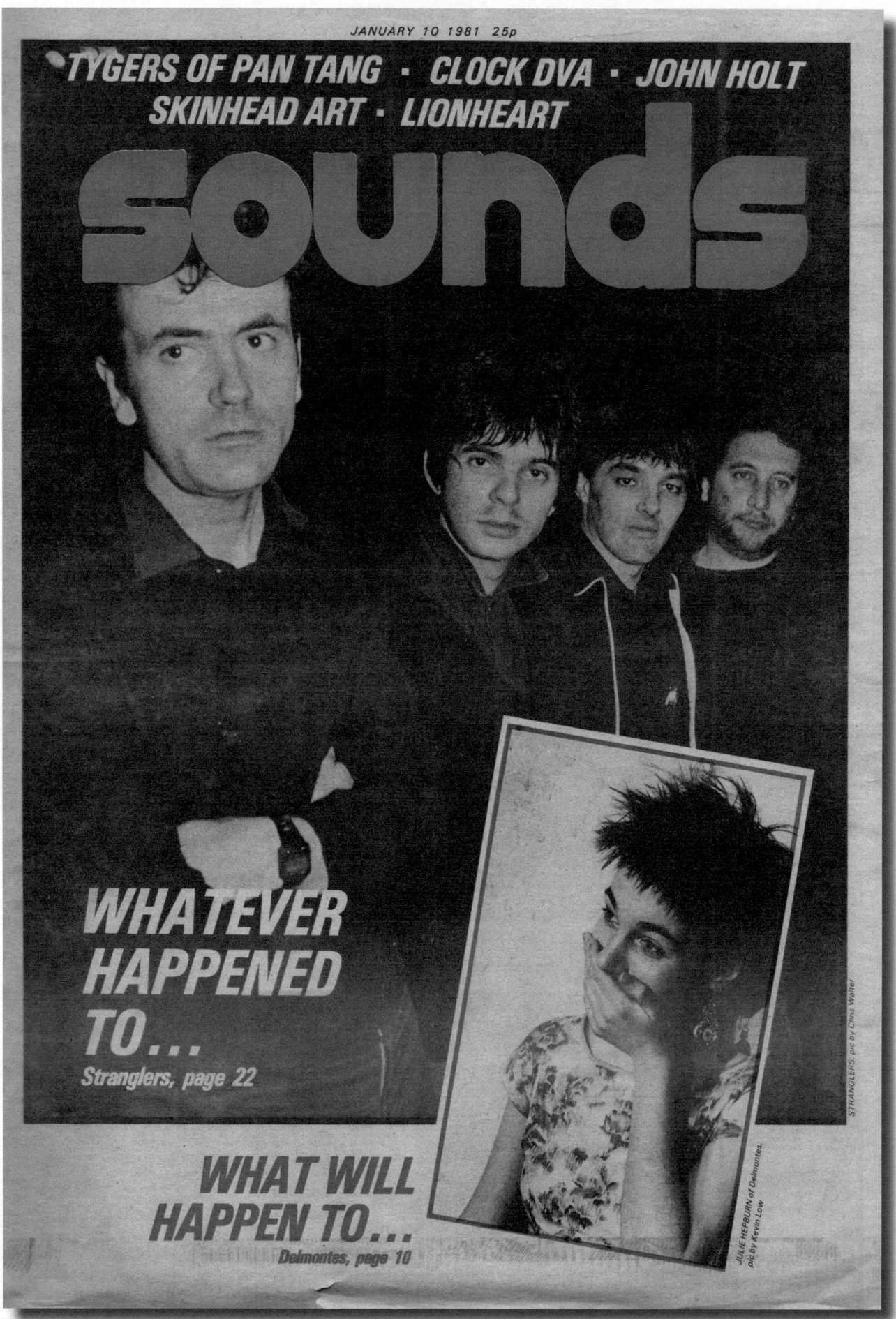

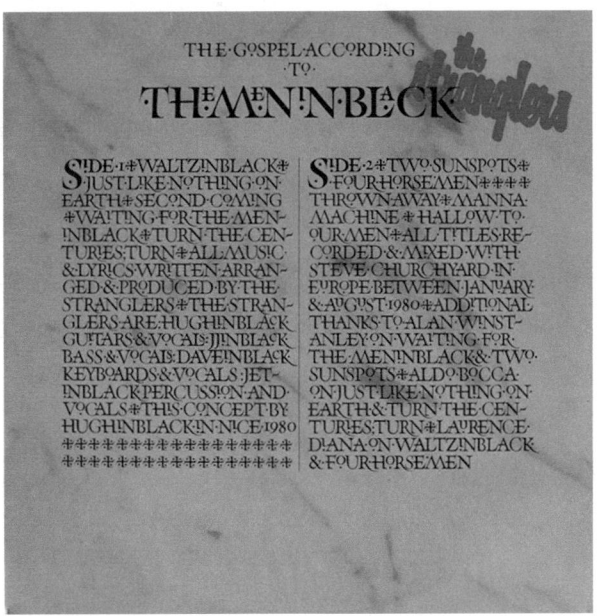

The Gospel According To The Meninblack

For many original fans this album was the straw that broke the camel's back it was just one step too far. They had tolerated the experimentation on *Black and White* and *The Raven* because both albums had their fair share of classic accessible tracks. Too many this album was too experimental, sounded too tame and had nothing they would call a classic on it and that was the opinion of many who actually bought it.

Many fans didn't bother to buy or even listen. Such a narrow-minded approach has made this album something of a hidden gem. The band decided to give full reign to their creative and experimental side, a side that was present on all of their previous albums but they had never gone for a whole album where every single track could be considered experimental or off the wall. What came to fruition was a unique collection of songs with considerable musical experimentation and quirkiness matched seamlessly to a complex conceptual idea.

Within a few months of *The Raven* being released the band were back in the studio recording what was to become *The Gospel According to the Meninblack*. *The Raven* had been a critical and to some extent a commercial success but nagging at the back of their minds, if not at forefront of them, was the group's failure to have a hit with their last three single releases.

The recording process proved protracted, and the band became virtual nomads as they flitted from studio to studio all over Europe. There were several reasons for the extended sessions, Cornwell's prison sentence following the loss of his appeal, then later in the year there was the Nice incident leading to the whole band being arrested and incarcerated. Add in a tour of the UK to promote a single, then tours in parts of Europe and a visit to the USA where all their gear was stolen, it was no wonder that recording took such a long time.

The album was trailed by two singles, 'Who Wants the World', a non-album track but in keeping with the Meninblack concept and then the album track 'Thrown Away'. Both, again failed to set the charts alight hitting 39 and 42 respectively.[1] 'Thrown Away' failing despite another *Top of the Pops* appearance. The band often complained about not being played on the radio and TV but the nation's favourite pop show can't be said not to have supported the band's cause above and beyond in this period of their career.

The album was finally released in February 1981, nearly 18 months after *The Raven* – again

Page 22 SOUNDS January 10, 1981

WELL, THEY SAID ANYTHING COULD H[APPEN]

Duff equipment, Close Encounters and bog-w[itches]. Stranglers In America, by SYLVIE SIM[MONS]

THIRD OF four nights at the Whisky and the audience is still dribbling in during the opening act. The Humans are on IRS and could just as easily be on the *Benny Hill Show* with their pop-eyed manners, ageing Knack's uncles tough-pop music, and Ronnie Corbett lookalike. By the time the Stranglers arrive at around 10.30 the crowd is still balding at the edges but ready.

Last time LA was Strangled was at the Starwood, a larger club where the kids were packed to the sweaty walls but managed to move in time to the music and the stripper like some automatic bath sponge. But that was two-and-a-half years ago, at the height of the (what number did we get up to?) British Invasion. Since then, while others have returned to evolve through the Civic to the arenas, the Stranglers in America have been pretty much buried like some mongrel that does a couple of good tricks before rolling over and playing dead — two albums in America, 'Black And White' their last Transatlantic breath.

Their resurrection tour (over 40 dates — Los Angeles is about halfway) is hardly the type on which conversions are made, except perhaps to the philosophy of Positive Thinking. Coming over to support their latest American elpee 'Stranglers IV' — a compilation album released on IRS records, Miles Copeland's label, that offered them a one-off deal of a record and tour support after the band dropped A&M two years ago with the immortal words on a telegram: FUCK OFF — they've had a roadie beaten up by cowboys in Texas, van tyres slashed by rednecks who've just learned to use cutlery and, best of the lot, a truck containing half a million dollar's worth of their equipment and instruments, half of it customised and irreplaceable, nicked while they were en route from New York to Washington only half a dozen dates into the tour.

Where others would go home and sulk, the brave band battled on with rented equipment, much of it proving merely an ability to self-destruct during shows.

At least the stuff they were using for the LA concerts (eight of them over a long, long weekend) is the same they've been using for a week or so, resulting in some kind of compromise as to its moods and eccentricities. But the basic hardware still sounds very different from their own (especially, poor Dave, the synthesisers) lending them the air of a *Top Of The Pops* Stranglers cover band. And one with a Max Bygraves frontman at that, Hugh Cornwell having to break off to chat to the audience and fill in a few minutes while the band and crew perform quick band-aid operations on the crumbling equipment. No chance to replace any of the old stuff either, with the insurance situation up in the air and pretty much all the band's money — at least every cent they earned off their last album in England — tied up in lawyers and advisors and various people trying to make sure that Jean-Jacques doesn't get put behind bars for the France fracas.

THE BAND weren't happy with tonight's performance but from the ground they sounded pretty good. They performed as determined and as tirelessly as a quartet of bridegrooms on their American honeymoon. Jet Black was purposeful, teaching the second-rate drums a lesson; beating hell out of them and providing the strongest sound. Dave Greenfield looked perplexed — often because what he played on the keyboards came out sounding sodden, the occasional high-pitch bleep breaking through the sludge for at least the first third of the set. Jean-Jacques played tensely, either loping back and forth across the stage or standing on one leg glowering. Hugh's vocals — praise the lord, his mike was at least working OK — cut through the sound that was mostly like a record player that's been dropped from a great height so often that only the bass button works with a loud, insistent buzz.

They played a couple of songs (or more depending on their mood) from the next album, 'Meninblack', due for release in Britain in February. This set started off with a new one, an instrumental synthesiser waltz *Carousel*-style, keyboards straining from low to fat to chirpy while the carnival sound became more and more spacey and moody before a hard, rocking bass line rescued it from the Twilight Zone. 'Just Like Nothing On Earth', another new one continued the interest in the little black men that pour out of flying saucers like their little green cousins (OK, Sammy Hagar, they can be little red folk too if you like) the world over.

The overall feel of the set is of long and interesting or monotonous instrumental sound punctuated by short, brilliant, gutsy rock and roll songs like 'Hanging Around' — this week, five years late almost, one of the most-played songs on a local rock radio station.

The audience was stuffy though, slow to respond. Hugh asked them if they were on quaaludes? Asleep? After all, it was a Sunday night. Eventually some of the younger kids at the front obliged with a perfunctory demonstration of the dance popularised by the *LA Times* article on rock and roll violence, The Slam (right foot up, raise it to his groin; left shoulder forward, aim it at the chest. . . .) in time for the last song and an encore — 'Dead Loss Angeles', what else? Hugh added insult to injury and recited a poem of great sensitivity he found on the men's bathroom wall (he should have seen what Sandra of Van Nuys said of his techniques in the ladies!) which summed up LA culture for him.

The crowd wasn't sure if it was being insulted, so cheered. The press knew they were, so gave the customary bad reviews, Angry Men Of Rock stuff. We were reading them at the start of our interview. The next and final night was their Royal Command Performance, there being various members of record companies present to help them, one hopes, in their search for a permanent haven in the United States and a chance to do another tour that will break them something other than financially. This won't be the one to do it, though not for lack of trying. When the Stranglers are good they are very good, and even when they're bad, through no fault of their own, they're still pretty good.

WE'RE AT the Tropicana motel, Dave's on the bed, Hugh's at the table, craftily perched so one eye can catch the television. Their manager's watching it and guarding the vodka bottle. Jean-Jacques and Jet have had their turn with the last customer, plus a go on the famous Rodney Bingenheimer KROQ show where he asked such wonderful things as oh wow, heard you were in jail, that must have been far out etc.

Though the attitude of the kids across America seems to be changing towards the band, it's been obvious that the media's hasn't. Newspapers have either come on blasé, having no idea who they are and not particularly caring, or digging up the tough punk clichés and touching them with all the relish of a pet tarantula.

Hugh's polite, tired, clever. Dave's your basic Nice Guy, all the above, and too nice to show it. Obviously the first question is, all things considered, especially the stolen equipment, why the hell go on with it?

"Well," muses Hugh, "it's like the Stranglers have never admitted failure. Right from the beginning we would never give up. This just makes us more determined, and it's always been like that."

But doesn't it all get a bit silly when you're battling on with bad equipment and can't really do a good show?

"It's a case of doing the best you can," Dave reasons. Adds Hugh, "You've got to weigh the pros and cons of carrying on and going back, and it just seemed like there were more pros to carrying on than going back."

The tour was Miles Copeland's idea. "Why don't you want to go to America?" he asked them. "It's not that we don't want to go, it's just that there's no-one there who will help finance the tour," they answered. So Miles said, "Well I've got a label and I think that your last album's really good and it's a shame it didn't come out in America, so how about putting something out on my label." They thought it a "reasonable idea" and packed their toothbrushes.

It's a one-off deal with the small label which runs from out of A&M's lot in Hollywood. Moving up to A&M seems to be the next step for a band that's learnt to walk on IRS, but it won't be for the Stranglers, whose telegram telling them to "Fuck off" following their last tour here over two years ago still hangs framed on a wall. All the gigs in major music bi[z] cities have a sprinkling of A&[M] men in the back rows.

"If there's another label which is interested in picking us up then they'll be putting out all the future things on us," says Hugh.

Their last tour here, they reckon, was even more screwed up than this one's turned out to be.

"They didn't know who we were or our music or anything," remembers Hugh. "We'd speak to journalists who weren't really aware of why they were there. Like, 'Why me? The editor sent me and I don't know who the fuc[k] you are and I'm not really interested anyway' and they ask stupid questions and we thought, God, A&M are supposed to be *helping* us. They didn't even send out an info to anyone before we arrived."

But with the two-and-a-ha[lf] year gap (not to mention an IRS bio that told you as much about the Stranglers as the Statue Of Liberty's welcome

A Musical Critique

January 10, 1981 SOUNDS Page 23

pix by Chris Walter

... The

s about America) ween visits, people still n't seem to know who they . Like the newspaper ncert reviews we were just ding, their reputation still ms to be as either mean d menacing jailbirds or oic-romantic jailbirds, ending on who's doing the orting.

"It doesn't matter what we " sighs Cornwell, "they're going to say we're like , and that's that."

A DUMB review in the *Herald Examiner* paper was based around the band's so-called lousy tude towards Americans, nething the band seemed e asking for by reading out t poem that summed up erican culture for Hugh.

"I didn't actually say mmed up". I said I'd found *example* of American ture on the wall and it really nulated my brain cells, and nyone had said that to me have taken it tongue-in-ek, but here they take rything so bloody ously. It was a joke, you w."

He recites with all the urish of a Shakespearean ct: *"There once was a guy med Cram/ Who but for cking cock wouldn't be rth a damn/ Ram it up his e, shove it down his throat/ l even give a blowjob to your Grandma's goat/ I've seen him on Santa Monica in front of every bar/ I've seen him up on Selma blowing guys in his car/ So if you need a knob-job or want to pork some ham/ Go to all the gay hotspots and ask for Mr Cram."*

"And I read that out and they took it seriously, like I was insulting America. They're all so serious about us."

They're probably too frightened to be anything else, what with the band's image as tough boys in black.

"They're going to hate us anyway, which is what they did."

Which brings us back to the original question: why bother then?

"Well, we thought it might be a better time to come out then two years ago," when anything with the remotest scrap of English heritage sold out shows. "And it definitely has been better. It's really surprising — we've had a large turn-out for a lot of the gigs, and they've been really into the music and they know about us and it's great. Some of the places have been really surprising, like little places where you think you're going to be a complete washout, and there they are, packed with cowboys and lumberjacks and bikers and just about everybody — like New Orleans where they're all shouting out the names of the songs and singing along with the numbers. New Orleans! It's amazing."

A regular little Rod Stewart show.

"We've got more of a following here than we thought we had when we came over," adds Dave, who says the whole thing reminds him of their early days in England, including the bad reviews. "It's surprising and it's refreshing really."

In England, they feel — to a certain extent — that their fans are so hardcore and loyal that they'd love them if they got onstage and blew their noses or sang Neil Young encores. "We're not scared of a challenge," swears Dave.

Generally speaking, they say, things have been going pretty well for them in England even though "We're hardly ever there . . . We've always had a basic die-hard following," says Hugh, "that has always been there, and adverse press reports that makes them even more die-hard and makes them distrust the press even more. Basically we get less and less airplay as time goes on and just get to be completely ignored. It's like they've got the philosophy in the media of, well if we ignore them they might go away, but here we are and here we stay . . . I think because our music appeals to a wide cross-section, no fashionable cliques.

"We started out playing everywhere where other groups feared to tread. We'd go to all the tiny corners in England where there were pockets of kids and they'd say 'Wow, we've never had a group out here, you're the first to come here' so they remembered that and when the record came out they all rushed out and bought it and it suddenly went into the charts without us being 'fashionable'. We're getting a cross-section audience out here too which is great, very healthy."

N OT TOO many women though?
"I don't know, I see a lot of women at our gigs, loads."

The manager suggests they're cowering at the back while the slammers slam away at the front. As for their not-so-good reputation among females in the past, Hugh sighs and says, "We've always been misunderstood".

So clear up the misconceptions then. The Stranglers are just four nice clean boys trying to earn an honest penny?

"Yeah, we always have been, it's just that people always took us the wrong way. An example of that is me reading out that poem and everyone thinks I'm anti-American just because I read out some filthy poem that I saw on a wall that titillated me. We just get misinterpreted. Maybe we just don't speak plain English enough or something. We got to be less subtle, more direct. Shall I commit suicide now or wait until after the last set?" he recalls with the words that upset the audience doing their little best on opening night.

What with Hugh's well-publicised spell in prison, 1989 hasn't exactly been The Stranglers' favourite year.

"There's always been problems before," says Dave, "but this year certainly had the worse. The years before kind of pale into insignificance beside it, but I think it's changing now slowly. The crew have got that feeling as well, I don't know why. Things are starting to pick up again, I feel. Our luck will get better".

T HERE'S ONE big hurdle first, the trial resulting from the so-called 'riot' in France, an expensive and frightening fiasco, the general feeling over there being that Jean-Jacques as a Frenchman should know what he was doing. Quite understandably this isn't the band's favourite topic of conversation. "It's just like living day to day at the moment," says Dave.

After this tour and the court case they'll sort out the equipment problems somehow, "then another tour, England and Europe maybe". They've chosen not to work in Europe for some time, feeling that the old homeland is "a bit more paranoid than it was, a lot of people out of work, so the music's getting more desperate with imminent destruction right on the doorstep".

It would seem that the Stranglers' music is getting more escapist in comparison, their next album 'Meninblack' being the nearest thing to a concept album they've done with a UFO-ish theme. "This album", says Hugh, "is the first one where all the tracks have a cohesion about them. They're all dealing with strange phenomena."

Dave: "And alternative ways of looking at religions through these extraterrestial phenomena. The nearest we've done to a concept album."

"We're not the men in black", says Hugh, reminding us of the MIB on the cover of 'Rattus' standing at the window in the back of the photo, and the song 'Men In Black' on 'Black And White'. "The men in black are a phenomenon that occurs all over the world, people seeing UFOs and sighting strange phenomena and getting visited by men wearing black suits and hats and open-toed sandals and drive around in Fifties cars and enter people's houses and speak to them and after half an hour or so they leave again and they put these people into trances with thought implantation or whatever —"

Dave: "Hypnosis. They impart information that if the people are saying too much about what they've seen, they won't say anything any more."

Hugh: "There's been lots of reports in the journals all over the world. They're sort of Close Encounters really. These guys have no facial hair and they sort of resemble human beings but aren't the bonafide thing." Sounds like the Knack to me. "These people never see flying saucers again, or they die or disappear afterwards or strange things happen to them. It is (he adopts a mysterious Doctor Finlay accent) a strange occurrence."

The music is appropriately spacey. "It's not just a collection of songs. It's very moody music and a lot of it's very spacey and more varied in style. You can't really talk about your music."

As for solo albums, "We haven't got much time at the moment. If we have we'll do them. I think Jean's been working on a few tracks," says Hugh. "I've got loads of ideas but there's no time, and we've got a lot of new Stranglers material to work on, so all of your ideas go into that. You only do solo stuff if you've got spare time and spare ideas and we've got niether." Dave will do one at the end of the tour once he's got new keyboards all in the right working order.

No plans to produce any local bands, though they've been given several tapes along the way, all the band listen to while in America. "I listen to very little American stuff," says Dave. "It's usually too dated culturally and musically."

Adds Hugh, "I've heard some nice things when guys come up to you and say, 'Hey I've got a band too' and give you tapes. The Lobsters (from San Diego) are pretty good."

They can't afford to be patrons of the art and support new bands either with everything that's gone on, despite their gold LP success in England which one would have thought would have given them at least some financial security.

"Charity begins at home," shrugs Hugh. "Of course it would be nice to help the whole world but we've got a lot of problems of our own at the moment and we have to sort those out first. Success in England doesn't mean money because of the taxes. Success in England just means success."

So what kind of success *are* the Stranglers after?

"The success that means buying some new fucking equipment. We'll deal with the rest as it comes."

The Stranglers 1977-1990

MIRACULOUS NEW ALBUM
THE·GOSPEL·ACCORDING
·TO·
·THE·MEN·IN·BLACK·

ALBUM LBG 30313
AVAILABLE ON CASSETTE
INCLUDES THE SINGLE 'THROWN AWAY' BP 383

THE TOUR
12TH FEB ODEON CANTERBURY · 13TH FEB TOP RANK BRIGHTON · 15TH FEB HAMMERSMITH ODEON LONDON · 16TH FEB ODEON BIRMINGHAM · 17TH FEB HANLEY VICTORIA HALLS STOKE
18TH FEB POLYTECHNIC SHEFFIELD · 19TH FEB ROCK CITY NOTTINGHAM · 20TH FEB UNIVERSITY LIVERPOOL · 21ST FEB APOLLO MANCHESTER
23RD FEB UNIVERSITY DURHAM · 24TH FEB PLAYHOUSE EDINBURGH · 25TH FEB APOLLO GLASGOW · 26TH FEB MAYFAIR NEWCASTLE
27TH FEB UNIVERSITY LANCASTER · 28TH FEB UNIVERSITY LEEDS · 2ND MARCH WINTER GARDENS CLEETHORPES · 3RD MARCH DE MONTFORT HALL LEICESTER

this was huge amount of time away from the music scene and potentially career ending. With only a couple of flop singles giving them any kind of a profile in 1980 the band's stock was low on the eve of release. The record scrapped into the Top 10 at No.9 in its first week but sunk like a stone after that. The release of a second single 'Just like Nothing on Earth' failed to halt the decline and was another commercial disaster as it missed the top 75, altogether the first time this had happened to the band.[2]

Two things became abundantly clear during the recording sessions one was Cornwell's term in prison for possession, drugs, particularly heroin and cocaine were a major issue for the band. The other conversely was a huge positive, collectively the band were experimenting sonically in the studio with many artistically stunning results. The process of experimenting in the studio in those days was long and drawn out as the processes were hugely labour intensive. Remember these were the days before computers, samplers and music software assisting recording. Things had to be done literally by hand when today a very similar although, not exactly the same effect, can be achieved by clicking a mouse.

The album had a concept which was credited to Cornwell on the sleeve but all the band bought into the idea wholesale and made contributions to the theme as well as the music. The premise was based around the mysterious Meninblack who made visits to people who claimed to have seen UFOs. Then add in aliens using the earth and humans as a laboratory and being complicit in creating organised religion and overall, you had a rather intriguing idea.

When the idea is dissected there are some inconsistencies e.g., the blurring of the meninblack's identity. Were they government officials, aliens, or both? To be honest this didn't really matter as the idea of the unexplained and malevolent extra-terrestrials just continued to gather pace amongst fans and the band. Today it would be called a conspiracy theory.

The packaging was lavish, a gatefold sleeve which gave the album the resemblance of a hymn or prayer book. The effect was enhanced by putting the recording credits and track listings on the front cover in a font that one would find in a medieval bible. The inside of the gatefold sleeve was taken up by Leonardo Da Vinci's *Last Supper* with an image of a Man in black next to Jesus whispering in his ear. The sleeve design was completed with a back cover which reproduced the lyrics to the final track, 'Hallow to Our Men' the band's version of the Lord's Prayer.

The group's logo was printed at an angle on the right-hand side giving the impression the album had been stamped Top Secret by some shadowy ministry in the bowels of Westminster. The whole cover concept was put together by John Pasche who had also been responsible for *The Raven* and the iconic handwritten lettering was done was done by Jim Gibson.[3] The only disappointing thing about the packaging was no lyric sheet or inner sleeve. The cost of this last item probably being perceived as a little too much especially as the album cost a king's ransom to record.

Once released, reviews were generally mixed to say the least and many critics thought the band had lost it, sales showed many fans felt the same. On the live circuit the band were still a big attraction, playing big venues and selling them out on extensive tours. The more enlightened and free-thinking members of the press got an inkling of what the band were doing but generally confusion and apathy reigned amongst the fourth estate.

Retrospectively critics have been kinder. Cornwell and Burnel are rightly proud of the work but in 1981 it only cut the mustard for a few. Indeed discussions on Stranglers social media about the album feature hugely negative comments and over forty years after the album's release, some fans still hate it that much.

Waltzinblack

For the second successive album in a row, proceedings start with an instrumental. This track has evolved into a signature tune for the band by becoming the walk on music for live performances for over forty years. In addition, it has been used as incidental music in TV shows, the prime example being super fan the late Keith Floyd using it for his show in the late eighties, *Floyd on Food*. This has meant the music has wider recognition than one would expect.

When you think of the context of it being used as a live intro soundtrack this adds to the idea of the song being an overture, a taster of what is to come and signalling to the audience the main event is about to occur. You can almost picture the audience taking their places or the listener at home settling into their seat with their headphones on studying the gatefold sleeve. The piece is a keyboard only and demonstrates Greenfield's mastery of his instrument. It's not only his technique that the track highlights but also his creative use of the synth to make new unworldly atmospheric sounds. The rest of the band contribute the Meninblack voices that are gradually revealed and build as the piece progresses.

The band have often challenged listeners and this track has a genuinely unsettling feeling partly due to the unconventional waltz time signature and the vocal sounds. Although essentially an instrumental with no discernible lyrics on the track, there is a celestial sounding choir to emphasise the religious context to the concept, and this increasing control also applies to the growing army of the manic and malevolent high-pitched voices of the 'Meninblack'. This menacing vocal effect was achieved by using a harmoniser and getting all the band members to laugh. Given that one of the themes of the album is aliens manipulating and controlling humans the idea of a gathering dark force boarding a spacecraft is realised.

*****

A keyboard only instrumental that expands on a simple idea in a 3/4 Waltz time. The sense of expectation is built as more synth sounds keep entering to build up the texture as each sixteen bar section repeats. The first section consists of just the bass notes and chords. The melodies that arrive on the second and third time have similar rhythms, but slightly different melodic shapes based on the chords with the melody for the third section having the long trill at the end.

It is, however, the two sounds that provides the contrast, yet both have suitable otherworldly timbres. The fourth sixteen bar section has the descending, rhythmically continuous melodic idea that contrasts with the previous melodies. Therefore, the multi-melodic layering texture that was crucial to the creative development of the band on the previous album is present here, although this is a completely different musical context, and the chords are clearly driving the music. The third chord in the four-chord sequence is a flattened second chord that resolves down by a semitone to the final, home key chord. This semitonal relationship has been used previously by the band and will often create a dark, almost menacing mood, as is the case here. But it is the sounds here that really define the piece. They are all different and all possess a macabre timbre that staunchly sets the mood for the album.

The second section arrives after the main section has been played four times and moves into the related major key but, because of the sinister sounds, there is no release from the previous atmosphere, but there is a sense of development within the song. The high pitched new constant keyboard sounds help to reinforce the texture where the main melody is occupying the middle EQ whilst all the other keyboard parts occupy the extremities of high and low thus reinforcing the sense of unease which is crucial to the piece.

The interesting 'A flat' chord arrives for the final chord, and this is the black note directly below the home chord to which it than resolves for the return of the main section. Moving by a semitone below creates a symmetrical moment as the final chord of the main section moved from a semitone above. But the relationship is far less common with the A flat to A and this cements the eccentric mood.

The unhinged choir like backing vocals at the return of the main section which abruptly come off at the end of each fourth bar add to this atmosphere, then the next repeat sees the disturbing high-pitched helium like alien voices which become more prominent as the second section repeats. The end of the fade out sees an extra beat added for the only time, giving us the impression that something is not quite right and out of step. Disturbing and delightful in equal measure.

Just Like Nothing On Earth

So, the story begins, the song announces its arrival with a space craft landing presumably populated with aliens. It's another Greenfield BBC Radiophonic style creation complete with a burbling, computerised sound signifying the extra-terrestrial nature of the track. As the burbling goes into the background but staying ever present, the pulsating beat of Black's drums set the pace with his three sidemen weave around his tribal space beat.

Unusually for a single and a short song the vocals don't come in until fifty seconds into the song. Cornwell delivers an alliterative tongue twisting rap at breakneck speed. It's done in a spoken voice and has a memorable hook using the song's title, Cornwell making it more memorable with his pronunciation of 'earth' as 'earrrrrrrth' as if he was emitting an unpleasant foreign body from his mouth.

The chorus is also notable as the Meninblack voice is used as a backing vocal to repeat the refrain. Technically the words don't actually rhyme but the alliterative process added to the meter of their delivery gives the impression of a rhyme. The words on paper that seem torturous to recite are actually a long tongue twister but get it right and they trip off the tongue and have a pace and rhythm of their own. The natural rhythm of the words and phrases put together is crucial to the song's pace and feel. The vocal delivery has the attributes of a rap. One description of rap and its delivery can be defined as "occupying a grey area between speech, prose, poetry, and singing" and also incorporating "rhyme, rhythmic speech, and street vernacular."[4]

Cornwell's delivery certainly fits this description — it's yet another example of the band being aware of what was going on around them musically and culturally. Rap was breaking out of the underground at the time but wasn't fully mainstream quite yet. Cornwell's delivery and technique was more complex than popular rap of that time. However more complex techniques of rhyme and rhythm were to evolve quickly in rap. At the same time as the album was released Blondie released their single 'Rapture', which was the first crossover hit for a rap and rock hybrid style. Coincidently the rap in 'Rapture' is a B movie scene about extra-terrestrials wreaking havoc in Brooklyn New York. Neither band could have known what the other was doing so it's one of those magical serendipities that music and art sometimes throw up.

The narrative is a series of close encounters of the third kind with aliens from around the world. We get a whistle stop tour around the globe taking in New Zealand, Japan and Austin, Texas (the location of the main motor mile). The three scenes described feature an alliterative approach to the description of the scene of a close encounter. Each scenario is resolved by a phrase that describes the victims experience as strange or something new. The words are more about the way they sound, rhyme work together and for their percussive effect rather than their meaning. Making exact sense of the lyrics is not the point although to Cornwell's credit there is a discernible narrative. The final verse in particular is a list of words that rhyme or sound good together to keep the rhythmic pulse established by the earlier verses but still add and make sense to the idea of a close encounter.

Released as a single after the album's release it was the first Stranglers single to not trouble the charts. Probably because it was an album track already and the album had gone down like a lead balloon with fans and critics. Not even a previously unreleased B-side could tempt fans into a loyalty buy. That's a shame as a loyal fan base could have got a chart position and then radio play. It was quirky enough to be noticed and had the possibility of being an unusual sounding hit single just in the way 'Golden Brown' did later in the year. Despite its failure to chart the band kept it as a regular live number until 1982 showing that at least the band had faith in the song.

*****

Just like nothing that has occurred on previous albums. This song really cements the departure for old punk fans as the band move away from the growling bass and organ and Cembalet based keyboard sounds. This departure had been clear on the previous album but has now moved even further away from the aggressive sounds of the first three albums. *The Raven* saw a significant change to the synth driven sonic landscape but still with an overall rock-based crunch from the four instruments. But now the move away from the four distinct instruments playing experimental rock is even more severe than before.

The bass in this song is now a texture that, at times is deliberately low in the mix and the notes are hard to identify but it still plays a crucial role in the drive of this song. The keyboard sounds are all linked to the otherworldly theme which had been previewed on the "Meninblack" song on *The Raven*. But here the sounds are far more clipped, and this gives space for the many other ideas to invade the space. The drums are a constant for the main section with an offbeat snare and continuous mid toms creating another fine example of Black's creative rhythmic backdrops. The bass is rumbling along on one chord with no specific melodic slant but highly effective in maintaining the drive. The keyboard riff is particularly melodious and the constant guitar playing has a random and angular feel. There are also other random riffs that appear in the middle of each phrase.

This all dovetails perfectly to accompany Cornwell's brisk rapping. The "Just like nothing on Earth" section sees the bass and keyboards pause and the constant toms drop out giving the guitar's last note in the phrase a prominence that sees it ringing in a sense of limbo whilst Black's hitherto unused hi-hat plays at the same time, all of which adds further instability to the listener. The high-pitched alien backing vocals at the end of the section remind us that we are in the realms of the supernatural. There are two quick clashing/dissonant chords that follow these alien vocals played on guitar and keyboards and this dissonance has been pervading the song which adds to the disorientating atmosphere.

When Cornwell says, "Just" with long held notes, the main drum rhythm continues along with the sumptuous keyboard riff type effect that started the song and has been present throughout. As Cornwell then delivers each word with long pauses, there is a repeating short keyboard riff where the final note changes, eventually moving upwards, but every phrase ends with all instruments coming off. These abrupt rhythmic stops obviously disturb the flow and yet are strangely beguiling whilst adding to the unsettling atmosphere as does Cornwell's vocal delivery on the word 'Earth' and the "It was just like nothing on earth" vocal line later in the song.

The song structure continues in the band's tradition of a tightly balanced approach with no filler moments, and there are also various instrumental moments that dominate but these seem more intertwined with the previously mentioned random vocals. It was no surprise that the album was a commercial failure as well as being the final straw for many original fans, but this song set up a fascinating experimental sound and the band were certainly not resting on their laurels.

Second Coming

The concept behind the album as well as dealing with alien visitation and alien control also turned it sights on Christianity and its control and manipulation of the populace. In interviews the band even went as far as to suggest that the bible and other holy books actually document alien life forms and their actions, and these actions are then portrayed as miracles or acts of God when recorded in the scriptures. The scenario in this song finds Cornwell positing the idea of the second coming of Christ and what might happen if he did return.

The tune has a jaunty feel and uses 'spaceship' sounds in background to keep the mood and theme present in the listeners mind. There are twists and turns but as is so often the case with the band they are stunningly effective and enhance the song which isn't deliberately uncommercial, but it doesn't fit the mould of what pop or rock sounded like. Three tracks into the album and we can see the band were clearly choosing to go out on their own in terms of music, lyrics, and production, happy to experiment and revelling in the possibilities of what could be done. There is even a musical joke as the track appears to fade out with monk like chanting but only for it to fade back in and back up to the original volume, a musical second coming.

The words are delivered in a deadpan manner which sometimes verges on being out of tune the vocals appeared to be double tracked but slightly out of sync which makes for an unsettling atmosphere. Cornwell proclaims to us that all over the Christian world people are eagerly awaiting Christ's return. In the first verse he appears to be describing the night before Christmas, which of course it would be if Christ was about to be reborn. People are so excited at this potential new Christmas day they are "sleeping awake in their homes" which takes the excitement and anticipation of the current Christmas Eve and applies it to the new Messiah.

Other Christmas images are also thrown in, for example shepherds and sheep are mentioned which has obvious links to the Christmas story. It also an indirect reference to people behaving like sheep when it comes to religion. When the rebirth doesn't occur Cornwell represents the disappointment as unwanted Christmas presents piled up in a corner and thus keeps the Yuletide theme in the forefront of the listeners mind.

The second verse deals with the anticipation of seeing a new Messiah and what will he look like and speculates on his personality. Will he be funny, or will his message upset people? Cornwell also makes the point that the second coming will be televised. One can picture the world's population around TV sets watching a talk show with the 'New Messiah'. The final verse entertains the idea that he won't be a perfect physical specimen with the writer suggest he may have disabilities or other issues and that being the case he may be rejected by the population because he doesn't fit the image of the Messiah the church has been portraying throughout history.

Cornwell gets up to his word play and innuendo tricks again with the title and chorus, "Second Coming". He doesn't pronounce "coming" in full initially but just sings "A second come... second coming" by emphasising "come" he signals to us a sexual innuendo which as we now know is a familiar Cornwell device.

*****

Most of the song is based around two conventional chords but the complexities of the song are considerable. The intro continues the otherworldly sounds established in the previous two tracks and the first keyboard riff has considerable delay and reverb then suddenly loses these effects on the second chord to create a completely dry sound. This dryness reinforces the feeling that something is suddenly closer after being a considerable distance away thus supporting the song's concept. Burnel's bass riff is rhythmically constant and relatively conventionally based around the two chords. However, this riff has considerable melodic shape to it, spanning well over an octave and once the vocal enters, the keyboard riff plays very low in the right ear with the same riff several octaves higher panned to the left ear. This riff has the same rhythm as the vocal melody but a different shape.

Meanwhile, the original keyboard continues in the mid-range. The holistic effect is slightly disturbing and yet faintly light-hearted, due in part to the arpeggio shape of the vocal melody and the actual sounds of the keyboards. Cornwell's guitar had been playing a continuous reverb and delayed riff from the intro and this continues whilst the bass, three keyboard sounds and vocal produce a six-part multi-melodic layering texture, which is, of course, continuing from the previous album. Yet at no point does the music sound cluttered due, largely to the thinner sounds and the proliferation of extremes of high and low sounds thus enable the vocal melody to being unencumbered in the middle of the sound.

Steve Churchyard clearly had great engineering and mixing skills, but this type of texture would not have been possible with the heavier bass and keyboard sounds of the first three albums. This timbral palette was a continuation of the previous two songs on the album and was exacerbated by Black's lighter eighties electronic sounding drums and, as was often becoming the case, with a rhythmic pattern that supported the texture rather than driving a song in a traditional way.

The rhythm here had the (very light) bass drum on every beat with another percussive sound panned left, whilst the hi-hat was panned right on every off beat. But the snare/handclap sound entered on the final off beat of the bar to add to the unconventional mood.

The structure is interesting as the verse and chorus are played three times with the third chorus developing into a long end section. There is no instrumental section following the intro and this was probably the first time that any song did not have a separate instrumental section. But it does not feel like a departure into a traditional verse chorus song due to the instruments continuing to have creative melodic strands to support the continuous vocal delivery.

In the third verse, another beat is added by a slightly heavier snare, again on the offbeat, this time between beats three and four. The chorus is a complete contrast where the continuous rhythms drop out and the bass and guitar engage in a call and response idea utilising new chords that are somewhat distant from the solid chordal base that was established in the main section. Cornwell's melody adds to the contrast by being clipped and again feeling dissonant in relation to the chords. The lower pitched melody almost has a spoken feel resulting in even greater contrast to the clear, well-shaped and high-pitched melody of the verse.

The pause like effect of this section helps to reinforce the doubt that the lyric portrays, whilst the whispered backing vocals at the end of the chorus maintain the alien concept that was established with the high-pitched backing vocals in the previous two tracks. The backing vocal harmonies that accompany the second and third verses add to the doubt by subtly clashing in an unconventional way but having the same rhythm as the main vocal. These backing vocals are adding to the extremities of pitch that were present from the start of the first verse.

The very long fade out occurs just over halfway through the song and gives the feeling of momentum as the drums have now established both off beat snares and shortly afterwards add the toms to now create another creative Black pattern that drives us on in an unconventional way. Greenfield adds descending trill like riffs panned right then left. When repeated, the final, lowest riff adds a particularly low and clashing set of notes.

Meanwhile the vocals are in a slightly clashing harmony and keep repeating. As the instruments fade out the vocals acquire more reverb with an ecclesiastic feel and are left on their own before we have the "second coming" of the instrumentation with a long fade back in before the definitive final fade out to a song that, like the previous song, is bursting with creative quirkiness.

Waiting For The Men In Black

The previous song dealt with the wait for a new Messiah on this song we are waiting again but this time for the mysterious Meninblack, according to the band these are the secretive officials who visit people after they report encounters with UFOs or aliens. We could be talking about the aliens themselves or that the Meninblack being in league with the extra-terrestrials, it isn't clear maybe because as the band admit themselves the recordings were conducted in a drug-fuelled haze.

The instrumentation has a futuristic feel reminiscent of pioneering synthesiser bands of the seventies and early eighties. The music gives the impression of waiting e.g., the repetitive guitar in the middle of the song sounds like a stuck record brilliantly giving the impression of a long wait.

The unworldly sound effects suggest a kind of space interference or the Meninblack themselves stirring and approaching. The long outro has Cornwell intoning the title phrase again and again leaving the listener with the general effect of a monotonous trance like a groove and suggesting a long interval of time is passing.

Whispered backing vocals through much of the song contrast with the high-profile harmonies on previous albums. In fact, the album as a whole takes an interesting approach to backing vocals on many tracks rather than using them in a traditional way to embellish a song in a higher register they largely abandon this traditional approach and the whispered voice tones add a sinister feel.

This is important as the song is about fear, fear of what will come and the music matches that. Cornwell's lyrics are minimal but by using repetition it again aurally adds to the idea of a long interminable wait. Despite the minimal words he still manages to paint some interesting pictures. We have people sitting on roofs and standing on hills looking at the sky for signs. He also gets over that the watchers are doing so with an understandable fear and trepidation.

With this scene we can draw parallels with many science fiction novels and films, for example *War of the Worlds* or *Day of the Triffids* in which the world looks to the skies with a fear of what might come. The atmosphere of fear is reinforced by the image of Cornwell clutching his teddy bear for comfort. This is an image that is traditionally used in literature, film, and everyday life to signify giving comfort in frightening situations. Michael Darling in *Peter Pan* takes his Teddy to Never Never Land being perhaps the most famous example.

*****

There is no let-up in the musical ideas as the concept rolls on with a structure that has the similarity of the previous song with a long end section but, for most of the song, has the more unconventional approach of short instrumental sub-sections interspersed with the main vocals that characterised 'Just like Nothing on Earth'.

The reflective feel from the long repeating ending of the previous song is upended when a guitar riff leads us straight into the vocal melody within seven seconds. The opening guitar riff has a strong shape to it and the main verse vocal line is derived from this. The bass riff is more prominent and has an important role in the overall soundscape, dovetailing effectively with the drum pattern that really drives the song. Toms carry the first three beats of each bar, followed by two snares on the last beat, thus creating yet another creative unconventional Black pattern.

Cornwell's vocal is, overall, in a low range and this is becoming the norm for the album. The higher pitched aggressive vocal lines deployed on the first three albums by both Cornwell and especially Burnel are now absent. The lower pitched main vocals add to the concept, especially as there are various instances of the highly effected high pitched backing vocals to contrast the main vocals and give space to each other in the mix.

The short instrumental section that follows "hoping that they're coming back" has another well shaped Cornwell riff with the bass riff here being similar. Keyboards add a slightly clashing moment whilst Black loses the snare but retains the toms. Using a brief instrumental riff-based interlude where the focal point for the chords change has been firmly established by the band throughout all their albums and is still present at various times on this album. Another example of this occurs a few moments later where once again an instrumental riff, this time played in unison by the bass, guitar, and keyboards, prepares us for a move into a new section, this time the whispered "Waiting" vocal section which, because of the instrumental creativity, has smoothly moved into a new key. Here Cornwell plays a guitar riff based solo underneath the whispered vocal.

When this section is repeated after the other sections have also been repeated, Greenfield now increases the alien soundscape by adding a gurgling type of sound that pans around in the headphones. There have been other higher held swirling keyboard sounds present in the background throughout the main section that also further reinforce the concept. At 2:51 there is a gratifying moment where Burnel, who has been biding his time on just two notes for the various repeats of "and I'm waiting for the Meninblack" seamlessly moves to his riff from the opening bar.

After many more repeats, Cornwell gives in to the high-pitched aliens who have been constant by reducing his line to "and I'm waiting" whilst the aliens threaten to overtake proceedings as Greenfields swirling keyboards also become more prominent. Finally, the relentless drum and bass pattern stops as the main vocal states "And I'm waiting" with only the swirling keyboards for company. Have they arrived? An ambiguous ending to a fascinatingly crafted yet hypnotic song.

Turn The Centuries, Turn

Side one draws to a close with another instrumental. The previous two tracks had been about interminable waits. Time and its role is an important factor in realising the album's concept. One of the premises the concept is built on is that religion and alien landings are linked and go back thousands of years. The history of religion, particularly Judo Christianity fascinated the band at the time. There is much evidence for these ideas they argue in terms of holy book scriptures such as the Bible, Tora and Quran. What really fascinated the band was the potential alien intervention may have had on religion and the history of humanity. In a nutshell alien technology could have influenced events recorded in holy books and may actually explain what have become to be known as miracles.

The idea and concept wasn't new. In the 1950s George King formed the Aetherius Society in London. He claimed to receive telepathic messages from the alien Master Aetherius and devoted his life to spreading the word of Aetherius. His ideas caught on and were developed further by authors like Erich von Daiken in his hugely popular 1968 book *Chariot of the Gods*.

The 21st century obsession with conspiracy theories generally and especially ones featuring aliens and UFOs can be traced from these ideas and theories. In 1980/81 the band were ahead of the game in terms of their interest in these ideas. They talked about it widely through the band's magazine *Strangled* so fans were well aware what was coming on their next album.

In the world of music there were other performers who were no stranger to ideas like this. Space rock was a musical movement in the early seventies with bands such as Hawkwind, Gong and Rameses espousing similar ideas, but with their hit singles The Stranglers probably had a bigger platform to espouse their ideas.

Probably the most hardcore of space musicians was found in the world of free jazz. band leader Sun Ra had been pushing the same agenda since the 1950s claiming his music was beamed to him direct from Saturn. The difference was that many of these exponents had their tongues firmly in their cheeks. Here was a band that truly believed or appeared to believe in the concept and unlike the free love and hippydom around space rock this was a vindictive force.

As a track 'Turn the Centuries Turn' is slow plodding tune with drums that sound like Jacob Marley's forged chains cranking around as he roams the earth as a ghost. It sounds world weary and old and tired which was exactly the effect the band were trying to achieve.

The subjects they were dealing and with on the album were centuries old and events were, in human terms slow to happen. The backwards guitar is a nice musical pun on the complex concept of time. By using the instrument in this way it suggests time itself can go backwards which is a theme so many science fiction novels films have used since H G Wells' *Time Machine* in 1895. The track has a soundtrack feel to it and one can imagine many film scenes where it would fit perfectly. A quick search of YouTube reveals some creative use of the track to footage from *Game of Thrones* and *The Name of the Rose*. It's a fitting closure to side one, with the concept suggesting the main denouement is about to happen.

*****

For many, this instrumental that considers the eternity of time, is too repetitive to be considered an effective song. The texture never changes in stark contrast to the opening instrumental to side one which builds so many different layers. Here we have over four and a half minutes of the same texture and sounds. There is a clear structure of an A section, followed by a B section, then a repeat of these but with the B section shortened, and a new section involving the effected guitar, the A section again and then a disintegrating long final section at 2:57.

But because of the same texture and sounds throughout and the drums repeating the same pattern for the whole song, (apart from a single one bar fill in the middle) the structure is of little significance. Perhaps the band sought to settle the listener after the previous three multi-faceted songs and the atmosphere here is certainly one of slow burn which enables us to draw breath and is in keeping with the title.

The bass brings us straight into the song with a rhythm identical to the *Eastenders* TV theme tune that first appeared four years later. But here we are clearly in the minor key to begin, although many would argue that the depressing nature of the *Eastenders* programme should have resulted in a minor key rendition of the theme tune. There are movements in 'Turn the Centuries Turn' towards the major key at points.

Interestingly, the fourth notes in the bass melody suffers from an uncustomary blip in timing. Because the melody is played on the bass, some engaging clashes appear that would not have sounded dissonant had they been played on a higher pitched guitar or keyboard. The bass taking the lead does enhance the drudgery that is implied by the title, as does the sustained keyboard sound. The other high-pitched shimmering keyboard sound is also constantly present and is a cross rhythm throughout, another of Greenfield's regular rhythmic features, but hard to spot here unless listened through headphones.

There are heavy chords played at the start of each bar with delay added to portray the relentless grind of the turning centuries and as the piece progresses, more guitar parts enter, firstly broken chords and then the reverse guitar effect. This develops into two layered guitars playing different solos and then the random and clashing nature overtakes proceedings including considerable moving of the panning flowing around between left and right.

The song becomes a different listening experience when using headphones and, for some, is a captivating, dreamlike sonic palette that aptly portrays the title to end side one, but others will find the lack of variety of both texture and sound over a long time-frame and repeating ponderous rhythm rather too much to be convincing, especially when clearer main sections disappear for the final third of the song.

Two Sunspots

The second part of the album kicks off with this sprightly tune. It wasn't recorded during the album sessions but dates back to May 1979 and the time of the Raven sessions. A slowed down version was used as the backing track for the song Meninblack. Despite being recorded much earlier the production and sound fits the album perfectly. If the song had been written and produced today, given its production, especially the synthetic sounding rhythm section, it would be consider a dance track.

Essentially the tune is a proto techno song to which Cornwell adds an energetic vocal. The original plan was for it to be a single and it certainly has a hook and driving pace, but the quirky and clashing guitar may have been too much for the pop picking public. Anyway, the plans were shelfed along with the song, only to see it quickly recycled in a different form and then in its original state as an up-tempo opener for side two.

The astronomical phenomenon of sunspots fit into the theme of the album. Sunspots are dark spots that periodically appear on the sun and according to some observers coincide or even lead to an increase in UFO sightings and extra-terrestrial activity. Recently some scientists have linked them to global warming and extreme weather.

On the surface the lyrics describe the perceived dangers around sunspots, so heat, blindness and weather change are all mentioned. However, Cornwell then talks about touching the sunspots which is of course impossible. However, it is possible because he has personified the sunspots into a woman's breasts or more accurately her nipples.

The second layer to the song is a man obsessed with a woman's nipples and when one reads the lyrics carefully the metaphor is obvious. It's typical Cornwell, saucy double entendre humour. In the last verse he is on the surface talking about stopping looking at the sun presumably to save his eyesight, by shutting out the sun.

Of course, on the other lyrical level it's a man obsessed by breasts trying to put them out of his mind by not looking at them but as he confesses, once seen he can't forget them. Cornwell magnifies his obsession with breasts or sunspots or more likely both, by repeating the phrase "just two sunspots" twenty times.

*****

A harbinger of what is to come on the forthcoming *La Folie* album with a fast-paced jaunty song that aims for commerciality with a standard drum pattern throughout that never changes. The structure is very conventional with verse and chorus repeated three times, an additional middle section, and a guitar solo. As was the case with 'Second Coming', there are no separate instrumental sections as the guitar solo is accompanied by the verse chords. The difference between the two songs is considerable as 'Second Coming' had many extra instrumental melodic strands and clear contrast between the two main sections whereas 'Two Sunspots' has no clear contrasts and limited instrumental melodic invention.

The constant high pitched and clipped keyboard sound is present throughout and this leaves space in the middle and lower range frequencies for Cornwell and Burnel to add considerably to the song. The guitar chords are very rhythmic which helps to drive the song, but they are also clashing at times, and this adds to the quirkiness of the piece, the offbeat chord that accompanies "two" in the chorus is a prime example of both the rhythmic and clashing features.

The bass rhythm also helps to drive the song and is keeping to the main root chord notes until the chorus where Burnel's trademark expansive melodic shapes begin to take hold, and these carry on into the second verse and during the end section. Because the keyboards and drums are maintaining a very functional rhythmic duty, the guitar and bass have the room here to develop these roles.

The vocal is also well shaped melodically, with a combination of a large range of low and high melodies, the latter of which has been very scarce so far on the album. The strong shape of the melody is becoming a feature of various songs such as 'Toiler on the Sea', 'Baroque Bordello' and, is to reach its zenith with 'Golden Brown' on the next album.

However, the chorus "Just two sunspots" is sung almost with an ambiguity of pitch, slightly between two pitches, or slightly clashing. This adds to the off kilter, yet jaunty feel and is perfectly complemented in the effective final section when Burnel repeats the backing vocal "Just two sunspots" in a soft tone mid-range whilst the main Cornwell vocal is fragmenting the phrase with these slightly off-tune notes.

Overall, one is left to ponder whether the lightweight feel established by the fast tempo of the very basic drums, the high constant keyboards, highly pitched vocals with the deliberately off-tune effect, and the predictable structure are too much of a departure from the weightier songs that have characterised the bands output despite Burnel's fascinating bass line and Cornwell's interesting clashing chordal guitar work.

These were the chords that were used and slowed down on the recording machine as the basis for the 'Meninblack' song from *The Raven*, and it is interesting to listen to two completely different pieces of music that are using the same chords to achieve different musical ends.

Four Horsemen

Greenfield steps up to the mic to sing his usual one song per album. He opts to use a more regular voice rather than his theatrical creepy villain voice of his previous outings, but he still manages to inject the terrifying subject matter with the necessary paranoid gravitas. He also plays a prominent part instrumentally as his keyboards dominate the track, making a complex and exceptionally listenable song which strangely seems to have been forgotten by many fans. The other members sympathetically and inspirationally compliment their bandmate in what had become classic Stranglers modus operandi.

The next chapter of the concept narrative unfolds linking judgement day with our alien visitors' theme. 'The Four Horsemen' of the title refers to the *Four Horsemen of the Apocalypse* first mentioned in the *Book of Revelations*. They represent death, famine, war and conquest. Although not mentioned directly in the lyrics such events are alluded to. Modern interpretations of the apocalypse revolve around nuclear war and the horsemen are associated with this when the writer talks of shielding eyes from the riders' robes i.e., a nuclear explosion. The four are compared to another biblical group the three kings. The kings brought gifts of joy and celebration to Jesus whereas the Horsemen's 'gifts' are various forms of destruction. The narrator in addition ponders another biblical character the devil and as to whether the four together are this entity.

Given the ever-present fear of nuclear war in the eighties its little wonder the idea of the end of world was a pressing subject matter in thought provoking art. Judgement Day whether in religious or secular form seemed constantly on the agenda from world leaders down. Given the band's history of mirroring their experience through their music it is no surprise they reflect these concerns of the early eighties. Ronald Reagan a hard-line right winger had just become President of the United States. Following the presidential election American missiles were planned to be deployed in Britain under an Anglo American agreement.

There was the so-called Star Wars project on the agenda bringing with it the prospect of space war. All this meant the idea of an apocalypse was not unrealistic and it was genuinely a daily concern for the general population in the 1980s. Musical contemporaries of the band reflected this in their music as well but their approach on the whole tended to be less subtle lyrically and musically than the Meninblack.

This often meant The Stranglers intelligent and different musical take on the world situation was often ignored. Interestingly post punk peers Killing Joke built a whole career around the themes of *The Gospel According To The Meninblack* and went as far as calling their third album *Revelations* to leave us no doubt where they were coming from.

The similarities between the two bands stretch to more than subject matter and it is uncanny the number of similar experiences the bands shared. Like The Stranglers, Killing Joke had serious trouble with the music press, they were also a band of exceptional and original musicians. In addition, the two bands careers have followed similar trajectories; initial critical and commercial success, then a barren period saved by a key hit single followed by a slow creative decline until a recent renaissance and critical acclaim. Sound familiar?

*****

Less than a third of the way into this sublimely disparate song, the vocals are finished, and we are left to ponder on the apocalyptic mood with a complex instrumental section that defies traditional song structures. The band had experimented with song structures from their first album, and this is therefore no surprise, but the vocal section that has preceded the instrumental also carries that disparate feel with chord sequences that really have no right to belong to each other.

There is very little in the way of conventional relationship from one chord to another with the previously used Tritone/devil's interval relationship also prevalent here. By the time Greenfield sings "Twas some product of mad man's minds" we have had six unrelated chords (including the intro) that support that sentiment from a musical point of view. We are halfway towards Schoenberg and his 2nd Viennese school's infamous twelve-tone technique where the music avoids having any sense of a home key. The vocal melody here obviously has an angular feel due to these unrelated chords, but it does retain a sense of belonging rather than disappearing into an inaccessible land far away from what most listeners to mainstream rock music can tolerate.

Greenfield adopts a tone that is less sinister than on previous songs but still adds to the disturbing mood by adding a second vocal throughout the section that almost sings in unison with the main vocal but slightly clashes at times exacerbating the challenge that the band is presenting the listener, whilst Black's unconventional cymbal crash on the half beat at the end of every second bar jolts us even more into agitation. The band has often challenged the listener with the dissonances of the black side of *Black and White* and the multi-melodic textures allied to unconventional drum patterns of *The Raven*. The chord pattern and the vocals here create a different type of challenge.

The instrumental section that makes up the bulk of the song has such variety that many fans will see this as one of the bands crowning glories in a long line of lengthy and complex instrumental passages. It begins by restoring a sense of chordal order after the vocal section, but Black spoils this by playing a fill on beats two and three that, once again, severely disturb any sense of rhythmic conventionality and Burnel further twists the rhythmic knife by also emphasising unconventional beats under a well-shaped keyboard riff based solo on a delayed sound that repeats notes.

After the initial riff is repeated, Black and Burnel settle down to provide a more conventional accompaniment. Meanwhile, Cornwell's accompanying guitar starts to flower into a rising riff at 1:30 that may go unnoticed but is typical of all the subtle extra creativity that is permeating the album. This is followed at 1:44 by a new instrumental section where the guitar, bass and drums play a riff in unison melodically and rhythmically which has a four-beat gap at the end whilst Greenfield plays a meandering solo on a delayed synth sound that incorporates his favoured crossed rhythm style.

The other three members of the band then add one extra note each time to their riff until they reach six extra notes and then they move back down to one again. A standard drum beat then breaks out as Greenfield continues to solo whilst Burnel adds extra high pitch bended notes and Black adds yet more irregular beats on the low toms. Burnel then moves the riff into a solo of his own at the same time as the continuing keyboard solo. Cornwell's guitar is also deploying melodic moments in the background and the result of this beautiful multi-melodic layered slow fade out is reminiscent of some of the Raven's finer instrumental passages.

Thrown Away

A nursery rhyme simple synth melody opens the song. It sounds like it's played on a pocket size Casio keyboard, but it is the Wasp synthesiser. Chosen as a single which appears to be a bit of an odd decision by the record company as to most people it seemed unlikely to be hit. If you were open minded there were potentially more likely singles on the album for example 'Two Sunspots' but to be honest all the tracks had their quirks.

So, the record company found itself between a rock and a hard place with nothing screaming out as an obvious hit single. A single was needed if there was going to be any chance of kick-starting album sales and therefore giving them a chance of recuperating the huge cost of recording the album. In the end the choice to go with 'Thrown Away' was probably made because the main synth riff was so simple and memorable but compared to what the band would normally do with

a song it barely registers.

Given the band's technical skills it is a bit of a surprise that the keyboards and the backing are so simple. However, such simplicity inadvertently gives the song a dance feeling. Had the backing track been made in the 1990s or even today it would be seen as a dance track. Burnel wrote the words and chooses like on many other of this album chooses to speak or growl them. Live the song was a different beast played with the keyboard melody line given more of a boast with bass frequencies to help it cut through which certainly made the song more powerful than its polite studio sibling. The live version actually emphasised how commercial the song could have been. It perhaps the only point on the album where the production let a song down.

Burnel's lyrics are more comprehensive than on previous songs on the album and there is a clear narrative. He keeps to the concept presenting himself as an alien looking at the earth and the mess humans have made of it. Choosing the growling vocal delivery puts him in character of an angry extra-terrestrial. Logic suggests if he wanted to play an alien, he should have chosen the Meninblack voice but as open minded as the band were at this time it was probably a bit too much of a leap of faith for them to apply that vocal strategy to yet another track and potentially damaged it commercially.

The words berate humans for wasting opportunities throughout history. It's as if he is a guardian akin to a Time Lord from the *Dr Who* series, a watchman character or even the silver surfer, the *Marvel* comic character. He muses that if he leaves them, they will waste even more opportunities. The clue to his alien status is made clear in the last verse where he says his stay is transitory and that when he departs, he will leave only 'false gods and hypocrisy' which essentially in a nutshell is the album's concept; All Gods are false and explained by alien visitations.

*****

Arguably the band's most simple song with the opening keyboard riff being the essence of simplicity both rhythmically and melodically with its scalic ascent and descent. The drums are in complete contrast to the previous song with a most standard rock beat and the guitar holds chords. The chords themselves are the three main chords used in popular music, again in stark contrast to 'Four Horsemen' and, indeed, the rest of the album.

When the bass enters, it too merely plays repeating root notes. On top of this the vocal is spoken in a very low and understated way that defied the decision to release it as a single. Many of the biggest chart hits have deployed simplicity but they will usually have had memorable hook lines and the spoken vocal in 'Thrown Away', along with the low range of the melody in the chorus, put pay to any ideas of top 20 material. The bridge and chorus do have well-shaped melodies with a new chord sequence that is relatively conventional yet considerably effective.

The keyboards add a much-needed textural change here as do the backing vocals and a rather heavy-handed low tom fill prepares us for the bridge and repeats at times. But the low range of the main vocals impacts on the commercial effectiveness of the backing vocals and the relationship of the two chords on "Thrown away" do not lend themselves to conventionally effective harmonies. Even the guitar riff after "away" suffers from its desire to keep company with the low register of the main vocal.

The second verse sees some textural additions in the shape of extra echo/delay on the guitar, hi-hats and high 'uhhs' on backing vocals but these features seem to be predictability reinforcing commercial norms. The structure is also the most simplistic the band had produced with verse bridge and chorus all being repeated before the chorus repeats to fade.

This also suggests pandering to commercial norms and is a long way away from most of the band's structures. However, following the complexities of the previous song and most of side one, the band are certainly providing an eclectic mix of musical experiences here. For that reason, this song seems to settle effectively onto side two on the album and its simplicity, doubled with the nod towards 1980's synth pop, does create a fruitful, almost mesmeric sound that supports the lyrical message and shows the band's considerable versatility. A song that will divide opinion amongst fans.

Manna Machine

A studio creation and a prime example of the recording studio being used as an additional instrument. A majestic shimmering piece of music which positively exudes heat and drips sweat. In line with the album's theme with an explanation of the biblical miracle of mana from heaven. The band's explanation was that the phenomenon occurred because of an alien machine. The bleeps and pulses of the soundscape create the impression of a living machine.

Key to the track is the loop tape of drum and sound effects Black created. The other members add inventive instrumental effects that support the image of the bringing the machine to life in the hot desert. The track fades in to give the impression of approaching and discovering the machine. Again, spoken vocals are the chosen mode of communication and Cornwell's delivery is like an adversarial barrister, assertive and quietly insistent with his key question 'Who did you kill?'

Some might argue that Pink Floyd got there first with their 1977 song 'Welcome to the Machine' which used synths to create a machine effect. However, that song is much more in the traditional song mode than this Stranglers track, with individual solos particularly on the keyboards and guitar making the Pink Floyd track a traditional song. Whereas on 'Manna Machine' The Stranglers as a group are as one throughout the track, they become the machine meaning there is no need for any soloing as it would destroy the concept of a single machine.

Lyrically the track neatly marries the two threads of the album's concept, ancient religious articles of faith and alien activity that may have shaped it. The premise of the song is to explain the oft quote biblical story of God providing manna from heaven. According to scriptures manna was a food, a type of bread that was supplied by God to help the Israelites during their forty year journey in the desert.

The song has its roots in a book published in 1978 called *Manna Machine* by two Cambridge university engineers Sassoon and Dale who took the events at face value but explained them not as acts of God but as a result of a machine created by extra-terrestrials. The lyrics take this premise and develop it further. As the song progresses, we learn that it is believed that the machine is still in the desert, hidden by the shift of sand over the years and still potentially viable.

Cornwell personifies the machine and at the same time weaves in historical allusions from the Middle East so we have references to "mummy" which works on two levels by name checking ancient Egypt whilst at the same time humanising the machine. Cornwell also makes the machine malevolent with the constant question "Who did you kill?" We also get a little of Cornwell's lyrical humour when he plays with the biblical measurements around forty choosing to mix his measurements by using days and years in the same line.

Later he's more mischievous when he muses if the machine can make cookies, presumably instead of bread. One last clever observation from Cornwell is when he uses the word caboose which was a noun originally derived from the word for a ship's kitchen, the mana machine was effectively a kitchen in the desert.

*****

The musical contrasts continue with gusto as an understated atmospheric piece with spoken words effortlessly glides into our consciousness after the simplistic yet, at times, engaging synth pop of the previous song. Greenfield's opening sound uses octaves and sliding of notes which maintains the alien concept and establishes a sense of key. Burnel also reinforces the key with his reverbed bass line that is two notes played at the same time, those two notes almost always being a fifth apart from each other.

Cornwell adds sporadic thin, clean delayed/echoed guitar licks that dissipate the sense of key established by Burnel and float around suggesting a more fluid chordal relationship. These guitar licks, along with the other keyboard effects, perfectly capture the intended mood of the song and enable Cornwell's spoken lyric to move in a fluid rhythm and delivered in a very low and introspective manner.

There are engaging moments in the bass part when Burnel alternates between the home key and a note one tone up during "And just one thing" and this note is to become an important foil at the end.

Another classic Burnel moment is the chromatic and rhythmically displaced run down before "And one more thing" which leads us back to the note one tone above from previously to accompany us into the long fade out over "disappear".

Another song that will divide opinion in a similar way to 'Turn The Centuries, Turn', as there is no obvious change of texture which results in a lack of a clear structure and this does, to some extent depending on opinion, affect side two as three out of the four songs so far have displayed essential simplicity and, compared to side one, the balance between these two sides is lacking in creative symmetry. Others will point to the beguiling, understated bass playing and accompanying sounds that capture a conflicting mood following 'Thrown Away' and leads us with the "Disappear" fade out into the grand finale.

Hallow To Our Men

Finally, to finish the album and draw a line under the concept the band create their own version of the *Lord's Prayer* but swap God for the Meninblack. Stranglers' albums had become renowned for finishing an album with long songs that have several distinct sections. 'Hallow To Our Men' doesn't disappoint in either respect, in fact it is their second longest song.

It has that classic Stranglers trademark for their lengthier songs, the long instrumental introduction before launching full tilt into the lyrics. The words are in keeping with the album's theme and are again minimal, efficient and thought provoking. Repetition of words or phrases are also present again in keeping with the rest of the album. The conclusion to the song is a synth created noise of a space craft lifting off into the cosmos.

The words are delivered in a spoken voice a style the album had already used several times. One could almost say it is a type of religious chant. Cornwell takes the *Lord's Prayer* and reworks it but keeps enough of the original style to leave us in no doubt that that the prayer is his inspiration.

The 'men' in the title are the aliens so by composing a prayer to them they are being treated as Gods which of course is the whole theme of the album. The first verse makes it clear Cornwell is talking of aliens by referring to a craft from above. In the second stanza Cornwell use his now familiar device of playing with and altering well know phrases. This is best illustrated by looking at the *Lord's Prayer*:

> Our Father, who art in heaven,
>
> hallowed be thy name;
>
> thy kingdom come,
>
> thy will be done
>
> on earth as it is in heaven.
>
> Give us this day our daily bread,
>
> and forgive us our trespasses,
>
> as we forgive those who trespass against us;
>
> and lead us not into temptation,
>
> but deliver us from evil.
>
> For thine is the kingdom,
>
> and the power, and the glory,
>
> for ever and ever. Amen.

If we simply look at the words and phrases Cornwell changes or borrows, this demonstrates the lyrics use the prayer as a template. Cornwell uses hallow in the same way hallowed is used in the prayer. The lyrics are a word play masterclass by Cornwell and illustrate his love of language and skill with words. To give a flavour of the verbal gymnastics around the new *Lord's Prayer* a few examples are required, "spacecraft" instead of a "kingdom" and "have fun" instead of "Thy (God's) will be done". The line "Give us this day our daily bread" Cornwell cleverly corrupts by saying "Give us this day some of your manna" which continues the bread image but relates directly to the album and its concept.

He adds his own original thoughts but keeps his theme within the prayer's parameters with human's overtly recognising their weakness and frailty when up against a Supreme Being or alien intellect. He finishes the lyric with "Forever and ever" repeated many times, which mimics and adds to with interest the end of the *Lord's Prayer*.

*****

This long song is largely an instrumental with a brief spoken lyric in the middle reciting the alternative *Lord's Prayer* delivered in one of Cornwell's casual tones. The song deliberately seems to want to construct itself upon repetition and the opening guitar riff strikes straight away after the atmospheric mood of the previous track. The guitar riff is repeated sixteen times with a thin octave based backing keyboard motif and although the drum beat and bass enter on repeats five and six respectively, the hypnotic feel of the song is reinforced by the refusal to develop ideas.

The bass and keyboards are both octaves based, played in constant rhythms, and reinforcing only one chord thus adding to the stubbornness to avoid deviating from the musical message. This is followed with no musical preparation in the form of a drum fill or instrumental riff into a resplendent keyboard riff, but the other instruments all play clear supporting roles over a standard chord progression to reinforce the clarity of musical thought for this opening section.

Black does employ some low toms in his drum pattern but the pattern itself, like the role of the guitar and bass have none of the complexities of many previous songs. By continuing the overall simplistic musicality developed on side two, the album seems to be ending with a clear head in preparation for the *Lord's Prayer* declamation, or so it seems.

The next section destroys the clarity of musical texture and musical simplicity with a section deploying five beats in the bar accompanying a curious keyboard riff supported by different bass and guitar riffs over Black's far more unconventional drum pattern. This section completely destabilises us as a listener as it has no natural sense of home key unlike the previous sections.

After a couple of four beat bars and a repeat, the clashing is ramped up even further at 1:47 where there two guitar ideas, bass and keyboard riff all move off in different melodic directions reminiscent of *The Raven's* most idiosyncratic moments. After twelve seconds, order is quickly restored with a two-chord phrase where all the instruments come off at the end for two beats. But then both these sections are repeated so we are being pulled from pillar to post regarding musical complexity and Burnel adds extra clashing high pitched riffs on the repeat of the two-chord section to add further uncertainty.

Suddenly we move, without any warning to the spoken vocal section in a completely unrelated key with one of the bands most clashing multi-layered melodic moments as the guitar, bass and keyboards all play riffs unrelated to each other. Whilst this is, of course, nothing new for the band that loves to throw away conventional melodic and chordal relationships, the fact that this song has already had passages of complete conventionality really does add to the feeling of disconcertion here.

Burnel then plays the identical rhythm to the spoken voice on "Give us this day" but with notes from a faraway musical galaxy. Black is adding to this glorious discord with yet another unconventional laid back off pattern to fit Cornwell's vocal drawl. There is an incongruity between this drawl and the highly unconventional and chaotic accompaniment that suggests this alternative *Lord's Prayer* is beyond the reach of mere humans. It is the antithesis of Sunday morning church services.

When Cornwell finishes the prayer and starts to repeat "forever and ever" we return to a previous instrumental section and then, after much repeating and some inspired reverbed toms that are drawing us in, Burnel very quietly pre-empts the return of the first keyboard riff while Cornwell subtly changes from "Forever" to "And ever". Then at 4:50 the bass notes to this riff start to become more audible before we return to that synth riff. This fades off slowly with many repeats in the manner of the first part of the song before the spaceship taking off sound effect finishes the album and, indeed, the concept.

The return of the main synth riff gives the structure a feeling of completeness and the different sections, some very repetitive, that veer between the conventional and the unconventional result in a profound musical experience that is not only a joy to listen to but also a fitting finale to the concept.

Musical Summary

The multi-layered melodic texture that was developed on *Black and White* and then mastered on *The Raven* is still the most crucial defining texture to this album and is fundamental to what sets the band apart from other bands. However, *The Gospel According To The Meninblack* simplifies the chords from which these melodic riffs branch out, and is preparing us for the forthcoming album, *La Folie*, in that regard.

The songs are built less around these multi layered melodic textures like they were on 'Genetix', 'Baroque Bordello' and "Ice for example from *The Raven*, but the simpler chords now form a backdrop from where the melodies develop. The dissonances/clashes from within these multi-layered textures are lessened and gone are the seriously dissonant songs like 'Do You Wanna?' apart from moments in the final song where the argument between musical conventionality and unconventionality is taken to the extreme with the length of the song enabling this argument to develop, and the song feels all the better for it.

The structures are, overall, less complex than on *The Raven* with 'Turn the Centuries, Turn' and 'Manna Machine' having very little change between sections thus resulting in less defined structures. 'Second Coming', 'Two Sunspots' and 'Thrown Away' have no separate instrumental sections but do have riffs that are central to the songs.

The overall structural effect is therefore one of less complexity than on *The Raven* but there is still much unconventionality to admire especially in 'Hallow to our Men' and 'Four Horsemen', and also in 'Waiting for the Meninblack' and 'Just Like Nothing on Earth'. Three of the songs on side two change very little in texture and there are more creative instrumental and vocal ideas throughout side one resulting in an imbalance where side one feels more creative than side two.

Whilst the textures are similar to *The Raven* and parts of *Black and White*, it is now the sounds themselves that are moving the band into another direction. Most of Greenfields Hammond organ, Cembalet and Mini Moog synth sounds have now been replaced by thinner, more eighties synth sounds, as well as some new swirling sounds that all relate to the otherworldly concept. Black's drum sound is moving very clearly into the fashionable eighties electronic drum sounds that will seriously impact future albums. And Burnel's bass sound has been completely transformed into a more synth sounding bass with the aggressive mid-range frequency punch now just a memory. Cornwell's guitar sound is still similar but on previous albums he employed an equal mixture of chordal and solo riff-based styles whereas on *The Gospel According To The Meninblack* there is very little chordal work. This is due in part to the lack of traditional rock sounds emanating from the other band members.

Vocally, there are less sung melodies than on any previous album with only two occasions, 'Waiting For The Meninblack' and 'Two Sunspots', where sustained melodies are central to more than one section in a song. The other vocal melodies in 'Second Coming', 'Four Horsemen' and 'Thrown Away' are central to only one section and this results in a less commercial album overall, with the emphasis more on the actual sounds that are supporting the concept.

This album therefore is the pivotal album in their career where the experimentation with multi-melodic layering, unconventional drum patterns and time signatures, unconventional bass and guitar playing are all still evident and there are moments on this album, especially on the middle three songs on side one to rival any other trio of songs.

But the sounds have changed and that new sound that exploded to life only four years ago has been replaced by an eighties inspired thinner, more electronic sound and, for this album, layered with less vocal melodies, weird keyboard and backing vocals to support the alien concept.

It is no wonder therefore that not only was the album a commercial failure, but it also resulted in many fans who viewed their roaring bass and keyboard sounds as a platform for their aggressive music disassociating themselves. A considerable number of diehard punk fans had already left following the complexities of *The Raven*, but *The Gospel According To The Meninblack* retained musical complexities and was an even greater step away from a harder rock sound with vocal tones also lacking in any earthy aggression.

But for many, especially in the world of hindsight, this album signified a band at the peak of their creative powers, prepared to shift significantly in a new direction and prepared to challenge their fans. Opinions will always differ whether it is for better or worse, but in terms of the musical journey the band took with *The Gospel According To The Meninblack*, it is undeniably a fascinating creative change of approach less than four years from the release of their debut album *Rattus Norvegicus IV*.

Album Summary

Hugh Cornwell speaking in 2022 sees the album as the artistic highpoint of his career. Stating that the whole band were at the top of their game. He then goes on to say that sales meaning nothing in this context adding, "It was a great concept, very inspiring and I think there are some moments of sheer poetry. And I don't think we surpassed it."

There is no doubt that as a concept the Meninblack was fully realised, even the B-sides fitted the mould. So, an artistic triumph but a commercial disaster. This led to the band becoming vulnerable to record company demands and they would struggle to get back the artistic freedom they had had. By 1981 they couldn't even buy a hit single and this after being something akin to bulletproof in the singles charts in 1977 and 1978. Now the bed rock of their support, album sales was being eroded. The album was just about a Top 10 hit but rapidly disappeared clocking up only 60.000 sales.[5]

Other problems hit the band, the long series of unfortunate events over the preceding two years and that perpetual destroyer of lives, drugs had tightened their grip on the band and were making things on all fronts very challenging. All were users but it was Cornwell and Burnel who had the bigger habit. On top of this, making the album had cost a fortune as the band had used so much studio time realising their musical experiments. It wasn't just the financial cost to the band, there was a great deal of emotional and physical energy expended as well.

However, they had created a monumental piece of work, a fully realised concept and a record if you listen to now makes one realise it has an uncanny contemporary feel, it is as the cliché says, timeless. The years haven't dated it at all, the production, the sounds and the playing all sound like they were done yesterday. Given the barriers in the band's way, some self-inflicted, others outside their control, and the amazing fact it was recorded in countless locations with countless engineers it is nothing short of a miracle that it is such a complete piece of work in every respect.

Having grudgingly won over critics with *Black and White* and *The Raven* the men and women of the fourth estate reverted to type by not making any attempt to understanding the concept and contented themselves by lazily writing it off as self-indulgent. To borrow from the concept of the album; prophets are seldom welcomed by their peers, and they are ridiculed and written off as having mental health problems because they say it as they see it and make no excuses for being direct.

The Stranglers made exactly the album they wanted and ignored doubters like producers, record company executives and of course the press. As time passes visionaries worth and their insight are eventually recognised and this to some extent has been the fate of this collection of songs although there are still many hard-core of fans who steadfastly refuse to be swayed to brilliance of the work. The album is actually a prophecy in its own right as it predicts the future sound of much of popular music and therefore it sounds contemporary.

Other than the music, it addresses the Green agenda before it was fashionable, confronts organised religion's hypocrisy and finally it predicts the rise and triumph of the conspiracy theory in the post truth world where the most straightforward of facts are questioned. Whether you love it or hate *The Gospel According To The Meninblack* it was decades ahead of its time and to a hardcore minority of fans an artistic and philosophical triumph.

The male meninopause

THE STRANGLERS
'The Meninblack'
(Liberty LBG 30313) ★★★

THE ONLY thing strange or otherwise in the least interesting about the Stranglers, in rock critical terms, was how good their last album, 'The Raven' proved. In every other sense they have towed the rockist (great new word!) line and steadily nose-dived, even as seeming proof releasing the obligatory rockist Awful Useless Live Artefact, the predictable precursor to that wholly unexpected juicy fourth album, truly their Indian Summer.

But that is all over now, it's back to towing the line and 'Meninblack' is the album that SHOULD have followed the live set. 'Meninblack' is far and away the Stranglers' worst album. It sees them tired and songless, churning out a jaded parody of, perversely, their best work, 'Black And White'.

Forget the meninblack, 'strange-happenings' attempted-spoof for it soon falls flat on its (albeit) half-hearted face and glaringly reveals itself as a would-be means of covering-up the loss, now critical, of Stranglers simplistic pop sensibility. Stranglers are a pop group run completely dry, getting desperate (or not it seems even that, there's so much lethargy here!) and handing the controls apparently completely to Hugh Cornwell (his 'concept', the sleeve says) who obliges gamely with the kind of very poor, bad Art School, anthropological whim that constituted his dreadful 'Nosferatu' rockist Solo Album of last year. Hugh on his tod doesn't work, it just proves eccentric.

Gone, collectively, is The Stranglers' black humour and, most of all, their naughty poprock flair. 'Meninblack' hasn't one good song. 'Thrown Away', the single, alone comes anywhere near that (and misses dismally through its daft flimsiness).

They are chiefly, most effectively a COMBINED unit, their (strong) personalities gell together, a kind of situation comedy Led Zeppelin (constantly their historic alter egos). But on 'Meninblack' three of the main characters are on their way out, there's no commitment or hunger here.

The Stranglers always threatened Led Zeppelisation, but instead they have turned into an aged, psychotic Chicory Tip. 'Meninblack' was made for the barren Woolworth's shelves. . .

It's all attempted abrasiveness, all humpy and bumpy, a weak Barron Knights parody of former true edge, all Media Personalities (a real struggle to be even that) blinking in the unfamiliar light of a studio again. And not a naughty song to sing. A pity. I liked them; a cartoon-pop laugh; an off-centredness; an esoteric satire. But now a pop dream in a state of fast declining Meninopause. . .

They even forgot to make a cheap 'laugh' out of Meninstruation.
DAVE McCULLOUGH

Additional Tracks: standalone singles and B-sides

Who Wants The World?

Every good Messiah needs a prophet to foretell their arrival and *The Gospel According To The Meninblack* got its messenger with this standalone single released in late May 1980. Without a big hit for nearly a year and three relative failures in its wake 'Who Wants the World?' was given a big push by the record company and the band. The band gave the company a highly commercial sounding song but with a sinister twist in the lyrics. Led by a catchy organ hook, a stomping beat and a singalong chorus, it was openly commercial but there were also things for hardcore fans to latch onto such as Burnel's threatening spoken backing vocals around the chorus.

The record company did there bit with a massive full page music magazine advertising campaign, a budget for a music video and a bargain price of 69p. Singles cost about a £1 in 1980 so this was some saving. There was also the unique human interest angle publicity to associate with the song i.e., Cornwell had been released from jail just before the release so there was a readymade opportunity to promote the record.

The band even did a series of dates to add to the promotion. Yet despite this concerted approach the single only scraped into the Top 40 at No 39.[6] Everything had appeared to be in place yet the chart performance was disappointing and it defies logic that it wasn't a bigger hit. Anecdotally lack of airplay was blamed and convinced the band even more they were victims of a conspiracy.

The cover, the adverts and the video put the Meninblack character centre stage, and this backed up Cornwell's lyrics. The band were overtly communicating to the fans that the idea of the Meninblack was going to be a serious concept. Fans might have thought it was a bit of a joke with *The Raven* album track and its slow pace and squeaky voices now they were being warned that it was to be a Stranglers trademark as much as the rat had been on the first two albums.

In his words Cornwell imagines aliens arriving in the UK, specifically the Midlands and trying out 'food' which is human flesh and of course a direct link back to the Meninblack track when humans were bred for food. Inevitably there is little Cornwell elements of humour with human and fleas tasting the same, trees not responding to alien communication and aliens going round with an earth tourist guide.

After a few days touring around the aliens leave in their spacecraft bitterly disappointed that the planet they bequeathed to humans has been ruined by them. The chorus amplifies the sentiment when Cornwell sings the question asked in the song title and then answers it himself in a down beat way with "Not me."

The song is another example of the band raising ecology issues before it was fashionable. Finally, Burnel's whispered contrary statements adds an element of mystery and potential threat and then friendship in the same line. It gives the listeners the idea that the aliens or possibly the humans aren't all the same in their approach some are violent, others want friendship. Nothing new in that thought but done in a way that gives a subversive air to proceedings and sets up the up and coming album perfectly.

*****

A highly conventional structure of verse and chorus repeated, an instrumental based on the verse stranglers and then a chorus to fade. The four instruments all have an equal part in ensuring the considerable drive of the song with the intro seeing two distorted guitar chords at the start of each bar whilst the organ replies in the gap with a busy chordal riff. Once the verse begins the drums, guitar and bass all play together on every beat whilst the keyboard continues a similar riff as before resulting in considerable energetic trust.

The song is based almost entirely upon two chords. The verse stays on just the one home key chord with the chorus alternating between the two, with a third chord for one bar only right at the end after the vocals have finished to take us back to the verse. But the song is unequivocally a 'chord' song rather than the multi-layered melodic approach that had been established on *The Raven*.

The chordal approach had signalled the success of most of their major hits and that was a reason why 'Duchess' was wisely chosen as a single from *The Raven*. As previously mentioned, 'Nuclear Device (The Wizard Of Aus)' was a lesser hit than 'Duchess' and the analysis of that song suggested reasons for "Nuclear Device's" lack of commerciality. The predominance of just two chords in 'Who Wants the World?' may impact subconsciously upon the listener to create a less commercial feel as a standard, widely used chord sequence will usually provide the necessary sense of movement towards a sense of climax and repose within a chord sequence, whether it moves towards the end of the verse, or towards the bridge or chorus.

The lack of chordal movement and chordal progression can therefore impact the song. There were so many other potential commercial aspects to the song: a fast-paced drum pattern, vocal harmonies throughout the second half of the verse and throughout the chorus, the spoken counter melody that infuses the "Not me" end to the chorus. Even the change of drum pattern from fast to half time in the chorus sustains an interest from a commercial angle. The hook line "Who wants the world" has a strength of melodic shape with the octave leap on the first two notes, but the melodic shape of the verse is lacking in development.

The backing vocals in the second half of the verse include a higher and a lower octave on the same notes and do provide interest but this does not replace the desire from a commercial point of view for a more varied melody. The stops in the music before we return to the second verse also add a musical piquancy and the song was straddling much of the style of earlier songs but with a tighter production.

Furthermore, all four instruments had clear roles to drive the song. All these musical features blended in highly effectively to produce a strong piece of music. The song appealed to most fans and is still rightly held in high regard. But the lack of both chordal movement and melodic development probably had a part to play in the surprising lack of commercial success.

The Meninblack (Waiting for 'em) (B-side of 'Who Wants The World?')

An instrumental version of the album track. Released six months before the album's release it gave fans a further taster of what was coming. It was a deliberate ploy like the A-side to indicate to fans what the future sound of The Stranglers would be. A prophecy of what was to come...

Top Secret (B-side of 'Thrown Away')

Lyrically, instrumentally and production wise the track fits the Meninblack concept. It would have fitted into the album seamlessly. Where the track falls down is that it is a little weak, the instrumental ideas don't appear fully realised and they don't quite gel. Add to this Cornwell's voice appearing to be out of tune in places and this all suggests it was rather hurried and ultimately unfinished.

The words unlike the tune are fully realised and Cornwell's version of the story of Nostradamus, The Stranglers favourite prophet. He ponders the burden of being a prophet and using astrology to make his predictions. We know from Nostradamus's writing that to say the least his predictions were disturbing and shocking. He wrote at night because by day he was an apothecary, which is best described as a Renaissance pharmacist. Cornwell pictures him as lonely with the predictions spinning in his head and no one to share them with, hence the title 'Top Secret'.

In fact, Cornwell calls this wrongly – Nostradamus did share his writings and they were popular at the time. Admittedly over the centuries he has gained far more popularity and notoriety. In fact, so famous he is known by a single name.

Despite the historical inaccuracies in the song the words and verses flow rhythmically. There are subtle nuances in the lyrics as Cornwell cleverly uses the words to gently suggest slight changes in the meaning and emphasis of the song e.g., for such a renowned soothsayer his life was surprisingly mundane.

*****

The thinner production of *The Gospel According To The Meninblack* album is evident in this potentially interesting yet flawed song. It results in an almost throwaway feel with the drum, bass and especially choice of keyboard sounds all emphasizing this lighter musical mood, which is somewhat at odds with the pensive lyrical message.

Cornwell's incredibly low vocal range at times and a dysfunctional overall melodic shape creates an off kilter feel to the voice which could even be seen to be out of tune, and several other slight clashes created by the guitar and keyboards add to this feel. The light mood is exacerbated by Cornwell's spoken delivery in the bridge/second section and the chords here are highly unconventional.

At 1:58 the song moves into an altogether darker mood when the original melody is now accompanied by a new, minor related chord. This idea of repeating the same melody (but at a different pitch here) whilst changing the chords that accompany it was pioneered by Debussy and others in classical music and the same melody is now engaged in much darker proceedings.

But the guitar and keyboards continue with their dissonance and the opportunity for an exciting developmental moment is lost as the piece becomes overwhelmed by the disparate threads and the overlapping vocals add more confusion to the overall sound.

Whilst the band had been producing a dissonant feel to many sections of music over the last three albums, the throwaway vocal tone allied to the harsh timbres of all the instruments and the clashing riffs of the keyboards, guitar and bass result in a less than satisfying experience that fails to realise any potential for the song.

Man in White (B side of 'Just like Nothing On Earth')

A song that although a B-side, is in keeping with the Meninblack concept. The subject matter was the then pope, Jean Paul II, and the influence of him, the holy office and the Vatican on the world. If any organisation is embroiled in conspiracy theory and secrecy, it's the Vatican, so the subject matter is hardly surprising in fact it's unthinkable that the band wouldn't have addressed this institution.

To add grist to the conspiracy mill Jean Paul II's predecessor, Jean Paul I, had only been in post a matter of days before dying mysteriously in September 1978. By 1981 speculation was rife about foul play because he was seen as too liberal. His successor, Jean Paul II although the first media friendly pope, was essentially a conservative and seen as restoring the traditional conservative values of the Catholic church that many felt had been potentially under threat with Jean Paul I.

So, when the band wrote the track all these factors were to the fore and the mystery and uncertainty around Jean Paul I's death came into play and the idea of the Catholic church covering things up, e.g., alien encounters, manipulations of the scriptures and control of the masses were becoming common currency. Since 1981 this questioning of the Vatican has snowballed and has run and run, with fanciful theories like Dan Brown's *Divinci Code* book in 2003 stoking the flames.

The first verse sees Cornwell ripping into the hypocrisy of the catholic priesthood, supposedly celibate but notorious for having secret sexual relationships and then either buying the silence or using fear to keep their lovers quiet.

There were strong rumours that Jean Paul II may have indulged in this way and he certainly covered up the systemic abuse of children by priests in the church. In the second verse he is attacking the slick PR around the Vatican. Jean Paul II was the first pope to use and exploit popular media and the first to widely tour around the world.

Cornwell makes the point that devout Catholics believe he is God's representative on earth and has a direct line to God by suggesting the almighty's telephone number is stamped on the Pope's heart. The chorus points out this is the man who has the power to get you to heaven when you die and implies that a small financial indulgence to grease the Vatican's palm might make the task easier.

The point being that surely only God can decide this not a corrupt organisation.

The track itself is as confusing as the papal conspiracy theories already mentioned. It's a busy song instrumentally with all four musicians keen to make an impression, it almost has a free jazz feel with each musician showing their chops in the hope that the alchemy would work and produce something sublime. The result is an interesting experiment that doesn't quite work. Added effects at the end which were recorded by Cornwell and engineer Steve Churchyard in Vatican City, feature an excerpt from a speech by the Pope and then a peel of celebratory St Peter's give a nice juxtaposition to the savage attack on the Catholic Church.[7]

*****

Musically the song lacks cohesion. Black's conventional fast paced rock beat accompanies a series of chords and notes that can't decide whether they should be rock, or jazz based where the melody note on (he'll help) "To" strongly suggests a Dorian mode which is a very common scale in jazz music. Greenfield's improvisatory meanderings throughout also utilise this note and suggest a freer form approach whereas the bass and guitar are moving in more rock-based scales and styles.

Fusion of styles can be invigorating but here the result is more confusion rather than fusion. An example of this occurs after Cornwell sings, "He'll help to get you there" where his guitar chords are clearly rooted in rock but Greenfield and Burnel move into a frantic experimental jazz feel. Another weak moment is the desire to fill the space after "When you die" with multiple different chord sequences which move the song into another sphere that is at odds with what we were becoming used to in the song.

Like 'Top Secret', the dissonance that the band successfully used is flawed here with the instrumental sounds being too harsh to culminate in an effective listening experience. The dissonance of 'Do You Wanna?' from the *Black and White* album and 'Genetix' from *The Raven* are examples where the moods are established from the beginning with unconventional drum patterns. A synergy is created in these examples with all four band members, even though they are often clashing with each other, but here on 'Man in White' the guitar and drums are clearly at odds with the keyboards and the bass keeps trying to straddle between the two as does the vocal melody.

Moreover, the early eighties thinner sounds that infused the bands overall soundscape were clearly less conducive to that synergy. Perhaps Black's locked his instinctively inspiring unconventional approach in another room to try to find cohesion with a simple fast paced rock beat, whereas this song may have benefitted from a slower pace and one of his more unconventional drum patterns.

Tomorrow Was The Hereafter (free single given away with *Strangled* magazine)

This song appears on reissues of the album although it was written and recorded a long time before *The Gospel According To The Meninblack* sessions. It was released in August 1980 by the band's fan club magazine **SIS** (Stranglers Information Service) and was written and sung by Burnel.

Burnel's voice is actually singing rather using his punky shout or whispered delivery. It demonstrates how effective his natural voice is. The song is from the early days of the band but the subject matter and the instrumental break signal the ideas that would bare so much fruit in the future.

The words and sentiments are hippy in style, the band were all old enough to have been hippies or if not hippies to be aware of them. The word 'hereafter' can mean two things it can mean "from now on" or it can mean "heaven or life after death". If we take latter meaning, which is the one Burnel intended, then the song actually fits into *The Gospel According To The Meninblack* concept because we have a religious theme.

The lyrics extoll the virtues of living for now because he is going to die very soon. Why? We don't know, but the words do allude to potential world destruction and maybe other species "Other worlds, other times". This is probably stretching things a little too far and the music and production is totally different to the rest of the tracks associated with the concept.

*****

The song is completely in keeping with their early pub days, when it was written. A fast-paced blues romp where most of the song is made up from the middle instrumental section lasting over two minutes. Many of their songs like 'Down in the Sewer', 'Sometimes' and 'Walk On By' had already incorporated long middle instrumental sections and here it is comprised of various small sub-sections lasting only a few seconds each, but all of them are in keeping with the blues rock feel with some typically melodious Cornwell guitar riffs and Greenfield's solos and riffs are also, typically exuberant.

The melody is well shaped for the style and Burnel's energetic, yet restrained delivery departs from his usual early days growling thus giving the song a slightly different feel to other songs of the time. That may be one reason why this pleasing song failed to fit into any early albums as the darker and aggressive nature of the first three albums would have possibly been compromised by this addition. 'Princess of the Streets' was similar musically, but the slower tempo necessitated a more atmospheric vocal delivery and an altogether darker feel. And by the time the more experimental *Black and White* and *The Raven* albums evolved, the pub rock blues days were a distant memory.

Footnotes

1. Official Charts Website

2. Official Charts Website

3. John Pasche website

4. Lynette Keyes, Cheryl (2004). *Rap Music and Street Consciousness*. University of Illinois Press.

5. Official Charts Website

6. Official Charts Website

7. *Song By Song* - Hugh Cornwell and Jim Drury

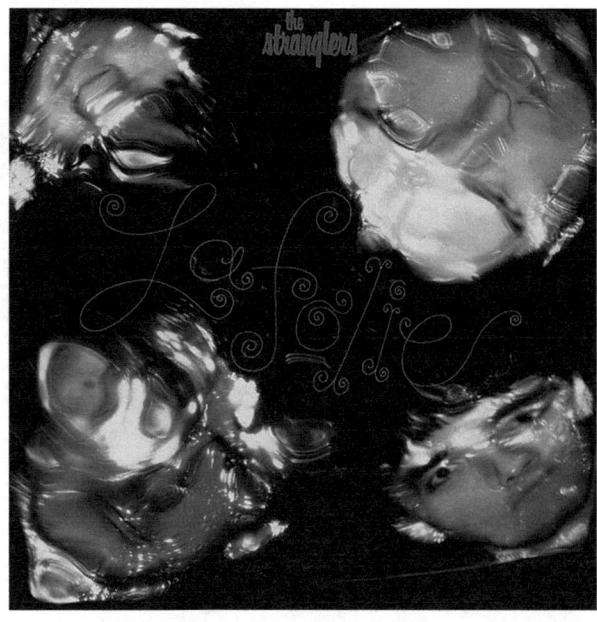

La Folie

By the middle of 1981 the band were not in a good place and added to all these circumstances they had a record company letting it be known that they were in the last chance saloon. An additional record company complication was that the band's label United Artists had been taken over whilst they had been recording *The Gospel According To The Meninblack* and that album came out on the new owners label Liberty Records.

The cost and commercial failure of *The Gospel According To The Meninblack* meant the messages coming through from their new masters were that things needed to change. The new owners were not best pleased with being left to pick up the considerable tab accrued from *The Gospel According To The Meninblack* protracted recording sessions. It might have been an artistic triumph, but it was a commercial disaster with the lowest sales so far of their career.

The other bad news was that they also appeared past their commercial peak in terms of singles with no top thirty hits for over two years. At the same time, they were still just emerging from a series of unfortunate events; Cornwell's imprisonment, inciting a riot and having all their gear stolen to name but a few. The band were resilient but it's hard to imagine such a set of circumstances not taking a toll in some way and effecting their decisions either artistically and commercially as well as taking a toll on the bonds between themselves.

Despite the challenging circumstances the irrepressible ensemble reconvened at Black's house in mid-1981 to begin writing with a new sense of purpose. The sessions were more business-like than the previous album and quickly bore fruit. They knew they had to deliver something their new bosses would be happy with whilst also keeping their artistic integrity and keeping their remaining fan base happy. The original concept of the folly love remained; the band would still be the producers but an agreement was struck with the record company that Tony Visconti would mix the recordings.

This was hardly a concession by the band as Visconti had an impressive CV of production credits, including T. Rex and David Bowie to name but two. Whatever the new album did commercially or artistically even before its conception it was clear it was going to be a turning point in the band's career. Knowing the chips were down they made a conscious attempt to sound commercial and contemporary. The band were completely aware of what was successful in the music scene during the early eighties and what the happening trends were.

As they were working on their songs there was a huge synthesiser/keyboard pop boom in the UK. The likes of Depeche Mode, The Human League and the Teardrop Explodes had all broken

through and were being very successful. As a keyboardist Greenfield in particular noticed this and began to use state of the art synthesizers more in his playing. The evidence for this is all over *La Folie* with the keyboard sounds at times referencing the sounds the trendy new bands were producing.

Other band members were also doing their musical homework in the quest for an innovative appealing sound. Burnel began to use a delay line on the bass more which he had in fact started to do on *The Gospel According To The Meninblack* album. It gave the instrument an echo sound which became a trademark on the *La Folie* album.

In terms of drums, Jet Black incorporated a lot of rim click work on the snare drum previously only heard on the song 'Don't Bring Harry'. Additionally, the drummer inspired by the drum sound he had created on the previous album led to him becoming interested in drum machines and their sound. Whilst not actually using them on this album he did on some tracks mimic their robotic precision.

Cornwell in turn developed a much more melodic, crooning singing voice rather than using his previous trademark sarcastic snarl. He was also using a new guitar with a longer neck than was usual which allowed him to explore higher registers on many of the songs. In terms of guitar sounds Cornwell had a long-standing belief that his guitar was always mixed too low. On *La Folie* the guitar is brighter and more upfront. Armed with these new musical approaches and the need for commercial success the band began writing and recording the album.

The band still had artistic control and stuck to their guns in terms of it being another concept album but this time rather than a narrative across the whole record they chose to base each song loosely around the idea of "La Folie" the French phrase which translates as "The madness of love" and the songs themes varied from romantic love, love of power and love of drugs.

The group had been planning to do something conceptually along these lines for some time and were mentioning it in interviews months before the songs were written. Concept albums were largely derided at this time and seen solely the preserve of dinosaur prog rock bands. By releasing *The Gospel According To The Meninblack* and now *La Folie* the band helped rehabilitate the idea of the concept album for post punk generation.

The idea had been forced underground when the musical tsunami that was punk hit the music industry. Concept albums were seen as the height of indulgence of the old guard of musicians and became deeply unfashionable. They still continued to be produced but bands weren't actually shouting about them. In reality and on the quiet there were a few notable punk/new wave concept albums floating around at the time: Sham 69's *That's Life* and The Skids *Days in Europa* being two examples neither of which set the world alight commercially but with the benefit of hindsight are now rightly held in high esteem.

Interestingly The Stranglers concept ideas rubbed off directly on Jimmy Pursey lead singer of Sham 69 when he went as far as to perform a modern dance interpretation of the song 'Meninblack' on the Riverside show in 1982. The Stranglers were happy to make no bones about the fact they were dealing in concept albums and in interviews at the time constantly referred to the fact the records had a theme and this championing of the idea started to make the idea of a concept album fashionable again.

The leadoff single 'Let me Introduce You To The Family' was released on 2nd November 1981 with the album following a week later which seemed an odd decision as the album was bound to take sales away from the single. Whatever the reason, the single stiffed at number 42 continuing the dismal streak of misses and the album looked set to struggle as well, debuting at 14 the first album not to crack the Top Ten.[1]

The massive success of the second single 'Golden Brown' meant the album got a fresh impetus and eventually peaked at Number 11.[2] The follow up to 'Golden Brown' was the title track 'La Folie'. It struggled to No. 47 failing to build on the success and momentum created by its predecessor.[3]

Choosing 'La Folie' as a single appeared a wilfully uncommercial choice, a long slow song sung in French seemed doomed to fail to tickle the fancy of the nation's pop pickers and it duly did. More importantly it could have destroyed the career resurrection 'Golden Brown' had achieved and it certainly didn't assist the albums performance, which disappeared from the charts after an 18 week run.[4]

'Strange Little Girl', originally a non-album track but has subsequently been added to the collection on reissues, was released in July '82 and became a top ten hit and regained some of the momentum the band had created earlier in the year.

The packaging of the album wasn't skimped on and although not a gatefold sleeve it featured a lavish inner sleeve with lyrics and artwork for each song. With *La Folie* being a concept album, the artwork was even more important and it didn't disappoint. The front cover features band members looking out from the cover with a black background sleeve. The faces are distorted as if they are looking in or up from a pond where the water has been disturbed thus causing a simmering distorting effect to their images.

According to sleeve designer John Pasche the effect was achieved by shooting the band's faces in black and white through water.[5] Their faces are ghostly white creating an ethereal mysterious feel. The pictures are hardly flattering which was a brave decision when image and cool were everything but again symbolises the band's contrary attitude to overt commercialism. The artistic statement was everything. The famous band logo adorns the sleeve as it has done on most releases since their first release. The album title is written in a thin red flowery font which has a childlike quality and according to John Pasche was an attempt to make it look whimsical.[6]

The back cover features a close up of what look like blood corpuscles in the top half. The track listing of side one runs across the top of the photo. Underneath this photograph is an out of focus picture of the band on stage lit up by white back lighting. The track listing for side two runs along the top of the live scene and the background the photos are set on is a dirty pink backdrop.

The inner sleeve is just as effective and though provoking as the outer sleeve. One side contained a drawing of that eternal symbol of love, a heart. However, it isn't a love heart it is an anatomical drawing of a human heart with all its main parts labelled like a school text book.

But it wasn't the names of the heart's components that adored the diagram but the credits for the record. It was a clever concept executed well and playing with love's traditional symbolism. The other side of the inner sleeve contained the lyrics which were illustrated by the design company *Shoot that Tiger!*, who deliver the concept in the same way they had done so superbly on the band's fourth album *The Raven*.

Each set of song lyrics gets its own discreet illustrations and artwork. The illustrations give clues and signposts to the lyrical content and meaning. It's a clever concept and it is executed with consummate ease. The inner sleeve artwork was certainly welcomed by fans and casual listeners alike as it was on *The Raven* because it was stimulating, informative and helped understanding.

It also featured cultural icons such as Leon Trotsky an old friend of course, Che Guevara, Marilyn Monroe, Leonoid Brezhnev, Ronald Reagan and an array nuns and homeless people and just to keep their controversial reputation going there is also a picture of Adolf Hitler.

Of course, the band toured the album playing to full houses again and plundering the new collection for five songs demonstrating their faith in their new opus. At the same time, they showed faith in the 'misses' from *The Gospel According To The Meninblack* by keeping three songs in the set. And with the success of 'Golden Brown' the band added extra dates in the New Year and rejigged the set to keep themselves and the audiences on their toes. The live reviews were highly complementary.

Reviews of the album on the other hand were not exactly effusive but neither were they damning, perhaps a sign that the band were now considered part of the musical furniture but were no longer seem as particularly relevant or as having their finger on the cultural and musical pulse of what was fashionable. The phrase condemned by faint praise aptly summed up the band's position in November 1981.

They were a band with a sizeable following, but they had their fifteen minutes of fame and there appeared no danger of them crossing over into the cultural mainstream. An interesting foot note is that despite the help of a gold plated and cultural iconic hit single and eighteen weeks in the charts the album sales were not that good particularly when compared to the first two albums and sales were actually more a kin to the much maligned *The Gospel According To The Meninblack*.

A Musical Critique

Non Stop

The album opens with 'Non Stop'. It should have been called 'Non Stop Nun' but the record company made a mistake with the printing. Without 'nun' in the title it does detract somewhat from what the point of the song was and the intended pun in the title but let's not let a record company administration error spoil the enjoyment.

From the opening bar of the opening track, we hear the new musical approach from the band. The sound is obviously perkier, and the melody played on a keyboard that sounds like a church organ helps emphasise the religious theme of the song. Without doubt it's a commercial opener to the album and showed the musical direction the band was moving to. The band judged it good enough to become the set opener for their up-and-coming tour in late 1981, a demonstration of the band's faith in their new material.

Cornwell's lyrics in terms of meaning are straight forward, finding him musing about the sexual feelings and sexual repression of a nun. Although the meaning is obvious the words are well chosen and trip off the tongue with a natural rhythm of their own. The lyrics and their delivery strike a tone of inquisitiveness and bemusement. He is asking a question that obviously intrigues him, a question about nuns and their sexual feelings.

Whilst there is a genuine inquiry in song, given Cornwell's sense of humour and mischievousness expressed in many other songs when he talks about sex, we can't help but imagine Cornwell with a secret grin on his face and a metaphorical tongue in his cheek as he sings the song. To add to the humour the lyrics on the inner sleeve feature a nun adjusting her stockings which has an obvious sexual element. Its classic Cornwell humour and imagery done with a nod and wink and the power of suggestion.

Its typical Stranglers, humorous and provocative and also a sign that the artists understands their fan base and realises they would enjoy such innuendo. The idea of a sexy nun has been a cultural phenomenon for a long time. That idea that a nun might not be quite as she appears. Feeding into this, another British oddity, such as vicars and nuns fancy dress themed parties which are an accepted norm and clearly Cornwell is exploring this peculiar vein of British culture.

As well as a saucy humour element, closer inspection of the lyrics reveals the notion of a romantic relationship between God and a nun, i.e., God as the nun's lover. The idea of a "bride of Christ" is presented as a metaphor and not literally by the church, however Cornwell is here presenting it literally as a physical relationship.

So, despite the obvious commerciality of the track in terms of its sound, melody, and the flowing lyrics he is making a controversial and challenging point about the concept of being a nun. Other artists have asked the same question one famous example being Ken Russell's 1971 film *The Devils* where amongst many controversial scenes one scene depicts the nuns masturbating with crucifixes. The film caused a storm and was banned in many counties or cut to ribbons by the censor. Cornwell isn't of course as graphic in his descriptions, but the implication is clearly there.

*****

A huge departure from *The Gospel According To The Meninblack* album with the obvious desire to court commerciality in the four areas of structure, chords, sounds, and melodies.

The structure is conventional with the short verse alternating at pace with the chorus. Whilst there is a new "And she gives up her own life" section, the brevity of these three sections with no separate instrumental breaks creates a lightweight feel as the chorus is played four times in total in a song that lasts less than two and a half minutes.

The most common three chords (1,4,5) form the verse and is an identical sequence to 'Duchess' with a slightly different number of beats for the chords. The organ riff that opens the song and is formed around these chords reinforces Greenfield's ability to produce those commercial moments. The chorus reinforces the chordal commerciality by simply using two of these three main chords. This will draw in a wider range of listeners as will the sounds emanating from the drums with its very standard patterns, rim click dominated for the verse then predictably switching to the snare for the chorus.

The guitar and bass also sound commercial friendly with the fashionable delay added to the bass sound. The "And she gives up her old life" section with its effective vocal harmony and more creative guitar and bass work adds much needed depth to the song. The main vocal melody in this section is pleasingly well shaped and an effective contrast to the spoken verses and low-pitched chorus.

Many new fans would have taken to this sound and there can be no denying the band's ability to move into new musical areas with yet another huge shift in direction. But for those craving either the classic early raw sound or attitude of the early albums, or those hoping for more of the glorious creativity of the three previous albums, there can only be disappointment.

Everyone Loves You When You're Dead

The song works in a similar way to the opener and uses the signature way the band operate, with instruments being introduced separately adding a sense of anticipation. The middle of the song is where a bitter sardonic sounding Cornwell makes his point about the disingenuous nature of the press and public once someone, particularly a celebrity has died.

The lyric also deals with the deification of dead celebrities which is so much part of society now. The late seventies and early eighties crystallised this obsession. Firstly with the death of Elvis in 1977 and then John Lennon 1980. After Lennon's death in particular the whole world seemed to stop for days to take in the wall-to-wall TV coverage of the event.

The song was inspired by Lennon's death and the reaction to it. His death had only happened six months before the song was written and it was still very much in the forefront of the peoples' minds. Cornwell's lyrics acerbically relate the tales of famous people who hadn't been well thought or appreciated for years then suddenly are canonised when they die.

This was particularly poignant in terms of Lennon who thanks to punk seemed irrelevant in the late seventies and early eighties. He had recently returned to music with the album *Double Fantasy* which on its release appeared to confirm he was an out of touch mega star and it certainly wasn't initially greeted with great acclaim from the post punk dominated music press and even the general public.

Soon after its release Lennon was murdered and suddenly he was presented as an infallible deity and the previously poorly received album suddenly sold in millions.[8]

The lyric sheet illustrates the theme perfectly by adding two more deities to the mix, old Stranglers favourite Leon 'ice pick' Trotsky and sixties revolutionary Che Guevara, both becoming revolutionary bedroom poster boys on their deaths and impeccable examples of icons who personify the idea proposed in the song's title.

Naturally there is undercurrent of Cornwell wondering how he will be perceived when his time is up. Who hasn't ever wondered about how they will be viewed after their death? There is a cynicism and bitterness from Cornwell in the song with his lyrics and his tone.

Without doubt there is an element of personal experience to the lyrics with references made to the band and fans He also takes aim at the press who one minute are punishing you for every little mistake made and then the minute you're dead canonise you as a saint.

Cornwell and the band were understandably very wary of both the music and the tabloid press, particularly in Britain, having been victims of sensationalist reporting following incidents in their career and private lives. As a band, the reporting of the Nice riot had vilified them all and then for Cornwell personally there were the reports of his drug conviction and subsequent prison sentence.

It is no wonder there is an edge to the song which Cornwell sums up with punning brilliance with the line, "The sun comes out and then you're read". The sun being British tabloid *Sun* newspaper and the rest of the line suggesting you have no control over this because "you're read" i.e., the act of reading a scurrilous story about yourself is done by other people which you personally can't control. It is no accident that "read" rhymes with "dead". "Dead" can be substituted for "read", Cornwell's point being that if you appear in the *Sun* its metaphorical death sentence for your private life.

*****

The instrumental intro is a throwback to *Black and White* and *The Raven* with the bass, keyboards and guitar returning to a multi-melodic texture with considerable clashing between the riffs. There is also a blurring of whether the piece is major or minor, heightened during the second half of the intro with Cornwell's chromatically descending riff.

Had this been on *Black and White* or even *The Raven* with their less 'polished' production and accompanied by one of Black's typically unconventional drum patterns then there could have been much to commend the overall effect. But here the very standard drum beat with the commercial sound production, alongside the more refined bass and guitar sounds, does not support the creative dissonance and multi-melodic layering. The entry of the vocals further exacerbates this with both its mellow tone and relatively weak melodic shape which relies too much on the chords that accompany it.

The "When you're alive" ending to this section cleverly halves the same chords that have just preceded it, a device that has been previously used, notably on their opening song on their debut album: 'Sometimes'. The upwardly rising melody here provides a more pleasing contrast and has a more effective shape.

A repeat of the instrumental opening helps the song to continue to move along on a pleasingly, musically contradicting path. Following repeats, the "Cos everybody loves you" new section effectively takes us further into a dissonant world with Cornwell's half spoken mildly sarcastic vocal accompanied by one of Burnel's finest bass moments on the album that has enough melodic incongruity to support the lyrical meaning. The guitar and synth provide a multi-melodic texture that contrasts with the two previous vocal chordal sections. Black's ride cymbal helps the mood but the main commercially standard drum pattern that has been present throughout the song is maintained here and this does not help the alternative edge that is trying to arise from the song.

The structure is less predictable than the previous song with three vocal sections and the reasonably lengthy opening instrumental section. The "Cos everybody loves you" section only appears once, in the middle of the song. But the bass line is used for the effective end instrumental section. When the second "When you're alive" section reappears at 2:09 there is an interesting twist as the accompaniment is now from the intro, but it then seamlessly changes to the original accompaniment.

Overall, despite the song's brevity at 2:42, there is a sense of wholeness and imagination from the structure where instrumental sections have a prominence that was, of course, a well-established feature of many previous songs and helps to give a more creative feel than 'Non Stop'.

The shifting of textures between chordal and multi-melodic layering is also effective but one can also point criticism at the commercial intent obvious from the predictable drum pattern and other instrumental sounds, plus some weaker vocal melodic shapes that reduces the impact of a song that carries a strong lyrical message.

Tramp

The first two songs had set a precedent they were short and catchy. 'Tramp' continues the theme in both these respects. The keyboards again are high in the mix and sound contemporary in terms of what was happening in the music industry in 1981. Greenfield demonstrating that he, like the other members of the band, was actively embracing new ideas. By the time 'Tramp' has finished we are barely eight minutes into the album and we have had three strong commercial songs, with pop sensibility but still maintaining the musicality than made the band stand out from their peers.

'Tramp' was without doubt commercial and quickly became a favourite with fans and therefore was mooted as a possible single to follow up the success of 'Golden Brown' but it never came to pass. Perhaps its pejorative title may have led record executives thinking they might have a radio play problem. Certainly it's hard to imagine a single being called 'Tramp' being issued today. The more likely reason it wasn't released was because of band politics and calls by Burnel for the title track to be released as a follow up to 'Golden Brown' instead.

Lyrically again the song is a narrative, and its meaning is very clear. Although the writing is very direct and to the point the vocabulary, turn of phrase and delivery make the words flow and come to life. They tell a tale of a man becoming homeless and living his life on the streets.

Cornwell muses about why this has happened. Maybe it was a failed love affair but at the same time the reality of survival is more immediate. The writer sums up this dilemma consummately with the following line: "A lost woman long ago, Does she miss him does he know? Does it matter in the snow?"

Such high-quality lines are not unusual in Cornwell's cannon and demonstrate he is a master craftsman in terms of song writing. In a song lasting three minutes the band had created a pop masterpiece with a killer tune that lyrically addresses love, pop's favourite subject and at the same time nailing the hardship and reality of being homeless.

*****

The commerciality that permeated through the opening track and parts of the second track is maintained with 'Tramp' with a very strongly shaped vocal melody for both the verse and chorus with a highly effective contrast in range between the two sections to lead one to wonder why this wasn't the choice for the follow single to 'Golden Brown'.

This is one of the album's strongest overall vocal melodies but there is also much of interest in the arrangement. The difference in sounds between the mellow guitar sound, the fuzzy keyboard sound, and the bass which, whilst not a complete throwback to the heavy mid-ranged punch of old, provides enough substance to please fans from newcomers to traditionalists.

Moreover, the melodic nature of this highly creative bass line during the verse sits in a thoughtful mix with the guitar chord-based riff and the keyboard's two distinct different sounds, the lower fuzzy and the higher more traditionally harsher Cembalet-like sounding riff at the end of each phrase sound. This multi-melodic layering texture of these different melodic strands in the verse is highly effective and this overall creativity results in Black appropriately taking a back seat.

The chorus changes from the multi-layered melodies into a chordal texture with a conventional chord pattern which gives the song a clear impetus and an effective contrast, aided by Cornwell's higher vocal melody. The drums are now on snare to add impact but this change of drums from verse to chorus is very similar to the opening track and, considering that the second track also had a highly predictable repeating drum pattern, we are seeing a more formulaic commercial approach for the album.

There is also a very conventional structure which also suggests that commerciality was the priority. The opening instrumental section promises much, especially following the unconventionality of the previous song. But when the verse is only sung once, lasting twelve seconds and we launch into the chorus, the intentions of the song to get to the "catchy bit" are clear and disappointingly so, as there was already much creativity to the song.

When the verse is repeated after the chorus, it is now, appropriately, double the length. A short instrumental section follows the second chorus and is a return to the multi-melodic layering texture with both keyboard and bass engaging in separate melodic solos at the same time that are unrelated to each other in key, providing trademark clashing and the little vignette of Greenfield's additional extra higher riff right at the end of this section is a marvel to behold.

Had this song been composed two albums earlier then we would probably have been treated to a longer instrumental section, but here we return, unsurprisingly, straight to a prolonged chorus to maintain the commerciality of the structure.

Despite these structural shortcomings, this is a strong song, successfully pointing the way forward as well as infusing creative delights of old.

Let Me Introduce You To The Family

The album had got off to a flying start with three short appealing tracks and the next song, 'Let Me Introduce You To The Family' attempts to hammer home this momentum ensuring there is no let up with Black's stomping disco beat drums starting the song off and placed very high in the mix by Tony Visconti.

This gives the listener a driving instrumental track that steams along like a train. Over the instruments Cornwell delivers a pacey, growling vocal with diametrically opposed high pitch backing vocals from Burnel and Greenfield. The song appears very busy, it's as if having set the accessibility and commercial bar so high with the first three tracks they are hell bent on keeping the advantage and try to do this by throwing a disco beat at the song, perhaps in an attempt to cover up commercial deficiencies elsewhere.

The lyrics on the surface are about Cornwell's wish for a loving demonstrative family but as is often the case with Stranglers' lyrics there is more than one narrative. Although a family can be a loving, nurturing bubble on the other hand they can be suffocating and controlling. Cornwell deals with both and uses the idea of matriarchy and patriarchy to do this.

We are left with the impression that matriarchically roles are seen by Cornwell as the most powerful with the mother controlling the progress of the narrator's life. Conversely on the male side the protagonist just sits on his father's knee, a nurturing image which contrasts with the idea of a domineering mother directing her son.

The cover picture on the single sleeve shows a sinister mafia family looking like butter wouldn't melt and adds typical Stranglers menace to initially what appeared a benign subject.

The final verse alludes to this by outlining the power and pull of the family and intimates the negative side of relations. The verse links with the picture sleeve as it describes the way a mafia family operates. As we know from popular culture the mafia is founded on family loyalty, an aspect that trumps everything else even if it involves criminal activity.

The final line of the verse "Let me introduce you to the family" followed by the multiple repeating refrain "I love the family" leaves one with a menacing atmosphere to the end of the song leaving the listener fully aware that you don't mess with the family.

There is a strong element of huff and puff and working too hard to be something different which means it doesn't quite gel and is therefore not loved by fans and the critics at the time. The song was chosen as the leadoff single which in hindsight does appear a little strange as there were more obviously commercial tracks on the album.

*****

A frantic song that gives the album a heavier, almost punk edge but why this was chosen as the first single seems a little mystifying, especially in the light of the obvious commercial potential of the previous song.

Almost one third of the song is given to the opening instrumental which is a series of furious bursts firstly from the bass with an elongated version of the opening bass of 'No More Heroes', and then the bass, guitar, and keyboards all together.

Meanwhile the drum pattern has bass drum on every beat with hi-hat on every off beat. The snare enters on the offbeat right at the end of every other bar reminding us of some of Black's more creative moments from previous albums. But this heavy fast paced intro would not have been endearing to most of the record buying public. Clearly the record company and the band considered that the verse that follows had an alternative commercial possibility, and it is a strong moment with the well-shaped vocal melody supported by traditional chords and the overall feel has an edge and vitality that may have caught the imagination of the public.

But it only lasts for fourteen seconds so the structure of the song weighs against the possibility of a successful chart placement. The following "I love the family" is too repetitive and the mixture of very high and very low vocal harmonies is too extreme to find commercial favour despite it adding an interesting timbre.

The new section later at 2:22 does move the song along with gusto. There is a key change to accompany the previous key changes from the instrumental into the verses and it is interesting to ponder whether these changes impact positively or negatively on the drive of the song. This is not a song where there is ambiguity of key as was the case in many previous songs from previous albums but consists of three distinct sections that have three clear different keys. But this new section also repeats the same lyrics, and this probably also adds to the reason why the song was not a commercial success. However, there is much to commend this powerful foray into a frenetic world, but there is also the nagging feeling of the song slightly lacking a sense of wholeness due to its repetitive vocal and instrumental features.

Ain't Nothing To It

There is no let-up in the relentless up-tempo nature of the album with the next track, the surreal, urgent, urban cool of 'Ain't Nothing To It' and a track that echoes the quirkiness of tracks on *The Gospel According To The Meninblack*. The song is propelled along by Black banging out an unremitting drum pattern high in mix. The other musicians weave around the metronomic rhythm creating a weird psychedelic soundtrack to match the subject matter.

The music and mood it creates is more challenging and obviously less immediate and less commercial than the first four tracks. The lyrics are surreal and appear to make no conventional sense. In fact, they are quotes from jazz musician Mezz Mezzrow, who played with Louis Armstrong and used the street language, jive talk, as a way of communication.

Mezzrow was white and Jewish but lived and work mostly in the black areas of New York. He referred to himself as "the link between the races" and used jive talk to cross the divide. Like all good street languages jive talk can only be understood by those who are meant to understand it. Mezzrow was a lifelong drug user and was arrested many times. He used the language when buying and selling drugs in an attempt to throw the watching police off the scent. The song is littered with drug references which are matched musically by the strong acid, psychedelic feel of the music.

The lyrics are all Mezzrow's and come from a conversation published in his memoir *Really the Blues*.[9] In the particular scene from his book, Mezzrow is standing on a corner selling marijuana. Cornwell took phrases from this conversation and stitched them together to create a feel for a street conversation. The jive talk delivered as if he's reading beatnik poetry or rapping. The whole idea is another example of an off the wall idea that shouldn't work but does. It's as if the band approached the song from four completely different directions, five if you add the 'cutup' lyrics and they all collide and somehow miraculously combine to make an outstanding song.

What's it got to do with love and the madness of love though? Well lyrically it's full of drug references and the love of drugs or more accurately addiction therefore fits the album's concept i.e., the madness that can't be explained by common sense or logic. If you listen carefully right at the beginning, you can hear Cornwell lighting up and taking a drag on what we would all imagine to be a huge spliff. More proof if it were needed that his prison sentence dished out by the authorities had not had the desired effect.

Mezzrow himself was added to the jive talk lexicon a 'might Mezz' was an expertly rolled reefer. Sitting with the lyric sheet trying to decipher the jive talk is fun and it is quite easy to get into the swing of it. However direct word for word translation doesn't work to get the meaning — you need to have a feel for it and some creativity.

For example the outro line, "She's faust to me, so skip it and forget it" Faust means "blind date" and once this is known you can fill in the gaps and give it a meaning. A possible meaning might be, she means nothing to me so let's move on. Another phrase used in the song is "She sleeps with her glasses on". It's an unusual image but the words of the phrase are standard but by applying a bit of creativity and surely the meaning is "the lady is alert and always on her guard".

A final example, "He's so tight he wouldn't buy a pair of shorts for a flea" is obviously describing a man who is 'careful' with his money, of course that could be totally wrong but the point is the lyrics within the song are stimulating and a challenge to decipher which as has been said before is part of the joy of musical appreciation.

It is also worth noting that at around this time the movie *Airplane!* contained a famous jive talk comedy scene that saw jive openly crossing into mainstream. Cornwell would undoubtedly been aware of this and it may well have been part of the reason for the track's inspiration. The language of jive is poetic and flows over the years, many words from it have come into common usage probably far more than most people realise. If you want an example of a seasoned practitioner of Mezzrow jive talk listen to an interview with Rolling Stones guitarist Keith Richards who uses Jive talk vocabulary in virtually every sentence, he utters.

The lyric cover artwork features a photograph of a black mother and child in obvious poverty. This fits life of the lyric writer Mezzo Merrow who although not black, identified with black people and referred to himself as black because of the harassment and poverty he witnessed and experienced. He lived his life in poor black communities.

It's often argued that this track doesn't fit the album because of its different feel musically. The album needed a gear change at this point, a different atmosphere and feel was needed to counter the commercial numbers so far and to prevent the album from lacking variety in terms of the music and its mood. 'Ain't Nothing To It' changes the feel totally as well as being an absolute classic for some fans.

*****

The track is a huge departure from the rest of the side due to its lack of commercial intent. For this reason, the song will divide opinion as newer fans may find the clashing between the instruments, coupled with the lack of both a sense of key and conventional chords at odds with the new order. Older fans will hear much of interest that could easily place this song on an earlier album. But does the song work as a whole and does it work within the confines of *La Folie*?

The structure is based upon three different sections that loosely repeat three times but with typical fluidity that avoids straight repeats, and this adds to the song. The opening section has a tantalising keyboard sound reminiscent of 'Just Like Nothing on Earth' with its sole reliance on the home note of D and its most common relation of A. The guitar riff reinforces the home sense of key but then Burnel enters with a constant and destabilising bass line that suggests a clashing/dissonant shift.

The song could have become relatively conventional from a key and chord perspective at this point but the new "Looks like" section shifts into a new key centre that reinforces the dissonant feel as the guitar plays a riff that is neither major of minor but suggests a whole-tone scale. This scale often sounds blurred and eerie and became more commonplace amongst the late romantic classical composers such as Debussy but is not commonly used in popular music.

Meanwhile Burnel and Greenfield provide riffs that skirt around the edges of this scale and the texture is once again multi-melodically layered with a more dissonant feel. This is ramped up further as we move into the third "Ain't nothing to it just here" section where all pretence of key has been abandoned in one of the bands most atonal moments.

The keyboards have dropped out leaving Burnel and Cornwell to play completely random melodies to the same rhythm of the spoken vocal. Playing the same rhythm gives the section some sense of togetherness but the third phrase is longer as Cornwell repeats "Ain't Nothin" and the whole phrase sounds rhythmically out of kilter as it is a cross rhythm over Black's relentless bass and snare on every beat of the standard four beats in a bar. There is no actual time signature change here, but the rhythm of the vocal lyric emphasises weaker beats, so this does challenge and excite the listener in equal measure.

These three sections repeat with some notable extra moments as in Greenfield's synth playing, an extra harmony on top of Cornwell's guitar riff towards the end of the second section on "She do and she don't", adding further impetus to the already established deviations.

Burnel's aggressive delay echoing towards the end and an extra harmony on the guitar during the fade really do cement a truly disconcerting feeling which is fully in keeping with the lyrical content. This is one of the band's final dissonant songs as future albums will move more and more away from these challenging clashing moments and the song needs to be played several times to be fully appreciated. There is a sheer energy about the song that develops and, although not to the liking of some fans, many others will bask in the ideas that shock and inspire in equal measure.

The Man They Love To Hate

Having been on a surreal acid trip 'The Man They Love To Hate' returns us to the more traditional songwriting territory. It's a powerful song and another of those longer album tracks that became another perennial live favourite.

Burnel wrote and delivered the lyrics. In his book *Song By Song* Cornwell says he asked Burnel to write the lyrics for the song and presents it as a ploy to tone down what he saw as Burnel's excessive bass riffing, reasoning quite rightly that singing and playing complex melodic runs is difficult. With the bass guitarist now more than game-fully employed singing, it gave Cornwell the chance to add his own stamp to the track with some majestic guitar.

Burnel fights his corner though, by using copious delay to devastating effect. Despite the musical squabbles the overall result is an amazing, listenable and innovative track. Not least the vocals which are spoken not sung. Burnel is a good singer, indeed a very good singer but around this time he was becoming a real shouter when singing lead vocals live.

Early Stranglers songs often required yelling and Burnel mastered the bad-tempered angry yowl perfectly, early songs such as 'Ugly' and 'London Lady' being the best examples. He could also sing well conventionally, the song 'The Raven' being proof of that. However, by 1981 his voice for whatever reason seemed less reliable in terms of holding a melody in a conventional way and the rumour was that he had lost confidence in his ability. To get over this speaking the lyrics in a poetic way was a practical and inspired decision. Of course, Burnel is not troubled now having resolved the issue many years ago and continues to be dual lead vocalist of the current Stranglers line-up.

Lyrically the song has elements of the autobiographical but not completely. On one level it's the tale of a man who is irresistible to women. Women just can't help falling in love with the guy when they meet him. He on the other hand is indifferent to them which appears to fit the approach of Burnel in romantic situations according to some band members.

However, there is a darker theme in the lyrics with illusions to domestic violence to children and women. There is also a reference to the songs protagonist's parents and a little word play with the title saying they're the people he loves to hate. It's not his parents he hates but their normal lives, which as Burnel was a young libertine punk, is hardly a surprise.

Later in the song he turns the tables with the suggestion that the narrator's father was violent to him and maybe his mother. As ever with many Stranglers lyrics they work on more than one level because when Burnel intones about "the city in the song" he is talking about London and its cultural elitism.

By placing the London in a song called 'The Man They Love To Hate' the city is personified, a place he hates but at the same time needs it as well. If any further clues were needed as to the content of the song the inner sleeve lyrics are accompanied by the ultimate men to hate Adolf Hitler and the devil. This song is probably die-hard fans favourite on the album as its feel, length and construction match the perennial live favourites like 'Toiler on the Sea', 'Down in the Sewer' and 'The Raven'. It is a fitting climax to side one.

*****

Finally, Jet Black throws off the shackles of commercialism and commences the song with a driving toms dominated drum pattern that, along with most of the drum patterns on the rest of side 1, never changes. The pattern does not have the unconventional complexity of other tom-based repeating patterns like 'Genetix' that are vital to the song but this one is the perfect fit for what is a standard set of chords that the guitar and keyboards play. The reliance on the toms helps to create a sonic base that is a pleasing contrast from the snare dominated songs that have preceded it. This is essentially a simple chord dominated song that contrasts strongly from the previous multi-melodic textured song.

The structure is simple which becomes the essence of the song as there are only two different sections from a point of view of the chords. The opening instrumental section has the same chords as the main vocal section. This simplicity is clear with little change in texture due to the constancy of the drums, keyboards, and bass. However, the subtle changes are key to the success of the song.

The sounds of the keyboards in the intro combine the rasping repeated sound that establishes the keynote and forms a backdrop and a sharper Cembalet-like sound for the chords played higher. Meanwhile the end of the intro sees Burnel deploying the very high register with delayed, echoed held bass notes which, like every other sound, fit perfectly into the overall mix as does the simple yet highly effective two note guitar riff that precedes it.

When the vocals enter, Burnel's 'matter-of-fact' spoken vocal delivery is accompanied by a melody on the keyboards that is almost the same rhythm and therefore could have been the sung vocal melody. This idea will become a key feature for various forthcoming songs on this and the following album. There is also a faint echoing of the main spoken vocal that pans right and then left and continues throughout the song thus adding more depth to the overall sound.

The skilful mix here is commendable as these sounds are heard in a perfect balance whilst the bass and rhythm guitar are unobtrusive yet crucial to driving the song. The fifth bar of the main section sees a typical Burnel bass inversion note that subtly helps to propel the section.

The new "He never wanted to suffer this fate" section commences with a well-proportioned guitar riff and when this is repeated to form the extended end section. Greenfield solos on top of the guitar to provide us with another moment of multi-melodic complexity. But, essentially, the power of this song lies in its simplicity where the four masters of their craft all contribute in equal measure to a powerful fast paced song.

This was to be one of their last heavier longer songs with a large proportion of instrumental sections. And it certainly gave added ballast to side one of the album. Fans from the beginning will look at this final crowning glory with misty eyes as the band moved away from longer instrumental-based rock songs and into a world of more experimental eighties pop.

Pin Up

Side two opens with 'Pin Up' a cheery song about poster girls that is pure pop in all its cheesy and kitsch glory. Essentially, it's a throw away song and It feels as if this was a deliberate choice by the band to be contemporary, recognising that synthesiser driven pop was all the rage at this time. It's a song reminiscent of the style of Depeche Mode who had by 1981 just started to pepper the charts with their consummate pop vignettes. 'Pin Up' at least matches the pop sensibilities of the new breed of pop stars.

Cornwell's vocals are high in the mix and take centre stage as he eulogises about the concept of poster girls. Stylistically this is what the new eighties synth pop bands were doing with no frills rhythm of a drum machine, simple bass synth notes and a twiddlely melody from the keyboard boffin and his computer. Black's drums imitating a drum machine foretold the future in terms of the band's rhythm master. He went onto adopt programmed drums on all subsequent Stranglers releases.

The lyrics are humorous and easy to understand, basically a straight forward narrative but Cornwell cleverly references nautical phrases throughout the song and sets the tale on a submarine, one of the pinup's natural habitats. In addition, there are clever allusions to the fairy tale Rapunzel. Whilst not directly referencing the song 'Baroque Bordello', the subject matter and imagery suggests links. More like a grubby bordello rather than a Baroque one.

The subject matter of pinups was not exactly unique at that this time in the pop world. Two bands had recently written about the subject. 1980 had seen the mod revivalists the Lambrettas attempt a mild critique of the pin up phenomenon with their single 'Another Day (Another Girl)' about that tabloid institution that was Page 3.[10]

Also in 1981 blues, pop rockers the J Geils Band had a massive worldwide hit with 'Centrefold'. This song was just a voyeuristic, leering celebration of the *Playboy* centrefold which unlike Cornwell's lyric contained not an ounce of wit, wisdom or irony in its words. On this track The Stranglers aped the approach of eighties synth pop very successfully but they were also doing it with knowing glances, witty lyric delivered with a dirty smirk.

It's nowhere near a classic in fact it's a very average song but was evidence that the band could play the pop game if required. The artwork on the inner sleeve is just as obviously 'pop' as in pop art, as the song, with Marilyn Monroe and her billowing skirt from the film *The Seven Year Itch*, possibly the most iconic pin up image of all time. She was the ultimate poster girl of the 20th century. An obvious but pleasing choice to accompany the lyrics.

*****

As with the opening to side one, side two commences with an undisguised attempt at the three-minute pop song with a simple structure. 'Pin Up' has the same drum pattern repeated throughout the song, very standard with bass drum and snare with an electronic repeated fast hi-hat throughout. The bass is barely audible, as there is a lower synth part as well, and it seems more like a synth bass.

The guitar enters on the second verse and then plays the chords to the same rhythmic pattern throughout. The keyboards combine predictable chord playing with percussive high pitched thin sounding sounds that repeat the same rhythm throughout. There is no change of playing at all from any band member with the impression that the rest of the band are going through the motions as session players. The chord sequence is conventional and the extra percussive keyboards in the short instrumental section after the second chorus add a morsel of variety.

The vocal melody and its tone of delivery are jaunty, and the effective vocal shape just about holds the song together. The band would often commence side two with upbeat moments and the previous album had the same type of song with 'Two Sunspots'. But that song had plenty of interest that is sadly lacking from 'Pin Up'.

It Only Takes Two To Tango

A barrelling instrumental backing track with a lyric about the Cold War making it just as relevant today as it was over forty years after it was written given the current situation in the Ukraine. Its main musical feature is the dual lead vocals of Cornwell and Burnel in close harmony, who represent the two to tango of the title with Greenfield on backing harmony. This musical arrangement gives the track a distinct Beach Boy feel.

It's another example of the band using incongruous juxtaposition to emphasise a point. The listener is treated to aesthetically pleasing soaring vocal harmonies singing about the potential of a nuclear apocalypse when the Cold War which was at its peak in 1981. The use of this device was probably the most effective thing about it if we are honest — a lacklustre song.

The vocals ascend over a repetitive loop like, rhythmic backing track from all the instruments making the vocals the main musical feature on this number. The vocal harmonies towards the end of 1979 single 'Nuclear Device (Wizard Of Aus)' are reminiscent of the Beach Boy style harmonies on display here. Throughout their career The Stranglers have made tight vocal harmonisation a feature throughout their albums and a track like 'Duchess' perhaps being the best example.

Lyrically the song refers to the Cold War but you would only probably get this because of the pictures of US president Ronald Reagan and USSR leader Leonid Brezhnev on the inner sleeve to accompany the lyrics. There also a reference to Adam and Eve and ancient history making it clear that war or the disputes that lead to them have always been with us.

The phrase "It takes two to tango" actually means both parties involved in a situation are equally responsible for it, which in a nutshell sums up the Cold War. The words are not specific, and the lyrics are minimalistic with one verse repeated and a long fade out with the repeated phrase "Better wait and see". That phrase sums up the attitude of the time, the world permanently on the edge of nuclear war but all the world's population could do was to 'wait and see' what the two most powerful world leaders would do. Would it be war or peace?

The early eighties were the height of the Cold War with few people able to see or imagine a potential solution. Ten years later the Cold War was over, and a time of hope ensued. Unfortunately this feeling didn't last long and as we know the world is in an even more dangerous place now than it was forty years ago. Unintentionally prophetic, however the song is exceptionally relevant over forty years after it was written.

With hindsight the song might also be a comment on the cracks appearing in Cornwell and Burnel's relationship and perhaps Cornwell imploring his songwriting partner to play more of a role as Burnel's songwriting appeared to be waning on *La Folie*. In Cornwell's eyes at this time, he wanted both parties i.e., him and Burnel to be responsible for the creative drive of the band.

*****

As with 'The Man They Love To Hate', Black's tom dominated drum pattern establishes the base for this song. Both songs have infectious drum patterns, but they never deviate, repeating throughout the song. Black's repetition of drum patterns throughout songs has become a key feature of the album. That said, the pattern here is highly engaging and both Cornwell and Greenfield's riffs swirl around the drums with very similar rhythms to create a striking backdrop. Burnel maintains the root notes of the chords with the same rhythm as the others as any of his trademark rhythmic or melodic embellishments would have impacted upon the established rhythm.

The structure is very simple with two verses, a key change section, then a repeat of everything before an instrumental fade out.

This is clearly a chord-based song even though those opening guitar and keyboard riffs have a telling effect on proceedings. The chords for the main section are the three most common chords (1,4 and 5) and this enables the band to develop their close Beach boys-esque harmonies. "You gotta begin" is particularly derivative with the harmonies coming in quickly rising one by one. There is an interesting key change on the "Ancient history" section which initially follows the same chord pattern as previously but then returns rather suddenly on "Better wait and see" to the original key with some interesting off kilter chords to follow as the same lyric repeats twice more.

After everything is repeated a throwback to many previous songs arrives with the long instrumental ending to the song following more repeats of "Better wait and see" with some more disconcerting chords and harmonies. Greenfield moves into a slowly meandering solo and Cornwell later joins on top with a riff based solo, both of which are rhythmically ponderous and as the main rhythmic pattern is relentlessly still moving on. One gains the impression that the groove was not particularly conducive to creative solos here as the song tamely fades away.

As the song begins to fade out, the drum pattern stays the same but shifts from the toms into a snare drum giving extra weight to the notion of a war-like footing which supports the lyrical content.

A song with a different groove and interesting moments which will not be to everyone's taste as the close harmonies combine both regular and irregular, distorted moments and the suggestion of differing musical styles will further polarise opinion. Is it ultimately effective? The use of multiple vocals throughout also suggests a group or army of intent and these distorted moments add another dimension to the meaning of the song and the "Better wait and see" prophecy.

Like 'Ain't Nothing To It' on side 1, "It Only Takes Two To Tango is an interesting deviation to the other songs around it, and it is sandwiched between two very clearly stylistically defined songs, providing a suitable contrast to the early part of side two but ultimately the song fails to ignite.

Golden Brown

With its iconic status both culturally and musically much has already been written about 'Golden Brown'. In fact, it has probably been discussed, listened and written about more than any other song by the band. The song is exceptionally well known by the general populace, who can quote the lyrics, regurgitate the famous facts that go with i.e., it's about drugs, it didn't get to Number One and it has an odd time signature etc.

There is an element of myth and disinformation about the song that needs to be unravelled. It's fair to say because of its iconic status most fans have a soft spot for the song, many seeing it as the pinnacle of their creativity and career whilst many others might not view it this favourably but recognise its importance in the band's history and career. The song, whether the band and fans like it or not has come to define the band in mainstream culture. It is undeniably a great song with a sublime melody and a subversive lyrics two elements the band have always excelled at.

Cornwell has gone on the record saying that the song is about heroin and about his then girlfriend. Reasoning that he could hide the drug references in the guise of a love song. The lyrics are clever and subtle enough so that the woman and drug motifs are completely interchangeable and seamlessly fit both themes. Cornwell personifies heroin as a woman saying she is as intoxicating and addictive as the drug and vice versa. The point being that both things make him feel good and by implication both are addictive.

The final verse see's the singer revisiting one of his favourite similes of comparing sex with a woman to a ship last seen on 'Toiler on the Sea'. If any song demonstrated Cornwell as a master craftsman songwriter, then it's this song. However, it wasn't all down to Cornwell as he pointed out in his statement following Greenfield's death where he paid tribute to his former bandmate stating, "He should be remembered as the man who gave the world the music of Golden Brown".[11] Greenfield had been carrying the tune around with him for ages trying to push it on to band at various opportunities. Finally Cornwell realised its potential during a break in recording after hearing Greenfield working on the tune yet again. He quickly wrote the words and the rest is history.

This contrasts with Burnel's contribution and view of the song; he was not a fan at the time and didn't even play on the track, the bass notes being provided by Greenfield's keyboard. Live the song caused a bit of tension between the two front men as according to the bass player, Cornwell struggled to play the solo accurately. These kind of tensions may well have fed into Cornwell's decision to leave in 1990. One suspects Burnel might now be a fan of sorts of the song, maybe not infatuated with it but thankful that it saved the band's career.

The song only got picked as a single because Black was a massive fan and became the song's advocate to the band and the record company. He eventually persuaded and bullied all around him into agreeing it should be a single and of course his judgement was proved spectacularly spot-on.

*****

The song commences with keyboards only and the irregular time signature immediately created huge interest when it was released. The band had been experimenting with irregular time signatures throughout every album and the irregularity here is no more experimental than on many previous songs. It is simply three bars of a 3/4 waltz like time signature followed by the final fourth bar adding one extra beat to create a 4/4 time signature. Some say it is in 13/4 time which is, to all intents and purposes the same as 3+3+3+4 time but the 3/4 waltz like feel is so ingrained therefore, from a theoretical standpoint, the 3/4 for three bars followed by one bar of 4/4 is more aesthetically correct.

This irregular rhythm only occurs during the instrumental intro and when this section repeats, and not during the sung verses. It is the harpsichord sound playing the chords in conjunction with a different keyboard sound playing a mid-range riff panned right, balanced with another similar sound but chords panned left on beats two and three as well as held bass notes on the keyboard (Burnel didn't play on the track) that create an unforgettable opening musical soundscape.

The harpsichord off beats on that final 4/4 bar complete the creativity of the phrase. The keyboards completely dominate musical proceedings rather like 'Outside Tokyo' and the multi-layered keyboards of 'Waltzinblack'. And, like those two pieces, the song is chord based, using, by and large, conventional chords. However, two principal reasons why this song became the bands largest hit were firstly, that simple commercial chord sequence which had the mesmerising feel of the multi-layered keyboard sounds and the sparkling moment of the offbeat time signature change and secondly, the beautifully crafted melody. It is the combination of these two musical features that resulted in a song that was both different and accessible to the chart buying public of 1981.

The large vocal melodic range falls in total over twelve notes in the scale and its three-part descent carries such a quality that the mood, aided by Cornwell's perfectly nonchalant vocal tone, draws the listener in over the more piercing sound of the harpsichord. It is this combination that creates the quintessential mood.

Other features of the music that perfectly encapsulate the mood are Black's drum pattern which, like almost all the other songs on *La Folie*, repeats throughout. This beat echoes the rhythm of the keyboards and his old jazz influences come to the fore with his soft snare and ride cymbal.

Cornwell's sublime guitar solo is the only time that the guitar is used on the track and has such consummate economy. It is divided into three short sections, the first of which has a repeating two note riff with the end of the phrase moving downwards on its repeat. The second shape starts on the same high note as the opening vocal melody and has another strong descending shape. Then the final flourish has an upward fast paced yet laid back moment of sheer enchantment underneath a return to the irregular time signature of the intro.

As with many Stranglers songs, the structure is subtly unconventional. The main vocal section is repeated but concludes well under halfway through the song without returning later. Instead, following the guitar solo the vocal then echoes two thirds of the solo without lyrics in a dreamlike state. This is followed by further dreamlike vocal musings enhancing the dual drug and love induced lyrical meaning, with the "Never a frown" line on multiple overlapping melodies heavily reverbed to fade.

There is nothing about this song that surprises experienced listeners of the band's output. It was a natural development of many musical features that had already surfaced in different guises on previous tracks: the irregular time signature, the multi-textured keyboard dominated sound, the slightly unconventional structure, the sumptuous melodies, the laid-back vocal delivery, the instrumentational ideas supporting the lyrical meaning, the strongly melodically shaped guitar solo. But all these features aligned with perfection to enhance Greenfield's simple chordal harpsichord idea.

There is an interesting comparison to be made with 'Norwegian Wood' by The Beatles. Both songs share the 3/4 time signature and have the same tempo. And both songs have an overall descending melodic shape for their main sections with a similar rhythm with the second "Or should I say" Beatles phrase similar to the "Throughout the night" Golden Brown phrase. These musical similarities lead to the thought that Cornwell may have subconsciously been influenced by 'Norwegian Wood' but there are so many other differences in the song that suggest that any comparisons are merely coincidental.

Significantly, whilst the Beatles had a distinctive sound (the sitar) near the start of the song, the melody played by George Harrison mimics the guitar melody that has already played which is also the main vocal melody to follow. The distinctive harpsichord opening to 'Golden Brown' is an independent section with a different melody in itself and is the main contrasting section to the vocal section.

This idea of an instrumental section being independent yet crucial to the song is a well-established feature of The Stranglers that was rare amongst other bands including The Beatles. 'Norwegian Wood's' contrasting section is the second "She asked me to stay" vocal section that cleverly moves into the minor key whereas 'Golden Brown' uses the time signature change to add interest and whilst it is also in the minor key, it is the related minor to the main vocal section whereas 'Norwegian Wood' is a more irregular minor.

The chords overall have no similarities with the opening chord of the main vocal section to 'Golden Brown' starting on chord 2 with a quicker descending melody creating a different feel to 'Norwegian Wood' which uses the home chord (chord 1) with a long note following by a higher note to start the main section. Melodically, whilst the overall descending shape is apparent for both songs, there is no close repetition of any specific phrases.

The greatest similarity between the two songs is that both are examples of musical creativity forging beautiful results.

How To Find True Love And Happiness In The Present Day

In this day and age the title sounds like it should be a self-help book or even better a title and premise for a doctorate thesis. The song lyrically and musically is another with a nursery rhyme quality. The keyboard sound is reminiscent of the effect Greenfield used at the beginning of 'Nuclear Device (Wizard Of Aus)', a squall like sound that gives a kind of bad tempered wasp feel to the melody.

This time it's Cornwell speaking the lyrics rather than singing. He delivers them in a measured deliberate way which emphasises there meaning. Each verse refers to a person he knows and what they love, be it money, power or life itself. Each character despite these loves realises there is something missing or wrong with their lives. It's tempting to say because of the album's theme and the song's title the missing part is love.

Laura Shenton in her book on the album *La Folie* comments that the lyrics are ironic, and the big clue is the sleeve art with its ubiquitous love hearts adorning the lyrics.[12] There is also an element of playful subversion in the pronunciation of the word "happiness". Cornwell pronounces it "hap penis" deliberately emphasising the genital aspect of the word throughout the song in the way a *Carry On* film might emphasise the double entendre.

This type of humour was a style Cornwell often employed and by doing so it neatly subverts the idea of love and presents it as a primal urge rather than a romantic concept. It's another

example of the band's using humour to subvert the norm. Unfortunately, as we have seen, not everyone, particularly the press, shared their sense of fun. However, you can imagine the band wanting it to get a single release so they could have a hit song with a rudely funny lyric.
Of course they had done this before in 1977 with 'Peaches'.

'How To Find True Love And Happiness In The Present Day' was the last song written for the album and although a good song with an interesting theme and feel, it is a little bit unremarkable. The subversive humour element just about pushes it over the quality assurance line. The band did air the song live on the *La Folie* tour and as with other songs e.g., 'Thrown Away' or 'Bear Cage' the song came to life when played live and was much more powerful and dynamic compared to the anaemic studio version. Searches on YouTube or the BBC *Live In Concert* CD release ably demonstrate this.

*****

The same musical device that was used in 'The Man They Love To Hate' is again evident here where the spoken lyric is accompanied by a melody on the keyboards on the same rhythm suggesting that this could easily have been the sung melody. This occurs both in the first half of the verse and throughout the chorus.

Greenfield's opening high pitched warped sound, similar to the opening of 'Nuclear Device (Wizard Of Aus)', adds to the light, almost throwaway mood here with Black's rim click dominated rhythmic pattern (similar to the opening song 'Non Stop') once again repeated without variation throughout the song. The added maracas in the bridge and congas in the chorus supplement the frivolous feel, as does Cornwell's precise delivery and the sparseness of the bass playing with many rests, and the occasional guitar riff in the bridge.

The structure to the song is very conventional with two verses followed by a chorus, another verse and chorus, a keyboard solo and then a fade out over the vocal hook line. The chorus vocal says "Tell him how to find true love and happiness" twice with the chords being subtly altered for the second playing.

All these features bring a certain charm to the song, once again showcasing the incredible diversity of style deployed by the band throughout the album. Greenfield's interesting solo towards the end of the song on the same warped sound becomes even more high pitched and utilises his traditional arpeggio shapes before settling on a fast three note repeating riff where the vocal re-enters this time with a sung melody that is accompanied by a guitar riff of similar shape with the congas and other Latin percussion completing the fade out.

Another song to divide fans as there is much to admire in the melodic interplay of the instruments and the overall playful feel. But some longer established fans will be disappointed that side two is displaying a lighter feel and the juxtaposition with more complex songs that occurred on previous albums is lacking.

La Folie

The album finishes with the title track and third single from the album. It's a gorgeous luxurious piece of music played at funereal pace. As the song shimmers the vocals relate a strange story of love.

The lyrics are in French and are again spoken rather than sung by Burnel in a conversational way. He worked on his French so that he got the accent perfect, and the result fits the music seamlessly. A melodic vocal line would have detracted from the wonderful backing track and in a sense by not singing in English but by speaking in French the unusual nature of this adds a natural subtle melody simply because the French language sounds melodic when spoken. The subject matter of the song is Issei Sagawa, a man who murdered his girlfriend and then ate her. Apparently, he loved her so much she was good enough to eat! La Folie... The Madness of love indeed!

The inner sleeve artwork has an anatomical heart as if it were on a butcher's slab and as the song references cannibalism, a popular theme in Stranglers songs, the link is obvious whilst at the same time because it is a heart it references love and the protagonist Issei Sagawa's claim that he was so in love with his lover the ultimate demonstration of his obsession was to eat her. Let's say it was an unusual single choice to follow 'Golden Brown'. Burnel is supposed to have talked Black and Greenfield into backing it as a single so Cornwell found himself outnumbered when he was pushing a more logical choice for a single, 'Tramp'.

To be fair it almost made the top 40 as over a period of a few weeks it slowly climbed the chart to the heady highs of number 47.[13] Such a decision could have been commercial suicide, a spectacular own goal after getting out of jail with 'Golden Brown'. Luckily the band bounced straight back with the top ten hit 'Strange Little Girl'. Some fans applauded the decision of releasing 'La Folie' thinking it was an artistic statement and also a very punk attitude thing to do i.e., sticking to their guns and as if the band were saying, we don't care about being commercial.

The reality of course was somewhat different. Band politics, bloody mindedness, artistic integratory whatever the reason for releasing it as a single it made no commercial sense and risked undoing all the good work 'Golden Brown' had done in raising the band's profile.

*****

The abundance of different musical styles that permeate the album grows even further with the final track. The song has links to 'Manna Machine' and even 'Turn The Centuries, Turn' from the previous album but is clearly a conventional chord-based song and focuses on the interplay between the guitar and bass to give it a more reflective and lugubrious feel.

Obviously the quietly intense French spoken delivery further exacerbates this mood. There are many reasons why it was unsuitable as a commercial follow up to 'Golden Brown' and somewhat surprising that it charted as high as it did at number 47. This was probably due to the 'Golden Brown' effect.

The structure is essentially very conventional with a long instrumental intro based around two guitar riffs, a verse and chorus which are both repeated, a middle section with a key change then another verse and chorus with an ending to fade that adds extra guitar ideas. The slow rate of change for all the sections and lack of discernible contrast in the texture and instrumentation result in a long atmospheric listening experience.

The sustained strings and light touch drum pattern start the song. Greenfield continues the sustained string sounding chords throughout the song and Black stays in the background yet subtly changes drum pattern from simple hi-hat and very occasional snare and bass to a more constant standard bass and snare rhythm in the chorus.

However, the first two lines of the chorus "Parce que J'ai La folie" Black unfurls a fill like pattern that is very subtle yet rather fascinating. It could be argued that there are more changes of drum pattern in this song than almost any other song on the album. But on this song, unlike most of the album, they are providing a supportive role rather than being at the forefront.

The verse sees Burnel speaking the lyrics whilst Cornwell's exquisite guitar riff competes for attention. Rather like the guitar solo on 'Golden Brown', there is a beauty in the shape that starts very high before descending over a large range with some interesting angular, unconventional leaps between notes. This shape is then followed by a return upwards in the same carefree manner. Burnel adds some high bass notes and upward slides rather than riffs with effects on the bass that add to the sonic mix, and these become more prominent as the verse progresses.

The chorus sees the guitar drop out completely and we are left with Burnel's very low sung vocal melody being almost echoed by his bass guitar with a few clashing notes that are, again, very subtle. The bass sound here has become one of the most mellow that he has produced.

After the second chorus, the song changes key up one semitone from the main verse with a high keyboard riff maintaining the reflective mood. After repeats of the verse and chorus the fade out incorporates a new guitar riff, again in keeping with the mood.

There are many who see this song as a beautifully thoughtful soundscape and others who will see it as rather too ponderous, over-relying on the monotonous sustained keyboard string chords to accompany the indulgent spoken vocal musings. Whichever viewpoint is taken, Cornwell's majestically crafted guitar work and the band's pursuit of a multitude of stylistic contrasts cannot be questioned. But it does leave side two lacking in substance and complexity, at odds with the closing songs 'Genetix' and 'Hallow To Our Men' from the previous two albums.

The Stranglers 1977-1990

Musical summary

Overall, it is difficult to sum up the album that contains such a plethora of different musical styles. Some would argue that this great variety demonstrates a major strength of the band, yet others will argue that the album lacks cohesion. Moreover, the obvious desire to produce shorter, more commercial songs will, again, divide fans. The more clinical eighties sound production and Black's insistence on repeating patterns throughout most songs that are almost replicating drum machines add more to the commerciality.

These two features were also a portent of what was to come on future albums. The drums are dominant for a majority of the songs and are, arguably, mixed too high with too much piercing snare, so the insistence on repeated, drum machine-like patterns compound the issue and affects the overall sound on the album.

Longer standing fans will be disappointed with these issues of repeating drum machine-like patterns, clinical sound production, shorter songs and, consequently, less stand-alone instrumental sections that wonderfully brought together the different instrumental prowess of the four band members. The result was that complex and weighty songs from the previous three albums like 'Toiler on the Sea', 'Curfew', 'Genetix', 'The Raven" and Hallow To Our Men' were absent.

There were still many clashing dissonances, especially on side one, and unconventional chord patterns that would have been appreciated by fans of the more experimental phrase of the previous three albums. The textures of many songs featured a combination of the chordal and the multi-melodic layering, but the latter, along with some of the dissonances proved to be less effective than on previous albums due to the more clinical production that failed to create the feeling of togetherness when the keyboards, bass and guitar were embarking on their disparate and often clashing melodic ideas at the same time.

A comparison of the first two minutes of 'Genetix' and 'Ain't Nothing To It' bears this out. Furthermore, the previous three albums all moved in different stylistic ways from the tumultuous opening two albums, but those three albums within themselves all had a strong sense of stylistic holisticness that cannot be applied to the more hotch-potch collection of *La Folie*. There are many triumphs for many fans: 'Golden Brown' of course, 'Tramp', 'The Man They Love To Hate', and for some, 'Ain't Nothing To It', 'La Folie', 'Let Me Introduce You To The Family', 'Everybody Loves You When You're Dead', and even 'How To Find True Love And Happiness In The Present Day'. But to reflect on the differences between these songs and the fact that most of these songs will divide opinion, adds weight to the feeling of lack of continuity.

Where to next? Releasing the single 'La Folie' as a successor to "Golden Brown was... ahem... madness. Was that the bands' joke? Did they want to maintain an unpredictability that had characterised their careers?

There were many fans accepting of the disparate collection of *La Folie* but feared for the predictability of further mainstream eighties pop. They wanted the band to maintain the unpredictability of releasing 'La Folie' as a single with a leaning back towards to the harder-edged sounds and extended instrumentals of old and they were about to be severely disappointed.

Album Summary

La Folie isn't a masterpiece and isn't universally loved like other albums in the band's back catalogue but has many merits including some classic Stranglers songs and virtually all the songs that were commercial and radio friendly.

As a concept it is fully realised although it was never intended to have a narrative like *The Gospel According To The Meninblack* but instead all the songs are all aspects of the "madness of love". 'Golden Brown' brought new fans into The Stranglers fold but despite a massive hit single the album struggled to match even the sales of the much maligned predecessor. To most fans it is probably a mid-table album.

It has been lazily confined to the band's commercial or 'gone soft' phase. The production or more specifically the bright sounding mix was seen by many as overtly commercial and not 'Stranglers'. It must be remembered that the band were in trouble prior to its release and there was pressure to deliver something that was more accessible. The songs and the mix certainly did this but as we were seen a lot of the band's trademarks were still there particularly in terms of their ear for melody and their subversion and their humour.

For these reasons it deserves to be held in higher regard. It is worth revisiting, putting it on the sound system and as George Michael famously said listen without prejudice and sitting back and discovering or rediscovering if not a classic but a first-rate body of work. It will be like discovering a lost gem that has been in plain sight all these years and those previously sceptical will ask why I didn't think that at the time. It is not just the album 'Golden Brown' comes from, it is a fully realised concept album with all the things fans of the band love them for, tunes, musicianship, humour and controversy. To any Stranglers fan it is essential not simply because it has 'Golden Brown' on but also for the catchy tunes of side one, the lost classic of 'Ain't Nothing To It' and the perverse, love it or hate it genius of the title track.

La Folie was a turning point in The Stranglers career. It marks them leaving the experimental and dark side of their previous albums to follow a more commercial orientated path. *La Folie* falls between two stools in that sense being neither fully experimental nor totally commercial. Falling between two stools is generally seen as a bad attribute. However, it could be viewed as positive as it showcases two distinct sides of their character. On the one hand the dark, broody feel of 'The Man They Love To Hate', 'La Folie' and 'Ain't Nothing To It' and then the poppy subversion of 'Non Stop' and 'Golden Brown'. The sound on the record was certainly clearer and brighter, particularly around the vocals however the subject matter of many songs was still, if you think carefully about it, challenging — e.g., sexual repression, cannibalism, drug use and death all tipped their hats as subject matter on the album. Although the band clearly desired commercial success with a more accessible sound they were still not afraid to challenge their listeners with the grimmer and seamier side of life.

In terms of the mix and sound, it's bright clearer and up front. Cornwall complains his guitars on this album and most Stranglers albums is too low. He might have a point but his job throughout the band's history much of time is to be the bedrock and come to the fore at the right time either for a solo or to drive the song with a riff. Despite Cornwell's minor reservations Tony Visconti had clearly done the job he was employed to do. Commercial only in the sense that is clean and clear sounding whilst at the same time still maintain the bands sense of studied surliness and malevolence.

With the band now free to sign to Epic and just like their previous three records they had an idea and a plan. The next album was going to show a radical change of direction musically and sonically. It was a risk, they had a strong loyal and tolerant fan base many of whom were going to be severely tested, but 'Golden Brown' had open up a vast potential market of pop fans who although hadn't fully bought into buying albums represented a huge potential market and a new career if the band could deliver.

Extra Tracks: singles and B-sides

Strange Little Girl (single 1982)

'Strange Little Girl' was the last record for UA/Liberty/EMI. The story was that the company failed to pick up their option to sign the band again after the release of *La Folie*. The contract stated that the record company had to agree in writing within ninety days of releasing each album. After *La Folie* they 'forgot' and conspiracy theorists suggest this was deliberate so the label could drop the band given the album's initial poor performance chart and sales wise.

'Golden Brown' was released before the ninety days were up but it didn't become a big hit until after the time had elapsed. As the ninety-day deadline closed *La Folie* the album was fast tracking out of the top 100 at number 88[14] in the charts and 'Golden Brown' was only at 25 in singles chart.[15] Given their recent singles chart history and expensive commercial album failures like *The Gospel According To The Meninblack*, the label chose quietly not to pick up their option.

This of course is speculation but whether it was label design or administrative inefficiency the band had become free agents and a lucrative deal with Epic beckoned. When 'Golden Brown' hit the jackpot a few weeks after the deadline the record label had second thoughts. Although they hadn't a leg to stand on as it was their decision or mistake to let the band go, they threatened court action to keep the band. A deal was struck, the band would provide one more single and sanction a greatest hits package.

This was an old song written by Cornwell and original member Hans Wärmling before Greenfield was in the band. In the ultimate of ironies, the song had been rejected by EMI when the band were trying to get a deal. EMI snapped the band's hand off when it was offered. Probably because of its commercial sound from the keyboard melody and Visconti's bright mix, it was a big hit finally giving 'Golden Brown' the commercial follow up success it and the band deserved.

The keyboards give the song a shimmering, luscious and haunting feel which had also been present to some extent on the original 1974 Wärmling demo. The 1982 version puts the keyboards to the forefront of the mix of the song which makes it more contemporary sounding and because of this contemporize sound it was automatically more commercial. Cornwell also alters the lyrics slightly from the original demo without significantly effecting the meaning.

The muse of the song is an old girlfriend of Cornwell's who used to leave the city to go and ride horses in the country. Cornwell has also said it references the French 19th century author Alain Le Sage who wrote what Cornwell describes as social realism with his novel *Gil Blas*. The reoccurring theme of the city being a bad and unpleasant place, forms the bedrock of the song's meaning. Although obviously commercial and gentle sounding there is a distinct undercurrent of menace and mystery to the track thanks to the atmospheric backing particularly the keyboards and haunting lyrics. Tori Amos recorded a cover version for her 2001 album *Strange Little Girls*. This version maintains the ethereal feel of the original but at the same time is tougher sounding with big drums to the fore in the mix.

As an extra track on subsequent reissues it fits the album perfectly, in terms of its quality and fitting the theme of *La Folie*.

*****

One of the reasons behind this song being the band's second highest chart placing was the wonderfully crafted chords and melody. There is a conventionality to the chord patterns but the subtle twists that move the song into a distant key for the chorus, and equally as seductive, the return to the second verse at the end of the first verse.

The descending bass that moves effortlessly throughout these two transition moments is also conventional yet superbly crafted. The actual chord patterns of the start of the verse and of the chorus are very conventional but these transitional sections allied with a haunting melody that contrasts highly effectively between the verse, bridge and chorus, result in a more than pleasing whole from a song writing point of view.

All that was left was for the soundscape to support the reflective atmosphere and Greenfield once again steps up with a sound that is equally as effective and crucial to the holistic sound of the song as was his involvement in 'Golden Brown'. The arpeggios that are played to accompany this haunting sound begin the sound and remain at the forefront throughout. The fourth chord during the verse after "look at you" has the highest note forming a ninth of the chord and this also reinforces the song's strength from a chordal perspective. The other instruments supplement this mood with understated roles, all adding to the commerciality that the band often moved towards during the *La Folie* album.

The concise structure is also reasonably conventional with an eye on the radio plays. After the first chorus there is no other verse but, instead a guitar solo that is a four-bar arpeggio-based riff repeated four times and another example of Cornwell's versatility and ability to produce memorable guitar moments that are entirely appropriate for the song. This lies effectively on top of Greenfield, continuing arpeggios from the verses. We then move back to the bridge and chorus to finish in a little over two and a half minutes.

Hans Wärmling, the original keyboard player before Greenfield, is credited as a songwriter and was responsible for the chords as the song was written before Greenfield joined. He sadly passed away in an accident in 1995 but will be remembered amongst fans as contributing to this beautifully well-crafted song. The song seemingly did not fit the profile of the band when it was unsuccessfully demoed to the recording companies in 1974, but, after all the stylistic journeys the band underwent in the short space of four years from '78 to '82, 'Strange Little Girl' finally found it's resting place at a more opportune time for the band.

Vietnamerica (B-side to 'Let Me Introduce You To The Family')

A song with a dreamy swirly feel thanks to Greenfield's meandering keyboard line and Cornwell's piercing lead melody. The new Razor guitar again allowing him to pick out precisely the high-pitched notes. Burnel's gruff sounding bass riff high in the mix adds some bite. The music is atmospheric rather than memorable giving a soundtrack to an imaginary film of devastation.

Lyrically its series of images related to America's invasion and defeat in Vietnam, with references to death and the atrocities of war. It is clearly judgmental of America and makes its point subtlety but at the same time doesn't actually pull its punches. Referring to the Americans as all powerful who have literally burnt the hands of the indigenous population with napalm and metaphorically had their hands burned as they lost the war. It was in contention for the album but didn't seem to quite fit, particularly lyric wise, with the love concept of the album. More work would have made it a better fit and perhaps it could have even been the twelfth track on the album.

*****

A plodding dirge that has Burnel and Black providing a most basic yet unconvincing rhythmic backdrop. The bass sound is a poor throwback to the earlier powerful mid-range sound with strange effects that sound distorted. The keyboards and guitar attempt to give the music some movement but with little success. The chords are also wholly unconvincing as is the melody and Cornwell's vocal tone and delivery completes the depressing picture.

Love 30 (B-side to 'Golden Brown')

Coupled with 'Golden Brown' 'Love 30' is an instrumental loop which was played backwards. Originally based on a bass riff. The band then added tennis racket shots noises and an umpire intoning the score hence 'Love 30'. The group rather ambitiously thought it might be used on a tennis highlight TV programmes and earn them a payday which to be frank given the quality of the track was pushing it a little bit too far. However the tune is of some merit and does have a bit of a groove feel after you have heard it few times. Not essential but of interest.

*****

This instrumental is an interesting piece, albeit too long, with a laid-back repeating drum pattern providing a swing groove with sound effects along Cornwell's held chords with chorus effects applied. The bass becomes more prominent as the piece progresses but never expands into a solo, instead playing the root notes at a quicker pace. This creates a feel not unlike the wondrous ending to 'Genetix' but Burnel never sways from the root notes of each chord.

Cruel Garden (B-side to 'Strange Little Girl')

The B-side to 'Strange Little Girl'. A jaunty, jazzy, acoustic number that signposts the way directly to the *Feline* album. It is the first band track to feature acoustic guitars. It's a sparse arrangement but the pacey instrumentation gives the song life and at the same time room to breathe. The piece pays homage to the Gypsy Jazz of the trail blazing Stéphane Grappelli and Django Reinhardt.

Lyrically the song adds a twist to the *Little Red Riding Hood* fairy tale and mixes in a bit of vampire and werewolf horror mythology for good measure. The predators are women or 'madams' and their prey by implication are men. There are lots of lyrical references to danger and being eaten. The being eaten reference is a traditional device for representing sex and in particular a sexual predator which of course is the uncomfortable sub text to the *Little Red Riding Hood* fairy tale.

The words were written and sung by Cornwell and the horror themes they present are familiar territory for the singer. This was after all the man whose first solo album was called *Nosferatu*. At the time the film *American Werewolf In London* was delighting and shocking the nation and bringing back into fashion old school horror movies with the age old theme of, don't go out when there is a full moon, which is alluded to in the lyrics. A simple but beautiful sounding acoustic guitar solo at the end belies the sinister lyrical content.

*****

A simple two chord song, seemingly rather throwaway in nature with the main body of the song over in less than two minutes. But this fast-paced jazzy swing song has much to commend it, with Black's brushes dominated pattern, Burnel's walking bass and Cornwell's acoustic guitar rollicking it along. The melody is well shaped, and both the guitar and keyboard breaks have an exuberance at odds with the darker subject matter.

Both these brief solos are so well crafted that we are left eulogising over Cornwell and Greenfield's talents and a desire for wanting more. But the song is only ever intended to be a brief foray into yet another stylistic world where, once again, the instrumental and melodic prowess of the band is to the fore. The backing vocal harmonies and Greenfield's counter melody over the chorus vocal melody are, unsurprisingly perfectly dovetailed, as is the call and response fade out by the guitar and the keyboards.

Nubiles (Cocktail Version) (B-side to 'Tomorrow Was The Hereafter')

Found on the opposite side to the 'Tomorrow Was The Hereafter' single which was a Stranglers Information Service release in 1980. Quite why it's on *La Folie* as an extra track is a mystery. To be frank there is not much merit in it. Basically, it is the band messing in the studio potentially trying to knock out a B-side by redoing an old song.

The studio banter is mildly amusing, and it is interesting juxtaposing of styles when compared to the version found on the *No More Heroes* album. The original song has an aggressive violent feel topped off with beeping, whirling electronics high in the mix. This in sharp contrast with the crooning style and jazz-lite rat pack feel of the backing of the 'cocktail' version found here. Perhaps most interestingly Cornwell can't remember the words to a song he wrote. The studio engineer has to keep prompting when the singer asks what the next line is!

You Hold The Key To My Love In Your Hands

A track that was first released on the compilation album *Hits and Heroes* in 1999 but was recorded at the time of the *La Folie* album. The lyrics have a double entendre feel in that *Carry On/* saucy postcard humour the band sometimes employed. Cornwell is toying with wordplay and puns again with what sounds like a real saying but is his own invention and is a smutty joke.

Basically the title means his penis being held in the hands of his lover and there is no need to explain the joke and innuendo any further! The original saying is "You hold the key to my heart", a noble loving sentiment that Cornwell undermines with what some might refer to as puerile humour. The lyrics describe oral sex in a way a heavy metal band would be proud of.

Although synths driven the really interesting thing about the track is the drums are real but sound robotic, like a drum machine, indicating the way the drum sound and playing of them by Black was going to go in the future Stranglers recordings. Cornwell himself is dismissive of it commenting 'It's probably the least interesting Stranglers song ever.'[16] That is probably all we need to know.

*****

An engaging little ditty where the simple bass riff and drums provide a fast-paced backdrop, and the guitar and keyboards play fast paced angular riffs at the same time with piercing sounds that provide the main interest. Just before the "If I scream" chorus the bass joins in with the angular riffs and all three instruments play the same rhythm but on different notes to entertaining effect. The last two chords of the chorus suggest a change of key but the defiant return to the original key provides another unconventional moment. Not a weighty song by any means but entertaining in its own way.

Footnotes

1. Official Chart website

2. Official Chart website

3. Official Chart website

4. Official Chart website

5 Correspondence with John Pasche June 2023

6. Correspondence with John Pasche June 2023

7. Official Chart website

8. Ironically John Lennon's own song 'Nobody Loves You (When You're Down And Out)' has similar sentiments.

9. *Really the Blues* - Mezz Mezzrow New York Review of Books (2016)

10. Daily British tabloid newspaper *The Sun* had photos of topless female models on page 3.

11. Hugh Cornwell statement re Dave Greenfield's death May 2020

12 La Folie – Laura Shenton Wymer publishing 2022

13. Official Chart Website

14. Official Chart website

15. Official Chart website

16. *Song by Song* - Hugh Cornwell and Jim Drury

THE STRANGLERS.

FELINE.

FEATURING THE SINGLE "EUROPEAN FEMALE"

ONLY 4.49 ALBUM OR CASSETTE.

HMV EXCLUSIVE AUTOGRAPHED ALBUMS AND TAPES (LIMITED AVAILABILITY)

TOUR DATES:

- January 29 St. Austell, Coliseum
- January 30 Poole Arts Centre
- January 31 Bristol Colston Hall
- February 1 Cardiff University
- February 2 Birmingham Odeon
- February 3 Birmingham Odeon
- February 4 Apollo, Oxford
- February 5 Nottingham Royal Concert Hall
- February 6 Manchester Apollo
- February 7 Leeds University
- February 9 Glasgow Apollo
- February 10 Aberdeen Capitol Theatre
- February 11 Edinburgh Playhouse
- February 12 Newcastle City Hall
- February 13 Sheffield City Hall
- February 15 Hammersmith Odeon
- February 16 Hammersmith Odeon

the HMV shop

More records. More tapes. More discounts.

Feline

By the late summer of 1982 the band were free of their previous record label, waving goodbye with a Top 10 hit. They were raring to go on their next album for their new label. Their new masters were Epic, an arm of the mighty CBS record company. The label's profile in the recording industry was high and they had a roster of big recording acts such as Abba, The Clash and Duran Duran. There was an air of positivity and a feeling of almost a kind of a rebirth aura around the group. As with the previous album the band decamped to Black's house to write the songs. This time there was no pressure to come up with an album to save their bacon and the atmosphere was relaxed and fertile with creativity. As ever the band had a plan, armed with their new acoustic guitars which they had already showcased on the B-side 'Cruel Garden', this album would feature a radical new sound. A brave decision given their previous output, but the band had never been afraid of taking risks.

Given the choice of instrumentation it was no surprise that the songs resulting from the sessions at Black's house were mellower and more laid back. *La Folie* had been brighter and largely more upbeat than its predecessor *The Gospel According to the Meninblack* but still had its foundations firmly in the punk/post punk style. The new style showcased on Feline obviously risked alienating long term fans, but the gamble was, this new style would pay dividends with their newfound audience following the success of 'Golden Brown' and 'Strange Little Girl'.

To facilitate this, as well as making the sound mellower there was a deliberate choice to strip down the sound and make it simpler. The band were aware since 'Golden Brown' they were no longer considered outsiders instead they were viewed as more mainstream, and the album's sound and the writing reflected this. and it was felt this was what was needed to appeal to a new and hopefully larger audience.

Tony Visconti mixed the album again, the sound he had brought to *La Folie* was considered a success and his work on 'Strange Little Girl' had enabled the band to consolidate their foot hold in the singles chart. This time Visconti had a new challenge as he was going to be working with acoustic and electronic instruments and also the band were operating in a different way.

The new songs were certainly less up front and far less aggressive than the past and were mostly synth led. The keyboards carrying the melody with the gentler acoustic guitar and the bass more in the background complementing and accompanying the song. Greenfield had a new Prophet Synthesiser and it was clear from the material that the songs were going to be keyboard led, if not dominated by them.

The bass playing is particularly interesting as it marks a distinct change in Burnel's style. There had been signs of the upfront driving bass riffs being lessened on both *The Gospel According to the Meninblack* and *La Folie* and they were lower in the mix on those albums than before. But the nature of the more laid-back acoustic songs led to Burnel's role becoming more restrained with less driving riffs and more of the traditional accompanying role. Even though there were still plenty of bass flourishes, they were less demonstrative, but they still helped to push the songs along.

The mix Visconti brought to the record allowed the songs and instruments space to breathe and subtlety enhances elements of the more stripped-down instrumentation and musicianship. Without doubt there is an 'easy listening' or 'easier listening' to the mix and the production, being the type of songs, they were they needed a sensitive and sympathetic mix to fully fulfil their potential.

Feline is often referred to as the European album and there are echoes of Kraftwerk and euro electronic in the songs. The band would have been aware of this and as we have seen on the previous album they were prepared to adopt, use and develop current cutting edge musical trends.

But rather than being copyists they put their own take on them. The approach of electronic drums and synth allied to acoustic guitar and acoustic bass was groundbreaking at the time. New Order, that most European sounding of bands, were experimenting with acoustic guitars and electronics around at this time but this didn't really come to fruition until their 1985 album *Low Life*. The European feel of the album is present in other ways, European capitals are mentioned in the titles and are referred to in other songs and travel looms big as a theme across the songs. In addition, the guitars add a Spanish flavour to certain numbers. The record was recorded in Belgium and a host of other European studios were used to produce B-sides for the single releases.

The album was also well received across Europe, it broke the band in France and hit the charts in Holland, Norway and Germany. Cornwell agrees in *Song By Song* that the instrumentation represented two Europe's – the drums and synth the North cold Europe – whilst the acoustic guitars represent the warm south.

The album was preceded by the customarily promotional single. 'European Female' was released a few days before Christmas. Presumably Epic wanted to avoid the song being lost in the Christmas deluge of festive tinged singles that always accompanied that time of year. They perhaps also hoped hard core fans would rush to buy themselves an early Christmas present and then it would be set for a New Year push as over the holiday people stopped buying novelty records.

The single hit the Top 40 in the first chart of the year and two weeks later with the help of Top of the Pops it hit the Top 10 making No.9 but like a star that burns brightly for a moment then disappears forever the single them dropped out of the Top 75 three weeks later.[1] The objective of a Top 10 had been achieved but the sales showed that the band were still a niche audience act. The audience had been added to with more fans of more mainstream music joining the ranks but fans from the early days were still haemorrhaging.

The record company also used the promotional tactics of a picture disc and a previously unreleased B-side but the initial momentum didn't build quite enough to fully crossover. The album was released on the day the single peaked in late January which probably took away the singles momentum holding back the LP a few weeks might have given the single additional life and found that post 'Golden Brown' wider audience again and a delay certainly wouldn't have harmed the albums sales.

The album went straight into the Top 10 peaking a week later at No.4[2] helped by the hit single and a free, limited edition, one sided 7-inch given away with the record, featuring the track 'Aural Sculpture'. It was a welcome return to the Top 10 but after three weeks the album began to slip down the charts. In an attempt to bolster its performance 'Midnight Summer Dream' was released as a 7-inch single in an edited form and an extended 12-inch mix.

Unfortunately, arguably the best track on the album didn't perform on the singles chart, despite the fan enticing different versions. Struggling to No.35 on the third week of its release it rallied the album a little around this time, but then it continued to fall and by early April was out of the Top 75 after eleven weeks in the chart.[3]

In the summer Epic had a last throw of the dice or was it a contractual obligation? 'Paradise' was released on 7 and 12-inch formats. It fleetingly reached the lower reaches of the Top 50 (No.48)[4] as again new songs on the B-side failed to bring in the fans.

Reviews of the album were again mixed; the best applauded the idea and intent but the material only garnered faint praise. The *NME* whose long hate campaign against the band was still in full swing opted to change tactics and moved from outright libellous insults to the literary device of a fictitious conversation between three 'trendy' young people who were obviously not NME cool cats.

The imaginary trio talk about the new record and the band and of course because they aren't cool, they love the group for the all the reasons the NME hates the band. The point paper was labouring to make was only unhip dimwits like The Stranglers. Admittedly the attempted criticism was more underhand and subtle than previous attacks. The review's headline was "Feeble!" which was a more apt description of the review rather than the album. The analyses of the album revealed yet again that the music press didn't understand or want to understand the band and much of their comments were lazy, uninformed, and cheap insults lacking wit.[5]

In terms of artwork the album front featured a black cover with a prowling black cat whose outline is picked out in white as is the album's title. The only splash of colour, the bright red of the band's name in the traditional font. The black back cover features the track listing and the red logo. The inner sleeve features the lyrics printed on one side and band information about The Stranglers Information Service with a picture of the SIS team.

The cover is classy and cool and reflects the music on the disc inside. Calling the album *Feline* was an inspired move as the subtle silky movement of a cat like creature represented the softer, delicate, and graceful music the band was now creating. Femininity is also associated with feline so again the idea of a softer side of the band is again being projected and the message is completed with the song 'European Female' who we are told is a feline who moves with air and grace.

As a first release for a new label, it had cleared a couple of hurdles, the band were back in the Top 10 of both the singles and albums charts and sales were respectable if not spectacular. It did also provide a solid base for the band to push on from. They had arrested the decline in sales and were nurturing a new part to their fan base. Sticking to previous habits the band had also flagged up their next move with the Aural Sculpture manifesto.

At this stage there was also an elephant in the room. The question of using a producer. The previous four albums had been self-produced and although renowned producer Tony Visconti had mixed the last two records, he could only mix what he was presented with. The issue was finally broached and both the label and band members, particularly Cornwell felt that using a producer would be a good idea. The feeling being whoever was given the producer's chair could at the very least just referee the arguments over musical ideas. The band seemed up for the challenge and with Epic firmly behind them their next work was going to see another change in style and approach.

Midnight Summer Dream

From the first bar where the long slow dreamlike synth enters, it's clear that this is a new sounding Stranglers with the ethereal atmosphere dominated by the keyboards. Cornwell delivers a spoken narrative for most of the song, but a melody appears to great effect towards the end. The vocal tracks are slightly offset from the lead vocal which makes it sound like an echo and they are sufficiently low in the mix and combine to give a ghostly déjà vu feel to the track.

There are three version of the song, the album version at just over six minutes, a remixed edited 7-inch single mix and a mighty 12inch mix clocking in at over ten minutes. All versions have their merits. The 7-inch begins with Burnel's bass, missing out Greenfield's extended keyboard intro. Cornwell's vocals have more reverb on them and the backing vocals, with the melody used in the chorus in the album track, are put higher in the mix. The spoken narrative that starts the song is soon overtaken by sung melody. The song fades out and it is obvious there is more to come if it wasn't edited.

To many the remix and the edit might be an issue, but it actually works and the song isn't any lesser for it. It combines being more commercial whilst retaining the essence of the song. The 12-inch extended mix brings out the full beauty of the piece. The extra length makes the song hypnotic and almost soporific and our potential slumber is disturbed by Burnel's occasion bass flourishes and the crack of Black's electronic snare. This mix actually adds something to the original. This is no mean feat as it wasn't something most 12-inch mixes did in the eighties.

The 12-inch mix was usual just a rouse for cynically extracting more money from loyal fans and a higher chart placing for the single. Usually, tracks were given added drum beats and fills, supposedly to make them more danceable. The typical result was to ruin the track and eternally damn the song by associating it with an eighties fad.

In the case of 'Midnight Summer Dream' the mix built on the song and accentuated its considerable positives. In fact, the band were well served by their remixers at Epic during their time on the label. All the singles received the extended mix treatment and Epic produced a retrospective in 1992 that put them altogether on an album called *All Twelve Inches* and they made for a hugely listenable album. Live the song also came to life with an extended instrumental ending featuring some Burnel bass play that then segues seamlessly into 'European Female'. Without doubt the song had a life of its own and always shone through whatever way it was altered.

The title sees Cornwell using his now familiar device of altering and playing with a well know phrase or saying. The title is a play on Shakespeare's *Midsummer Night's Dream* based on a mispronunciation of the play's name by his then girlfriend. The lyrics are a straight narrative of a conversation between Cornwall and a friend of Black's at the drummer's house, the famous off licence where the band lived in the early days. The words have a surreal and hallucinogenic quality which is not surprising as Cornwell's was describing the events from the point of view of his own bad acid trip.

The lyrics have a conversational feel to them and contain some interesting and beautiful poetic images for example "Beauty hidden in our foreheads" suggesting humans struggle or are frightened to share their dreams and visions and instead as he points out in the next line just show their unpleasantness. The lyrics use a great deal of impressionistic and imprecise language, as if the narrator can't fully or really remember what happened, and all this contributes to the dreamlike atmosphere of the song. Towards the end of the song the old man has departed the scene the narrator awakes from his slumber and briefly searches for his nightime companion thus giving the idea that the conversation didn't really happen and it was just a fantasy.

*****

The same feature where the spoken vocals are accompanied by a keyboard melody of the same rhythm that dominated 'How To Find True Love And Happiness' and 'The Man They Love To Hate' from the previous album also appears here. But here the idea completely dominates proceedings with the long, dreamy string synth intro being a slowed down version of the melody that will accompany the main spoken vocal section. Then, after nearly five minutes, as we think the song may be moving slowly towards a long fade, Cornwell breaks out into the sung melody that echoes Greenfields keyboard version in the background to the spoken vocal that remains. This moment resonates deeply with the mood and, despite being less than thirty seconds long, provides the song with a much-needed climactic boost.

Black has now abandoned real drums in place of drum machines and, as in most of the songs from *La Folie*, is happy to play the same repeated pattern for most of the song. This is a very standard drum pattern with an extra tom placed on the end of the eighth bar. This tom then remains, replacing one of the snares on the fourth beat of every bar. There are slight variations with an extra tom at times, and additional bass drum in the section prior to the climactic sung vocal section.

The most notable rhythmic moment is when the band all come off firstly just before "Woke up in an armchair" at 2:22 and then just prior to the climactic moment. In both cases Black produces a higher electronic tom fill that captures the understated mood with suitable composure. But, for most of the time the drums repeat the standard pattern with very little variation and this lack of textural change is also the case with the other instruments.

The structure therefore lacks definition as there are no discernible instrumental contrasts between sections and the spoken vocal does not provide any contrasts either. The structure is based around three different chord patterns with 1:35 and 2:02 providing subtle changes to the main section. The patterns are all conventional apart from the penultimate chord in the third section at 2:17 which is a flattened second chord that will become a feature of the album. It evokes a European, primarily Spanish folk feel, and is used very occasionally in popular music.

It has been used before by the band with its appearance at the end of the main section of 'Outside Tokyo' on the *Black And White* album, the intro of 'Shah Shah A Go Go' and during the second half of the main section of 'Don't Bring Harry' both from *The Raven* album all creating different moods. All these moods are tinged with a dark feel and its pivotal use in 'Waltzinblack' was possibly the darkest. But the use of the chord on *Feline* will be to create the European feel rather than the darker mood.

There is a dreamlike beauty to Greenfield's opening with the melody that will become the main feature of the song slowed down to half the speed using a vibrato-like swirling sound. The texture is chordal with conventional chords that accompany Greenfield's melody. The old multi-melodic textures that characterised many of the previous albums and were one of the principal thrusts of the band's creativity, are conspicuously absent from the song suggesting that the album will move more towards the accepted commercial chordal texture.

So Burnel's aggressively melodic bass lines and Cornwell's superbly crafted melodic guitar riffs are completely absent here. Cornwell's guitar contribution in 'Midnight Summer Dream' is limited to strummed acoustic chords in the background and Burnel keeps a very conventional steady bass line that follows the chord with the occasional inversion of the chord on the fifth and sixth bars of the mains section "A midnight summer dream". Burnel's slightly more urgent bass line at the same time as Black's extra bass drums with new chords at 4.38 signals a change and, indeed, does pre-empts the previously mentioned climactic section. But, overall, there will be many fans lamenting the passing of these multi-melodic moments where each member of the band seemed to disappear into their own worlds, often clashing musically with each other yet maintaining a unified whole.

That is not to say that the song does not have charm and strength. It certainly does and is an undoubted highlight of the album with the climax of the sung version of the keyboard melody an immensely satisfying moment. There are various chordal sections that flow pleasingly into each other, and the song is heralding yet another change of musical direction for the band. For better or worse, this stylistic shift demonstrates the bands' desire to keep developing, and there is much to admire from the continuing melodic wonder of Greenfield's keyboards and his ability to choose sounds that create such defining atmospheres. It is a shame that the other instruments seem to be moving further away from their dynamic pasts.

It's A Small World

Having set their stall out with the opening number the band press home the fact that this is a band that is now ploughing a different musical furrow with an acoustic guitar picking start and icy keyboards. The bass is given a bass synth effect to match the synthetic drums. The vocals in the verse have a mechanical almost robotic feel.

Hearing it now, one can't help thinking of a mid-eighties New Order. The drums have a 'Blue Monday' feel and sound, particularly the drum fills, and the snare splashes that dominate the beat. The keyboard sound on the track also predicts what New Order were to become famous for sounding like, and Cornwell's vocal delivery is detached, a style that New Order's Bernard Sumner mined enthusiastically in the eighties.

How does one account for these obvious similarities? It might be tempting to think the explanation could be plagiarism however this is unlikely. At this time bands were using the same limited electronic equipment especially the new models of synths that were appearing and soon to become ubiquitous, so it's far more likely there would be some unintentional similarities based around the instruments pre-sets and also what producers thought sounded commercial. It is important to remember The Stranglers were there at the dawn of electro pop/ rock and they made their point then moved on.

The common usage of the saying "It's a small world" is to describe an unlikely meeting with an acquaintance in an unusual or unlikely place. There is another meaning, that the world can be effectively made smaller by the improvements in methods of travel therefore anywhere on the globe can be reached within twenty-four hours. It can also refer to the idea that the earth is a small celestial body when compared to size of the universe.

There are of course other ways the phrase can be interpreted if one pauses to think, and the multiple meanings of the saying are reflected in Cornwell's lyrics. Another example of his words working on different levels and containing double meanings. The song contains some of Cornwell's most poetic phrases and the first verse sees him addressing the different interpretations of the song title's meaning, so we have a travel motif and an example of coincidence. One of the messages of the song is that the world and all it has to offer can easily be discovered on your doorstep if you know how and where to look, and the inference being it's all in your head. Followers of mindfulness and meditation would recognise the wisdom of this assertion.

There is a cryptic meaning to the lyrics that is signposted by Cornwell when he uses solving a crossword to make the point. The puzzle is resolved in the final verse of the song which sees him escaping from a pleasure garden after drawing lots with his "friends" to see who escapes first. Cornwell confesses in *Song By Song* that this was him alluding to contemplating leaving the band. The band as a pleasure garden is an interesting image, we as listeners can imagine.

You don't need much of an imagination to think of the pleasures of being in a band but at the same time we can also see such a world can lead to overindulgence and it is a matter of record that the guitarist and Burnel were still using heroin. The final line of the verse in which "a flower dies of thirst" suggests that being in the band was at times sapping his creative energy and a period that was genuinely unhealthy for him. His decision to jump ship seven years later and the reasons for leaving basically revolved around Cornwell feeling trapped, thus making the words of this song all the more poignant.

*****

There is no doubt where the album is heading musically as this song builds upon the electronic drums, acoustic guitar more subtle string-based keyboard sounds with a non-aggressive vocal delivery. The old bass sound would have been completely out of place within this sonic palette but there are moments in this song where Burnel's contribution feels as though it would have been more suitable to the *Black And White* album.

Indeed, the song is a confusing mix where there are occasional clashes throughout with the bass line in the verses not always agreeing with the acoustic guitar and the keyboards, or the vocal line. This inconsistency moves on but because it is surrounded by ultra conventional moments like the chords at the start of the chorus but the "out" melody note sounds jarring as well so this exacerbates the situation.

Another example is at 2:04 on the "It's a small world too" melody line at the end of the very conventional two chord sequence that has a Spanish feel because it has a semitonal relationship, but the vocal line has clear clashes. Clashes in music are almost always challenging to the listener but if they are stylistically consistent then the listener will either take it or leave it. This song is stylistically inconsistent as there are many moments of complete conventionality juxtaposed immediately next to these wholly unconventional moments.

The acoustic based guitar chords of the introduction are another example. There is an agreeable quality to this intro as the chords give a floating feel with a major key flavour whilst the keyboards and bass provide an ethereal quality, but this is immediately extinguished by the clear minor key and rather bulky mood of the verse.

When this introductory section is repeated after the first chorus, the keyboards are clearly playing in a minor key whilst the guitar has reverted to the major. This does not work because immediately afterwards the conventional minor key verse lumbers straight back in. The vocal melody does not help matters with a very strict rhythm to the verse and a shape that is very chordal, and the tone is unconvincing, so the overall vocal melody lacks fluency.

The rhythm of the second line also results in an awkward moment when the "prise" of surprises is emphasised which feels unnatural. The chorus melodies, supported by the breathy backing vocals and Cornwell's more urgent vocal tone have more craft to them.

The drums add to the inconsistency. The potentially enticing atmospheric is ruined by the very hard electronic snare sound that occasionally punctuates the music. And Black's desire to maintain an eighties euro type pop feel is at odds with Burnel's bass lines. Some will say that these clashes work. That is a difficult case to answer from a point of view of stylistic consistency.

The lyrical content and some of the melodies help the music to move along with a good degree of purpose, but trying to reproduce the old clashing challenges for the listeners wrapped up in a far more nondescript groove that is trying to be commercial is unconvincing, as is the vocal delivery overall.

Ships That Pass In The Night

A jaunty, nagging, catchy song with many Spanish musical references which direct the listener to the European theme of the album. The whole song has a subtle laid-back feel but can be linked to 'classic' Stranglers longer songs in the vein of 'Toiler on the Sea' and 'The Raven'. The band's approach and sound is different to previous longer Stranglers songs but they still have the tension build up, the familiar lyrical images and the interesting instrumental breaks, but the feeling is more laid back cool than the driving urgency we have become used to. Cornwell's lead vocals and the harmonies are rich and melodic giving an added warm lush feel to the music.

In terms of imagery, we are in familiar territory the motif of a ship is again used to make the point of the song. Cornwell also chooses to use a familiar lyrical technique by working with a well-known saying as the title and a component of the chorus.

The phrase "Ships that pass in the night" was originally a Henry Wadsworth Longfellow quote from his poem *The Theologian's Tale*. The title is a popular one in rock, Jimi Hendrix wrote a song with the same title and seventies rock band Be Bop Deluxe recorded a song called 'Ships In The Night'. The saying is a simile for loneliness and certainly Cornwell's lyrics reflect that. To expand further on the literary device one can, add in the idea that the image is about a missed opportunity, for example unrequited love. In addition, it could refer to a brief meeting or recognition that might never be repeated or a regular meeting, but no significant communication occurs. In the latter case a failing or troubled relationship could be thus described.

Cornwell addresses more than one interpretation of the saying using the simile to comment on romantic love, religion, politics, and health. The implication being that despite potentially offering hope any contact with any of these is fleeting and unfulfilling. Contrast this with the chorus when an approaching "ship" can be a danger but on this occasion proves to be benign and the threat sails safely by. It could well be the singer is also commenting on life in the band and signifies the band were growing apart and becoming more distant from each other. Yet again because of the impressionistic nonspecific nature of the words the listener has the joy of imposing their own personal interpretation on the song.

*****

The mix becomes even drier with a riff on a soft bass sound light years away from the sound of just four years earlier. The electronic drums accompanying are a very conventional pattern but with extra percussive shaker sounds at the end of every second bar helping to further establish a Spanish feel. The acoustic guitar enters after one round of the four-bar bass pattern with the exact same riff except for the two chords at the end of the second bar.

This stripped-down sound is then the ideal foil for the keyboards entering with a subdued brass/string type, sustained sound, that simply moves up by scale on the start of every bar. This is played over six repeats of the four-bar bass and guitar riff and each time the starting note is a little higher and it also develops in full chords thus lasting over forty seconds in total.

This simple scalic idea has been deployed by the band in previous guises: the vocal melody "Se-cond com-ing" on 'Second Coming' and the opening keyboard solo on 'Toiler on the Sea' being two examples. It is fascinating to compare those three examples and to realise that the band underwent such dramatic changes in their style in a relatively short space of time.

Following this long section there is another short instrumental section that serves to move us into the verse. It utilises the semitonal and flattened second chordal relationships that was deployed in the previous two songs therefore further emphasising a Spanish flavour to side one.

Greenfield's synth trumpet sound riff played in harmony certainly adds to this feel as does the continuing use of the acoustic guitar. This moves cleverly and seamlessly into the verse with the help of a diminished chord which, along with the main key chord are the only two chords in the verse.

The vocal melody is particularly well shaped here and, after the long intro, gives a sense of balance to the song. The following chorus section returns to using conventional chord patterns and a another well shaped and contrasting melody complete with backing vocal harmonies and the continuing trumpet keyboard sound with a different melody on top of all the vocals thus moving the songs into a denser texture following the stripped back opening.

Burnel's bass playing is at times, during the end of the intro and in the verse, reminiscent of previous definitive moments but with a much more subtle tone, and the main bass riff also has a strong groove. Cornwell again restrains himself to acoustic guitar, but this is fairly high in the mix and helps to drive the song in the verses with much off beat playing to complement Burnel's subtle melodic flourishes. Black's patterns are generally conventional, but the verse does have some highly effective fills that, again, throwback to more expansive times.

The return to the older structures of longer instrumental sections has significance here. The opening and closing instrumental sections account for two thirds of the length of the song with the middle part having verse one, chorus, verse two and chorus before a synth trumpet riff enters too close to a parody of traditional Spanish folk norms and taking the European feel too far.

The strong melodies, contrasting sections, and the instrumental interplay of the verse fittingly links the old style with the new, but the song never quite fulfils its potential as the instrumental sections that are key to the song's success are too predictable and never quite capture the complex originality of old.

The European Female

Flourishes of Spanish guitar from Cornwell gently embellish the subtle Burnel bass to glide the song along. Ghostly sounding keyboards drift around the song like aural mist with drums grounding the whole thing with a metallic crunch.

Burnel wrote the words, one of only two song lyrics he provided for the album, so he takes vocal responsibility serving up a quiet hushed understated performance which certainly enhances the eerie erotic feel of the song. Initially there is no surprise in the lyrical content as in the first two verses Burnel appears to be singing about a woman from Europe. As he had a French girlfriend at the time this is no surprise. Burnel excels with the poetic and lyrical lilt of his lines, in particular the second verse, which has a sublime lover's description of his sweetheart just speaking:

> She speaks her, lips are kissing
> The air around her face
> I don't always understand her
> I love her air and grace

In addition to the wonderful erotic image of the words, the "air kissing" can work on another level as such a gesture is a typical way of greeting someone, particularly in France. The "I don't always understand her" line could be literal as his lover speaks French but also allude to a man finding it difficult to understand the motivation and ways of women.

However, as we have come to expect from Burnel and from Cornwell their words are rarely straight forward one-dimensional narratives. After luring us into think it's about his lover the actual fact is there is a deeper meaning. The words actually compare the continent of Europe to a love affair with a woman.

Given Burnel's fascination and passion with the concept of a united Europe first demonstrated on his 1979 solo album *Euroman Cometh* it isn't a stretch to think he would personify Europe as a woman he loves. If this is done the lyrics are more significant and ironic "We'll be together for a thousand years" and "Do you feel you might fall" intones Burnel.

After recent events i.e., Brexit and the current war in the Ukraine this is clearly not the case. Being together with Europe for a thousand years is no longer a truism for citizens of the UK thanks to Brexit. Additionally, the war in the Ukraine is a threat to the whole of the European continent and its unity. So, as is, so often the case words written over forty years ago are given more significance as the cyclical nature of history returns us again to circumstances that seem all too familiar.

The song was an obvious choice as a leadoff single and duly made the Top 10 but sadly proved to be the only hit single from the album.

******

Burnel returns to the breathy vocal tone that served so well in the song *The Raven* but here, a little over three years later the mood is considerably different. The bass underpins the song but with Burnel's now customary much softer tone, Cornwell's acoustic guitar and Black's electronic drums. Greenfield's keyboard sounds are also much softer, and all this creates a sonic palette that was commercially friendly as the single release achieved top 10 status.

The structure of the song is also highly conventional with repeating verses, bridges and choruses, a short instrumental section linked to feel of the verse and the chorus, and then two more choruses with an instrumental chorus to fade.

Cornwell plays the classical guitar rather than the acoustic, restraining himself only to melodic fills in contrast to the previous songs on side one where there was much chordal strumming. The overall sound of 'European Female' is therefore softer than the previous song, 'Ships That Pass In The Night' where the harder edged acoustic guitar chords were prominent. Greenfield's keyboard sounds are also softer than in 'Ships That Pass In The Night' and Black also contributes to the softer sound with a less abrasive snare sound.

The song continues the chordal theme of the Spanish semitonal and flattened second relationships from the previous songs on side one and is exaggerated even further becoming a crucial part of the song as there are only two chords for the verse, and these are the semitonal relationship of the flattened second to the home chord.

The chorus also has a minimal use of chords with only three being deployed, the final two of which, once again provide a semitonal relationship. The spareness of chords and the semitonal relationships, coupled with the general texture, provides an uncluttered soundscape that enables Cornwell's guitar work to flourish and reinforce the Spanish mood with his frequent use of slides. Interestingly he always plays at the end of the vocal phrases in the verses and choruses so there is none of the unconventional melodic layering that was so crucial to the songs on previous albums.

The brief riff that accompanies the repeated "fall" lyric is used as the basis for the instrumental section after the second chorus which now becomes a fascinating instrumental section as Cornwell's riff has a feel of being a cross rhythm and Greenfield now provides another cross rhythm on top. Alas, this beautiful moment where the bass and drums are rhythmically at odds with, separately, both the guitar and the keyboards only lasts thirteen seconds. Yet another example of the transformation of the band from those long and complex instrumental sections of previous albums into shorter, more commercial friendly sections.

Melodically, the bridge passage is a weaker moment where the vocal melody is in unison with the rising bass line, but the melodies of the verse and the chorus are particularly well shaped and memorable. Greenfield's contribution is also significant with the trademark arpeggios making a welcome return from the intro and throughout the verse, albeit in a much softer tone than, for example, in 'No More Heroes'.

There is a second twinkly sound in the intro and verses that borders on the irritating but provides a sheen that complements the mood. The chorus has a melodic keyboard line that echoes the melody line whilst there is a soft sustained sound that is also in keeping with the laid-back mood. The little riff at the end of the bridge passage is a charming moment as is, of course, the solo during the brief multi rhythmic instrumental section after the second chorus.

Rather like the previous song, there is much to commend about the song, and it certainly ticks the boxes regarding commercial appeal. But, to the fans who wallowed in the instrumental and structural excesses of the earlier albums, there was also the feeling of what might have been had the song been allowed to breathe into a longer piece with additional more complex textures. The last chorus, for example, commences just under two thirds of the way into the song and then somewhat meekly fades out with nothing else of interest to maintain our attention.

Let's Tango In Paris

The track kicks of side two and it's a song that shows, if further proof were needed, that the band had totally mellowed and were all romantically involved in long term relationships. Again, the track is keyboard led with the synthesiser emulating an accordion and flute to add the required Gaelic flavour advertised by the title.

The name of the song is more evidence of Cornwell's panache for word play. *Last Tango In Paris* was a film made in the early seventies and starred Marlon Brando. It was notorious for its sex and death themes and scenes. Cornwell by just changing one letter from the first word of the film title changes the meaning completely but the fact that it is still so close to the film's title mean the listener still has its seedy content and connotations at the back of our minds. Cornwell even pronounces "let's" as "last". These peripheral ideas help save the song from just being a softly romantic, crooning unremarkable love ballad and give it a slightly darker edge.

The lyrics are essentially a collection of archetypical, clichéd romantic images. So, we are treated to candlelight, flowing wine and dancing the night away in the capital of love, Paris. Not exactly an original approach but if you are in love then you forget the cheesiness and unoriginality of the cliché.

As suggested, there is a potentially darker side to the song and there is the waltz time, a key change and some lush backing vocals but they are not enough to save the track from being at best an average song in terms of memorability and meaning. Its style and sound fit the album, but it doesn't grab your attention and is a weak start to the second side.

It didn't even have single potential as it lacked a killer melody and the lyrical ambiguity of a song like 'Golden Brown'. It has all the attributes of a filler, and the trouble was that the band weren't overrun with quality material at this time and the songs they had in pencilled in for B-sides didn't fit the album.

Of the extra tracks they did have 'Vladimir and Olga' was a joke song, 'Permission', a reggae number with urban realism as its theme which simply didn't fit the album and 'Pāwshēr' atmospherically may have worked but had no lyrics. So effectively the song had to be on the album. It is a well-crafted number, and it is not a bad song but it is not that special.

*****

When one has feasted to the riches of the complexities of the music of the band's previous albums, it is something of a disappointment to be subjected to the opening track of side two having very little to offer in terms of complexity of structure or texture, or development of ideas. The structure of verse and chorus repeated with no linking sections is a particular weakness.

The opening chord sequence is interesting and Greenfield, as is often the case on the album, is at the forefront of setting the almost ghostly mood with, initially, the quick changing chords played sustained, followed by the fast arpeggios to accompany the verse vocals. The verse consists almost exclusively of these quick but subtle arpeggios with the soft held bass notes at the start of each bar, a bass run down on the eighth bar, and very soft tubular bells accompanying the fifth, sixth, and seventh notes of the vocal melody.

The main vocal melody has rhythmic similarities to the verse of 'It's A Small World' but is taken even further here where every note is lasting one bar of the fast three beats in a bar. There is a strong melodic shape and whilst the effectiveness of the rhythmic restrictiveness is open to debate, it does add to the rather eerie mood.

The chorus adds more texture with an acoustic guitar strumming on beats two and three of each bar panned right whilst another guitar is playing on every beat and is panned left whilst the keyboards continue in the same manner as the verse.

Burnel now plays a root note on every beat of the bar whilst Black supplies one lonesome snare on bar two of each four bar sequence. The vocal melody has a certain charm but is strictly repeated and the song needs more than this.

Finally, there is a textural development in the second chorus where the drum pattern is now busier with trademark Black unconventionality to it. However, apart from the backing vocal repeating phrase fading in, that is it as the song fades out and we are left even more unsatisfied with the lack of development than on some of the songs on side one.

The repetitiveness of the vocal melodies, the rhythmic restrictiveness, the lack of interest in the musical arrangement and the very basic song structure result in the conclusion that this song has an allure from the mood it sets, but is, for a band that has bristled with creativity on many of its previous songs, considerably undercooked.

Paradise

Paradise piques the interest once again after the lack lustre opening to side two. Perhaps one of the most unlikely Stranglers track ever and over the years there have been a few contenders for that title. With a jerky high pitched Burnel vocal over a world music, ethnic wooden percussion reminiscent of the sound of the Gamelan with a reggae influence sound and feel. Then add to this Burnel using a variety of vocal tones which, along with the contrasting female vocal tone, help to emphasise the change in mood of the lyrics as the song progresses makes the track virtually unique.

Given the instrumentation and arrangement it gives the impression of a tropical island, the stereotypical idea of paradise for many people. It is a quirky masterpiece and was almost an unlikely hit single. The record company's thinking being it's so odd but so catchy it could be. Sadly, they were wrong and a summer release in August failed to catch the public's imagination despite a 12-inch release with previously unavailable tracks.

The percussion Gamelan behind the track is very similar sounding to the Tears for Fears hit single 'Mad World'. 'Mad World' was released in late September '82. And became a Top 10 hit in late 1982. *Feline* had been recorded in September and it is possible The Stranglers liking what they heard were influence by the sound Tears for Fears used but there is no concrete evidence to suggest this.

More likely two band's working independently came up with a very similar sound and idea. This was probably because producers, engineers, tape operators and bands where sharing state of the art recording techniques and also using the same make of equipment thus accounting for the musical coincidences.

If nothing else, it demonstrates how intertwined the record company majors were in the 1980s. A prime example of this was the ubiquitous nature of the Fairlight digital synthesiser in the mid-eighties or more accurately particular effects. Unleashed in the mainstream recording world by Peter Gabriel and Kate Bush in 1980 in a creative and innovative way, by the mid-eighties it seemed every mainstream record had a Fairlight effect, often string sounds, on it.

The overuse of this particular technology is part of the reason why eighties recording output is often judged so harshly. Thankfully The Stranglers and Greenfield in particular, resisted the temptation to follow the Fairlight fashion. In terms of percussion Black might now have been insisting on programmed drums on recordings but was savvy enough to resist the dreaded gated drum, another sound every mid-eighties record seemed to incorporate.

Burnel provides the words for the song the second and final time on this album. He uses his favoured technique by giving us a narrative in an economic but poetic style. It's clearly autobiographical as he relates a tale in the first person. He is a troubled soul looking for happiness, who initially thinks he has found his true love when he discovers a woman who is the subject of the song.

Burnel's then Parisian girlfriend is in fact his muse and she even provides backing vocals. The story has a sting in the tale though, as Burnel realises he hasn't found his soul mate but instead she lies and tries to control him. He uses the image of his emotional and intellectual freedom being restricted by comparing this situation to being in chains.

This image harks back to his masterful lyric on the *Black And White* song 'Curfew' where he referred to freedom being a chain. One wonders what his then partner must have thought of this when she read the lyrics. He goes on to bemoan the fact that moments of complete happiness can't be preserved forever in time. He also employs the life as a movie device to make his point and the ideas of the freeze frame. Ultimate it's a world-weary cynical view of love that relates back to the concept of the previous album – *La Folie*, the madness of love. The images are poetic and there is some clever and witty world play in the song. Take the first verse:

I went in search of paradise
They said it would be good for my head
So I went in search of paradise
But she took me by the head instead

In the first line he is saying his lover will be good for his mind but finishes the verse saying she controls his mind. However, by using the phrase 'took me by the head' as well as being about the mind it is also an obvious reference to oral sex. So, the verse works on several levels. Is the lover controlling his thoughts or is it a sexual experience? Most likely it is both, sex and control.

In addition, we get comments on the cities of Paris and London. The implication is that both can be glamorous, but they can also provide despair. Or because of the order of the words. Paris is glamour and London is despair. We know from past songs that Stranglers were not fans of London and had a love hate relationship at best with the capital.

The delivery of the words are done in a high pitched yelp in a staccato rhythm going against the flow of the rest of the song. In the final verse he lowers his register to give the vocals a whispering croon. The different styles help emphasise the change in mood of the song's lyrics as it progresses. Finally, the choice of the title "Paradise is interesting as it is close in spelling and pronunciation to Paris, perhaps another cryptic clue to the meaning of this glorious curio of a song.

*****

The drum pattern sets the backdrop for the song and, apart from a few subtle additions, remains essentially the same throughout the song. It has a mixture of electronic bass drum and hi-hat mixed with electronic wooden world music percussion that provide the main thrust of the beat. From this a guitar with considerable effects enters on the beat playing the two chords that constitute the intro and verse, followed by the keyboards playing the chords on the 'off' or weaker beats giving a slight reggae effect.

When the keyboard ceases the offbeat chords and moves onto a melodic riff, the acoustic guitar enters playing the chords in a less 'off beat' pattern. This keyboard riff is, once again, similar to previous recent songs like 'Midnight Summer Dream', 'The Man They Love To Hate', and 'How To Find True Love And Happiness', where it foreshadows a vocal melody with a similar rhythm whilst the lead vocals speak, or in this case, shout but here there is a semblance of a two-note melody.

This vocal provides more of a texture than a traditional melody. The shouting is restrained and is not at the forefront of the mix which successfully manages to meld all the disparate sounds together. Even though there are only the two (conventional) chords providing the basis, the song is effective as the other ideas have space to breathe.

A severe contrast occurs from a vocal point of view in the bridge "Paris, London" section where two different female vocalists sing in unison, one panned right and the other panned left. Again, there are only two conventional chords that are different chords to the verse, and the two guitars, bass and drums carry on as before. But the keyboard melody that was clearly linked to the main vocal has now become a counter melody that is completely different to the new female vocal melody. This keyboard melody starts with the same rhythm as the keyboard melody from the verse but then it alters, signalling a brief return to the multi-melodic layering of previous albums.

The chorus is, initially, an instrumental with a new keyboard melody which has a simple repeating rhythm to it but, as was the case with the female vocals, has the same melody panned left and right. This melody is initially in unison at octaves but then becomes a harmony. There are, once again, conventional chords but more than two chords for this section.

Following repeats of the verse and bridge and instrumental chorus and the verse and bridge again the chorus this time has the sung vocals with Burnel now in his breathy tone. This is a highly effective section as not only does the keyboard melody marry well with the new vocal melody, but there is also another string-based melody weaving smoothly around the vocals thus creating a three-part multi-melodic layering texture. This section becomes a long fade out with a feeling that a new instrumental section could have broken up the repetition thus providing the gratification that always accompanies a chorus that later returns.

The song is somewhat of an enigma with elements of the band's well established musical ideas, but enough difference to set it apart from any of their other songs. The conventional chord sequences were (unwittingly) a main reason why the record company chose this as a single, with the hope that the disparate musical ideas would appeal.

The shouted main vocal was probably a step too far for the mainstream singles buying public, as was the quirky structure of the main vocal chorus only appearing at the end of the song. But that does not stop this song having an appeal to many as one of the strengths of the album. The combination of the band's established musical ideas to produce a fresh sounding experience is what draws in the listener here and, despite the questionable structure, there are enough ideas to formulate a song that sounds complete, something that is somewhat lacking with other songs from the album.

All Roads Lead To Rome

Another track and another surprise, this time the band appear to go completely synthetic and produce a track that is basically a homage to Kraftwerk both in terms of sounds and themes. As we have already learned the drums are electronic but here the repeating bass sounds like a sequencer. There appears to be no discernible guitar which leaves Greenfield full reign to give the track a synthetic soundscape and add a melody that could be straight out of Depeche Mode's synth pop textbook.

The overall feel of the music is one of movement and increasing momentum. Cornwell speaks the lyrics in a voice that is mannered to give the impression of being 'European'. It's supported in the chorus by melodic backing vocals. The band and particular Burnel were Kraftwerk fans and they pay further homage to the iconic Germany synth masters by using similar lyric themes such as travel, cityscapes and the near future.

Lyrically Cornwell is playing games with us again this time he leaves intact a well-known saying "All roads lead to Rome" but don't expect a literal meaning because this of course is not a song about Rome but about New York. The titular saying, which incidentally stems from a medieval French scholar, not Shakespeare or the Roman's themselves, is used as a metaphor meaning all roads lead to the world's capital city, in ancient times this was of course Rome but in the modern era New York is probably the most iconic city in the world and considered by much of the world's population as an unofficial capital of the world.

Further evidence for this argument is that the UN headquarters are also located in the Big Apple. New York is effectively the new Rome and in the early eighties Cornwell was spending a lot of time there because of his American girlfriend. He was thus inspired to pen his lyrics about the city that never sleeps.

The clues to the location are in the imagery of the writer's words with descriptions of the skyscrapers in Manhattan as "steel fingers clawing the sky". He also uses "yellow chariots" to describe New York taxis but by using the word chariot with its Roman connotations Cornwell is toying with the listeners trying to fool us into thinking we are in Rome again. A beautiful little literary ruse.

Cornwell's visits to New York in the early eighties was at a time when the city was a dangerous and literally bankrupt place, not the tourist idyll it is now, and the lyrics reflect the seedy underbelly of the city referring to peasants and poverty.

He also describes peasants' eyes turning from grey to green to blue suggesting the sadness the poor may feel, and also the envy they have for the rich. By using the word peasants, Cornwell hints at Rome again, a city that was always aware of the danger of the poor as a revolutionary force so much so the cliché but truism of 'bread and circuses' as a domestic policy was born.

The track has a travelogue feel with its propulsive advance and lyrical themes that mix the technical and historical and the diversity of people peasants, tycoons and passing observers all delivered in a detached emotionless tone reflecting the fact the writer is an outside observer, an alien in the city.

In terms of style and topic the track suggests another musical contemporary that of early eighties Simple Minds who produced the ultimate travelogue album in 1980 with *Empires And Dance*. The Stranglers were certainly allowing their present-day influences to flow and drive their creativity.

On a final note, the band made a video for the song and the film's location is clearly New York. The director secured a "yellow chariot" for the shoot but sadly it wasn't an iconic New York yellow cab which rather missed the point. Making a video usually suggests the song was being considered as a potential single. In fact, it was never a contender and the film was made by a fan/friend who loved the song and talked the band into appearing in it.

*****

The first section of the song is a rare moment on the album where the music is defined by the multi-melodic layering texture rather than being chordal. Another feature from previous albums is the two instrumental sections in the middle having more time to expand with new ideas which is welcome as the album has lacked independent instrumental sections. This is needed as the rest of the structure is highly conventional with the main section being repeated three times before the instrumentals and once after with a new section developed from the end of the main section when "All roads lead to Rome is repeated" at the end.

The style is moving into the Kraftwerk inspired eighties synth genre. The bass plays an effective opening idea but after fourteen seconds the bass deploys a typical eighties synth feel and sound. Another throwback to previous albums is Black's drum pattern. It is a drum machine, and the bass drum is on every beat to fit the style whilst the hi-hat and snare are very conventional, but the toms that accompany the verse spoken section have an offbeat unconventionality that was so crucial to many earlier songs. There are also other sharp percussive sounds panned both left and right which add to the movement of the song.

The contrast between the spoken vocal at the start of the main section and the smooth tone of the higher backing vocals in the second half of the section is typical of the way that the band had used backing vocals throughout each album. Harmonies were often used, but merging those clear contrasts was always a clever textural device and it is, once again, used to good effect here.

The bass synth rhythm is constant quavers throughout which enables Greenfield's main two riffs of the verse, the first lower and the answering one higher to smoothly sit on top of the mechanical rhythm provided by the drums and the bass. The only time the bass rhythm changes is towards the end of the song where the lyric "Touch your face" adds the word 'frightened' and here we then have a rewarding moment where the interplay between the spoken vocal and Burnel's breathy backing vocals fuse in tandem with the backing vocals incorporating vocal harmonies and accompanied by rich strings.

The instrumental section after "Weigh the scene" is a complete contrast as the sharp keyboard sound dominates with a solo but then merges into a different chord pattern with another keyboard riff complementing to high effect.

There will be some fans who would have reacted with dismay to the direction this song took from the roots of the early albums. Many older fans would have been able to cope with most of the songs from *Feline* and applauded the band's desire to develop their stylistic creativity. But this song was so clearly aimed at fitting into the eighties synth pop style and that would have been anathema to them. But regardless of one's opinion of this style, there is substance to this song with the returns of previously used features being an interesting development in this different song.

Blue Sister

'Blue Sister' continues the musical style set by the preceding song but with the guitar and bass now sounding authentic again. As the song unfolds Black pushes the song along in a Krautrock motoric style. The track was similar in feel to Krautrock and psychedelia of the seventies in places, with its dreamy synth sections, but this is contrasted by the up tempo phases which reflect the synth pop boom that was occurring in the early eighties.

Whilst the band might have been influenced by current musical trends and to some degree trying to ape them, perhaps in this case they are trying a little too hard. Given the synth pop boom of the early eighties the number undoubtedly had some commercial potential with its tumbling synth and Cornwell's crooning vocal that caresses the words in style reminiscent of the Human League's Phil Oakey but ultimately it doesn't feel quite there as a song.

Lyrical Cornwell uses the age-old image, so common in rock music which is to relate sadness to the colour blue. The singer narrates the story of a woman who is sad because her lover has left her. It's not initially entirely clear why he left but he was "taken" by friends.

The unsaid narrative is that maybe they and her lover are up to no good. The second and final verse are revealing saying this isn't a new experience and there is a specific drug reference with the phrase "their lines are old to". The band were still using a lot of cocaine and heroin at this time. Cornwell later revealed that the lyrics were about Greenfield's girlfriend who was worried about him because of his newfound habit of drug taking with Burnel and Cornwell.

With this revelation it's clear the "friends" referred to are other band members who had already enthusiastically embraced the opiate culture. There is a plea and a veiled warning in the words to 'Blue Sister' urging her not to drive her lover away as this could be potentially fatal for him. Whether this would be because of drugs or something even more sinister like suicide is not entirely clear.

Interestingly one of the lines of the verses, repeated three times throughout the song is the narrator expressing that he cares about 'Blue Sister'. A sting in the tail perhaps? A secret declaration of love for her? Or more likely just empathetic reference to her situation and worries. The drug references though admittedly vague were probably the reason why it wasn't considered as a single although of course they had managed to get away with it before with 'Golden Brown' also it was an atypical Stranglers number so might have confused fans and any potential wider audience.

*****

The style of the song blends in with the previous songs on side two but with a different feel that is immediately established by the heavy delay on the keyboard chords and then the held guitar which also uses considerable delay.

The bass and drums have more of a natural sound to them. The low keyboard riff which is then followed by the fast drum pattern being established and then has another riff on top of the keyboard riff. This riff has vocal "ahhs" and the guitar in unison and the extended intro with different sub sections lasts almost one minute, reminding us of earlier albums where such intros were commonplace.

But the entire intro is based around two chords and is lacking in real melodic invention until the backing vocals enter after forty-three seconds, relying instead on the sounds being created. A comparison of this intro to most of the longer intros on *The Raven* for example highlights the richness of melodic invention on that album and, at times, the paucity of ideas on *Feline*.

There is, however, a sense of expectation from the overall arrangement of the intro but the rest of the song does not live up to these expectations. The vocal melody does not sit with ease over the instrumental accompaniment with a lack of stylistic consistency that was not the case with the two previous songs, 'All Roads Lead To Rome' and 'Paradise'.

Furthermore, there are unusual weak performance moments. Vocally, the first note "Blue" and the last note "Cry" of the first phrase for example are unconvincing, as is some of the timing by the bass in the intro and the keyboards in the middle instrumental section where the band all play the same chords and rhythm.

The unconvincing chord pattern for the second "That scene's not a new one to you" section further destabilises the song as it jars with the potentially interesting melodic shape of the vocals. For once, Greenfield's choice of sound for the chords in this section does not help the song to flow in a way that the intro was clearly developing.

The following instrumental section where all the band are performing the same rhythm contains, as already mentioned, performing inaccuracies which are highlighted by the general mix being very dry. Furthermore, this section is too similar to the instrumental section in 'Four Horsemen' from *The Gospel According To The Meninblack* album, but inferior as the latter song had cascading keyboards over the top, as well as the interesting rhythmic changes and the more forgiving, less dry, mix.

When this instrumental section is repeated there is a more convincing feel with the extra chordal effects and entry of the drum pattern. And the end of the song returns, thankfully, to the intro but with an added guitar solo that seems a little half hearted, a few backing vocals and the delayed keyboards finally taking centre stage. These additions almost seem like an afterthought as the song is already fading out, whereas a more prominent final section would have benefitted the song.

Never Say Goodbye

For the final track on the album the band go back to a more obvious musical arrangement of acoustic instrumentation with electronica found earlier on the album. The three preceding tracks had seen electronics dominating. This had an arrangement that saw more of a balance between the two styles similar to a song like 'European Female'. The band had a reputation for finishing an album with inspired longer songs that often became live favourites e.g., 'Down in the Sewer' and 'Genetix'.

Even less favoured album closers like 'La Folie' or 'School Mam' had an edge or an interest to them so 'Never Say Goodbye' had some tough acts to follow. The band appear to be trying to do what they had done so brilliantly earlier in their career by bringing in different musical ideas but here it doesn't quite meld together, and the result is that the ideas are not fully realised. To be frank as a closing song it is a little too understated and underwhelming.

The words refers to past friends who have passed and to previous lovers and the fact that even after the end of a friendship, a death or the end of a love affair, the relationship isn't totally finished because they will be reunited either through memories that pop into the mind or as the lyrics imply in an afterlife.

It's interesting that Cornwell is prepared to countenance an afterlife, or some form of continuation given his scientific background, however it shouldn't be a surprise as he does have clear interest in religion and spirituality as many of his songs attest. The idea for the lyric is potentially interesting but compared to many other album closers it is a little insipid and sentimental.

The overall result is that the elements to make it a great Stranglers song are present but it lacks a magic spark of creativeness, it all feels as if they are all trying a bit too hard to make it happen and result is the song feels forced rather than inspired the outro sums this up with attempts to create a dynamic finish like "Genetix but in the end there just a fade out as no one can find the definitive finish.

*****

Like 'It's A Small World' on side one, there is an understated acoustic guitar chord-based intro but here this mood leads us fittingly into the verse section. This section links us back to the semitonal chordal relationship that dominated side one and gave the Spanish feel and Greenfields's piano riff reinforces this mood. The vocal melody also carries the semitonal flavour and, rarely for this album, Burnel produces a bass line of melodic interest.

The three-part melodic interplay of the piano, vocals and bass at the same time move us towards the multi-melodic textures of old and the verse consequently moves along apace.

The chorus continues with a similar multi-melodic texture, but the chords have become more conventional.

The bass continues with a more melodious line under the conventional chorus chords which, whilst raising a question as to whether a more conventional root-based bass line would have been more appropriate due to the cleaner, laid-back feel of the song, reminds us of many wondrous moments from previous albums.

The piano riff in the chorus with its triplet cross rhythm helps to bind the song along with the prominent acoustic guitar chords. The drum pattern is conventional with bass drum on every beat throughout the verse and chorus, standard hi-hat and snare, every fourth beat in the verse and doubled to beats two and four for the chorus.

One simple fill at the end of the chorus where the bass drum plays quick notes leaves us feeling underwhelmed and pining for one of Black's more complex fills and a more complex rhythmic pattern that could have added much more to the verse. The end of the chorus leads us briefly into a backing vocals moment which, once again, has a question mark over its effectiveness as it seems to be another attempt to use a musical device to move the song on.

The instrumental section that follows the third chorus starts promisingly as the two initial chords are unconventional and reinforce the Spanish feel. But they are followed by a forced set of chords that move down semitonally and, once again, suggest throwing in a trusted musical device to fill a gap. The final chorus does finally see Black producing a series of different drum fills that add momentum to the long fade, but the lingering feeling remains that the bass is jarring with the more conventional piano riff and acoustic guitar.

There is considerable interest within the song especially with effective melodies and piano riffs supported by the interest of the bass, but it lacks a sense of dynamism and that hinders the album having an effective climax.

Musical Summary

The change of direction resulted in newer fans now on board following the success of 'Golden Brown'. And the chart success of 'European Female' following on from 'Golden Brown' and 'Strange Little Girl' meant that three singles had achieved top 10 status, following the previous seven singles all failing to reach the top thirty.

This resurgence in singles chart success resulted in *Feline* being one of their bestselling albums. But some older fans who had struggled with the idiosyncrasies of *The Gospel According To The Meninblack* and the three minute pop songs of *La Folie* were really stretched to breaking point and for many the laidback, acoustic approach of *Feline* was the final insipid straw.

The distinctive sound that created the early success for the band had disappeared. The aggressive mid ranged melodically driven bass had been replaced by a much softer sound that now played mainly the root notes of the chords in traditional rhythmic patterns. There was very little electric guitar, never mind any beautifully crafted melodic solos that so distinguished Cornwell's instrumental contribution on the earlier albums.

Black's drums had become completely electronic and were often repeated conventional patterns, the antithesis of the unconventional patterns that frequently changed during previous albums that were crucial to the overall soundscapes of those songs.

Greenfield's keyboards remained to the fore but with the other three band members softening up, his choice of sounds inevitably had to move in that direction as well. Occasional use of harder keyboard sounds like during the second half of the main section and the ensuing instrumental section of 'Blue Sister' now jarred with the overall sound. Clashing dissonance was also far less frequent and suffered a similar fate in sounding out of place within the overall less edgy sound. Most of all, the aggressive vocal delivery that blended to these sounds with so much energy had completely vanished.

The songwriting was varied and some of the devices that made the songs stand out as different to the norm on the previous albums were fleetingly used. The creative multi-melodic layering texture was now employed far less. Time signature changes were absent. The long varied instrumental sections were, overall, shorter with more of these sections being related to verse or

THE STRANGLERS
'Feline'
(Epic EPC 25237) **½

I ALWAYS get Stranglers albums to review. It is like a habit. And it has become as boring in every sense that the word implies. Stranglers, like (sort of) SLF, are (sort of) punks who have counted out time quite successfully since the days of threat were over. You wish they'd have disappeared by now. (Sort of) embarrassing.

'Feline', quite simply, is Stranglers continuing their present blandness. That is, blandness-that-they-hope-isn't-blandness. They try to suggest a dark threat still in the last few singles and albums. 'It only looks like a sell-out kids, but it's still black and evil and just you wait!'

It's more to do with luck, of course. It was a brace of fluke lachrymose 45s that set Cornwell and co off on their end of career sentimentality.

'Feline' is immensely passable — it is like an untalented Steely Dan cruising through some b-sides — but it shows the two distinct ways in which you can look at the Stranglers these days.

Firstly, superficially, 'Feline' (an album asleep on its feet) reveals Cornwell and Burnel, burned by their erstwhile solo LP flops, still hanging on to the vestiges of their former (in vain) intellectualizing (Burnel's European ideal, Hughie's mysticism) whilst admitting, in harness with the other two, that they really have hit on an easily turned out gold-mine in the formula revealed in 'Golden Brown'. It's called eating your cake while you theorize on its texture.

And it really is a gold-mine! What with the boys now getting quite aged, such low-paced cruising as 'Feline', wherein not a drop of sweat is shed, is a nice way of making a living while — especially for Hugh who, as on the last, has the majority of the spotlight — your morals don't get too shaken.

In truth, the 'mysticism' of 'Feline' is superstitious hokum. Most of all, its accompanying bland and obvious and determinedly uninspiring backing track renders it conservative, middle-class and rather parochially English Eccentric. Like a bad episode of The Avengers.

Hugh's cerebralizing, in the end, is as relevant and as ironically Mary Whitehouseian as a Fiftie's episode of Tonight or Probe.

On the other hand — the hand that habit makes me go naturally for — 'Feline' can be seen, just as ABC's and League's current postulating can be seen, as successfully marking out time, keeping your end in there and fighting, while we're all waiting for another punk rock to come.

Stranglers have not essentially 'sold out'. They are still clinging to some semblance of career continuity like good 'uns. There are still ideas there, just as a fluke.

'Feline' is Stranglers' engine ticking over so slowly it's practically stuttering to a creative halt. It's still going though, and this leaves room for a sudden (Next album? One after that? Will it still be me?) inexhaustive revving up to full, first album power again.

Certainly, with the luck they have had this far, they are entitled to their own slice of immortality. Old superstitious Prof Cornwell will be pleased!

DAVE McCULLOUGH

chorus sections thus giving a sense of filling out songs rather than injecting them with new ideas. The chords themselves veered more and more towards the conventional and the overall mix was in a far drier eighties style. Most of this had begun to be signposted on the previous album, *La Folie*, but whereas that album had been seen as a mix of the old and new, *Feline* was undisputedly camped in the latter.

It is difficult to compare the strength of songs when faced with the completely different styles of the first five albums although many would agree that, overall, the songs were weaker than on *La Folie*. There were, of course, some standout songs where enough of the older musical devices were convincingly married to the new style and 'Midnight Summer Dream', 'Paradise' and, to a lesser extent, "European Female, celebrated this new approach.

One can never accuse the band of resting on their laurels and one can only applaud their stylistic changes that marked each album following the first two albums that were essentially the same style. And *Feline* had some commercial success. But the band were defined by those established musical devices mentioned above and consequently stood out from the crowd up until now.

Ultimately, *Feline* was virtually a new band sound, and many would have preferred the approach of the musical evolution of *Black And White* and *The Raven* rather than a musical revolution of *Feline* which led to the band sounding very similar to many other bands of the time.

Album Summary

So, a new label, a new musical direction and a new album but some things remained stubbornly the same particularly in the UK despite a top 10 hit to proceed it, the album failed to set the world alight with sales. It broke into the Top 10 and was the band's best opening week chart performance since *The Raven* but then a familiar tale of only selling to a niche market continued.

Further single releases failed to resurrect the albums decline. However, the album did break the band in France and it charted in other countries like Germany, Netherlands and Norway for the first time, with respectable rather than mega sales in those territories. Clearly there was interest in the album in wider Europe hence it's one of the reasons why it became known as the "European" album also many of the song had a European themes and musical styles.

The important thing from the band's point of view was that they had made a clear statement – they had radically changed their style and were saying to the world this is what we are now. It can't be overemphasised what an incredibly brave artistic and commercial decision this radical change of style was. The rock 'n' roll arena is littered with the corpses of bands who decide to change direction with a radical transformation of style or a weird concept album which then destroyed their career and had the music press queuing up to butcher their ambition and fans deserting a band as if it were a sinking ship, refusing to hand over their hard earned cash on what they consider a huge indulgence.

The Stranglers had embraced both of these ideas, the weird concept album and the radical change in style and had continued to sell records and gain new fans. This was no small achievement and many of their contemporaries weren't so lucky. The Skids got away with one concept album but when they tried another, a Scottish folk album called *Joy* it bombed, despite being an artistic triumph and the result was the band split within a couple of months.

Magazine lost their seminal guitarist John McGeoch the resulting album without him in a new style couldn't get them arrested in terms of sales and was further damaged when lead singer and lyricist showed no faith in the new material and left before it was released, These are just two examples of bands destroyed by failing to take the fans with them when they made a significant artistic change.

The sound and feel of the album has worn well over the years. Only the excessive sound of the electronic drum programming particularly the snare grates and dates it. The originally Idea to work with acoustic guitars and electronic keyboards and drums is not fully realised across every track.

Tracks on side two are more electronic based which again supports the concept of the album being "European sounding". It's a gentle slow burner of a record which rewards with extended listening. It does lack a strong up tempo number that all previous albums had had but this was a deliberately ploy as the band were keen to show off their subtler, gentler side and perhaps the product of both the fact all the band were in love and the recreational drugs they were using.

Although there are great songs on the album, for example the three singles which were all in a new style. Other tracks were very good, 'All Roads Lead To Rome' and 'Ships That Pass In The Night' whilst others were less memorable, well-crafted but lacking a bit in inspiration.

In addition, there wasn't the quantity of tracks to choose from when putting the track listing together. Looking at the B-sides coupled with the singles, only 'Permission' was a high quality song. 'Pāwshēr' could have been great but without a proper lyric it was merely a filler. Was the band's creative well drying up?

These issues and others needed addressing. Sales were a potential issue but with the album breaking into new territories there was no real record company pressure at this moment. The band must have thought about who their audience actually was now, a large part of the old guard stemming from punk was still with them and perhaps the biggest contingent, but it had waned considerably since the days of the first two albums.

There was a newer audience which arrived with 'Golden Brown' who appreciated the softer side of the band. Unfortunately, the new fan base wasn't large enough to replace those that had fallen by the wayside since 1977. The band still had a considerable following and despite a rocky patch in the very early eighties seemed able to once again guarantee hit singles and albums something many other bands would have killed for.

But America still remained a pipe dream despite their new record company being American owned. The stumbling blocks to crack America were considerable. First there was their reputation of being difficult, then there was them being unprepared to put in the time touring there extensively. Finally, there was their name. Bible belt America was unlikely to embrace a band with such a shocking name. In this country the band had managed to lose the shock value of the name. It was an outrageous name in common sight that because of the band's longevity and mellower later material had totally lost its shock value.

Another concern for the band was that Burnel was becoming less productive as a writer. On *Feline* and *La Folie* combined he had only brought a total of four songs to the table, but their quality was undeniable however it meant the song writing and lead singing burden was falling more and more to Cornwell.

In the studio Burnel was still having his say on the material as a whole but there was a noticeable change in the style of his playing. He was less upfront and the runs were less complex and driving. He was becoming a more traditional bass player, accompanying the songs rather than driving them. At the time this was fine as the softer material needed this. His accompanying bass on 'Midnight Summer Dream' and 'European Female' are to key to making them stunning songs. At the same time the creative dynamic was changing, inevitably they weren't the same gang from the early days, the all in it together approach was changing.

Cornwell lived in different part of the country to the others and working together required a lot of travel for him. Also because of their proximity Greenfield and Burnel were becoming closer and collaborating more which bore fruit in later band recordings and in their own collaborative album *Fire and Water*.

The question for the band was did they carry on with the acoustic/ electronic approach which to be honest they hadn't maintained over *Feline* or did they take some elements of that approach and build on that with another new slant added in. There was also a question of a producer. The band had effectively not had a producer for four albums. Maybe now there was need for a person with fresh ears and a detached approach to get the most out of any new material, act as a referee when it was needed and suggest new ideas which might be out of the bands comfort zone. The record company weren't insisting on a producer but certainly wouldn't stand in the bands way if they wanted a name producer.

B-sides

Savage Breast (B-side to 'European Female')

A dreamy floating keyboard melody allows the song to drift along. In the background the programmed electronic drums contrast to this feeling operating in an unrelenting almost restless way. It jars against the soothing melody and creates a tension.

Lyrically Cornwell is again working on more than one level with his words and also indulging his passion for taking well known sayings and putting them in song titles. The phrase in the title is from restoration playwright William Congreave from the play *The Mourning Bride*. The original quote was "Music has charms to soothe a savage breast" (often misquoted as savage beast). So Congreave is talking literally about the healing power of music. Cornwell on the other hand is initially talking about the healing power of music at the start of the song, however in the same verse he changes the emphasis, making it clear that music is an image for a woman he is in love with and whose love can sooth his savage breast.

A great example of The Stranglers using word play and as with so many songs the meaning isn't quite what you might have originally thought. It's the literary equivalent of what they do with the musical accompaniment on so many songs there is far more to it than one might have originally thought both lyrically and musically.

Although the song was the B-side to 'European Female', in truth it was more than good enough to have made the album. It fits the theme of the album perfectly as does the acoustic and electronic arrangement. Allied to this with the quality of music and lyrics and it's a better song than the straightforward 'Last Tango In Paris'.

*****

A change of time signature accompanies the intro, a rare event for the band these days. Three beats in bar one followed by four beats in bars two with conventional open fifth chords on guitar and bass. Once the vocal enters, the music reverts to four beats per bar. The well-shaped vocal melody over a fairly wide range is well supported by the held guitar chords, with effects including considerable delay.

The bass is interestingly reminiscent in parts of earlier reflective bass lines like 'Don't Bring Harry' and 'Outside Tokyo' but with a now standard soft tone. There is a soft swirling keyboard riff allied to the bass and vocals helping to create something of a multi layered melodic feel that adds to the dreamlike atmosphere much established by the mellow vocal tone, as does Black's electronic drum pattern. This has some interesting different patterns on the toms and avoids some of the sharper sounds that arguably jarred on some of the songs on *Feline*.

Unfortunately, the song fails to develop as the chorus retains the same texture and the ensuing repeats are the same texturally with a rather unimaginative spoken vocal halfway through to accompany the intro repeat. The final third of the song is a long fade out over the one-line chorus but with an accompanying slow rising keyboard scale on a rather harsh sound but, thankfully, low in the mix. Some backing vocals enter as the song is well into the fade which should have entered earlier and been given more importance. It's a shame that the creativity that clearly stands out in this song was not supported with a few more additional ideas as this could have transformed it into a highly effective piece.

Pãwshēr (B-side to 'Paradise')

Atmospheric dreamy and mixes electric guitar with synths. It basically an instrumental despite 'Pãwshēr' the only word on the track being intoned at various intervals. As the track progresses the guitar gets more processed and busier and it's in the background of the mix providing a soundscape. It is very reminiscent of the style of Charlie Burchill from Simple Minds. It's one of the few times we really hear Cornwell play like this and use guitar effects to such a degree. The result is a hypnotic backing track that is crying out for lyrics.

'Pãwshēr' or Porcia was the wife of Brutus and was immortalised in Shakespeare's *Julius Cesar*. So potentially there was fertile ground for an interesting lyric which sadly didn't come to pass. The name is also associated with expensive fast cars (Porsche) and indeed Cornwell stated that the backing made him think of the car. He sings the word in a swooning style which one can imagine being used in a lifestyle advert for the car.

The delivery implies a lost in love state and fantasising of owning your dream car. It also implies a longing for a woman called 'Pãwshēr'. In addition by choosing to spell the name this way Paw....sher we also get an oblique reference to the album title. The name suggests a feline state and the spelling obviously can relate to a cat's mitt. An interesting musical experiment but was only ever destined to be a B-side.

*****

The bass is in a major tonality whereas the keyboards are clearly minor, but the difference is subtly effective. The electronic drum pattern begins very conventionally but soon adds interesting toms and then remains repeating throughout as does the bass. The guitar adds textures with various riffs all of which have considerable delay on them and there are always two different guitars, one panned hard left and the other panned hard right, thus reinforcing the dreamlike, swirling quality.

These riffs change throughout, often high pitched and then often low pitched, occasionally more conventional chords but more often clashing and the two guitars are always playing similar ideas. It may have been interesting for Cornwell to have combined a high-pitched idea in one ear with a low-pitched idea at the same time, but this may have detracted from the soothing, dreamlike atmosphere.

Because the bass, drums, vocals, and the string sound of the keyboards are constant, the guitar has the space to move around in pitch and style with the different sonic ideas thus providing the gradual sense of movement within the piece. The repeating vocal riff of two long softly sung notes add more lush harmonies as the piece progresses.

The keyboard string sound and chords are very similar to 'It's A Small World' and is in the same key. On the one hand, an effective soundscape with subtle guitar layers that create a pleasing dreamlike quality but, on the other hand, the lack of new sections or ideas are out of step with most of the band's instrumentals and leave a sense of wanting somewhat more from almost five minutes of music.

Permission (B-side to 'Paradise' 12-inch)

A reggae influenced track, which as we have already seen is not unusual for The Stranglers. Some of the classic reggae instrumentation and sounds inhabit the track. In places Cornwell's guitar emulates a melodica sound beloved of reggae great Augustus Pablo and then on the keyboards the bass heavy synth sound, so key to Bob Marley's sound and break through. There also elements of dub with use of echo and reverb.

What we have here is an unusual item, a Stranglers' protest song. A few songs in the past for example fit this bill but not many. They had written songs that reflected protests of a kind about personal issues – 'London Lady', might match that niche. However, they had not written such an obvious anti-ruling class song, it could be The Clash circa *London Calling* or *Sandinista* in style and content.

Lyrically we have references to police brutality, tear gas and rioting. This reflects Britain of the early eighties when cities erupted in protest against government policies and heavy-handed policing. Choosing reggae as a medium to make their point echoes the times as well as their musical peers both black and white used reggae to attack the system.

Reggae was the language of protest cutting its revolutionary teeth in its birthplace, the island of Jamaica from the early seventies. In the late seventies reggae found an ally in punk and a hybrid movement. Punky reggae grew up with bands like Misty in Roots, Steel Pulse, The Clash and the whole Two-Tone movement riding this wave.

These bands dealt almost exclusively in diarising the urban protest of the time. As we have seen, The Stranglers were also influenced by this movement which was reflected in the style on some songs and in 'Permission's' case the lyrics as well.

There was also a European revolutionary angle to the song as well. The band and their fans had experienced heavy-handed policing in Nice in France first hand following a riot after a promoter failed to provide proper power resources for the gig to go ahead. The lyrics allude to this event in what appears to be a clever Cornwell pun:

But when the trouble hits the fan
they never shed tears for the banned

The obvious reading of this is that as a protest progresses and turns sour the authorities have no sympathy for the protesters and the treatment meted out to them by the police. However there is potentially another interpretation to the lyric. The key words are "fan" and "banned". The first line appears to be a polite way of saying "When the shit hits the fan" and image of excrement flying everywhere.

However, give fan its other meaning i.e., fanatic, a fervent supporter of a cause or organisation or a band and the line has a different meaning. It becomes a fan of the band being hit by a third party, the police.

In the next line turn "banned" into "band" and you have the idea of the police having no sympathy and no compassion for the band following their arrest in Nice. This maybe stretching things but it certainly an interesting line of thought whether it was intentional or unintentional. The title is an ironic one as it is basically implying protesters have to ask permission to be allowed to make their point but the whole point of protest is that it is not about asking for permission.

The use of the single word and the whole point of lyric is that protest is a right that no one, including the police have a right to deny it. The sad fact is that such an approach by the authorities, as Cornwell accurately observes, "turns protest into pain".

The song is a hidden gem secreted on the B-side of a failed single. It is worthy of a much higher profile. However great a song it is, it clearly doesn't fit the *Feline* vibe or style. A shame such a quality song has been missed by so many fans.

*****

At last Black's drums sound more natural again for the reggae inspired groove. Burnel's bass line is also typically reggae with the very first riff employing the triplet cross rhythmic feel that is very common for this style. There is a surprising lack of 'off beat' guitar to reinforce the style but the keyboards make up for this with two different parts panned left and right at the same time. The second half of the verse, "I try to thread the needle's eye" moves the rhythm into more complex moment where Greenfield adds a triplet idea and Black adds toms so there is now a subtle complexity to the different cross rhythms.

The chorus sees Greenfield move onto new ideas, still playing two different riffs panned left and right, on one of his harder synth sounds that blends in here to high effect. The added backing vocals produce an effective harmony and blend in with the style as do the conventional chords.

Cornwell's almost deadpan, at times precise delivery belies the protest nature of the song which was common for the style. But the song is too long. It moves along jauntily for three verses and choruses to reach exactly the halfway mark of two and a half minutes. A brief instrumental and repeat of the chorus would have been sufficient but the second half of the song is much ado about nothing and the opportunity for a highly effective song becomes lost in the uneventful, protracted second half.

(The Strange Circumstances which lead to) Vladimir and Olga

(B-side of 'Midnight Summer Dream')

The first song of what was to become a series of songs featuring Vladimir. The others in the series appeared as B-sides on future singles except one of the series which appeared on Burnel's and Greenfield's side project album *Fire and Water*. It's The Stranglers being humorous, and the idea was to make the story ongoing through future tracks. Greenfield leads the melody which is ongoing through future tracks with an Eastern European musical backdrop.

The story recounts a bad acid trip during a road trip. Vladimir and Olga are travelling to Odessa in the Ukraine which was then part of the Soviet Union. The hallucinations are caused by mouldy bread the two travellers consume. The narrator's senses are heightened by chemicals he has imbibed, and he starts to question the normality of his life. The sensory experience is added to by studio effects and deep-toned manic laughing giving similar unsettling effect found on 'Waltzinblack'. An interesting curio and an archetypical B-side.

*****

There are various similarities between this quirky piece and 'Waltzinblack' from *The Gospel According To The Meninblack* album.

It is primarily an instrumental but the with spoken word over it. It is in 3/4 waltz time. It commences with just keyboards using an eccentric sound and builds up adding more layers with various repeats. Even the ending has the laughing backing vocals. The main difference is that 'Waltzinblack' was a pure instrumental whereas the music here is clearly composed to support the bizarre spoken message, so both the chords and melody therefore have an eastern European folk song feel.

Like 'Waltzinblack', the chords are, in the main, conventional and the crucial third chord (the flattened second) at the opening of 'Waltzinblack' that gives the pieces much of its eerie flavour is present here as well over the "I'd worked hard" lyric.

Another similarity between the two pieces is the keyboard playing octaves of the same, or similar melodies. In 'Vladimir and Olga', the main melody is played in octaves from the very start and is panned with the lower octave left and the higher octave right. On "Some simple fare" the keyboards split into harmonies and continue with another soft mysterious sounding keyboard providing another melody.

So, as in 'Waltzinblack', the different melodies are building up at the same time. Following "The old wives' tale of bread mould madness" the bass joins in the melodic layering with an interesting subtle descending line as other spooky keyboard sounds are introduced.

On "I laughed and ate" further keyboard ideas enter, once again in a very similar vein to 'Waltzinblack' with the high-pitched chordal arpeggios albeit less piercing here than in 'Waltzinblack'. Black joins in with a simple mid-range tom on the first beat of every bar but as the next section arrives, he moves to a quicker bass drum as the piece becomes more and more disturbing or mouldy bread drug inducing.

An echo added to the voices appears to add to the disconcerting atmosphere. The final section sees the piece fading out over an even more urgent drum tom pattern and the "lahs" and rather manic laughing.

Musically there is much to admire about this comedic song and anything that transports us back to the glory of the opening of *The Gospel According To The Meninblack* album is well worth a listen.

Aural Sculpture Manifesto (single track 7-inch single, free with initial copies of *Feline*)

Another humorous track and the band once again pointing to the future with the title and concept of their next album. Worth noting that perhaps more than any other band The Stranglers appeared to have a career plan for releases, this was the fourth time either on record or in the press the band had overtly talked about future releases whilst promoting their current album.

Cornwell berates the pop music scene in a received pronunciation accent in a sketch which is a surreal joke done in the style of *Monty Python's Flying Circus* or *The Goons*. One can imagine John Cleese or Peter Sellers delivering the speech. Of course, it's meant to be funny but at the same time makes the valid point about lesser musicians corrupting music by not really understanding now it works.

It echoes an album released at the time by the Hafler Trio, *"BANG" - An Open Letter*. This record and subsequent releases by the group contained manifestos with a similar theme as the 'Aural Sculpture Manifesto' by warning about the danger of sound if it isn't handled by experts, quoting scientific and technical papers and experts to back up their assertions. The Hafler Trio were later to reveal it was all a hoax and their sources and scientific evidence were all false.

Greenfield talks through the technical spec of his synth in a slightly speeded up voice adding to the humour and making it even more like a *Goons* or *Monty Python* sketch. The backing musical track featuring Greenfield on synthesiser.

It probably fooled a few people into taking it as a serious statement rather than a surreal joke. It is witty in a clever way but not exactly belly laugh material or essential listening.

*****

There is very little music of note with just a series of random, bird like quickly played keyboard dissonances until Black gives us a simple snare pattern to herald Greenfields triumphal heavy chords at the end. Perhaps a wasted opportunity to provide a witty musical backdrop that was successfully achieved with 'Vladimir and Olga'.

Footnotes

1. Official Chart website

2. Official Chart Website

3. Official Chart Website

4. Official Chart Website

5. NME February 1982 Simon Dell archive

Aural Sculpture

The band began working on the follow up to *Feline* in late 1983. At around the same time Burnel and Greenfield released their collaborative album *Fire and Water* which scrapped the bottom reaches of the album charts No. 94 for a week.[1]

In terms of further group activity formal recording for what was to become *Aural Sculpture* began in February 1984. The band were in an industrious creative phrase and producing themselves. They finished eight songs in three weeks, were still writing material and so with more in the tank they booked further time in the same studio in Belgium for the early summer. However, there was a spanner in the works, on hearing the work in progress Epic rejected what had been produced and basically told the band they needed a producer. Potentially this could have been a flashpoint between band and label, but the band and particular Cornwell felt it is what they needed. A few names were mooted but the band quickly agreed to Epic's first choice Laurie Latham.

Latham was a name producer cutting his teeth in the late seventies with Ian Dury and the Blockheads album *New Boots And Panties* and their number one single, 'Hit Me With Your Rhythm Stick'. In 1983 he produced Paul Young's album *No Parlez*, a huge international smash with production and sound that defined the eighties with its heavily synthetic textures particularly around the drums, bass and brass.

After *No Parlez* every big record seemed to have the splash of the plastic Simmons drum kit and the warbling wobble of the fretless bass. Bringing Latham and The Stranglers together was certainly going to be interesting. Because of his work with Paul Young and its associated commercial success Latham was 'the' producer of the time. A talented individual who also combined being an engineer with being a producer. Initially he worked on 'Skin Deep' which was deemed a success by all parties, so Latham was brought on board for the whole album.

One of Latham's first suggestions was that some of the songs would benefit from a brass section. The band had used a single saxophone on a couple of tracks in the past ('(Get A) Grip (On Yourself)' and 'Hey! (Rise Of The Robots)' but a three-piece section on three tracks was a totally new departure.

Brass was very much in vogue at the time in pop music and if it wasn't actual brass, it was that very eighties sound of synths imitating brass. The band embraced the change in style, so much so that they took a brass section on tour with them to promote the album and even rearranged old favourites such a 'Nice 'N Sleazy' and 'Down in the Sewer' so they had a brass component.

Adding a new dynamic to classic songs was not universally popular with sections of the audience who perceived it as ruining a classic song. The brass section flitted in and out of the set and were often booed as they walked on stage by part of the crowd.

The album was preceded by the single in September 1984. 'Skin Deep' released in 7 and 12-inch formats with extra tracks and a remix of the title track on the 12-inch. The single performed respectably reaching No. 15.[2] The album arrived in November peaking at No. 14 in the first week but then dropped like a stone the following week to No. 44.[3]

However, the album then hung around the bottom reaches of the charts eventually clocking up ten weeks in the chart. 'No Mercy' was released in December 1984 in 7- and 12-inch formats, the latter containing the ubiquitous remix. The single hung around for seven weeks but only reached No 37.[4]

A December release is always a gamble, it could lead to extra Christmas sales but also the more likely scenario that it gets lost in the Christmas deluge especially as there was no obvious festive theme to the song. The relatively disappointing chart performance of the single meant it failed to bolster the album sales which by early January 1985 now slipped out of the chart altogether. The record company made another chart bid in February with 'Let Me Down Easy' but despite previously unreleased tracks, remixing the title track and being on both vinyl formats the single it only made 48 in charts.[5]

The concept was loosely the idea of *Aural Sculpture* outlined in the 'Aural Sculpture Manifesto', the track that was released as a free single with initial copies of *Feline*. The idea was in reality a joke with the band taking a swipe at their contemporaries who weren't as musically capable as the Meninblack themselves.

The songs thematically didn't follow a particular concept like the madness of love on *La Folie*. Instead, it was in the way they were constructed, meaning each individual song was a type of aural sculpture. The band members and Latham were the sculptors metaphorically bending and chiselling the sound. The aural sculptures on show were in actual fact much simpler than many of the songs on previous albums.

Songs like 'Genetix', 'Ice' and 'Baroque Bordello' were musically sculptured by the creative structures which incorporated long instrumental passages with melodic ideas, often multi-layered. These songs would seem to be the epitome of aural sculpture. The band of course realised the new songs were nothing like as complex of much of their earlier songs, the band playing another joke on the listener.

The album cover reflected the idea, picturing the band standing with a piece of sculpture entitled *Aural Sculpture*. Interestingly the band had commissioned the work from an artist who happened to be a member of Cornwell's family. The shoot for the cover had occurred months before because the album had originally been planned for a mid-1984 release but following Epic's rejection of the initial tapes saw the album released in late 1984 instead.

The back cover featured four close ups of an ear of each band member just to ensure that the listener gets that the theme is aural. The inner sleeve featured the lyrics on one side and the other side following on from *Feline* there was SIS information and a new photo of the staff but to be frank, apart from the front cover picture the packaging and art work was rather uninspired.

In terms of reviews some of the British press didn't hold back: Sean O'Hagan in the NME continued the vendetta against the band who they basically felt had outstayed their welcome, referring to the songs as "ugly, uninspired and vacuous".[6] Other reviews were kinder but hardly effusive. The music press was still influential at this time and can to some degree be seen responsible for the albums below par chart performance.

As far as band relations went things were different it wasn't exactly a conflict, but issues were starting to get in the way. For instance, Black was now adamant he wouldn't play live drums on recordings. This became a bone of contention with other members as it gave an artificial sound to the recording and meant the other instrumental performances were in perfect time but sounded too clinical. The instruments didn't breathe or ebb and flow like they did on earlier albums.

Using programmed drums had been an interesting musical experiment on *Feline* but for it to become a rigid approach that was never going to change was potentially disheartening, especially as *Aural Sculpture* heralded a return to a more live feel in other areas. Another issue was that Burnel's involvement and writing contribution had become patchy largely due to his father's terminal illness and death during recording.

Cornwell was happy to have the exposure for his songs but ultimately the lessening contribution from Burnel was worrying in terms of the variety and quality of the songs and the pressure it put on the guitarist in the future.

As well as these concerns working in the studio was vastly different than the early days, when the band together worked on songs. Even on later albums like *The Gospel According To The Meninblack* there were strong elements of group collaboration.

In his first act as producer Latham had taken Greenfield to Belgium to work specifically on the keyboards as time went on this was to become the norm with band members working individually or in pairs on songs in the studio. On the plus side drugs were now becoming much less of a problem the cocaine and heroin that had been around the band lessened and then disappeared.

Ice Queen

Approximately two minutes and ten seconds in and BOOM! The brass arrives signalling to the music industry and fans that the band are back with a new musical direction. It's interesting to speculate the sense of surprise fans must have got when they heard the brass stabs so high in the mix. It's almost the band saying 'Boo! That scared you didn't it!' Basically, a musical joke and those naughty mischievous Stranglers shock you again but in a new and different way.

The shock of the brass is made even funnier as although the introduction is dynamic it might have lured some fans into thinking they were getting *Feline* Mk 2, rather than the brighter and upfront collection of songs on show here. The surprise is made even more effective because the instrumental break it arrives in has already been played three times in the song with no brass, but the fourth occasion is a totally different story. The brass can be described as metaphorically roughing up the listener.

The ice queen as an image presents several possibilities it can be a woman who is emotionless or doesn't show her emotions, it can also be an image of death and malevolence as for example the white witch/ice queen, from *The Lion, the Witch and the Wardrobe* who symbolises pure evil. More often such women are often portrayed as being beautiful. Cornwell incorporates much of these tropes into his lyrics. Presenting himself as getting emotionally involved with a woman and this causes her to start to respond emotionally, illustrated by the use of the word melt. He uses a card game as a metaphor for the relationship. The vagaries of good and bad luck in a game represents the topsy turvy nature of all relationships.

Traditionally card games are often used as a metaphor for the jeopardy and used to illustrate a life and death situation e.g., playing poker with the devil for your soul is another age-old literary device. Cornwell isn't quite moving into this area, but the words do hint at it. A card game is about winning so we can transfer that to the situation with the writer actively trying to win over a woman that keeps her emotions a secret.

The main thrust of the song is obviously about a former girlfriend of Cornwell's. He makes some frank confessions admitting to not playing fair in the relationship, we can speculate maybe he cheated on her or maybe he knew she was besotted with him, and he used this to his advantage, but it is not made clear. The word blues is used to describe her, so this implies an unhappy woman. In addition, knowing Cornwell's propensity for sexual innuendo and the fact the song is about woman words used like "laid" and "ride" are deliberately chosen.

The song plays another musical trick late on with a false ending to catch out the first-time listener. All in all, a great and dynamic introduction to the band's new direction. The use of the brass stabs gives the song an element of Stax soul. On other songs on the album there are elements of soul, even those without a horn section but to call it a 'soul' or 'type of soul' album is rather over egging things. The song also demonstrates the difference a producer makes. It was Latham's idea to use the horn section not the band's and it seems unlikely they would have considered such an musical option without him.

*****

The opening chord of 'Ice Queen' immediately exposes a shift away from its electronic and drier sounding predecessor replaced by a more live feel with the emphasis in the intro of the rising scalic organ riff and the held guitar chords. The telling fact is that the keyboard sound is an organ, and the guitar is electric, coupled with Burnel's low rumbling bass riff that could so easily have been from one of the earlier albums, except for it being lower in the mix.

Even Black's drums, whilst still clearly in the electronic camp, have a more live feel about them with a few more fills and changes of patterns from the norm of the previous album. The overall production is a warmer, less dry sound and the song itself has an alternative feel being different from anything on *Feline*.

At the start we have a feel of the multi-melodic layering that so distinguished some of the earlier albums with the vocal melody working in conjunction with the slow rising organ riff and that low bass riff in the background. Because of the very low pitch of the bass, organ and the vocals, the overall sound could have been rather muddy with only Cornwell's occasional sustained guitar strum providing any higher sounds.

But the mix here is superb and Black's choice of electronic drum sound helps the song to rattle along and avoid any low-pitched fog. The following "I didn't have time" section sees the organ move onto more pronounced quick changing chords to help the drive of the song, and the bass accompanies with conventional root chord notes. The creative organ part is highly effective and moves into a higher range here as does the vocal halfway through but then they all drop back to impressive effect to the opening lower range on "I thought I'd just" with the vocal melody being in unison with the bass and harmonised by the keyboard creating an impressive rhythmic urgency and is crucial later in the song. It feels alive, sounds live and the band are moving forward as one.

The fast-changing chords continue in the new "I knew the Ice Queen" section maintaining the drive but there is also a deliciously subtle unconventional chord pattern here that is hidden by the smooth and conventional vocals with added vocal harmony. There are two additional keyboard sounds, a percussive chord with multiple delay and a well-crafted melodic riff just after "I knew the Ice queen". These additional ideas help the song to continue moving with purpose and creativity. When this section is repeated, the melody is the same but is sung faster with the accompanying chords shortened in length.

Suddenly the brass enters, playing the "I thought I'd just" riff that was previously played in unison. Another impressive mix here as the brass section really do cut in with high effect, accompanied by Black's snare in rhythmic unison. Whatever fans views of the use of the brass, there can be no disputing the effectiveness of the way the different sounds are melded together, and it does, in an instant, move the album further away from the electronic feel of the previous album into a more live feel.

These different sounds move along to great effect with the new brass riffs at the end of each vocal phrase having a slightly dissonant, clashing quality whilst the two low held brass notes add further textural complexities.

There is so much going on and a song that perhaps would have melted into the background with the icy Euro pop *Feline* treatment, is brought to life here with the energetic arrangement allied to the traditional melodic creativeness of the band and the additional brass. After the "I knew the Ice queen" section is repeated Burnel adds a welcomed presence with a return to songs of old, with some exuberantly restless higher pitched reverbed notes and slides.

This is immediately followed by everyone, including the brass, engaging forcefully in the "I thought I'd just" riff followed by four beats of silence and then the highly effective low held brass notes return to take us to the fade out whilst Greenfield treats us to some distorted high pitched keyboard notes, reminiscent of sounds from *The Gospel According To The Meninblack* album, that are panned quickly from ear to ear.

The structure is inventive with the additional ideas ensuring no moments of loitering which drives 'Ice Queen' successfully along, successfully integrates the brass, and develops the song into a wonderfully creative and complex piece of music that sets the new direction of the band in full flow.

Skin Deep

Latham shows what else he could bring to the table as a producer and engineer with the majestic simmering 'Skin Deep'. This was the first track he worked on with the band and more specifically Greenfield. When Latham heard the original recordings, the band had produced for the album he decided that this was the song he could make most difference to. Working with Greenfield he came up with the track as it is here. The band and the record company were knocked out by what he had added. On the back of passing this audition Latham was awarded the prize of doing the whole album.

It is without doubt a beautiful song and the production is stunning, delicate and brittle it's like a sonic honeycomb. The keyboards and tremolo guitar give the song a lustrous pulsing, simmering sheen whilst Cornwell's crooned up vocals perfectly complement the music effect giving the song its distinctive simmer. To many the pièce de résistance, a piece of pop perfection topped off with soaring backing vocals.

We have mentioned the backing vocals several times before but it needs emphasising how technically good Burnel, Cornwell and Greenfield were in close harmony. It's almost like a secret weapon and one the casual listener doesn't expect the band to have, but as we have already seen they have used it countless times before to devastating effect and would continue to do the same throughout their career.

'Skin Deep' is the zenith/high water in terms of backing vocals and harmonies on a song the backing vocals bring a discernible extra dimension to the beauty of the sound that makes the track into a wonderful pop song. Conversely to some listeners the backing vocals on display were too sugary. Although it should be remembered the band were deliberately attempting to be more commercial and weren't going to apologise for sounding so accessible.

Of course, the first single off the album it became a top twenty hit. A hit but disappointingly not top ten or higher despite a picture disc release and a 12-inch mix. Such a stunning piece deserved better. Perhaps fans felt it wasn't Stranglers enough and was too soft and too poppy.

The idiom "Beauty is only skin deep", in other words a person's character is more important than their look is the lyrical drive of the song. Cornwall delivers the message as a warning imploring us to "Watch out for the skin deep" meaning be wary of superficial people in life, don't be taken in by appearance.

Again he plays with a well-known saying not using the whole phrase but enough of it to give us the key to understanding the song. The lyrics aren't specifically about a relationship with a lover or any other kind of relationship but being so unspecific they can fit any situation the listener cares to suggest. The key message is to be wary, be careful and use your judgement and do not fall for shallowness.

The verses and the chorus are beautifully written with a natural flowing rhythm. The lines are written in monorhyme i.e., all rhyme with each other but there is no sense of this being forced or clichéd but just sound naturally poetic because of the careful choice of words.

*****

After the complexities of texture in the opening song, 'Skin Deep' is a very simple song in many ways, not dissimilar to some of the songs from *La Folie*. The chords are very conventional with the main three chords (1,4,5) being used for the majority of the song. The arrangement is also simple with Greenfield's higher pitched riff based on those three chords which is an effective contrast from the lower ranges of 'Ice Queen'.

Cornwell maintains the sustained electric guitar chords, similar to the start of 'Ice Queen' but alternates this with a lower simple riff. The bass and drum parts are simple throughout with the 'kick in' of the fuller lower bass and the introduction of the snare for verse two. The vocal melody has limited shape, but the lyrical message is a strong one that is supported highly effectively by the notion of simplicity.

The addition of the backing vocals for the chorus adds a welcome texture and provides a strong higher melodic foil for the main lower vocal melody, and further contrast is provided from the verse with the guitar replacing, momentarily, the keyboard riff with continuous arpeggiated mid-range chords. The second half of the chorus sees an added high piano riff alternating with the main vocals and the backing vocals still in the higher register.

This adds a layer of commerciality, and it was no surprise that the song was chosen as a single, achieving reasonable success. There is an argument that the high-pitched backing vocals are too twee and could have prevented a higher chart placing, and lower backing could have enhanced the subtly brooding mood of Cornwell's vocal tone in the verses.

The ending sees the main keyboard riff alternate between the major and minor chord whereas it had previously been almost exclusively major. The structure is also very simple with a verse and chorus repeated with nothing else except for another repeat of the second half of the chorus. But the sections are long, and the chorus has two parts to it, so the end result is proportionate. Simple is effective with both the strong lyrical message, the well-shaped backing vocals providing a contrast in pitch to the main vocal, and the effective musical accompaniment proving, yet again that the band had an obvious propensity for stylistic shifts within the first two songs of the album to produce strong outcomes.

Let Me Down Easy

Another beautiful sounding song dealing with the darkest subject, dying. Cornwell wrote the words for Burnel when the latter was going through the trauma of his father dying. Essentially a simple song musically but brilliantly put together, so it is memorable and poignant. There are swaths of synthetic strings which at times give the song in places a peaceful style which actually suits the subject matter perfectly. Greenfield's use of an organ and the deep tone of the backing vocals are reminiscent of ecclesiastical music and singing and places the listener in church during a funeral which perfectly matches the sentiments of the lyrics.

Black's drumming is straightforward, and the sound is softer and wholly appropriate for the subject matter. Interestingly male session singers were used on backing vocals for the first time. In the past the band had occasionally used female backing vocals when required but using a trio of male backing singers was a new departure. It is not clear why session musicians were used as Greenfield and Burnel had dealt admirably with such duties on previous albums and Burnel's contribution to 'Skin Deep' was divine.

According to the album credits Greenfield does no singing at all on the album. Maybe it was thought a few songs needed an added boost or simply it was a sign of the growing distancing of band members and that Burnel and Greenfield weren't around in the studio to add backing vocals. Certainly, the recording process in the band had changed more to individual band members working with the producer on their parts.

The dynamics of the instruments shine through. For example, the piano which punctuates the track sparingly but dramatically adding gravitas. The dynamics of the arrangement are Latham's work. His production and engineering skills enhances a song into a much more interesting listening experience. The words are straightforward, but heart felt. The title alludes to the desire for death when it comes to be painless.

The theme of the song uses the familiar metaphor of comparing death to sleep and Cornwell speaks for us all in his hope that death is a peaceful painless process. The lyrics are sparse and simple but perfect for the sentiment of the song. The constant repetition of the title as the chorus gives the impression of the singer pleading as if pleading for a painless peaceful death to happen. Cornwell also uses the image of a ship sailing on a calm sea and the idea of weightlessness which are common images for death. The combined effect of all the songs element creates a sympathetic and caring memorial for the passing of a loved one and contrasts sharply with that other eulogy song, 'Dagenham Dave' which is no less heartfelt but made in a much more strident even harsher way.

The song was the third single to be released off the album coming out in February 1985 coinciding with the Aural Sculpture tour. It was release in two formats 7 and 12-inch with a special mix on the 12-inch. There were two unreleased tracks, 'Achilles Heel' was on both formats and 'Plaice De Victoires', an instrumental of the title track was added to the 12-inch.

Determined to get a hit Epic also released a double 12-inch special edition of the single which added 'Vladimir Goes To Havana' and the now unavailable 'Aural Sculpture Manifesto' as the other tracks. Despite such inducements for completest fans to buy the single, the release failed to set the charts alight and despite coinciding with the tour it stalled just inside the Top 50.

*****

The bass riff that opens the song uses two minor chords as its basis but when the piano and then guitar enter, they are clearly playing riffs based on major chords thus inducing a clash that continues throughout the song. The vocals are also clearly in the major key. The bass is playing at a low pitch and with a smooth tone, so the clash is not too evident, but it is, nevertheless, an interesting moment for a song that is completely chord based. The clash does not occur in the verses when Burnel retreats to conventional playing of the main notes of the chords.

The conventional chords have a slight twist on the fourth chord of the opening section once the piano enters which is major rather than the traditional minor. The low range of the bass, piano chords, organ riff and the vocal "uhhs" all combine to darken the mood thus supporting the grievous lyrical message.

The only higher pitched sound is the electric guitar which, after a well-crafted opening riff, reverts to two notes being repeated. The main vocal is also low in pitch but the backing vocals that enter along with the start of the main vocal on the "Let me down easy" section are an octave higher and add a slightly haunting quality. The holistic sound therefore contributes to the sombre mood which is necessary as the band chose a mid-tempo groove and the drums are very conventional.

There is an argument that an arrangement without a steady drumbeat could have added poignancy to the song and it would certainly make for a haunting piano solo instrumental as the melodies and subtle chordal shifts are impressive. An example of the subtle chordal shift occurs when the verse is repeated but the chord is different on "Into a calmer sea" than it had been in the first verse. The chord adds a lift due to it being a major third chord rather than the traditional minor so it could be argued that word painting is evident here.

The reinforcement of the low piano sound and the higher backing vocals at the end of the first part of the verse sung with long notes and in harmony on "ea-sy" help to maintain the poignant mood. These backing vocals tempting us into the realms of an ecclesiastical choir. The presence of the organ helps to add to this reverence. The addition of higher strings on "My body slips away" further perpetuates this mood. And the organ solo in the instrumental section that follows also fits the semi religious mood although the fast scalic playing is also reminiscent of the sixties organ solos and invites further comparisons with The Doors. This is probably the first time since 'Walk On By' that the rather tenuous and tedious comparison could be applied.

The vocal melody is effective as is the soft tone of delivery. These create a reflective mood and the "Let me down ea-sy" phrase produces more word painting in both its descending melodic shape after "weight of a hundred years" on "Let me down ea-sy' and also with the spacing out and slowing down of ea-sy.

The fade out highlights the low piano, the opening organ riff, and the mix of main and backing vocals to high effect and the spoken "com-on" at 3.34 sounds particularly heartfelt. The backing vocals repeat "Let me down me down me down..." and there is a higher violin idea which takes the first note of the vocal melody as its starting point which adds to the reflective mood as the song fades, befitting the sad nature of the lyrics.

The song has effective melodies and chord patterns, but the overall subtle and slightly haunting nature of the arrangement allied to the low vocal melody made it a strange choice for a single. It will bring a lump to the throat for many fans understanding the grief of their bass guitarist and, indeed, their own losses.

No Mercy

Another basically simple song which was made great by Latham's arrangement and also his skill at separating the instruments in the mix so that all the parts can be heard making a complete listening experience. We have conventional guitars, electronic drums, real horns and then a variety of synth sounds as well as the session singers that play a significant part in the overall mix. It might not have worked so well if Latham hadn't marshalled the sounds so well and ending up with a sense of spaciousness across the whole album.

The song starts with a simmering synth lick working with Black's programmed rim click that makes the listener think they might be getting a Trans Europe Express Kraftwerk experience. Then the other instruments arrive, and things move in a different direction. Greenfield again is a busy man providing a vibraphone effect at various points as well as peculiar sounding synth riffs.

Lyrically Cornwell tells a tale of life's travails in terms of work and love. "Life has no mercy" meaning life can be cruel and difficult. The first verse finds him discussing being a slave to work for little reward, which could be a swipe at record companies.

In the second verse he wonders if he is getting it right with his lover and suggests that she might have affections for someone else "Will she sooth your brow with kisses only meant for thee?" In later verses he muses that even when things are going well you worry about when things might go wrong, In the verses towards the end of the song Cornwell becomes a kind of agony uncle telling listeners not to worry if their fantasises don't come true, and if you are lucky enough to find love consider yourself fortunate. As a Cornwell lyric goes it straightforward but the words as ever trip nicely together.

The song is ridiculously appealing and therefore was a shoo-in for a single release. It was released in early December 1984 and hit the top 40 in mid-December but then got buried in the Christmas rush despite being released with an innovative 12-inch mix, extra unreleased tracks and a picture disc.

Hopes of a big hit were high. It also received a fair amount of radio airplay but unfortunately only just cracked the Top 40 on the third week of release. It did hang around the bottom of the charts over Christmas for another four weeks which is unusual for a minor hit.[7] Normally after peaking such records drop like a stone and are out of the Top 75 chart within a week or two at the most.

It suggests the sales could have been there to make it a bigger hit if the record company had targeted their promotion in a more efficient way and thought about the timing of its release. The Stranglers never really cracked the single release around Christmas with the failure of 'No Mercy' this time and 'Don't Bring Harry' five years before. However, the releases just after Christmas had spawned two big hits 'Golden Brown' and "European Female. The mid-eighties were also the time when record companies were using a huge amount of different formats and mixes to get fans to buy multiple editions of a single to get all the mixes and unreleased tracks.

There were four formats, including a picture disc used by Epic which was conservative when you compare it to contemporaries Frankie Goes to Hollywood who's record company ZTT released their iconic smash, 'Relax' in a plethora of formats including three different 12-inch mixes.

*****

The introductory sound on keyboard takes us back to *The Gospel According To The Meninblack* album with Black's bass drum on every beat. Cornwell's guitar riff is also something of a throwback to earlier albums, especially with his use of the repeating of the riff but one bar later whilst the first riff continues. This is accompanied by a different, very low, rasping keyboard riff which suggests that the live Brass may have been considered for this song. Black's drum pattern has more of a live feel with the fills that he deploys.

When the vocals enter, the rasping low keyboard riffs continue and halfway through on the "Will it be as tough" line a xylophone or Marimba sound enters adding further interest to the overall sound. Cornwell's delivery is somewhat more agitated than the obviously reflective tone of the previous song and this is a pleasing shift as both 'Ice Queen' and "Skin Deep also have more energy than most of Cornwell's delivery on the previous album, *Feline*. There is a pleasing shape to the melody as it rises in the second half of the verse towards "No mercy".

The chords are static for the first half of the verse and then become more frequent as the verse develops but staying on the side of conventionality. Burnel's sound is more aggressive than in previous songs and albums and, allied to the more live feel of the drums and the vocal delivery, cements the album's considerable move away sonically from *Feline*.

The addition of the backing vocals in "have to wait and see" are unobtrusively softly sung an octave higher than the main vocals. The backing vocals become a central force as the song develops. The second verse sees "Ahhs" followed by rich lower harmonies on "No mercy". As we then enter the second section, the backing vocals add prominent, gospel like harmonies on the final "No mercy".

It is interesting that the band deliberately sought to add new voices into the overall sound and not to use their own distinctly different three voices that had been used on many occasions for backing vocals on previous albums. This certainly adds a new colour to the sound on this and the previous track although it is debateable whether the overall contribution of this new injection adds to the overall sound.

The second section also has an interesting, slightly clashing keyboard riff on a typical Greenfield disturbing sound that also throws us back more to *The Gospel According To The Meninblack* and *The Raven* albums. This riff dovetails neatly with the main vocal and then the "life shows no" line changes again with the return of the xylophone and a more crafted melody to blend in with the backing vocals. These different sounds help the song to move along.

After obvious repeats the long outro sees the backing vocals to the fore, an effective change of the bass note down a tone at 2:57 and an additional floaty guitar chordal idea to add even more to the mix. Perhaps, in days of previous albums, we would have seen some of the instrumental sounds developed into more defined sections, but the band here seem content to continue with the far more conventional pop song structures that have now become the norm. There are many ideas contributing to a strong song and the vocal melodies gave the song potential for chart success but some of the sounds like the otherworldly synth and even the guitar, bass and drums sounds seemed to suggest an effective album track as opposed to the previously successful singles 'European Female' and 'Skin Deep' where every sound had an eye on commerciality.

That said, despite the similarity of tempi for most of side one, each song carries subtle differences of sound and groove to help develop a strong side.

North Winds

A plaintive piano opens the closing track to side one. The guitars and synths combine to provide a beautiful icy atmosphere. As the instruments intertwine Burnel intones in a doom-laden Lou Reed style voice a tale of worldwide woes, half spoken for the verses with a clear melody for the chorus. Having such a minimal vocal melody gives the subject matter added gravitas. Its Burnel's one lyrical and singing contribution to the album as he was understandably preoccupied with his father's terminal illness.

Greenfield punctuates the song with a keyboard instrumental break that combines electronic and string sound effects. In the outro he is back on piano with a flourish, playing some epic piano work to build the song to a finish.

Burnel's lyrics are a heartfelt observation of the horrors of war and an intense critique of the institutions that wage them. The tone is one of disgust and bewilderment with human beings, a theme that links back to some of his other songs e.g., 'Meninblack' and 'Thrown Away', songs in which he was also openly critical of the stupidity and cruelty of the human race. Around the time of the writing in 1984 the Iran Iraq conflict was raging and there were bloody civil wars in Sri Lanka and Eritrea. These events that were reported daily in the news with disturbing footage of the carnage.

The lyrics despite describing scenes of death and destruction are beautifully poetic. The first verse evokes an apocalyptic war that references scenes from the *Terminator* film with machines personified and turning on human beings. In the second verse Burnel turns to the Second World War and the genocide of the Jews and the subsequent birth of Israel.

The chorus is a powerful statement using the metaphor of the north winds blowing as a cleansing force blowing away evil and the destruction. The fact that Burnel states he wishes this is what would happen suggest it is forlorn hope and will not happen, and the winds will not blow away wars because humans' inability to actually want to resolve conflicts. Another take on these lines is to interpret the north winds as the evil force themselves, possibly Hitler like wreaking havoc in the world. Once again, the different the views on lyrics sparking interesting debate and thought.

Much of the imagery used is graphic, he refers twice to young people on fire which brings to mind the Vietnam War and the iconic film of a child suffering napalm burns and a Buddhist monk's protest at the war with self-immolation.

Burnel also appears to target religion after initially saying he wishes he was a believer but then posits what do you believe? A person with a belief is a nonbeliever to another person with a different faith. The listener is left with the metaphorical picture of Burnel holding out his hands in anxiety and shaking his head in disbelief at this insoluble conundrum. In the end he concludes for his own sanity he looks and listens to the ocean to give him inner peace.

The listener can see him in their mind's eye standing on a shore watching and listening as the wind blows in from the sea. One can't help thinking of Raymond Brigg's nuclear holocaust graphic early eighties novel *When The Wind Blows* as any modern war has the capability of going nuclear and the fear of a nuclear wind was prevalent in all human's consciousness at this time.

It also suggests a different, even darker underlying meaning to the piece which is the' 'cleansing' power of a nuclear winter wiping out selfish humanity.

The song brings side one to a natural ending. The Stranglers throughout their career have excelled at closing the first half of an album with a piece that provides a natural break, a song that requires the listener to pause and take stock. For example, 'Hanging Around' and 'Toiler on the Sea' closed side one of their respective albums, giving a rousing finale to the first act. 'North Winds' although more understated does exactly the same and is an extremely well executed and thought-provoking piece from the band and Burnel.

*****

This strength of each song on side one serving up slightly different sonic palette is brought to its consummate conclusion with the final song, 'North Winds'. There is a sublime sparseness to the opening with the quickly arpeggiated piano chords accompanied by the soft rustling of the wind. The choice of a pure piano sound here really adds a reflective authenticity to the proceedings and the entry of the bass and drums are so simple and over just two chords to maintain the sparseness. The guitar chordal riff is also perfectly restrained and is accompanied by two new keyboard sounds, but all the while promoting nervous restraint that seems to predict the doom-laden message that is about to arrive. The calm before the storm.

The entry of the vocals build upon this restraint as Burnel sings in a self-controlled anguished tone and the melody feels half spoken but it is the combination of the restricted notes, often repeating the main chord note, and also the rhythm of the melody that creates this half-spoken feel. It is on the "On a generation" line where the chords change, the melody now moves higher and Burnel's tone becomes more impassioned. And when this is repeated on "the chosen people finally went back" we are led into the chorus with true conviction.

The chorus is beautiful in its simplicity with a highly effective melodic shape that is split into two. The longer notes of the opening phrase "North winds blowing" are contrasted by the quicker and slightly lower "I wish they would blow" phrase. The accompaniment is simple with prominent sustained string keyboard sounds echoing the main melody and plenty of reverb on the main vocal thus merging with occasional moments from the opening piano chords. The last "away" has a momentous low held keyboard chord to add even more depth to an already profound song. The previous restrained guitar chordal riff then merges to great effect with the extra string keyboard parts to bridge us back into the verse.

After the second chorus we are exposed to another of Greenfield's superbly melodically crafted keyboard solos, this time on a violin sound with a lower answering phrase at the end to add even more to this moment. The choice of violin can be associated with a searching emotion in a different way to brass for example and this befits the mood of the song at this point. It feels almost like it is over too soon, but the nature of the song demands brevity and restraint.

The verse then repeats with Burnel impassioned tone sweeping us along with his emotion. The chorus is then repeated to finish the song but here the tension is ratcheted up by the more prominent backing vocal harmonies, including a very low harmony, as Burnel starts to improvise the main vocals, becoming more pained and higher in pitch, whilst the high piano sound from the intro embarks on a solo, becoming even higher in pitch and which contains considerable use of cross rhythms. The final held chord is, appropriately, not the main chord so we are left in a sense of limbo, to ponder on the dystopian message.

Along with the track *The Raven*, this is Burnel's finest vocal from his post aggressive songs as his delivery carries the perfect blend of emotion and the choice of sounds, that start and end with the haunting 'real' piano and use swirls of backing vocals, strings, and guitars. The lack of complex riffs is well judged, and the keyboard violin solo embodies the restraint of the track that, although lasting four minutes, seems to maintain an impressive brevity. This all results in the perfect complement to the strong vocal message to create a highly emotive song.

Uptown

Side two begins with the attention grabbing 'Uptown', a raucous stomping piece which sees Cornwell going back to his early harsher urgent vocal which suits the subject matter of a horse race. The guitar is acoustic, but it's strummed with vigour. There are other embellishments to this simple song with Beach Boy style harmonies in the bridge and robust bottom end synth brass. However, If that wasn't enough there is a radio commentary of a race in the middle to add to the frenzied atmosphere. The number noticeably fades out just as Greenfield appears to be warming up for a solo. The fade outs suggest that the band probably didn't have an ending for the song.

The subject matter appears straight forward as Cornwell describes the excitement of a horse race. It's basically in the style of fifties rock 'n' roll possibly another nod at making an attempt to appease the American market and their American record company. It also demonstrates Cornwell and the band's love for the style of music as they will have all grown up listening to – fifties American rock 'n' roll.

As ever with Cornwell the meaning is not quite what it may seem the underlying meaning becomes clear when you realise the title uptown is street language for a person on cocaine a substance Cornwell was coming off at around this time. Cornwell states that he is going "uptown" which could also be a reference to going to buy drugs similar to the way the Velvet Underground used the phrase in their paean to scoring drugs, 'Waiting For My Man'.

Conversely the opposite term downtown is slang for a person on heroin, another substance the Cornwell was still using. The reference to speed in the lyrics are again euphemisms for cocaine use. Cornwell revealed this in his book *Song By Song* when he corrected his co-author's assertion that the song was about horse racing. The song is littered with the vocabulary of equestrianism e.g. saddle up, crop, steed and jockey so a superficial listen would lead to this conclusion. He is employing a similar device to what he did on 'Golden Brown' and hiding the meaning of the song. Perhaps we should have realised that The Stranglers were unlikely to have written a song about the sport of Kings, horseracing.

However, it must be said this is one of Cornwell's more cryptic metaphors it is hard to garner the subtext of the lyric without the inside information Cornwell's thoughts in his book provide.

This writer was initially taken by the surface meaning and took the metaphor in a completely different way i.e., it's not about horseracing it's about car street racing, the horse analogy is just a poetic way to refer to cars.

The style is fifties rock 'n' roll just as in the song 'Greased Lightning' from the movie *Grease* which is about a car street race. Of course, given the intended meaning of the words this last assertion is faintly ridiculous at best and at worst hilariously inaccurate. The point is, as has been said, the joy of song interpretation and decoding oblique lyrics.

Each fan will have their own view or theory about a song's meaning and the fun and passion of these discussions after listening to a song is the very essence of a love of popular music. A disagreement with a writer's intention is nothing new and one suspects Cornwell and indeed Burnel welcome it, as it demonstrates they have stimulated a creative act and of course it adds an aura of mystery to the group that all great bands thrive on.

Having said all this, the lyrics have a natural poetic flow and with Cornwell's skilled delivery there is a pleasing smooth run to the symbolism throughout the whole song. The juxtaposition of an up-tempo fifties' American music style with what we now know is dark subject matter gives the song an unexpected edge. A commercial up-tempo song with a good time feel which had the potential to be a single but was maybe a bit too far away from their core fan base taste to risk, although as we have seen before this didn't always stop them.

*****

Side two commences jauntily with a simple, conventional chord sequence played by a combination of acoustic and electric guitars with standard bass and drums. The forthright 'off beat' rhythm of the chords helps to immediately hook in the listener. And the main vocal melody that follows has a stylistically fitting shape that throws us back to the band's early pub rock songs, albeit with the band's eighties sound.

However, the song falls away from its promising beginning as the next section has a questionable unconventional angular chord sequence that really challenges the continuity of style. This song could have been moving into an eighties realm of 'Tank' but, instead, tries to shift stylistically but the lightweight nature of this song results in a dilution of the promising opening.

The band had taken to snappy pop like openers to side two with three of their previous four albums with the slightly morose and undercooked 'Let's Tango In Paris' from the previous album *Feline* being the exception. This song, however, creates a similar mood to 'Two Sunspots' from *The Gospel According To The Meninblack* and 'Pin Up' from *La Folie*.

Both those songs maintained a consistency of style even though 'Pin Up' in particular lacked development but 'Uptown' suffers for the attempt to diversify and should have been a forthright pub rocker. 'Ice Queen' successfully bridged a stylistic shift as it was, essentially, a strong song. And the shift made it into an outstanding record.

Every other song on side one had its own style and groove that differed sufficiently from each other but settled into their stylistically consistent grooves. Here we see an attempt to add complexity to the song via a stylistic shift chordally with the second section, but it doesn't quite work. It also seems a shame that the brass section was not live here but played on keyboards (first heard at the end of the second section and continued into verse two) as this would have added to the up-tempo live rock feel and therefore maybe adding continuity to the stylistic feel.

The "we're all meeting at the track uptown" section also fails to convince, and it is interesting to note that the guest backing vocals who added an interesting new dimension with their different tone were not used for this section. Perhaps the lack of real brass and guest backing vocals were down to time constraints as, in both cases, they were drafted in the studio for one day only.

The rest of the song is straight repeats of these three sections with an uninspiring fade out where new musical ideas would have given the song a much-needed new dimension. The added racing crowd noises feeling like an attempt to add impetus to the song but is no substitute for new ideas and feels like padding.

The additional textures on the highly atmospheric long repeat of the chorus in the previous song, 'North Winds', or the explosive introduction of the brass on 'Ice Queen' were examples of new musical impetus that would have benefitted the highly promising opening groove of Uptown.

Punch And Judy

If the last track could be deemed unusual Stranglers territory then Punch And Judy is even further out of the zone in the hinterland, the outlands of The Stranglers musical zone. Led by a big sounding brass intro it's an up-tempo soul number. The brass intro is reminiscent to the sound Dexy's Midnight Runners were using in the early eighties with their soul revival sound. It also nods to the big part brass played in the popular Ska based bands of the time such as Madness and Bad Manners.

Brass was a go to sound for many bands in the early to mid-eighties particularly for the more obvious pop bands like Modern Romance or Wham! It seemed that every hit single at that time had to have at least a sax solo, think of Spandau Ballet with 'True', Orange Juice with 'Rip it Up' and even band's without brass used synthesisers to get a brass sound. A prime example being Europe's mega hit 'Final Countdown' with its hugely catchy synthetic keyboard brass sounding introduction. And now here were The Stranglers fully embracing the trend as they sort to widen their fan base and wider their existing fans musical tastes. It is without doubt a sprightly tune and veritably swings along.

Cornwell with his flowing alternate rhyming, updates the traditional domestic violence saga Punch And Judy to the modern day. In the first verse the two characters stories are told separately by Cornwell's clever use of alternate line rhyming. By numbering the lines of the song we are able to see Punch's narrative is on odd numbered lines and Judy's tale is on the even numbers. Cornwell keeps the characters stories on alternately separate lines until halfway through verse two where Judy's story takes over the rest of the verse.

He final unites the two protagonists on the same line, which coincides with a musical crescendo two thirds of the way into the song. Having done this he continues his rhyming scheme in the final verse incorporating both characters in the same lines using rhyming to intertwine the character's story together in this verse its Punch's story that dominates but Judy is constantly referred to or referenced.

Cornwell relates a tale of Mr Punch returning home from a stretch inside prison looking to get reacquainted with wife Judy and stay out of trouble hence the line about keeping his large nose clean. We can surmise that domestic violence is the reason he has been in prison given the historic plot of *Punch And Judy* shows where Punch is portrayed as a wife beater. Such a story line has obvious links to Cornwell himself given he served time in prison and the controversial lyrics of 'Sometimes' which describe a domestic violence event.

There is also an undercurrent of violence later in the song with the phrase "Hitting on her" which of course colloquially means being sexually attracted to someone but again could be a pun relating to domestic violence. Amazingly even today day domestic violence is still part and parcel of the historic children's puppet show.

Cornwell yet again using his lyrical trademark and toying and playing with words, their meanings and their inferences. He does again in this song by using parts of Punch's traditional costume, the truncheon and the hat. By drawing attention to it the writer is quite clearly implying this modern-day Punch might be a policeman which cleverly by implication links the song to police brutality.

This was a hot topic in 1984 with the miners' strike in full swing and also the band's own experience with the police. There are multiple layers to the truncheon symbolism. Cornwell by mentioning it draws our attention to the weapon. It is a traditional prop of a *Punch And Judy* show and of course it is also a traditional phallic symbol. The mischievous writer enjoying the double entendre this puts in the listeners head and this is something that won't have occurred accidentally to the writer. Cornwell will have absolutely intended it, particularly as the song has already allude to sex several times.

Earlier in the song Cornwell has cast himself as Punch and on his return from incarceration is playing to an audience which of course Cornwell did himself when he returned to live shows after his prison term. Judy is presented as a loyal wife with a playful twinkle in her eye, keeping the home tidy whilst Mr Punch does his time and equally looking forward to returning to having sex. But is there an ulterior motive to her polishing those stairs for her husband's return? Whatever theories the listener might think it is made clear by the repeated line "See soul and beauty in Punch and Judy" that it was a passionate and loving relationship, despite the darker implications.

*****

Whereas 'Ice Queen' saw a fascinating fusion between the brass and the strong instrumental ideas of the band, 'Punch And Judy' is all about the brass and less impressive for it. The band members serve to become backing musicians with the guitar playing a rather rhythmically cumbersome chordal accompaniment and the keyboard for the main part being held organ chords. Both these parts are very low in the mix and, as a result, the first verse lacks punch.

The bar room piano fills do add considerable interest and Greenfield once again hits the stylistic spot with ease. The drum pattern is conventional, although the snare fills sound heavy handed and a little too high in the mix, and the bass is an unadventurous walking bass under, for the most part, the twelve-bar blues rock 'n' roll chords. No flourishes here for Burnel.

However, the brass arrangement gives the song considerable impetus. There is considerable skill in the arrangement of these brass riffs in the main verses with variety and some highly impressive clashes that really cement the style and one can presume that the brass players and Laurie Latham had a large hand in the composition and arrangement of these riffs.

The intro which also serves to become the chorus is less impressive as the brass arrangement amounts to rather laboured arpeggios and the main vocal also uses arpeggios and therefore lacks a little ingenuity. The backing vocals do help to create a wall of sound that contrasts from the verses. Cornwell's main vocal in the verses delivers the message with an assured tone that does help the song to move brightly along and with a shape that is restricted in keeping with the bluesy style.

The impressive saxophone solo after the second chorus has an effective raspy tone but it is a shame that Cornwell's guitar riff that enters just prior to the saxophone becomes so low in the mix that is never develops. A trade-off between guitar and sax could have really lifted the moment and it is typical of this song that, whilst the brass riffs in the verses are something special, the rest of the band are not giving themselves the time and space to develop a deeper sound and groove. Furthermore, to finish the song on a sax solo to fade after the second chorus suggests that the bluesy style had stifled the band's creativity.

For fans who had considerable doubts about the prominent use of brass on the album, 'Punch And Judy' will be a song to quickly gloss over. But for others who had more open minds about the brass, this song certainly has some interest with those stylish riffs.

Spain

The surprises continue with the next track out of the traps. The first surprise is there is no brass but there is cowbell, fretless bass and castanets. The song is called 'Spain' so it is a bit of a surprise there is no Spanish guitar but there is steel/slide guitar.

Elsewhere the band and producer spare no expense to give the song a Spanish vibe. As well as the drums Black makes use of castanets and a tambourine as well as the aforementioned cowbell to add to the Hispanic vibe. Greenfield provides a quirky sounding keyboard riff that sounds like it should be fronting a holiday programme which perfectly fits the topic which is essentially a whistle stop cultural guide to Spain. Just in case we have forgotten we are in Spain the track fades out with muted Spanish trumpets and crickets chirping.

In terms of subject matter Cornwell's flowing delivery takes us first to rural Spain and emphasises the equestrian history of the country painting a picture of Gauchos riding in the Iberian heat. Interestingly as he gallops through his lyrics, he again references America as he has done several times on the album already, by mentioning John Wayne. The point being there were cowboys in Spain before their more famous cousins in the USA.

In the second verse he emphasises the links between the two countries again by comparing Spain to California. The Spanish were the first Europeans to settle in that part of the USA. By referencing the USA throughout the song and for that matter the whole album Cornwell was perhaps hoping to make the band more appealing to America. As we know if this was the strategy, it wasn't hugely successful. The pronunciation of the word Spain in the chorus is unusual and draws the listener's attention. Perhaps it is Cornwell poking fun at the way a British tourist and ex-pats might pronounce the country's name.

In the third verse he dispenses with the American references and finishes with a warning. Spain at this time was less than ten years out of the fascist dictatorship of Franco. He implores the Iberian inhabitants to learn from their neighbours' mistakes and finishes with an allusion to the Spanish civil war concluding that freedom and democracy would have occurred then if it hadn't been for Franco.

Cornwell concludes by describing the fascist victory as "like the bull in the china shop" thus cleverly referencing Spain with its national symbol the bull, by using a well-known idiom which describes chaos and destruction.

There is another sting in the tale as the spoken Spanish female backing vocals are the words of Franco's young daughter after the civil war with a propaganda message for Spanish children and the children of the world. Having made an effort to give the song a Hispanic feel it is almost lost at the last with the incongruous English football terrace chanting of 'Spain' during Greenfield's Hammond organ solo.

Overall It's a classic example of how subversive the band were, on the surface a very commercial and upbeat track but just below that surface was a serious message people just needed to listen carefully.

*****

The electronic cowbell on every beat and the prominent maracas establishes a groove that is then built upon with a held bass and low swell synth sound in unison whilst the guitar enters with considerable effects including delay that becomes the sonic backdrop for the song. These repeating delays from the guitar carry on for most of the song whilst the bass then plays a continuous rhythmic pattern underneath Greenfield's first keyboard riff which is a simple arpeggiated riff, but the subtle drive of the rhythm provided by the constant bass, maracas and delayed guitar moves the song pleasingly along.

The chords are standard, and the vocal melody has an appropriately combative tone with an echo/delay on the vocal that helps to create a slightly restless feeling. The low swell synth sound from the intro returns with a riff at the end of the first verse that utilises pitch bending and, along with the echoed vocals, helps to create a slightly disconcerting feel. Greenfield then adds extra organ chords to build the texture for verse two.

A sudden departure from the verse occurs with the second section where Cornwell's sustained, delayed, and reverbed guitar is prominent, and the chords change into an interesting pattern that starts with a minor chord but the third (major) chord is unrelated to the first chord thus creating an ambiguity of mood that befits the interesting addition of the spoken Spanish voice.

This sudden change in texture may, to some, be considered as too much of a contrast. However, the multiple voices on "We knew that it" that soon split into a harmony are an effective bridge to relieve the mood as the rhythm pauses, before starting up again to impressively take us back to the verse. After repeats of these two sections, there is an interesting Greenfield solo on an organ sound that has a bluesy urgency that, whilst seeming a little incongruous to the style, effectively moves the song along, as the backing vocals repeatedly shout Spain. Whether this solo moving straight back into the Spanish vocal section works is a matter for conjecture but the song is moving along with impact, so it is a moot point.

Repeats follow until the song begins to fade out over another organ solo and Burnel provides some discerning melodic flurries until the very end as we only barely hear a Spanish-like trumpet and some insect noises to remind us of the subject matter.

An effective song that has a sense of wholeness. The spoken Spanish vocal will, to some, have a negative impact by grating on the overall sound, but there is much to admire about the quietly assertive groove and the melodic and textural impact of the song. As was the case with all the songs on side one, there is, despite the contrast of the second section, a consistency of style within the song and a contrast to the other songs which benefits side two after a mixed start.

Laughing

A plaintive soulful, brittle, ballad and a song that has space and starkness and a sound that perfectly fits the subject matter. A classic case of less is more. The most memorable sound is that of the drum machine an unusual choice of instrumentation which might seem a little odd as the band possessed a great drummer. It also perhaps says something about where the band were in terms of some of their relationships and working practices.

In actual fact the use of the drum machine in this case was inspired. The group were again reflecting a musical fashion of the time with many bands producing sparse electronic tracks around an interesting drum machine pattern. Billy Idol had a big hit with the atmospheric 'Eyes Without A Face' in 1983 which had a distinctive drum machine pattern and Phil Collins' 'In the Air Tonight', although famous for the iconic drum break is actually led for the majority of the song by a distinctive drum machine pattern. Bands were embracing and experimenting with the new technology and The Stranglers were no different and with Latham as producer they had a person that was at the cutting edge of the technology.

The lyrics are once again oblique. It is clear there has been a tragic death but deciphering anything concrete is very difficult to do. So, turning to Cornwell for clues he states in *Song By Song* the lyrics are is a tribute to Marvin Gaye. The drum machine sound used in the song are also a cryptic clue to the song's subject as they are the same sound as the one used on Gaye's worldwide 1980s hit 'Sexual Healing'.

Knowing this makes things much clearer, the opening two lines deal with Gaye's tragic death. Not for him the iconic rock 'n' roll death in a plane like Buddy Holly, Richie Valens and Big Bopper alluded to in the first line but tragically at the hands of his father in a drunken argument. Cornwell's nibble wordplay again at play equating Gaye's shooting to lead poisoning.

The song may be a tribute but in the second verse it doesn't shy away from the darker side of the soul singer's life documenting his drug use and indulging with prostitutes in seedy motel rooms. The third verse refers to Gaye's famous song 'Wherever I Lay My Hat (That's My Home)' using it to make the point that unlike many artists the singer was not obsessed by fame and never really courted it. It also shows Cornwell at his roguish best as he is taking a sideswipe at producer Laurie Latham and singer Paul Young.

Latham had just help make Young a worldwide star by overseeing his cover version of Gaye's 'Wherever I Lay My Hat (That's My Home)'. Cornwell denies it's a put down but also admits to not talking to Latham about it.

*****

The electronic bass drum and toms that begin the song are a musical reference to Marvin Gaye's 'Sexual Healing' with a little more off beat rhythm than Gaye's classic opening rhythm. Black continues his penchant for constant electronic hi-hat or maracas in previous songs on the album with the continuous hi-hat here throughout the entire song.

A strange clanging sound appears for one beat six seconds in but, other than that, the arrangement is sparse to let the very melodious vocal breathe, and Cornwell delivers in a soft, reflective voice with some highly effective low tones. This is potentially a beautifully crafted song with some debate as to whether the arrangement helps or hinders this potential beauty. There are moments where the keyboards feel a little too sugary for example the riff after "didn't seem fair" sounds like many other song releases in the mid-eighties.

Black not only has the hi-hat throughout but also adds a clave/woodblock on every beat throughout the song giving the impression that the 'click track' has been inadvertently left on. Furthermore, a rather abrasive snare type sound, not dissimilar to the one-off clang in the intro, appears at the end of every second bar during the verse and at the end of every bar in the chorus. Many years later we could argue that the electronic sounds were overused but the band, like most other artists of the time, were succumbing to the great force of eighties pop drums.

Despite the eighties drum sound influence, the more live snare that enters for the chorus gives the song a discreet lift. Greenfield continues with the cliched sounds in the chorus with a metallophone and the guitar plays held strummed reverbed chords during the second halves of the verses and this has become a common occurrence during the album.

Greenfield's choice of violin for the solo does lie effectively above a low string arpeggiated sound. The synth sounding bass has an impressive sense of movement, not unlike the bass in 'Don't Bring Harry'. And some of the lower keyboard sounds provide a slightly haunting feel. But this song is about Cornwell's mesmeric melodies and his harmonies in the chorus are superbly judicious.

The chords combine highly conventional with some typically off kilter moments as in the first two chords in the verse which have been used before, as in the completely different feel of the opening to 'Curfew' when the drums enter. And Cornwell maintains the impressive melodic flow despite the incongruity of these two chords which helps to add a curious nature to the song. The movement chordally into the chorus "You're laughing" is sublime when we are fooled into thinking that the song has changed key. This also adds to the curiosity of the mood.

It would be fascinating to hear this strong song with a non-eighties electronic arrangement but, even with some of the arrangement bordering on the predictable, there is so much to admire.

Souls

A beautiful melody gently fades into your consciousness with the whole band deftly picking out their lines with unerring precision. Cornwell's warm soulful croon skips around the lyrics. Latham again creates a spacious celestial ambience that allows the song to float, breathe and gently pulse. After two and half minutes it fades out as if it were an ethereal entity that had just passed through spreading its wisdom. The fade out and for that matter the fade in are a deliberate choice and not as mentioned in the appraisal of 'Uptown' a disguise for a lack of ideas. The instrumental break with the keyboards imitating a vibraphone was a ubiquitous eighties production effect used by the band on a number of occasions.

In terms of understanding, the narrator is relating a tale of losing the love of his life and is struggling to come to terms with life after the event. He is unable to function and feels totally bereft as all he can do is offer his love. This lover is given God like status and is referred to in reverential tones as an idol and a deity whose dwelling is a temple.

The music and production mirrors the idea of a Goddess with its floating beautiful harmony and the fact it passes briefly through before moving on to another destination. The music is therefore the antithesis of our jilted lover who is distressed and potentially suicidal without the lover he has put on a pedestal. The protagonist's lover is a Deity who takes what she needs from her suitors and then discards them "she eats souls" opines the singer. Cornwell's effortless poetry perfectly sums up the eternal strife and power dynamic of a broken relationship when one party clearly has the whip hand over a still besotted former lover.

*****

Why the official CD album version leaves out the second verse that appeared on the original vinyl is a mystery. The song is short enough even with the additional verse and benefits from the repetition of the perfectly shaped melody that contrasts so well with the bridge.

This is an example of the time-honoured technique of the verse being sung in a low register with a shape that has an upward feel being then opposed by the bridge that has a higher register thanks to the backing vocals, and a downward shape.

And the chorus provides another contrast with longer held notes whereas the verse and bridge had quicker length notes. This song could potentially have had a considerable impact on the charts had it been released as a hit. The chords are very conventional, and the bass part is littered with highly effective inversions of the chords in the bridge and chorus/intro.

Burnel apparently didn't like the song but that seems strange given his quietly impressive work that helps to subtly drive this simple yet effective song. The feel created by the acoustic guitars and the wonderfully softly swirling opening keyboard riff reminds us of *Feline*, but Black's drum sound and fills are veering towards a live feel here with the song feeling all the better for it. Would a similar 'live' treatment for the drums on 'Laughing' and one or two other songs on the album added to the overall mood on the album?

The overall texture has much to commend it, with those swirling yet restrained keyboard riffs at the start setting the tone: the first riff is in the lower register and the second answering phrase being higher in pitch. Throughout the song, Greenfield has constant fast repeating chords on a piano-like sound in the background helping to gently move the song along and when the main vocal enters, the riffs stop, leaving us with the economy of the soft constant high piano chords with the bass and acoustic guitar.

Some high chords play on the first beat of each bar in the bridge, which, along with the backing vocals sung in unison but an octave higher creates an effective contrasting flow. The keyboard riffs from the intro return for the chorus and dovetail perfectly with the long held vocal "so-uls" melody.

The instrumental section is lacking somewhat and along with the lack of second verse, culminates in a song that just needed another spark, perhaps instrumentally, to move it into another gear to enhance what is already a subtly strong song. Furthermore, extra instrumental invention to lengthen some of the side two songs would have resulted in the option to mercifully cull the disastrous final song to follow.

Mad Hatter

It's fair to say Mad Hatter was the final straw for many old fans of the band. A swing number with a xylophone effect leading the melody, Doo-wop backing vocals provided again by session singers and a trombone solo! Not to mention a fretless bass providing that ubiquitous, dated bass sound of the mid-eighties. The band were famous for iconic end of album songs; 'Down in the Sewer', 'Genetix' and 'Hallow To Our Men'. To many fans this wasn't a song worthy of being the last of the album or even worthy of being a Stranglers song. Even on an album that introduced a new style 'Mad Hatter' sticks out.

Whatever fans thought of the song and the styles it incorporates there is no doubt it is a well-crafted, well executed song with some 'interesting' ideas. Also it carries on The Stranglers tradition for challenging their listeners. Previously they had done via complex melodic interplay, unusual rhythmic patterns and controversial lyrics. Now they were challenging our expectations with what might be described as an easy listening track.

Sonically we have Black's galloping programmed drums sounding real for once. Greenfield puts the xylophone pre-set on the keyboards and comes up with a vibrant riff that gives the song that light jazz/easy listening feel. Burnel with a fretless bass sound which makes it appear like he's auditioning to be in Paul Young's band. As Young's producer Latham was probably responsible for this. Cornwall chips in with chirpy semi-acoustic jazz chords on rhythm. The whole instrumentation results creates a merry romp.

Cornwell joins in with the fun with a flow of words to match the vibe. In the first verse he checks just about all the participants at the Mad Hatter's tea party in *Alice in Wonderland*. On initially hearing the song the listener might be tempted to take the words and the music as just a tribute to *Alice In Wonderland* as it was one of Cornwall's favourite books. However, listening carefully it isn't just a homage to the said book but Cornwell likening a party he attended to the Mad Hatter's tea party hosted by a larger-than-life character who became a friend.

The strange concept of the tea party and the consuming of various hallucinogenic substances by Alice in the book means it's not a big leap to assume the bizarre behaviour and scenes describe are drug induced. Indeed, one of the many phrases used in street slang to describe a drug dealer is 'mad hatter'.

Another angle on the interpretation is the song is describing a show featuring an entertainer or a comedian who has an 'off the wall' sense of humour. The word mad is often used as a way to describe this kind of humour e.g., mad cap humour, note the hat reference, meaning comedy that is not the norm. It is commonly used to describe surreal off the wall or absurd humour.

Mad could also be a description of the music, for Stranglers fans the music was 'mad' i.e., totally unexpected. The song is clearly a joke in its subject matter, the way in which it was performed and the chosen musical style. As we have seen, humour in songs has been a common theme throughout the band's back catalogue.

A Musical Critique

✶✶✶✶✶

The previous three songs: 'Spain', 'Laughing' and 'Souls' were all strong songs with contrasting grooves and moved side two along with a gratifying sense of purpose but perhaps lacking in a harder edge. So, the decision of the band to finish with a joke song, laden with cheesy sounds was one of the greatest mysteries of all their albums. Being the final song on the album, it cements the two new textures of the brass and the guest backing vocals, but in an extremely negative light.

The song utilises the twelve-bar blues chord pattern until the middle "Mad as the mad hatter" section which moves off into a terribly contrived chord pattern. The main instrumentation is Greenfield's vibraphone sound alternating with the live brass whilst Black plays his constant snare pattern, Burnel plays a walking bass and Cornwell contributes occasional, high clean guitar chords and a suitably 'throw away' vocal tone.

The 'Doo-wops' from the backing vocals and low interjections from the brass add to the jocularity and all that is needed to complete the contrived fun is a trombone solo which duly arrives. Enough said.

Musical Summary

The expanse of different styles is considerable, and the fusion is, at times, impressive. Not only were the band moving away from the colder, acoustic electro pop of *Feline* into a more live feel but still retaining a degree of the commercial eye with short songs with conventional chords and conventional structures, but they threw the two new ideas of a brass section and soul-tinged guest backing vocals into the overall sound.

The success of these two new additions is debatable. There was a practical benefit of having the guest backing vocalists as the main four band members were often not present at the same time during recording. Ironically, some of the best moments from the backing vocals for example in 'Skin Deep', 'North Winds', and 'Souls', come from the band members and the appearance of the guest backing singers in 'Mad Hatter' undermines some of the positivity from their appearance in 'Let Me Down Easy' and 'No Mercy'.

The same can be said for the brass which fuses magnificently in the opener, 'Ice Queen', but the other two songs feel, at times, like a vehicle for the brass as 'Punch And Judy' is not a strong song and 'Mad Hatter' is a woeful end to the album which leaves a bitter taste in the mouth. Although the brass contentiously shifted the stylistic approach for some of the album, they did contribute to a return to the more live feel.

Burnel's sad personal circumstances and probably a growing disillusion with the musical direction led to him withdrawing into his shell, leaving Cornwell to pursue the less acerbic side to the band. That said, Burnel still contributed many superb bass moments, but they were altogether more understated and quieter in the overall mix than on the earlier albums, but this had been the case anyway for the previous two albums prior to *Aural Sculpture*.

Black's drum machine sounds turned more towards a live feel after *Feline* and the album felt warmer as a result, but many would have loved for him to pick up the sticks again. Greenfield continued, as always, to produce a vast array of different sounds, some of which were clearly moving into the mid-eighties synth pop conventions, but there was much to admire in the sheer breadth of different sounds as well as the quality of the melodies and riffs and the return of the organ made a huge difference on 'Ice Queen'.

There will be many lamenting how the original sound had disappeared almost entirely from view but the mid-eighties possessed a completely different musical landscape to the late seventies and most bands underwent fundamental changes in sound. Those who didn't often suffered with lack of chart success so the fact The Stranglers transformed their sound was not unique or surprising.

The way the earlier songs were composed with the longer instrumental sections, the multi-melodic textures, the unconventional use of chords, time signatures and structures reduced during *La Folie* and even more during *Feline* points to the band's feeling the pressure to have commercial success. Furthermore, the pooling together of creative ideas by individual band members within

AURAL HYGIENE

THE PRESS Office, Epic Records, Soho Square, London. The bout — a three round middleweight eliminator between a representative of the reigning champions (a maninblack, a black belt in karate), and some urchin from a scurrilous music weekly (black belt in stamp collecting).

The Sounds man makes the first psychological move by trendily arriving several minutes late, but it's all to no avail as the Strangler arrives even later — one up already and we're not even in the ring yet.

Burnel takes my hand in a vice-like grip (just which vice remains to be seen) and advances to within six inches of my body, eyes levelled straight at mine. The traditional black of his uniform is tempered by a green corduroy jacket, a sure sign that the mellowing process is well under way. The stage set, we leave for the scene of the impending battle.

ROUND ONE. And so the dauntless gladiators enter the arena, a fabled shrine of pugilism, fiendishly masquerading as an up-market wine bar. In a nausea-inducing striped corner sits the champ, and in the other corner of the same couch sits the chump. With trepidation I accompany Burnel to the bar.

"Chablis," he asserts. Only after ordering do we consult the wine list — £9.25 a bottle. My heart sinks, but the decision is made — in any case, who am I to argue?

As he points out, "I am French, after all."

With their reputation for physical intimidation in the process of rehabilitation, I accuse the bass Strangler of financial intimidation. However, the terrifying prospect of having to resort to the use of my Abscess card (your flexible funeral) is offset to a large extent by the sensation of the golden grape juice sloshing past a parched larynx. Jean-Jacques indulges in some lyrical waxing.

"Chablis is a good, fruity, reliable wine from a not-too sunny part of the world. I prefer Burgundy and Beaujolais, though I find Bordeaux and what the British call Claret to be rather heavy."

With that impressive combination, the Gaul has established a commanding lead on points. With Burnel demonstrating his fancy footwork, and easing off on the obligatory opening exchanges, I take my opportunity to snatch a breather.

What about that reputation (which saw other, better-informed Soundsters taking prodigious steps backwards as I recklessly stood my ground, a kind of kamikaze volunteer interviewer)?

"Some interviewers are real arseholes, and they get a bad time accordingly," cautions JJ. "They go away and write a derogatory article, and the reputation is perpetuated — it's a vicious circle. But the Stranglers don't live in a vacuum — it's a pleasure to meet new people. We're confident, and I think this is sometimes mistaken for smugness, which just isn't the case.

"Maybe people take us too seriously, or perhaps we're only funny to ourselves. We've always felt we had a lot of humour in what we've done. I think our 'Aural Sculpture' manifesto is one of the funniest bits of plastic ever made, and yet critics said it was one of the most pretentious, arrogant statements that anyone could possibly make.

"I think the blurb (with the new album) is wonderful. I'm really proud of it. I don't know who's the more pretentious — us, or the people who get uptight about us."

The new album is altogether pleasant on the ear, by turns soulful and gentle, if not particularly original.

"The person who says he's totally original is an idiot," chides Burnel. "David Bailey once said there are two kinds of artists — those who copy, and those who imitate. The bad artist copies, but the good artist imitates."

And into which category do the Stranglers fall, I wonder?

ROUND TWO, and it's my turn to purchase the plonk. With a heavy heart and a tear in the eye, I wave goodbye to two dearly beloved fivers — like losing a couple of sons. Heigh ho, back to the fray.

Do you feel the music press have the knives out for you?

"Quite possibly, but I don't really blame them. I'd have it in for someone if they kicked me in the legs, or stomped on me, or gaffer-taped me to a girder of the Eiffel Tower — wouldn't you?"

Has anyone ever tried to physically take you on?

"A few times. If they were trying to prove something to me, they've never succeeded. Having a black belt doesn't make you invincible, though, it merely improves you from what you were originally."

How would someone with an equivalent level of attainment in, say, Judo fare?

"Oh, they'd get bollocked, of course! Judo's a sport, karate's a Martial Art. By the time they'd grabbed hold of me their skull would be broken. If I can smash breeze blocks, a skull should be no problem."

Time to talk music? Perhaps not...

"I don't really know why you're interviewing me, if you write for a music paper — I renounced music 18 months ago, as did my three colleagues. I'm an Aural Sculptor! That's the end of the interview!"

ROUND THREE. JJ picks up the tab, and we enter the sprawling slurring section of the encounter as a female friend of the bassist enters into the conversation.

"God, is this an interview?" is the unbiased observation as we tackle vital issues such as England's recent boshing of the Turks ("That'll teach them to invade Cyprus") and human relationships ("it's time we had a new sex"), and so I re-direct the flow of the conversation to more pertinent subjects, namely Sex! Bingo! Grace Jones!

JJ in protective mood: "Contrary to what the papers might say, I'm not marrying Grace. She's just a really nice person — she's real, and doesn't pretend to be diplomatic or all smiles."

How did you meet her?

"Through Kenzo, the designer. I don't like to publicise the fact that I'm friendly with all these people, it just so happens that they're the most fashionable people — eat your heart out The Face! I think it's a laugh, as the Stranglers are the least fashionable band you could possibly imagine! That's healthy irony, don't you think?"

We talk private lives at some length, with the result that I now know a lot of extremely interesting things about JJ ("I'm a cad," he confesses) and the boys, but I like my legs in their present configuration, and don't feel inclined to have them remodelled, so I'll keep stumm.

After ten years together, do the Stranglers feel like the Status Quo of New Wave?

"Status Quo with a big S and a big Q?" blasts an incredulous Jean-Jacques. "What you should say is that we happen to have got on with each other for longer than most people do.

"If anyone feels they can't say what they want to say within the structure of the group, they're encouraged to do things in other fields. That's happened on three occasions to date."

Time to broach the subject of the new long player. I venture to suggest that elements of the record have a French film feel.

"You mean French New Wave? And here we have five seconds' silence from Francois Truffaut. Dave and I actually did a soundtrack for a French film called Fire And Water, which came out last year."

And I gather Roman Polanski has expressed an interest in directing the next video?

"Yes, he telephoned us a few weeks ago and said he was still interested in doing it, work permitting. Obviously we couldn't do it in this country, though."

How do you rate 'Aural Sculpture'?

"I think it's a good album, different from all our others. It's not radical, but it does break new ground for us. It's not wallpaper music, which is more than I can say for most music today."

Did you say music?

"Well, of course — it's not music at all! It's not wallpaper sculpture, that's what I meant to say! Oh, what a giveaway!"

The final bell, the end of the contest and I've come out virtually unscathed. Regardless of the outcome, I'd be prepared for a re-match any time — wallet permitting...

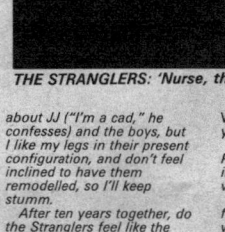

THE STRANGLERS: 'Nurse, the screens!'

THE STRANGLERS' J J BURNEL gives Andy Hurt an ear bending!

songs was, lamentably, dissipating.

Ultimately therefore, the album feels less like the band coming together as a creative force with Cornwell having a greater songwriting input than on previous albums. But most of Cornwell's songs are strong and delivered with skill and assurance. All of side one and 'Spain', 'Laughing' and 'Souls' all have much to offer on side two. These eight songs all have their own stylistic contrasts, yet they flow well into each other.

Despite Cornwell's strong songs, the dissolution of the creative togetherness of the band that had epitomised their earlier albums cast a disheartened shadow for many but at least the return of a more live feel and more rhythmically driving and emotive songs than on Feline would have pleased the older fans.

Album Summary

The idea of change and a new direction had been laid by *Feline* but by the end of that album it felt like a cul-de-sac and the band had accomplished all they could. The quality of some of the tracks on *Feline* felt inferior to the past and the experiment of acoustic with electronics had only produced half an album the rest being more electronic which hadn't been totally successful.

The band seeing a dead end turned to a producer and this kick started another new direction. This was a brave but necessary decision and success was far from guaranteed. In fact, commercial disaster was far more likely as it again risked alienating their fans.

Having changed direction once and got away could be deemed pushing you luck, but doing it again might be regarded as foolhardy and tempting fate but feeling they had no other choice the band dived in with both feet, embracing a producer for the first time in six years and the sound and ideas he bought.

Latham brought a new contemporary sound with his production and engineering skills and it was also his idea of using brass. Despite dividing fans most notably at gigs the brass was here to stay for the next two albums and tours. The album rebranded the band as they were setting their stall out as an edgy rock pop band with a contemporary sound. Unlike many eighties albums the sound doesn't sound dated or cheesy. The album can't be described as timeless and the main reason for this is the drums which whilst mostly doing what they should do by sitting in background and keeping perfect time they occasionally grate on certain tracks particularly some of the tracks featuring brass. Their perfect time keeping stifling the rest of the band's playing the one exception where the drums work perfectly is 'Ice Queen' because they personify the cold icy atmosphere of the song. Elsewhere their plastic sound doesn't sit well today.

The album did reasonably well abroad with chart placings in Europe and New Zealand and 'Skin Deep' was a Top 20 in six counties including New Zealand and Australia. Although this was progress it wasn't the breakthrough that was hoped for.

In the UK the sales and chart placing of the singles and album were disappointing despite their quality, older fans weren't rushing back or picking up legions of new fans. Unlike *La Folie* there was no 'Golden Brown' to bolster an album making its way south in the charts.

The company tried with quality singles 'No Mercy' and 'Let Me Down Easy' linked with extra tracks and various gimmicks but to no avail. Things weren't helped by a press reaction that wasn't particularly positive. With papers openly questioning why they still existed. This was a time of music papers i.e., *NME*, *Melody Maker* and *Sounds* and pre the glossy music magazines such as *Q*, *Mojo* and *Uncut*. The papers all tried to out hip each other and set new trends. Anything that had been round more than five years was fair game.

The Stranglers had been around for ten years and added to their difficult reputation they had virtually no friends in the papers. Their bravery in changing artistic direction was given little or no credit. Music magazines were a year away from starting with the iconic *Q* being the first in 1986. From their off the magazines operated a more considered and mature approach, judging what was in front of them and had no trend setting axe to grind. Unfortunately, *Aural Sculpture* was a year too early to benefit from this positivity. If we skip into the modern day where there are no papers and only magazines the band's recordings from the mid-eighties are given a fair and considered review.

The USA remained a barren territory for the band. There were tours but not hugely extensive ones which meant breaking into the market was virtually impossible. The Aural Sculpture tour in the UK played the usual big city venues and the band brought some new ideas to their live set. Firstly of course the brass section for the new album's numbers, as well as brass arrangements for selected classics. The instruments and PA were wireless giving them a bit more freedom on stage and there were also huge white sheets over the amps which under lightening gave an impressive impression on an ice scape.

In terms of relationships professional and social there was some strain. Burnel was contributing fewer songs. Black was insistent on programming his drums and his intransigence on the matter caused consternation. Greenfield showed no signs of pushing himself forward to sing again and was just content happy getting sounds out of his synths using pre-sets rather than creating pioneering, innovative sounds himself.

Cornwell whilst writing the bulk of the material was getting less ambitious in his musical approach and his colleagues who in the past had taken some of his basic ideas and ran with them were now merely accompanying him with admittedly some beautiful ideas but nothing that was cutting edge.

The album was a qualified success keeping the fan base giving the band a new direction and making some in roads into new territories. The band had again changed style and pulled it off achieving the notable feat of still keeping a sizable following sales wise and particularly live.

Most bands would have sunk without trace with such radical changes in direction. Who would have thought in 1977 that seven years later The Stranglers would be promoting effectively a pop, soul-tinged album with their own brass section?

Despite the difficulties starting to surface in relationships, critical indifference and commercial stagnation the band went straight back into recording the next album with Laurie Latham at the helm.

Extra Tracks

Here And There (B-side of 'Skin Deep')

Burnel had only produced one lyric for the album, but he was more involved in the songs that didn't make the album or were recorded specifically for B-sides. 'Here And There' is clearly his song given the lyrics with their European references. Burnel's vocal performances across the band's albums are interesting as he uses a variety of styles and it's often hard to recognise them as being from the same person. Cornwall on the other hand is always instantly recognisable whatever style he chose. With Burnel there is the shouting aggressive punky style of 'Ugly', the whispered almost talking timbre of 'The Raven' and the high pitched staccato of 'Paradise' to name but three styles. On this track it's a rich sounding croon.

Greenfield provides a very bright tune which has an almost Caribbean feel. Given the subject matter of the song, which is essentially European such musical sounds seem a little out of place. The rest of the instrumentation is rather unspectacular, and the production makes Burnel's croon the main focus for the listener.

The lyrics are packed with European references and languages. It signals Burnel returning to his Europe obsession outlined in his solo outing in 1979 *Euroman Cometh*. There is a clear love song element to the words. The phase "I miss you" is translated into French, Dutch and Flemish. The female backing vocals provided by Dagnar Krause, add to the love mood as they suggest a dialogue between Burnel and a woman.

On the face of it the lyrics appear in places rather random, for instance in the first verse there is a reference to the lack of available housing in Holland. This almost certainly refers to a high profile 1980s campaign in the Netherlands by squatters which led to violence and the authorities even using a tank to restore order.

In the second verse Burnel refers to a campaigns in Belgium about the arguments for use the French or Flemish in the country. Some campaigners even arguing for partitioning of the country. He then adds the perspective of a conflict in his country, presumably the UK, where people are fighting for survival which is clearly a reference to the miners' strike of 1984-5. In the third verse there is an obscure reference to the then still standing Berlin wall. Burnel's point is that if something like use of a particular language can create conflict then you don't need a structure like the Berlin Wall to perpetuate conflicts and differences as they are already there.

The implication being if this is the case, what hope for the human race is there? Whilst these heavy social issues are raised each verse still has a romantic strand of the song with the words 'I miss you' regularly repeated.

*****

There is a disjointed feel to the three different sections that comprise the song. The instrumental opening has a bright, almost garish feel with the synth brass and xylophone sounds with a simple snare and bass drum pattern on every beat and bass enters halfway through with equally simple continuous root bass notes low in the mix.

This is followed by the chorus "Here and there" section with an immediate key change and then when the verse section commences, there is another key change, this time in the minor following two very distinctly major key sections.

The drum pattern changes for sections two and three to incorporate much use of the snare similar to 'Bear Cage' and the female backing vocals provide a further major sheen. Burnel's crooning tone compounds the feeling of disjointedness although the drums, female vocals and continued xylophone and brass keyboard riffs maintain some semblance of continuity.

The change of key on "Savner dig" does not help matters and the continuation of competition between the keyboard brass and xylophone sounds and the prominent snare grates on the proceedings as they are all piercing sounds that seem at odds with the lyrical content. Whilst the guitar is present throughout, Cornwell never seems convinced as to what his role is and, subsequently, it is low in the mix.

The melody has an interesting shape and could have been a basis for a potentially strong song, but the keyboard and guitar sounds, the vocal tones, and the constant shifting of key struggle to produce a unifying outcome.

In One Door (B-side of 'No Mercy')

Another keyboard led song with an agreeable melody. It feels more of a group collaboration than 'Here And There'. Lyrically Cornwell is opining about wanting to escape the world he inhabits, the petty arguments and uncertainty. He wants to seek solace with his lover. Some of his lyrical images link back to 'Baroque Bordello' with talk of having his body bathed with exotic oils.

The lyrics are a metaphor for the band situation which as already alluded to had started to fracture. Cornwell sounds inpatient and frustrated but he's not upset with his lover that is not the problem, he just wants to be with her enjoying life. The problem is his other obsession, the band. Whilst remaining a united front publicly in interviews and especially at gigs in the recording studio the cracks were showing.

With a producer at the helm it was far more likely the majority of the work would be the producer working one to one work with each musician. Thereby giving the other band member's time on their hands. This inevitably led to separate interests and socialising.

The Stranglers were not unusual in this scenario throughout rock history such working practises have led to many bands losing the last gang in town mentality and becoming distant and eventually dysfunctional. The most obvious example in the early eighties were The Clash who in the end were not even speaking to each other. The process of separation began with The Stranglers as soon as they started work with Latham, who's first act in the producer's chair was to spirit Greenfield off alone to work on 'Skin Deep'.

It was never a plan to start splitting the band, that wasn't Latham's intention, but the traditional working practices of a producer meant there was a good chance it would lead to bonds loosening between band members.

The line about fussing and fighting sums up Cornwell's feeling about the band. As time progressed more and more of his lyrics would reflect this concern.

Ironically given the subject matter of the lyrics this is a Latham produced track and would have been in contention for the album. The song has some nice touches, but it was the right the decision to relegate it to a B-side as it isn't a remarkable piece and surpasses nothing on the original running order of the album.

*****

An unremarkable song regarding the melody and the chords. There is a conventionality regarding the chord pattern that requires something to lift it beyond the mediocre and both the shape and, most of all, rhythm of the melody is uninspiring. Black had reverted to a very conventional electronic snare on beats two and four pattern after displaying more adventure with some of his other patterns around this time and the drums are too high in the mix, so this adversely affects the song.

Burnel's bass sound is one of his more aggressive offerings for many songs and this helps the song to move along as do the delay affected guitar and the various piano and bell like keyboard sounds. There is a randomness about the guitar and keyboards that helps the song to have another dimension as the vocal is delivered in a smooth tone with predictable harmonies creating a pop song feel.

The chorus has a slight sixties feel with the vocals sung in a 'round' and the twee keyboard flute type sounds leaving the effectiveness of this section debateable. Black finally delivers some impetus to the song with some effective tom fills as the ending delivers a mix of ideas, but not enough to extinguish the bland feel to the song.

Head On The Line (album outtake, released on CD version, 2001)

Another annoyed lyric from Cornwell over a persistent stabbing keyboard. He delivers the words with a snarl and almost a sense of desperation. The backing is to be frank uninspired and rather clichéd and sounds like a group searching blindly for inspiration to back their animated singer. The rising harmonies towards the end are reminiscent of the harmonies of glam rockers the Sweet's biggest hit 'Blockbuster' and represent how short of musical ideas the band were.

The singer berates a friend/colleague and demanding they get their act together and stop wasting opportunities and accept their responsibilities. The spectre of substance abuse is the elephant in the room and it's hard not to think of tensions in the band are the muse for the words of this song. By this time Cornwell was clean of drugs but others weren't.

The title of the song uses the old Cornwall device of messing with a well-known idiom or maybe two well-known idioms. One saying is "put your neck on the line" and another about "put your head on the block". Both have the same meaning i.e., the jeopardy of taking a risk.

By combining them it gives the words more power and also emphasises Cornwell's exasperation at the situation. The singer displays a distinct lack of sympathy for the character he is describing and unlike most of his song lyrics it is very direct and straightforward. One wonders if band members realised what he was saying or convinced themselves it was a lyric about a relationship with a woman as the lyrics can be also fit this scenario.

Despite the song's strong lyrical sentiment, the music meant it was destined that the song would be an outtake and add to Cornwell's increasing frustration.

*****

The arrangement and choice of sounds typifies the problems that the band had been enduring for a while. The song is not particularly strong but, with a rawer live feel then it could have passed muster.

Cornwell's vocal tone clearly suggested that an aggressive approach was the intention, but the backing severely lacks punch with its underwhelming synth brass sounds throughout which dominate the mix with the much-needed distorted guitar unable to rise above the morass of synth sounds. The choice of snare with a softer crack than could been chosen from the array of electronic sounds at their disposal further dilutes the aggression and any qualities to the song are taken out of reach by these sonic decisions.

Black does program some tom fills that do help to add more intensity, but these are somewhat lost amidst the clutter of the previously mentioned sounds. The middle section "So have a drink" is preceded at 1:16 by the most contrived 'cabaret' semitonal riff on the synth brass and then Cornwell's vocal melody echoes the chords and the bass line which is almost often a bad decision and severely weakens the section.

This middle section is followed by repeats of "Your heads on the line" which is accompanied by backing vocal "Ahhs" which sound like a mixture of live and synth vocal sounds and, once again, reduce the aggression that the song needs. This should have been followed by a distorted guitar solo but instead we are subjected to a few weak synth brass riffs that typify the muddled thinking behind the intentions for this potentially punchy song.

Achilles Heel

Fans might be lured into feeling they know 'Achilles Heel' better than they actually do and that's because the opening riff is very similar to opening riff of 'Choosey Susie'. The similarities with the past don't stop there as the band revert back to their early years sound. The keyboards use the old sounds of piano and organ. Burnel's bass is busy but doesn't dominate he song. Cornwall's voice has a gruff, although not angry tinge to it. A tone which is a bit of throwback the past. The backing vocals are simple but effective. Towards the end the voices and instruments ascend to a peak once and then a second time. The tension is building to what feels could be a multiple melody free for all. Instead, the musical peak is reached, and the song finishes on a resonating crash. Good but could have been even better.

An Achilles' heel, according to mythology is a weakness in a strong person that can lead to their downfall. So what weakness is Cornwell referring to in his minimal lyrics? The words show the narrator recognising he has a weakness and it's sung as a warning to himself. If this is the case, it's Cornwell recognising the dangers of his previous cocaine use. He was clean of opiates at this point but like all addicts knows he will have an inherent weakness all his life, the Achilles heel of the title.

The lyrics are short and sweet but they emphasis the traps and seduction of drugs. With a bit more care and love the track could have been even better as it is it doesn't quite fulfil its obvious potential.

*****

The opening guitar riff starts identically to 'Choosey Susie' and then the song continues in a similar vein, albeit with an eighties sound. But the mood and the drive of the two songs are very similar. The vocals start on the same note and the backing vocals also have similar functions at the end of the first phrase and throughout the respective songs. The more live feel of 'Achilles Heel' with a more prominent electric guitar and 'real' keyboard piano and organ sounds and drum pattern with frequent snare fills gives the song a feel-good factor and Cornwell delivers in a semi-Elvis tone that suits the mood.

The second section changes key to move the song effortlessly along and the two climactic surges towards the end of the song are equally fitting. It is somewhat surprising that this song was not chosen for the *Aural Sculpture* album, in place of 'Mad Hatter' or 'Punch And Judy' as the semi blues/soul feel would have been effectively augmented by some rasping brass riffs, especially the final surges. And it would have also been another reminder that the old and new could blend effectively.

Hot Club (Riot mix) (B-side of 'No Mercy')

A jaunty instrumental with the sound effects of a busy bar/club. The effects were done in the studio by the band and consists of clinking bottle and discussions which turn a bit more rowdy as the track progresses hence the sub title 'riot mix'. The result is to create a Gypsy/Roma inspired melody and another bit of fun by the band. There is a version without sound effects called 'Hot Club'.

*****

A fast-paced folk type instrumental with standard chord patterns but both the chords and the melody use the flattened second chord on occasions to add a little more Eastern European feel to the piece. This chord was used with much frequency on the *Feline* album and its stylistic impetus has now shifted from West to East.

The opening also has a guitar playing in balalaika style, a Russian folk guitar. The arrangement consists of the melody being played on an acoustic guitar sound but possibly being played on the keyboard rather than an actual guitar. And there is another keyboard playing a constant higher harmony in the background.

Place de Victories (B-side of 'Let Me Down Easy')

Straightforwardly an Instrumental of 'Let Me Down Easy'. The band had used this tactic before by using an instrumental of 'Waiting For The Meninblack' on the B-side of 'Who Wants the World?'

Without words it allows the listener to concentrate on the instruments and their melody. This reveals what a beautiful tune and arrangement the backing track is. The band were not alone in releasing instrumentals of existing songs. It was in fact common place at this time, they were particularly used on 12-inch versions of single releases. In most cases these mixes were a pointless aural exercises designed specially and cynically to milk fans for more cash.

In this case The Stranglers are a notable exception as were Simple Minds both of whose instrumentals unearthed hidden musical depths and placed on show the exquisite quality of the instrumentation.

*****

The instrumental version of 'Let Me Down Easy' has an additional track of Greenfield on organ replacing the vocals. When the riff is repeated at thirty seconds, the notes change slightly from the previous playing and some notes now clash in a questionable way. Other than that, the mix is slightly different but uninspiring compared to the original vocal version.

Vladimir And Sergei (From *Fire and Water* by JJ Burnel and Dave Greenfield)

In the interests of completing the Vladimir story this is part two of the saga. It is not an official Stranglers release as it appeared on the *Fire and Water* album by Burnel and Greenfield. The music is suitably Eastern European and Burnel narrates the story.

There is an element of sexism in the tale as Olga is punished for getting fat and sent to a health spa. Vladimir then embarks on a gay affair with sailor Sergei. It is actually a serious criticism on the USSR's regime who had an incredibly poor human rights record against LGBT people as well as many other people they saw as dissidents. Intellectuals fell into the dissident group and the lyrics comment on that aspect of USSR society which was still alive and kicking at the time of this recording.

Vladimir And The Beast (Part 3) (B-side of 'Skin Deep', 12-inch)

Part 3? What happened to Part 2 you ask? In actual fact Part 2 Vladimir and Sergei appeared on Greenfield and Burnel's album *Fire and Water*. Having involved Cornwell in Part 1 he wasn't involved on this episode and it was Greenfield and Burnel who came up with the track.

Like the other Vlad tracks the music was created by Greenfield in the style of Eastern European folk music and is in fact rather engaging. Burnel narrates the story in his version of a Russian accent.

This time we find Vladimir being released from a Gulag having spent two years being 'rehabilitated' following a gay relationship with Sergei and having doubted the Communist revolutionary philosophy. His travels take him to the war in Afghanistan following the Russian invasion. What follows is a series of atrocities, drug taking and Vladimir finally taking a shine to a camel. The lyrics and scenarios are humorous and made more so by Burnel's dead pan delivery. At the same time it shows the band commentating on world events on a topic that was a major threat to world peace and like much of the political humour of the time as now it was clearly anti-Russian.

*****

After ten bars of two beats per bar the music shifts into a waltz like three beats per bar and this change occurs at various points during the piece. Other than that, the chords are very conventional in a folk like way with the predictable reappearance, first at 1:17, of their well-used flattened second chord similar to 'Hot Club' and, of course far more effectively as the third chord in 'Waltzinblack' and on much of *Feline*.

This chord was also used in 'Vladimir and Olga' and the chords overall are similar, but this part three version lacks the instrumental melody that part one possesses other than the "la la" stereotype of traditional Eastern European folk song. Musically limited to say the least.

Vladimir Goes To Havana (part 4) (B-side of 'Let Me Down Easy', collectors' edition)

Part 4 picks up where Part 3 left off with Vladimir in more rehabilitation. This time he has a gay experience and a cocaine binge. The name of the characters Burnel creates are straight out of the *Carry On* school of insulting double entendre so we have Vladimir Andropyournosin and Doctor Mikhail Buggerovsk. Burnel was nothing if not creative in his Vladimir stories.

The Vladimir series gain a cult following amongst fans. It is worth listening to them all in order including the missing Part 2 (on *Fire and Water*) as they provide an entertaining twenty minutes both musically and humour wise.

It also demonstrates the band had a world view and were able to articulate it in a witty and interesting way without resorting to political posturing or protest which was very much the fashion amongst musicians in the mid-eighties and explains why they got virtually no coverage for the highly politicised music press of the mid-eighties.

*****

The same typically Eastern European folk song chords that occupied the other Vladimir songs with more tempo changes than in previous songs. Cornwell employs some fast guitar strumming to imitate the balalaika. Greenfield's riffs are accompanied by the vocal "Laas" in unison and Black's bass drum and snare on every beat all adds mock authenticity to the proceedings.

The Beast

An instrumental released in 1992 but recorded in 1984. It had lyrics written by Cornwell but they were left off. It's a beautiful piece of music and then the musical journey then goes off piste and becomes a techno track largely thanks to Black's programmed driving drums and a simple bass riff.

We then return to the earlier keyboard break. It feels like a lost opportunity as the music is inspired, particularly the second part and could have led to three different songs given the different sections on show here. Burnel eventually used the music on his *Un Jour Parfait* album in 1988 adding lyrics in a spoken voice and a melody for the chorus.

*****

This intriguing instrumental begins with a Cornwell Spanish guitar solo in free time (lacking a specific sense of pulse) based over two chords which has a convincing allure. The first change of chord to the key chord after three seconds sees the melody clashing to a semitone below the key note which leads us into thinking that we may be about to embark on a mysterious dissonant journey but the piece settles down with two riffs that are wholly attractive.

The first of these is based on a rising chord that, when repeated, extends to five beats instead of the previous four beats. The second, lower riff at 0:41 also has an extension of an extra beat when repeated but because the whole section is in a free time, it is somewhat inconspicuous.

After this evocative opening, the mood is completely dissipated by Black's Techno drumbeat, first on bass drum only, and then with hi-hat added, with Greenfield now repeating the two guitar riffs but with no extensions to the beats in the bar as the drum pattern is definitively four to the bar.

Greenfield then adds other riffs which are still performed over the same two chords as before until the end of the section where one of the two repeating chords is now subtly changed from a minor to a major chord at 2:22 adding an interesting twist. This section is then repeated but with Black now introducing the snare and occasional toms. One could argue that the drums are cumbersome and that a dialogue of a softer keyboard sound and Spanish guitar may have resulted in a successfully atmospheric piece. But the band had different ideas and wanted to build the instrumental up by adding one instrument at a time.

So, the bass enters next over the added keyboard riff and then the keyboard drops out to leave just the bass (and drums) playing a slightly expansive continuation of the two main chords. The keyboards then re-enter with a rather hackneyed low synth blues riff at 2:54 which, mercifully, is only played twice.

After several bars of just drums, a jangly and delayed guitar enters continuing the same two chords. Suddenly, after nearly three and a half minutes of the same two chords, a new sequence is played accompanied by vocal hums but, with the guitar, bass and drums now all motoring along, a sense of drive is developing. What follows next is rather unexpected as Black unfurls some heavy electronic fills, panning around left and right followed by a keyboard sound that sounds more like it belongs to an eighties cop movie especially as it is based on one chord.

More repeats of the vocals and more explosive random drum sounds follow before the opening riff returns to add a sense of continuity. The delayed guitar chords and extra guitar riffs add a pleasing sense of movement to this return. The end section adds another rarely used chord by the band at 5:18 which, again, sounds like it belongs to an eighties TV show and, along with Cornwell's delayed guitar, finishes the piece.

Six minutes long and with many different facets to it, one is left to muse on its holistic effectiveness. Clearly a product of its time which leads to awkward moments, but also with much to commend it. But there is also a convincing argument that the atmospheric opening could have been developed and become the main stylistic force of the piece whilst manipulating the different beats in the bar, accompanied with more subtle keyboard sounds, drums and bass.

Footnotes

1. Official Chart Website
2. Official Chart Website
3. Official Chart Website
4. Official Chart Website
5. Official Chart Website
6. Sean O'Hagan, NME September 1984 provided by Simon Dell's archive
7. Official Chart Website

The Stranglers 1977-1990

Dreamtime

In late 1985 the band reconvened with Latham to begin work on the follow up to *Aural Sculpture*. Although not a huge commercial success the album was successful enough artistically and in terms of relationships for all parties, including the record company, to carry on working together.

The sessions began at ICP studios in Belgium which was also where *Aural Sculpture* had been recorded. What followed was a tortuous a few months of work which led to only three tracks being anything like finished and according to Burnel weren't worthy of being on an album – one was even an *Aural Sculpture* left over.

There wasn't a massive fall out, but Latham had other projects to go to and mentioned that he thought the songs needed more work which surprised the group. It was mutually agreed to end the relationship.

The band reconvened in Cambridge with Mike Kemp as co-producer along with the band. Kemp had worked with Greenfield and Burnel on *Fire and Water* so was a relatively known quantity. The co-producer used a young Owen Morris as engineer who of course later found fame and fortune by producing Oasis's multimillion selling first albums.

In terms of the producers, it is tempting to see Kemp as a Burnel's and Greenfield's man, and the pendulum of influence in the band swinging to them and to Burnel in particular. For a start he contributed much more in the way of songs than his single lyric and one vocal performance on *Aural Sculpture*.

Burnel saw Latham as Cornwell's man and as we have seen, almost said as much when reflecting on *Aural Sculpture*. With Latham no longer at the helm maybe the band might realign along lines of the early days where there was a vying for the spotlight and to be heard, which spurred the two songwriters onto to great creative heights and productive collaboration on songs that were genuinely jointly written.

There was potentially a window of opportunity that could have been good for the band in terms of quality, productivity and collaboration. But in truth the opportunities of working on songs was getting less and less as the two songwriters turned up to the studio with songs already completed and there was little opportunity to add ideas.

It was in reality another sign that things were not well in the band's camp. Instrumentally things weren't looking up either. Black insisted on programmed drums again and consigned the band to being perfectly in time but stilted. In reality many bands were now recording drums in a similar way.

Greenfield continued to explore the pre-set button on his synth and although as ever still a brilliant player the unique sonic innovator of the early albums had gone AWOL. Burnel continued to play it safe with his bass lines and bass sound. That dynamic, driving, aggressive playing allied to complex melodic runs seemed to be a thing of the past.

Cornwell, a man who had constantly claimed his guitar was not high enough in the mix seemed content to just add subtle understated colour to the sound the others created. Even on his own songs he played simple, but admittedly quite effective guitar lead runs, building on the style he developed on the previous album, and was now a trend.

The band's new direction was musically safer and simpler and was obviously a conscious decision, the days of inspired musical experimentation were gone. However, they chose to continue using brass or brass sound effects on a number of songs. Whilst not exactly experimental it was still a brave choice as it was fair to say the use of brass had split the opinion of long-term fans. The band were not backing down over this as they felt it was where their future lay and they also continued to use a brass section whilst on tour.

The group previewed the album with the release of the single 'Nice In Nice' in August 1986. A chirpy tune but it underachieved and only just cracked the Top 30 (No.30).[1] The record company quickly tried to correct things by immediately releasing 'Always The Sun' in mid-October. Lightning struck twice as the song also stalled at No.30[2] despite being a classic and has consistently appeared in their live sets for forty years.

The failure is a mystery as the song got copious airplay and was given a variety of releases from 7-inch, 7-inch double pack, and 12-inch with of course, each version containing previously unreleased tracks or mixes.

The song did well internationally and was a hit in several countries as well as getting a good deal of radio play in the USA — the first time this had happened for the band. Could this be the start of an American breakthrough? Epic released the album in early November and hopes were high although the lead off singles hadn't set the world alight chart wise it had created a buzz in the industry about the band and that they were back on form with quality material.

There was genuine consternation in the industry and elements of the press that 'Always The Sun' hadn't been a bigger hit. However, despite the positive feeling around, and inside the band, these hopes were unfortunately unfounded. The album scraped into the Top Twenty albums, debuting and peaking at a disappointing No16.[3]

Then like its predecessor it dropped alarmingly and by late November, only four weeks after its release, it was Number 91, and then dropped out of the chart.[4] A commercial disappointment and possibly a commercial disaster. It returned to the very low reaches of the charts for two weeks in late January.

The single 'Big In America' had been rushed out in mid-December to try and reignite the album but The Stranglers Christmas single curse struck again, and despite six weeks in the chart it only just cracked the Top Fifty (No.48)[5] in the first week of January. The single's minor hit status possibly breathed a little life into the corpse of *Dreamtime*, causing it to make that brief reappearance in the very lower reaches of the Top 100.

The record company then tried to revive the album with a fourth single in early March, 'Shakin' Like A Leaf'. The single fared worse than its predecessors only managing four weeks and a highest position of 58.[6] Epic were nothing if not persistent and had 'Was it You?' lined up as a potential fifth single but thought better of it and shelved the release.

Abroad the album failed to build on the foundation *Aural Sculpture* laid, and only made fleeting appearances in the lower reaches of Australia, New Zealand, Canada and the Netherlands. There was an appearance in the US album Top 200 peaking at 172, a small breakthrough but hardly a ringing endorsement.[7]

The title *Dreamtime* was based on the Aboriginal cultural/ religious idea. According to the art website Aboriginal Contemporary Dreamtime is described thus: "Dreamtime is the period in which life was created according to Aboriginal culture. Dreaming is the word used to explain how life came to be; it is the stories and beliefs behind creation. It is called different names in different Aboriginal languages, such as: Ngarranggarni, Tjukula Jukurrpa'.[8]

The band didn't base the whole album around the concept like they had done with albums in the recent past. This time only a few of the tracks linked directly to the concept. The artwork however, both inner and outer sleeves utilised the concept. The front cover — a beautiful photograph, had four Aboriginal people in silhouette against a desert sunset.

The symbolism of the cover works on another level, four figures being chosen perhaps to represent each band member and as they are in silhouette they appear as MeninBlack. The back cover shows a parched cracked desert floor of the outback. The inner sleeve used Aboriginal art to illustrate the lyric sheet. The lyrics themselves were made to look handwritten and although not in aboriginal language the calligraphy effect with the artwork gives an indigenous feel to the design. The sleeve was designed by Jean Luke Epstein who had also worked on *Aural Sculpture*. Epstein was also responsible for the related singles of both albums.

The Stranglers were not alone in being interested in the concept of Dreamtime. It was a bit of musical theme in the eighties with Kate Bush releasing the groundbreaking album, *The Dreaming* along with its title track as a single in 1982.

It was coupled with a B-side called 'Dreamtime'. The tracks used aboriginal instrumentation as well as the concept of aboriginal mysticism. The Cult's 1984 debut album was also called *Dreamtime* and dealt with the mystical concept of indigenous North American people. In addition, there was the global rise in the mid to late eighties of Australian eco rockers and Aboriginal champions Midnight Oil.

The point being that The Stranglers were now firmly on mainstream territory with their latest album and for once were maybe a little late to the party. Even The Jam in 1982 had a track called 'Dream Time' with a backward tape intro that evokes the altered consciousness state associated with the Antipodean spirituality.

If it was reviewed, the reviews tended to condemn the album with faint praise, which appeared to be a bigger insult than a hatchet job from one of their enemies in the music newspapers. Adverts were put in the press and there was a tour to accompany the album which in UK terms showed them still to be as popular a live attraction as ever. They also toured in Europe extensively and played dates in the USA which kept the band busy into late 1987.

Reviews of the album when it was reissued aren't particularly effusive either with comments like "too smooth" and "time filler" jumping out. In terms of musical style, the album is a trifle schizophrenic with the band trying all kinds of styles such as swing, jazz, skiffle and even samba.

This accounts for the general consensus that there isn't enough continuity of style or subject matter to make the album work or hold together.

It is the first time the band seemed to lack a viable concept for an album with perhaps only the artwork being the most realised theme. Given the number of countries referred to by name and musical style used it could maybe be subtitled 'What we did on our Holidays'.

Always The Sun

Destined to become a signature tune for the band and released twice, each time cracking the Top 30 but going no further despite a big push by the record company on both occasions. There was even a *Top Of The Pops* appearance on the week of release, but it failed to inject the necessary momentum.

The 1990 version was released after Cornwell had left and is little different from the original single save for some minor twiddling from John Ellis newly promoted from touring band member to full member. The album version is nearly five minutes long whereas the 7-inch single was edited, shortening Greenfield's atmospheric keyboard introduction to make it more radio friendly, because remember, the pop picking public can only cope with songs just over three minutes long.

There was a 12-inch mix which clocks in at nearly six minutes. The band mixed this version themselves and added a few minor flourishes like an instrumental break towards the end which does enhance the experience for the listener. This version of the track shows once again that when it came to the 12-inch format they themselves or the remixers they chose were masters at adding to the listening experience something that most other name bands at this time were unable to do, opting instead for addition drum fills in an effort to allegedly make their tune more danceable.

On the album version Greenfield provides a long introduction with a keyboard soundscape that metaphorically creates a sunrise with lush chords. The guitar simmers, whilst the bass accompanies in the background in a sympathetic way. Black's subtle programmed rim click sets an atmosphere that this is a song where the listener needs to take note of the lyrics.

Cornwell begins with a series of questions which challenge the inequality of the world. During the song he takes sideswipes at politicians for cynically and deliberately failing to deliver social justice because it would upset the status quo. In a gentler way he makes a jibe about weather forecasters being unable to accurately predict the weather leading to disastrous unpreparedness for some serious weather events in the eighties.

There are other ecological elements to the song with allusions to a drought in the first line which also fits in with the theme of the cover artwork. The song essentially celebrates the omnipresence and continuity of the sun whilst at the same time imploring people to think about the implications of a permanently sunny climate.

The mid-eighties were a time when the world turned its attention to the horror of drought and starvation thanks to conscience pricking news reports and of course the pop industry with its fund raising and awareness raising campaigns of Band Aid and Live Aid. An interesting aside to the pop industry's fund raising is that the band were not invited to be involved in either event. This was very surprising given The Stranglers had a fair degree of longevity and recognition by 1985 and were still regular visitors to the charts, even if it was only to graze the lower reaches of the Top 40.

Their absence can perhaps be best be explained by their past history and behaviour, which was still a ball and chain around their media persona. Then factor in that they simply didn't have the right friends and it isn't difficult to see why the invitation never came.

When Cornwell makes an allusion in one of his lines to people losing their money via gambling, he cleverly uses the word "lads" to describe the recipients of your hard-earned cash but it's not just young chancers he's referring to. The "lads" are *Ladbroke's* the bookmakers. Although a song obviously about the sun i.e., the celestial body, the sun is often used in references to nuclear explosions.

A book about the making and using of the atomic bomb by Robert Jungk was entitled *Brighter Than A Thousand Suns*. A book title that fellow music travellers, and like The Stranglers, serial baiters of the music press, Killing Joke borrowed for their 1986 post apocalypse concept album.

Nuclear war was a cultural obsession at this time and Cornwell nails the issue with his "pushing the knob" phrase i.e., pushing the nuclear button, a phrase in common usage throughout the decade.

It is Cornwell's song despite the full band credit and was brought virtually complete to the group who made no alterations to what they were given. This was becoming more and more the norm for the way the band worked.

Burnel brought his songs to the table complete as well and there were only three songs where there was a genuine collaboration between the principal songwriters. The song is very well thought of outside the band's fan base and has become one of their signature tunes. It's a genuine mystery as to why it wasn't a mega hit.

*****

Sustained chords on a soft keyboard synth pad sound open the song but an echo feature soon enters after a few seconds on the keyboards, that provides a rhythm and the movement for the entire song. The drums and bass soon enter, and the chords settle into a very conventional pattern using the main three chords.

The keyboard sound is so enveloping in an almost hypnotic way that the listener cannot help but be drawn into the music's simplistic charm. The result is similar to 'Skin Deep' where a simple song uses the three main chords but with a sonic palette subtly driven by a keyboard sound with bass, guitar and drums all playing a conventional supporting role.

The difference is that 'Always The Sun' deploys softer sounds especially on the guitar with its clipped chords that are hardly noticeable as they blend with the keyboard sound to add an extra delicate rhythmic push whereas on 'Skin Deep' the guitars deliberately added a contrast in sound.

The programmed drums are softer here as well as is the vocal tone. This is one of Cornwell's most breathy vocal performances and it dovetails effectively with the instrumentation to enhance the dreamlike nature of the song. As with many of the band's songs, this atmosphere is at odds with the sentiment of the lyrics. The only chord that defies conventionality is after "man with the gun" which could be seen to be word painting as the sudden shock of the chord is after the word "gun". This harsh change in chordal movement moves us into a brief bridge and then the chorus, but both these sections restore chordal conventionality with the related minor chord of the chorus providing the necessary lifting contrast.

Further similarities between the two songs involve the melodic shape which, in both verses, is understated with a sense of reflectiveness which, in both cases, contrasts highly effectively with the choruses, both of which have strong shapes and sing-along hook lines. Both songs also deploy high pitched, breathy backing vocals in the choruses. 'Always The Sun' displays a particularly deep contrast in pitch between the low musings of the verse and the rising repeating hook line of the chorus, supplemented by Burnel's breathy high pitched backing vocals.

All these features add to the obvious commerciality and the overall blend of sound married to the vocal tones results in a highly effective song. It is no surprise that it continues to be a staple of the bands set and always produces the desired sing-along as well as the cheers and flashing lights when Greenfield's 'off beat' chiming sound enters during the second and subsequent verses.

Cornwell's guitar solo is one of his most melodic, of which we know he is so capable and yet guitar solos have been in such short supply over recent albums. The accompanying high backing vocal "Aahs" that punctuate the solo are also crowd-pleasing moments.

Another difference between 'Always The Sun' and 'Skin Deep' is that the latter followed such an intriguing and contrasting opening song in 'Ice Queen' to establish an adventurous feel to side one of 'Aural Sculpture'. 'Always The Sun' opens the album *Dreamtime*, and its equanimous quality does create a different mood for the opening of the album and it is followed by another strong, yet temperate song.

Dreamtime

The title track is a good song but most of the keyboards, drums and indeed the guitar are victims of the studio production of the eighties and therein lies a problem of not just this song but a lot of the album.

If the listener can get past the dated garish production, the subject matter of the song is Aboriginal mysticism. And whilst the bass and guitar create a genuine atmosphere the drums and the keyboards are too bright and clean and give a clinical, antiseptic feel to proceedings.

Compare this to Kate Bush's homage to Aboriginal culture with her 1982 song 'The Dreaming', where she successfully combined indigenous instruments and eighties synthetics to create a 'real' sounding, earthy, trance like piece of music that doesn't sound processed, despite using the ultimate musical processer, the Fairlight.

Bush admittedly had a bigger budget, endless time and could hire who and what she wanted but The Stranglers weren't exactly being starved of cash either and had already spent considerable time in the studio working on the album.

Bush's vision and ability allowed her to create a timeless, challenging but ultimately satisfying piece of music. The Stranglers in their pomp could have done the same. As it stands it's a good song, but it could have been great with a more sympathetic ear and a resistance from the producer and band to the sound of 1985.

The whole concept of Aboriginal Dreamtime is timelessness and the sound on display here is dated and anything but timeless. The vocals, lead and backing, as well as the lyrics salvage the song giving it dynamics and a peak.

The song marks a return to an Aboriginal theme for the band who first visited the theme on 'Nuclear Device (Wizard Of Aus)'. Cornwell's lyrics are minimal but extremely effective. There is a natural groove to the song created by the entire band with the percussive marimba sound leading the way.

Cornwell's vocal locks into the groove and this makes the song mirror the philosophy of Aboriginal culture. The first nation peoples' way of life was all about being in harmony with the environment and the singer's lyrics reflect the oneness with the earth.

Put very simply Dreamtime is what Aborigines believe to be their creation story, but it is much more than that and is an essential belief a philosophy and a way of life. The environment and humans' relationship to it are a cornerstone to the Aboriginal way of life. Stones and stone structures alluded to in the lyrics are key important mystical objects in the religion.

Cornwell's lyrics can't sum up in detail a whole religion in a few verses, so he adopts an impressionist approach to give listeners a flavour, so important elements like the significance of the earth are mentioned but not in detail. He also drops on a couple of other concepts which show the complexity of this ancient first nation culture when he uses the phrases "total clock". Aboriginal people had detailed and sophisticated mathematical ways of measuring time even though they didn't have clocks. Cornwell also uses his wordplay to make a telling pun re-Australian, and first nation culture in the line:

> The only thing for us to do
> Is walk about and then appreciate the view

On the surface he is just talking about a tourist moving about but by choosing his words carefully the two words "walk" and "about" he is also referring to a deeper meaning because by putting the two words together one gets the word 'walkabout'. Walkabout is an Aboriginal mystical rite of passage which involves young males surviving and having spiritually enlightenment in the outback for up to six months.

This concept crossed over into mainstream first world culture with Nicholas Roeg's film *Walkabout* staring David Gulpilil and Jenny Agutter. The meaning and concept of the film was somewhat ambushed by Agutter's nude scene which caused a storm at the time and today it would not been allowed as she was only seventeen at the time.

Despite the notoriety, the film was one of the first mainstream films to deal with Aboriginal culture in an equal and non-judgemental way and also feature a first nation actor as one of the stars. Cornwell would undoubtedly been aware these references when he was writing the song.

*****

The title track has a lengthy instrumental built around a rather subtle bass riff and, initially, two guitar chords. There is a keyboard solo with two different sounds panned right and left and played in octaves and the sounds have a World music feel, with the lower octave right panned sound being a wooden percussive xylophone/marimba, to reinforce the aboriginal roots on which the song is based. The bass sound and Cornwell's short clipped dry guitar riffs also lean towards a similar feel.

This is a welcome return to the multi-melodic layering textures that has been far less prevalent over recent albums. The keyboard solo has strength and yet it is somewhat subdued by being low in the mix at the expense of the drums and guitars that are, arguably, too prominent. The end of the instrumental introduction sees a new chord pattern which uses a descending chromatic idea and will become the verse chords.

Further fast repeating descending keyboard chord notes on the xylophone/marimba sound add to the World music theme. The keyboard solo now becomes a repeating riff under the vocal melody. The melodic shape of the vocal is limited yet highly effective in its low register and is complemented by Burnel adding a high breathy "Dreamtime" backing vocal harmony to the end of the phrase. The chorus moves, effectively, higher in the vocal register with multiple vocals, some pitched an octave lower to add richness and with a continuation of the background keyboard riffs and clipped guitar.

Verse two sees the low vocal now sung an octave higher to good effect which adds urgency to the song, and the addition of the new "We won't have to touch" section after the second chorus introduces a significant slightly clashing lower backing vocal harmony that also reminds us of the earlier, more dissonant times.

Black's sturdy snare led drum fill at the end of this short section also reminds us of the older drum patterns whilst Cornwell's rising melody provides a sense of symmetry following the previous descending pattern and culminates in one of his quirky vocal tones on "view".

The ensuing short keyboard solo has another keyboard part very soft in the mix which potentially creates intriguing clashing notes towards the end, but the second part is too low in the mix to highlight this.

More repeats of all the sections follow and the ending is signalled by a pause on the instruments in the chorus on "Time" with the lower backing vocal taking more prominence, before all the instruments stop with a guitar and keyboard echo quickly fading out.

This is a strong song melodically and chordally, and the arrangement coated with the World music sounds, whilst not to every fan's liking, has plenty of interest with multi-melodic layering all the more welcome.

Was It You?

After two subtle songs to open the album the mood is totally changed by the explosive brass riff that leads this piece. This is only the second time brass had opened and carried the main melody of a Stranglers' song and added to the muscular bass riff it gives the song a real swagger.

The backbeat of the drums ensures the song is moved along at a frantic pace The chiming guitar work peaks with a strangled lead solo that resembles Dave Davis's solo on 'You Really Got Me' by The Kinks. The song was earmarked to be a single and there was a second version of the song, the 7-inch edit which was subsequently released when the album was reissued.

Burnel employs a plethora of his singing styles in the song virtually singing each line in a different style, so we get the whisperer, the snarler, the crooner etc. Such diversity serves to add to the lyrical theme which is about a conspiracy of collaborators.

Burnel brought the song complete to the band and that signifies a return of confidence and form for the bassist with a raucous piece which deals with the big issues of the mid-eighties in a conspiracy theory way with a dose of humour thrown in. So, there are references to AIDS, the famine in Africa, and the conspiracy element is that he links these world shattering issues to the secret services of the USA and the then USSR i.e., the CIA and KGB respectively.

The song title is an accusatory question. Burnel's answer is that he doesn't really know what is going on and as a result he feels he is losing control which should be interpreted as him getting angry and feeling powerless at world events. As ever with The Stranglers despite dealing with a serious issue there is an element of humour with the incongruous line.

The 7-inch edit of the shelved single features the line "Meat and vegetables, was it stew?" a meaninglessly line in the context of the song but an undoubtedly humorous image. Some lyric sites print this particular line as it is in the title phrase i.e., "Was it You?" However careful listening reveals the correct wording of the line is the culinary dish.

There is no doubt the writer engaged in the word play to catch the casual listener out. A little joke at the listener's expense and also to check they are actually listening. The proposed single was a heavily edited and rearranged version of the original song found on the album. The length of the song was cut, new lines of lyrics were added, and others moved around. For example, the "stew" line was the first line of the song on this version.

There was also a lyric edit with the phrase "genital disease" replaced with the more radio friendly "general disease". Interestingly STDs have been a theme of Burnel's in his songs over the years, e.g., 'Crabs' from his solo album *Euroman Cometh* in 1979.

The instruments appear more separated. Burnel's vocals are clearer allowing the lyrics to be showcased and the jokes to be signposted. Black's drums are more conventional and added to different backing vocals in the middle section all combine to make the song more effective. The single edit had a great deal of effort put in to making it sound current and commercial.

There was also an inventive dance orientated 12-inch remix prepared known as the hot mix done by the band themselves. It would have been the fifth single off the album but was shelved when Epic effectively called time on trying to promote the album. The 7-inch and 12-inch mix pandered to what was fashionable in the charts and the fact that there was so much wholesale tinkering with the song perhaps suggests the band and the record company didn't really have faith in the song to be a hit single.

*****

After the more laid-back feel of the opening two songs, there is a change of gear with the bands' most aggressive song for many albums but with the addition of the brass that had debuted on the previous album. The opening main section is riff-based rather than chord-based, and the brass plays the most prominent role with a repeating high riff whilst the guitar, keyboard and extra brass play a contrasting rising riff.

The bass plays a third riff and these three multi-layered melodies do have a slight clashing feel. The vocal melody is part sung; part spoken with Burnel playing with different forceful vocal tones, avoiding an overly aggressive tone but opting instead for a more questioning approach to suit the title.

Meanwhile Black keeps things very simple with the snare drum on every beat, a pattern that was used frequently on the earlier albums, accompanied by plenty of snare and tom fills, designed to sound live. The section ends with a return to a chordal texture on "I don't really know" which provides an effective contrast, and the final chord is suitably unconventional (or uncontrolled) to support Burnel's vocal melody "losing contrololol" word painting.

Does the overall effect work? Had this song adorned one of the first three albums with its rawer and more aggressive instrumental sounds then the song probably would have carried considerable weight, but the more pop sounds that had fused through their previous two albums and the first two songs on this album presents a dichotomy that is not easily resolved.

Whilst the brass clearly has a powerful tone, it is debateable whether it is suitable for this type of song, but the brass is only part of the conundrum. The band had travelled so far away from their sonic roots, so the song ultimately results in confusion. Burnel needed more aggression within the overall sonic framework, including his own bass sound, to support his assertive vocal tone.

The problem of stylistic uncertainty is exacerbated by the slightly incongruous middle section after the second "losing control". A conventional chord sequence accompanies a keyboard solo with a sound that doesn't dare to be too aggressive and a shape and a rhythm that is uninspiring, especially compared to the creativity of the shapes of the previous song. The lower brass notes add to the uncertainty of what this section is trying to achieve. When this section is repeated later there is a strange spoken voice, but the words are inaudible, so its effectiveness can be questioned.

Cornwell adds an aggressive impetus with his solo that deliberately lacks melodic intent. But with the brass present and then playing the opening riff an octave higher, this casts further evidence to doubting the effectiveness of the song. Another barely audible voice speaks right at the end of the fade "Or maybe it really was… you".

Their most aggressive song since the *Black And White* album. 'Let Me Introduce You To The Family' from *La Folie* had similar moments and the disco beat drum pattern negatively affected that song. Here, the brass feels similar as it seems to get in the way of a possible rawer sound had the distorted guitar and some harder synth been given space to give the song the aggressive backdrop it needed.

You'll Always Reap What You Sow

A big, lush ballad written by Burnel but sung by Cornwell. Sung by Cornwell as the rest of the band felt his voice fitted the song better. Cornwell does sing the song beautifully it's a restrained and heart felt performance for the most part and when he cuts loose in the chorus he still always appears to be in control.

The rest of the band are restrained and provide a sombre backing track to match the bittersweet tone of Cornwell's vocal. The pedal steel work by session musician BJ Cole adds a melancholy atmosphere. Given it's a slow song and not particularly musically inventive it is over long clocking in at over five minutes, a bit of judicious editing would not have gone a miss.

Indeed, several songs on the album suffer a similar problem as if the band were trying to eke out their material. It's also a symptom of the mid-eighties CD boom where the new format offered groups up to seventy minutes music on one disc. Vinyl didn't offer the same ability. The album clocks in at nearly forty-six minutes which was pushing vinyl's sustainable sound quality.

Other bands used the new format to add more tracks and write longer songs which didn't mean the additional time led to greater quality. The first six Stranglers albums clocked in at around forty minutes or even less. Sometimes less is more.

Lyrically it is very interesting not for the turn of phrase, but the smouldering vitriol Burnel holds for someone. The received wisdom is that it was about Cornwell but that's pure speculation. The circumstantial evidence is strong as the two had been moving further apart. Song collaboration wasn't really happening like it did in the old days and Cornwell's material was starting to dominate more than it had done in the past.

On *Aural Sculpture* Burnel had really only brought one song to the table on *Dreamtime* he had come up with three strong songs and had despite differences, collaborated with Cornwell on three others. In terms of the vocals the rest of the band and producer Mike Kemp opted for Cornwell to sing the song which must have been a bitter blow for Burnel, particularly as the lyrics were obvious heartfelt, and there was clearly a strong message to somebody whether it was Cornwell or not. If the song is about Cornwell, then Burnel was following in a grand rock 'n' roll tradition of band mates criticising each other through a song.

A classic example being John Lennon's 'How do you Sleep?' which was directed at Paul McCartney following the acrimonious breakup of The Beatles. Carly Simon called out film star Warren Beatty in 'You're so Vain'. In the post punk world PIL picked up the baton with John Lyden's scathing attack on former manager Malcom McLaren through the song 'Albatross'.

The Stranglers themselves early in their career also set the pace with songs like 'Sometimes' and 'London Lady'. Clearly Burnel was mining a rich seam of rock and band history and tradition with his scornful attack on an unnamed individual.

There is a demo version featuring a Burnel vocal take on YouTube that is fascinating to listen to. It demonstrates that Cornwell followed almost completely Burnel's vocal melody and phrasing. The big difference is the chorus where the bassist delivers a no holds barred emotional roar of a performance. It was the chorus in particular that was felt to be wrong by the band and so the take was confined to the vaults. Many fans who have heard this demo actually prefer Burnel's performance even if it has slight technical flaws compared to the one that eventually made it onto the album.

The Burnel vocal version lacks the pedal steel guitar of BJ Cole, and it also has an inspired whistling outro which may have prompted him to think of using a pedal steel guitar on the final version. Both versions owe a great deal to Roy Orbison's vocal crooning style with perhaps Burnel especially with the delivery of the chorus emulating the Big O at his best.

*****

A shift in tempo and instrumentation where three different guitar sounds of sustained echoed chords, the faster background strums and a relatively low-pitched thin riff dominate the soundscape in the introduction.

With Cornwell singing the song and having such a prominent instrumental focus, many would mistakenly believe that he wrote the song, but Burnel's less conventional chord patterns are to the fore here and, as a result, the song has less sense of a home key with each section suggesting a subtle key shift culminating in a desired drifting, almost timeless, effect.

This supports the mood of the song and the band's decision to have Cornwell's more soulful tone adds to the sense of drift. The domination of the guitars is increased by the addition of BJ Cole's pedal steel guitar from the second verse onwards. This reinforces these drifting, timeless moods as this particular guitar is able to easily slide up and down through notes and Cole utilises this device to good effect here.

There is limited instrumental input from the other three band members and Burnel's bass is delayed until the second verse ("You had no reason") and even then, it is low in the mix despite it having some interesting shape and rhythm. Prior to this, a keyboard enters on the first "You'll always reap just what you show" performing a low bass like riff that, along with the backing vocals, "It only goes to show" do stand out and are questionable in their effectiveness to the overall sound which is busy enough already.

This low keyboard bass idea continues at points mainly after "It only goes to show" and competes with the bass at times leading to both sounds creating melodic layering but they are so low in the mix, partly due to the steel guitar, that the potential effectiveness of this melodic layering is somewhat reduced.

The softer toned backing vocals are in harmony with the higher harmony sitting rather awkwardly. The new section, "I didn't think of vengeance", has a suitable lift with keyboard held strings merging with backing vocals to provide a sustained sound as the strumming guitars now provide a gratifying sense of momentum as does the slightly unconventional chord pattern where "And now it's time" has the same melody as "I didn't think of vengeance" but the chords are different, reinforcing the fluidity of the mood.

The first guitar solo at 2:55 is yet another example of Cornwell's superb ability to produce such strong melodic moments during his solos and the second solo that fades out the song is Cole's much higher solo which, at first is almost too high but becomes a suitably impressive fade out. Burnel nibbles at some interesting bass movement right at the end of the fade almost teasing us to ask why he didn't do this earlier. Of course, we wish he had.

This is an underrated song and Burnel once again shows a side of his songwriting where he effortlessly produces strong melodies over highly effective, slightly unconventional fluid chord patterns. The arrangement is less convincing and open to debate. Is the proliferation of guitars too much? Do the low keyboard bass sound and backing vocals work? Overall, it is tempting to say that such a strong song could have been stripped down a little more in parts as it did not need so much instrumental input.

Ghost Train

Cornwell makes no bones about it in his book *Song by Song* that the song is about the band and their lack of direction, their arguments and the burden and resentment he felt at being the main songwriter.

Ironically given the subject matter it's one of three songs on the album that he and Burnel collaborated on. One might expect it to be an aggressive no holds barred song but what we get is a heavily synthesised pop song set to a skiffle beat and Cornwell delivering his anger in subtle wordplay which meant the designed recipients of the message probably failed to grasp its meaning.

The song suffers from eighties production techniques, probably more than any other Stranglers song. The processed train sound and the toy town train whistle sound incredibly dated and embarrassing. However, they weren't the only ones using train sounds badly with electro popsters OMD delivering the dreadful 'Locomotion' which given it predates 'Ghost Train' by eighteen months might have influenced the band to go down this track.

If you want a good example of a band using the mid-eighties music fetish for trains check out A-ha's Kraftwerk inspired 'Train Of Thought'. Given A-ha were a self-confessed pop band their train motifs carried far more gravity than 'Ghost Train' or 'Locomotion'. The Stranglers weren't the only ones using skiffle elements at this time earlier in 1986. Indie band It's Immaterial had a big hit with the chugging skiffle rhythms of 'Driving Away From Home'.

It is conceivable that this influenced Cornwell as he kept a close eye on the music scene and its fashions and fads. *Dreamtime* contained a variety of musical styles which had become a band trait since *Feline*. It's as if they were searching for what would bring them a big success to move them onto the next part of their career. The point being, as Cornwell suggests in his lyrics of 'Ghost Train', the band lacked direction and therefore more likely to fall prey to musical fads in the hope of finding inspiration. "Ghost Train is a classic example of this for a band that specialised in timeless classic this is possibly their most dated song.

Using the image of a 'Ghost Train' to portray the band does actually work and then using a skiffle shuffle to deliver the message is on the surface inspired. Skiffle has a long association with the railways, the rhythm itself is inspired by tempo of a steam locomotive and much of the subject matter of the songs were inspired by travelling on trains. The most famous example being Lead Belly's 'Rock Island Line' made famous by proto rock 'n' roll guru and King of Skiffle Lonnie Donegan. Donegan sped up the original and in one foul swoop invented skiffle and landed himself a Top Ten hit on both sides of the Atlantic.

As an image the ghost train conjures up ideas of lack of control, fatalism, a journey to nowhere and an unreal situations. There are also many oblique references to the band's situation such as the use of the word "passengers", which is what Cornwell must have been feeling about the rest of the band, given he felt he was doing the lion's share of the work.

He also refers to himself as the "driver" and is critical of himself in that role with references to his drug use clouding his judgement when he uses the phrase "snow blinding the driver" and also his inability to take good advice: "driver not listening when the weather is fine".

By the same token he could also be criticising other band members because with the exception of Greenfield, all the other band members saw themselves as drivers of the band at various times. For example, Black's intransigence over the continued use of programmed drums and then Burnel's forthright opinions and judgements on other musical aspects.

The band's view was if someone held a strong opinion and wouldn't back down then that opinion stood. Greenfield was no shrinking violet either but perhaps not as insistent or intransigent as the others. Making his point, remember it was Greenfield's persistence and refusal to bin the idea that eventual gave them and the world 'Golden Brown'.

Towards the end of the song Cornwell's vocals become more histrionic and can be taken as a sign of the frustration he was feeling. Rather ironically, given the guitarist's past complaints about being too low in the mix, there are some outstanding guitar flourishes out front which seem wasted on such a muddled song.

Finally the song ends with a whimper with a weak simulated train whistle as it fades out into the distance which probably tells the listener all they need to know.

*****

Percussive sounds and a train whistle greet the listener for the final song on side one. Not the most auspicious of openings for the ending to a side that has contained contrasts in style and considerable quality. But this song really lets the side down as, despite the title, it hardly goes anywhere, instead being stuck in a dubious groove based on a limited chord pattern.

The repeating keyboard riff, clean guitar licks and repeating bass riff all contribute to the sense of train-like movement, the idea of which is questionable. The vocal delivery has a languid tone, and the reasonably shaped opening phrase is followed by a spoken phrase which further reduces the effectiveness of the song.

The second half of the verse "Wondering where" continues the spoken vocal with a predictable chord shift which seems lacking in creativity as the final two chords seem 'stuck on' to enable us to return to the start of the next verse. Things disintegrate further in verse two with the softly sung backing vocals and a harmony on "arrive" in an attempt to enhance the quality. But the mood has become too saccharine despite the guitar riffs that do provide some moments of quality.

The next section "It's been a long, long ride" finally moves the song up a gear and there is much promise to this section with Cornwell's impassioned high vocal delivery of an effective melody and suitable chords but unfortunately the groove and accompanying sounds are unable to support the voice to the necessary degree, so the impact is subdued. Instead, Black introduces some extra panned hi-hat sounds to further imitate the train movement. We didn't need them to start with and we don't need them now.

What is the point of the song? The lyrics are, on the surface, one of the most banal ever written by the band and to accompany it with various sounds linked to trains along with the inoffensive repeating ideas, the soft vocal tone, the insipid backing vocals, and the spoken vocals results in a very questionable experience despite the potential from the more aggressive vocal section and the guitar riffs. By the time the long, five-minute journey fades out, the band has long since entered a dark tunnel and derailed as side one comes to a close.

Nice In Nice

Side two of the album springs into life with the sprightly swagger of 'Nice In Nice'. Another commercial sounding song chosen as a single and a mystery as to why it didn't perform better, especially as it was also accompanied by a witty and striking video. The tune owes a lot to Greenfield's synth playing as he underpins the song.

As it's an up-tempo song Black's crashing computer generated snare drum give it that distinctive eighties sounds. Burnel's restrained cooing, whisper-singing of the lyrics gives a sneering effect to match the target of his lyrics. In terms of a style the band are aping the fashion of the time, electro pop, to try and sound contemporary and the production certainly gives it that feel.

As we know Nice is notorious in Stranglers folklore being the scene of their incarceration following a riot at a gig. The song is nothing to do with that but the band reference the incident with the picture sleeve featuring a photograph of the band in handcuffs with Burnel waving his chained hand in defiance.

The prison allusion is continued as the 12-inch mix of the song was called the Porridge Mix. The video then tops off the incarceration in Nice motif with the band dressing up in convict uniforms complete with balls and chains looking for all the world looking like extras from the film *Papillion*. The group are clearly having fun save for Black who gets a conciliatory pat on the back in a line up as he clearly thinks the whole video thing is ridiculous.

Part of the video had Burnel dressed as a woman, which is only revealed at the end and playing the part of the main character of the song. It has to be said he plays a convincing woman and yet more evidence of the band's consistent theme of referencing traditional British humour. Throughout theatrical history men have dressed as women for comic effect. The link goes back to Shakespearian times and comes through to the modern day with pantomime dames, *Carry On* films and drag queens.

Burnel and indeed Greenfield had already dragged up for the cover of their 1983 single 'Rain And Dole And Tea' from their *Fire and Water* album. Cross dressing was a bit of a theme in the eighties with Boy George for example, and Queen in their 1984 video 'I Want To Break Free' that had taken cross dressing to a worldwide audience. Further interest is provided by the unique sight of Greenfield standing up and grooving with those fashion items of 1980s — a keytar — a synthesiser strapped to him like a guitar..

Lyrically the song appears to be a straightforward description of an entitled rich French girl who gets everything she wants from her father. A girl of staggering arrogance and fully aware of the hold she has over her suitor.

Then the complexity comes in because the song is Burnel writing about his wife, and they were still very much in love. Perhaps so much in love he was able to poke fun at her without causing offence. The title is an amusing play on words the first word of the title is using the word to mean pleasant or attractive and the last word of the title is the city of Nice in southern France. "So Nice in Nice" can be paraphrased as the attractive girl from Nice. Then there is also the irony of the title for the band as things were certainly not nice in Nice for them in in 1980.

The title ends any further literal allusions and basically the lyrics just describes the girl and her demeanour. One gets the sense that on this album Burnel is easing himself back into song writing just producing simple narratives and description to make his point rather than going for fancy literary devices he used earlier in his career. It's understandable given on the previous album he had been a virtual no show as a songwriter.

*****

Side two commences with this undeniably commercial toe tapper. The eighties sound is omnipresent, and the very high mixed electronic drums are almost piercing to listen to. Add the low synth riff from the introduction that remains throughout most of the song and the jangly chorded guitar sound and there is a proliferation of treble throughout the mix which was certainly a product of its time but is now somewhat jarring to the ear.

This trebled mass is further reinforced by Burnel's breathy vocals and the equally breathy backing vocals. The chord pattern nods to the commercial norms but overall, the song has strength and good contrasting qualities between the sections, and it was probably somewhat of a disappointment to see the song, like 'Always The Sun', only reach number thirty in the charts. The chorus hook line was, perhaps, not quite strong enough for the audience of 1985 and the treble fuelled production was, ironically, possibly overcooked.

Greenfield's extra keyboard arpeggio riff after "It wants this lady" are also a little grating to the ear as are Black's weighty fills in the chorus even though both of these moments have their merits. Cornwell's guitar riff after "from her dad" is a simple one chord idea that does add to the impetus and, overall, the song, with its simple structure rollicks along effectively.

The middle eight "Don't ever tell me", after the second chorus, is a highlight but it's unconventional chord pattern and change of key reduces the commerciality as does the new keyboard sound here which has *The Gospel According To The Meninblack* album otherworldly effect. Burnel's dreamy vocal delivery effectively supports the song's rather biting sentiment at this point.

Both Burnel with this song and Cornwell with 'Always The Sun' had composed highly effective songs that were designed to have chart success, but that success was limited, and this probably did not help the growing tensions in the band.

Big In America

Chosen as a single but failing to set the charts alight, but there was no doubt the band were trying to sound commercial and were throwing the proverbial kitchen sink at trying to have a big hit to reignite their career. The listeners are treated to an array of typical eighties pop techniques.

So, in a seemingly endless list we have quirky keyboards, brass effects on the synth, an actual saxophone solo, slide guitar, a big riff that sounds like Killing Joke's guitar innovator Geordie, big beat drums and Burnel's supporting bass. All the instruments match the title and are big sounding. Greenfield uses a plethora of keyboard effects and gives the song its best moments. The big theme is further hammered home with the 12-inch mix which is spacious, thunderous, and named the Texas mix, remember everything, is bigger in Texas Man!

The video of course follows suit featuring a model Manhattan skyline complete with Empire State Building complete with a King Kong lookalike, draped in the stars and stripes in a style reminiscent of the pop art of the sixties. Like the song the video is far too busy and combined with the music one reaches sensory and cultural overload.

The overload of imagery continues with the lyrics which are multi-faceted with every line offering more than one layer of meaning. The title itself refers to the band's desire to crack the USA. Big in America is a famous music business cliché and an aim all bands and record companies look to achieve. It's the music business version of the American Dream.

Lyrically Cornwell goes through a series of scenarios of people wanting to be successful in America. In the first verse he refers to a roach wanting to live in a tree. Superficially he's talking about an insect but by using the word 'roach' there is an obvious drug reference. On another level the word roach has often been used to describe migrants into America particularly those from Mexico.

Mexicans entering the US legally or illegally to get a better life and thus become big in America and has been a political football for decades. The migration to America theme is supported by keyboards at the start and various other points when they mimic a ship's horn as it pulls into dock. One can picture the ships pulling into New York past the Statue of Liberty full of migrants.

In the second verse he references Vietnam Vets, a group ignored and disowned by the American public since the mid-seventies. Soldiers who lost a war were not to be honoured or held in high esteem. These people weren't big in America they were persona non grata. There is a reference to a vet ((Vietnam veteran) being in overdrive, suggesting mental health problems and indeed many Vietnam vets suffered serious psychological damage.

One of the best cultural representations of this is the film *Rambo First Blood* (1982) which deals with the issue sympathetically but also points out the wider implications and effects such people can have on society.

In 1985 a second *Rambo* movie was released with a much less sympathetic and more gung-ho approach. It was a huge success and the character crossed over into the mainstream as a one-man army dispatching anyone who didn't buy into the American dream and being Big In America.

The video of the song actually features a cartoon sequence of the Rambo character. By choosing this character and the references to roaches in the first verse Cornwell is subverting and exposing the uncomfortable truth of the concept of being big in America and the American Dream and that these ideals are only open to particular types of people.

The third verse references Cornwell's then American girlfriend, an assertive woman who controls people, especially men. The line "She wore the pants across the big expanse" is supposedly her controlling him from across the Atlantic but just as easily a slight put down of her being a large woman. He also refers to her whipping particular men which suggest an element of BDSM coming into play and also a nod towards one of his favourite songs 'Whip It' by Devo.

Cornwell in a music paper when asked to review his favourite songs listed 'Whip It' in his Top 10 and famously added "What your right arm for?" The last verse has Cornwell articulating his desire which on the evidence here appears to be to make it in America and then go and live there.

With a transatlantic partner at the time this was probably the singer's preferred option. Cornwell's pronunciation of America in the chorus is mannered and appears to imitate the pronunciation of the Louis Gossett Jr's character Fiddler in the iconic slavery TV mini-series from the mid-seventies, *Roots*. In an iconic heart to heart scene the wise old man informs the young newly arrived slave that there is no going back, and he is in America for good. "You in Ammmerica now Toby".

A poignant reminder that there has always been forced migration as well migration with an element of choice. Another interpretation of the pronunciation is it sounds like 'Americure' as if Cornwell is ironically saying that America was seen as the cure for everything. Another example of the joys of individual interpretations of lyrics. A song full of instrumental sounds, lyrical ideas and visual concepts if one includes the video but ultimately this is to the song's detriment as all in all there is too many superficial elements going on to make the song as memorable or innovative as it could have been.

*****

Cornwell unfurls his Elvis tone to support the sentiment of the lyrical content of the song and the change of groove to the 'swing' rock feel is a repeat of 'No Mercy' from the previous album. Like the previous song 'Nice In Nice', there are question marks over the production as the trebly drums are again to the fore and this time are augmented by the low brass riff mixed with low keyboards with an accompanying keyboard pulsing percussive effect to give movement to the song, but, along with the continuous electronic hi-hat, feels a little too much.

Certainly, the mix is better appreciated with headphones where the low brass riff has a little more space to breathe. Cornwell's sliding high guitar riffs imitate BJ Cole's presence from 'You'll Always Reap What You Sow' and gives the song a further nod to the lyrical content theme as the sound conjures up American images.

Cornwell's chord pattern for the second section "And when you're big in America" strays from his recent songs and involves a less conventional feel with the Tritone/devil's interval relationship between the first two chords. And the build-up of Greenfield's arpeggios during the second half of the section reminds us wistfully of 'No More Heroes' days. The chord after the two-beat break at the end of the section is not the home chord that we are expecting as Cornwell's vocal pronounces "Americure" to add fuel to the anti-American sentiment, and this unconventional chord adds to the feeling that America is out of step with many other world views.

The expected home chord duly arrives two bars later with a rasping and highly effective sax solo. After further repeats there is an instrumental ending with a new chord pattern which moves the song effectively towards it's fade out but perhaps this would have been even more effective had there been other melodic riffs.

Overall, some interesting ideas and sounds with the sax solo clearly having a positive effect on the song. The lower brass riffs suffer somewhat from a lack of clarity in the mix, perhaps they were simply too low in pitch. But the song is simply not strong enough overall, and the album is now beginning to struggle following the poor end to side one.

Shakin' Like A Leaf

Third song of side two and the third single in a row and another musical style ticked off in the search for that elusive big hit and this time it's a swing jazz number with a big brass sound. Being a single it got a 12-inch extended track called the Jelly Mix which was actually done by Burnel. He does a good job by stripping out some of the clutter and adds a harmonica break that works surprising well in the context of the song.

It is actually another Cornwell song and another song title and chorus that borrows an English language idiom. The phrase is used to describe fear or nervousness in a person. The simple rhythm and the cadence of the words embellish the idiom of the title and the simple but memorable melody give the song an allusion of familiarity. Sadly, this wasn't enough to make it a hit. Maybe fans baulked at the idea of a swinging Stranglers big band sound.

Cornwell's words in one layer of meaning interprets the saying as a fear of nuclear war and by making the fourth verse about 'villains' he is referring to politicians on news broadcasts who either stoke up the fear via the medium or don't answer the question.

Although the title is a saying for dread, given Cornwell's recent life experience at the time i.e., coming off drugs the song can actually just as easily be seen about the physical effects of drug withdrawal something that Cornwell was all too familiar with. Withdrawal from cocaine and particular heroin, which Cornwell found more difficult to do, literally can lead to uncontrollable shaking. In the first two verses he also suggests the inability to sleep another symptom of withdrawal.

The second verse also deals with not being tempted to take just one more hit to ease the pain of withdrawal when the singer asks for respite. In the third verse there is a reference to the enhanced sensual perception former addicts' report when clean of drugs with an allusion to the sound of autumn.

The reference to TV villains may initially seem at odds with this interpretation but can also be given another layer of meaning as people in recovery often refer to watching TV during cold turkey as it was the only thing, they were capable of doing.

Despite the failure of the song to become a hit it was regularly played live in Cornwell's final years with the band, possibly to ensure the travelling brass section was not underemployed but also in a live format the song came to life much more.

*****

The brass continue their side two presence with some predictably jolly riffs with this swing rhythmed, big band influenced song. The brass is not as prominent in the mix for the intro as it was in 'Punch And Judy' from the previous album, another song where the brass set up the mood of the song during the intro.

The first verse sees Cornwell's vocal sung very low with an echoing vocal sung an octave higher with some delay on but a little muddy in the mix whilst the guitar and keyboard parts accompanying the conventional bluesy minor key chords are not entirely convincing. The second "Oh silent night" section produces an effective chordal and melodic contrast whilst Greenfield's arpeggios once again provide suitable momentum. There are some strange voices in the background under "like a leaf", barely audible and, as in 'Was It You?', its inclusion has to be questioned as it is so low in the mix.

The song bubbles along effectively as the main section returns, this time with Cornwell's vocal an octave higher and the brass interjecting effective riffs in the gaps in the voices whilst the echoed, barely audible, backing vocals are still present. The return of the "Oh silent night" section continues the momentum but, again, the brass is a little lost in the mix. As was the case on the previous song, 'Big In America', we now have a section where the brass has solos. It was saxophone only for 'Big In America' and this time it is the full brass section playing riffs rather than a solo.

But then a tenor sax does solo highly effectively over the brass riffs. Rather surprisingly this ends the song as there was the potential to bring the whole texture down one more time and then push towards a final climax in the Swing Jazz tradition as we were only two and a half minutes into the song.

Another song that will divide opinion. One can't help tapping a toe to the infectious swing rhythm and expansive brass, and the higher vocals in the second verse are effective. But the rather short time length perhaps lends itself to the thought that the band was unable to develop the song beyond its two main sections, so once the instrumental section had occurred, there was nowhere else for this style of song to go. As a result, there is an overall lightweight feel to the song.

Mayan Skies

Cornwell writing about yet another country having treated fans to songs about Spain and America this time the subject is Mexico. The song is a Cornwell and Burnel collaboration. Greenfield gives us a floating introductory riff which suggests a sunrise to match one of Cornwell's lyrical themes in the song.

The dominant instrument that carries the melody is a trumpet in the style of the Mexican Tijuana brass of Herb Alpert exquisitely played by Martin Veysey. The music sounds ethereal giving the impression of a sunrise and a country waking up. With such a pastoral sounding piece of music that deals with a phenome of nature, the track is crying out for real drums that would have made for a more organic and natural sound. The Mexican theme was later revisited by Cornwell in 2013 with the release of a Tex Mex version of 'Golden Brown' featuring the group Mariachi Mexteca.

The Mayan skies of the title reflect the history of Mexico's first nation people the Mayas who lived in what is now southern Mexico from 2600 BC therefore making a direct link to the other first nation themes on the album and the title track 'Dreamtime'. Lyrically there are three short verses in which Cornwell impressionistically sketches a picture of Mexico commenting on its beauty but also as he has done in his other songs about countries, he juxtaposes this with a darker side and the history of misery around one of Mexico's natural resources, gold.

He also explores the torture and suffering in Mexico's past from Mayas, Aztecs and Conquistadors through to the Mexican revolution in the 19th century. The line about youth respecting and embracing the old relates to the day of the dead in Mexican culture when families gather and believe the dead's souls visit to commune with living relatives. The colours Cornwell refers to in the song are the colours of the Mexican flag and with a deft touch he links those colours red, green and yellow to the Mayan skies at sunrise and sunset. This also links of course to the albums cover with its antipodean sunrise which shares the same colours as Mayan skies.

*****

The start of the song sees the band playing in rhythmic unison, a feature that characterised parts of 'Blue Sister' and 'Four Horsemen'. Unfortunately, the electronic drum snare sound feels a little too harsh as does the drum fill as the title suggests something a little more reflective. This is soon replaced by a keyboard solo on a sweeping sound over a very interesting chord pattern with Burnel utilising inversions as is often the case with the less commercial songs.

Every chord is inverted here, Greenfield adds another constant percussive pulsing rhythmic sound, and Cornwell adds another timely texture at the end of this mini section with his held jangly chords. The guitar then leads into the verse with a simple two note riff and, although the intro is only a little over half a minute, we are reminded of the many previous occasions where the band had complex multiple sections to their instrumental introductions.

The vocal melody has a strong yet simple rising scalic shape which has a rhythm on "colour of life in a..." at the end of the phrase which cuts across the music in an effective cross rhythm. The texture here is augmented by the backing vocal harmonies, again simply a third higher (conventional) but sung and mixed with a restraint that impressively adds to the dreamlike quality suggested by the lyrical content.

The sudden introduction of the solo trumpet at the end of the phrase becomes a feature of the song and adds to the world music authenticity with its use of the flattened seventh note that creates a mode (mixolydian) typical of the style, and also the frequent use of crescendos during held notes and vibrato.

This main section is built around very limited chords and the band display a deftness of touch with the arrangement here that dovetails highly effectively with the sweeping vocal. Burnel's bass line, for instance, helps to drive the song in a subtle way as does Cornwell's simple two chord repeating riff from before. The change of chord on "Mexico" also flows perfectly well.

Following repeats, the short trumpet solo is the third brass solo in successive songs on side two but here it is busy yet underplayed and again enhances the already laid-back flow of the music.

A new "Mayan skies sleep talk" section arrives with the same chords from the start of the intro, but this time played with a much slower rate of change. This clever link further enhances the song, and this section is also characterised by the constant backing vocal harmony and Greenfield's panning constant electronic otherworldly sound which also rather surprisingly enhances the mood of the song. The rhythmic unison intro returns but this time the accompanying trumpet softens the moment and the backing vocals "up above" also add to the mix.

The overall structure of the song has a slight unconventional feel as the four minutes seem to pass by quicker than on many recent songs that have relied on far more traditional verse/chorus structures. And there is a pleasing complexity to the music generally with many different sounds occupying the landscape to form a pleasing whole with just the heavy-handed opening being a questionable decision.

For the band to arrange all these sounds and complex chords over a relatively simple but effective melody was an achievement and resurrected side two to lead us with purpose to the final song.

Too Precious

In The Stranglers grand tradition, a long strong song to finish the album. A laid-back samba feel pervades the song and it's punctuated by long beautiful instrumental passages and is rhythmically complex. The instrumentation reflects the musical direction chosen since *Feline*. It's subtle and beautifully crafted. The bongo drums are understated and all the better for that and they sound real even though they are actually programmed and in the background they gently move the song along.

The other members of the band ply their trade with restrained but complex melody lines. Nothing instrumentally slaps you in the face and any musical changes are seamless and smooth and don't jar. This approach is perhaps a sign of musical maturity or a band coming to terms with their position in the rock and pop world. They were no longer the aggressive but musically gifted bad boys of rock but now more considered thoughtful craftsmen. Their feeling being you can't be angry and contrary forever. The band were playing the game as they had over the previous two albums, but they still could subvert the norm with the musical skill and lyrical allusions.

Cornwell catches the mood of the instrumentation with his restrained but intense vocal performance. The title 'Too Precious' meaning being too revering of something and behaving in such a way that it is to the detriment of others and oneself. So, what is Cornwell defining as too precious? As ever with Cornwell there is more than one layer to his writing.

In the first verse he is clearly painting a picture of oppression where a small minority hold power and wealth whilst the oppressed majority might be materially poor but morally rich. He uses shining rocks as an image which one can take as diamonds. So, it's 1986 and the listener is in a country where a wealthy minority rule a poor oppressed minority and the biggest wealth provider is diamonds. This puts us firmly in South Africa. Apartheid was at its height and resistance was growing ever more violent. Nelson Mandela was still in prison and years away from freedom. The too precious of the title refers to the white majority of South Africa trying to hold onto Apartheid and their privileged wealthy lives.

The second verse continues the diamond image with the writer commenting on the country saying it is built on a rock, but the foundations are unstable i.e., rubble. The rumours mentioned in the verse refer to world pressure and from pressure inside South Africa. Cornwell explains that this pressure from without and within are a cancer that will ultimately destroy the regime as they can't be suppressed forever.

The final line is a warning, with Cornwell personalising his feelings about the country by using the word "baby". This also works on another level and is a nod to a lover who is too precious about something maybe the relationship or maybe in a symmetry of the metaphor a diamond ring.

The song was the result of a third collaboration on the album between Burnel and Cornwell. It is the best song on the collection and is a reminder about the creativity and quality that often resulted when the band worked more collaboratively.

*****

The song builds on the complexities of 'Mayan Skies' and, between them, deliver a strong end to the album, albeit in an understated way. It is interesting to note that these two songs were, along with 'Ghost Train', the only songs written by both Cornwell and Burnel and, in the musical arrangement and juxtaposition of main and backing vocals, we are once again reminded of the strengths of the pair of them writing together as well as lamenting that this was becoming a rare occurrence.

It is the band's third longest proper song (discounting 'School Mam') after 'Down in the Sewer' and 'Hallow To Our Men' and the space the song is afforded is not only surprising but also extremely welcome. The instrumental prowess of the band has been given limited scope over recent albums and this song is a reminder of their abilities to build beautiful non vocal passages.

Unlike 'Down in the Sewer', the song is not broken down into different sections but flows with such purpose that one feels the song could have gone on for even longer.

There is no preamble but a wonderful Cornwell guitar riff over chords that have a chromatic movement, likened by many comments to the James Bond theme and it is interesting to speculate that this chord pattern is rarely used in popular music due to its close association with 007. Cornwell's rhythmic impetus at the end of the phrase further strengthens the impressive riff.

This series of chords does add a little flavour of mystique which is in keeping with the song and the sounds of the intro as well as enhancing the loose concept of parts of the album. Here the sweeping synth held chords provide the bass resonance whilst the bass embarks upon a series of riffs commencing with very melodic high-pitched riffs that could have been a notch up in the mix at the expense of a slight dip in the drums.

Having said that, Black creates an energetically soothing pattern with much use of the electronic conga that does move the song effectively along. Almost half a minute flies by before the guitar dips out over new chords whilst the bass provides the limelight but in a very understated way. The guitar then re-enters with a riff that will become a focal point for the verse whilst the bass continues to provide melodic impetus and the keyboards provide slightly random, almost jazz like chords on a harder sound thus returning to a multi-melodic layering texture, and we feel all the better for it, especially when the main vocal then provides another strong melodic layer.

The higher octave backing vocal on "Beauty led to the blinding" is yet another gloriously subtle yet assured texture. The melody then rises by step into the "Somebody should tell you" section which is higher in pitch and flows highly effectively from the lower previous main vocal melody. This then leads to a repeat of the main verse section but this time Cornwell, having risen in pitch, sings it an octave higher. This device of singing the second verse an octave higher has been used three times, having been used on 'Dreamtime' and ''Shakin' Like A Leaf and, yet again, it proves to be effective, moving the song up in intensity, as does Burnel's even more effusive bass. For example after "You must have heard all the rumours" and the instrumental strength of the band is shining through here. Burnel's run down on "They won't disappear" finishes off an intensely sublime passage.

The "You're, baby too precious" section is yet another moment of subtle intensity where the held low synth chords provide a platform for Cornwell's slow vocal melody whilst Burnel and Greenfield provide extra background riffs until the held keyboard chords and vocal 'Ahh' adds a brief climax until they are suddenly replaced by the instrumental section.

What follows next is almost two and a half minutes of instrumental that rivals any moments from the band. This is the last great instrumental flourish that the band will produce, following in a long line from the earliest songs like 'Down in the Sewer' through to 'Toiler on the Sea', 'Hallow to Our Men' and now here, no less in majesty but in a slightly more discreet style that befits the song.

Cornwell commences with a fairly low riff and then Greenfield interjects, and they both play in harmony with hollow sounding intervals that add to the 'light touch' world music feel. At three minutes, Burnel, who has been prowling away on low melodic riffs to great supportive effect, adds more expansive high pitched bass chords to great flowing effect.

At 3:04 Greenfield moves into a different feel with a new high-pitched riff using the well-worn cross rhythm idea whilst Cornwell holds notes. At 3:17 Cornwell moves into a new cross rhythmed idea with his three-beat phrase going against the four-beat pattern, a rhythmic feature that the band has always been comfortable in deploying. Greenfield joins in with a harmony and the complexity of the rhythm here (at 3:31) is stunning yet elegantly flowing. More interplay between Greenfield and Cornwell at 4:06 and then 4:20 with new riffs maintains the cascading beauty and Burnel at 4:20 repeats the bass riff that will link them back to the introductory section with another sublime moment.

After a return of the vocals, we are treated to another instrumental section where Cornwell uses and develops the riff from the end of the introduction an octave higher and blazes away whilst Greenfield provides melodic musings on a very soft sound and Burnel continues to rumble away melodically to such great effect. This slowly fades out and we have witnessed the very essence of the bands instrumental magnificence allied to a superbly crafted song. This is the last time that we will see such a song and one is left to ponder whether other songs from recent albums might have risen beyond the claws of commerciality to produce longer instrumentals with similar results.

Musical Summary

There are many moments to savour on *Dreamtime* that continue to shine a light on the bands' musical attributes, but the overall sound was now entrenched in its time. The two previous albums had moved in different directions musically but were guided by ideas that were deemed fashionable in the early and mid-eighties. But the sound that accompanied the first five albums was unique and was the overarching reason why the band stood out.

It is hoped this book will highlight the many other musical features including multi-melodic layering textures, long complex instrumental passages with clashing notes, unconventional chords, time signatures and structures. But it was the actual holistic sound led by the keyboards and bass and superbly backed up by the guitar and drums that the four disparate band members created that enabled the band to stand out as being so different in 1977.

On *Feline*, *Aural Sculpture* and now on *Dreamtime*, the band had fundamentally moved towards a mainstream sound with electronic drums, preset synths, softer bass, and softer guitar (often acoustic rather than electric). The band blended in with most other bands of the mid-eighties so lost its potency for being different.

When there is a conscious decision to reduce the influence of those musical features for more conventional chords, structures, and textures then the ability to stand out from the crowd will be even further reduced. Moments like the beautifully interweaving long solos on 'Too Precious' match the quality of any instrumental passages gone before even though the change in sounds will not be to every early fans' liking.

'Mayan Skies' also had plenty of textural and structural variety in keeping with the older unconventional songs and 'You Always Reap What You Sow' carried much melodic and chordal strength. But 'Was It You?' needed the sounds of old to be totally convincing and the single choices: 'Always The Sun' and 'Nice In Nice' suffered from being too 'produced' in order to try to impact the top 40, and ended up with holistic sounds that, ironically, did not stand out enough from the plethora of other songs of the time.

The biggest hits in the eighties almost always had defining sounds. Sounds are equally if not more important than chord patterns or melodies in terms of chart success. There are, in simple terms, two types of pop music creations — songs and records. A song will have strong melodies and appropriate chords and will not rely on extra production, for example, Elton John's 'Your Song' or Paul McCartney's 'Yesterday'.

Records on the other hand are 'produced' with sounds to stand out from the crowd. 'Relax' by Frankie Goes To Hollywood is a strong example where the melodies and chords are severely limited, but the production is exciting and different. One would never hear a soloist with just piano or guitar singing 'Relax' but McCartney's 'Yesterday' or Elton's 'Your Song' will be forever performed.

That is not to say that the record is better than the song or vice versa. All bands output will contain a mixture of the two notions with the examples mentioned being at the extremes, and most pieces of popular music will have elements of both notions within them.

The Stranglers were no exception. 'Peaches' is a good example of a record. Everyone will remember the sounds created, but the melodies and chords are very limited. 'Golden Brown', on the other hand, is a song that stands on its own and will have been performed on countless occasions by soloists with simple piano or guitar accompaniment. But 'Golden Brown' also had the harpsichord sound which made it stand out from the crowd, not to mention the change in time signature.

When the sound of a band fits in with the norms of the time, then the songs will have to be particularly strong. 'Dreamtime' suffered from trying to fit in with the sounds of the day as the collection of songs is, overall, as strong as most of their albums but the sounds were fitting in rather than standing out.

Album Summary

Epic were a big company with a lot of commercial muscle but despite being given three commercial and contemporary sounding albums and a series of very marketable radio friendly singles they had failed to break the band big in the UK and had done nothing for them in America. The album sales showed the band were still on a commercial decline.

The band's coverage in the music press was virtually nil however despite this as a live attraction the band could still pull the crowds into big city theatres. The live album *All Live And All Of The Night* released in 1987 covering the *Dreamtime* and *Aural Sculpture* tours demonstrated a still potent band with a brass section fully bedded in, seeming to point the way forward and to the future. They just need to covert this loyal live following into studio album sales.

The album lacked a focus with a loose theme of First Nation civilisation, mysticism and ecology which was only present or alluded to on a few tracks. The rest of the album was a collection of different musical styles and unrelated subjects. The production made the band sound contemporary rather than the timeless and unlike their early albums they didn't stand out from the crowd anymore and this been true of the last two albums.

The songs were in the most part good but neutered by the recording process and the desire to recreate the fashionable sound of the time. In terms of lines in the sand it now appeared that the brass, which first appeared on *Aural Sculpture*, was here to stay for the time being. The question for the future was would they continue to ape current musical genres and continue to flit from genre to genre or would they settle on a particular style?

Being fluid between musical genres may have kept anticipation high as the world wondered what style the band with adopt for their next single and it demonstrated flexibility and musicianship, but it didn't help the record company marketing it. Marketing departments in big record companies want consistency of style as it easier to sell. Without doubt the company would have wanted a more cohesive sound and style. Fans also wanted the security of a recognisable style. Long term fans were getting a bit lost with a consensus growing that the band had gone soft and overtly too commercial. On the other hand, newer fans would enjoy a particular song in a certain style but then find there was nothing else like that style on the album. The band seemed uncertain of its identity.

Within the band there were tensions with the song writing collaboration and even musical collaboration seemed a thing of the past although when it did happen the results were often spectacular. Witness 'Too Precious'. Cornwell was resentful as he felt he was shouldering too much responsibility in terms of song writing and vocals. However, there were signs of a Burnel revival in terms of quality and quantity of his songs. Black was never going to budge from his use of programmed drums which irked the rest of the band but none of them would make a stand. Greenfield kept his counsel and seemed to go with the flow but appeared at times to have lost his way when it came to creating innovative sounds and was happy just to accompany and add flourishes to the songs.

The tour for the album lasted well into 1987 and then it was time for a new album. Work was started on what was to become *10* in early 1988 but it wouldn't see the light of day until late spring 1990. Which meant the gap between albums was three and a half years. In those days only bands like U2 and Dire Straits seemed to be able to make comebacks successfully from such long layoffs. Those groups had massive fans bases throughout the world and were touring globally during the album gaps thus keeping up their profile. The Stranglers did not have this luxury.

B-sides and extras

Since You Went Away (B-side of 'Nice In Nice')

A pleasant tune led by an organ riff. One is left with the feeling that the song was recorded quickly and would have benefited from a little more work particular around the lead and backing vocals which are a bit too low in the mix. Conversely the drums are at right level and avoid the skull crushing battering that at times featured in the band's sound. Cornwell's guitar is unusual high in the mix and better for it. Vocally Burnel gives it his best Roy Orbison impression which certainly conveys the emotion of the subject matter.

The subject matter is simple enough, a broken love affair between a young man and older woman. Burnel uses the familiar image of how time appears to move slowly once the affair is over whilst during the relationship it flew by.

The chosen topic and tune demonstrate where the band were at, and that the softer side of life and music was now their default setting. Burnel has always been one to document his love affairs in a very direct way e.g., 'London Lady' and 'Choosey Susie'. As ever he leaves us in no doubt as to the way he is feels about his muse.

*****

This song had the potential to enhance the *Dreamtime* album but lacks a sense of rigour regarding the structure and the arrangement. It is still an engaging fast paced simple song but lacks clarity between the sections. The main three chord pattern occupies most of the song apart from a convincing departure midway through the song with the high vocals "Whereas before well time flew by" which could have been the basis for a chorus.

Instead, the song meanders with the vocal melody changing slightly to move towards that high pitched moment but blurring the phrases as it repeats the main sections. This vocal melody also suffers from a simple rhythm that lacks variety which meant that the shape needed to be more defined to provide contrast.

Instrumentally the guitar has a pleasing spotlight whereas the only drum fill arrives after the vocal line "To watch me cry" with a little rhythmic re emphasis just prior to this. Otherwise, Black maintains the same rhythm throughout as does Burnel with his incredibly restrained bass line. Arguably, this keeps things simple but surely a song with such rhythmic drive as this needs more embellishment from its rhythm section and such flourishes would certainly have added to a more 'live' feel which could have enhanced the song and the album.

Greenfield's participation is also limited but highly effective with the opening organ riff and the arpeggios during the higher middle section "Ever wanted to hurt someone" catching the eye. The emotional drive to the song was there as the pace and chords and guitar really help to move the song along with conviction. But the song needed the sections being defined by a clearer melodic shape and by different sounds which could have resulted in a highly effective song.

Norman Normal (B-side of 'Always the Sun')

Seek and ye shall find! A gem of a song hidden on a B-side with a killer tune and unsettling lyric. Even a cursory listen makes you wonder how it never made it onto an album and a more detailed study reveals a song of hidden depths. It is in actual fact a left over from *Aural Sculpture* and would have made a great finale to the album instead of the vilified 'Mad Hatter'.

A Laurie Latham production and his stardust is sprinkled all over it, particularly on Cornwell's beautiful chiming twelve-string guitar figure. Elsewhere the backing vocals are sumptuous the drums are restrained and serve the song. The keyboards build and give the song a cinematic feel. Burnel's vocal have a similar feel to Cat Stevens' 'Matthew and Son', both songs use the same chords this isn't suggestion plagiarism with only a limited number of musical notes similarities are bound to occur.

The song is more than a just a great tune as Burnel provides a sinister and subversive take of an underworld gangster possibly, given some of the references, one of the Kray twins. As the title suggests Norman appears to lead an everyday life with a wife family and pets but underneath, he is a serial criminal who ends up in prison whilst his gang of cronies escape to Spain.

He has another secret in that he is also gay and enjoys cross dressing which has an obvious association with East End gangsters of the 1960s – the Krays who both identified as gay or bi sexual. The sting in the tail at the end is that Norman himself is the victim of a hit, killed by a car bomb presumably because he was seen as a danger to his gangland boss.

Burnel opts for a story telling narrative, a device that was his preferred lyrical style. He tells the tale with aplomb so much so one can imagine it being a film in the style of those great dark British gangster movies of seventies and eighties like *Get Carter* or *The Long Good Friday*.

The track has a psychedelic feel but through an eighties production filter and given some of the subject matter the song is comparable to Pink Floyd's 'Arnold Lane' and The Kinks' 'Lola', but with more lyrical teeth and controversy.

*****

Another interesting song that could have been considered for either *Dreamtime* or *Aural Sculpture*. The arrangement has a very eighties feel with the jangly guitar and brass synth chordal stabs but it is the juxtaposition of the main and backing vocals that really help to drive the song.

Burnel's opening vocal to the main verse has a wide range with only two (conventional) chords accompanying it but the second part to the main section "He was read his rights" has an innovative chordal pattern suggesting two changes of key but then flowing effortlessly back to the main two chords. Burnel's penchant for these types of chordal patterns were occasionally too severe but, in this case, as with 'You'll Always Reap What You Sow', the chord patterns provide intrigue and an unconventionality that really help to move the song up a gear.

The vocals for this section are divided between the higher softly sung melody and Cornwell's spoken word that has echoes of 'Midnight Summer Dream' in its style of delivery and provides a highly effective contrast to the main vocal which promptly returns. There is a feint backing vocal on all the main higher opening vocal phrases which is barely audible but, after a short instrumental section involving keyboard a fast-repeating synth chordal effect and the guitar chords, the opening melody is now slightly adapted to become the main chorus vocal phrase "Take me much higher".

This time, however, the backing vocals are more prominent, and this creates a highly effective moment that will be expanded as the phrase is repeated later. At this moment, the phrase is only sung once and is immediately followed by the "Norman Normal" phrase that also indulges in a prominent vocal harmony in a similar vein to the previous phrase but with a different and effective chord. So much has occurred by this moment at 1:23 and the rest of the song perhaps suffers structurally a little from being a touch too overlong, although the way these main two vocal phrases intertwine at 2:26 is fascinating.

But this is only just over halfway through the song and the rest of the song feels like a long and slow outro, complete with the musical device where the instruments drop out at 3:02 and just the vocals and drums remain for all the instruments to come surging back. The band did not use this device very often, but it was a very common idea that often added to the commercial sing-along nature of hits. Cornwell's jangly chords quickly fade in and then suddenly disappear a couple of times before returning permanently.

Overall, despite it being a little laboured in the second half of the song, and overall sound dominated by eighties style guitar, synth and drums, there is much to admire in the way the vocal melodies work together.

Multi-layered melodic textures were a distinct strength of the band but here they avoid adding more melodic ideas on the instruments but maintain a chordal accompaniment in order for the vocals to have the space to play off each other. This B-side song should have had a higher profile.

Dry Day (B-side of 'Big In America')

A track that quintessentially sums up 1980s music production and saw the band indulging, probably unintentionally in yacht rock. Hall and Oates could have written this song. The elements of classic yacht rock are all there so here they are an obviously glossy production exemplified by the processed drum intro, a cheesy sax riff over the top, the ringing, meant to sound funky rhythm guitar, wind chime sounding keyboards, string effects and a bouncy bass guitar riff.

That's an exhaustive checklist in fact it's a masterclass of eighties, of popular sounds and personified. It's a song that would have enhanced any episode of *Miami Vice*. The band pull the sound off perfectly and although speculation, the song had all the traits and potential to be a transatlantic hit.

However, the band's name and previous history might have got in the way. If Epic had been creative, they should have created an alter ego band to sell the song. This isn't just idle speculation as around the same time post punk band XTC generated the Dukes of the Stratosphere alter ego to sell their psychedelic style pop songs which were atypical of the band's usual releases. Ironically Dukes of the Stratosphere records sold better than XTC's. A track that is as smooth as a baby's bottom, one the yuppies would have loved it they had ever got to hear it.

Cornwell uses the weather and specifically rain as a device for expressing emotion, so the threat of rain represents potential tears and upset. The narrator is asking the subject of the song are they going to be able to cope, can they avoid getting upset? In contrast to Burnel's preferred lyrical approach of a straight narrative, Cornwell sketches impressions and encourages the listener to add more detail. It's tempting to fill in the gaps with the story of a failed relationship and moving on which is classic yacht rock material.

The whole recording is convincing and professional and was more proof at how adept the band were at imitating other musical styles whilst searching for a new style of their own. It may well have crossed the band's mind that their future could be multiple styles and writing to order with whatever was musically fashionable at the time rather than creating their own hybrid style.

*****

The intro of just under a minute exposes the song as a pastiche of many of the eighties sounds. The saxophone opening riff is the melody of the later chorus and the funky dry guitar licks and bell like keyboard sounds are all predictable late eighties staple sounds. There are two very conventional chords for the verse and the chorus predictably moves to chord five and then retains conventionality with a well-trodden pattern.

The melody also predictably rises to a higher phrase for the chorus following the lower pitch of the verses. The equally predictable saxophone solos after the second chorus fulfilling the, once again, predictable structure. Cornwell even throws in higher vocal embellishments as the song fades.

The song lasts exactly five minutes and is an entirely respectable roll call of musical features used during this period. But why the band wanted to indulge in these features is a shame considering their ability to create original soundscapes only a few years previously. Maybe this desire to conform to the chart styles of the day is another example of the muddled musical thinking that was growing within the band.

Hitman (B-side of 'Shakin' Like A Leaf')

If ever a song was meant to be a B-side it was 'Hitman'. An obvious experiment and another musical style. This time we are in the territory of Heaven 17 circa 1981 mainly because of Greenfield's synthesiser which apes the sound used by that band on their seminal album *Penthouse and Pavements*.

The drum machine pattern used by Black also reproduces the patterns many synth pop bands used for their own experiment B-sides. Initially it sounds like Black is just randomly pressing the demonstration button on his drum machine. However, a little bit one of exposure to the song i.e., more than one listen and there is a nagging insistence about the jarring beats. Greenfield's random soundscapes have a similar effect and added to Cornwell's best Lothario croon and there is a surprising ear worm quality about the song.

Lyrically the title gives the listener plenty of scope. Hitman as in assassin, hitman as a top music producer or hitman as Casanova figure hitting on women. The actual truth according to Cornwell is hitman as in a photographer and he combines this with the hitman as assassin metaphor referring to getting a woman in his sights. Sights of a camera but given the title and refrain he is presenting the protagonist as an assassin and hunter.

*****

The electronic drum pattern never changes during the song but there is an interesting moment moving into the chorus at 1:22 where the music seems half a beat ahead of the drum pattern thus placing the two loud cracks onto the half beat at the end of the bar and the first beat of the following bar, whereas they had previously been on the fourth beat and the following half beat but this is not clear due to the poor mix.

Burnel's bass often seems to be playing half a beat before the start of the beat during the verse but is too low in the mix and all the electronic keyboard riffs have a sense of a random rhythmic feel that, along with the drum pattern that reinforces off beats, creates an overall stuttering backing to Cornwell's vocal line that has a smoother rhythm and a reasonably strong shape.

But the most unedifying aspect to the song is that the main vocal is too low in the mix, as is the bass, and they are overpowered by the keyboards and drums, both of which have very piercing sounds. Cornwell's economical tone further exacerbates the problem.

There is interest from the sparse guitar riffs, but they seem to be competing with the keyboard riffs at times and the sparsity compounds the disjointed rhythmic approach. There doesn't seem to be any instrumental sound gluing the groove together although this will have a hypnotic charm for some.

The chorus, apart from seeming a half a beat out of sync, does not quite blend as the distorted power chord guitar has little support as the disjointed rhythm continues. The chords have an interesting twist with the sixth chord taking us a little into a darker mood, but the melody is lacking here, as is any attempt to change the texture from the verse.

Although the song has its merits, the mix does not support the band and the attempt to move wholeheartedly into a different genre ultimately grates with too many piercing sounds and, just like 'Dry Day' before it, we are left to wonder whether such a departure was necessary. The feeling of trying too hard to search for a late eighties identity invades both these songs.

Burnham Beeches (B-side of re-release of 'Always The Sun', 1990)

A lush Instrumental include on the 2001 release of the album. It's a pleasant piece of music and was a good enough tune to merit a lyric if someone had had the inclination. Pressed into service to provide a B-side for the reissue of 'Always The Sun' after Cornwell had left the band. It was recorded during the *Dreamtime* sessions and originally planned to be the B-side for the shelved 'Was It You?' The inspiration for the track is Burnham-on-Sea a seaside town in Somerset. An additional guitarist Sil Wilcox was used to fill the track out.

An Evening With Hugh Cornwell (B-side of the Official Bootleg of 'Shakin' Like A Leaf')

A postscript to the extras — not a musical release but a hilarious eighteen minute long collection of Hugh Cornwell's banter with the audiences on the Aural Sculpture tour e.g., "What's wrong? What's happened? Has it been a depressing day in Sheffield… again". It is classic Cornwell and genuinely funny, well worth seeking out.

*****

Based on three different chord patterns, this instrumental never really goes anywhere as the arrangement stays more or less the same for all three sections with a slight increase in both texture and pitch of the guitar melody for the second section.

The chords are fairly conventional with a slight twist for the final chord of section one and the third chord of section three but, overall, the nondescript guitar sound and soporific backing from the repetitive slow drum pattern, the plodding bass and the held string type keyboard chords result in a lacklustre performance with the highlight being the repeating keyboard chords at the end that remind us of the far more alluring and uplifting moment at the start of 'Always The Sun'.

Footnotes

1. Official Charts Website

2. Official Charts Website

3. Official Charts Website

4. Official Charts Website

5. Official Charts Website

6. Official Charts Website

7. Billboard Charts Website

8. Aboriginal-contemporary-dreamtime website

10

A planed break of a couple of years between albums would have been a good idea given band dynamics and relationships. It would have given members chances to pursue their own projects and if managed properly the band members could have then returned refreshed and reinvigorated. Instead, an unplanned break of nearly four years occurred which was potentially career destroying.

One of the four years, 1987, was spent touring. Then virtually straight off the back of touring the band went into the studio in 1988 to produce their next album, however it wasn't to appear for another two years. The band delivered the album to the record company in time for a late 1989 release. It was self-produced with the help of the soon to be famous producer Owen Morris acting as engineer.

Epic didn't like it and insisted it was rerecorded thus delaying any release by another six months. The band had kept in the spotlight to a degree because they managed a top 10 hit (No.7) at last with a one off single. Sadly, it wasn't their own song, it was a cover of The Kinks' 'All Day And All Of The Night'.[1] The single was a precursor to a live album released in early 1988 called *All Live And All Of The Night* which ironically was well received and performed better than the previous two studio albums. It hit No.12 in the album chart and hung around for six weeks.[2] In early 1989 their old record company helped give the band achieve a bit more profile with the reissued '(Get A) Grip (on Yourself)' which reached No.37, and a singles compilation album, *Singles (The U.A. Years)*, which made No.57[3]

Whilst a live album and a hit single kept their profile up in 1988 the band were hard at work on *Dreamtime's* follow up. Cornwell states "... and then spent the whole of 1988 recording tracks in Cambridgeshire".[4] At the same time Cornwell was working on his solo album *Wolf* which was recorded in early 1988 and released in June of that year.

Although signed to the major record label, Virgin, the album and singles failed to trouble the charts. Despite this there was potential for a tour in the US where the album picked up a bit of airplay. Rather unfortunately Cornwell was dropped by Virgin and actually in the USA setting up a promotional tour when the news broke.

Burnel and Greenfield were also busy working on their covers blues band the Purple Helmets, gigging and recording. If you are wondering about Black, he was building the recording studio the band would use in Burnel's back garden, whatever was happening the band weren't resting or recuperating.

The plan seemed to be to carry on regardless, and don't mention potential burnout or diminishing sales. The band needed sympathetic management and that appeared to be lacking. By 1988/9 they had been on the tour album, tour album carousel for eleven years with no discernible break, producing nine studio albums, two live albums, four solo or collaborative albums and hundreds of gigs.

It's no wonder that frustrations were building, little things became big things and so on. The rejection of their tenth album must have been a bitter pill to take although Epic did have form in this area. They got the band to use a producer on *Aural Sculpture* after three previous self-produced albums. Laurie Latham then took on working on *Dreamtime* but walked away questioning the song quality and the time being taken to record, leaving the band to co-produce with Mike Kemp. This time Muff Winwood, Epic's head of A and R told the band the songs needed a producer. The company's choice was Roy Thomas Baker who had made his name producing Queen in the 1970s. Queen were big in America, and this formed the main thrust of Epic's sales pitch to the band. The promised stateside breakthrough might finally be on the cards.

The songs were re-recorded with Baker who eventually produced a bright pop rock album with his trademark technique of multi tracking guitars stamped all over it. The album was released in March 1990 having been preceded by the top twenty (No.17) hit '96 Tears'.[5]

The single wasn't a band original, it was another cover, the second time they had used another band's material to get in the singles chart. It smacked of desperation and suggested too many that the band had no faith in their new material. The song was a ? And Mysterians track, a cult sixties garage rock band from the states. The album peaked on the first week of release at No.15, one place higher than *Dreamtime* but then bombed out of the Top 100 within four weeks. Proving to be anything but the return to big commercial success the company and the band hoped for.[6]

The album cover was a source of interest and potential controversy and best described shall we say, of its time. It was designed by Jean-Luke Epstein and Grant Louden. Epstein had also designed the covers of the previous two albums. The cover features the band dressed up and made up as ten prominent world leaders. Burnel cross-dressed to represent Margaret Thatcher and Benazir Bhutto. That wasn't an issue it was the fact that several of the leaders on show had been 'blacked' up by the makeup artist.

Without doubt had it been done in today's world there would be controversy and perhaps there was in 1990. *The Black and White Minstrels* had been consigned to history in 1978 by the BBC. The corporation had stopped broadcasting the show because of its offensive stereotypes of black people and the grotesque make up used to black up the actors. Therefore, one would have expected by 1990 nobody in their right mind would consider using makeup to attempt to get a likeness of a racial group. Apparently, this wasn't the case, maybe some kind of defence of such a stance was that the makeup wasn't grotesquely stereotypically. A better defence might be to look at other cultural norms from the time and the early 21st century.

Comedian and champion of minorities and inclusiveness Matt Lucas wore black make up to play a character in *Little Britain* in the early 2000's to little or no public concern. Harry Enfield who again was seen as a right on individual dressed up as Nelson Mandela as late as 2007 and appeared to receive little or no public concern.

Since those times society has moved on and in a more inclusive and representative society such portrayals are quite rightly seen as offensive. One is left with no doubt that such an album cover would not now be produced. In 1990 it may have been pushing the boundaries of good taste but was by no means seen as taboo. Perhaps an indicator of how much society has moved on. *Dreamtime* had seen fewer musical collaborations but *10* saw the band starting to move back more to working this way at the same time both writers were also confident enough to bring fully formed songs to the party.

Burnel built on his increased productivity seen on the previous album with more songs and vocal performances on the album. Relations between the band members appeared to be calm, united by the fact that their record company appeared to be losing faith in them. Conversely the band felt the company weren't doing their job properly having failed to break the band back into mainstream popularity despite being delivered a series of commercial singles and albums. Now they had a company rejecting their album and imposing a producer on them and they seemed determined to prove the suits wrong.

The album was conceived in 1988/89 when the musical cultural movement called Madchester was gathering pace. It was based around indie and rock bands becoming more dance orientated fuelled by the drug Ecstasy. Bands like The Stone Roses, Happy Mondays and The Charlatans burst on to the scene. The organ driven sound of The Charlatans wasn't a million miles away from early Stranglers and the burning question was would a long in the tooth established band like The Stranglers be able to compete with the new kids on the block or would they be seen as dinosaurs, just like they had viewed the orthodox musical fraternity of the mid-seventies?

There was the usual large tour of big city venues in the UK and a whole series of dates across Europe which were topped in London at Alexandra Palace in August. Following the date on 11th August at the Palace, Cornwell announced he was leaving the band thus lowering the curtain on the first phase of The Stranglers.

Sweet Smell Of Success

Unlike the previous album which started with a gentler, reflective number, the band opted for an up-tempo number, hopefully attention grabbing. Ever aware of what was going on around them in the musical world there is a jazzy dance groove to the song. Chosen as a follow-up single to '96 Tears' it failed in its mission to crack the charts reaching only No. 65 and spending only two weeks in the Top 75.[7]

A huge shame is as it has all the elements of a really commercial song. Greenfield dusts off his organ to lead the song. Interesting to note that around the same time The Charlatans were breaking big with their organ sound and were soon followed by the Inspiral Carpets, but Greenfield was there first so maybe the band were setting trends again or probably more likely the organ sound was fashionable again.

Elsewhere his beautiful jazzy piano reflects another music fashion of the time which was to use piano on dance/club tracks. Elsewhere Burnel's bass is up front and settles into a riff that's not a million miles away from The Doors classic 'Riders On The Storm' bass line.[8]

Cornwell cuts in with trademark skinny guitar. Roy Thomas Baker asserting his role as producer gets in on the act by bringing in Stuart Brooks to perform a muted Miles Davis-esq solo to add a subtle jazz feel. The subtlety is enhanced by the producer getting Simon Morton to add congas over the drums which somehow lightens the effect of the heavy back beat.

Like the track from the previous album, 'Big In America' there are many different styles being used but this time all the techniques and nuances serve the song rather than becoming merely ballast. The video places the band in a jazz nightclub casino peopled by the world leaders depicted on the record sleeve.

The leaders are depicted gambling, the implication is clear, world leaders in cahoots deciding and betting on the future of the world while the band plays on.

Cornwell's words don't quite match the video director's interpretation but are so impressionistic there is a wealth of ideas as to what the song maybe about. The collection of images Cornwell assembles are about striving for success and then wanting even more of the trappings and luxuries of success. Basically, we have a 'sex and drugs and rock 'n' roll' song which of course is traditional success criterion for any band.

There are of course drug references with the use of words like "trip" and "stuff". Burnel and Cornwell were open about their use of cocaine and other pharmaceuticals and what they saw at the time as their potential benefits. By the time of this album, they were no longer indulging so the song is perhaps a voyeur or former drugs traveller looking in on the rock 'n' roll drugs scene.

The band were able to indulge in drugs because of the success of the first two albums which will have provided much disposable income. Perhaps the most pithy view of the freely availability of drugs in the music business world was voiced by the band's musical contemporary Sting who once said of using cocaine, "It's God's way of telling you you've got too much money". A quote that rings true to this day. If drug use was a symbol of success The Stranglers certainly ticked this box.

Elsewhere in the song there is a reference to an alluring woman which covers the sex base as criteria for success. It is also an image for the temptation the drive for success brings. Success breeds the drive for even more success and the trappings that go with it. Gambling is another theme Cornwell explores; he could be meaning it in the literal sense i.e., that making pots of money can trigger a gambling addiction.

One can see this by looking at premier league footballers or any other very successful subgroup who have more money that most people can imagine yet seem more likely to fall into gambling addiction than most other groups.

Alternatively, it could be the suggestion that to achieve further success you have to take career gambles which of course may well not work out. The parallels with the band are easy to see, who had certainly, in the latter years taken all kinds of gambles with their career with varying degrees of success.

The song is a Cornwell-Burnel collaboration with Greenfield for once having a sizeable say in things. The title comes the 1950s film of the same name. Interestingly the film deals overtly with the perceived stigma of using marijuana, which was a daring and edgy topic at that time. One of the main characters is an immoral newspaper owner, an irony that would not have been lost on the band given their history with the press. Another key character in the film is a jazz musician and given this knowledge creates a nice symmetry to the way the song sounds, its lyrical content, and the video representation.

*****

The tighter, more powerful 'live' sound replaced the softer palette of *Dreamtime* with an immediate return to a bass infused soundscape in the introduction. Whether the prominent live congas add to the overall experience is a matter for conjecture as the band seemed to be wanting to strip back to a more 'live' sound hence the proliferation of distorted guitar and bass. Greenfield also stripped back to use, for the most part, real piano but, this was at odds with their original signature sound that set them apart. However, this was 1990 and the band sound had evolved many times since the early days.

The music of the intro is promising with the opening guitar chords played with rests in between and in unison with the bass. The relationship between the second and third chords is the tritone/devil's interval, the unsettling relationship that had been used far more frequently during the early albums, but the rest of the chords fall into the conventional patterns. These intro chords are then repeated but played with less of a gap between each chord and then again with no gap.

Sandwiched between these chords is four bars where the bass plays a rumbling and highly effectively riff whilst the distorted guitar reverts to the old days of discordant chords. Black's drum pattern allows congas to be centre stage for the opening and then enters with a conventional pattern with a typically late eighties snare, but, mercifully, less of the grating treble timbre that had dominated the sound on occasions in the previous album. Even though they are electronic, there is the sense of a live feel to augment the other instruments. Greenfield's organ sound is very low in the mix and then the piano enters with an effective, bluesy solo. This is accompanied by a different yet equally effective bass riff that becomes the mainstay for the rest of the song.

Cornwell's vocal delivery is reverting slightly back with a hint of menace for the first low pitched phrase, but the second contrasting higher phrase is more commercial, especially when on the repeat, "But is the trip", there is an effective harmony, but this does soften up the overall feel to the song. The bridge has an obvious chord pattern and drum fill that takes us to the hook line accompanied where the bass riff reappears, having changed to follow the chords for the bridge but with some inversions and a heavy slide down when the other instruments stop that really does induce heartwarming thoughts of earlier albums.

The piano appears with solos in between sections and then a muted trumpet solos using the blues scale with an impressive range that gradually gets higher in pitch whilst Cornwell shouts "Fallin" and Burnel adds momentary melodic fills.

Cornwell's answer to this climax is to deliver a breathy, spoken "You check your hand" with an amusing swagger.

There is much to be excited about with this opener, not least for the return of the self-assured bass, the distorted guitar, and a more live feel. But the highly mixed congas and the muted trumpet are debatable in their effectiveness, and they arguably dilute the intended heavier feel although the trumpet really does add a creative texture.

The song also feels a little light in terms of melodic and structural invention with the feeling that with extended heavier distorted guitar, bass and or organ instrumental sections could have moved the song up to a higher 'live' level. Nevertheless, a promising start to the album.

Someone Like You

Almost immediately the second track is upon the listener it's not quite a segue but almost and reminds one of those great gigs where there is no discernible gap between the first few songs as the headline act attempts to grab your attention. It's another up-tempo number with an obvious feel-good vibe.

The sound that immediately jumps out again is Greenfield's organ and with Cornwell's guitar sound harking back to earlier times you could almost be forgiven we are returning to 1977 but the production and instrument separation is too slick. Baker's production creates a shiny pop garage style which is summed up by Black's rattling backbeat drums which suit the song and the feeling providing a strident clatter perfect for the garage pop style production and clearly an attempt to write a commercial sounding number.

Lyrically we find Cornwell in love and giddy with excitement about his new squeeze. The love is described using dramatic natural disaster phenomena e.g., earthquakes, whirlpools, and hurricanes. There is nothing particularly original about Cornwell's descriptions of love. These are all nouns and images that are traditionally associated with the initial all-consuming passion of a new love or romance.

His description of life pre the love affair with his new flame is engaging and humorous intimating he was sleepwalking through life until she arrives and turned things upside down and breathed life into his soul. Cornwell delivers the vocal in a joyous almost euphoric style and why shouldn't he? He's head over heels in love.

It's a good stomping happy go lucky song with a number of catchy hooks and humour to pull in the listener but in all honesty, it is a bit too lightweight. It's a song that feels it would have been better a better fit on *La Folie*. The production, its brevity and obvious commerciality gave it the potential to be a single, but it is probably a bit to close in feel, sound to '96 Tears'.

*****

The live feel continues with the organ taking centre stage, ably supported by the distorted guitar and bass, the electronic drums also serving up plenty of Black inspired snare dominated fills adding to the live atmosphere. Added to that, we are also treated to a rare, distorted guitar solo that has a typically appealing Cornwell shape but is all over a little too soon as the gods of commerciality are still rearing their ugly heads.

The song is rather simple with very conventional rock chords until the "All alone at night" section where the two previous chords are now developed in a sequence moving upwards with passing key changes giving a sense of momentum. Cornwell produces an effective melody over these sequenced chords and finishes with a vocal flourish on "(What else can I) DO" to take us into the guitar solo.

The song itself is not the strongest but does have an appeal. The bass line is restricted, the reliance of the "Someone like you" group vocals is overused, and the organ is a little predictable at times and seems to be preparing us for the next song, '96 Tears', which arrives with hardly any gap in between. A little mystifying that the band is preparing us for an uninspiring cover version. But the song has some appeal, especially the fourteen seconds of guitar solo and the final organ chord glissando.

96 Tears

Hot on the heels of the previous track Greenfield's Farfisa kicks off the third up tempo number in a in a row as the band carry on their assault to gain the listeners attention. It's strikingly similar in sound to 'Someone Like You' with the use of the organ high in the mix and the now trademark clattering drums, pumping bass and gnarly guitar. The only slightly difference is the use of brass to punctuate the song.

The song is a cover version of the ? And the Mysterians 1966 Billboard No.1. Although The

Mysterians were a garage band their version was a laid-back subtle recording. The song was also covered in 1977 by Eddie And The Hot Rods on their 'Live At Marquee' release. The Rods version is engaging, being high in energy and commitment but with no organ to highlight the tune. As the two bands were fellow travellers on the pub rock scene there is every possibility the Stranglers were aware of this version of the song and stored the memory away as a potential number to cover. In fact the band actually take from both versions of the song, using the energy of the Rods, particularly with the drums but then taking the organ sound of the original and placing it high in the mix to drive the song. The production made it a natural choice for a single and for the second time in a row they hit the Top Twenty with a cover version.

On the downside they hadn't had a top twenty hit with one of their own songs since 'Skin Deep' in 1984. Putting a cover version that was already available on to album perhaps said more about the quality of the other original material they had for the record.

Lyrically the song has an edge with a spurned lover wanting to settle a score with the protagonist wanting his former paramour to feel same hurt he is feeling after she walked out. The song was also covered by Madchester Farfisa fans Inspiral Carpets in 1988 and released as part of the *Plane Crash* EP.

In the spring of 1990 both bands were releasing albums, the Inspiral's with their debut *Life* and The Stranglers with the aforementioned *10*. The chart performance of the records tells the story of the changing fortunes of the two bands. *Life* from the Inspiral Carpets was released on 24th April 1990 and had glowing reviews. It peaked at No.2 in the album charts in early May and spent twenty-one weeks in the charts.[9] It confirmed their rise from barely know cult act to mainstream success inside a few months.

In contrast The Stranglers' *10* released a few weeks earlier to critical indifference in mid-March had disappeared from the chart by the time the Inspirals released their album. Confirming that they were no longer a major power in the fickle world of pop music. A symbolic musical changing of guard had taken place.

*****

Quite a faithful rendition of the 1966 original by ? and the Mysterians with the opening organ riff and later organ riffs being identical. The repeated bass riff is initially identical with higher notes at the end, whereas the opening thunderous snare fill and subsequent snare sound is an addition that adds a harsher edge than the original.

Cornwell's guitar is less strummed with distorted guitar played on the first beat only of each bar and is fairly low in the mix compared to the keyboards bass and drums and also compared to the softer strumming guitar in the original. And the tone of the vocals is a little more pointed and less crooned than the original. The other main difference in the opening section is the addition of backing vocals that was absent in the original.

The second section where there is a departure from the two repeating chords to the related minor chord displays a structural change where there are less bars than in the original and the single chord that occupies this section is embellished with a welcome bluesy flourish to the chord on keyboards and guitar with an additional echo to the spoken vocal.

This was a questionable section in the original and by shortening it and adding these features, The Stranglers have arguably improved the section. On the return to the main section the brass enters, another addition from the original. The low sliding tenor sax note and the higher trumpets in harmony of thirds are stylistically adhering to the sixties blues and soul brass arrangements and the brass continues for almost all the rest of the song.

Quite why the band decided to cover this song was something of a surprise given that it has such limitations with chords and contrasting sections. Many people regard the original as a classic, but it is the overall sound, led by the organ, and the vocal delivery that defines it.

The success of the band's cover of 'All Day And All Of The Night' the previous year, which resulted in their second highest single placing (along with 'Strange Little Girl') perhaps influenced them and/or the record company to continue the idea that had begun with 'Walk On By' ten years previously.

But to aim to have two singles chart successes within close proximity sets a dangerous precedent, suggesting that the band had begun to run out of ideas of how to impact on the singles charts with their own songs. This was the first time that a cover version had appeared on a Stranglers album and placing it as the third song following two similar sounding songs of their own didn't really move side one along and stalled any possible momentum.

Furthermore, 'Walk On By' was the band's original unique aggressive sound and vocal delivery pervading a beautiful yet laid back song of the sixties.

'96 Tears' was the bands late eighties sound that was anything but unique and the cover seemed like an simple update for the late eighties and many other bands could have produced a similar result which clearly was not the case for 'Walk On By'.

In This Place

The atmosphere of the album changes radically with the fourth track. A slow haunting ballad sung by Burnel in perhaps his most histrionic vocal performance ever. Producer Baker realised he had three excellent singers in the band and decided to play that strength. Baker had the same experience with Queen where three members of the group were excellent vocalists, and this allowed the producer to create the wonderful harmony sound that became their trademark.

He now did the same with The Stranglers and creates a choir of harmonies that is reminiscent of many Queen songs. The Queen ideas weren't finished either with the lush backing vocal arrangement, as Baker used other recording tracks for Cornwell to add more guitar creating a sound very similar to Queen's Brian May. Greenfield adds some inventive atmospheric spooky effects and Black's percussion is suitably sombre.

Lyrically Burnel is in a dark place trying to come to terms with the end of a relationship, is it with a woman or as has been speculated, was it about the failing relationship with Cornwell? Cornwell didn't ask the bassist and said it wasn't necessarily about their relationship.[10]

Burnel is not specific enough for one to be certain who he is referring to. The bass player again takes a narrative style and by referring to and naming all the seasons he demonstrates the passage of time and that this is not something he can get over quickly. He creates an image of an empty lonely house full of ghosts from the past which is then brilliantly complemented by all the instrumentation.

Cornwell's insistent riff is like a tap dripping and personifies the passage of time. The backing vocals are longing and added with the Greenfield and Black's empathetic playing a ghostly lonely presence is magnificently created. If we are hoping for a happy resolution with the arrival of summer Burnel brutally informs us the summer has been and gone and his torment remains. An achingly beautiful sad song.

*****

One of the potential highlights of the album where Burnel's distinctive songwriting skills are again to the fore. In some ways, this is similar to 'Don't Bring Harry' from a musical point of view with the slow tempo, minor key and idiosyncratic chord patterns. Some of the chords used, for example the flattened second, are present in both songs but it is the arrangement that is vastly different. 'Don't Bring Harry' has a beautiful piano part, languid yet unconventional bass lines, a glorious guitar solo and drums that supported these musical features with a subtle delicacy.

On 'In This Place', the wash of backing vocals at the start in a musical canon (the frere Jacques idea used on occasions by the band and as early as on 'Goodbye Toulouse' on the guitars from *Rattus Norvegicus IV*) allied to sustained keyboard sounds seems a little too dominant for the sonic landscape and, partly due to Burnel's soft vocal delivery, the beauty of the melody and chords, is perhaps reduced. Whereas the arrangement of 'Don't Bring Harry' allowed the strength of the song to shine through.

There is, however, still significant merit in the arrangement, especially in the clipped distorted guitar arpeggios that cut through the plethora of sustained sounds and are interestingly panned between left and right although this sounds like a Baker inspired moment as there is a touch of the melodramatic Queen feel to this moment of electric guitar sitting on top of a bed of backing vocals.

The soft drum tom heartbeat carries on throughout the song and provides the most subtle sense of movement but there are other guitar and keyboard parts that are somewhat lost in the overall sound. For example, there is a barely audible staccato keyboard quick rundown at 1:32 that is lost whereas the high-pitched keyboard soft arpeggio part that is present through most of the entire song seems to add to the already overloaded sustained sounds, as does Cornwell's occasional ringing guitar chords at the start of the verses.

The chorus "All the words" section, Burnel's voice changes to a more impassioned delivery and the vocal melody line is equally impressive, this time rising in contrast to the falling shape of the verses. At the end of the phrase after "Said", the guitar and bass play a highly effective chromatic descending riff in unison and Burnel's repeating "Carefully laid to rest" in the second chorus is one of those sublime moments that delivers such emotion. Perhaps this should have finished the song as we could have been spared the vocal effects very similar to Queen's *Night At The Opera* on the fade out, suggesting another Baker influential moment.

With a less intrusive arrangement and more space for some more instrumental interplay, then 'In This Place' might have been seen as one of the highlights of the bands entire output, something that Burnel's songwriting skills for this song deserved.

Let's Celebrate

Perhaps in the starkest of musical contrasts in their recording career we go from the incredibly sombre, funereal, reflective sadness of 'In This Place' to a party as The Stranglers go disco. I kid you not! The title gives us a clue to whence this came: 'Let's Celebrate', not a million miles away from 'Celebration' the good time track by disco funksters Kool and the Gang.

The band aren't just imitating a musical style it's actually a full-on tribute to the New Jersey band's signature song. The evidence isn't hard to find the same 'Whoo! Whoo!' backing vocals, the brass stabs, the subject matter, and the good time lyrics. The song has a heavy danceable swagger whilst Kool and the Gang opted for something a little lighter and funkier, but the overwhelming similarities are there for all to see.

The band took the song on the road and a live version can be seen on YouTube. The footage is very revealing showing Cornwell for the first time ever as the archetype solo vocalist. His guitar is a mere prop during the track and instead of playing the instrument he engages in expressive hand gestures, like so many vocalists, to gee up the song and the crowd. The guitar duties are handled by new live recruit John Ellis.

Returning to the studio version and we find there is a bit more grit musically as the song progresses with a restrained, and meant to be raucous guitar solos, one of which sets up a neat Greenfield solo. Bizarrely the song fades with a distant wailing sax solo that does sound rather good and the listener is left feeling that the saxophone break fade out was an opportunity missed.

Words wise this is not one of Cornwell's most taxing or poetic songs to unlock. A straightforward party song celebrating the joy of sex with multiple partners. The singer borrows from the Heavy Metal thesaurus to portray sex so there's a great deal of references to "honey" and "tasting" it, "riding" and "tailgates" that leave little to the imagination.

The spoken seductive female voice, which was actually producer Baker's wife, adds an even more lascivious feel to proceedings. One is left with the feeling that Cornwell is mocking the overtly sexual lyrics found in so many rock and pop songs. He wasn't mocking Kool and Gang as they were less carnal in their lyrical meaning, as apparently Kool's song writer, Ronald Bell, says his idea for 'Celebration' came from reading the Quran and the description of angels celebrating God.

*****

The obvious potential of the previous song had laid something of a foundation for the remainder of side one. Unfortunately, the formulaic pop sounds that burst onto the track with accompanying inane brass immediately dissipates the potential that had built. In total the riff is played twice on the guitar followed by a further five times with no extra musical development on the brass which suggests that, once again, the commercial forces are dominating thoughts here.

The guitar carries on the riff over one chord as the vocal enters with a predictably upbeat melody to support the celebratory feel. The extremely restrained bass and the drums provide a basic support with no keyboards at all during the verse and just a smattering of organ in the intro. The obligatory backing vocals enter to some effect on "If you wanna come don't hesitate". But then they hit a nadir with the following "Let me get to chase your honey child", with the high pitched "Woo woo" and "Honey Child".

More "Woo Woos" follow in the following section where, finally, the chord changes and the brass returns with more predictable riffs. Following the second chorus, a spoken female vocal arrives in a semi sultry tone to espouse the positivity with a strange proclamation about honey whilst swirling keyboard sounds, and a change of chord pattern at least provide a musical interlude from the previous offerings.

This section really does feel like padding to fill out the song and seems a little pointless. Fortunately, there is an upturn as Cornwell launches into an effectively shaped rising guitar solo but, once more, Baker's influence is clear here as it seems like Brian May has entered the room.

Greenfield's bluesy organ solo follows and is typically exuberant. The guitar solo returns as the song starts to fade and a saxophone eventually takes centre stage with a strangely dissonant and unruly solo as the other instruments fade out. A confusing end to a song that has little to offer other than a toe tapping groove and some quality soloing. The songwriting is weak and the arrangement with those backing vocals and the brass is almost unpalatable in its search for a commercial formula.

Man Of The Earth

A hidden gem languishing on side two of a much-maligned album — it's an absolute diamond of a song. A ringing guitar riff introduces a song about the mundanity of life, particularly working life. The arrangement showcases the guitar and the vocals with the bass and brass providing a pleasant melodic bottom end sound. Whilst the organ also adds depth and gives the song a sixties Kinks like feel. Producer Baker turns to the tried and trusted trio of vocalists to provide more body and dynamics and nails the beat group sixties aesthetic with a nineties shine.

Cornwell shows us again with his wordplay that he has an affinity with and a love of Ray Davis. The Kinks man is a brilliant chronicler of everyday life and was able to turn ordinary experiences into strikingly beautiful and poignant songs.

Cornwell here demonstrates as he had in the past, he has the capability to do exactly the same. It's Interesting to note that he and Ray Davis to all in sense and purposes were writing as outsiders. They hadn't really any recent experience of modern life drudgery being residents of the glittery pop world, but both clearly have empathy and sympathy with people who led ordinary lives.

Cornwell delivers the words in a resigned way which creates a suffocating feeling of mundanity and of being crushed by the expectations of everyday life. As the verses progress, he details the shackles that restrict the protagonist's life, the boring office job, the annual package holiday, and the family gatherings where he has to get drunk to numb the pain and boredom. The one escape route appears to be if he could become some sort of writer that would enable a route out of his private hell.

Several times the listener is given the clear impression that the main character will do anything to get out of the rut he is in. Cornwell cleverly alludes to Shakespeare and his character's aspirations of being a writer by referring to the protagonist's desire to write sonnets which was the bard's magical shorthand way of communicating his passion. The hero of the song has the air of a flawed tragic Shakespearian character and may be his flaw is not appreciating what he has.

The end of the song is bleak with the narrator contemplating old age and death or possibly a terminal disease. The title and off repeated refrain "Man of the earth" conjurers up several ideas. The title of the song is often used in English language to describe workers in agriculture. Or is Cornwell referring to someone wanting to be involved in ecology and save the planet? Or is he playing with the idiom "Man of the world" i.e., a man experienced in the sophisticated ways and pleasures of society.

Substituting "earth" for "world" merely to ease the rhyme and therefore suggest the song's character desires the cosmopolitan exciting life associated with being a man of the world. The latter suggestion is the most likely, particularly as Cornwell himself would recognise that he has been lucky enough to experience all the things his character desires.

Cornwell's clever use of rhyme and repetition shouldn't be underestimated. It may seem simplistic but the full rhymes, half rhymes and internal rhymes within the verse structure make the story flow giving it a natural momentum. The repetition builds to a crescendo end where it is used six times in seven lines giving an impression of an aching longing for and desire for the life of a man of the world.

The song was due to be a single and certainly had the potential to be a surprise big hit if a sympathetic radio station had attempted to try and break the song. However sensing diminishing returns on the band due to the albums disappointing performance the record company chose to cancel the idea.

*****

Side two continues where side one left off with another predictable up-tempo song which also seems to be striving for commercial acceptability but, once again, lacks any sense of emotion or creativity. The jangly guitar chords that open the song have too much treble and Baker's idea of multi-tracking the guitars many times is questionable here.

The electronic snare adds to the EQ woes with yet more treble and the bass sound cannot possibly complement this soundscape by being anything but bland. The song itself has conventional chords and the appearance of the flattened seventh chord ("He wants to be done) which can often add a tougher blues feel, fails to add any bite and the anodyne stepwise guitar riffs between vocal phrases fare no better. Greenfield meanwhile is left to play sustained chords on the organ very low in the mix but there is a change of texture on the "He wants to be done" line where the organ is higher in the mix and the multi tracked guitars drop out.

But it is the mawkish melody and backing vocals that really do extinguish any positive thoughts for the song. The backing vocals repeat the stepwise guitar riff from earlier and the result is even more trite. The overall saccharine result seems to perfectly fit the line "The Easter Bunny brings Christmas cheer".

The middle "Words become the man" section introduces a new conventional chord pattern with the organ again a little higher now in the mix and replacing the multi-tracked guitars thus repeating the textural change that occurred during the verse and reinforcing the lack of creative thinking. The melody continues to be predictable and banal, this time in a higher register, as do the backing vocals with their block of harmonies that are now grating to excess.

Various exact repeats and then a fade out over the second half of the verse add to the uninspired feel and Cornwell's insipid delivery features an unconvincing "Yeah" at 3:04 that seems to sum up the mood. The contributions by Burnel, Greenfield and Black could have taken mere minutes to compose and is indicative of how they were not operating as a band anymore, but often becoming merely session musicians for each other's songs.

Too Many Teardrops

Then with a bang we return to the bright shiny garage rock. This time it's a bluesy number but the rhythm section gives it a dance feel reflecting the musical fashion of the late eighties and early nineties. Greenfield's organ and piano comes to the fore as his sound and playing dominates the track.

Burnel and Greenfield's stint in their second band the rockabilly, blues and soul covers band The Purple Helmets serves them really well on this track enabling them to completely slot into the vibe. The keyboard player in particular, demonstrates yet again that he is a master in these genres as well as post punk.

The lyrics are about emotional exhaustion, someone who has cried so often in the past and has nothing emotionally left to give, not even tears. A person beaten into submission, emotionally scared and brutalised. However, the protagonist still has the awareness to realise he should care and that if he could, he might be cured.

However, the last line is bleak, seemingly offering no hope of redemption. The familiar references of emotions to water and weather are present, a signature device for Cornwell's lyrics. Most definitely an album track, not quite a filler but not a song that would ever enter that very exclusive club of Stranglers' album tracks that have become classics and have been performed regularly throughout the band's long career.

'Too Many Teardrops' was never destined to be loved like 'The Raven', 'Toiler on the Sea' or 'Tank' and illustrates perfectly the bands issue in 1990. They no longer had an embarrassment of riches in terms of material and were trying to squeeze what they could out of what can best be described as uninspiring songs.

*****

A welcome return to the harder edged bass and prominent organ that dominated the early part of side one. Cornwell also has a harder edged guitar sound in the intro with a slight move away from the over produced slickness of the recent riffs, and back to less conventional and slightly clashing ideas.

But the opening to the vocal is the blocked harmony backing vocals yet again and these continue to have a dominant presence throughout the song. Once again, the influence of Baker seems to be at play here and not necessarily for the best.

The chords are conventional but fit the bluesy style and the main vocal melody has an effective shape and consistent flowing rhythm that does work effectively against the repeating backing vocals. There is an interesting if not wholly convincing keyboard part that develops in the verse. The piano sound combines with the organ from the intro and the second half of the verse sees the piano on "Soothing water" play a solo underneath the vocals that ends with the cross rhythms for which Greenfield had make his mark on the early albums.

The new "Night and day" section is initially disappointing with its restricted stepwise melody, seemingly spruced up by, no surprises, blocked vocal harmonies. But the end of the section: "But they're gone" has an effective feel with the faster constant bass riff complementing the simple vocal melody and the stopping of all the instruments is a particularly strong moment because when they return, the guitar sound has an earthy edge that enhances the improved band sound.

Cornwell then sings "Too many teardrops" thankfully on his own instead of the backing vocals, and now plays the vocal melody from the verse on guitar. Whilst this is pleasant enough, the opportunity for a more embellished solo might have further lifted the mood which is not really going anywhere. This opportunity is also squandered on the fade out and seems systematic now of the band that a return to rambunctious instrumental passages of yesteryear is off limits as this was not the 'done thing' in the late eighties.

Where I Live

An autobiographical good time tune piece with Burnel as the motorbike outlaw riding around the Cambridgeshire countryside on his bike. The tune is competent enough and the production is big and beefy like the rest of the album and initial listening is pleasant enough.

Burnel sings in yet another different voice sounding as if he is from Mid-West America rather than the home counties of England and given the freewheeling motorcycle images one is put in mind of the film *Easy Rider* but unfortunately this tune doesn't have the impact and swagger of Steppenwolf's 'Born to be Wild' that was part of the *Easy Rider* soundtrack.

Lyrically the words are much more interesting than the tune as we get an insight into Burnel's huge passion for motorcycles. He had recording history in terms of bikes having used his Triumph Bonneville engine ticking over of to provide the rhythm for the track 'Triumph (Of the Good City)' on his solo album *Euroman Cometh*.

In this song he addresses his obsession in a direct way. As had become the norm with Burnel's lyrics we get a straight narrative from the bass man detailing a series of japes and scrapes on his excursions around middle England. We get beer drinking, pulling local girls and the consequences when their father's find out and forcing the bass man to leave town after being faced with the prospect of a shot gun wedding or worse.

What comes shining through is Burnel's love of where he resides. His lyrics verge from the poetic "Church spires stab the clouds" to the comic sexual innuendo "two big balls a cap and a bat" and to the inept with references to "a dog and cat" to get the lyrics to scan. Despite all this it is a jolly jape of a song, a definite filler or more obviously a should have been B-side of a 12-inch limited edition single.

*****

A return to the more piercing treble EQ for the guitar opens the piece. Although this is Burnel's song, there is still an attempt to conform commercially as was so blatantly the case with 'Man Of The Earth' and 'Let's Celebrate'.

Burnel employs a more throwaway vocal delivery as opposed to one of his breathy or aggressive tones, with part of the delivery being half spoken. As a result, there is a lightweight feel that was absent from his previous offering on the album, 'In This Place'.

This vocal tone could been seen to have an endearing quality but, equally, it reduces any substance that the song may be trying to portray. The chords are far more conventional than for some Burnel patterns that twist and turn. Backing vocals are present but less prominent and there is an interesting twist on the middle "The way the old church spire" section where the melody moves around combining two quick different ideas, although the sustained brass notes don't really add anything.

But this mini section certainly helps to move the song along. Despite the lightweight feel and piercing guitar, the song has a pleasant groove with the off beats at the end of each phrase of the verse starting on the lyric "Beer", and this helps Black to program a more interesting drum pattern with more interesting fills, and soon after even more so on the three repeats of the word "mine" which helps to propel the song along.

The ending manages to retain our interest with an impressively shaped guitar solo over brass riffs whilst Black continues the fills. That piercing opening guitar riff is still present and just about avoids overtaking the other features as the music fades.

Out Of My Mind

A big production standard rock song that doesn't really go anywhere. There are plenty of guitars wailing away in various channels and they create a committed noise without being very inspiring. The most interesting bit is the soaring solo which appears to be Bill Nelson inspired, another artist Roy Thomas Baker produced. Sadly, being placed at the end in the fade out it is totally wasted. Black and Burnel drive the song with a simple propulsive repetitive rhythm. Elsewhere Baker uses the 'secret weapon' of backing vocals with reverb to create that those ethereal backing vocals sound. There are many technical sound effects on show on the track but the key element the song quality wasn't there. The band and producer are left papering over the cracks by over producing songs.

Lyrically the song is more interesting than the backing track, it is multi-layered in meaning. Again, we see Cornwell taking a well-known cliché "I can't get you out of my mind", and immediately he tinkers with the saying by swapping the stem of the sentence with the end of the sentence.

By doing this he draws attention to the statement and thereby makes it more powerful and actually stand out. It therefore makes the new sentence far more effective and actually no longer a cliché. In terms of subject matter, it seems simply to be a eulogy to a lover, a person Cornwell appears to be addicted to and this allows him to use his often-tried device of comparing the effect of a woman to a drug.

Of course, the song is also actually about drugs as well. The title 'Out Of My Mind' is often used as a reference to tripping on LSD and add to this the psychedelic recording effects e.g., backwards guitars, reverb, ethereal voices and the conclusion blindingly obvious.

The song also deals with the age-old wisdom that love can heal all ills, for example just the sight of his love can cure a hangover and in the same breath implies she can cure substance addiction. Presumably the excessive drinking the narrator refers to has been caused by him not being with his love and needing to drown his sorrows. The joy of the experience sees Cornwell using one of his favourite images of the sun, in this case the sunrise is compared to his paramour and lights up his life.

*****

Baker's influence opens the song with a slowing down of the backing vocals effect, similar to Queen's 'One Vision' (although he did not produce that song) that tries to set up the psychedelic mood, before Black's constant drum pattern has every half beat emphasized but with additional toms panned left and right.

Meanwhile the guitar has considerable effect on it and, coupled with the swirling organ keyboard sound leaves virtually no room for the bass riff which sounds interesting but is barely audible. Another example of 'producing' the more traditional sound of the band for the late eighties and not really succeeding.

This is followed by the "Out of my mind" section where the vocal harmonies, one low and one high with plenty of reverb, deliberately clash with each other enhancing the psychedelic feel as does the additional backward guitar. The overall effect is disconcerting, in keeping with the lyric at this point but it is debatable whether the opening is effective overall. All the psychedelic swirl is then stripped back for the verse, and we are left with bass root notes, two only, in unison with a clipped guitar, under the vocals with a simple accompanying drum pattern.

Do these extremes in texture work? Does the melody work when it reaches for the seventh note in the scale on "Over". It is certainly a break from the formulaic offerings that have accompanied much of the album. The next "But when you smile" section sees a less conventional chord pattern which was a rarity on the album. The pattern moves effectively towards a return of the opening instrumental. The whole song then repeats with additional backward guitar on the second verse "I'm high from talkin'".

The structure of the song is a letdown as there could have been room for creative instrumental expansion, considering the subject matter. But the merging of the psychedelic feel with the heavy, constant drums along with a very economical main vocal tone results in the song not really finding its identity. A more unconventional drum pattern would have helped, but, once again, the producer's influence has a negative effect on the direction that the band wanted to take this song.

Never To Look Back

The last song of the album and another autobiographical piece from Burnel but a more serious reflection on his life than 'In This Place'. Instrumentally it's another big production number, synthetic strings from Greenfield, as well as a melody led by a bell like synth effect.

Then the producer, just to make sure the listener has got it, sprinkles lush vocal harmonies over the top of the track and we have yet another track that has the whole shebang, but this time it is the right thing to do and adds to the song.

The words from Burnel are incredibly honest and reflective. Despite his own advice Burnel does look back at some of the most controversial aspects of his life and career. The point being he needs to look back one last time so he can make his peace and move on.

The main assertion of the lyrics is the accusations that Burnel had right wing / fascist leanings. This probably stems from his exploration of controversial Japanese artist and right-wing nationalist Yukio Mishima on the *Black And White* album. In a beautifully constructed couple of stanzas, he lays forth the charge and his defence:

> I had a black shirt
> But I wasn't one
> All my loving is not enough for that
> I had a black shirt
> But I wasn't one
> I had black thoughts
> But now they're undone
> Thoughts are easy

Blackshirts was the name given to Oswald Mosely's British Union of Fascists in the 1930s. Given the band wore all black from 1980 and had an album with that image in the title and were often referred to as the Men in Black in the music press. Therefore, it is not surprising that in their bid to settle old scores from the punk explosion, the music press of the early eighties couldn't resist combining the Mishima interest and the dressing in black to reach a simplistic inaccurate conclusion.

The band's cause wasn't helped either by their thuggish history. The circumstantial evidence gave the music press the small burden of proof they needed to have the band banged to rights as right wing extremists. It was a classic case of adding two and two together and coming up with five. The accusation wasn't overtly reported or directly printed because the band would have sued but an unpleasant whispering campaign followed the band around like a bad smell.

Add to this the fact that the music newspapers effectively stopped covering the band in 1984 and in today's terminology they were effectively cancelled.

Burnel wasn't the only one to be a victim of unfair labelling. In the late seventies and early eighties some sections of the music press operated like they were part of Stalinist Purges making unfounded accusations on band's that didn't tow what they deemed the correct ideological line.

Other bands were unfairly labelled and struggled to free themselves of the stigma. In 1979 Stranglers post punk apprentices The Skids released their second album *Days in Europa* complete with an original poster from the 1936 Olympics of an Aryan athlete on the front sleeve.

The packaging of the album and potentially a couple of the songs were a little naive but there was no intent to support or glorify Fascism as the band were committed socialists. However, the press and particularly the NME were merciless in their accusations resulting in lead singer 19 year old Richard Jobson having to defend his and the band's reputation in an *NME* interview in late 1979.[11]

Another band to suffer at the time were Factory band A Certain Ratio, based on ridiculous circumstantial evidence of a record sleeve and the band's name. It was alleged the band's name had been taken from a speech by Hitler about what makes a person Jewish.

Perhaps the best know victims of these smear campaigns were Joy Division / New Order who suffered similar slurs for their choice of name. Like Burnel these bands faced a whispering campaign from the music press. The accusations were regularly aired throughout the 1980s and even today the accusations were still being discussed a fact Burnel wryly address in the song with the line:

> The truth is changed by
> The memories we have

Going back to Burnel's lyrics he is brutally honest admitting to dark thoughts which to be frank anyone would have after reading Mishima and his sado-masochistic philosophy. The bassist is almost saying he can see where his critics were coming from with this admission but as he points out 'Thoughts are easy'.

Who in the world would want to be judged by their stream of consciousness, the random involuntary thoughts that cross your mind? Every person has dark thoughts they wouldn't want to be public, and it is simply part of the human condition.

Burnel also bemoans the collective memory changing the facts and them being changed to suit some peoples' narratives. Ultimately, he concludes looking back just adds to the myths and lies. His rather gloomy conclusion is that whatever good or love he shows in the present will not erase the false received wisdom other people have of him. It is hard not to think of this final track, on the last recording of the original line up as an unintended insight in what was about to happen to the band.

Burnel's vocal in places is understandably emotional and in other places resigned. It's as if he is having an existentialist debate with himself on what is real. It is a very good song and a worthy of the honour of being the last song on the album and the last song of the original line-up. What a shame it's imprisoned in 1990 production values and sounds.

*****

This is the only moment on the entire album where Greenfield's synth sounds take centre stage as his other major contributions were on piano and organ sounds. And the song is so much the stronger for it with a real sense from the outset of the band blending as one where all four instrumentalists can be clearly heard. Burnel's bass has more of an old edge to it, the drums are not striving for the quintessential late eighties snare sound but actually trying to sound like real drums. And the guitar, which commences the song with a quick, raw distorted chord, maintains the power chords throughout, albeit in a supportive role.

The opening synth riff has a highly effective shape with the second half chromatic run down complementing the opening slower rising melody. It is a dominating sound and a clear throwback to previous albums where the multitude of various synth sounds would permeate entire albums. Greenfield's choice of sound and his imposing riff immediately establishes the mood of the song and is a springboard from which the song develops, something that had been lacking for much of the previous three albums.

The chords are conventional as is the texture and the structure, but it is the way Burnel's almost pleading, heartfelt vocal delivery backs up the strong lyrical message with that rawer band sound which, in this case, gives credence to the "Save the best til last" notion.

Moreover, the self-reflecting lyrical mood, coupled with the fact that this was to be the original band's line-up's final album song begged for an ensemble sound effort where all four instruments blended with such force. The only potential 'fly in the ointment' regarding this song being a fitting culmination is the over produced backing vocals. The "uhhs" that arrive soon at the verse are replaced by "Ahhs" and then followed by multiple harmonies on one of the most emotive and climactic lines: "All my lovin", thus reducing the emotive impact of a single, pleading voice.

Once again, the album is being let down by the proliferation of backing vocals as this takes away the space for the instruments to have an impact. This song needed very few backing vocal textures as the instruments had such a vital part to play and the electric guitar in particular suffers from under-exposure due to a crowded texture.

The middle section, "How could I think", moves the song into another dimension to a high degree of effect. This is due, once again, to Burnel's penchant for the unconventional chordal patterns. Here, it is the tritone/Devil's interval relationship between the first two chords on "How could I think".

There has already between a sudden key change and this unconventionality is continued as the following two chords on "never like this" are changed when the phrase is repeated on "Ever exist". This necessitates a change one semitone lower on Burnel's vocal melody on "exist" compared to the previous line on "this".

And, finally, we are free of backing vocals for this section which clearly enables the main vocal to display more emotion. Instead, Cornwell adds higher pitched sustained distorted guitar notes which adds to the distraught and confused emotion that engulfs this section so successfully.

But it is the dysfunctional chords that really embed the emotion and remind us that these types of chordal moments were still a part of the band's armoury but, sadly, infrequently exposed in the latter albums. One reason why these chords work so well here is that the overall sound has an older rock-based ambience. A comparison with 'Was it You?' from the previous album bears this out as there were unconventional chord patterns also deployed in that song, but the proliferation of brass and the more eighties drum sound left no room for either Cornwell's distorted guitar or Greenfield's prominent synth. The overall sound on *10* was more live than on *Dreamtime* so more synth and distorted guitar could have enhanced some of the songs.

There are well proportioned repeats, but another slight gripe would be that the ending and fade out seemed to be calling for a more structured guitar part following on from Burnel's vocal repeat of "never to look back". It is still an interesting set of splintered riffs and maybe there is a symbolism in the fractured nature of the guitar as the song (and band) fades into the distance. But the riffs displayed such potential for one last hurrah of Cornwell's organised, aggressive distorted beauty – one can never have too much of a good thing.

A fitting musical and lyrical statement to end the original band's canon.

Musical Summary

The album is, ultimately, a considerable disappointment where the cracks in the band's relationships affected the quality of their songwriting. These were the weakest set of songs that the band composed. Allied to this was the pressure laid on the band to produce a commercial sound and so the contributions of Roy Thomas Baker had a considerable influence on the overall sound, an influence that was unfortunately not always a positive one. There was a deliberate attempt to refocus the sound from the softer approach of the previous album, *Dreamtime*.

But Baker and the band moved towards an organ based 'live' feel and this proved to be limited and did not draw upon the great individual skills of the band members, especially Greenfield who seemed to be reduced most of the time to padding out sounds rather than dominating them. Greenfield's organ sounds were largely predictable and most of his parts on '96 Tears' were exact replicas of the original. A comparison to his organ parts on 'Walk On By' leaves one feeling thoroughly despondent.

How many of the backing vocal moments were initiated by Baker is hard to say. The band had always used backing vocals judiciously, but this album is caught up in the late eighties backing vocals vogue and maybe the band were happy to see this happen. They replaced synth and guitar parts as a defining texture for many sections on the album thus reducing the effectiveness of songs as half of the band were, to some extent, having their wings clipped.

What made Baker's finest production moment, 'Bohemian Rhapsody', stand out was the judicious use of backing vocals contrasting at the appropriate time with the input from the piano and guitar. The opening, rather like Talking Head's 'Road To Nowhere', was specifically for block vocal harmonies, as was the middle, 'operatic' section. But this contrasts sublimely with the harder guitar led rock band sections and the piano led ballad sections where the solo voice was left to outpour the emotion. Backing vocals at these points would have reduced the emotional effectiveness.

The guitars were multi-tracked many times to also provide a more 'in vogue' sound but this, like the backing vocals, also affected the overall space within songs as there were frequent occasions where the wash of guitar sound was overpowering. Compare that to the first six albums where the guitar sound made such a vital contribution by being rather piercing in timbre and, of course, by often deploying melodic lines rather than the predictable chordal ideas that invaded *10*.

By including the cover version and then releasing it as a single and using this sound to promote the album, this almost admitted defeat in promoting their own songs especially after their previous single was also a cover version. When the band finally produced a strong song that included an integral synth sound that blended in with the harder, live feel, the result was supreme, suggesting what might have been. But it was the last song on the album and the damage had been done.

There is an inevitability in that most bands where songwriting duties are shared will suffer insurmountable creative conflicts. When a single person is responsible for most of the band's songwriting, like Sting in The Police or Mark Knopfler from Dire Straits, then these bands can often continue for as long as the major contributor wishes due to the arbitrary factor.

When a band like Queen has four songwriters but with all four members being largely responsible for their own songs then that again provides, at times, an arbitrary state although cracks are often likely to appear sooner rather than later.

When the music is composed by one person and the lyrics by another, like Glenn Tilbrook and Chris Difford in Squeeze then there is perhaps more scope for sustainability as each member has defining roles. But when the music to songs is jointly composed then creative sparks will fly more quickly, especially when the talents of the two main songwriters are augmented by the crucial contributions by Greenfield and Black.

Furthermore, analysis of the band's songs has highlighted the differences of approach favoured in chordal construction on the later albums by Burnel and Cornwell which may add more fuel to the fire.

Perhaps we ought to celebrate the fact that bands like The Stranglers managed to survive as long as they did as the fusion of that creativity was, like with The Beatles, never going to last. The fact that all songs were attributed to all four band members sets a clear statement that they wanted to be considered as a true band with equality and we should marvel at the results and accept the split as almost inevitable rather than search for the protagonists with contempt.

Album Summary

The album wasn't the commercial break through the group and record company had craved. The band had acquiesced to record company pressure and rerecorded the record with a name producer. They had listened to further advice and recorded a cover version to get a hit single to trail the album. However, the album like its recent predecessors had failed to ignite the charts in the UK, aboard and certainly not in America.

There was no doubt the band had given the company quality commercial material for years even if it wasn't classic Stranglers fare. Despite having a great deal of commercial material, the band made little commercial headway. In fact, the evidence from sales was their audience was shrinking and had been since *Aural Sculpture*. They had to all intents and purposes delivered saleable products, and the company were backing the band with a large promotion budget. Epic released a plethora of singles on multiple formats in order to boost sales, a large advertising campaign in the press and provided funds for videos but despite all this, sales were poor.

The single biggest reason for this commercial failure was perhaps the quality of the raw material i.e., the songs and the way they were produced. One is left with the impression that the band was perhaps trying too hard to sound contemporary and the result was it all sounded a little too forced. There was perhaps an element of the record company despite pouring money into a sales campaign did not understanding the band or their history.

The commercial team lacked imagination and an eye for clever and effective marketing. The band's history and reputation had not helped them in the early to mid-eighties but by 1990 the truth was that they were part of the music business furniture and needed someone to recognise this and play on it.

Ironically by 2004 and the album *Norfolk Coast* their management and record company realised they were now an institution and exploited that to successfully raise their mainstream media profile with interview appearances on TV including mainstream middle England shows like *Good Morning*. In 1990 Epic failed to realise this potential angle to sell the band. In terms of America there was no change despite tours their name and reputation meant they were never going to break big there.

The album has a big sound, the drums clang around, the guitar for once is high in the mix as are the keyboards particularly the organ. Its Burnel's bass that suffers being rather indistinct and also lacking the attention-grabbing runs of the pre 1983 albums.

The vocals and backing vocals are rightly to the fore however it's all a bit shiny and made for the CD age and this is hammered home even further with the booming big band brass on many of the songs. A few songs have a garage rock feel, but shiny happy production loses the grit the genre requires to appear genuine. The preceding album *Dreamtime* although a child of the brash sounding eighties had a subtler warmer production.

As we have seen subtly in the right places has always part of The Stranglers game lyrically, musically and production wise. Roy Thomas Baker's production had never been famous for its nuances and so what the listener gets is a designer in your face raucousness which doesn't quite ring true. A sound made for the age of the Yuppie, all show but no substance or what substance there was masked by the mix.

Owen Morris's production on a couple of B-sides showed what the album could have sounded like, but he probably blew his chances with the record company of them accepting his mix with the disastrous mix of 'Poisonality' (see the extra tracks section).

Of course, the band took the record on an extensive tour where they could still be relied on to sell out big city venues but nothing approaching an arena. There was still a solid, if confused fan base out there, ever faithful who had even accepted the brass section who went on tour for the third album in a row. The tour climaxed in the second week of August with a big showpiece gig at Alexandra Palace and the rest is history.

Hugh Cornwell left The Stranglers the morning after a gig at London's Ally Pally on 11th August 1990 feeling the band had run its creative course and feeling the pressure as the main songwriter.

To be fair Burnel was coming back as a productive songwriter but in 1990 perhaps both writers' quality was not quite up to previous standards. Inevitably after fifteen years together there would be grudges and perceived wrongs which with hindsight with a bit of distancing i.e., a sabbatical and good management could have been overcome these difficulties. At the time Cornwell was adamant the others didn't work at persuading him to stay and so just like that, in an instant, the most creative innovative line up of the band was done.

Cornwell went on to pursue an eclectic and critically acclaimed solo career in music and writing but never coming close to the same levels of popularity he had with the band. The rest of the band chose to carry on, which was initially a bone of contention with Cornwell but what else could they do?

They had commitments a career and a brand. The remaining members recruited then touring guitarist John Ellis as a full-time member and Paul Roberts on vocals. They continued to tour and record but to an ever-shrinking audience. By the end of century and the beginning of the new millennium their time appeared to be coming to an end. Ellis felt so and left the band but in a masterstroke, he was replaced by Baz Warne who appeared to breathe new life and enthusiasm to the other members.

The result in 2004 was a stunning return to form with the chart bothering *Norfolk Coast* album. The music press even turned full circle and started to rave about the band. Burnel and Warne's song writing relationship flourished meaning Roberts was effectively frozen out of the band, leaving in 2006. The new four-piece recorded another three critically acclaimed albums culminating in 2022 with *Dark Matters* perhaps their strongest collection of songs since the late seventies and early eighties.

Sadly, in the last few years two legends of the band departed this life. Dave Greenfield died in May 2020 from Covid and Jet Black passed away in 2022. Greenfield was still an active member of the band when he was taken too soon and can be heard on *Dark Matters* with some of his most inspirational keyboard work.

Black had ceased to be a playing and recording member of the band due to ill health after 2012's *Giants* album but was still up to his death, very much involved albeit in the background. Indeed when Greenfield died Black was adamant the remaining line up continue and made his feelings clear to Burnel.

Extra Tracks

Instead Of This (B-side of '96 Tears')

A Burnel song that was apparently a contender for the *10* album. Certainly, it's much better and heartfelt than much of *10*. The subject matter chronicles the end of a relationship and therefore an unintentional symbol or even a realisation of a coming to an end to Cornwell's time with the band. Or is it the end of a lovers' relationship?

The words aren't specific enough to be conclusive. A laid-back bongo rhythm sets the tone with a nice groove deftly complimented by Greenfield's keyboard washes. Cornwell's guitar beautifully accompanies the song, playing lines off the rhythm of the words.

Burnel begins the song in a world-weary whisper where he captures perfectly the 'can't be bothered to argue and just go away' tone perfectly. He gets a little louder as the song progressed but brilliantly maintains his resigned withering tone. The final verse recounts what the exiting partner could have had. Burnel's delivery is so good that he could be singing about anything or even nonsense and you would know exactly what he means simple by the tone. One can picture the morning after a raging argument with both parties exhausted and resigned to it being over, this song exemplifies what such a situation feels and sounds like.

The production is by the then little-known Owen Morris who was soon of course to make his reputation with Oasis. The sound is sympathetic to the song with space and ambience unlike the cluttered sound Roy Thomas Baker's created on the album. If the rest of Morris's tapes had all sounded as good as this then the company's decision to order a rerecording would seem very strange. However, as we shall see, not all the other tracks he produced did sounded like this.

*****

One can understand why this song was not chosen to be on the album. Burnel's very low-pitched vocal line, the subdued texture that never changes, and the subtlety of the unconventional chord pattern were all deemed to be opposite to the direction for the album. But these elements all resulted in a raw emotion that was sadly lacking on the album. Burnel had contributed to the two most emotive songs on the album in 'In This Place' and 'Never To Look Back' and this song had the potential with some creative arranging to emotionally match those two songs. Perhaps it is a little ungracious to state that it was too subtle for the record company and Baker to have the creativity of thought as to how they could transform this song into their sledgehammered commercial approach.

The song has moments of beauty with the shifting keys, provided by the unconventional chord patterns, adding to the reflective, almost dreamlike mood. Burnel's vocal delivery also augments this mood and by the time he sings, "I don't want to fight about it" in the second verse he is lost in his controlled despair.

The bass provides a constant movement whilst the guitar adds sporadic licks before settling on a more chordal riff when the sustained keyboard chords enter, the two chords alternated descending each time. As the vocals enter the keyboard chords combine upwards and downwards shapes whilst the congas inspired drum pattern provides a suitable understated rhythmic backdrop.

The new "You could have had all" sees the keyboard chords sound become softer whilst Cornwell has higher pitched single note that complement the soft keyboard pad. The guitar in particular becomes infectious in its role, but the structure is affected by the lack of another idea to give the song a more complete feel. It is a shame that no one was able to tweak the instrumental arrangement here and there to create a slightly more coherent approach whilst retaining the dreamlike emotion for this strong song.

Poisonality (B-side of '96 Tears', 12-inch and CD single)

A chameleon of a song looking for a proper identity. The main question is are we in AOR/Yacht Rock territory again or are we in the heavy rock hinterlands? In parts the song wants to be rough, ready and heavy with the rock singer vocals and the heavy guitar, but they are too low in the frankly muddy mix to make a lasting impression.

If it's AOR the band are trying for then the instrumentation and sounds are there, but the mix is so poor and there is no hope of a smooth sound. One is left with a song that falls between two stools. Another case of throwing everything into the mix and seeing what sticks and to be honest not a lot sticks, and a metaphorical pile of mud is left on the studio floor. There is no space for the instruments or vocals to breath.

One assumes they were all recorded with clarity and precision, but the mix shackles them and doesn't allow them to shine except for the synthetic brass melody of the keyboards which to the song's detriment dominates the sound. The song is effectively drowned by the musical circus that is going on so despite all that is happening it doesn't make for a satisfying listen.

The song tries to have a certain swagger but sadly it is flailing around looking for a direction. The track was produced and mixed by Owen Morris and having made such a good job on 'Instead Of This' he rather blots his copy book here. If the album the band presented to Epic sounded similar to this then it's no wonder, they demanded it was re-recorded with a name producer.

Lyrically Cornwell demonstrates he is capable of writing a very competent heavy rock song. In the first line he borrows from AC/DC's 'Whole Lotta Rosie' when he informs the listener, he wants to tell us a story about a woman. He then goes to use his heavy rock thesaurus unashamedly giving us a string of heavy rock clichés used to depict women.

Let's start with her name, Poisonality, a woman's name made in hair metal heaven and perfect for the vibe this song was trying to create. Or maybe it's what describes what the woman does i.e. poisons the well of a stable relationship.

Both concepts are the meat and drink of heavy rock. Whatever the intention it doesn't really matter, and he carries on mining this very narrow seam of rock creativity portraying the woman as a snake with a long body, a slithering tongue and crawling through the grass stalking her prey which of course happens to be Cornwell.

The metaphor is flogged even more, as when she embraces him it's a serpent tongue in his ear and an anaconda grip of his body. The sexual imagery is thankfully exhausted and topped off with the money shot image of her 'poison' tasting good. All standard hackneyed heavy rock metaphors for describing women meaning the song's lasting effect is to leave the listener with a heavy metal wet dream story about a woman.

*****

The song revolves around the two conventional chords for the vast majority of the song. There is a slight change of chord pattern after the second chorus "Her poison tasted good to me" but the previous two chords still dominate this pattern so any hope that this may lead to a much-needed shift in direction are quashed.

The texture follows an equally monotonous path where the shift into the "Poisonality" chorus merely omits the previously dominating high synth brass chord sounds and replaces it with sustained guitar chords whilst the bass and drums continue almost identically as before. The melody is also very repetitive with the opening vocal phrase then repeated twice where the first note moves up one note each time scale and the other notes repeat. This could be mildly effective if there was another melody that provided contrast, but the "Poisonality" chorus is only a short hook line and limited melodically and still has the main note from the first section dominating.

There is a small contrast provided on "The poison tasted" section but nowhere near enough for the song to have a coherent sense of development. But, most of all, it is the unchanging texture with the synth brass and drums dominating. There is a guitar riff buried in the middle of the mix and some strange vocal effects and screaming sounds. Plus, there are backing vocals accompanying the main vocal most of the time, but the mix is so muddied by the synth and drums so the holistic sound is too cluttered for anything to display clarity. And for this to continue for most of the song, with only very minor changes, results in a tediously repetitive and less than gratifying listening experience. A shame as the song has an effective main section that needed extra musical development.

Motorbike (B-side of 'Sweet Smell Of Success')

In a similar vein to 'Where I Live' Burnel gets on his motorbike and takes us on another road trip. It's a pleasant enough song but very little to challenge or excite the listener. Morris does a good job brightening up the rather perfunctory tune. There are some nods to late-stage Velvet Underground in the sound.

Lyrically we get another homily to the joys of motorbiking and the Triumph Bonneville with the odd sexual innuendo thrown in. Clearly this is Burnel's greatest passion and if he really likes someone, they get the ultimate accolade of being allowed to ride his bike or are we missing a double entendre? To be honest it doesn't really matter and if ever there was an archetypal B-side this is it.

*****

Although the mix is, thankfully, far clearer than on 'Poisonality', there is an insipid feel to the song where the relentless ultra-conventional drum pattern continues throughout. The opening chord pattern is unconventional but flawed as it paves the way for the verse with, largely, two very conventional chords repeating that is at odds with the opening chords. The guitar that takes centre stage for the intro consists of a lower sustained conventional echoed chord followed by a higher, slightly clashing chord which again fails to convince.

This is followed by sustained organ and guitar with an extra lower guitar riff but low in the mix, as is the bass which has some interesting shape at times, but this is lost in the overall sound. It all sounds mundane and Burnel's breathy tone only exacerbates this mood. The melody is very limited and predictable and seems to stop just after "Bikes cliches" at the end of the second verse for no reason.

There is a change of chord pattern for the next "Black leather jacket" section which at least provides respite from the two-chord domination of the previous section and Burnel adopts a more urgent tone which adds a little impetus.

This however is followed by a rather painful organ solo over the two verse chords. These are chords one and four and this is a very common relationship that can sound rather hackneyed depending on the context and the organ solo certainly obliges in this respect here. There is a new section "And if you ride my motorbike" where Burnel increases the energy in his vocal tone with a higher pitched melody over a different conventional chord pattern, but this is less than convincing and is soon interspersed with a return to the lower breathy vocal "You might have guessed it anyway" and the possible impetus of a more driving section is lost.

Burnel's vocal tone does become more impassioned as the song starts to fade but one cannot extricate oneself from the banality of the arrangement, the chords and, most of all, the lyrics.

Something (B-side of 'Sweet Smell Of Success' 12-inch and CD single)

A slow blues written by Burnel and probably inspired by his work in his side project with Greenfield the Purple Helmets. Cornwell contributes a nice suitable bluesy solo at the end. Lyrically Burnel extols the joys and responsibilities of parenthood and his baby son. It's done with love and humour. Ironically the bass player issues some warnings to his son of things not to do in later life, things that did come home to roost and were revisited by an older and wiser Burnel on the track 'Lines' on the 2021 album *Dark Matters*.

*****

There is merit in this slow swung blues song, especially the impact of the "But I love this little stranger" chord pattern to the slightly unconventional minor four chord supporting Burnel's emotive vocal at that point, and in Cornwell's guitar solo at the end which starts to move up the gears but is cut off by the quick fade just when he seems to be getting into his stride.

The chord pattern follows the typical blues patterns but seems to be trying too hard and lacks a coherence as too many different chords are used. The first six bars all have different chords and the sixteen bars that form the main section have no repetition within them. Usually, four bars will be repeated at least once but by having no four bar repeats within the section as a whole, the result is that the listener is unable to really latch onto the familiarity that is necessary for a song to succeed, especially when the blues melody is often of a random, half spoken nature, as is the case here.

Furthermore, there are moments when the melody simply follows the main note of the chord, for example in the second phrase "to my love quite recently". This will usually result in a weaker shaped melody. Burnel's vocal does successfully become more impassioned towards the end of the second verse and there are some interesting keyboard sounds to accompany the "Don't play around with my feelings" section at 2:20 which could certainly have added a more original slant to the overall sound had they been developed.

But the chord pattern starts with that unconventional minor four chord that successfully spiced up the main section, so the effect is diluted for both moments now. And the slightly unconventional major third chord that was also a feature of the main section, being the fourth chord, immediately follows and once again reinforces the incoherent chordal pattern. But the arrangement, with the electronic piercing snare drum, preset synth sounds and lack of prominent riffing from the guitar casts a shadow on any attempts to create an emotive Blues feel.

You (B-side of 'Golden Brown' reissue, 1991)

Released as a B-side to a reissued 'Golden Brown' after Cornwell quit the band. The release was part of an attempt to restart the band's career. A repetitive riff drives the song with different guitar melodies around it and Cornwell's vocal performance is heartfelt.

The words describe an obsessional relationship and what it is like it is to be all consumed with someone. Cornwell's familiar device of comparing emotions to the weather are out in force again. Generally, the song's sounds are good, and it has a late eighties early nineties pop feel, However one is left with the feeling that it is not quite finished and needs a few more lyrics and a bit more inspiration around the accompanying music.

Owen Morris produces again and does a good job with what he has got but one can see a major record company suggesting it needs more work to be a complete.

*****

Once again, the late eighties sounds weaken the potential for the song. There are some twee moments with the predictable bass and keyboard chord rhythm alongside the continuous guitar riff has a sound that helps to create a pleasant mood but lacks any cutting edge. This inoffensive mood continues as the main vocal melody enters accompanied by softly strummed acoustic guitar, occasional sporadic higher electric guitar licks and sustained organ chords.

The bass is barely distinguishable the soft snared electronic drums add to the innocuous feel which is reinforced by the melody making use of the fourth note of the scale which is supported by a suspension chord for example at 0:46. This chord is more frequently used in ballad pop music rather than rock.

The change of chord sequence at 0:31 is also conventional with preset synth pads including a low vibraphone sound adding to the predictability and the scalic run down at 0:36 on the lower synth is highly formulaic of late eighties keyboard moments and adds to the general malaise.

When the main verse returns, higher backing vocal 'uhhs' punctuate the end of the vocal phrases rivalling the previous keyboard parts in their sickliness. There is a change of mood with the new, more urgent "Oh You" section but this potentially interesting section with slightly unconventional chord patterns that suggest a change of key seems to lack any real semblance of melody here.

This is followed by a rather pointless return of the verse section without vocals but with strummed guitars high in the mix. This section is longing for a solo rather than superimposing an 'on trend' late eighties guitar sound. More repeats and a fade with nothing added points to a song that had strong potential had the arrangement delivered more bite and less commercially predictable pleasant sounds.

All Day And All Of The Night (1987 single)

The song would arguably fit better on the *Dreamtime* reissue but ended up on the *10* reissue which makes no sense in terms of release chronological. It's a straightforward cover with nothing new added to the song apart from eighties production values and a brass section beefing up even more that famous monster riff and the drums of course have that late eighties harshness.

Cornwall gives the lyrics his best sarcastic snarl and does a passable take on Dave Davis's wild solo.

By this time the record company were desperate for a hit. Four singles from *Dreamtime* had been released but no big hit had occurred. The company were going to release 'Was it You?' But eventually it was decided a Kinks cover was a better option. With a live album in the wings the original plan was to release a live version of the Kink's classic. However, it was felt the live recording of the song didn't pass muster so a studio recording took its place. The song did its job and was a Top 10 hit (No. 7)[12] and thus teed up the live album to sell pretty well and in truth better than *Dreamtime* or *Aural Sculpture*.

*****

Unlike their cover of 'Walk On By' the band decided to give a faithful rendition of the original Kinks song with exactly the same structure and very similar sounds when taking into account the improved recording process two decades on.

Cornwell's solo deployed a similar style and similar shapes to the original solo, but he starts with the higher riff that occupied the second half of the original and then he moves to the lower riff which had been at the start of the original. The only additions were Greenfields humming sustained chords in the chorus and the addition of brass which, again, is debatable as it simply provides an additional texture, reinforcing the main riff and adding held chords. Why is it there?

Is the band now saying here we are, no longer a four piece but a fully-fledged seven piece so we need to give them something to do? They certainly didn't provide any extra creativity to the song. Other than that, the band chose very wisely to cover this song as it was ripe for the late eighties' treatment. This says a lot about the original song and less about The Strangler's and their record company's confidence in their own songs, especially as its release was followed up with another sixties cover version: '96 Tears'.

Viva Vlad (B-side of 'All Day And All Of The Night')

The song continues the epic adventure of Vlad with our hero after misfortunes and various unfortunate events ends up in Mexico. The lyrics are written and spoken by Cornwell and it's no surprise we are south of the border as Mexico is clearly a country, he loves given the songs he has written about it and references within other songs.

The tune meanders pleasantly along supported by a booming drum as the singer regales us with more of Vlad's adventures.

This time Vlad, having been set adrift and shot at by the police arrives in Mexico where he enjoys the hospitality and realises, he is not far from the fleshpots of Miami which seems to be drawing him ever nearer like a moth to a flame. Cornwell takes time to note the Mayan culture in his words building on his songs on *Dreamtime*. He also takes a sideswipe at American and German tourists using disparaging language to describe their ethnicity.

*****

There are echoes of 'Waltzinblack' here as the piece is in a three-beat time with the 'Om pah pah' feel, and all the sounds are keyboards apart from the perfunctory drum pattern. Unlike 'Waltzinblack' however, the three main keyboard parts all enter at the start and continue throughout. There are two parts that are more chordal keeping the waltz feel whilst the main riff is an effective, Eastern European folk type melody in keeping with the Vlad music from the other songs in the series, as are the jovial backing vocals.

The chords that accompany the spoken story are very interesting as they regularly shift in direction to de-stabilise the main key and the culmination is landing on the 'D' chord after "Senor, you are in Mexico" to slide back down to the semitone below for the return of the main section.

This relationship was a common recurring pattern for the band and was the crucial relationship that coloured 'Waltzinblack' from the third to the fourth chord. But here it is slightly different as it is returning to a section as opposed to being in the middle of a chordal pattern. If one was to place these chords in a different style and context, either in a heavier rock or a ballad like song, then it could be the basis for a strong piece of music. Once again, the band's penchant for twisting chord patterns that like to meander down an unsettling path are to the fore here.

Footnotes

1. Official Charts website

2. Official Charts website

3. Official Charts website

4. Song by Song - Hugh Cornwell and Jim Drury Sanctuary Publishing 2001

5. Official Charts website

6. Official Charts website

7 Official Charts website

8. Song by Song - Hugh Cornwell and Jim Drury Sanctuary Publishing 2001

9 Official Chart website

10. Song by Song - Hugh Cornwell and Jim Drury Sanctuary Publishing 2001

11. *NME* interview with Richard Jobson, November 1979, Simon Dell archive

12/ Official Charts website

A Musical Critique

Overall Musical Conclusion

There is a fascinating musical journey over the ten albums. The raw and instantly recognisable sound that attacked listeners on *Rattus Norvegicus IV*, the opening album, was continued in much the same vein on *No More Heroes*, the second album. Allied to this highly original sound were many instrumental sections that were new ideas within songs, not merely adding solos to repeats of previous sections. This resulted in unconventional structures to many songs where these new instrumental ideas would enhance the momentum.

There were moments on these two albums where the future complexities of multi-melodic layering textures and more complex rhythms and chords were present, but it was on the third album, *Black And White*, where these complexities came to the fore. The chords now incorporated many clashing / dissonant moments, the rhythmic patterns were often more complex, and frequent use of the multi-melodic layering resulted in a more challenging yet exciting listening experience.

The fourth album, *The Raven*, saw a significant change in the overall sound, principally from Greenfield's shift to more synth sounds and the blending in of the other instruments, allied to a greater range of vocal tones. The multi-melodic layering was now widespread as were the unconventional rhythmic patterns, creating a more complex overall effect. This divided fans, with some seeing the album as the band at the peak of its powers and other older fans losing faith in the lack of bristling aggression.

The fifth album, *The Gospel According To The Meninblack*, saw another huge shift to a cleaner and dryer sound with the experimental songs to fit the clear concept. It was a stage too far for many older fans and there were very few new fans on board as the album defied commercial norms. In retrospect, some will argue that the album was a creative tour de force but many more will disagree and suggest the band indulged too much and alienated their core of fans.

The sixth album, *La Folie* was a means to an end following the commercial disaster of the previous album and saw the band, with record company pressure, attempt to compose archetypical three-minute pop songs with the drums now setting out a clear path towards an electronic feel with many standard repeating patterns and hardly any of the complex patterns from the previous two albums.

The previous complexity created by the separate instrumental sections and the multi-melodic layering were on the wane as they did not fit into the commercial ideal, so the bass and the guitar now adopted more conventional roles with less melodic interplay. The result was a mixture of the old and new which, due to the chart success of 'Golden Brown', brought new fans on board.

The seventh album, *Feline*, attempted to build on this commercial success but with a change of style into a softer, more acoustic, euro pop feel. Most of the sounds were adapted to this style with an abundance of acoustic guitar, softer synth sounds, the bass becoming more conventional in its style and the drum machine all trying to integrate into this style. The band were no longer leading the way but following other fashions.

The eighth and ninth albums, *Aural Sculpture* and *Dreamtime*, tried to address the insipid feel that had permeated the previous album but continued to be swayed by the fashions of the eighties and turned to brass and guest backing vocals to inject a more live feel. The albums both had much to commend with many well-crafted songs but the raw sound and musical features that had dominated the first five albums were severely diminished and the two new injections were debatable in their success. The final album, *10*, unfortunately fell away due to the poorer quality of the songs and the muddled attempts to produce a commercial sound.

As with any band, there were many moments of good and bad, and the last five albums saw the band blending in with the eighties' styles with some success, but for those first five albums, there was a glorious mix of creativity centred around multi-melodic layering, separate instrumental sections, and unconventional and dissonant chordal and rhythmic patterns which was allied to that unmistakable original dynamic sound.

These first five albums had many different stylistic developments and for many, the results were, and continue to be memorable and unforgettable.

David Rodgers, September 2023

The Stranglers 1977-1990

THE PRODIGAL SONS

HUGH CORNWELL: back in black — Steve Double

THE STRANGLERS
Edinburgh Playhouse

NEVER BEFORE has the old adage 'like audience like band' proved so true. A year ago at the Dominion in London, The Stranglers were a gruelling spectacle, distant, dreary and tame. A year ago, they were quite plainly going through the motions.

But tonight, amidst a virtually hysterical atmosphere – making even the most debauched of London gigs seem funereal – the band stalk into their revitalised set with an obvious lusty glint in their eyes. Cornwell is sleek and sinister, JJ Burnel taut and supple, Jet Black solid and reliable, and Dave Greenfield, a raven-haired dandy in matching sweat-shirt and long johns, a wee bit odd, but there you go.

To begin with, it looks dicey. Greenfield's keyboards splutter and die, only to burst back into life then fizzle out yet again. But the sheer exuberance of the event itself eventually overshadows, then banishes these initial problems altogether.

Songs from the new and surprisingly vibrant 'Dreamtime' LP are received already like old friends, as is the suave and gently psychedelic current single, 'Always The Sun'.

Latter-day Stranglers material – tunes like the exquisite 'Strange Little Girl', stuff that's revealed the group to be highly competent brute balladeers – doesn't quite click as it should within the live environment, but the snarlers work like magic.

'Nice 'n' Sleazy' sees the stage invaded by 30 or so would-be JJs, each mimicking the bassist's curious karate kicks and hip-swivels with a rabid eye for detail, turning the performance into more of a family get-together than the big pop concert I'd been expecting. Cornwell's smiling face says it all.

It's good to see so many people not caring about who's hip and what for and why. It's also nice to find The Stranglers putting out their best music in years, getting to grips with it and having fun. They never actually do anything *startling* but that's possibly where their strength lies: they excel at being artfully ordinary. I'm almost converted.

MR SPENCER

Final Thoughts

When originally planning this book, it seemed certain that there would be an extensive conclusion. However, as the book progressed and evolved it became clear that by summing up each album at the end of a chapter that writing an extensive conclusion would merely duplicate a lot of what we had already said. That said there are of course wider themes to address and tease out, but these probably don't need a lengthy analysis so hence rather than a conclusion we opted for what might best describe as 'Final Thoughts'.

Hopefully as the reader proceeds through the book they will get a sense of which albums and indeed which songs we consider essential or in common parlance, classics. They should also hopefully deduce albums and songs which are not essential. Finally, the reader will also recognise works that can be considered competent or good but aren't quite essential but most certainly aren't bad.

It will also be clear as mentioned in the introduction the co-authors do not always agree. Again, emphasising the point that long held opinions, some might say prejudices are all part and parcel of the joy of music appreciation. To be fair as co-authors there was a huge amount of agreement around albums and songs. If we hadn't had so much common ground, then writing the book might have proved impossible or appeared as a bad-tempered argument over several hundred pages of text, which would probably have confused any readers and the authors themselves!

The reason for us sharing broadly similar views is that over the last forty years we have regularly shared our opinions with each other. This book was a labour of love over a full year, so what can be construed from such a forensic examination?

One thing that shines through this whole period across all albums is the quality of the lyrics. Burnel and Cornwell are excellent writers. Burnel with his favoured direct narrative approach but not averse when necessary to using more complex techniques to make his point. Cornwell is more impressionistic and his playfulness with idioms and subtly changing them gives his lyrics a real depth.

Both writers ensure their lyrics in most cases have different layers of meaning which mean the songs can mean different things to different listeners. 'Nice 'N Sleazy' and 'Threatened' are two examples of this, where quite legitimately, completely different interpretations and conclusions can be made about the songs.

Both writers regularly employ humour in their lyrics, a fact that critics have ignored throughout their career. They share a love and are influenced by bawdy humour and delight particularly in the double entendre. At the same time the humour is not always so obvious and once again they were often fell victims of reviewers missing their subtlety. Even when perhaps the music of the song doesn't have particularly inspiring the lyrics have at least been interesting and, in some cases, inspiring. 'Never To Look Back' and "Man Of The World' being prime examples of the lyrics saving an average tune.

The era 1977–90, or the Cornwell era, produced ten albums and after living with those albums day and night for the last twelve months and going over them in considerable detail it is possible to put them into particular phases that show the band's evolution and career phases.

The first part of their career can be called the New Wave Phase. However, despite what we as co-authors think, to many it with always be labelled the punk era, even though so many of their songs were complex and more ambitious and so obviously not punk.

The albums in this phase would be *Rattus Norvegicus IV* and *No More Heroes*. The second era of their career most certainly should be called Post Punk Phase and features the albums *Black And White*, *The Raven* and *The Gospel According To The Meninblack*. The band should be recognised as pioneers of this field of music, if not the creators of it. Most of the tracks on these records pushed the musical envelope, a key trait of the post punk genre and an approach first personified by *Black And White*.

The third era should be called The Commercial Experimental Phase and features *La Folie* and *Feline*. These albums demonstrated a deliberately more commercial sound but both albums still had plenty of innovation and experimentation.

The final chapter, Corporate Commerciality Phase and feature the last three albums of Cornwell's tenure, *Aural Sculpture*, *Dreamtime* and *10*. This era was a concerted attempt to embrace the commercial pop scene of the eighties using any marketable, musical means necessary to be successful.

This final phase failed to deliver sustained commercial success so it can be judged as a relative failure. It will also be no surprise that artistically and aesthetically it is the least rewarding for the listener. We are sure people with disagree with this grouping and perhaps for most people there are only two groups worth considering, good albums and bad albums! However, by having more groups we are trying to recognise the nuances within in this part of their career.

Having lived with some of these records for over forty years and in the last twelve months even more so, my opinion on the albums and the songs has in many cases been confirmed but in other case my ears have been opened to songs and albums I previously didn't rate.

In the early eighties the first six albums were my go-to listening experience and yes that does include *La Folie*. You might be surprised at my ranking in terms of favourites (can you guess) but all had merit and could fit a particular mood I might be in whether it be angry upset or the need to escape.

In truth the albums after *La Folie* I barely knew however listening to them extensively over the last years has revealed previously hidden delights in terms of songs with every album having tracks that were special. In terms of whole albums, *Aural Sculpture* an album I had previously written off, and most of *Dreamtime* are excellent listening experiences.

Even albums I am not particularly fond off had highlights and to me indispensable songs. The 12-inch mix of 'Midnight Summer Dream' is a fabulous piece of work and the mix of 'Sweet Smell Of Success' is immense.

Our critique ends in 1990 when Hugh Cornwell left the band but this as we know wasn't the end of The Stranglers and they entered a new era of their history which in itself could be split into phases but that's a concept for another book!

However, it's worth dwelling on the fall out of Cornwell's departure for the band and fans. The band chose to carry on which seemed to initially surprise Cornwell but he came to terms with it and remarked at gig to promote his book *A Multitude of Sins* in 2004 that he was happy for them to keep performing the songs as it brought him income through royalties.

In reality what else could the rest of the band have done but carry on? They were three quarters of the original group and had all contributed to the songs and they still had a writer in their ranks. Some fans said that having chosen to carry on they should have changed their name. Maybe, but in reality, why? The Stranglers as a band were bigger than the individuals in it. The other three had every right to carry on.

Fans disagree over the decision and there are different camps of opinion. Some think Cornwell leaving was the end and refuse to engage with the post Cornwell era. Others have never forgiven Cornwell and constantly bad mouth him whilst barely able to give him any thank for his fifteen years in the band and the songs he wrote.

Others are only interested in the post Cornwell era, hard to imagine I know, whilst others fondly remember vocalist Paul Roberts and love that era almost exclusively era. Personally, I celebrate all the eras and every ex-member of the band from Hugh Cornwell, Hans Wärmling, John Ellis and Paul Roberts. They all brought something to the band.

I fondly remember seeing the Paul Roberts and Baz version of the band in 2004 having not seen the group for ten years and joyful realising they were still a proper band and were still relevant.

Hugh Cornwell is still, thankfully for such a prodigious talent, making quality music and touring regularly, playing a mix of his new material and old Stranglers songs for which he must rightly be very proud. Recently following the deaths of Greenfield and Black there is now only one original member. Baz Warne has been with the band twenty years and is a full-time songwriting member as well as vocalist and guitarist.

There are two newer full-time members, Jim Macaulay on drums and Toby Hounsham on keyboards. Being full members is key as it keeps band cohesion, The Stranglers are still a gang, a going concern and most of all a band. They are not a backing band for one original member unlike so many reformed bands on the live circuit today and therein lies another critical point The

Stranglers never split up unlike any other of their peers they carried on through thick and thin.

Eventually things turned full circle. Artistically 2021 saw them release one of their strongest albums of their career with an extensive tour of big venues to support it. In 2024 they celebrate their fiftieth year with a tour that already has sold out venues. At this point the band's legacy and standing has never felt stronger.

Mark Finnigan, September 2023

Appendices

Solo Albums and Collaborations

Whilst the band were recording and touring between 1977 and 1990 there were of course the obligatory side projects with band members wanting to pursue their own personal music and conceptual visions Of course there was also an element of ego involved and there had been whispers of solo careers.

These albums are not Stranglers albums so there isn't the same detailed analysis of the music or the lyrics, but an extended view is required as they do have an influence on band recordings either directly or indirectly. The proximity of some of these albums meant some of them were being recorded whilst the band were working on Stranglers albums.

The product the band collectively produced from early 1978 to June 1979 consisted of two group studio albums, a live album, two solo / collaboration albums, a standalone single and a plethora of non-album B-sides.

Such a work schedule was bound to lead to cross fertilisation between the projects intentionally or unintentionally. It is amazing where they found the time to be so productive when you add the amount of time, they spent touring including the far-flung shores of the USA, Australia and Iceland. The creative pressure cooker atmosphere bore fruit for the band and individuals. They were a creative tap that couldn't be turned off.

As with the group albums each release will be taken in chronological order so there is a context, a narrative, and an understanding of their effect on the band.

Mark Finnigan

"IF WOMEN WANT RESPECT WHY DO THEY STILL THROW THEMSELVES AT US?"

THE STRANGLERS INTERVIEW PART 2: DAVE McCULLOUGH TALKS TO HUGH CORNWELL.   PIC BY JILL FURMANOVSKY

I SPENT 3 hours on the train to Birmingham in the hope of finding Hugh Cornwell. He wasn't there. He'd gone to Ipswich.

I nearly got beaten up at Euston Station that morning, I spilt hot tea on my arm in the swaying train on the way back and had a contretemps on the boring journey home, this time with some tubby businessman. And I was tired. It's a good thing I'm a highly paid, hip rock writer, ha ha, elsewise I might have been getting a little cheesed off.

My search for the missing Strangler continued through the rest of the week. Then on a chilled, sunny Saturday afternoon, my wonderlust in the wake of countless 'H.C.'s' scrawled on countless walls all over the country ended in a cosy cafe in deepest Covent Garden. The following is a transcription of what I think proved an interesting few hours conversation;

What's happening with your solo album?

"It's going to be finished in two months time. It's got eleven tracks on it and it's going to be me doing everything except drums, which Robert Williams, Captain Beefheart's drummer, will be doing. He's really excellent. I saw him play last summer and I knew he was the guy I wanted to do it. At Christmas I was really bored, so I rang him up and said I'd be over tomorrow. So we did a lot of jamming and started it just after Christmas. Seven tracks have been done so far, there's three or four more to do, plus vocals."

What sort of sound can we expect?

"It's different. I mean, it's not like The Stranglers. There's a few weird instruments on it that we found, percussion instruments that Robert could play. He plays drums the way I need for the album, melodic, playing the drums like an instrument and not just a time keeping machine which is what so many drummers do. He did the arrangements of all the tunes between us."

What's your reaction to the accusations of star-tripping self-indulgence?

"Well, I think It's a shame that they just can't dig on it. It's a shame they can't take it for what it is, which is just a band with too many ideas trying to get them out. We've literally got musical diarrhoea at the moment. I mean we can't stop being creative just to think, y'know, 'oh, people might think we're ... oh, we better not do that.' That's crazy, y'know."

Were these same musical ideas not there in the early days when you were writing something as tight and commercial as 'London Lady'?

"Um ... no, they weren't. Then we were struggling hand to mouth. It was a different situation when you're living in an ice-cream van for 7 nights a week all over the country, getting 50p a night pocket-money, I mean, you haven't got the time to think about it. The only thing you're aware of is that you have to stick together as a unit in order to go that one step further."

What about gigging? Are you going back to America for instance? But, then, you hate the States ...

"I can stand California. It's more European than the rest. I hated New York, it's like the east end of London with skyscrapers, it's a complete wreck of a city. We'll probably be going back in October or something."

I can't see why you're going back if you hate the place so much, frankly.

"You've got to understand we get a lot of letters from kids saying 'We really loved you last time, now all my mates want to see you next time here in Cleveland', why don't you come back?' Well, I think we should go back again. The media completely ignored us the last time, and it's such a big place that even if you do a few gigs like we did it's just a drop in the ocean. I'm sure if we were over gigging in the mid-West we'd be huge over there by now. But, I don't want to spend three months in America, Jesus!"

But do you really think in terms of those few kids? Is it not really a case of the usual trying to 'break it' in America?

"I can relate more to those people writing me letters. We can't really look at it as, y'know, (assuming a suitably excruciating mid-West accent) 'it's a big market over there. We just shipped 3,000 units' ..."

Turning to the new live album. Do you not think it's a sure sign of serious sterility in a band's career when they release a live l.p. at this stage?

"Oh, is it really? A couple of bands have released live albums that have been their best albums, like The Mothers and The Stones. Our's is just like a complete gig, a set. We spent a lot of time on it. It would have been easier for us to release a new studio album. We sat for hours and days and weeks and when there's 10 takes of 50 songs that's a lot of time. We ended up with 21 tracks which were good enough to release."

Jean was talking to me last week about the size of the band's debts.

"Yeah, we've been ripped off."

How close do you think those problems brought you to a break up of the band?

"We would never let the people do that to us. We discovered it because they just weren't working for us anymore. It was obvious what was happening."

Were you that naive early on?

"We were green. That's why we only found out what was going on until recently because now we're not so green."

I notice the 'Stranglers In Nude Woman Shock Horror' headline on the cover of the new album. Don't you think it's taking the band's sexist image to ridiculous and quite unwarranted lengths?

"It's not a made up headline. We couldn't believe that after so long people could STILL write headlines like that! It's very tongue in cheek putting that on the cover. We see a lot of the hysteria as being very funny. It's a good laugh. I saw a good joke the other night in the paper of two girls sitting on the beach in bikinis, and these two guys walked past and didn't even look at them, and one of the girls said, 'if there's one thing I hate more than being treated as a sex object, that's *not* being treated as a sex object.' I think that sums up so much. Rock and roll has a very animal like quality to it and you're never going to separate that from sex."

Do you not think, in rock and roll for example, woman is the victim of repression to a very great degree?

"Not at all. The woman who are in rock and roll are very UNREPRESSED. They're sex symbols. That's why Poly Styrene is the great white hope of the BBC. She represents the fat, ugly girl in England. 'Here you are people' they say, 'she's fat, she's ugly and yet she's made it. Don't lose hope.'

"Most girls want to be fucked. It's true, man. They stare into your eyes and say 'fuck me', which is a shame ... so many bands use naked women to promote their product. We've never done that, yet we get all the stick. There's something definitely wrong somewhere; that 'Big Bottomed Girls' Queen single, for instance, and all the Roxy Music albums ... the press totally ignore those bands just to make a point about us. But ours is a very tongue in ... ah, *clit* type of humour! (laughter) ... we've got a song on the new studio album called 'Two Sunspots'. It's a guess-what-we're-talking-about song."

Are you serious about when you say 'all women want is to be fucked'?

"When you get loads of woman coming up to you with 'that attitude' we think, y'know, god, all you want is that in the end, so how can you expect any sort of respect? If you really want to build up a new image of yourselves why do you STILL, y'know, 'throw yourselves'?"

Do they all 'throw themselves' at you?

"Yeah, most of them, otherwise they don't bother to try and meet you."

Do you not think that even SOME women might want to communicate with you on a level apart from the sexual?

"Well, there're the ones who write the letters. I suppose we excite. We once got sent a rubber from a girl who wrote and asked us to fill it, y'know. Maybe to be ugly and scraggy like us is in vogue. Maybe we're creating a new fashion.

"I accept that women are really into sex and I do my duty. I enjoy it, they enjoy it and everyone's happy. It's a shame that women have this insecurity about enjoying themselves. They've got a terrific inferiority complex that they've invented themselves. It's been built into their physchology since the beginning. They don't know why they've got it but they've got it."

Sometimes I think it's The Stranglers that have the in built inferiority complex and that the macho image is the natural reaction against that.

"We're taller than most people. We've always been confident and arrogant. If you don't believe in what you're doing how do you expect anyone else to?"

What about gigs for the future in this country, and in particular, London, where you appear to be finding it literally impossible to play at the moment?

"We want to try and do a British tour some time in the summer or early autumn. It would be nice to find a venue we could use, somewhere like The Alexandra Palace for instance. We can't get a gig here that's the right size. We'd like to get six or seven places around London, that would take two to three thousand, and, y'know, go round them for a week. We hate playing residencies. We tried that the last time but we just couldn't find the venues."

Do you ever feel the pressure of trying to remain an accessible band?

"It's hard as you grow in popularity to, y'know, maintain that. That's why I like being in London because I don't have a car and I just bum around in tubes and buses and it brings your feet down to the ground again."

What's your attitude towards the other new-wave bands that are now playing The Hammersmith Odeon?

"I think the new wave has disappeared up its own arse. Good luck to them ... all the bands suddenly turning round and saying 'we're not new wave' y'know, which is like Thoreau's old statement 'beware of anything that wear a uniform'."

What do you think of the bands that are going about at the moment?

"Nobody knows what to try next. I've seen most of the 'tipped' bands recently. I didn't think much of them. I think a lot of them are really overrated."

Have you ever thought of starting your own label?

"Possibly. It's too early to say. I mean, we're nearly broke. Of course I've got three Rolls Royces! I've got a car that blew up last week."

We know about a lot of Jean's interests outside the band, but what about yours?

"I'm really into production. I'm interested in how sound is produced. I've produced The Snakes and a couple of Pop Group sessions which got them a recording contract, which was good, I'm really into films too. I did a film of the Battersea gig."

AND SO we finish our coffees and head off like two lonely lost waifs to Leicester Square tube station. Hugh is tired. He's heading off to Southampton for another local radio interview. As he hops into the taxi we shake hands and then go our separate ways.

It's a cold Saturday night scene in London by now, and, as I scramble down the tube station steps, I think about the man in black. A strange man. A fusion. Like The Stranglers themselves. Real and unreal. Cool and uncool. Inside and outside. A future that's black and white, or a future that's no future at all? We'll see.

A Musical Critique

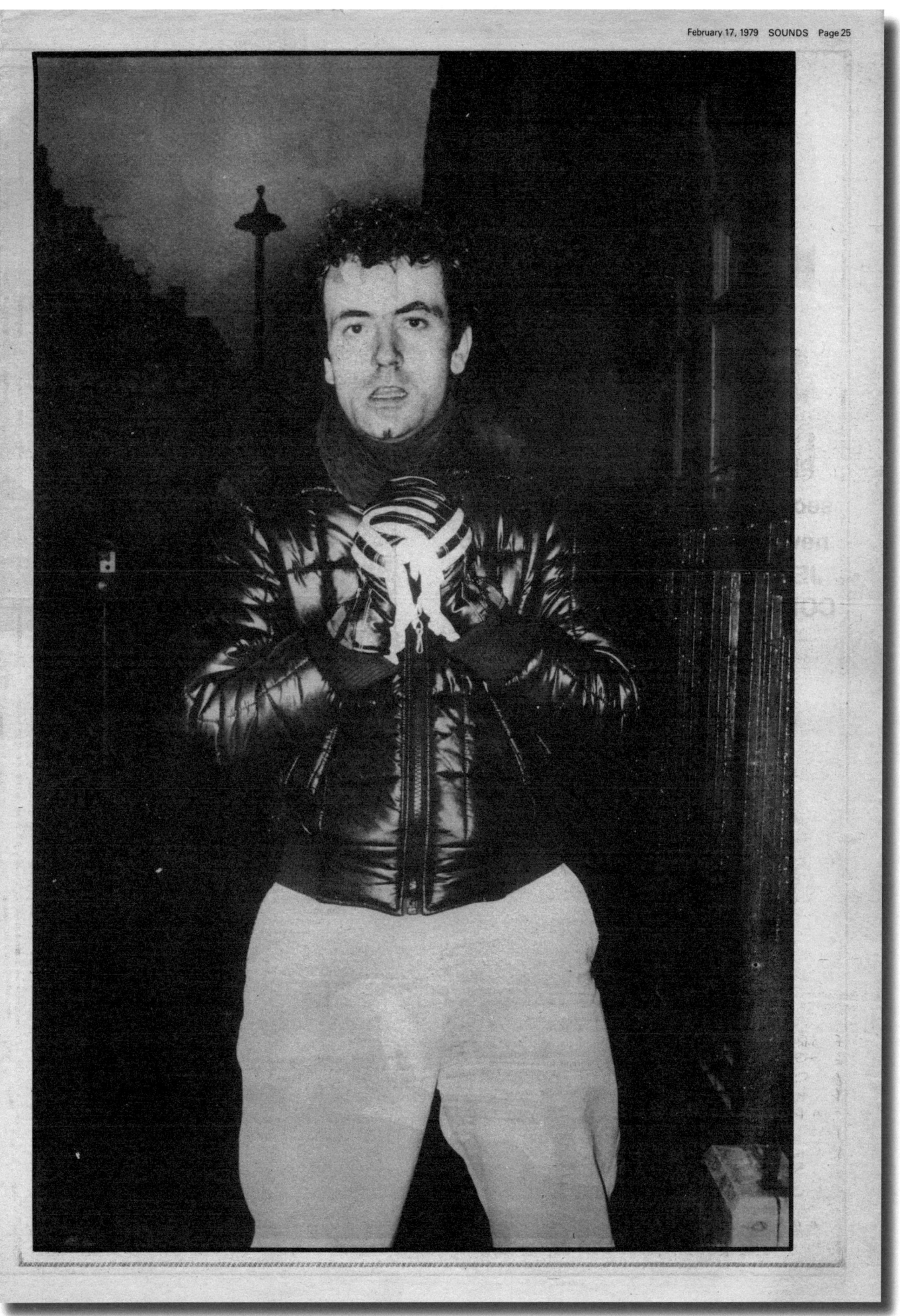

Euroman Cometh
(Jean-Jacques Burnel)

Whether the band would admit it or not there seemed to many, to be a bit more than a healthy rivalry in the band in late 1977. Burnel as the youngest, with the movie star good looks and the wild reputation was being touted by some as a solo artist or as a face to front a project.

Rumours gathered a pace especially after the controversy around Burnel being placed centre stage in a mock-up of a *No More Heroes* album cover (see the *No More Heroes* chapter). It was a sign of egos in the band. Following the recording of *Black And White* there were rumours of a split. Then the rumour changed and becoming a story about a couple of solo projects by Burnel and Cornwell. At this point things appeared very fluid in the band and the solo outings had the potential to make or break the band pending on their success.

The first solo record to appear was Burnel's *Euroman Cometh*. There was a big promotional push behind it, full page adverts in the music press, a promotional video for a single and a big tour of big venues. Despite the push the album didn't really ignite the charts peaking at No 40.[1] The single failed to chart and the tour played to half empty halls.

If a solo career had been a plan, then perhaps it was better to think again. That said the album is a creative triumph and Burnel took considerable risks with the songs, the way it was produced and with the concept itself. As with much of The Stranglers early work *Euroman Cometh* has aged well. Recorded by Burnel in downtime during the *Black And White* sessions. He was actually living in the studio having become temporary homeless due to an episode documented in the single '5 Minutes'.

The concept behind the album was a united states of Europe which ironically and prophetically is obviously still a contentious subject in this country. In 1979 when the album was released Britain had been part of the Common Market, otherwise referred to as the European Economic Community (EEC) a forerunner of the EU, for six years. It was a contentious subject in the seventies with the country holding a referendum in 1975 – only two years after the then British Prime Minister, Edward Heath had signed the European Communities Act 1972 – to see whether the UK stayed in Europe.

The issue of Europe and Britain's part in it has rumbled on ever since. Over the years Europe has become bigger and more powerful and is effectively now a united states of Europe. A united states that the United Kingdom is now not a member of. By choosing this concept, which incidentally was close to Burnel's heart, has by default remained completely relevant. The sleeve featured a striking photo of Burnel outside the Pompidou centre in Paris. The inner cover features maps of historical European empires in the blue and yellow and the EEC (European Economic Community) flag of yellow stars on a blue background. Also on the inner sleeve was a track listing and playing credits but no lyric sheet.

Sound wise, it's a distant cousin of *Feline* predicting the so called 'European' album released by the band in 1983. Burnel's love of European music meant there are also elements of Krautrock experimentation and an innovative use of electronics and other instruments running throughout the album. The bass playing which one might expect to dominant and be show stopping is anything but, it serves the songs creating sonic textures to complement the other instrumentation.

The fact he virtually plays all the instruments sets certain parameters so with no drummer he used drum machines. The drum machine which sounds like ones that were built into home organs in the 1970s and give the tracks a primitive almost homemade sound. It's not just the subject matter that make the album contemporary but sonically it still sounds fresh and exciting over forty years later.

The Stranglers 1977-1990

THE SOLO SINGLE FROM J.J. BURNEL

C/W OZYMANDIAS (NOT ON ALBUM) UP 36500

FREDDIE LAKER (CONCORDE & EUROBUS)

JJ BURNEL

APRIL TOUR
Sun 15th GLASGOW Pavilion
Mon 16th MANCHESTER Apollo
Tue 17th LIVERPOOL Eric's
Wed 18th DERBY Assembly Rooms
Fri 20th BIRMINGHAM Digbeth Town Hall
Sat 21st BRIGHTON Dome
Sun 22nd BRISTOL Locarno

Mon 23rd CANTERBURY Odeon
Tue 24th PORTSMOUTH Locarno
Wed 25th HEMEL HEMPSTEAD Pavilion
Thur 26th NEWCASTLE Mayfair
Fri 27th EDINBURGH Odeon
Sat 28th BRADFORD St Georges Hall
Sun 29th ILFORD Odeon
Mon 30th LONDON

FREDDIE LAKER (CONCORDE & EUROBUS) IS TAKEN FROM THE ALBUM EUROMAN COMETH · ALBUM UAG 30214 CASSETTE TCK 30214

Euroman

Sung in French sees Burnel setting out his manifesto as he name-checks past empires of Europe. The music is all about atmospherics, a creeping guitar refrain in the background bolstered by a simplistic but effective bassline. As the song progresses the K-Tel drum machine beats speeds up to match Burnel's increasingly quicker delivery an increasingly imposing narration dominates the track. The recording quality is lo-fi and whether intentional or not gives the song, and incidentally the whole album a naive but innovative feel. The closest contemporary musical references would be Cabaret Voltaire who were producing similar sounding records at this time.

Jellyfish

Immediately changes the atmosphere with a jaunty little guitar motif dominating the mix whilst the drum machine and trademark growling bass propel things along at a lively pace. Electronics add some spikey spice to contrast against the jolly guitar riff. Lyrically it's about Burnel absorbing his influences just like a jellyfish.

Freddie Lake (Concord airbus)

Track three brings along the album's single and perhaps the most Stranglers like song on the collection. Kicking off with an aggressive bass riff which could have graced any of the band's first three albums. The vocals are distorted making it a strange but brave choice for a single.

The subject matter also precluded it being well received in the USA with its scathing attack on what Burnel perceived as an America conspiracy against European entrepreneurship and ingenuity in the aerospace industry with the pioneering development of cheap transatlantic air fares by British airline entrepreneur Freddie.

In addition, it comments on the development of supersonic passenger airliner Concorde. The USA in both cases did everything they could to ban or make life difficult for these two innovations. For Burnel these commercial battles crystallised the need for a united states of Europe to combat such economic strategies from a dominant USA. There was even a video shot for the song indicating the record label were supportive of Burnel and were hedging their bets on a Burnel solo career if the band broke up.

Euromess

Prophetically named and whatever your stance on Europe happens to be the phrase, Euromess, would be an apt description of the Brexit process. It begins with creeping, atmospheric instrumentation skulking into view and Burnel using vocal distortion and an array of other instruments, including a treated melodica to create a chaotic electronic soundscape. He intones his warning "Don't rely on lies" creating a genuine feeling of claustrophobia and paranoia that reflects the confusion of post war Europe.

Deutchland Nicht Über Alles

This track ends side one of the original album with a repetitive insistent guitar motif accompanied by a syn drum and a simple heavy simple bass riff set the sombre tone. Electronics then flit in and out to add to a hypnotic instrumental track that is far more complex than it initially feels.

Burnel demonstrate his Euro credentials and linguistic prowess by singing a 'new' German national anthem in German. By putting "Nicht" into the title Burnel changes the meaning completely so instead of 'Germany above everything' the famous Deutchland über alles opening line expressed in the current national anthem. By adding "Nicht" the meaning becomes 'Germany not above everything' a rather different sentiment.

The Stranglers 1977-1990

A Musical Critique

February 10, 1979 SOUNDS Page 25

EUROMAN COMETH IN THE FORM OF STRANGLER JEAN-JACQUES BURNEL AND DAVE McCULLOUGH COWERS IN THE FACE OF:

MISHIMA, MACHISMO AND MACHETES

PIC BY JILL FURMANOVSKY

SOMETIMES I get to feel so mean. Somebody's standing in my way. Somebody's gonna have to pay. I walk up and down Oxford Street for a good half an hour. I'm getting annoyed with myself. I've been given directions to find publicist Alan Edwards' office amid this busy, throbbing heart of the metropolis and I'm lost. Completely lost. And Jean Jacques Burnel is probably waiting for me, no doubt angry and incensed at my tardiness.

Oh boy. Everybody I ask the way seems either stoned or retarded or foreign or all three. I bet he leaves in a temper before I arrive and singles me out for a good thrashing some night at a gig. Well, I mean, after all, that's what these Stranglers chappies are reputed to do, isn't it? I'm frightened. I realise that my 'angry' (sic) and tortured self is expected to give J.J.B. 'a hard time'. I suppose I'm doing all right so far, I surmise, as I head up the stairs of the agency that I've at last and rather miraculously stumbled across a goodish half an hour late.

HE'S NOT there of course. It had to be. It's got to be. I sit down and chat with the publicist types and drink tea out of a cracked mug. The room is drab and squalid and dark. I sip and wait and wonder. The cover of the new Stranglers live album sits beside me, the actual vinyl instigator of this forthcoming confrontation.

The band leave for Japan in a few days' time, gigging there before heading on to Australia for some dates. The album that they are leaving us, I notice, has all the goodies on it . . . 'Something Better Change', 'Grip' . . .

Suddenly the door bursts open and a cold breeze lifts my hair as I turn sharply round and see the wiry figure of Jean Burnel, inevitably leathered and insanely grinning.

"I want you to know that I think all journalists are pigs. You are a pig."

Yeah? His voice is a blend of refined fury and cheeky good humour. I can't take him seriously but I'm still wary of him. And then something happens mid insult:

"I know you. I never forget a face."

He scratches his chin and I resolve his confusion by telling him that we'd met briefly at the end of the last tour in Belfast.

"I never forget a face . . ." he grins triumphantly. "I wish I hadn't agreed to do this now."

He doesn't clarify that statement and I head into the adjoining room a little confused and baffled myself. This is going to prove interesting, I ponder, as I put down my cold tea. Interesting, indeed.

JEAN BURNEL has a theory about the rock press. He thinks they're all out to get him. The transition that I've made personally, therefore, namely from the fanzine to the music press world, is thus roughly, in his estimation, tantamount to selling my soul to the highest bidder. You can't dissuade him from that conclusion.

The ensuing conversation with Jean was punctuated at frequent intervals with a grave reminder of The Stranglers' grievance at "two years of being constantly slagged off by the press."

For the moment Jean is content with a heated exchange between himself and photographer Jill Furmanovsky. He informs her of the fact that she hates him. Jill protests and departs to do some shopping. Jean smiles confidently as he launches himself on to the narrow window sill above me, from where he looks down at me like a hungry, energetic young lion eyeing its crippled prey.

I feel uncomfortable. This is stupid! I hate people being what I expect them to be! Jean, do you think I hate you? He peers down upon me and his smile stretches further across his face.

"I like to think everyone hates me. Then I know where I stand. Paranoia? No, paranoia is when you *think* everybody hates you."

He doesn't laugh. Neither do I. I gulp and inquire rather obviously about the new live album.

He's clearly anticipated the theme of my next question, namely that a live album at this stage in a band's career is an accepted symbol of sterility and laziness. Superficially, in The Stranglers' case, the situation is, if you like, worse. It's as if they've maintained their separateness from The Business (which they have, despite their giddy success) for so long, only to now undermine it with a plethora of solo albums and a live effort. Well, J.J.?

"If I thought it was that kind of business type, 42 track style album I would have thought we didn't need to do the album. It wouldn't have gone out."

He goes on and I must confess my cynical 'uptightness' about the motives behind the live LP were more or less vanquished by the deadly seriousness of his voice and the almost *pleading* expression on his face. It was as if he hadn't even *thought* about the album in that manner before.

"We could have brought out a compilation album, like The Doors did. I think a live compilation is better than a studio one 'cos there's lots of tracks that haven't been released on albums before. It's very rough. There's bits of verbals between tracks, bits of punch-ups and things. You can hear what Hugh's voice sounds like when he's talking."

Conversation steals its way rather uncertainly, seeing we're in a rather too formal interview situation (at Jean's insistence) for my liking, to the subject of The Stranglers and politics. I suggest that the band have opted out of positive, committed policies in comparison to bands like The Clash and The Jam.

"I think we've been more political than the other bands." He becomes incensed at the thought. "The fact that we walked out at Guildford, the fact that we did it a year before anyone else, the fact that we've been to prison a couple of times, the fact that we've had managerial splits without any undue publicity, whereas other people rip off for the sake of 'liberating the people' . . . I think it's pathetic."

He shuffles back up the sill. To Jean, The Stranglers are explicitly the victims of their own worthy non-conformity. He lays down his feelings in a general form:

"We've always been on our own and that's what has made us, don't you agree?"

Ah, yes. The Robin Hoods of the New Wave.

"We've been on the outside all the time and that suits me fine 'cos all my life I've been on the outside."

He is still smiling.

"I know where I am."

THE STRANGLERS have a dignity about them. They have great respect for themselves, their music and their audience. But how much of this *feeling* is real and cleansed of tinsel sentimentality or self-deception? It's hard to tell. I mean, do you actually, returning to your former quote, think about anything as hazy as 'liberating the people'?

"Not much. I think it's a presumption that any people who consider themselves as writers would like to . . ."

He tails off, unsure.

"I mean, a lot of people have got into Mishima (Yukio Mishima that is, the fervently nationalistic Japanese writer who committed ritual suicide) since we've written about it".

He speaks of The Stranglers as "part of an underground movement" when I refer to the band's history of pulling out of gigs and being the incumbents of GLC prohibitions.

"I don't regret it at all, man, 'cos I think it shows that we're part of an underground culture."

Yet, how can you account for something as plainly 'overground' as being (until Elvis Costello's recent domination) the undoubted 'acceptable side of punk' in many respects, the first album still proving The One Punk Record To Have by those unconverted to the genre?

"The acceptable side of punk? Yeah?"

I suppose I'd qualify as 'having a go' at him at this stage. He's leaning over at me, chattering with menace. He's changed the subject (again) to the press's habit of talking above the heads of kids and pseudo-intellectualising. What about the lyrics on the second side of 'Black And White'? Aren't they a trifle obscure for the average 'punter', as he likes to put it?

"Of course, you can't thrust it down people's throats. We could have been a lot more obvious."

Checkmate, I think.

'STRANGLERS IN Nude Woman Shock Horror'. That's what it says on the sleeve of the new album and it forces me to dredge the depths of the the band's reputation for that hoary old party trick, yes, you've guessed it, sexism.

"It's what one of the Glasgow papers wrote," he explains. And then pleads, "What's sexist about The Stranglers?"

That front cover for a start.

"Don't you think it's taking the piss out of all you guys?"

I remain steadfast and serious; some women would be offended by it.

"A lot also wouldn't. There's also a lot of blokes who would be offended by it. They adopt a cause or an image."

I must admit, this aspect of the band makes me laugh a lot (I'm very sexist myself). I mention an article in *Monotony Maker* against sexism in rock and roll recently.

"Shit man! If you want to be insulted you go out of your way to be insulted. Those people are sub-intellectual."

Do you not agree with the point that woman is in many ways a repressed victim of rock and roll; it *is* more difficult for a woman to make it in rock and roll than a man, after all.

"It's very difficult for a woman to have a cock between her legs. I think folk-music's more for women."

TALK MOVES inevitably on to the subject of Jean's solo album, 'Euroman Cometh' which will be in the shops, as they say, in a few weeks time.

The album came about as a result of "certain political things which I can't assume the rest of the band to be involved in. That's the European flag, which I'm a great believer in. It's also come about 'cos I don't have a pad of my own so for a time I stayed in the studio overnight playing with myself."

J.J. describes the music on the album as 'Eurorock' ("I believe there's an actual style of music called Eurorock, going back to Can and, nowadays, people like Jean Michel Jarre") and other sources tell me that the only Stranglers material it sounds similar to is 'In The Shadows' from the last album.

"I just did it when I was in town. It was basically to keep me off the streets, so I could have a place to go at night."

J.J. Burnel's social life does appear rather hectic and violent in nature; he tells me of one "pad" he had where three stabbings and a rape occurred, the latter prompting his writing of '5 Minutes'.

"I got a place last Christmas and it got smashed in too".

Sounds like a violent existence.

"Yeah, a fair bit."

He looks at his fingers, his head bowed dramatically. Silence.

"It doesn't help much, violence. I must admit. It doesn't solve problems. Fair dues, I've been trying."

He refers to an article he wrote for one of the music weeklies recently.

"Until recently, I've been trying. But you get frustrated after two years of being slagged off."

His interest in physical well-being (shall we call it?) started at primary school, when as a 'foreigner' in the other kids' eyes, he'd a rough time.

"I didn't think of myself as French until much later. I just wanted to be like everybody else. I couldn't understand why I kept getting beaten up."

His dad gave him boxing lessons and, well, as he puts it himself: "I wasn't getting beaten up as much."

I link this personal experience of Jean's to his adult attitude towards the frailer sex. Can't he relate to their physical disadvantages in terms of those early hardships?

"Oh yeah, I'm very gentlemanly with women. You don't understand that I treat them in the way that a lot of the modern ones want to be treated. They might find the old fashioned way patronising, but if you treat them rough with aggressive male vibes they mightn't dig that, so either way you lose out."

Which do you try first then?

"I try to be myself."

Jill returns with French rolls and more tea. And the hassling over photographs begins again. Hmmm.

GRADUALLY JEAN starts to be more at ease and his conversation becomes less wary and stylised. He talks about the two American tours that the band now have under their belts and of his revulsion at the place. Why didn't you leave for good after the first visit if you hated it that much? I can't resist asking.

"We're being sued by seven people as it is! We're in hot for quite a lot."

I'm intrigued and he goes into details that are astonishing and unprintable. Suffice to say, the band are relieved to be free of Albion management, whom Jean talks of as building their current relative success of The Stranglers' "backs" and off their "success".

"For the past twelve months we've been through a lot of hassles and we planned to bring out this live album . . ."

Those two statements I found interesting in juxtaposition and he anticipates my curiosity:

". . . but we're even more in debt through doing it now!" There shall be no 45 taken off the album ("even though we'll be pressurised to do it by the record company").

"Now we're being sued right left and centre. We've not publicised or capitalised on it before 'cos it's 'in' cliquey type of business, which I don't think is of interest to the punter."

We talk finally of gigs for the future. Jean's Euroband will be doing a short tour round the country, dates including Glasgow and Liverpool's Erics, the band line-up constituting Jean on bass, Brian James (of Dimmed fame) on guitar, the Drones drummer, an as yet unannounced girl keyboards player and possibly the reknowned Lew Lewis, who plays on the album, on harp.

But what about Les Stranglers themselves? Nothing is planned yet, but the band are eager to play dates in London, Jean, however, confessing that "Battersea was a mistake". He's clearly wary of playing too many open air gigs, risking alienating the band from their audience.

I agree heartily with the caution. The last thing we want is *another* of the bands that championed the cause of the new wave in those dim days of the past lighting up matches along the scatterbrained rows of The Hammersmith Caves.

Jean leaps down from the window sill and shows me a book on Mishima before heading down to the ladies loo on the next floor for some photographs with a relieved Ms Furmanovsky. Mmm. That didn't hurt now, did it David? his expression seems to say. Yeah, that's the great thing about The Stranglers. They always surprise me.

Do The European

Opens side two with a title that makes it sounds like a new dance craze that is sweeping Europe and which on reflection is a good metaphor for the song's sentiment. A call for the populations of Europe to embrace being European and also a comment on national identity and racism.

These sentiments are expressed over a cosmopolitan backing featuring European police sirens and abundant electronic effects. Burnel adopts a Gary Numan style voice to express the song's refrain. In fact, the vocal style was generic to post punk bands and Numan was one of several singers with this type of vocal delivery however he became synonymous with the style when he smashed onto the scene just after Burnel's album was released.

In contrast there is an urgent punk vibe to the verse vocals and the effects put on them make them sound like they're being delivered by a bull horn in the middle of a riot.

Toute Comprehendre

A simple arrangement with electronic effects impersonated bird tweets over a fuzzy bass line, a drum machine driving things along and a distorted guitar adding a break mid-way through the song. Burnel sings the song in both French and English and the title which translates as "understand everything" sums up perfectly the lyrical drive of the song.

Triumph Of The Good City

An instrumental tribute to the town of Hinckley made famous for producing Burnel's favourite bike of the time the Triumph Bonneville. The track is inspired by the rhythm of the bike's engine ticking over, which shows its incredible reliability by keeping in perfect time with the drum machine. Guitars and electronics clank around the perfect rhythm section making the track a tension filled mood piece that could be used in a film in a depicting a scene where characters are waiting apprehensively before pulling off a heist.

Pretty Face

Rhythm and blues on speed played by an actual band which featured amongst others Lew Lewis on harmonica and Brian James of The Damned on guitar. There is a Dr Feelgood vibe about it and Burnel was a friend and onetime flatmate of Wilco Johnson, but also there is early XTC atmosphere going on in there as well. The song is a little out of place given the genuine experimentation and use of electronic on the other tracks.

Crabs

Led by the home organ rhythm box which sets up a simple, almost twee synth-based melody. The bass is in the background but muscles around giving much needed bottom end. The lyrics are Burnel's sorry tale of catching an STD and being quick to apportion the blame for who passed on the condition and caused his predicament.

Eurospeed (Your own speed)

The slide guitar over a drum machine gives a laid back sleazy easy feel to the track. A call to people to do their own thing and not be tempted to follow allegedly more glamorous paths. The title is a blatant drug reference, speed fuelled the punk music scene and as we have seen The Stranglers were not afraid to document or draw attention to their drug use.

Ozymandias

A B-side to 'Freddie Laker' and was basically the poem by Shelley put to a manic drum machine led backing track. Burnel delivers the poem in a thespian on speed type voice. One can also see a direct link to the later Vlad series of tracks The Stranglers produced from the mid to late eighties. The poem appeared to strike a chord with Burnel as he also directly references it on the stark track 'Ugly' found on the band's first album. 'Ozymandias' and its sentiments clearly meant a great deal to the bassist.

Summary

The CD reissue contains a nine-track live performance from Hemel Hempstead in 1979. It's a fabulous complement to the album. A real band brings the songs to life. The drum machine is present, but the addition of a live drum toughens up the songs. It also sees the appearance of John Ellis on guitar, who had played on some of the album tracks.

Ten years later of course he became a member of the live Stranglers band before joining them full-time following Cornwell's departure. To be honest Ellis is a bit too flashy on guitar on the live tracks however this doesn't detract too much from the whole band performance.

A close listen reveals that the band Burnel put together was very tight and more than competent. Sadly, the size of venues chosen were a little ambitious for a solo tour resulting in poor attendances and some shows having to be cancelled.

Listening to the crowd response at Hemel Hempstead it is clear the hall isn't full, and the crowd is a little confused possibly expecting some more familiar numbers. But Burnel stuck to his artistic guns and played no Stranglers songs meaning the set lasted only forty-five minutes. The tour got a good deal of flack in the press with the album and concerts being seen as an

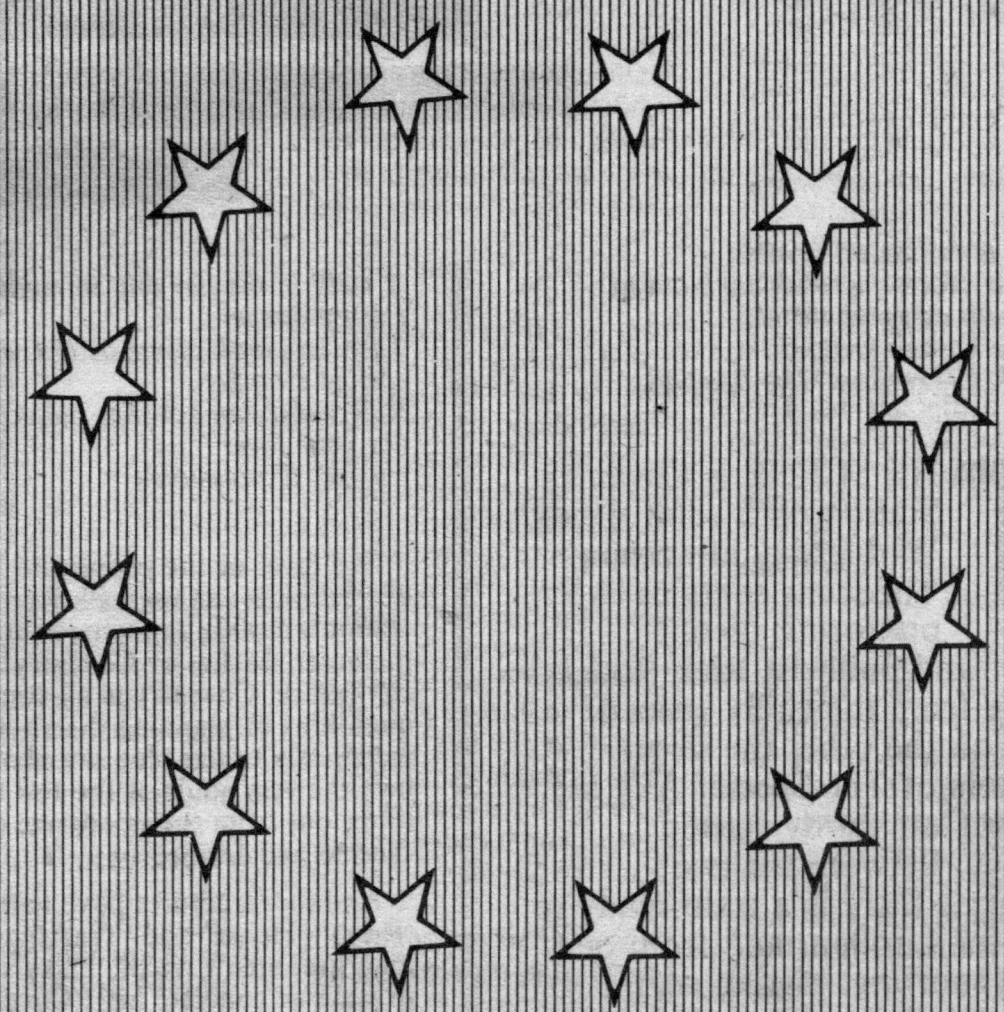

indulgence but on this evidence, they were decent gigs and to an open minded audience a worthwhile experience.

The studio album was a brave departure at the time and primarily because of that has aged well. It has a lo-fi charm and certainly points to some future Stranglers tracks, particularly the songs found on side two of *Feline*.

It also enabled Burnel to scratch that nagging itch of potentially going solo and perhaps made him realise that it would be a tough road and that being in a band was a better bet even if there would be some compromise. It must have added to his confidence and as he did all the songwriting and played virtually everything on the album, making it a real achievement.

Postscript

Girl From The Snow Country (withdrawn single)

A proposed solo single slated for release in 1980 but it was withdrawn before being released. Less than a hundred promo copies were pressed up and the cancellation of the release has made it the rarest, most expensive and most sought-after Stranglers related release.

Copies exchange hands for hundreds of pounds. *Discogs* records a highest price paid of £365 and a lowest price paid as £174. Fewer than one hundred copies were released before they were recalled. The song's rarity means it was bootlegged several times and those pressing are also illicit a very high price.[2]

The song is available to hear on YouTube but no formal CD release has ever occurred. The song wasn't actually finished it was just a demo but someone at the record company exceeded their authority and pressed up copies with two tracks from the Euroman Cometh tour recorded at Hemel Hempstead, 'Ode To Joy' and 'Do The European' on the B-side. Burnel pulled the plug on the release.[3]

The song is similar to tracks on *Euroman Cometh* and has a feel of Neu with a travelling motorik beat. The vocals are whispered and the whole effect combined is essentially to create a bright poppy song. However as is often the case with Burnel there is a darkness to the lyrics as towards the end the singer reveals himself as a killer.

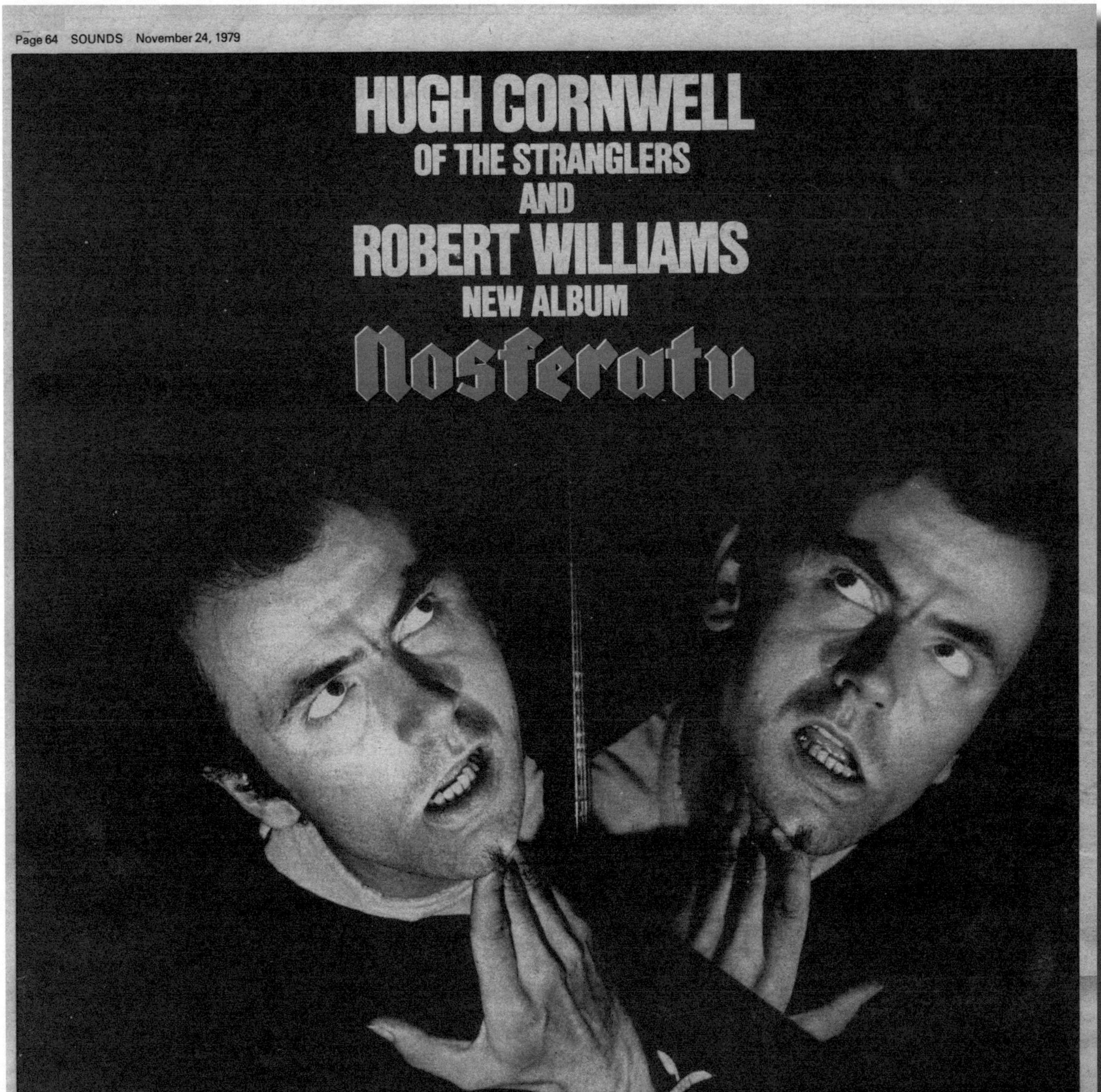
Page 64 SOUNDS November 24, 1979
HUGH CORNWELL
OF THE STRANGLERS
AND
ROBERT WILLIAMS
NEW ALBUM
Nosferatu
Nosferatu
ALBUM
UAG 30251
CASSETTE
TCK 30251
INCLUDES THE SINGLE WHITE ROOM
cw LOSERS IN A LOST LAND (INSTRUMENTAL)
BP 320

Nosferatu
(Hugh Cornwell and Robert Williams)

With Burnel recording a solo album it was inevitable Cornwell would also get a rhythmic itch he needed to scratch. Cornwell met Robert Williams when he finished a tour with The Stranglers. Williams was a drummer in Captain Beefheart's band, the two hit it off and spurred on by Burnel's solo record Cornwell suggested recording an album together.

Most of the recording was done in studios in Los Angeles. The album was written in the studio because it was such an off the cuff idea that neither had any material prepared. As with Burnel's album United Artists agreed to foot the bill for the recording and to release the album. Again, as with Burnel there was a proper advertising campaign with full page adverts in the music press and a leadoff single, 'White Room'.

The loose concept of the album was to provide a soundtrack for the classic silent F W Mernau movie *Nosferatu*. The album was produced by Cornwell and Williams with help from various engineers. Although the title and concept were linked to the silent movie, at around the same time film director Werner Herzog was releasing his cinematic version of *Dracula* called *Nosferatu the Vampyre* starring Klaus Kinski. Herzog's version visually owed a huge debt to the original film most notably in the iconic look of *Dracula* with Kinski's bald, demonic look being taken straight from the original. A coincidence that the album was named *Nosferatu* or did it influence the musicians' concept?

The packaging for the album saw no expense spared in terms of the quality of material used to depict and make the album cover. On the front cover there is a brilliantly atmospheric still from the silent film, depicting *Dracula* approaching his castle via a boat. On the back, a superb up shot of Cornwell and Williams looking every inch like Vampire hunters Professor Van Heilsing and Jonathan Harker.

The inner sleeve provides musical credits liner notes and has a close-up picture of a sinister ritual mask depicting the devil. The flip side of the sleeve has the lyrics overlaid over a photograph of a woman circus performer a link to the song 'Wrong Way Round'.

The album was released in November 1979 but despite the commercial campaign the album and the preceding single with promotional video didn't trouble the charts. There was no tour planned and this was perhaps the reason why it failed to take off. But in reality, it wasn't really expected to – it was too niche and artistically challenging for most Stranglers fans to want to part with their money.

Nosferatu

The title track gets things rolling at breakneck speed with a frenzied bass drum pattern. The instrumentation and the lyrics make the song sound like a chase and William's adds to this singing in an urgent desperate voice.

Cornwell contributes another of his nagging insistent guitar lines. The atonal title chanted as a chorus add to the desperate chaos and suitably Gothic keyboards round off the short but dark opener as Nosferatu escapes the dawn. The track would not have been out of place on the *Black And White* album.

Losers In A Lost Land

The music creates an aimless drift of a tune and Cornwell's vocals follow suit occasionally quivering to unsettle the listener. He relates a story of old actors or is it victims of vampires? The feeling of the song catches the idea of the undead and terminal sickness particular Cornwell's brittle guitar and the deliberately off-key vocals. The bass adds some excitement and sounds as busy, quirky and punchy as Burnel. It isn't a million miles away from Stranglers and perhaps a cousin of 'In the Shadows.

White Room

A cover of The Cream song written by Jack Bruce and Pete Brown. It's a suitable song to cover given the concept of the album and the lyrics conjure images of the dead. Initially it's a stripped back version almost deliberately anaemic to symbolise the undead. That is until Williams' immense tom toms crash in and leave the listener shaken and wishing all drums from this era sounded like this.

Cornwell's chaotic guitar solo at the end is inspired, cocking a snook at the studied respectful blues solo by Eric 'slow hand' Clapton on the original. The video shot almost exclusively in black and white places the two musicians in the titular white room giving the impression of an asylum and a direct link to the *Dracula* novel where the unfortunate Renfield is tormented by the count. The duo wears voluminous *Dracula* like black clothes and their pale make up gives the impression ghostly vampire spectres. The only real colour is a red filter applied to Cornwell halfway through done to obviously symbolise blood. An inspired visual interpretation giving a real edge to the song.

Irate Caterpillar

Another example of being ahead of the curve as the ambient industrial sound at the start predates Joy Division's epic track "I Remember Nothing. Cornwell adds a circular guitar and with a spoken vocal on top, the track has a real sinister surreal feel.

Given the subject matter one immediately thinks of sci-fi films like *The Fly* or the shockingly tasteless *Centipede*. The lyrics paint a picture of a bad acid trip and hallucination. Elsewhere a fuzzy neat guitar solo and some inspired bass drum work give the track an even more psychedelic tone.

Rhythmic Itch

The closing number to side one. A jerky, jaunty discordant piece of post punk made even more quirky by the skilled used of a variety of percussion instruments. Sung by Williams in an urgent hyperactive voice that was a style that defined early post punk records. Members of Devo add keyboards to cement the quirk factor.

Wired

Side two opens with the frantic 'Wired', the song appeared as a Stranglers B-side on the 'Don't Bring Harry' EP and is probably after 'White Room' the most commercial sounding song on the album.

Despite that it does have an agitated free jazz sax riff over the pacey instrumentation. The song creates space with a stop start instrumental breaks which create a feeling of paranoia. The paranoia is embellished by Cornwell's drug reference lyrics. The "something got up my nose" line are references to his increasing cocaine habit.

Big Bug

The subject matter is the story of Trotsky during the wars of intervention and the civil war in revolutionary Russia. Trotsky commanded the Red Army and was fighting the war on many fronts against a plethora of enemies. He travelled on an armoured train. the 'Big Bug' of the title, to the many different fronts to direct military strategy.

Despite no military training he masterminded the Bolsheviks victory. The story is close to Cornwell's heart, and he has referred to it on several occasions during his career. The lyrics find

Cornwell at his most poetic the bug metaphor is continued throughout the song. Revolutionary Russia is presented as a red leaf the bug is protecting. It eats white cabbages, a suitable image as the white armies were the name of the Bolsheviks enemies.

The process of metamorphosis is alluded to which of course links it to the earlier song on the album 'Irate Caterpillar'. The sting in the tail, to use an idiom appropriate to song, is that the bug metamorphoses not into a beautiful butterfly but a fly. Clearly a comment on revolutionary Russia becoming a totalitarian regime rather than a land of utopian socialism.

The song starts with an extract from a Trotsky speech and instrumentation imitates the sound of a train. It then becomes funky with a fluid bass pre-dating the indie industrial funk pedalled by so many bands in the early eighties. The song has at least three phases making it a mini post punk, prog epic.

Mothra

A memorable percussion led track mostly instrumental that stops and starts, the only vocal is the intoning of the track's title. Mothra is a fictional giant moth monster that was invented by the Toho Japanese film studio and first appeared in 1960 in the eponymous movie. It's the third track on the album with an entomological theme.

Wrong Way Round

The song has a distinct fairground feel with it cheerful tune started with a pipe organ toot and then led by Cornwell's trademark needle sharp repetitive guitar riff. Ian Dury plays the part of a fairground barker drumming up business for a woman in a circus side show. Cornwell's lyrics which on the surface describe a woman in terms of a freak show but as is so often the case with Cornwell the lyrics have other layers.

The images relate to a lover who has a contrary or rebellious side. It features metaphysical conceits, paradoxes and is Jonathan Swift like in its description of a body and bodily functions. Inevitably there is a suggestion of sexually innuendo and kinky sex lurking in the background.

Puppet

A synthesiser led idiosyncratic but charming melody with deliberately atonal chanting vocals. Cornwell's lyrics follow the traditional literary image of individuals being controlled by malevolent forces. The force appears to be the need for money and the puppets in question are musicians at the beck and call of record companies. The album memorably finishes with a percussive tune on tuned tom toms by Williams. The CD reissue of the album added the B-side to the 'Wired' single, an instrumental of 'Losers In A Lost Land'.

Summary

There is no doubt the album is a challenging listen as some reviewers at the time said. However, it is sticking with it that will eventually reward the listener with sonic hidden depths layered lyrical meaning.

It was a genuine collaboration between the two musicians which is often forgotten, Robert William contribution was key and in many places, it is him taking the lead and even providing vocals on several tracks.

The guest musicians are integral to the creative process, and all added distinct and memorable parts. The loose concept around Vampires holds up over the first side but then appears to morph into a fascination with entomology, which does actually fit in with the *Dracula* story, which in turn is a metaphor for the effects of drug use.

Given the lyrical themes and the style of music on show there is a strong argument to say this is the first proper album of the genre we now refer to as Goth. Recorded in 1978 and early 1979 it certainly predates any other band from this genre with the possible exception of Siouxsie and the Banshees who's debut was recorded at a round the same time.

As with Burnel's solo work there are direct links and influences to future Stranglers albums particularly *The Raven* and *The Gospel According To The Meninblack* not only because of the experimentation and innovation shown here but also lyrical and sonic themes.

Well corny

HUGH CORNWELL AND ROBERT WILLIAMS
'Nosferatu'
(UAG 30251) **

ELSEWHERE Hugh Cornwell has said that 'Nosferatu' was 'something I did on my holidays', that it was unconnected with the Stranglers and what they were doing.

In other words it's yer standard Solo Album, and not a very exciting prospect to boot. The album is allegedly pegged around FW Murnau's 1922 'classic' horror film, though the listener, unfamiliar with the movie, is hard pushed to string together any overall general or cohesive style going on. The music is mainly lumpen or intricate or self-indulgent or all three. There's scant sign of Stranglers' melodic flair, and missing is the kind of compensatory sense of humour or dark wit you might associate with Cornwell. Above all, however, 'Nosferatu' fails, in grand Solo Album fashion, through a lack of central direction. Too many strands come from too many angles at the same time, and there's not enough indication of where they're coming from.

What you get is two sides of listless jazz funk, beginning brightly with the title track, a slick speedy model, the awfully twee 'Losers In A Lost Land' soundtrack and the unsubtle reading of 'White Room', before the album withers down into highly involved yik yak, best estimated by its own titles, 'Irate Caterpillar', 'Rhythmic Itch' and 'Mothra', rounding off with two diluted 'Shah Shah' types calling themselves 'Wrong Way Round' and 'Puppets'. Sub Weather Report, sub Beefheart at his lightest, sub Hugh Cornwell in his most profitable place as a creative Strangler, subordinating the interest of (you) the fan to personal, eccentric ambitions.

Hugh Cornwell on 'Nosferatu' is like Bruce Forsyth on Broadway, he's his own loser in his self-willed lost land, and he'll come out of it a far less worthy a figure than he's gone into it.

The most astonishing aspect of all is the dark duo's production chore which presents the whole crackly, cobwebbed and antiquated Nosferatu theme in a glossy matt-finish, all spick and span and incongrously Modern.

Really, I thought the days of dry ice and Rick Wakeman were finished, and I feel obliged to end, in the true mood of 'Nosferatu', by self-indulgently using Hugh's review space to tell you about the wonders of the new Lurkers' single and the new Fall album. That's *my* Solo Concept for this morning, y'see.

DAVE McCULLOUGH

Fire and Water (Ecoutez Vos Murs)
(D Greenfield and JJ Burnel)

Living close to each other in the Cambridgeshire countryside meant it was only a matter of time before the two musicians, as well as collaborating in The Stranglers, would also collaborate on their own album. In 1983 the two musicians were asked to produce a soundtrack for the film *Ecoutez Vos Murs* (Listen to your Walls) directed by Vincent Coudanne. The soundtrack was released on the band's label Epic, but the film didn't see the light of day.

The album was named after two of the four elements of nature in Greek philosophy. A wild guess would suggest Burnel was fire and Greenfield water. The cover artwork represents the elements by using the colours red and blue to represent the natural elements. The elements are named in the title in three languages English, French and German. On the back cover there is a suitably enigmatic quote from Einstein about the meaning of life the universe and everything. There was also a single, a remix of the track 'Rain And Dole And Tea' and the album actually troubled the charts reaching No.94 for a single week.[4]

Liberation

A track that definitely puts us in soundtrack cinematic territory and has more than just a feeling of Kraftwerk and the experimental British synth pioneers such a Gary Numan and John Foxx. It has a pleasing, but edgy melody tied down to an early eighties robotic drum machine. It wouldn't have been out of place on an album by any of aforementioned bands and Greenfield intoning a quote from Einstein halfway through gives the impression of a found sound and emulates a technique used by another pioneering band of the time Cabaret Voltaire.

Rain And Dole And Tea

Rather a surprise after the European vistas created on the first track. This track imitates a Phil Spectre sixties girl band with Maggie Reilly's vocals doing a great job of emulating Ronnie Spectre and the Ronettes.

The backing is all drum machine and synth led which predicts a musical technique and fashion in the eighties and nineties which was used to relaunch divas like Dusty Springfield, Petula Clarke and Shirley Bassey.

Maggie Reilly was no stranger to the pop world having sung on many of Mike Oldfield's records in the early eighties. Her best-known collaboration being the international smash hit 'Moonlight Shadow' in May 1983. Lyrically it's the tale of two poverty-stricken lovers, not quite 'Leader Of The Pack' but along those lines. It was later remixed and released as a single.

Vladimir and Sergei

The missing 'Vladimir' episode from The Stranglers cannon. This is actually the second in the series that started with the B-side to 'Midnight Summer Dream'. For a more detailed analysis see the chapter on *Aural Sculpture*.

Le Soir

An atmospheric jazz tinged instrumental with a walking double bass line. One can imagine it being used to accompany a nighttime Paris street scene as the protagonists of the film stroll through back street Parisian cafes.

Trois Pedophiles pour Eric Sabyr

An atmospheric piece with three distinct parts. The rhythm track is a percussion frenzy with the drum machine pattern reminiscent of the random drum machine backing for The Stranglers song 'Hitman'. The drum effects date the song as they mix the splashing snare sound so beloved of the eighties and the *EastEnders* denouement tom-tom pattern.

After almost two minutes other instrumentation kicks in with a second musical section of reverb drenched synths. The third part loses the electronic backing to leave Greenfield's poignant beautiful Satie influenced piano.

Dino Rap

A new genre of rap, Mockney old school gangster hip hop! In reality an attempt by Burnel to pay a kind of tribute to a crew member. It is a joke track but doesn't really work. It sounds dated and even at the time it is clear the duo don't really understand rap / hip hop. Peers Killing Joke with their 1988 track 'Stay One Jump Ahead' had the same problem.

I'm afraid this song has more in common with Morris and Minor and the Majors 'Stutter Rap' than anything happening in the real rap world like Grandmaster Flash and the Furious Five's 'The Message'. The Stranglers made a better effort of the genre with the outro to 'Nuclear Device (Wizard Of Aus)' and the track 'Ain't Nothing To It'.

Nuclear Power (Yes Please)

Ever the ones to take a contrary stance against fashions in the music world, whilst every serious rock group in the music world stood against nuclear power The Stranglers duo took the opposite view choosing to champion the energy source. History appears to back their stance as Britain and the rest of the world now sees nuclear power as the solution to global warming and the energy crisis. Across what can be described as a proto techno backbeat Burnel espouses his tongue in cheek contrary tribute to nuclear fission his main argument appearing to be its here to stay.

Detective Privee

With a jolly tune reminiscent of the future Stranglers track 'Hot Club' Burnel in his best *La Folie* inspired French accent narrates a story of his past love conquests and given the title translation 'private detective' maybe he's out to entrap a serial Casanova.

Consequences

Beautiful, layered, cascading synth melody give the album a fitting finale.

Rain and Dole and Tea (remix)

The reissue CD contained the remixed single version of this track which took out the multi-track vocals of Maggie Reilly concentrating on her lead vocal melody pushing it to front of the mix. A video was shot featuring our heroes yet again as drag queens and a full four months before Queen released a similar video for 'I Want To Break Free' which of course was a worldwide hit selling millions but yet again demonstrates even in solo and collaborative works The Stranglers or parts of them were ahead of the curve.

Summary

As an album it is an interesting curio which has much merit. There is the odd failure, 'Dino's Rap' is a bit embarrassing, but all the other tracks have good points. Greenfield gets to showcase his new synths, instruments that will dominate the forthcoming Stranglers albums.

It is a genuine soundtrack album with atmospheric, layered instrumentals dominating and allow one to easily picture the cinematic scenes they might accompany. Never destined to sell by the lorry load so breaking the top 100 was an achievement and something The Stranglers in the late 1990s would have killed for.

It also showed their new record company Epic, for it was them who released it, had huge faith in their new charges and were prepared to fund the recording and proper promotion of the record. The album also linked to the European theme the band had been following since *Black And White* and later on *Feline* which had been released the previous year.

D GREENFIELD & JJ BURNEL
'Fire & Water (Ecoutez Vos Murs)'
(Epic EPC 25707)***

I CAN'T help wondering what Vincent Coudanne will make of the lyrics Dave and JJ have added to the fairly reverent score they composed for his film *Ecoutez Vos Murs*. For despite the sleeve's rampant symbolism, this is probably the closest any of the Stranglers will come to making a comedy record.

The I Ching hexagram depicted on the sleeve is Wei Chi: fire over water, which relates to the fact that Dave is a fire sign, Aries, while Jean Jacques is Pisces, a water sign. You might imagine there was a concept at large here, but it doesn't appear to extend any further than this.

Side one opens by quoting Albert Einstein which may be intended as an introduction to the Fire & Water philosophy but the album quickly becomes a great eternal riddle in its own right as 'Liberation' then swings into a straightforward electro-rocker.

No prizes for guessing that 'Rain & Dole & Tea' is about London or, especially, the heartwarming tale of a chic young Parisienne and her poor-but-proud English bloke. Session lady Maggie Riley guests on what is essentially 'Da Doo Ron Ron' meets 'He's A Rebel'.

But the straight pieces are, for all their sensitive keyboards and digital mixes, lost in the novelty value of it all. Certainly 'Fire & Water' would be more listenable had the instrumentals been grouped together.

Returning to the I Ching for a minute, fire, which flares upwards, over water, which flows downwards implies that no conclusion is reached, that nothing is achieved — and that's really how this album strikes me. Two strong forces pulling in opposite directions. I can see Stranglers fans buying it, but I can't imagine it getting played.

LUAKA BOP

The Stranglers 1977-1990

Wolf
(Hugh Cornwell)

Cornwell secured himself a solo deal with Virgin and released an album in June 1988 before the band were due to record a follow up to *Dreamtime* later in the same year. Produced by Cornwell and Ian Ritchie with some help on some tracks by Clive Langer and Steve Churchyard it featured numerous musicians including Jools Holland.

The production reflects what was fashionable in the eighties and featured a good deal of programming of drums and bass which gave the album a dance feel. There was a taster single 'Another Kind Of Love' and a further attempt at the charts with a follow up single 'Dreaming Again' released after the album's release but alas none of them troubled the charts. Ironically there was the most interest from that Strangler release graveyard, America. There was even talk of a tour, but it all came to nought when Cornwell was dropped by Virgin.

Another Kind Of Love

Listening to the opening track now and we can be in no other time zone but the eighties, a world of processed drums and programmed backing tracks. Cornwell adds some trademark guitar over the galloping backing. There are also eighties trademark brass stabs, copious backing vocals and even a honking sax break thrown into the cluttered mix. It's certainly commercial and was released as a single. Lyrically, it's Cornwell in his bachelor pad entertaining a lady friend.

Cherry Rare

Not as in your face as the opening track but despite the slower laid-back vibe there is a huge amount going on. Cornwell returns to his favourite subject sex and the guitar effects gives it a synthetic blues feel so beloved of producers in that age.

Never Never

'Lucy In The Sky With Diamonds' keyboards stand out from the chaotic mix which has far too much happening. The words refer to Never Never Land an idiom based on the children's novel *Peter Pan*, a saying that has been adopted to mean having unrealistic expectations. Cornwell lists his wishes realising it won't happen and to think it will, is living in a fantasy world.

Real Slow

A yacht rock sax defines the song. For once there is a little more space in the mix, but we still have to suffer the eighties percussive effects. Lyrically Cornwell is dealing with the album's title as he espouses a series of traditional lupine imagery and sets it all in a relationship song. The imagery is rather sinister but unfortunately this tension is lost by the Mister Mister 'Broken Wings' sounds and the 'Careless Whisper' saxophone.

Break of Dawn

A sparser arrangement compared to most of the album creates a sense of atmosphere, but we are propelled along at a pace. Cornwell provides a laid back relaxed vocal delivery a technique he has mastered throughout his career it is almost conversational and therefore draws the listener in. Another gentle love song enhanced by subtle, soft female backing vocals. The protagonist is portrayed as magician, a master of the art of love. An excellent song and a standout track.

Clubland

The title is all the clues one needs to tell us where this album saw its target audience. There is a dance / clubby vibe to the whole album. If you want a direct reference for this song, think of Cameo's 'Word Up!' It's funky, danceable and it's got wah-wah and disco guitar. Just to complete the dance set, add in a banging snare sound, synthetic brass keyboards, and if that wasn't enough there's an eighties disco plastic guitar solo it could almost be Prince. After all that instrumental stimulation the lyrics simply describe scenes in a club.

Dreaming Again

Another welcome break in the album in the maelstrom of techno instrumentation. A gentle ballad with a Hammond organ solo adds a much-needed earthy feel to the synthetics which allows the song to drift along. On the surface a song about sleeping but of course Cornwell isn't that straight forward in reality it's hoping and wanting a better world.

Decadance

Back to a big production with a mid-paced number. The listener can smell the whiff of corporate rock. The title is a deliberate misspelling of the word 'decadence' which is a comment by Cornwell on the ubiquitous dance sound and club culture that inhabited the charts at that time. However, the irony is that the sound and subject matter of Cornwell's album can be seen as decadent with its overindulgence of instrumentation.

All The Tea In China

The familiar tactic of Cornwell using an idiom to set up a song. It begins with just an acoustic guitar and Cornwell's voice. Dreamy synth and ethereal backing vocals. One of the best songs on the album and along with a couple of other tunes a classic example of less being more.

Get Involved

A delicate Kraftwerk keyboards intro but spoilt by the clumsy drums which detract from the subtle setting created. Then the synth starts to double down, and we get a clumsy lumpen mess. The female lead vocals don't really help and give the track a syrupy feel. Another processed guitar solo is thrown over the top of the molten treacle sound and in a nutshell that's the problem, the instrumentation lacks depth and is superficial.

Summary

If he was aiming to produce something totally different to his previous work Cornwell certainly achieved that target. The album is of its time and unfortunately damned by its production. In truth there are some excellent pop songs here, but it is very hard to see the woods for the trees because of the OTT production. Lyrically it lacks the sophistication and interest of his Stranglers work.

The sound of the album is generic eighties pop and apes the sound of successful acts of the decade from Alison Moyet to A Flock of Seagulls but to be frank any act who recorded for a major label in the eighties have albums that sound like this. The albums often contained songs but are forever cursed by their production.

It also puts into perspective The Stranglers as a group in eighties who certainly had that period sound particularly around the drums and keyboards, but we should be thankful they weren't as highly programmed and processed as *Wolf*.

Cornwell was probably testing the water for a solo career. On reflection the first single is a good song and could have been a hit as it ticked all the right boxes of the time, an up-tempo dance orientated, and synthesiser sounds in abundance with a bit more luck and promotion it might have been a hit although to be fair there was a fair amount of promotion by Virgin. They tried again with another single 'Dreaming Again' which again failed to create any traction in terms of chart action. Virgin then cut their losses and pulled the rug from under Cornwell's feet.

Were people whispering in his ear? Go solo Hugh you're the main man, just as they had done after the first two albums. When the album disappeared from view Cornwell very quickly returned to The Stranglers fold, but one still has a sense of the dye being cast and that he wouldn't be in the band for much longer. The sparser songs on the record are the ones that have stood the test of time best, and this was a lesson the singer took on board for his solo career both in the studio and when playing live.

Un Jour Parfait
(J J Burnel)

This solo outing was released in autumn 1988 between *Dreamtime* and *10* and just after Cornwell's *Wolf*. The album sees the bass player fully embracing his French roots with all but one song sung in French. Epic released the album but only in territories that embraced the French language. In the UK it was available on import.

The songs are beautiful gentle pieces of pop and are fleshed out considerably by Greenfield however this time unlike *Fire And Water* it wasn't billed as a collaboration but as a Burnel solo album. Burnel produced it with the assistance of a young Owen Morris as engineer who was also helping the band work on *10*. Never likely to trouble the charts there were two singles culled from the record.

Un Jour Parfait (Thème)

A beautiful lilting piano theme.

Si J'étais

In English 'If I was' which was coincidently the name of a solo hit for Ultravox's Midge Ure in 1985. A pleasing pop song driven by keyboards over programmed drums. The sound of the synths make it recognisably eighties and with Burnel's soft croon the song has a dream like quality.

Weekend

A song originally written by Belgian band Glaciers George and reworked by Burnel and the Belgian band to create a different song. It begins with fat brass synth lines but as the song progresses the sound metamorphoses into a beautiful heavenly choral sound.

Triste Ville Ce Soir

A jaunty bass riff leads in a Latin jazz influenced melody and Burnel's breathy vocals give the impression of a late night Parisian jazz club and given the title translates as 'sad city tonight' he certainly captures that vibe. There are a couple of nice instrumental breaks from a raunchy sax and Greenfield on organ.

Un Jour Parfait

Builds on the earlier theme – 'Un Jour Parfait' which translates as Perfect Day. The backing has an up tempo beat with a subtle, deft lush keyboard melody leads the song embellished with a few trademark bass parts that are recognisably Burnel. The bassist opts to speak the lyrics which gives the song a story telling quality. The music was original meant for a Stranglers track with lyrics called 'The Beast'. The group were never happy with the track and dumped it. Burnel took back the music for the title track of his solo album. The Stranglers track was eventually released as an instrumental in the nineties.

Via Dolorosa

The drums high in the mix drive the song at a fast pace and there is a raunchy guitar riff running through the track. Greenfield adds some trademark keyboards, and a brilliant piano break and brass is used to beef things up. Burnel gives it his shouty punk vocal and the combination of all the elements create a cohesive rock track. It is perhaps the most Stranglers like sounding track on the album and certainly wouldn't be out of place on *10*. The title translates as 'painful way' which this track certainly isn't!

Le Whiskey

Beginning with the click, click of ice in a glass and the pouring of a drink, Burnel takes us on a lonely drinking session over an efficient, laid-back delicate tune dominated by Greenfield's keyboards whilst the rim click drum, jingling guitar and gently swooping bass add texture. A mixture of spoken vocals which become melodic and imploring in the chorus. An atmospheric piece as the listener can almost smell the Whiskey and the Gitane cigarettes.

Crazy (She Drives Me)

A layered track featuring a heavy back beat with a musical agile bass and guitar dancing around the beat to soften the percussive blows. Again, the bassist opts for a half-spoken, half-song approach before cutting loose in the chorus.

Garden of Eden

Sung in English and sees Burnel at his narrative best. He sings over a slow paced almost dragging, chugging reggae instrumental track dominated by Greenfield's keyboards. A synth for ethereal background chords, a piano to play the melody in unison with the bass and then out of nowhere a delightful organ break. Lyrically there is a great reference to Queen Elizabeth II and her infamous bedroom intruder with Burnel as the intruder taking swipes at her parasitic children.

Rêves

Most definitely a Euro feel to the track with an eighty's funky bass line. Probably the least remarkable track on the album.

Waltz

A pleasant instrumental that signals the end of the original album. It features some beautiful keyboard and guitar interplay between Burnel and Greenfield.

Extras CD reissues

Le Whiskey (12-inch mix)

I haven't been able to track this down. We welcome any links to the song.

Elle Assure

Not on the original album and released as a standalone single. A New Order style song, 'Truth Faith' being the closest reference combining big beats and synthesisers with guitar and at least matching his Manchester peers in intent and effectiveness.

Rêves (12" mix)

Another missing link.

Les Mensonges et les Larmes

Still missing in action please post us a link.

Summary

A very listenable album that reflects the times it was recorded and demonstrated Burnel was able to mix it and compete with the more lorded and fashionable peers. Although he set out to produce something that paid tribute and reflected his strong French connections an English language version would have been a welcome edition and potentially commercial. The quality of the songs was good and certainly better than some of the songs he would bring to The Stranglers in the late eighties. Vocally we get a full range of the Burnel styles from punk to crooner, to spoken word and a good deal in between. In places it is a little Euro pop but to be honest that adds to its charm.

Live albums Compilations, Session Albums and Bootlegs

There are a considerable number of official live releases from the period 1977–1990 and they are worth investigating as they all demonstrate what consummate musicians the band members are and why they were head and shoulders above so many of their peers.

They also accurately reflect the different musical phases the band went through and how as time went on they adapted old favourites to reflect that band as they were at that particular moment in their history i.e. the addition of brass, new synthesisers and an additional guitarist.

The albums below are not an exhaustive list of all that is available rather they are just tasters of what might be considered essential listening for committed fans. Any further suggestions are more than welcome.

Live (X Cert)

The band's then label United Artists released their first live, album in early 1979 mainly to fill in those days, a long gap between the studio albums *Black And White* and *The Raven*. Culled mainly from the infamous Battersea Park 'strippers' gig in 1978 and also some from the Roundhouse gigs in 1977.

The CD reissue added other tracks from The Nashville in 1976 and Hope and Anchor in 1977. Reviews were generally positive but not outstanding. Some people felt the mix was wrong and the song choice could have been more ambitious or more singles orientated.

The reality is that unlike many live albums it does capture the band accurately in all their aggressive multi melody glory. As well as the music it introduced fans, who hadn't seen the band live, to Cornwell the crowd banterer maestro with his acid comments, particularly at the *Daily Mail* demographic and its view on the punk movement.

All Live And All Of The Night

The next official release was on Epic Records in February 1988 capturing the band from various shows between 1985 and 1987 with its touring brass. The brass section obviously employed to recreate the brass arrangement used on *Aural Sculpture* and *Dreamtime* however this would have led them somewhat underemployed, so the band took the opportunity to rearrange some of classic songs and add brass arrangements – well demonstrated by the version of 'Nice 'N Sleazy' found on this album.

The CD reissues added more tracks from more shows including shows from the last tour to feature Cornwell in 1990. On these extra tracks the brass section is showcased on more classic songs so the listener gets to hear 'Peaches' with a brass arrangement as well more selected tracks from *Aural Sculpture* and *Dreamtime*. It demonstrates the band's evolution and that they were thinking hard about freshening up numbers they had played hundreds of times. It was released to fill the long gap between studio albums *Dreamtime* and *10*.

Live At The Hope And Anchor

Once Cornwell had left the band in 1990 more live releases flowed from their early career. In 1992 this set was released. It had already been used to source 'Tits' for the B-side of the free 7-inch white vinyl 'Walk On By' single given away with initial copies of *Black And White* in 1978. The recording had also provided two tracks, 'Hanging Around' and 'Straighten Out' for the *Hope And Anchor Front Row Festival* album released in 1978. The live tape also includes 'In the Shadows' as a B-side for the 'Don't Bring Harry' EP in 1979. To finally have the whole set on an official release (it was of course available as a bootleg) was a joy as the band were on searing hot form that night. Produced by Burnel and an excellent document of their sound in the early years.

Saturday Night Sunday Morning (Ally Pally 1.8.1990)

Released in 1993 and is a document for Cornwell's last ever performance with the band. It of course features the brass section and touring guitarist and soon to be full member, John Ellis. Listeners can catch up with a brass arrangement of 'Down in the Sewer' and if they really want it, a live version of the bemusing disco influenced 'Let's Celebrate'. There was a VHS release and later a DVD release with unhelpful variation in the track listing between the audio and visual releases.

The Stranglers And Friends

Released originally in 1997 and subsequently reissued a couple of time, it chronicles the Rainbow Theatre concerts in April 1980 when Cornwell was in prison for drug offences and friends rallied round the band so they could perform.

The friends that came to the rescue came from all corners of the musical universe showing, despite reports to the contrary the band were well liked and respected. From the Prog world Robert Fripp, Steve Hillage and Peter Hamill. The pub rock world sent Ian Dury, Larry Wallis and Wilko Johnson. Whilst the new wave / post punk world added Richard Jobson, Robert Smith and Toyah.

This list isn't exhaustive and many more stepped up to the plate vocally and for guitar duties. Given the hasty pulling together of musicians and limited rehearsal time the album is somewhat of a curate's eggs with some performances a little shaky, but worthy of a listen given the star-studded nature of the line-up and the unique circumstance it documents.

Live In London

A controversial release from 1997 and covers the *Aural Sculpture* tour. Controversial as it isn't actually from London and detective work from fans suggests the gig was in Zurich. In addition, the material would put it sometime in 1985 whilst the photo on the cover is circa 1978, Cornwell is pictured in light coloured clothing and by the mid-eighties all black was de rigour for all band members. However, it is worth seeking out as it's the first outing for the brass section.

A Musical Critique

Live at the Hammersmith Odeon
BBC in concert 1981

Released in 1998 but wrongly named **as** the concert was in 1982. It is from the second leg of the La Folie tour which was put together to build on the success of 'Golden Brown'. The recording quality is fantastic and comes from BBC live broadcast. The band are capture in their early eighties pomp when no one could touch them as a live unit.

The set list is classic Stranglers contrariness, despite being recorded by the BBC with a potential audience of millions they opted for classic album tracks, which would be unfamiliar to casual listeners rather than a greatest hits set. They only chose to include a couple of hit singles to pacify the uninitiated.

So, fans and potential new fans were treated to 'Down in the Sewer', 'The Raven', 'The Man They Love To Hate' and 'Genetix' with only 'Golden Brown' and 'Duchess' being the only discernible hits. Interestingly some of *La Folie's* weaker tracks come to life, for example 'How to Find Happiness And True Love In The Present Day; really positively thrives live because of the interplay of the musicians onstage. On record it seems a bit of a throw away filler and a little sterile but here it evolves into an edgy tour de force.

Other singles were played but they are relative chart misses, 'Just Like Nothing On Earth', 'Who Wants The World' and 'Let Me Introduce You To The Family' – great songs but not hits but hard core fan favourites. And we wonder why they weren't mega stars!

Compilation albums

The Collection 1977 - 1982

Released in 1982 and does what it says on the tin and issued as part of their deal to break from EMI. Not unsurprisingly it was a good seller.

Off the Beaten Track

Released in 1986 and gathers together all the stand-alone singles and all the B-sides from the United Artists / EMI years which were then difficult to get hold as the singles were all deleted. It actually charted at number 80 for two weeks.[5] A sign of the loyalty of the band's following.

The Singles

A more comprehensive releases than *The Collection 1977 - 1992* release. It is a good place for a total beginner to start. '(Get a) Grip (On Yourself)' was remixed and reissued as a single with 'Grip 89' added to the title. It hit a chart peak of 33 bettering the 1977 release but still alluding the fun Top 30. The album peaked at 47.[6]

Greatest Hits 1977 – 1990

Another re-hash of the EMI hits released at the end of 1990, Again the hits package performed well on the charts peaking at No.4 and spending nearly a year on the charts.

All Twelve Inches

Released in 1992 the album gathers together the 12-inch mixes of all the singles and proposed singles from the Epic years. It is a surprisingly good album mainly because the mixes on the whole are creative and in many cases inspired.

The 'Midsummer's Night Dream (extended version)' is essential and even the 'All Day And All Of The Night' mix of The Kinks' number is of interest rather than sacrilegious. Elsewhere the band do some of their own mixes demonstrating they had an interest in the mixing process whereas most bands at the time just seemed to allow a remixer free reign and offer very little input themselves.

Here & There:
The Epic B-Sides Collection 1983-1991

For those desperate to get all the Epic B-sides this is the album for you although it doesn't contain the legendary 'An Audience with Hugh Cornwell'. Of course, it a curate's egg of a record containing some gems like 'Norman Normal' and some stuff that can be best described as work in progress e.g., 'Hitman'. It does bring the Vladimir stories together and to many, this alone is worth the price of admission.

Session albums

The Early Years - 74-75-76 Rare Live & Unreleased

A 1994 release and worth listening to for the very early versions of some of their best-known songs plus a live recording from the Hammersmith Palais in 1976. Noteworthy for the first version of 'Strange Little Girl' and a demo of a couple of previously released tracks 'Wasted" and My Young Dreams'.

The Sessions

1995 issue and features BBC sessions from 1977 and 1982. The BBC sessions don't really do the songs the full justice compared to the subsequent album versions. However, it's very interesting to hear the songs in a much more stripped back version.

Footnotes

1. Official Chart website
2. Discogs website
3. webinblack.co.uk/JJ_Burnel_Interview
4. Official Charts website
5. Official Charts website
6. Official Charts website

The Authors' Journey

Co-writing this book has led to a huge amount of editing with much material left on the cutting room floor. There are many reasons for this, the most obvious being the writing wasn't quite what we wanted or the writing style on reflection wasn't what the book required. In addition, some of this now discarded material served as a kind of warm up session helping getting me in to the right state of mind to write my part of the book.

At the start of the project, I had a great deal of ideas and opinions about The Stranglers that I was desperate to share. In attempting to write an introduction I produced a huge piece work that was very passionate, opinionated and very personal. However, after some reflection I realised it wasn't right for an introduction and also not right for the book.

The piece had served a purpose though as it helped order my thoughts about the band, the albums, and the songs. It also had allowed me to hone my style to write the book. However, when I re-read it there were sections in the piece about the band's live shows that still resonated. I was struck that when I put, what were essentially live reviews, all together they actually told the story of my relationship with the band and the love I feel for their music.

It still doesn't quite fit as an introduction and it is a bit random in places but as a standalone piece in the appendix it gives a full insight into my passion and motivation for co-writing the book.

Mark Finnigan, June 2023

Finally in June 1980 I took the plunge to go and finally got to see The Stranglers. The band were fresh out of jail following the not nice in Nice incident where they were accused of causing a riot at a concert. They announced a quick fire tour in Britain to raise their profile in a positive way and to support the just released of the 'Who Wants The World' single. Three of us went down to the ticket office of the Apollo in Ardwick Green, in downtown early eighties Manchester. We struck lucky and got seats virtually at the front. In truth we wouldn't really be needing the seats on account of us intending to pogo the night away. Great! I thought, well in truth I thought, oh shit! As we were right at the front we would be right in the middle of what modern day parlance refers to as the mosh pit with all those tartan wearing, mohican sporting tough punks. But there it was I was finally going to see The Stranglers.

I look back on that gig over forty years ago and despite attending hundreds of live shows in my time this is still probably the best concert I have ever attended and certainly the best opening I have ever experienced. At the time I wouldn't quite admit it as I had seen my favourite band The Skids a few months before and they were brilliant but The Stranglers were on another planet. Although if you'd have asked me then I'd have denied it and said The Skids were just a little bit better. I was lying to myself; The Stranglers were the kings of live performances at this time. So what was it that gave them that X factor, when that expression X factor, meant something outstanding and not some dodgy middle of the road family entertainment.

So there we are at front of the stage at Manchester Apollo surrounded by Greater Manchester's Native American inspired punk tribe feeling a little intimidated but hugely excited about the concert ahead. The support band Liverpool's Modern Eon had done a good job and had received a warm reception from the crowd, not something Stranglers crowds were renowned for. Then after what seemed an interminable wait the lights went down, the orange lights on the amps pierce the dark with a throbbing glow and the track 'Longships' suddenly booms over the PA. A fast instrumental with swirling organ sounds, a sharp guitar riff and depth charge drum and bass sounds.

Then a cheer goes up, quietly at first, as only the front rows can see the band in the gloom of the wings. Hand torches scan the stage like searchlights to find a pathway through the myriad of cables and gear. Then a crescendo of cheers erupts as the whole hall can now see their heroes appearing from the wings to pick up their weapons. They stride on confidently, as if they own the place. In reality they do own the place, the stage is their turf. Then the clunks and fizzes of the connection of the instruments to the amplifiers and they start to play.

I am speechless as we, the crowd, start to pogo furiously as if we were one entity, one animal, a single rabid dog. The song is 'Threatened' from the album 'Black And White' and sung by JJ Burnel. We are literally just underneath him as he does his karate inspired bass dance. The menace in the air is palpable, Burnel's jaw jutting out in a 'fuck you' look as he intones the words in what is one of his darkest songs.

Cornwell to the right of the stage is singing an amazing backing vocal which sounds like he is singing another song at the same time as Burnel. The effect is in equal measure amazing, magnificent and disturbing. Years later I discovered Cornwell was singing the word "malfunctioning" over and over again but sung in a startlingly creative way with a series of nuances which give the effect of a phrase being sung rather than a single word.

The bass is growling away and Burnel plays it like he is wrestling with it as if were some kind of foe. Hitting the guitar body and neck to get it to boom like a cannon during the bridge of the song. Cornwell's guitar rings out with a dangerous spikey sharp as a porcupine quill riff.

Jet Black impassively drives the song with a galloping drum pattern and the keyboard god, Dave Greenfield is the glue that holds it altogether as his other worldly keyboard lines weave between the other instruments to bind the song together. The song finishes with the chilling last line delivered acapella style "Bring me a piece of my Mummy she was quite close to me" followed by a last rendition of the riff and a sudden end. I am speechless I can't believe the power of what I had just seen and heard. It was indescribably brilliant, a religious experience a coming of age, a musical orgasm.

Unbelievably after such a staggering start, they then built on that foundation and take events to an even higher part of the stratosphere with the next two songs, 'The Raven' and 'Toiler on the Sea'. The crowd is carried along on a massive wave of euphoria, it's no wonder these three tracks are part of my all-time Stranglers Top 10. The truth is it didn't even stop there, the whole concert was just as exciting in terms of the emotions, the song choice and most off all the playing and musical interaction of the band.

I have never before or since seen a band keep the atmosphere as high throughout a whole concert. The excitement was enhanced by the menace from the stage and the same emotion coming back from the audience, creating a mix of danger, excitement and sheer joy. When I look at the set list now there was only one hit single played all night and this from a band who had many to choose from. Simply staggering and the first spark in inspiring me to write this book.

After seeing them play live they quickly returned to Manchester to promote *The Gospel According To The Meninblack* album – another stunning show to cement my belief in my new faith. If someone put a gun to my head this album is probably my all-time favourite, it is a masterpiece.

My third live experience followed with the tour supporting *La Folie* at the same venue.

Manchester Apollo, 25th November 1981

As soon as *La Folie* was released the band took it out on tour. My Strangler fan friends, were more than excited about the gig especially as we felt the new album, *La Folie* was more accessible than their previous album *The Gospel According to the Meninblack*. It was my third Stranglers Apollo gig in just over a year and testament to the band's popularity and live reputation that they could play this often and still sell out big venues.

My previous experience of the band live had been electric. The sound and sight of them opening my first gig with a blistering version of 'Threatened' is still my greatest ever gig experience. A mixture of awe, excitement, fear and joy. As a band they were at the peak of their live powers in 1980 / 81 in fact they were absolutely on fire, live and dangerous summed up their gigs.

Before we get into The Stranglers set its worth relating the whole experience. Seeing a gig then was a totally different experience than it is now. In 1981 going into Manchester city centre was potentially a very dangerous experience. The summer of 1981 had seen serious rioting in Manchester, particularly in Moss Side a stone's throw away from the Apollo in Ardwick. Tribalism in music was still rife and could lead to you being beaten up if you met people from an alternative music tribe.

The Stranglers were still identified with punk in 1981 and still had many bondage and

Mohican followers. The band had a reputation for being tough and able to handle themselves and because of this attracted an aggressive element as part of their crowd. That was the feeling at a gig in 1981 and it wasn't just Stranglers gigs where you felt it might all just kick off at any moment. The things that gig goers today take for granted, like stage times, disabled access, a 10:30pm curfew and helpful polite security were alien concepts in those days. Basically, if you got out of gig without an injury, altercation or being threatened you'd had a good night!

Stranglers' gigs were also famous for their support band or more accurately the reception they got. The group were champions of new music and gave support slots to up and coming and soon to be great bands like The Skids, Human League and Simple Minds. All these soon to be big hitters supported The Stranglers in their early days. Many other bands trod this path and benefited from the band's patronage and went down well with their audience. However, Stranglers fans also had a reputation for being more than harsh to bands they decided weren't good enough, punk enough or loud enough. If they considered the support band were below standard, then implements might be thrown. At Manchester Apollo in November 1981 all aspects of a support band's lot on a Stranglers tour were on show.

First up were Taxi Girl. They are from France and had the added bonus of being a JJ Burnel favourite so much, so he had even produced their then most recent album *Seppuku*. Burnel even roped in Jet Black for percussion duties on the album following the death of the band's drummer. With at least two Stranglers behind them the band had every chance of success surviving the support slot. They manage to pull it off with an energetic songs and performance.

The keyboard player is the star of the show playing his organ like XTC's Barry Andrews with the keys pointing at 45 degrees to the stage so allowing him the opportunity to dance as well as play. The standout song from their spikey new wave was 'Cherchez le Garcon' which had been a hit in France.

The band exacted moderate applause from the audience and after a short set escaped to the wings with what in football jargon could be described as an away draw. In terms of their further career the band carried on until 1986 but it was probably this time in 1981 that their career was at its height. *Seppuku* was their most successful album; it was given a big push in the UK at the time and the support slot with The Stranglers was their big break to achieve wider acclaim outside their homeland. It didn't quite work out that way but like their live set the band gave it a good go.

Now normally after one support band you expect the headliners to be on next on but not on this tour. There was another delight to be had, Dr Spratts 20th Century Popular Motets. Around six people arrive at the front of the stage and start to sing acapella style. The words are sounds rather than recognised language. It's a bit like scat singing, a motet I learned later is a vocal composition. The voices harmonise with each other, well they did for the first ten seconds of their set. Then the crowd erupts with a torrent of abuse, saliva and flying objects towards the stage.

Dr Spratts, to their credit try to carry on but after two minutes they call it quits and beat a hasty retreat to lick their wounds and brush off the spittle. The atmosphere had changed the audience were impatient, distracted and even angry. The headliners couldn't come soon enough. The lights dim, then the intro music, 'Waltzinblack' starts, and the crowd starts to cheer enthusiastically. Then the audience volume erupts to great heights, into a primeval noise as the band hits the stage and kick into 'Non Stop' in emphatic fashion. The audience like me have been doing their homework as they sing along to the brand-new song. It's a feather in the cap for the *La Folie* album because choosing a new song as an opening number can be a risky business but with an emphatic thumbs up from the crowd the gamble has paid off.

Keen to build on the momentum they segue straight into 'Threatened', my personal favourite, with all its brooding menace. I'm in heaven and the atmosphere is completed by an impressive, minimalist, back lit white light shows which enhances the atmosphere of malevolent euphoria. The visual spectacle before me recreates the live shot on the *La Folie* back cover. That is why forty years later that photo is still imprinted on my mind, it brings back all the feelings I have alluded to and means I can remember the gig as if it were yesterday.

What follows in the next hour or so is my perfect Stranglers set, it's well balanced and rich with tracks from *The Raven* and *The Gospel According To The Meninblack* whilst also visiting older albums for fans' favourites. Songs like 'The Raven', 'Just Like Nothing On Earth' and 'Nuclear Device

(Wizard Of Aus)' drive the set with relentless momentum.

La Folie has more than its fair share of songs, demonstrating the confidence the band had in it and also what an excellent album it is. In addition to the album opener the band plunder their new work for four other songs 'The Man They Love To Hate', 'Tramp', 'Let Me Introduce You To The Family' and 'Golden Brown'. The highlight of the new songs is a blistering version of 'The Man They Love To Hate' with Burnel growling his way through the narrative as his colleagues tear it up instrumentally.

The set finishes on a massive high with 'Genetix', with its amazing crescendo finish. It's a natural song to finish with and would become a traditional set closer for many years. The great thing about a Stranglers gigs then and now is they always play a great deal of their classic album tracks rather than hit singles. They don't go for all the greatest hits overload. This is an excellent trait artistically and for the fans as they often get a surprise when an old but much-loved album track is played.

The band encore with 'Bring On The Nubiles' with a 'Cocktail Nubiles' introduction which might explain why many years later 'Cocktail Nubiles' was included on the *La Folie* reissue. Other encores included 'Duchess' and 'Hanging Around'. The crowd want more and there is a momentum created for an unprecedented third encore. In response the sound engineer plays the title track 'La Folie 'through the PA and the stage is slowly invaded by dancers / performance artists who set about human sculpting the name of the album. A bizarre end to a storming gig. I leave the gig excited and buzzing, the band had really smashed it and my friends, and I chat excitedly about how good the gig was in the back of my dad's car. A magnificent, exciting gig and we got home without being punched, threatened or abused! Result!

It is worth noting that the tribalism that gave gigs such a malevolent atmosphere began to evaporate from this time. From 1982/3 gigs seemed much less threatening to me. This possibly coincides with the rise of U2 who somehow crossed the divide and united the musical tribes, the metal heads, punks, mods and rockers and any others you care to mention.

I saw all those tribes in the audience and getting along fine at a U2 gig in 1982. The concert was at the dangerous Manchester Apollo and was amazed to have overheard two bouncers bemused at the diversity of tribes attending the gigs and the peaceful atmosphere. Bono has many critics, and I am one of his harshest but helping uniting the waring music factions is probably his greatest achievement. If only his music was better!

Set list: Waltz in Black (Intro music), Non Stop, Threatened, Just Like Nothing on Earth, Second Coming, The Man They Love to Hate, Meninblack, Who Wants the World, Baroque Bordello, Golden Brown, ramp, Thrown Away, Tank, I Feel Like a Wog, Let Me Introduce You to the Family, Nuclear Device, Genetix.

Encore: Cocktail Nubiles segues into Bring on the Nubiles, Duchess.

Second encore: The Raven, Hanging Around.

Third encore: La Folie played over the PA whilst performance artists spell out La Folie.

When 'Golden Brown' tore up the charts in early 1982 the band went back on the road to promote it. They rejigged the running order of the set and added a couple of numbers. They opened with 'Down in the Sewer', and added from *La Folie*, 'How To Feel True Love And Happiness In The Present Day'. They dropped 'Threatened', 'Bring On The Nubiles' and 'I Feel Like A Wog'. More evidence if it were needed of a band constantly evolving and more than happy with their new work. A good document of this part of the tour is *Live at the Hammersmith Odeon*. A BBC recording originally released by the corporation and later reissued by EMI.

Then there was a lull, I lost the faith a little and also went to university. Whilst I was busily drinking and accumulating vinyl at the University of Sheffield and I might add at the taxpayers' expense thanks to my student grant, the album *Feline* slipped out. Several student friends who hadn't been fans until recently acquired the album. Being a musical snob, I was miffed others were discovering the band in the light of 'Golden Brown's' success. Where were they in the lean days around the arrest in Nice, the failed hit singles and the poor sales of *The Gospel According To The Meninblack*? I remember one of these acquaintances inviting us to a 'premier' of *Feline* in his hall of residence room with a group of new fans. I have to say I was underwhelmed by the album. To be honest I was determined not to like it. It has taken writing this book to make me appreciate the album properly. It isn't my favourite but the vision behind it and different styles employed makes it a pleasing rewarding listen.

I briefly reconnected with the band on the *Aural Sculpture* tour at Sheffield City Hall. Another stunning gig this time with the addition of a brass section, a controversial move that was not met with unfettered joy by many fans. Personally, I thought the brass was an inspired decision and actually enlivened the new songs and breathed life into some of the older songs.

Despite attending the gig and seeing the band were still relevant and hungry I wasn't inspired to buy the album. A decision I now regret as I see the album as a pop masterpiece particularly thanks to Laurie Latham's production which doesn't cross the line into the bright but banal eighties production values that blighted so many bands then. I will even go so far as to say that I can even see merit in the track 'Mad Hatter'. A track that holds a special place of loathing in many Stranglers fans hearts.

The gig did however finally encourage me to buy the first two albums, despite having heard them countless times. Rather surprisingly I hadn't actually bought them. Resorting to my 'home taping is killing music' copies instead as my student finances couldn't quite stretch to albums, I had already recorded onto C90 cassettes. If only I had applied such logic in the new millennium and the Spotify era, as I'd be a millionaire!

Instead, I have a record collection that would rival a second-hand record shop. After *Aural Sculpture* I kept a watching brief on new Stranglers material, being aware of the singles but never really engaging with the new albums preferring instead to play their older albums particularly *Black And White*, *The Raven* and *The Gospel According To The Meninblack*. However, getting acquainted with the later material has been somewhat of a revelation and I was pleasantly surprised by now much quality there was. Post *La Folie* feels like a different band with an attempt to sound more commercial whilst at the same time having subject matter and music that still challenges.

My true return to the fold came via the *Norfolk Coast* album in 2004 which was an inspired return to form. I went to see them again for the first time in nearly twenty years and found they had lost none of their venom and musicality. I even got to review the gig for the Sheffield Telegraph and was immensely pleased and proud to get on the guest list.

I thought I'd made it and expected a life as a hip music journalist and trend setter to lift off. Ala's life got in the way, and it took another twenty years for me to get my act together to co-write the book I had always wanted to write. Dave Greenfield's tragic death was the trigger. I spoke to my lifelong friend and Stranglers fan Rog (David Rodgers) and we came up with the unique idea of doing a musical appreciation of the band using his expert musical theory knowledge and my limited experience of being a rock music hack.

We decided to do every song of the Hugh Cornwell era. For each song we decided to give it a short impressionistic review as a music magazine of paper might do then analyse the lyrics and then deconstruct the music. I concentrated on the review and lyrics and Dave had the mammoth task of the music. Initially we went at it great guns but gradually we ran out of steam no publisher and life events sapping our energy so reluctantly we put the project on hold.

Then in the summer of 2022 Laura Shenton published her book on *La Folie* and I was inspired to do my own version (part on which you can find in the *La Folie* chapter). Determined that my writing about that album would not just be an academic exercise I sent the manuscript to Laura and to Jerry, her publisher at Wymer. A correspondence ensued and I am immensely grateful to Laura for her encouraging positive comments.

A face-to-face discussion with Jerry on Zoom as we call it now led to an offer to write the book. I immediately contacted Dave who I had been drip feeding my thoughts to try and get him to take up writing again. I sensed it was working and now with a publishing deal and a deadline in the bag he was back on board. Since then, it's been a breeze.

Co-writing logistics can make things challenging but we have met the challenges including many differences of opinion on songs and albums, but we still remain firm friends, thank goodness. With this book, we wanted to stimulate debate and get fans to enter the fray with their firmly held opinions just like myself and Dave did when working on the book. We want to hear about their prejudices and their secret never expressed confessions about songs and albums.

Speaking of which I am sure there are fans out there who, believe it or not don't actually like *Rattus Norvegicus IV* or others that have a secret love of *10* and some who can't stand 'Golden Brown'. With the analysis of the music there could be a degree of discovery and education for some non-music fans and for the real musicians out there who are aware or unaware of the band there are fascinating explanation of how the songs work.

Mark Finnigan

The first proper gig I ever attended, aged fifteen, was to see The Stranglers on October 25th, 1979, at the Manchester Apollo. My friend and I were anxious as the reputation of the band's gigs was well known to us but fortunately our parents were unaware of this.

When the house lights went down, the roar ratcheted the febrile atmosphere up to breaking point as Dave Greenfield's three high swirling chords of 'Shah Shah a Go Go', followed by JJ Burnel's simple yet ridiculously powerful octave bass guitar and Jet Black's constant bass drum, was almost overwhelming. The final piece in the sonic jigsaw of Hugh Cornwell's piercing guitar was 'job done' in memories for life. Even before the snarling vocals entered, that opening sound from forty-four years ago can still be tasted as if it were happening right now.

During the second song, 'Ice', a large green haired Punk aggressively barged past me and several others, and exited the gig swearing at the top of his voice as he wanted a one hundred percent punk sound.

Fortunately, I conquered my fears about what else might happen over the next two hours, and soon became completely immersed in the power of the live sound mesmerised by all those melodies building up on top of each other. Ice is still one of my favourite songs and I wish I could magically meet the punk today to diplomatically explain the folly of his actions.

David Rodgers

Acknowledgements

The authors would like to thank the following:

Peter Grimes, Rob Jones, Cliff Howarth, Mike Howarth, Dan Finnigan, Pauline Lyons, Simon Dell and his amazing archive! All the family and friends who supported and encouraged us along the way — you know who you are!

And most of all to Sue and Debs for all their patience and support.

Bibliography

The Stranglers La Folie In Depth - Laura Shenton, Wymer 2022

Peaches A Chronicle of The Stranglers: 1974 – 1990 Robert Endeacott, Soundcheckbooks 2014

A Multitude of Sins The Autobiography - Hugh Cornwell, Harper Collins 2004

The Stranglers Song by Song – Hugh Cornwell and Jim Drury, Sanctuary Publishing 2001

Strangled Identity, Status, Structure and The Stranglers – Phil Knight, Zero Books 2015

The Stranglers The Classic Album Series Rattus Norvegicus and No More Heroes – Chris Wade, Wisdom Twins Books 2022

The Stranglers No Mercy The authorised and Uncensored Biography – Dave Buckley, Hodder and Stoughton 1998

Burning Up Time – The Unofficial Stranglers and Hugh Cornwell Forum Facebook site

Stranglers Memorabilia: The Premier Stranglers Collectors' Forum

The Simon Dell Music Press Archive 1977 1990

The Stranglers Chris Twomey's band biog online on thestranglers website

Other titles from Wymer Publishing that you might like:

978-1-912782-69-7	*Elvis Costello This Year's Model: In-depth,*	Laura Shenton
978-1-912782-85-7	*The Stranglers 1977,*	Laura Shenton
978-1-912782-88-8	*The Stranglers Then & Now,*	Alan Perry
978-1-912782-91-8	*Antmusic: An unofficial biography of Adam and the Ants,*	Mark N. Redmayne
978-1-915246-01-1	*Talking Heads Remain In Light: In-depth,*	Laura Shenton
978-1-915246-02-8	*The Stranglers La Folie: In-depth,*	Laura Shenton
978-1-915246-08-0	*Lively Arts: The Damned Deconstructed,*	Martin Popoff
978-1-915246-23-3	*Punk Rock A Visual Biography,*	Andy Francis
978-1-915246-24-0	*Siouxsie and The Banshees - The Early Years,*	Laurence Hedges
978-1-915246-27-1	*Wild Mood Swings Disintegrating The Cure Album by Album,*	Martin Popoff

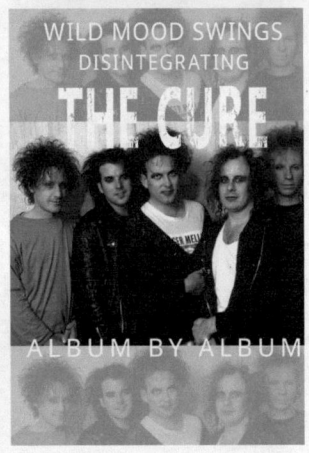